KV-638-355

Microsoft® Certified Systems Engineer

Windows® NT Server 4.0 Exam Guide

Microsoft® Certified Systems Engineer

Windows® NT Server 4.0 Exam Guide

Written by Steve Kaczmarek, Andrew Dahl, Theresa Guendling, Michael LaBarbera, Leslie Lesnick, James O'Connor, with contributions from James Blakely

Microsoft Certified Systems Engineer Windows NT Server 4.0 Exam Guide

Library of Congress Catalog No.: 97-65540

ISBN: 0-7897-0990-2

This book is designed to provide information about Microsoft's Windows NT Server 4.0 exam. Every effort has been made to make this book as complete and as accurate as possible, but no warranty or fitness is implied.

The information is provided on an "as is" basis. The author(s) and Que Corporation shall have neither liability nor responsibility to any person or entity with respect to any loss or damages arising from the information contained in this book or from the use of the discs or programs that may accompany it.

00 99 98 6 5 4 3 2 1

Interpretation of the printing code: the rightmost double-digit number is the year of the book's printing; the rightmost single-digit number, the number of the book's printing. For example, a printing code of 98-1 shows that the first printing of the book occurred in 1998.

Que is an independent entity from Microsoft, and not affiliated with Microsoft Corporation in any manner. This publication and CD-ROMs may be used in assisting students to prepare for a Microsoft Certified Professional Exam. Neither Microsoft Corporation nor Que warrants that the use of this publication and CD-ROMs will ensure passing the relevant Exam.

Credits

Publisher
David Dwyer

Executive Editor
Mary Foote

Marketing Manager
Kourtnaye Sturgeon

Managing Editor
Patrick Kanouse

Acquisitions Editor
Nancy Maragioglio

Development and Technical Editor
Robert L. Bogue, MCSE, CNA

Production Editor
Patricia Kinyon

Editors
Kristen Ivanetich
William McManus

Software Product Developer
David Garratt

Assistant Marketing Manager
Gretchen Schlesinger

Manufacturing Coordinator
Steve Pool

Book Designer
Ruth Harvey

Cover Designer
Ruth Harvey

Production Team
Jenny Earhart
Maribeth Echard
Brian Grossman
Heather Howell

Indexers
Ginny Bess
Cheryl Jackson

Composed in ***Bembo*** and ***Avenir*** by Que Corporation.

To my partner, Bill Glewicz, who has supported and encouraged me throughout this and many other efforts; to my Cairn terrier, Scruffy, who contentedly warmed my feet while I typed away at my computer; and to my parents, Donald and Pearl Kaczmarek, who fostered in me the pursuit of knowledge and a determination to succeed.

—Steve Kaczmarek

I want to dedicate this book to my wife and partner, Leslie Lesnick, and my son Benjamin.

—Andrew Dahl

Acknowledgements

Steve Kaczmarek would like to thank the following for their support during this project:

Don Essig, Nancy Maragioglio, Pat Kinyon, Lisa Wagner, Dana Coe, and Sarah Rudy at Que Corporation, who made this book possible. Also, Rob Bogue for his editing contributions.

Pam Bernard, Pam Riter, and Elaine Avros at Productivity Point International for their support and assistance, especially when balancing training and writing schedules.

My fellow authors for agreeing to undertake this project with me and for sharing their expertise and their time to make it a reality.

My fellow partners and trainers at Productivity Point International for their assistance and expertise when my mental active RAM failed to work properly.

Productivity Point International, a truly world-class training organization, for its ongoing investment and conviction in me and for offering me such an exciting career opportunity.

Andrew Dahl acknowledges the following:

More than any other book that I have been involved in, this book could not have come to be without the efforts of many other people. Thanks to all of you.

About the Authors

Steven D. Kaczmarek, MCSE, MCT, has been associated with Productivity Point as a training consultant since October 1991. During that time, he has focused on providing operating system, network management, and personal computer support training to its clients. Since January of 1996, he has also provided independent consulting services. He holds training and professional certifications (MCT and MCP) from Microsoft Corporation for Windows 3.1, Windows for Workgroups 3.11, Windows 95, Windows NT 3.51, and Windows NT 4.0, Microsoft Systems Management Server 1.2, and TCP/IP, as well as the Microsoft Systems Engineer certification for both Windows 3.51 and Windows NT 4.0. Later this year, he plans to begin work on another book tentatively titled *Understanding and Implementing Microsoft Systems Management Server.*

Prior to joining Productivity Point, Steve provided a variety of client personal computer support services through the IS departments of Heller International, McDonald's Corporation, and Continental Bank, which included purchasing and installation of personal computer hardware and software, network management, maintenance and help desk support, and customized training. He jokes that he started working with personal computers when they were in their "terrible twos" and has survived them into their "teen years."

Steve has a Master of Science degree from Loyola University with a specialization in computational mathematics.

Steve can be reached through e-mail at **sdkacz@aol.com** (America Online) or **105000,1756@compuserve.com** (CompuServe).

Andrew Dahl is a noted author/consultant in the fields of Web technology, Internet commerce, and groupware. Dahl is coauthor of *Internet Commerce, The Lotus Notes Administrator's Survival Guide* (Lotus Domino/Notes is the market leader in groupware), *Connecting Netware to the Internet*, and *Building Successful Internet Businesses.* He specializes in helping companies develop new software critical to their business operations.

Theresa Guendling launched her career over twenty years ago and has successfully managed a career of technical training, corporate consulting, and authoring. Taking advantage of a solid educational foundation, she has been able to play a leading role in corporate projects including systems analysis and design, expert systems development, and enterprise level networking systems.

Teri holds an undergraduate degree in Computer Science and a Master of Science degree in Management Information Systems. Studying as a doctoral candidate, she was able to develop graduate level courses in the design and implementation of corporate expert systems. Teri was a tenured instructor of Computer Science and taught undergraduate as well as graduate courses. She is a Microsoft Certified Systems Engineer (MCSE) and a Microsoft Certified Trainer (MCT).

Teri began her career working on large-scale mainframe systems. Her career progression has paralleled technological advances, positioning her for enterprise networking consulting, authoring, and technical training. Her special areas of interest are Microsoft Windows 95, Microsoft Windows NT, Systems Management Server (SMS), and SQL Server.

Teri is a published author, having authored *SMS 1.2 Administrator's Guide* (SAMS Publishing) and another venture with Que, *Microsoft Windows NT Exam Guide*. Additionally, she has edited several books on these topics and has developed and taught courses for Productivity Point International (PPI).

Teri resides in the Chicagoland area with Bill, her husband of over thirty years. As founder and owner of TMG & Associates, she has developed a widespread reputation within the computer industry and is recognized as an industry expert. She can be reached at **102415.3262@COMPUSERVE.COM.**

Michael LaBarbera, MCPS, MCT, has successfully combined over 14 years of experience and knowledge with hardware and software ranging from high-end main frames to low-end controlling logic circuits. He configures, installs, upgrades, and supports networks, hardware, and primarily Microsoft operating systems. With over seven years' experience in the technical education environment, Michael has worked closely with design and technical engineers in order to develop, maintain, and train proprietary courseware. He has developed numerous impromptu seminars and workshops for his clients.

Michael began his career with computers and software from his fascination with electricity and a hobby analog computer. Michael graduated with honors from DeVry Institute of Technology in Digital Electronics.

Michael has several years' experience as a Microsoft Certified Trainer and Product Specialist.

James P. O'Connor, MCT, is a Corporate Technical Trainer for Productivity Point International and is based out of Hinsdale, Illinois. Since working for PPI, Jim has conducted Microsoft-certified courses on Windows NT 3.1 through Windows NT 4.0, Windows 95, Windows 3.1, 3.11, plus numerous PPI Windows NT and Windows 95 courses.

Prior to PPI, Jim was employed by Burroughs/Unisys Corporation for 28 years. The first 13 years were spent as a field engineer supporting numerous mainframe and peripheral equipment throughout the state of Wisconsin and within the Minneapolis district. The last 15 years of Jim's career with Burroughs/Unisys were spent in the training department in California and Illinois where he taught classes and developed courses on Burroughs/Unisys proprietary mainframe and peripheral equipment. Jim has also taught classes in England and Australia. The last two years with Unisys were spent conducting Microsoft NT, Windows 3.1, Windows for Workgroups 3.11, and DOS classes.

Jim resides in Bolingbrook, Illinois, a Chicago suburb, with his wife, Donna, and two daughters, Nicole and Michelle. His Internet address is **joconnor@ppiptc.com**.

Productivity Point International (PPI) provides integrated computer software training and support services to the corporate market. PPI's more than 110 state-of-the-art training centers throughout North America serve the needs of both computer users and information technology professionals in subjects such as end-user applications, local area networks, application development, system migrations, and client/server computing. PPI offers results-oriented training in more than 500 seminar topics, created by a staff of experienced curriculum developers and delivered by more than 1,000 professional instructors.

Since launching its computer training network in 1990, PPI has trained more than four million students from thousands of companies. PPI specializes in designing and delivering customized solutions that fulfill its clients' specific computer training needs. Its roster of blue-chip clients includes leaders in manufacturing, financial, and other information-intensive industries, as well as government institutions.

PPI offers a unique, proprietary methodology—*Productivity Plan*—which integrates the software training process, products, and services under an umbrella of strategic planning. This consultative methodology delivers a customized productivity solution for people who use software as an integral part of their jobs. *Productivity Plan* consists of three components: DISCOVERY (needs analysis and skills assessment), DESIGN (training plans, products, and support services), and DELIVERY (implementation and evaluation).

PPI has developed proprietary, objective evaluation, and measurement techniques that quantify the results of *Productivity Plan* and the return on investment. PPI's evaluation system also provides a formal method of channeling feedback into the Discovery process, delivering a "closed loop" process that lets the client company refine its software productivity solution through time. These results yield a number of important benefits:

- More cost-effective use of training dollars.
- Improved skill retention and transfer to the job.
- Better employee time-utilization.
- Increased on-the-job productivity.

We'd Like to Hear from You!

Que Corporation has a long-standing reputation for high-quality books and products. To ensure your continued satisfaction, we also understand the importance of customer service and support.

Tech Support

If you need assistance with the information in this book or with a CD/disk accompanying the book, please access Macmillan Computer Publishing's online Knowledge Base at **http://www.superlibrary.com/general/support**. If you do not find the answer to your questions on our Web site, you may contact Macmillan Technical Support by phone at **317/581-3833** or via e-mail at **support@mcp.com**.

Also be sure to visit Que's Web resource center for all the latest information, enhancements, errata, downloads, and more. It's located at **http://www.quecorp.com/**.

Orders, Catalogs, and Customer Service

To order other Que or Macmillan Computer Publishing books, catalogs, or products, please contact our Customer Service Department at **800/428-5331** or fax us at **800/835-3202** (International Fax: 317/228-4400). Or visit our online bookstore at **http://www.mcp.com/**.

Comments and Suggestions

We want you to let us know what you like or dislike most about this book or other Que products. Your comments will help us to continue publishing the best books available on computer topics in today's market.

Nancy Maragioglio
Acquisitions Editor
201 West 103rd Street, 4B
Indianapolis, Indiana 46290 USA
Fax: 317/817-7448
E-mail: certification@mcp.com

Please be sure to include the book's title and author as well as your name and phone or fax number. We will carefully review your comments and share them with the author. Please note that due to the high volume of mail we receive, we may not be able to reply to every message.

Thank you for choosing Que!

Contents at a Glance

Appendixes

Table of Contents

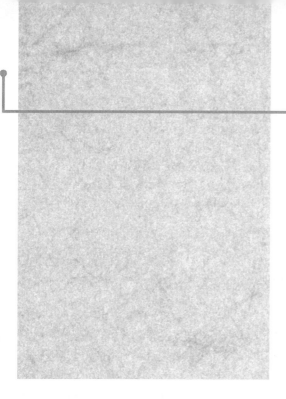

Introduction

This book was written by Microsoft Certified Professionals, for Microsoft Certified Professionals and MCP Candidates. It is designed, in combination with your real-world experience, to prepare you to pass the **Implementing and Supporting Microsoft Windows NT Server 4.0 (70-67)**, as well as give you a background in general knowledge of Windows NT Server 4.0.

The reader should already have a strong working knowledge of the following subjects before beginning a study of this product:

- *Windows NT version 4.0 user interface.* Windows NT Workstation and Server share the new Windows 95 interface; you should be comfortable using this interface to access configuration options.
- *Basic networking concepts.* Any network operating system relies upon the network running at peak efficiency to produce the best results. Even if you're not familiar with all of the networking technologies, you should understand the basics of Ethernet, Token Ring, and routers.

As of this writing, the exams cost $100 each. Each exam consists of 50 to 100 questions and are timed from one to two hours each. Depending on the certification level, you may have to take as many as six exams, covering Microsoft operating systems, application programs, networking, and software development. Each test involves preparation, study, and, for some of us, heavy doses of test anxiety. Is certification worth the trouble?

Microsoft has co-sponsored research that provides some answers.

Benefits for Your Organization

At companies participating in a 1994 Dataquest survey, a majority of corporate managers stated that certification is an *important factor* to the overall success of their companies because:

- *Certification increases customer satisfaction.* Customers look for indications that their suppliers understand the industry and have the ability to respond to their technical problems. Having Microsoft Certified Professionals on staff reassures customers; it tells them that your employees have used and mastered Microsoft products.
- *Certification maximizes training investment.* The certification process specifically identifies skills that an employee is lacking or areas where additional training is needed. By so doing, it validates training and eliminates the costs and loss of productivity associated with unnecessary training. In addition, certification records enable a company to verify an employee's technical knowledge and track retention of skills over time.

Benefits Up Close and Personal

Microsoft also cites a number of benefits for the certified individual:

- Industry recognition of expertise, enhanced by Microsoft's promotion of the Certified Professional community to the industry and potential clients.
- Access to technical information directly from Microsoft
- Dedicated CompuServe and The Microsoft Network forums that enable Microsoft Certified Professionals to communicate directly with Microsoft and with one another.

- A complimentary one-year subscription to *Microsoft Certified Professional Magazine.*
- Microsoft Certified Professional logos and other materials to publicize MCP status to colleagues and clients.
- An MCP newsletter to provide regular information on changes and advances in the program and exams.
- Invitations to Microsoft conferences, technical training sessions, and special events program newsletters from the MCP program.

Additional benefits, depending upon the certification, include:

- Microsoft TechNet or Microsoft Developer Network membership or discounts.
- Free product support incidents with the Microsoft Support Network seven days a week, 24 hours a day.
- One-year subscription to the Microsoft Beta Evaluation program, providing up to 12 monthly CD-ROMs containing beta software for upcoming Microsoft software products.
- Eligibility to join the Network Professional Association, a worldwide independent association of computer professionals.

Some intangible benefits of certification are:

- Enhanced marketability with current or potential employers and customers, along with an increase in earnings potential.
- Methodology for objectively assessing current skills, individual strengths, and specific areas where training is required.

How Does This Book Fit In?

One of the challenges that has always faced the would-be Microsoft Certified Professional is to decide how to best prepare for an examination. In doing so, there are always conflicting goals, such as how to prepare for the exam as quickly as possible, and yet, still actually learn how to do the work that passing the exam qualifies you to do.

Our goal for this book is to make your studying job easier by filtering through the reams of Windows NT Server technical material, and presenting in the chapters and lab exercises only the information that you actually need to *know* to pass the Microsoft Windows NT Server Exam (plus a little bit extra). Other information that we think is important for you to have available while you're working has been relegated to the appendixes and sidebars.

How to Study with This Book

This book is designed to be used in a variety of ways. Rather than lock you into one particular method of studying, force you to read through sections you're already intimately familiar with, or tie you to your computer, we've made it possible for you to read the chapters at one time, and do the labs at another. We've also made it easy for you to decide whether you need to read a chapter or not by giving you a list of the topics and skills covered at the beginning of each chapter, and describing how the chapter relates to previous material.

The chapters are written in a modular fashion, so that you don't necessarily have to read all the chapters preceding a certain chapter to be able to follow a particular chapter's discussion. Don't forget about the lab exercises. You can practice what you read on your PC while you are reading. Some of the knowledge and skills you need to pass the Windows NT Server exam are best acquired by working with Windows NT Server.

How This Book Is Organized

The book is broken up into 24 chapters, each focusing on a particular topic that is an important piece of the overall picture.

- Chapter 1, "Microsoft Certified Professional Program," gives you an overview of the Microsoft Certified Professional program, what certifications are available to you, and where Windows NT 4.0 and this book fit in.
- Chapter 2, "Understanding Microsoft Windows NT 4.0," provides an overview of the features and functionality of Windows NT including the new Windows 95 interface and networking models.
- Chapter 3, "Windows NT Server 4.0 Setup," discusses the installation process, step-by-step, from planning considerations to actually answering the installation dialog box questions.

- Chapter 4, "Configuring Windows NT Server 4.0," explores configuration settings, both basic and advanced.
- Chapter 5, "Managing Users and Groups," discusses users, groups, and profiles.
- Chapter 6, "Security and Permissions," explores security and access control lists. It also covers shares and setting permissions on shares.
- Chapter 7, "Policies and Profiles," delves into system policies and user profiles.
- Chapter 8, "Remote Server Management," covers the Network Administration tools and what platforms support them.
- Chapter 9, "Managing Disk Resources," discusses FAT versus NTFS, and the different partitioning options that NT supports.
- Chapter 10, "Performance Monitor," shows how to use the Performance Monitor to evaluate performance and tune the server.
- Chapter 11, "Printing," examines the printing process and how to add a printer, including information on printer spooling and setting priorities.
- Chapter 12, "Windows NT 4.0 Architecture," dives into the guts of NT, discussing the difference between user and kernel modes.
- Chapter 13, "The Windows NT 4.0 Boot Sequence," discusses the different stages that NT goes through when booting.
- Chapter 14, "Network Essentials," is a brief review of the basics of networks and how they impact Windows NT.
- Chapter 15, "Windows NT 4.0 Trusts," discusses how security works in a multi-domain trusted environment.
- Chapter 16, "Domain Models," discusses the Microsoft reference models for domains which are used on the exam.
- Chapter 17, "Windows NT Networking Services," examines the basic structure of network connectivity and how browsing works.
- Chapter 18, "TCP/IP and Windows NT," shows how to configure DHCP, WINS, and DNS for Windows NT in a TCP/IP environment.
- Chapter 19, "Novell NetWare and Windows NT," delves into connectivity with Novell NetWare environments, including migration options.

- Chapter 20, "Network Printing," shows how network print jobs are handled, and how to print to various network connected printers.
- Chapter 21, "Remote Access Support," explains how to set up RAS for NetBEUI, IPX, and TCP/IP.
- Chapter 22, "Multiprotocol Routing," discusses the options that must be set to get Windows NT to perform routing functions.
- Chapter 23, "Network Monitor," delves into how to see exactly what information is being passed on the network.
- Chapter 24, "Advanced Troubleshooting," examines Stop Errors and using the kernel debugger.

Following these chapters are the Lab Exercises. You can do these exercises at your own pace, when you want to—you're not tied down to the computer for every chapter.

All of the Microsoft Windows NT Server exam objectives are covered in the material contained in the text of the chapters and the lab exercises. Information contained in sidebars is provided to give you additional information that may help you in answering exam questions, but are not necessarily part of the exam objectives.

Finally, the many appendixes in this book provide you with additional advice, resources, and information that can be helpful to you as you prepare and take the Microsoft Windows NT Server exam, and later as you work as a Microsoft Certified Professional:

- Appendix A, "Glossary," provides you with definitions of terms that you need to be familiar with as a Microsoft Certified Professional.
- Appendix B, "Certification Checklist," provides an overview of the certification process in the form of a to-do list, with milestones you can check off on your way to certification.
- Appendix C, "How Do I Get There from Here?" provides step-by-step guidelines for successfully navigating from initial interest to final certification.
- Appendix D, "Testing Tips," gives you tips and pointers for maximizing your performance when you take the certification exam.
- Appendix E, "Contacting Microsoft," lists contact information for certification exam resources at Microsoft and at Sylvan Prometric testing centers.

- Appendix F, "Suggested Reading," presents a list of reading resources that can help you prepare for the certification exam.
- Appendix G, "Internet Resources for Windows NT Server," is a list of places to visit on the Internet related to Windows NT and other BackOffice products.
- Appendix H, "Windows NT 4.0 Overview," discusses important components of Windows NT which aren't necessarily on the Server exam.
- Appendix I, "Lab Exercises," is a set of hands-on labs that demonstrate key concepts discussed in the book.
- Appendix J, "Self-Test Questions and Answers," provides performance-based questions designed to test your problem-solving capabilities.
- Appendix K, "Using the Self-Test Software," gives you the basics of how to install and use the MCSE Windows NT Server 4.0 Exam Guide CD-ROM included with this book, which includes skill self-assessment tests and simulated versions of the Microsoft exam.
- Appendix L, "TechNet Sampler," contains samples taken directly from Microsoft's TechNet. TechNet is the technical resource for IT professionals seeking information about Microsoft products. TechNet provides critical information for deploying applications, minimizing downtime, and building technical expertise. The Microsoft TechNet trial CD-ROM, included with this book, contains over 400M of Microsoft technical information, including the Microsoft Knowledge Base.

Special Features of This Book

There are many features in this book that make it easier to read and make the information more accessible. Those features are described in the following sections.

Chapter Overview

Each chapter begins with an overview of the material covered in that chapter. The chapter topics are described in the context of material already covered, and material coming up.

Notes

Notes present interesting or useful information that isn't necessarily essential to the discussion, but will enhance your understanding of Windows. Notes look like this:

Note Microsoft posts beta exam notices on the Internet (**http://www.microsoft.com**), and mails notices to certification development volunteers, past certification candidates, and product beta participants. ■

Tips

Tips present short advice on quick or often overlooked procedures. These include shortcuts that save you time. A tip looks like this:

Tip

Use the Windows NT Task Bar to quickly switch between open programs and windows.

Key Concepts

Key Concepts present particularly significant information about a Windows NT or IIS function or concept. Count on this material being on the test. Here's an example of a key concept:

Key Concept

When you share a resource in Windows NT, the default is to provide Everyone with complete access to the resource. If you want additional security, you must add it yourself by restricting access with permissions.

Sidebar

Sidebars are used to provide additional information and enhance the discussion at hand. If a particular topic has a different twist in Windows NT server, it will be discussed in a sidebar. A sidebar looks like this (but longer):

Network Monitor on NT Server

Another useful performance tracking tool is packaged in with Windows NT Server 4.0. It is called the Network Monitor and provides network packet analysis to the administrator.

Caution

A Caution is meant to draw your attention to a particularly tricky twist in a concept, or to point out potential pitfalls. Cautions look like this:

> **Caution**
> If you do not keep your Emergency Repair Disk up to date, and you use it to restore Registry information, you can wipe out your existing account database by overwriting it with the old information.

In addition to these special features, there are several conventions used in this book to make it easier to read and understand. These conventions are described in the following sections.

Underlined Hot Keys, or Mnemonics

Hot keys in this book appear underlined, like they appear on-screen. In Windows, many menus, commands, buttons, and other options have these hot keys. To use a hot-key shortcut, press Alt and the key for the underlined character. For instance, to choose the Properties button, press Alt and then R. You should not study for the MCP exam by using the hot keys, however. Windows is a mouse-centric environment, and you will be expected to know how to navigate it using the mouse—clicking, right-clicking, and using drag and drop.

Shortcut Key Combinations

In this book, shortcut key combinations are joined with plus signs (+). For example, Ctrl+V means hold down the Ctrl key, while you press the V key.

Menu Commands

Instructions for choosing menu commands have this form:

> Choose File, New.

This example means open the File menu and select New, which in this case opens a new file.

This book also has the following typeface enhancements to indicate special text, as indicated in the following table.

Typeface	Description
Italic	Italic is used to indicate new terms and variables in commands or addresses.
Boldface	Bold is used to indicate text you type, and Internet addresses and other locators in the online world.
`Computer type`	This command is used for on-screen messages and commands (such as DOS copy or UNIX commands).
My Filename.doc	File names and folders are set in a mixture of upper- and lowercase characters, just as they appear in Windows NT 4.0.

Chapter Prerequisite

This chapter has no prerequisites, other than a desire to become a Microsoft Certified Professional.

1

Microsoft Certified Professional Program

As Microsoft products take an ever-increasing share of the marketplace, the demand for trained personnel grows, and the number of Microsoft certifications follows suit. As of April, 1996, the team of Microsoft Certified Professionals increased in number to over 40,000 product specialists, over 8,000 engineers, and over 1,600 solution developers—there also were over 4,900 certified trainers of Microsoft products.

This chapter covers the Microsoft Certified Professional Program and describes each certification in more detail. Microsoft certifications include:

- **Microsoft Certified Professional**
- **Microsoft Certified Systems Engineer (MCSE)**
- **Microsoft Certified Product Specialist (MCPS)**
- **Microsoft Certified Solutions Developer (MCSD)**
- **Microsoft Certified Trainer (MCT)**

Exploring Available Certifications

When Microsoft started certifying people to install and support its products, there was only one certification available: the Microsoft Certified Professional (MCP). Over time, demand for more specialized certifications were increasingly being made by employers and prospective customers of consulting firms.

There are now five certifications available in the MCP program, as described in the following sections.

Microsoft Certified Systems Engineers (MCSE)

Microsoft Certified Systems Engineers are qualified to plan, implement, maintain, and support information systems that are based on Microsoft Windows NT and the BackOffice family of client-server software. The MCSE is a widely respected certification because it does not focus on just one aspect of computing, such as networking. Instead, the MCSE has demonstrated skills and capabilities on the full range of software, from client operating systems to server operating systems to client-server applications.

Microsoft Certified Solution Developers (MCSD)

Microsoft Certified Solution Developers are qualified to design and develop custom business solutions with Microsoft development tools, platforms, and technologies, such as Microsoft BackOffice and Microsoft Office.

Microsoft Certified Product Specialists (MCPS)

Microsoft Certified Product Specialists have demonstrated in-depth knowledge of at least one Microsoft operating system. Candidates may pass additional Microsoft certification exams to further qualify their skills with Microsoft BackOffice products, development tools, or desktop applications.

The Microsoft Certified Product Specialist *Areas of Specialization* (AOS) that lead to the MCSE certification include:

- **Networking** This AOS requires the candidate to pass the Windows NT Server exam, one desktop operating system exam, such as the Windows NT Workstation 4.0 exam, and one networking exam, such as the Networking Essentials for BackOffice exam.

- **TCP/IP** This AOS requires the candidate to pass the Windows NT Server exam and the Internet working TCP/IP on Windows NT exam.
- **Mail** This AOS requires the candidate to pass the Windows NT Server exam and the Microsoft Mail (Enterprise) exam.
- **SQL Server** This AOS requires the candidate to pass the Windows NT Server exam and both SQL Server exams.
- **Systems Management Server** This AOS requires the candidate to pass the Windows NT Server exam and the SMS exam.
- **SNA Server** This AOS requires the candidate to pass the Windows NT Server exam and the SNA Server exam.

The Microsoft Certified Product Specialist product-specific exams are your first steps into the world of Microsoft certification. After establishing a specialty, you can work toward additional certification goals at the MCSE or MCSD level.

Microsoft Certified Trainers (MCT)

Microsoft Certified Trainers are instructionally and technically qualified to deliver Microsoft Official Curriculum through Microsoft authorized education sites.

Understanding the Exam Requirements

The exams are computer-administered tests that measure your ability to implement and administer Microsoft products or systems, troubleshoot problems with an installation, operation, or customization, and provide technical support to users. The exams do more than test your ability to define terminology and recite facts. Product *knowledge* is an important foundation for superior job performance, but definitions and features lists are just the beginning. In the real world, you need hands-on skills and the ability to apply your knowledge—to understand confusing situations, solve thorny problems, and optimize solutions to minimize downtime and maximize current and future productivity.

To develop exams that test for the right competence factors, Microsoft follows an eight-phase exam-development process:

1. In the first phase, experts analyze the tasks that make up the job being tested. This job-analysis phase identifies the knowledge, skills, and abilities relating specifically to the performance area to be certified.
2. The next phase develops objectives by building on the framework provided by the job analysis. This means translating the job-function tasks into specific and measurable units of knowledge, skills, and abilities. The resulting list of objectives (the *objective domain*, in educational theory-speak) is the basis for developing certification exams and training materials.
3. Selected contributors rate the objectives developed in the previous phase. The reviewers are technology professionals who currently perform the applicable job functions in their own employment. After prioritization and weighting, based on the contributors' input, the objectives become the blueprint for the exam items.
4. During the fourth phase, exam items are reviewed and revised to ensure that they are technically accurate, clear, unambiguous, plausible, free of cultural bias, and not misleading or tricky. Items also are evaluated to confirm that they test for high-level, useful knowledge, rather than obscure or trivial facts.
5. During alpha review, technical and job-function experts review each item for technical accuracy, reach consensus on all technical issues, and edit the reviewed items for clarity of expression.
6. The next step is the beta exam. Beta exam participants take the test to gauge its effectiveness. Microsoft performs a statistical analysis, based on the responses of the beta participants, including information about difficulty and relevance, verification of the validity of the exam items, and a determination as to which items should be used in the final certification exam.
7. When the statistical analysis is complete, the items are distributed into multiple parallel forms, or versions, of the final certification exam.

   Also during this phase, a group of job function experts determines the cut, or minimum passing score for the exam. (The cut score differs from exam to exam because it is based on an item-by-item determination of the percentage of candidates who answered the item correctly.)
8. The final phase—Exam Live!—is administered by Sylvan Prometric™, an independent testing company. The exams are always available at Sylvan Prometric testing centers worldwide.

Note Microsoft posts beta exam notices on the Internet (**http://www.microsoft.com**), and mails notices to certification development volunteers, past certification candidates, and product beta participants.

Tip

If you participate in a beta exam, you may take it at a cost that is lower than the cost of the final certification exam, but it should not be taken lightly. Beta exams actually contain the entire pool of possible questions, of which, about 30 percent are dropped after the beta exam. The remaining questions are divided into the different forms of the final exam. If you decide to take a beta exam, you should review and study as seriously as you would for a final certification exam. Passing a beta exam counts as passing the final exam—you receive full credit for passing a beta exam.

Also, because you will be taking *all* of the questions that will be used for the exam, expect a beta exam to take significantly longer than the final exam. For example, the beta tests for Windows NT 4.0 have, so far, had a time limit of 4 hours each and more than three times as many questions as the final versions of the exams!

Note If you're interested in participating in any of the exam development phases (including the beta exam), contact the Microsoft Certification Development Team by sending a fax to (206) 936-1311. Include the following information about yourself: name, complete address, company, job title, phone number, fax number, e-mail or Internet address, and product areas of interest or expertise.

Microsoft Certified Systems Engineer Core Exams

To achieve the Microsoft Certified Systems Engineer certification, a candidate must pass four required "core" exams, plus two elective exams. There are two possible paths, or tracks, that lead to an MCSE certification—the Windows NT 4.0 track and the Windows NT 3.51 track.

Microsoft Windows NT 4.0 Track to an MCSE

The Microsoft Windows NT 4.0 track to an MCSE is significantly different from the earlier Windows NT 3.51 track, although there are still four core exams. These first two exams are required:

- Implementing and Supporting Microsoft Windows NT 4.0 Server (70-67). This exam covers installing and supporting Windows NT 4.0

in a single-domain environment. Passing this exam also qualifies a candidate as an MCPS.

- Implementing and Supporting Microsoft Windows NT 4.0 Server in the Enterprise (70-68). This exam covers installing and supporting Windows NT 4.0 in an enterprise computing environment with mission-critical applications and tasks. Passing this exam does *not* qualify a candidate as an MCPS.

The third required core exam can be fulfilled by one of four different exams:

- Microsoft Windows 3.1 (70-30). Legacy support.
- Microsoft Windows for Workgroups 3.11 (70-48). Legacy support.
- Implementing and Supporting Microsoft Windows 95 (70-63). Tests a candidate's ability to implement and support Microsoft Windows NT 4.0 in a variety of environments, including as a network client on Novell NetWare. Passing this exam qualifies a candidate as an MCPS.
- Implementing and Supporting Microsoft Windows NT Workstation 4.0 (70-73). Tests a candidate's ability to implement and support Microsoft Windows NT Workstation 4.0. Passing this exam qualifies a candidate as an MCPS.

The fourth core exam can be fulfilled by one of the following:

Note This exam is waived for those candidates who also are Novell Certified NetWare Engineers (CNE) or Banyan Certified Banyan Engineers (CBE).

- Networking with Windows for Workgroups 3.11 (70-46). Legacy support.
- Networking with Windows 3.1 (70-47). Legacy support.
- Networking Essentials (70-58). Tests the candidate's networking skills that are required for implementing, administrating, and troubleshooting systems that incorporate Windows NT 4.0 and BackOffice.

Note Microsoft has retired some of the above exams, which means you won't be able to take them. However, if you've previously passed one of these exams, Microsoft counts it toward your certification, until it is withdrawn from the program. If the exam is withdrawn before you complete your certification, you will need to take a replacement course. Once you are certified, you are not affected when a course is withdrawn.

Windows NT 3.51 Track to the MCSE Certification

Most current Microsoft Certified Systems Engineers followed, or are following, this track, which will continue to be a valid track.

There are four core exams. The first two, the Windows NT 3.51 exams, are required:

- Implementing and Supporting Microsoft Windows NT Server 3.51 (70-43). This exam covers installing and supporting Windows NT Server 3.51 in a variety of environments. Passing this exam also qualifies a candidate as an MCPS.
- Implementing and Supporting Microsoft Windows NT Workstation 3.51 (70-42). This exam covers installing and supporting Windows NT Workstation 3.51. Passing this exam qualifies a candidate as an MCPS.

The third required core exam can be fulfilled by one of three different exams:

- Microsoft Windows 3.1 (70-30). Legacy support.
- Microsoft Windows for Workgroups 3.11 (70-48). Legacy support.
- Implementing and Supporting Microsoft Windows 95 (70-63). Tests a candidate's ability to implement and support Microsoft Windows 95 in a variety of environments, including as a network client on Novell NetWare. Passing this exam qualifies a candidate as an MCPS.

The fourth core exam can be fulfilled by one of the following:

Note This exam is waived for those candidates who also are Novell Certified NetWare Engineers (CNE) or Banyan Certified Banyan Engineers (CBE).

- Networking with Windows for Workgroups 3.11 (70-46). Legacy support.
- Networking with Windows 3.1 (70-47). Legacy support.
- Networking Essentials (70-58). Tests the candidate's networking skills required for implementing, administrating, and troubleshooting systems that incorporate Windows NT 4.0 and BackOffice.

Electives for the Microsoft Certified Systems Engineers

Besides the core exam requirements, you must pass two elective exams to complete a Microsoft Certified Systems Engineer certification. The list of electives in Table 1.1 was current as of March, 1996.

Table 1.1 Microsoft Certified Systems Engineer Electives

Exam	Number
Microsoft SNA Server	70-12
Implementing and Supporting Microsoft Systems Management Server 1.0	70-14
System Administration of Microsoft SQL Server 6.0	70-26
Implementing a Database Design on Microsoft SQL Server 6.0	70-27
Microsoft Mail for PC Networks—Enterprise	70-37
Internetworking Microsoft TCP/IP on Microsoft Windows NT 3.5	70-53

Continuing Certification Requirements

After you gain an MCP certification, such as the Microsoft Certified Systems Engineer certification, your work isn't over. Microsoft requires that you maintain your certification by updating your exam credits as new products are released, and old ones are withdrawn.

A Microsoft Certified Trainer is required to pass the exam for a new product within three months of the exam's release. For example, the Windows 95 exam (70-63) was released on October 9, 1995. All MCTs were required to pass exam 70-63 by January 9, 1996 or lose certification to teach the course.

Holders of the other MCP certifications (MCPS, MCSD, MCSE) are required to replace an exam that gives them qualifying credit within six months of the withdrawal of that exam. For example, the Windows for Workgroups 3.10 exam was one of the original electives for the MCSE certification. When it was withdrawn, MCSEs had six months to replace it with another elective exam, such as the TCP/IP exam.

From Here...

This chapter discussed the Microsoft certification program. You should make sure to check out Microsoft's Web site (**www.microsoft.com**) for any changes before beginning your studies.

The next chapter, "Understanding Windows NT Server 4.0," is designed to help you become familiar with the new interface and explore how to modify the configuration.

Chapter Prerequisite

The reader should already be familiar with the basic operation of either Windows 3.x or Windows 95. While a brief overview of the new Windows NT 4.0 user interface is provided in this book, it is essential that the reader have a strong working knowledge of basic networking concepts and terms.

2

Understanding Microsoft Windows NT 4.0

Before beginning a detailed discussion of Microsoft Windows NT 4.0 Server, an overview of the NT product line is provided for a clearer understanding of what is included in the product line and how it can be used within an organization. This chapter then covers the features and functionality of Microsoft Windows NT 4.0 Server.

Topics that are discussed in this chapter include:

- A list of features and functionality common to the NT product line, past and present, and an in-depth exploration of certain specific characteristics.
- An explanation of when a Windows NT Server installation is appropriate, given the needs of the clients involved, the level of administration desired, and the level of security required.

- An introduction to the basic architecture of the NT operating system and an explanation of the features and functions that are new to version 4.0.
- A comparison of Microsoft's workgroup model with its enterprise model of network communication.

Exploring Windows NT 4.0's New Features

Microsoft Windows NT is a 32-bit operating system that is designed to provide fast and efficient performance for power computer users, such as software developers, CAD programmers, and design engineers. Figure 2.1 displays a glimpse of the features common to both Windows NT Workstation and Windows NT Server (versions 3.51 and 4.0, respectively). Because it provides better performance for existing 16-bit applications (both MS-DOS and Windows), as well as 32-bit applications developed specifically for the operating system, NT is increasingly found on the desks of business users. These performance enhancements include:

- Multiple platform support
- Preemptive multitasking
- Expanded processing support
- Expanded memory support
- Expanded file system support
- Enhanced security
- Network and communications support

FIG. 2.1⇒ These features are common to both Windows NT Workstation and Windows NT Server.

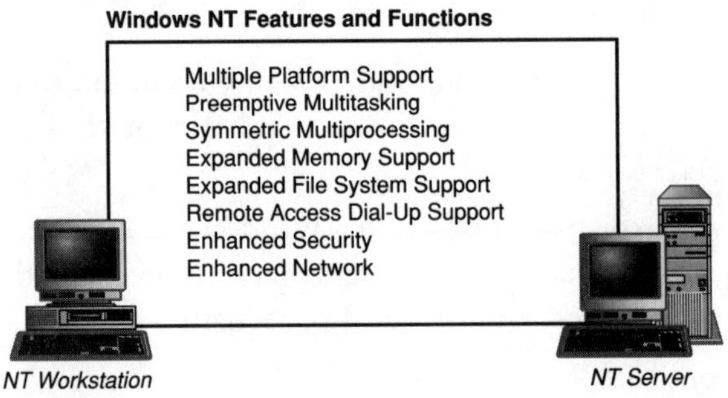

Multiple Platform Support

Microsoft Windows NT is engineered to run on several hardware platforms. The *Hardware Abstraction Layer,* or HAL, component of the NT architecture isolates platform-specific information for the operating system; for example, how to interact with a RISC-based processor as opposed to an Intel x86 processor. This architecture makes NT a highly portable system. Only a few pieces of code, such as the HAL, need to be recompiled. NT supports Intel x86 and Pentium-based computers, as well as RISC-based computers, such as MIPS R4000, DEC Alpha AXP, and PowerPC. Future support will be limited to Intel and Alpha machines.

Preemptive Multitasking

All processes in NT are given at least one thread of operation. A thread represents a piece of code relating to a process. For example, loading a file may require several "threads" to carry out the process; in other words, locating the file on disk, allocating RAM for the file, moving it into that allocated memory space, and so forth. Many processes and applications written for Windows and NT have multiple threads associated with them.

NT can treat each thread of a process independently of the others, providing a greater degree of control over the overall performance of the system. Each thread also is given a processing priority based on its function. For example, an operating system process, such as memory allocation, receives a higher priority for its threads than a file-save process.

Each thread is given a specific amount of time with the processor. This sometimes is called *time-slicing*. Higher priority threads are processed ahead of lower priority threads. All the threads of one priority are processed first before those of the next priority, and so on. This process is called *preemptive multitasking*. In addition, certain threads, primarily those that are system related, are processed in the protected mode of the processor (known as ring 0) and, thus, are protected from other processes and crashes.

Other threads, those relating to application functions such as file printing, run in the unprotected mode of the processor. This means that, while they may be given their own memory space, other "poorly written" applications (and their threads) might try to "butt in" and cause what is generally referred to as a *General Protection* or GP fault. Microsoft has taken several precautions to ensure that this does not happen in NT. These threads, and the precautions Microsoft has installed in NT, are discussed in more detail later in this book. Supporting both multitasking and multithreading gives applications excellent processing support and protection against system hangups and crashes.

Expanded Processing Support

Microsoft Windows NT provides *symmetric multiprocessing* with support for OEM implementations of up to 32 processors. Every process that runs under NT has at least one thread of operation or programming code associated with it. A process might be either user-generated, such as the writing of a file to disk or printing a document, or system-generated, such as validating a user logon or providing read access to a file.

Symmetric multiprocessing enables the NT operating system to load balance process threads across all available processors in the computer, as opposed to *asymmetric multiprocessing*, in which the operating system takes control of one processor and directs application threads to other available processors.

Expanded Memory Support

Windows NT supports computers with up to 4 gigabytes of RAM and theoretic file or partition sizes of up to 16 exabytes (though this number will vary depending on the type of hardware you have). An exabyte is one billion gigabytes. You might consider that to be a theoretical number, and to a certain extent it is. However, it was not that long ago that MIS departments debated the wisdom of purchasing 10-megabyte disk drives for their users' computers because they felt that the drives would never be filled up.

Expanded File System Support

Windows NT provides support for the MS-DOS FAT (*File Allocation Table*) file system, as well as its own NTFS (*New Technology File System*). Previous versions of NT also supported OS/2's HPFS (*High Performance File System*).

Key Concept

Version 4.0 no longer provides support for HPFS.

NTFS provides a high level of security in the form of file- and directory-level permissions similar to those found in other network operating systems, such as trustee rights that are used in Novell's NetWare. NTFS also provides transaction tracking to help recover data in the event of system failure, and sector sparing, which identifies potentially bad disk storage space and moves data to good storage. NTFS also provides data compression implemented as a file or directory property. For more information on NTFS, see Chapter 9, "Managing Disk Resources."

Enhanced Security

Security begins with NT's WINLOGON and NETLOGON processes, which authenticate a user's access to a computer, workgroup, or enterprise by validating their username and password, and assigning each with their own security identifier. In addition to this mandatory logon, NT offers share-level resource control, security auditing functions, and file- and directory-level permissions (in NTFS partitions).

Network and Communications Support

Windows NT is designed to provide several internetworking options. The NetBEUI, NWLINK (IPX/SPX), TCP/IP, AppleTalk, and DLC protocols are all supported and included. NT is also supported on Novell NetWare networks, Microsoft LAN Manager, IBM LAN Server and SNA networks, Banyan VINES, and DEC PATHWORKS.

Through *Remote Access Service* (RAS), NT offers a secure dial-up option for clients and servers. RAS clients can remotely access any shared network resource to which they have been given access through RAS' gateway functions, such as shared folders and printers.

In an NT network, valid workstation clients include Microsoft Windows NT Workstations and Servers, Windows 3.x, MS-DOS, Windows for Workgroups, Windows 95, OS/2, Novell NetWare (client/server), and Macintosh.

Choosing Windows NT Workstation or Server

The difference in choosing when to use NT Workstation or NT Server is not necessarily the difference between desktop and enterprise computing. Both NT Workstation and NT Server provide the capability to make resources available on the network and thus act as a "server." For that matter, an NT Server can be made part of a workgroup of NT Workstations to act as the resource server for that workgroup. Choosing between NT Workstation and NT Server really comes down to the features specific to each product and the type of network model that will be implemented. The following sections discuss the differences between NT Workstation and NT Server.

Microsoft Windows NT Workstation

Microsoft Windows NT Workstation is designed for the so-called *power user*, such as developers or CAD designers, but increasingly is becoming the desktop operating system of choice for end-user business computing because of its robust feature set, as described in the last section. In addition to those features and functions that are common to both NT Workstation and NT Server, NT Workstation offers the following specific characteristics (see Figure 2.2):

- Unlimited outbound peer-to-peer connections.
- Ten inbound client connections for resource access.
- It can be either a RAS client or server, but supports only one remote dial-in session.
- Retail installation supports two processors for symmetric multiprocessing.
- Acts as an import server for Directory Replication Services.

Microsoft Windows NT Server

Windows NT Server is designed to provide file, print, and application service support within a given network model. Figure 2.3 illustrates specific characteristics of NT Server. While it also can be used as a desktop system, it is engineered to provide optimum performance when providing network services; for example, by optimizing memory differently for application servers than it does for domain controllers. In addition to the features and functions described previously, NT Server offers the following capabilities:

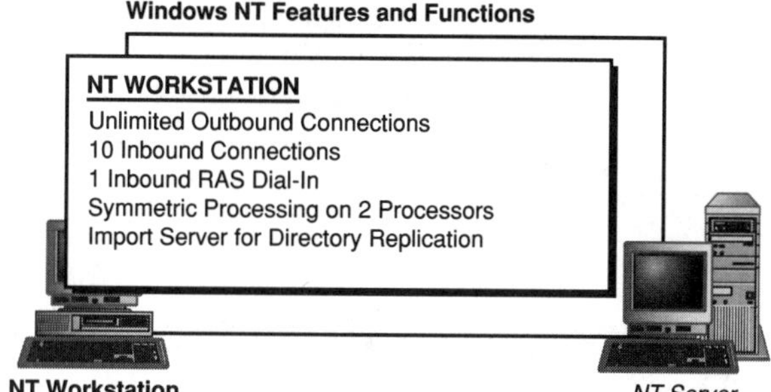

FIG. 2.2⇒ Windows NT Workstation features and functions.

- Allows as many inbound connections to resources as there are valid client licenses (virtually unlimited).
- Support for as many as 256 remote dial-in RAS sessions.
- Retail installation supports as many as four processors for symmetric multiprocessing.
- Provides a full set of services for application and network support, such as:
    - Services for Macintosh that enable client support for Macintosh computers.
    - Gateway Service for NetWare that enables NT clients to access Novell NetWare file and print resources.
    - Directory Replication Service for copying of directory structures and files from a source NT Server computer to a target NT Server or Workstation computer.
- Provides full integration into the Microsoft BackOffice suite, including System Management Server, SNA Server, SQL Server, and Microsoft Exchange Server.

The Microsoft Windows NT Server product can be installed as either a server that provides only network-accessible resources or as a domain controller that additionally provides centralized administration of user accounts and resource access. These concepts are reviewed later in this chapter.

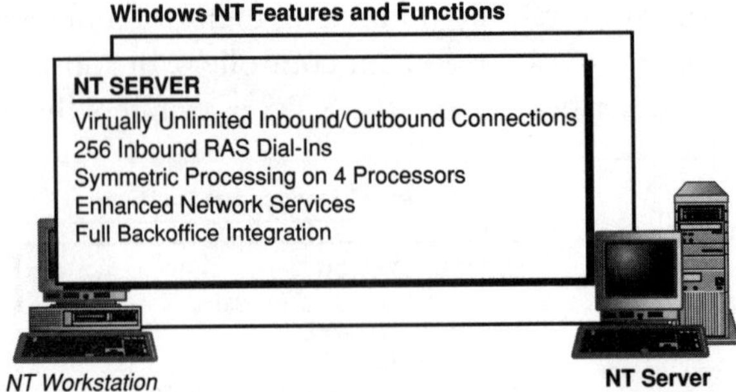

Windows NT Features and Functions
NT SERVER
Virtually Unlimited Inbound/Outbound Connections
256 Inbound RAS Dial-Ins
Symmetric Processing on 4 Processors
Enhanced Network Services
Full Backoffice Integration
NT Workstation
NT Server

FIG. 2.3⇒ Windows NT Server features and functions.

New Features and Functions in Windows NT 4.0

This newest version of Windows NT continues Microsoft's commitment to reliable, performance-driven, network-ready operating systems by incorporating the power, features, and functions of the NT operating system with the object-oriented Windows 95 user interface. Enhanced features and functions common to both NT 4.0 Workstation and Server include:

- Windows 95-like user interface
- Windows Explorer
- Hardware profiles
- Enhanced dial-up networking support
- NDS-aware client services for Novell NetWare 4.x
- Integrated Windows Messaging engine
- Internet Explorer 2.0
- Web services

Windows 95 User Interface

All the basic features of Microsoft's Windows 95 interface have been integrated into Windows NT 4.0. This includes updated or enhanced system utilities, such as the Performance Monitor (called the System Monitor in Windows 95), as well as additional utilities, such as the Windows Explorer, Network Neighborhood, Briefcase, Desktop shortcuts, Microsoft Network support, and the Recycle Bin.

Windows Explorer

This feature of the interface replaces the File Manager utility. It provides excellent browsing capabilities for management of drives, directories, files, and network connections. The Explorer presents the user's data-access information as a hierarchy of drives, desktop, network connections, folders, and files. The browsing capabilities of the Explorer offer not only browsing of file and directory names, but also of data strings within files. Throughout this book and its labs, you will use Windows Explorer to access files and folders, set permissions, create and manage shared folders, and so on.

Note Though Windows Explorer replaces the File Manager Utility by default, File Manager is still available and can be launched by the user.

File Manager can be run by following these simple steps:

1. Choose Start from the Task Bar.
2. Choose Run from the Start menu.
3. Enter in the File Manager file name: winfile.exe
4. Press OK.

Microsoft recommends using File Manager only until you become comfortable with Windows Explorer. File Manager is still made available only for transitional purposes.

Hardware Profiles

Perhaps one of the most useful enhancements to Windows NT 4.0 is the support for multiple hardware profiles. First introduced in Windows 95, this feature enables you to create hardware profiles to fit various computing needs. The most common example of using hardware profiles is with portable computers. You can create separate profiles to support the portable computer when it is in use by itself, and for when it is positioned in a docking station.

Note Plug and Play is a feature of Windows 95 that is much appreciated. Note that, while the Plug and Play service has been included with Windows NT 4.0, "hot" plug and play (the capability for the operating system to recognize a configuration change on-the-fly and implement it) will not be fully supported until the next major release of Windows NT. Windows NT 4.0 does, however, recognize some hardware changes when it restarts. For example, additional memory or a new hard disk will be automatically detected by NT the next time you boot up.

Enhanced Dial-Up Networking Support

The RAS Client service now is installed as Dial-Up Networking. In addition, NT 4.0 provides the Dial-Up Networking Monitor for monitoring user connections and devices, as well as Remote Access Admin for monitoring remote user access to a RAS Server.

NT 4.0 also offers Telephony API version 2.0 (TAPI) and universal modem driver (Unimodem) support, which provides communications technology for FAX applications, the Microsoft Exchange client, the Microsoft Network (MSN), and Internet Explorer.

API provides access to the signaling for setting up calls and managing them, as well as preserving existing media stream functionality to manipulate the information carried over the connection that TAPI establishes. This allows applications to not only dial and transfer calls, but also to support fax, desktop conferencing, or applications that use the telephone set dial pad to access voice-prompted menus.

NDS-Aware Client Service for Novell NetWare 4.x

Microsoft provides an enhanced version of its Client Services for NetWare (CSNW) with NT 4.0, which supplies compatibility with Novell NetWare servers (versions 3.x and later) running NetWare Directory Services (NDS). This enables users to view NetWare-shared resources that are organized in a hierarchical tree format.

Integrated Microsoft Windows Messaging

Microsoft Windows Messaging is Microsoft's newest electronic mail product. Windows Messaging has been included with NT 4.0, which enables users to send and receive mail, embed objects in mail messages, and integrate mail functionality into Microsoft applications.

Internet Explorer 2.0

Microsoft's Internet Explorer 2.0 is included with NT 4.0 to provide users access to the Internet. However, Microsoft now has Internet Explorer 4.0 available through its various Internet sites (**www.microsoft.com**, for example). Watch for Microsoft to continue to enhance this product and make upgrades widely (and cheaply) available.

Internet Explorer requires that the TCP/IP protocol be installed and a connection made to the Internet.

Web Publishing

Microsoft includes Web publishing services in NT 4.0 that enable you to develop, publish, and manage Web pages, as well as FTP and Gopher services for your company's intranet or for smaller peer-to-peer networks. With NT 4.0 Server, Microsoft provides Internet Information Services (IIS) designed for heavy intranet and Internet usage. With NT 4.0 Workstation, Microsoft provides Peer Web Services (PWS) for smaller workgroup-based Web publishing.

Integrated Network Monitor Agent

NT 4.0 includes a version of the Network Monitor utility, which is included with Microsoft's System Management Server BackOffice product. Network Monitor provides a full range of network-analysis tools for tracking and interpreting network traffic, frames, and so forth.

Last but Certainly Not Least

Of all the features contained in NT 4.0, there is one from which you will obtain the most productivity. It also is an example of enhancements made to NT's Open GL and direct-draw video support. This is, of course, PINBALL! Yes, there is a new game added to NT 4.0 and it is quite an addition. As mentioned, it does take full advantage of changes to NT's architecture and enhancements for video support. Try it out!

Note Pinball is installed in the Games folder, which can be found by choosing Start, Programs, Accessories, Games. If you have not installed your games, you can use the Add/Remove Programs applet in Control Panel to add them. In the applet, choose the Windows Setup tab, highlight Accessories, choose Details, and select Games. Choose OK. Be sure to have your source files or CD handy because NT will prompt you for them.

In addition to these features that NT 4.0 Workstation and Server share, Windows NT 4.0 Server offers the following list of specific features and functions:

- Microsoft Internet Information Server
- DNS Name Server and enhanced support
- Integrated Support for Multiprotocol Routing
- Enhanced support for BOOTP and DHCP Routing
- Remote Reboot Support for Windows 95 clients
- New remote server administration tools for Windows 95 clients
- Installation Wizards for most utility program installations

Distinguishing a Workgroup from a Domain

There are two distinct types of networking supported by Windows NT: workgroup computing and the domain model. As you plan your network, you need to distinguish between these two and decide which model best meets your networking needs. The next section compares these two models.

Workgroup Model

The workgroup model of networking is more commonly referred to as the *peer-to-peer* model. In this model, all computers participate in a networking group. They all can make resources available to members of the workgroup, and can access one another's resources. In other words, each computer acts as both a workstation and a server.

Computers using Windows NT, Windows 95, and Windows for Workgroups have the capability to participate in a workgroup network model, as shown in Figure 2.4. In fact, both Windows NT Workstations and Windows NT Servers can be members of a workgroup. However, only Windows NT Server offers the added capability of providing user-level security for network resources.

Note Windows 95 can provide user-level network resource security by using an NT (Server or Workstation) or Novell Server. However, this requires that one or the other be present on the network.

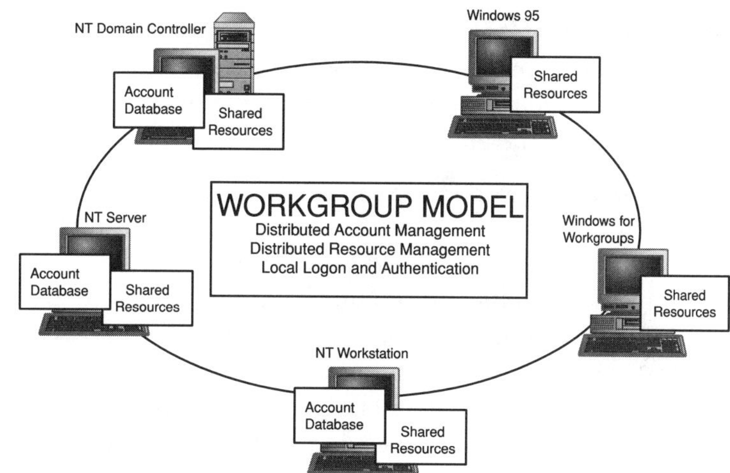

FIG. 2.4⇒ An example of the workgroup network model.

Ch 2

On computers using Windows NT, access to resources is provided by authenticating the inbound user at the resource computer. Each Windows NT computer participating in a workgroup must maintain a list of users that will be accessing the resources on that computer.

Potentially, this means that each computer will have at least as many user accounts as there are participating members in the workgroup. Account administration in a workgroup thus is considered to be distributed, as is resource administration. In other words, the responsibility for maintaining the integrity of user accounts and resource access generally falls to the owner of the computer. A workgroup model, then, might be construed to have limited security potential.

The workgroup model works quite well within smaller networks where the number of users requiring access to workgroup resources is small and easily managed. This number has been suggested to be between 10 and 20 computers/users. As mentioned before, a Windows NT Server can participate in a workgroup. If a larger number of computers or users is required within a workgroup model (more than 20), the more heavily used resources might be located in a Windows NT Server participating in the workgroup. This can help simplify the management of large groups of users accessing resources. Nevertheless, the main characteristics of this network model are distributed account management, distributed resource management, and limited security.

Domain Model

The domain model of networking, also known as the *enterprise* model, was introduced by Microsoft as a response to the management challenges presented by the growing workgroup model.

Unlike the workgroup model, the domain model (see Figure 2.5) maintains a centralized database of user and group account information. Resource access is provided by permitting access to users and groups that are members of the domain, and thus appear in the domain's account database. Recall that in the workgroup model, each computer maintains its own account database, which is used for managing resource access at that computer. In the domain model, by virtue of their participation in the domain, the resources utilize the same central account database for managing user access. Resource managers also enjoy a higher level of security for their resources.

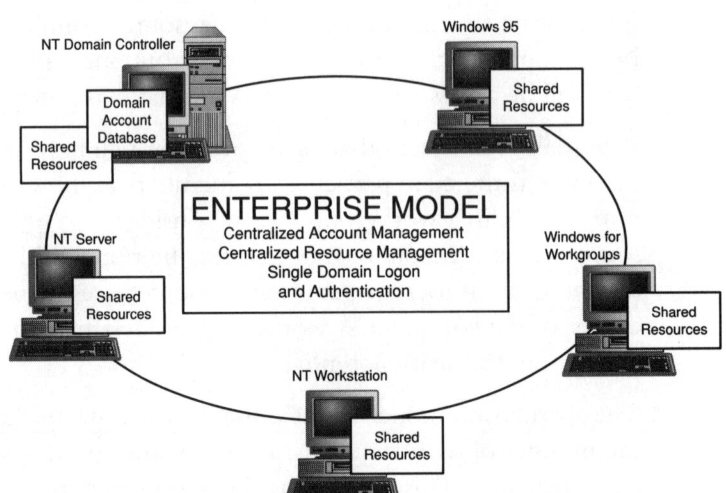

FIG. 2.5⇒ An example of the domain network model. The domain model answers what Microsoft refers to as the "enterprise challenge."

Organizing an Enterprise Network

When planning a large wide area network for an organization—hereafter referred to as the *enterprise*—Microsoft advocates implementing a structure that answers the following challenges:

- A single network logon account for the user, regardless of the user's location or domain affiliation
- Centralized account administration
- Easy user access to network resources, regardless of the location of the user or the resource in the enterprise
- Focusing network resource administration in the hands of the resource owner or administrator
- Synchronization of account and security information across the enterprise

The structure should be capable of supporting enterprise networks of varying size, with servers, computers, and users in a variety of geographic locations. It also should support, and in some cases utilize, a variety of network architectures, protocols, and platforms to provide a completely flexible and open architecture.

Microsoft responds to this challenge with its Directory Services solution. Windows NT's Directory Services provides a domain model of enterprise computing that centralizes account information and management into a single domain account database, while focusing network resource management with the owner/administrator of the resource.

A *domain* can be thought of as a logical grouping of computers in a Microsoft network. A *domain controller* establishes the domain's identity and is used to maintain the database of user, group, and computer accounts for that domain. Besides the domain controller, a Windows NT domain can include member servers and workstation computers. A member server might be a Windows NT 4.0 Server configured as an application server, a database server, a RAS server, a print server, or a file server. Workstation computers might run Windows NT Workstation 4.0, Windows 95, Windows for Workgroups 3.11, MS-DOS, Apple Macintosh System 7, or LanMan 2.2c for DOS or OS/2.

All of the computers that identify themselves as belonging to a particular domain are part of the same logical grouping. As such, they have access to the account database on the domain's domain controller for authenticating users as they log on, and for creating access control lists (ACLs) for securing network resources stored on those computers. An enterprise may consist of one domain, or several domains, following one of the domain models suggested by Microsoft. See the section, "Domain Models," later in this chapter, for more information regarding these models.

For example, a domain might be centered around the organizational hierarchy and reflect its departmental structure. Perhaps the MIS department has assumed all responsibility for maintaining user and group accounts, while placing resource management within each department. Possibly, the enterprise is organized according to regional areas, such as the West, Midwest, and East domains. The domain structure might even be global in nature, reflecting the enterprise's international presence. Windows NT's Directory Services provides a fit for each of these structures because Windows NT domains are logical groupings of computers; therefore, they are extremely flexible. While the physical layout of your network may affect the type of domain model that you choose to establish, domains simply don't care what the network topology looks like.

Single Network Logon

The concept of a single network logon is really quite simple: Provide the user with a single logon account that can be used to access the network from anywhere within the enterprise. An account executive based in Chicago should be able to fly to her company's office in London, use her same account to log on to the network at any computer in the London office, and access the same resources she has access to when in Chicago.

Windows NT 4.0 Directory Services is designed to provide just that capability by combining the domain model of networking with a security relationship called a *trust*. Briefly, a trust relationship enables users from one Windows NT domain to be granted access permissions to the network resources in a second Windows NT domain.

Assume that a trust exists between the London and Chicago domains. If the account executive's account is maintained in the Chicago domain, she can still log on to the company network at any computer in the London domain. Directory Services enables the account executive's log-on request to be passed through the trust, back to the Chicago domain for authentication (see Figure 2.6). This process of passing the logon request back through the trust to the account domain is called *pass-through authentication*. After her account has been validated, she can access any resource in the enterprise to which she has been given permission. Note that she needs only one logon account and password to access the network and its resources. Her physical location is not important, nor is the location of the resources.

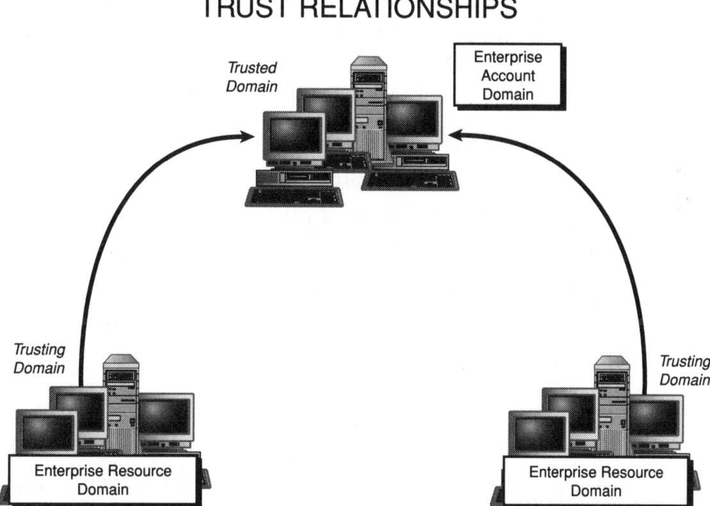

FIG. 2.6⇒ UserX's logon information is passed through the trust relationship to be authenticated in the appropriate domain, as depicted here.

Centralized Account Administration

Recall that in a workgroup model, account administration tends to be decentralized to the desktop of each member of the workgroup. Each user might maintain their own workstation's account database, making it difficult to establish or maintain consistency or security.

By contrast, in a domain model accounts are centralized on a specific domain server called the *domain controller*. The domain controller for the domain establishes the domain's identity in the enterprise. In fact, a domain is established by the installation of a *primary domain controller* (PDC). The PDC maintains the master account database for the domain. The PDC can also authenticate users on the network (or log on users), but its primary function is to maintain the domain's account database.

While a domain can contain only one primary domain controller for managing accounts and authenticating users, the domain can include one or more *backup domain controllers*, or BDCs. The BDC receives a *copy* of the master account database maintained on the PDC. Its primary function is to authenticate users who are trying to log on to the network.

Windows NT 4.0 includes two utilities that can be used to manage user, group, and Windows NT computer accounts: User Manager for Domains and Server Manager.

▶ **See** Chapter 5, "Managing Users and Groups," and Chapter 8, "Remote Server Management," for in-depth discussions of the User Manager for Domains and Server Manager, respectively.

Briefly, User Manager for Domains enables an administrator to manage the account database from any computer in the enterprise that supports the utility. This includes, of course, any Windows NT Workstation or Server, but also can be a Windows 95 or Windows for Workgroups 3.11 computer by using available add-on server-management tools. Remote server-management tools are discussed in Chapter 8, "Remote Server Management."

Similarly, Server Manager enables the administrator to use directory services to remotely view and administer domains, workgroups, and computers. For example, administrators can use Server Manager on their Windows NT 4.0 workstation desktops to start and stop services on a Windows NT 4.0 Server, or to synchronize account databases among domain controllers in a domain.

Network Resource Access

Through a combination of single logon accounts, centralized administration, and trust relationships, a user can easily access any resource that they have been given permission to use, from anywhere in the enterprise. For example, return to the account executive in Chicago.

The account executive has an account in the Chicago domain that she uses to log on to the company's network. She regularly accesses a SQL database of client information that is located on a member server in the Chicago domain, and to which she has been given access permission. She frequently visits the company's London office, which has its own domain and its own SQL database. There is also a trust relationship between the Chicago and London domains.

As previously discussed, when she sits down at a computer in the London domain, she can still log on to the network by using her same logon account and password, just as if she were sitting at her computer in Chicago. Also, because of the trust relationship and pass-through authentication, she can still access the SQL database on the member server in the Chicago domain (see Figure 2.7). The entire access process is transparent to her—as it should be for every user in the enterprise.

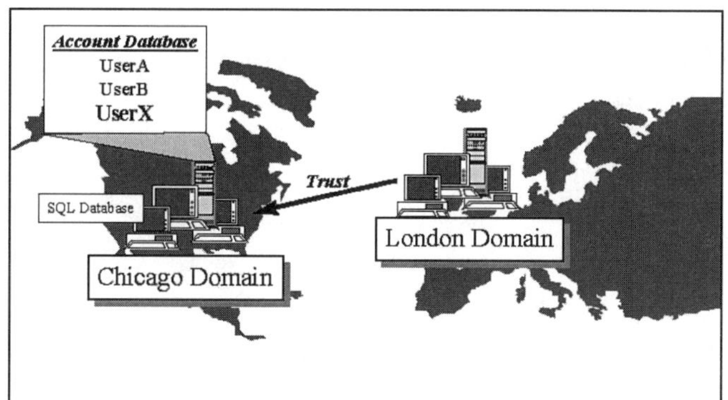

FIG. 2.7⇒ When UserX logs on, whether in Chicago or in London, she has access to any resources to which her account has been given permission, such as the SQL database.

This concept can be taken a step further by giving resources their own domain. This means that, in most organizations, each department, unit, project team, and so on, usually has its own set of resources that they want to manage. Human Resources manages the company's Employee Handbook in Lotus Notes and maintains a SQL database of employee performance reviews, résumés, and other confidential information. Finance manages the company's budget spreadsheets, including the investment options for the retirement fund.

Each department wants to securely manage their own resources, ensuring that only authorized persons have access and that the level of access is controlled. But, they do not want to deal with day-to-day account management, such as forgotten passwords, locked out accounts, new users, users changing group memberships, and so on. In a large organization, the number of resources and resource managers may make a single large domain impractical.

In this particular scenario, each department could be given its own domain for the purpose of managing their own resources, as shown in Figure 2.8. Account management would still be maintained in the account domain. By establishing trust relationships between each resource domain and the account domain, the resource managers can use the account domain's account database to create access control lists for each of their resources. Users can still log on to the network with the same single logon account and password, and access any resource to which they are given access permission. Everyone utilizes the same account database, yet account and resource management is centralized where it should be—with the appropriate account and resource managers. This is called a *master domain* model. Trusts are covered in detail in Chapter 15, "Windows NT 4.0 Trusts."

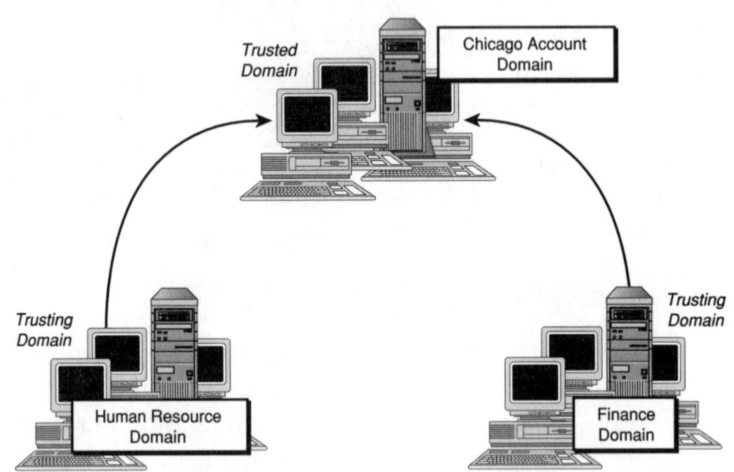

FIG. 2.8⇒
The trust relationship between each resource domain and the account domain enables resource managers to use one central account database to secure access to their resources.

Once again, Windows NT Directory Services provides a flexible set of options for resource management that can fit the needs of most enterprise models.

Synchronization of Account and Security Information

As previously pointed out, a domain is established by the installation of a primary domain controller (PDC). As with all security objects in Windows NT, such as user and group accounts, trust relationships, and computer accounts, the creation of a PDC establishes a security identifier (SID) for the domain that is used for any security-related function, such as establishing trust relationships, implementing backup domain controllers, and effecting account synchronization.

Creating a domain controller is an implementation of Windows NT Server 4.0. Besides establishing the existence of the domain, the primary role of the PDC is to maintain the account database for the domain, hereafter called the *master account database*. If the PDC is the only domain controller created for the domain, it will also serve as the validation server to authenticate users' requests to log on to the network.

In most networks, however, in addition to the PDC, one or more backup domain controllers (BDCs) are created for the domain. The primary role of the BDC is to authenticate users' logon requests. To do so, it must receive a copy of the master account database from the PDC for that domain. In fact, when the BDC is created, you must tell it to join a specific domain as a backup domain controller. A security relationship is established between the PDC and the BDC, and they share the same account database. The relationship between these domain controllers is so integral that any local group created on the PDC is considered local to *all* the domain controllers for the domain.

Key Concept

Any change that is made to the account database for the domain affects only the master copy maintained by the PDC. Changes are never directly registered on a BDC. BDCs receive only the copies of the changes made to the master account database, according to a regular schedule.

If you are using User Manager for Domains on your London desk's Windows NT 4.0 Workstation, and the PDC for the domain you are administering is located in Chicago (accessible through a dedicated line), your change requests will be sent through the connection to the PDC in Chicago, even though you may have one or more BDCs located locally in London.

This is easy to test. Shut down your PDC temporarily. Then try to use User Manager for Domains to add a new user account. User Manager for Domains will display a blank screen. It can't open the master account database because the PDC is not currently active. However, as long as there is a BDC available on the network, the users will continue to be able to log on successfully and access any resource they have permission to access, provided the resource is not on the PDC that is down.

Caution
If you try this test, be sure that you restart your PDC!

As stated earlier, the BDC receives a copy of the master account database and any changes made to it, according to a regular schedule. On a regular interval, every five minutes by default, the PDC checks the master account database for changes. When it detects a change, it sends a notification to the BDCs in the domain. This notification interval is called a *pulse* and can be modified in the PDC's Registry. More about setting this and other Registry values related to synchronization are found in Chapter 4, "Configuring Windows NT Server 4.0."

When the BDC receives a pulse from the PDC, it copies the changes from the PDC. In networking terms, this is called a *pull* operation because the BDC copies the changes instead of having the PDC send them. Until the BDC receives the changes, however, its copy of the master account database still contains "old" information.

Consider the following scenario. The administrator in London has added three new user accounts for three new employees that have joined the London office. The administrator uses User Manager for Domains to add the accounts, and these changes, as you already know, are registered in the master account database on the PDC in Chicago. You also know that, by default, it will take up to five minutes for the PDC to note the change and "pulse" the BDCs, including the BDC in London. Add the additional time it takes for the BDC to copy the changes. Depending on the amount of other network traffic, the BDC may not get the changes immediately. In fact, if the new employees are particularly motivated to get on to the network to start working, and they try to log on before the changes reach the BDC in London, they won't be able to log on because the BDC will still have the old information, which doesn't include the new employees.

The Server Manager utility includes two functions related to the synchronization process. Briefly, the administrator can force a synchronization to take place at any point in time between the PDC and any specific BDC, or between the PDC and all the BDCs. If the PDC is down, access to the master account database is unavailable and synchronization cannot take place. The administrator in London can use Server Manager to have the London BDC synchronize with the Chicago PDC as soon as the new user accounts are created. Then, the new employees can log on as soon as they want.

A domain may have no BDCs or several BDCs. The number and location of these BDCs likely will be determined by the number and location of the users in the enterprise, as well as by network performance and traffic concerns. For example, if the domain consists of 1,000 users who are all located in the same building, with little or no routing taking place, then the domain might consist of the PDC and perhaps 1 or 2 BDCs. On the other hand, if your network consists of the same 1,000 users dispersed in 10 regional offices, connected by various WAN connections (RAS, T1, 56K, and so on), your domain might then consist of the PDC and one BDC located at each regional office. Number and placement of BDCs is more likely driven by issues of performance than by the number of users.

However you plan for your BDCs, the synchronization process ensures that the master account database maintained on the PDC is kept up-to-date on each of the BDCs, enabling your users to log on to the network from wherever they are located in the enterprise.

Types of Domain Models

There are four types of enterprise domain models:

- Single Domain Model
- Master Domain Model
- Multiple Master Domain Model
- Complete Trust Model

Single Domain Model

In the Single Domain Model, there are no trust relationships. All users and all resources are contained within one enterprise domain. Figure 2.9 illustrates a Single Domain Model.

This model is common for small businesses, or in situations where the computers do not participate in a larger WAN environment.

Master Domain Model

In this model, there is one domain that maintains the account database, and one or more domains that administer resources (see Figure 2.10). The account database contains all the users, groups, and NT computer accounts that are members of, or participate in, this domain. Resource domains generally do not contain lists of users and groups. Instead, they identify who can use their resources by obtaining the list of users and groups from the account domain through the creation of a trust relationship between the resource and account domains.

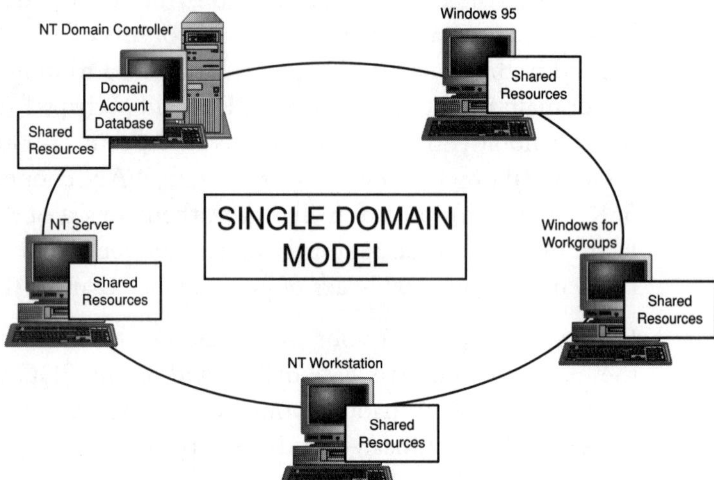

FIG. 2.9⇒
Single Domain Model.

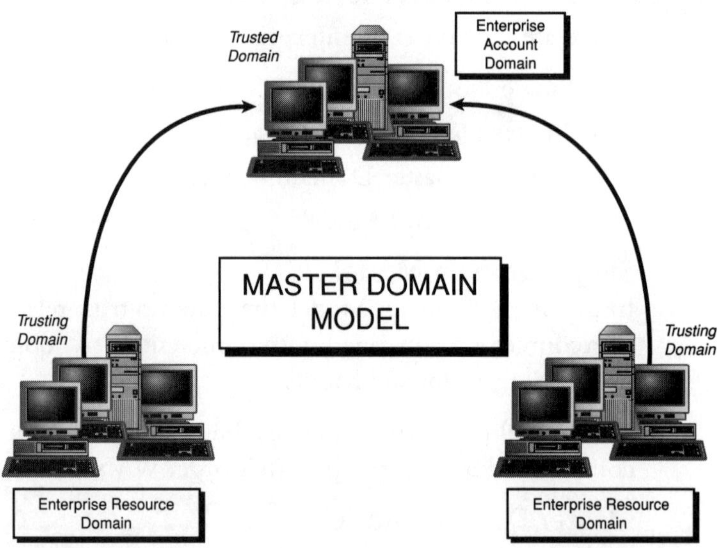

FIG. 2.10⇒
The Master Domain Model—centralized account database management.

This model is common in organizations where resources belong to various departments, and those departments maintain authority over access to their own resources. They do not need to maintain user accounts, just access to their resources. They maintain access by populating their resource access control lists with users from the account domain's database.

Multiple Master Domain Model

This model is similar to the Master Domain Model. The difference is that, in the Multiple Master Domain Model, the account database may be distributed between two or more account domains. This may be a result of the way users are distributed through a WAN (wide area network), the size of the databases, the type of server computers, and so on. Figure 2.11 illustrates a Multiple Master Domain Model with its trust relationships.

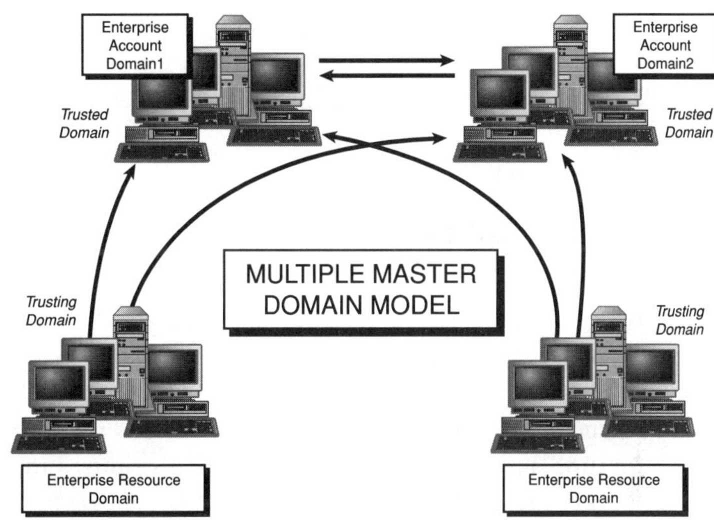

FIG. 2.11⇒ The Multiple Master Domain Model—distributed account management.

In this model, each resource domain trusts each account domain. In addition, the account domains trust each other. In this way, any resource manager can provide resource access to any account domain user.

Complete Trust Model

This model is perhaps the simplest to describe, though it provides perhaps the least amount of security. It is graphically displayed in Figure 2.12. In this model, every domain trusts every other domain, and every domain maintains a copy of its own account database. Resource administrators can provide resource access to users from any other domain. However, resource access is potentially only as secure as the "worst" administrator. This is not to say that this model has not been successfully implemented in several large organizations. It does, however, require a greater degree of control to remain secure.

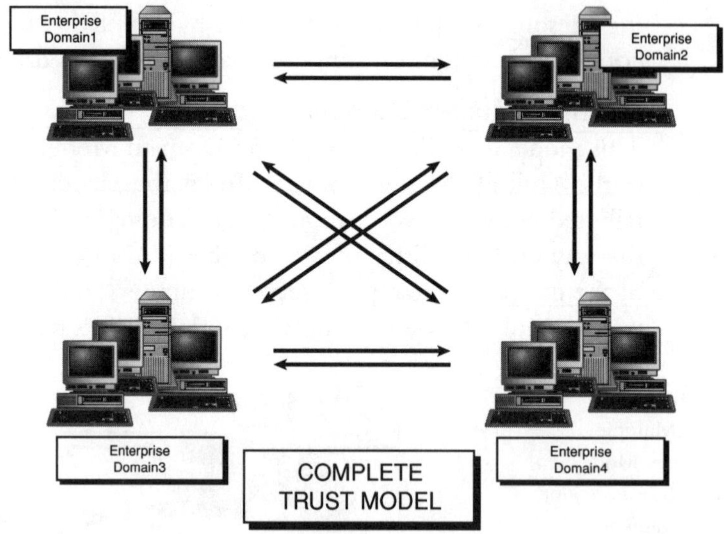

FIG. 2.12⇒
The Complete Trust Model—domain based account management.

Which Model Is Best?

Choose your networking model according to the number of users and the type, frequency, and so forth, of the resources the network will provide. Networks with relatively small numbers of users who are accessing specific resources on specific computers are easily accommodated and administered by the Workgroup Model. Recall that, in this model, both account administration and resource management are distributed to each member of the workgroup. Each computer maintains its own accounts database. As the workgroup grows, the number of users in each computer's database grows proportionately.

Networks with large numbers of users who require a single point of log-on, centralized account administration, and centralized resource management, benefit from the Enterprise model. The type of domain model that you choose for the enterprise depends on how those users and resources are distributed within your organization.

Taking the Disc Test

If you have read and understood the material in this chapter, you are ready to test your knowledge. Insert the CD-ROM that comes with this book and run the self-test software, as described in Appendix K, "Using the Self-Test Software."

From Here...

The next chapter discusses the system requirements for Windows NT 4.0 and the installation procedures.

Chapter Prerequisite

You should already be familiar with the basic workings of your computer system, particularly how to boot it, its current operating system, and the basics of BIOS, memory, hard disks, CPU types, serial and parallel ports, network adapters, video adapters, and the mouse.

3

Windows NT Server 4.0 Setup

This chapter explores the Windows NT 4.0 Server installation process. It concentrates on three primary components of the installation process: preparation, execution, and completion. The following specific topics are addressed:

- Understanding NT 4.0 Server's system requirements, as well as other data you will need to have ready to smoothly complete installation.
- Exploring the NT 4.0 Server Setup Program and Installation Wizard, including a look at the various setup options available.
- Completing the setup process and starting Windows NT 4.0 Server.
- Discuss the process of performing an unattended installation.
- Discussing some installation troubleshooting tips and techniques, including how to uninstall NT 4.0.
- Exploring how to migrate applications and settings from earlier versions of Windows to Windows NT 4.0 Server.

Preparing to Install Windows NT 4.0 Server

The installation of the Windows NT 4.0 server actually is pretty straightforward and relatively painless. However, there is some information that you need to collect ahead of time to make installation even smoother. Before you begin your installation of Windows NT 4.0, do some detective work. There basically are two questions that you need to ask yourself:

1. What is the system configuration of the computer on which I am installing NT 4.0?
2. What kind of an installation am I implementing?

System configuration includes such information as the make and model of the computer, the BIOS type and date, bus architecture, video card and monitor, network adapter, modem, memory, processor type, disk controller and drive, sound card, and so forth. System configuration also includes the current operating system, installed applications, available disk space, and so on.

Beyond choosing from amongst the Typical and Custom options, you also need to know in which kind of network model, if any, the computer will be participating, the location of the installation files, the number of blank formatted disks you need to have ready, and so on. A more exhaustive checklist will follow later in this chapter.

It sounds like a lot of detective work. But, if you think about it, you probably know the answer to most of these questions right off the top of your head. NT does an excellent job of detecting most of this information for itself. What you should be most concerned with here is discovering the nuances of a specific configuration that can throw a speed bump into the installation process. For example, if you have MS-DOS 5.0 or higher installed on your system, you might use the Microsoft Diagnostics utility to provide some of the more subtle details, such as interrupt and DMA settings. After you have installed NT server a few times within your own organization, you will begin to understand and appreciate the nuances that your particular computer and network configurations bring to the installation process.

Windows NT 4.0 Server System Requirements

Table 3.1 outlines the basic hardware requirements for a successful installation of Windows NT 4.0 Server.

Table 3.1 NT 4.0 Server Hardware Requirements

Component	Description
CPU	32-bit Intel 486/25 or higher, Intel Pentium, Pentium Pro, or supported RISC-based processors such as MIPS, Digital Alpha AXP, Power PC
Disk	118M *free* disk space required for NT System file partition (149M for RISC-based computers)
	Cluster size also is important. Microsoft recommends that a Windows NT Server with 32K clusters have at least 200M of free space
Memory	12M RAM minimum required; 32M strongly suggested (16M for RISC-based computers)
Video	Display adapter with VGA resolution or higher
Drives	CD-ROM drive and 3.5 inch disk drive if installing locally. CD-ROM required for RISC installs
Network	One or more supported adapter cards if member of a network or if installing over the network
File System	A FAT partition (recommended, but not necessary) on an Intel-based computer; a minimum 2M required FAT partition on RISC-based computers

The most important characteristic of the computer's configuration, and the one that you should pay the closest attention to, is the hardware's compatibility with the Windows NT 4.0 server. For most organizations, the compatibility of the hardware probably is not a big issue. However, if one piece of hardware is incompatible, expect your installation to have problems. In fact, if you have a hardware failure during installation, your first thought should be "incompatible hardware," probably followed by some sort of stress-reducing phraseology.

Microsoft works very closely with most major hardware manufacturers to ensure the compatibility of its products with Windows NT. To this end, Microsoft regularly publishes and updates a Hardware Compatibility List (HCL). If you have any doubt at all about the compatibility of the hardware, consult this list. Pay particularly close attention to network adapters, SCSI adapters and drives, especially CD-ROM drives, video drivers, and sound and game cards. For example, video-driver support has changed significantly with NT 4.0, rendering earlier version drivers inoperative. Also, do not take for granted that, just because your computer model is BrandName TurboX and it appears on the HCL, that all the internal components (especially those just mentioned) are also supported. It is reasonable to assume that all internal components *are* supported. However, if your installation fails due to a hardware problem, check the failed component against the HCL as your first troubleshooting step.

Note There are several ways of accessing the HCL. If you subscribe to Microsoft TechNet, or the Microsoft Developers Network, you will find a copy of the HCL there by searching for **Hardware Compatibility List**. You also can find the most up-to-date versions by accessing Microsoft's World Wide Web site at: **http://www.microsoft.com/ntserver/hcl/hclintro.htm** or Microsoft's FTP server at **ftp://microsoft.com/bussys/winnt/winnt_docs/hcl** ■

The second most important consideration is third-party devices and drivers. Once again, Microsoft provides a tremendous list of support drivers for most major third-party products. Even though Microsoft provides most of the drivers you need, if there is any doubt, be sure to have an NT-compatible driver available just in case. You generally can obtain these relatively easy from the device manufacturer.

Tip

If you are installing the Windows NT 4.0 Server as part of a major roll-out within your organization, you should consider performing a test installation on sample computer configurations from within your organization. At the very least, perform test installations on those computers that can be identified as "iffy" in regard to their compatibility.

Choosing a Server Role

There are three server roles, from which you must choose one before installing NT Server. The three possibilities are:

- **Primary Domain Controller (PDC)** Contains the master copy of the directory database (which contains information on user accounts) for the domain. There can be only one primary domain controller per domain, and the primary domain controller must be the first machine installed.
- **Backup Domain Controller (BDC)** Helps the primary domain controller. The primary domain controller copies the directory database to the backup controller(s). The BDC can authenticate users just as the PDC can. If the PDC fails, the BDC is promoted to a PDC. However, if a BDC is promoted, any changes made to the directory database since the last time it was copied from the old PDC are lost. A domain can have more than one BDC.
- **Member or Standalone Server** A standalone server is a Windows NT Server machine that doesn't participate in the system of domain controllers of the domain. A standalone server can provide all Windows NT Server functions (file service, print service, Internet service, or whatever) but it doesn't maintain a copy of a domain accounts database and cannot authenticate domain users.

  A standalone server can be part of a domain or a workgroup. Standalone servers that are parts of domains are called *member servers*, which are useful because keeping a file or print servers free from the overhead of authenticating users often proves cost-effective. You cannot change a standalone server into a domain controller after installing it; your only option under such circumstances is to reinstall Windows NT and change the server type to domain controller during the installation process.

After you install a PDC or BDC into a domain, it must remain in that domain, unless you reinstall Windows NT, because you can't change the Security Identifier (SID) for the domain after setting it during installation. You can, however, change the name of a domain; change the domain name first on the PDC, then on the other network machines. Windows NT simply maps the new domain name with the old SID for the domain.

Preparation Checklist

After collecting the computer's hardware information, ensuring its compatibility with Windows NT 4.0 server and that it meets the minimum installation requirements, there is some additional information that you need to know before executing the setup process. For future reference, use this checklist as a guide for preparation. With the exception of the first four items, this list represents the information that is requested during the setup process:

- Read all NT documentation files.
- Assess system requirements. See Table 3.1.
- Assess hardware compatibility. Verify by consulting the Hardware Compatibility List.
- Gather device driver and configuration data:

• Video	Display Type, Adapter and chipset type
• Network	Card type, IRQ, I/O Address, DMA, Connector, etc.
• SCSI Controller	Adapter and chipset type, IRQ, bus type
• Sound/Media	IRQ, I/O Address, DMA
• I/O Ports	IRQ, I/O Address, DMA
• Modems	Port, IRQ, I/O Address, Modem Type

- Backup your current configuration and data files.
- Determine which type of initial setup will be performed. (You may need three blank, formatted disks before running Setup.)
- Determine the location of the source files for performing this installation. (Are they on CD-ROM, on a shared network location?)
- Determine on which partition the NT system files will be installed.
- Determine which file system you will install.
- Determine whether you will create an Emergency Repair Disk. (If so, you need 1 blank disk available before running Setup.)
- Identify your installation CD Key.
- Decide on a unique computer name for your computer.
- Determine which workgroup or domain name the computer will join.
- Identify network connection data: IP addresses, IPX card numbers, and so forth.
- Identify in which time zone the computer is located.

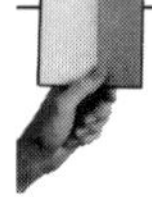

Tip

There are well over 90 text files that contain additional information specific to individual devices, such as network cards and video drivers. These can be found by browsing for .TXT files in the subdirectories for your specific platform. For example, on an Intel computer, look in the I386 platform directory on your NT 4.0 installation CD-ROM under the DRVLIB.NIC subdirectory for a subdirectory with your network card's name, and in that directory, look for and read the files with a .TXT extension.

There are certain other files that warrant close examination. In the platform directory, I386 for example, look for SETUP.TXT. It contains general information regarding devices and drivers that are used and required during installation. There are also three compressed files that contain release-specific information: readme.wr_, printer.wr_, and network.wr_. These can be expanded and read with the Windows Write program or the Windows 95 WordPad program. From a DOS prompt, switch to the platform directory and enter the command by using the following syntax: **expand file.wr_ c:\target directory\file.wri**. For example, if you've created a directory called readme on the C: drive, expand the network.wr_ file there by typing **expand network.wr_ c:\readme\network.wri**.

Executing the NT 4.0 Server Startup Process

So far, this chapter has concentrated on pre-installation detective work and preparation. It now turns your attention to the actual setup process and begins by discussing the five major phases that occur during this process:

1. The setup begins in what is referred to as DOS or text mode. If you have installed Windows before, this blue text screen format will look familiar. During this mode, several screens appear, asking for various pieces of information about the computer configuration for the NT 4.0 Server. These screens include:
   - A menu of startup options
   - Detection and configuration of storage devices, such as SCSI drives
   - Initial hardware verification
   - Choice of the installation disk partition

- Choice of the file system for the installation partition
- Installation directory name

2. This information is used to reboot the computer and load a mini-version of NT 4.0. This is a 32-bit multithreaded kernel that enhances and supports the setup process.
3. As the computer reboots, NT hardware detection takes place. This event discovers and initializes hardware devices for use by NT. These devices include:
   - SCSI adapters
   - Video adapter
   - Mouse and Keyboard
   - Disk drives
   - CD-ROM drive(s)
   - Comm and Parallel ports
   - Memory configuration
   - Bus adapter
4. A GUI interface is installed and the NT 4.0 Setup Wizard is displayed. The Wizard walks you through the rest of the installation process, asking for information such as:
   - Personal information
   - Unique computer name
   - Network card information
   - Network configuration information, such as protocols
   - Workgroup or Domain membership
   - First user account and administration information
   - Whether to create an Emergency Repair Disk
   - Time Zone
   - Video display setup
5. Finally, any additional support files are copied to the NT system directory, configuration information is saved in the NT registry, and the setup process completes and restarts the computer.

The following sections discuss each of these phases in more detail by walking through an actual installation of Windows NT 4.0 Server. Read through the process carefully, and then try it yourself in the lab.

Note The setup process is essentially the same for Intel-based and RISC-based computers. The process described here will apply to Intel-based computers. Any variations that apply to RISC-based computers will be noted as they occur in the process. ■

Beginning Setup

The setup process begins by locating the installation files. If you intend to install NT locally, you will need, at the very minimum, a compatible CD-ROM drive and, optionally, a 3.5 inch disk drive. If you are installing NT over the network, which will largely be the case in most organizations, you will need to have an active network connection and at least read access to the location of the installation files.

It's interesting to note that you don't have to have your installation files on an existing NT computer and you don't need to be running the Microsoft network. Indeed, the installation files can be loaded on a Novell NetWare server and the computer that is going to have NT installed can be running the NetWare client software. So long as the NT computer-to-be can access a network drive, the setup process can be initiated.

The first phase of the setup process, by default, requires the creation of three startup disks. NT copies all the basic boot-configuration information, as well as the mini-NT kernel, to these disks and then uses them to start the process. If you are installing NT locally and have the original setup disks and CD-ROM, you probably have a set of startup disks in the NT box. You can use these or let NT create a new set for you. If your computer does not have a compatible CD-ROM drive, you need to use these disks to begin the setup process.

Note According to Microsoft's technical documentation for the Windows NT 4.0 Server, if the BIOS of your computer supports the El Torito Bootable CD-ROM (no emulation mode) format, you can begin Setup from the NT CD-ROM directly and let NT prompt you to create the startup disks. However, problems have been reported with various compatible CD-ROM drives that may require you to use the packaged setup diskettes to begin Setup. ■

Generally, if you are installing NT over the network, you will not have access to the disks that come in the box and you will need NT to create them for you.

Another purpose of the startup disks is to provide a means of starting NT for repair or recovery purposes if you cannot later boot. If you intend to create and keep current an Emergency Repair Disk, you can use this disk only if you first boot by using the startup disks.

However, it is not essential that you create these disks during the startup process. You can save some time by performing a diskless installation of NT. This is particularly useful when performing an over-the-network installation, or rolling out NT on a large scale.

The NT Setup executable on the Intel platform is named WINNT.EXE. If you are installing NT for the first time on a computer, you use this executable. If you already have a copy of NT installed on the computer (for example, NT 3.51 Server) and intend to upgrade to NT 4.0 or install a new copy of NT 4.0, you can use an alternative executable called WINNT32.EXE. This is a 32-bit version of the setup program and will run with increased performance.

Setting Up NT 4.0 Server on RISC-Based Systems

On RISC-based systems, the setup process begins a little differently. Remember that on RISC-based computers, you must have a minimum 2M FAT partition created before proceeding with NT Setup. This partition holds the two hardware-specific NT boot files: OSLOADER.EXE and HAL.DLL. If you do not have a FAT partition, you must run the ARCINST.EXE utility located on the NT Installation CD-ROM in the platform subdirectory. When you boot your computer, choose RUN A PROGRAM from the ARC menu and enter the path to the ARCINSTALL.EXE utility. After the utility starts, choose CONFIGURE SYSTEM PARTITION and follow the screens.

The following general steps begin the installation process on a RISC-based computer. The rest of the setup will proceed generally as described in this book.

WINNT.EXE and WINNT32.EXE offer a variety of setup option switches that give you more control over how the installation proceeds. The syntax for using either executable is as follows:

```
[WINNT¦WINNT32] [/S:sourcepath] [/T:tempdrive] [/I:inffile] [/O or
/OX] [/F] [/C] [/B] [/U[:scriptfile]] [/R or /RX:directory]
```

Table 3.2 outlines these switches.

Table 3.2 WINNT.EXE Option Switches

Switch	Explanation
/B	Performs setup without creating startup disks. Instead, it creates a temporary directory on the hard disk with the most free space, called WIN_NT.~BK. This requires an additional 4-5M of free disk space above the 114M installation minimum.
/O	Creates the three installation startup disks. Note that with this switch, these disks can be created at any time. This switch CD-ROM installation.
/S:	Specifies the full drive or network path of the NT sourcepath installation files.
/U[:script]	Used with /S, it provides an unattended installation by skipping the screen that asks for the installation file location. When used with an optional script file, Setup will not prompt the installer for any information during setup.
/T:tempdrive	Allows you to specify the location of the temporary files. If not specified, NT will choose a drive for you.
/I:inffile	Specifies the filename of the setup information file. The default file is DOSNET.INF.
/C	Skips the free-space check on the startup disks. This can save a little time.
/F	Skips file verification as the files are copied to the startup disks. This can save a little more time.
/R	Specifies an optional directory to be installed.
/RX	Specifies an optional directory to be copied.
/UDF	Uniqueness Database File. A Uniqueness Database File (UDF) lets you tailor an unattended installation to the specific attributes of specific machines. The UDF contains different sections, each identified with a string called a uniqueness ID. Each section contains machine-specific information for a single computer or a group of computers. You then can use a single answer file for all the network installations, and reference machine-specific information by providing the uniqueness ID with the /UDF switch.

You now are ready to start the setup process. As stated at the beginning of this section, Setup begins by locating the installation files, as follows:

1. If you have access to your CD-ROM drive on your computer, switch to the CD-ROM drive and locate the directory that pertains to your system type (I386, MIPS, ALPHA, PPC) or connect to the network location of the installation files by using your DOS client-connection software.

   If you do not have access to your CD-ROM drive, try booting from the startup disk provided in the NT 4.0 Server box.

2. Type **WINNT**, with any desired option switches. The text mode phase of the setup process will initiate.

Note If you are installing NT 4.0 Server from an existing installation of NT, simply choose Run from the File menu choice in Program Manager or File Manager and enter **WINNT32**, followed by any desired option switches.

Text Mode Phase

Recall that the DOS or Text Mode phase of Setup has the following six basic events:

- A menu of startup options
- Detection and configuration of storage devices, such as SCSI drives
- Initial hardware verification
- Choice of the installation disk partition
- Choice of the file system for the installation partition
- Installation directory name

Each event will now be explored in more detail.

Startup Menu

The first screen that appears welcomes you to the Setup process and presents four different ways to proceed:

Tip

On all Setup screens, a pretty useful help dialog box is available by pressing F1. Also, you can exit Setup at any time by pressing F3.

1. To learn more about NT Setup before continuing, press F1.
2. To set up Windows NT now, press ENTER.
3. To repair a damaged Windows NT version 4.00 installation, press R.
4. To quit Setup without installing Windows NT, press F3.

These are fairly straightforward options, and are mirrored in the white status bar at the bottom of the screen with their keyboard shortcuts.

Of these four options, the one which may raise a question is the third option, repairing a damaged installation of NT. This is the option that you use with the Emergency Repair Disk to restore configuration information. The Emergency Repair Disk contains data from the NT Registry—more about that later.

Mass Storage-Device Configuration

The next step in the setup process is the detection of mass storage devices, such as CD-ROMs, SCSI adapters, and so forth. The detected devices are displayed on the screen. IDE (Integrated Device Electronics) and ESDI (Enhanced Small Device Interface) drives are also detected, but generally not displayed in the list.

If you have a device installed that is not shown on the screen, you can choose to add it by pressing S. Otherwise, press ENTER to continue with Setup. Of course, you can always add the additional devices after Setup has completed from the NT Control Panel. If you do press S, be sure to have your drivers disk available.

License Agreement

Setup will present you with a multi-page license agreement. This is the standard type of software agreement that Microsoft presents, warning you to install a valid copy of NT and not a borrowed copy from somebody else. You will need to page down through the license screens to accept the agreement and to get to the next step of the installation.

Verifying Hardware

The setup process next displays the basic list of hardware and software components that it detected, including:

- Computer
- Display
- Keyboard

- Keyboard Layout
- Pointing Device

If the list matches what you have installed in the computer, press ENTER. If you need to make a change, use the up or down arrow to highlight the component that needs to be changed, press ENTER, and then choose the appropriate item from the list.

Partition Configuration

The next screen involves choosing the disk partition on which the Windows NT system files will be installed. This is referred to as the system partition. The system partition can be an existing formatted or unformatted partition, or it may be an area of free space on the hard disk. Setup will display the partitions and free space that it detects on all physical disks. Use your UP and DOWN arrows to select the partition or free space where you want to install NT.

If you select an area of free space, you will need to press C to Create the partition. A new screen will display, telling you how large the partition can be, and asking you for the size you want. Enter your choice for the size of the partition and press ENTER. NT will create the partition for you, return you to the Partition Configuration screen, and display the new partition in the list. Select the new partition and press ENTER to continue.

If you are using an existing partition as the NT system partition, select it and press ENTER.

You also can select and delete partitions from this screen. This is useful if you need to free up some space and then create a larger partition for NT.

Note In either case, be sure that there is at least 118M of free space available on the selected partition. This is a *minimum* value; more free space will help performance. For example, you will need space for a pagefile for virtual memory management. Recall that the default initial size for a pagefile is 12+ the amount of physical RAM installed in your computer.

Do not install NT on a compressed partition. Disable compression before Setup begins.

If the partition is mirrored, disable mirroring before Setup begins.

If any partition is labeled as Windows NT Fault Tolerance, do not delete these partitions because they represent stripe sets, volume sets, and mirrors that, if deleted, could result in significant loss of data.

Formatting the Partition

The system partition contains all the NT system drivers, hardware configuration, security information, the registry, and so on. There is also a primary or boot partition into which NT copies its boot files. The next screen allows you to choose with which file system—FAT or NTFS—you want to format the proposed system partition. If you select the wrong partition, just press ESCAPE to return to the previous screen.

Your choice of file system depends on several factors. The following is a list of considerations for choosing NTFS:

- NTFS supports NT file and directory permissions security and access auditing; FAT supports only the Read Only, System, Hidden, and Archive attributes.
- NTFS supports transaction tracking and sector sparing for data recovery; FAT does not.
- NTFS supports partition sizes of up to 16EB and file sizes of 4-64G, depending on cluster sizes; FAT supports a maximum file size of 4G and is inefficient for partition sizes greater than 250M.
- NTFS provides file and directory compression implemented as a property; FAT does not.
- NTFS is recognized only by NT on that computer; FAT is recognized by NT, MS DOS, and OS/2.

If you are installing NT on a new computer, and do not also intend to run MS-DOS or Windows 95 on that computer (called "dual-booting"), then simply create the partition and format it as NTFS or FAT.

If you do intend to dual-boot with MS-DOS or Windows 95, be sure that it is installed already and that the boot partition is formatted already as FAT. If you install NT on the boot partition, NT will modify the master boot record (MBR) with its boot information and will maintain a boot pointer to the MS DOS system files. If you install NT first, format the partition as FAT and *then* install MS-DOS, the MBR will be altered and you will not be able to boot NT successfully.

RISC Partition Formats

NTFS can be used on RISC-based computers. However, NT requires at least one FAT system partition of 2M as a minimum size for its boot file information. Create this partition, as well as another system partition of appropriate size, for NTFS by following your RISC-based computer's documentation.

Ch 3

Dual Booting Windows NT 4.0 Server and OS/2

Windows NT and OS/2 can coexist on the same computer. If you have installed OS/2 and MS-DOS on the computer and use the OS/2 boot command to switch between operating systems, NT will configure its boot up to dual boot between itself and whichever of the other two operating systems you had running when you installed NT.

As NT 4.0 no longer supports the HPFS file system, if you intend to keep OS/2 on HPFS, you must install NT in another partition. Similarly, if you are using the OS/2 Boot Manager, the NT installation process will disable it upon completion. You must re-enable it by marking the Boot Manager partition as the active partition by using NT's Disk Administrator utility. If, after working in OS/2, you choose to boot to NT, use OS/2's Boot Manager to mark the NT partition as active and then reboot the computer.

Dual Booting Windows NT 4.0 Server and Windows NT 4.0 Workstation

For testing, instruction, or development purposes, you may choose to have both NT 4.0 Workstation and Server installed on your computer, or perhaps even different versions of NT. The Setup program detects the existence of another installation of NT, Windows 95, Windows for Workgroups, or Windows 3.1, and displays that installation's system directory as an upgrade directory for your current installation. Simply press N for "New Directory," as offered on the screen, to install this version of NT in a different directory. The Setup program keeps the other version(s) intact and installs this version in its own directory. Setup also modifies the boot menu to display this new version at the top of the boot menu and as the default boot-up operating system.

Installation Directory

Setup next asks for the name and location of the NT system files. NT displays the path and default name of the directory for you on the selected partition. The default directory name is WINNT. You may change the name to whatever you want, but it is recommended that you keep the name recognizable, such as WINNT40, especially if you have other versions of Windows or NT on the computer.

If you do have an existing version of Windows, Windows 95, or NT on the selected partition, Setup will detect that and display that directory as the installation choice. Setup assumes that you want to upgrade the existing operating system.

Final Screens

The next screen of the text mode phase informs you that Setup will examine the disk for corruption. It offers two types of exams: basic and exhaustive. The basic exam, initiated by pressing ESCAPE, is best used on new partitions that do not have data stored already. The exhaustive exam, initiated by pressing ENTER, runs slightly longer, depending on the size of the partition and the amount of data stored. Even though the exhaustive exam does take a little extra time, it is highly recommended if you are installing Windows NT 4.0 server on an existing partition with existing data.

After you make your selection, Setup displays a dialog box showing the status of the process as it copies files to the new NT system directory.

When the files have been copied and the directory structure created, Setup informs you that the text mode portion has completed and that you should press ENTER to restart the computer. At this point, you can press ENTER or, if it is getting late, you can just turn off your computer. Actually, it often is suggested that you do power off the computer and then power back on to reset all the hardware devices, particularly network cards, for NT.

Restart, Lock, and Load!

When the computer reboots, if you watch very closely, you will see the NT boot menu appear briefly with a choice for NT installation. This is the default and will start automatically. If you are quick with your fingers, you can press the UP or DOWN arrow keys to disable the default time and boot to MS-DOS or Windows 95. There will be a menu entry for either MS-DOS or Windows 95, depending on which operating system has been installed. Otherwise, just let NT take over.

It is during this phase that NT loads its 32-bit multithreaded kernel, which enhances and supports the setup process. As the computer reboots, NT hardware detection takes place. This event discovers and initializes hardware devices for use by NT, such as SCSI adapters, video adapter, mouse and keyboard drivers, CD-ROM drives, comm and parallel ports, memory configuration, and bus adapter.

You next see what will become a familiar set of boot-up screens. The first screen will be a black screen that loads system drivers (white consecutive dots), followed by the infamous blue screen—infamous because it is here that you see screen dumps related to unsuccessful boots of NT. Most of the time, however, this screen simply outlines the progress of various boot tasks. If you have chosen to format or convert a partition to NTFS, you will see messages to that effect as conversion takes place. Also, NT will reboot the system once again for the file system to be recognized and take effect.

Once this process is complete, NT loads the GUI portion of Setup, which is called the Windows NT Setup Wizard.

Windows NT Setup Wizard

The Setup Wizard is a much streamlined and intuitive interface for gathering information pertinent to the configuration of NT on the computer. Essentially, the Setup Wizard asks you configuration option questions during the display of several Windows GUI dialog boxes. After you have made your selections and provided the appropriate information, the Wizard loads the necessary drivers, updates the registry, and completes the installation.

Tip

Each Setup Wizard dialog box has BACK, NEXT, and HELP buttons to make it easy to move back and forth amongst the screens and to reselect options before committing yourself.

The very first screen you see outlines the standard Microsoft license agreement. You must select OK to this agreement before continuing with Setup.

The next dialog box outlines how the Wizard will proceed. There are three parts to the Setup Wizard:

1. Gathering information about your computer
2. Installing Windows NT Networking
3. Finishing Setup

Gathering Information About Your Computer

The Setup Options dialog box offers four installation options: *Typical*, *Portable*, *Compact*, and *Custom*. Table 3.3 highlights which components are installed by default for each setup option.

Table 3.3 Default Components Installed by Each Setup Option

Component	Typical	Portable	Compact	Custom
Accessibility Options	Yes	Yes	No	Selectable
Accessories	Yes	Yes	No	Selectable
Communication Options	Yes	Yes	No	Selectable
Games	No	No	No	Selectable
Windows Messaging	No	No	No	Selectable
Multimedia	Yes	Yes	No	Selectable

The Typical and Custom options are very much the same as the Express and Custom options that most users have encountered when installing Windows and most Windows applications. The two setup options new to NT 4.0 are the Portable and Compact options.

Typical setup is the default, as well as the recommended option. It installs all optional Windows components, including Microsoft Exchange and, of course, the games. It asks few questions and automatically configures component settings.

Custom, on the other hand, gives the most control over the installation and configuration of options.

The next two dialog boxes prompt you for a user name and company name for registration purposes, as well as a Product Identification number, or CD Key. The number usually is included on the CD-ROM case or in your NT installation manual. In some organizations, depending on the type of installation being performed, you may not need this number because your organization has negotiated a company-wide license for distributing the software. You must enter something in both of these dialog boxes to proceed to the next dialog box.

The next dialog box asks you to specify a licensing mode. There are two options:

- **Per server license** Clients are licensed to a particular server, and the number of concurrent connections to the server cannot exceed the maximum specified in the license. When the maximum number of concurrent connections is reached, Windows NT returns an error to a connecting user and prohibits access. An administrator can still connect after the maximum is reached, however.

- **Per seat license** Clients are free to use any server they want, and an unlimited number of clients can connect to a server.

If you can't decide which mode to select, choose Per Server mode. You have a one-time chance to convert the per server license to a per seat license by using the Control Panel Licensing application.

The next dialog box asks for the computer name. This is the name that NT uses to identify this computer internally and for network and remote communication. It must be a unique name if the computer will be a member of a workgroup or domain. This name can be up to 15 characters long.

Tip

While a computer name may contain spaces, it is not recommended. In a large network, users connecting to computers can become confused as to the presence or absence of spaces in a name. In fact, in a large corporate network, a standard naming convention for computer, workgroup, and domain names will greatly simplify the configuration and maintenance of your network.

On the next screen, you must specify whether the computer is a primary domain controller, a backup domain controller, or a standalone server. These server-type options are discussed earlier in this chapter.

The next screen references the Administrator Account and asks for a password for that account. The administrator account is a built-in account that NT creates for managing the configuration of the computer, including security and account information. The name of the administrator account is ADMINISTRATOR and the password can be up to 14 characters. You need to enter the password twice, once to confirm it.

Caution

Passwords in NT are *case-sensitive* so be sure that you type it in correctly and then *remember it!* If you forget your password during the course of installation, *you will not be able to access NT.*

You may have read or heard that certain Pentium-based computers have a faulty *floating point* module. In very specific circumstances, this sometimes can produce inaccurate results when dividing certain values. If Setup has detected that your computer has such a problem, the next screen will give you the option to disable the module and let NT perform the math. This results in a decrease in performance for floating-point operations. However, if your applications heavily rely on floating-point arithmetic, such as complex Excel macros, then you may prefer to choose YES to this option.

The next screen involves the option of creating an *Emergency Repair Disk*. The Emergency Repair Disk contains setup information relevant to this installation of NT, including the location of source files and computer configuration and security information from the registry. It can be used to replace corrupted or missing boot files, recover account information, and restore NT to the master boot record of the computer boot partition if it has been modified. To use this disk, you must have a startup disk with which to boot and then choose R for "repair" from the startup menu.

If you choose to create an Emergency Repair Disk, be sure to have a blank disk handy, and choose YES.

Tip

If you choose not to create an Emergency Repair Disk at this time, you always can create one later. NT provides a command-prompt command called RDISK.EXE, which is used to create a new Emergency Repair Disk and to update an existing disk.

Depending on the type of installation you choose at the start of the Wizard, you may see a dialog box that lets you choose which optional components to install. You may choose one of two options: Most common, or Show a list.

If you choose Most Common, Setup will proceed to the next portion of the Setup Wizard process. If you choose to Show a List, you will see a new dialog box with a list of options. This is the same dialog box that you see when selecting optional components in Windows 95.

The truly fine thing about this dialog box is the way that it presents you with component information. You will see a list of five or six main components. Most of these actually are component areas that are composed of a list of component items from which you can choose. As you select each main component, a description box to the right explains what functionality each provides, as well as how many of the component items have been selected for installation. If you select the DETAILS button, another dialog box will display the checklist of component items. You may select or deselect these items as you want and then return to the main dialog box. As you select items, the description screen notes how many items you selected, such as `12 of 14 items selected`. You also see just how much additional disk space is required for the items in question.

As you select NEXT, the Wizard takes you to part two of its setup process: Installing Windows NT Networking.

Installing Windows NT Networking

The next few dialog boxes reference information regarding the configuration of network-related functions and components. Your first choice is to indicate whether you are implementing network features at all, and if so, whether you will be Wired to the Network through a local interface, such as a network card, or if you have Remote access to the network through a modem connection, or both.

If you have chosen Wired to the network, the next dialog box will prompt you to detect and install the network card. Choose Start Search to begin Setup's detection process. The dialog box will display a list of all detected network cards. You can choose to configure any combination of cards by selecting or deselecting their check boxes.

If Setup cannot detect the card, or you have a driver disk available, you can install the card from your disk by choosing Select from list, and then the Have Disk button.

Note Remember to check the Hardware Compatibility List to be sure that your network card is supported by NT. (See the Preparation Checklist earlier in this chapter.)

You can install additional cards, or change card settings, later on from NT's Control Panel. ■

The Setup Wizard, most likely, will next display a configuration option dialog box for the specific card(s) you selected. This dialog box, or series of dialog boxes, ask for the correct IRQ, I/O base port address, and memory buffer address settings, as well as any other card-specific settings, such as on-board transceivers, thin versus thick coax, and so on.

Note Please note that NT will display the manufacturer's proposed or factory settings in these dialog boxes. As some cards are software-configurable, the actual settings on the cards may not match the manufacturer's settings. To avoid conflicts, especially the failure of NT to initialize the card and network settings on your computer, be sure to know your card settings ahead of time. (See the Preparation Checklist found in the section titled "Preparation Checklist.")

The next dialog box asks for Network Protocol choices. By default, NT selects TCP/IP and NWLINK IPX/SPX as your protocol. However, you may select any combination of TCP/IP, *NWLINK* (NT's 32-bit implementation of IPX/SPX) and NETBEUI. Additional protocols may be added by choosing Select from list. Other protocols that can be installed include AppleTalk, DLC, and Point-to-Point Tunneling.

Tip

Here's a tip for those who are installing large numbers of NT clients where TCP/IP will be the protocol choice. If your clients already use TCP/IP, then you know how easy it is to misconfigure TCP/IP when installing it, especially the subnet mask and default gateway. If you are installing over the network and have copied the install directory (that is, I386) to the hard drive, you can modify IPINFO.INF.

IPINFO.INF is a template for TCP/IP configuration parameters. It's a fairly large file, but you're interested only in the section that begins with [DefaultIPInfo]. The file mostly consists of comment lines, so make sure that you have found the section that does not have each line preceded by a semicolon (the comment indicator).

After you find the [DefaultIPInfo] section, you can modify the following parameters:

- `NumberOfIPAddress = x` *x* is the number of IP Addresses to be assigned. For most computers, this should simply be set to `1`.
- `IPAddress1 = 'xxx.xxx.xxx.xxx'` Because this parameter changes from client to client, you might not want to fill this in.
- `SubnetMask1 = 'xxx.xxx.xxx.xxx'` All of your clients probably will use the same subnet mask, so it is smart to set this default.
- `DefaultGateway = 'xxx.xxx.xxx.xxx'` Again, all of your clients on a particular subnet should use the same default gateway (router), so it is also smart to set this default.

Of course, users can still override this information during an installation, but at least they won't be guessing parameters out of the blue.

The next step is to select the *Network Services* that are appropriate for your computer. By default, five services are installed with NT networking and cannot be deselected. These services are: *Computer Browser, RPC Configuration, NetBIOS Interface, Workstation,* and *Server.* Again, additional services such as Client Service for NetWare, Microsoft Internet Information Services, Remote Access Services, and so on, can be installed by selecting Select from disk, or from disk by choosing Have disk. Network services will be discussed in Chapter 17, "Windows NT Networking Services."

At this point, you have made all appropriate choices and the Wizard will give you a choice to continue and install the network components, or go back and alter your selections. Choose Back to make changes and Next to continue.

The next dialog box displays the *Network Bindings.* Think of bindings as being the network "paths" that determine how services, protocols, and adapters interact to effect network communications. You can adjust the bindings by changing their order, enabling them, or disabling them. NT has selected the optimum bindings based on your network component settings. If you need to adjust them later, you can do so from NT's Control Panel. A further discussion of bindings appears in Chapter 17, "Windows NT Networking Services."

Each card that you install may have protocol-specific information that is required. For example, if you choose TCP/IP, you need to specify a local address, router information, WINS address information, and so forth, or specify DCHP configuration. These dialog boxes then will be displayed as the Wizard completes the setup of network components.

Note If you began your installation as an over-the-network type, and you did not power off your computer after the text mode, you may see a message stating, to the effect, that NT cannot verify the card settings and asking whether it should use them anyway. The answer you should choose is YES! use the settings. The reason for this message is that, in a warm boot such as NT performs after the text mode setup, all device settings, particularly network card settings, are not reset. Thus NT is detecting that those settings are already in use. A cold boot, on the other hand, involves powering off the computer. This, of course, resets all device settings, including the network card settings that triggered the message in the first place. ■

If NT is unable to initiate network communication, you will have the option either to go back and check your settings or to continue on without configuring the network.

As you select NEXT, the Wizard takes you to part three of its setup process: Finishing Setup.

Finishing Setup

There are just two more dialog boxes to consider before the Setup Wizard completes the installation. The first dialog box displays the Date and Time utility. Adjust the settings to reflect the time zone of the computer and to ensure that the system time is correct.

Note Several interprocess mechanisms, as well as certain applications and Microsoft BackOffice products, rely on time stamps and time synchronization among computers. Inaccurate time zones or time values can result in process failures, and in some cases, an incomplete processing of data. ■

Finally, the Display Properties dialog box pops up. This dialog box enables you to configure your video display by changing settings such as pixel resolution, color palette, refresh frequency, and font size, as well as by changing your video driver information. Before you complete this screen, choose TEST to see whether you actually can read your display with the settings you chose. After testing, you can choose OK.

A status dialog box now is displayed, showing the progress of files copied from the temporary directory (WIN_NT.~LS). When this is complete, the Wizard asks you to remove any floppy disks and to press the RESTART button to reboot the computer. As before, at this point you can safely turn off your computer.

If you let the computer restart, and have chosen a dual-boot configuration for your installation, you will see NT's boot loader menu. Your new installation of Windows NT 4.0 Server will be first in the list, and it will be the default operating system, unless you choose the other operating system option within 30 seconds. If you choose NT, it will load with all the options you chose, and present you with the WELCOME screen.

Troubleshooting Installation and Setup

If you have carefully read this chapter, you will have relatively little problem, if any, with your installation of Windows NT 4.0 Server. In fact, installing NT 4.0 is rarely troublesome if you have done your detective work. It is designed to detect and configure as much on its own as possible. Nevertheless, this section runs through a couple of tips, suggestions, and reminders, beginning with the Preparation Checklist, just in case you encounter problems:

- Read all NT documentation files.
- Assess system requirements. Refer to Table 3.1.
- Assess hardware compatibility. Verify by consulting the Hardware Compatibility List.
- Gather device-driver and configuration data:

• Video	Display Type, Adapter and chipset type
• Network	Card type, IRQ, I/O Address, DMA, Connector, and so forth
• SCSI Controller	Adapter and chipset type, IRQ, bus type
• Sound/Media	IRQ, I/O Address, DMA
• I/O Ports	IRQ, I/O Address, DMA
• Modems	Port, IRQ, I/O Address, Modem Type

- Backup your current configuration and data files.
- Determine which type of initial setup will be performed. (You may need three blank formatted disks before running Setup.)
- Determine the location of the source files for performing this installation. (Are they on CD-ROM, on a shared network location?)
- Determine on which partition the NT system files will be installed.
- Determine which file system you will install.
- Determine whether you will create an Emergency Repair Disk. (If so, you need one blank disk available before running Setup.)
- Identify your installation CD Key.
- Decide on a unique computer name for your computer.
- Identify network connection data: IP addresses, IPX card numbers, and so forth.

- Identify in which time zone the computer is located.

Perhaps most critical to a successful installation of NT 4.0 Server is the compatibility of your computer's hardware. The following are two reminders:

1. Be sure that your computer meets the minimum requirements necessary for installing and running NT 4.0 Server.
2. Be sure that you have checked *all* hardware components in your computer against the Hardware Compatibility List for NT 4.0 Server.

These two actions alone will significantly increase your success rate.

Next, become familiar with the hardware settings for installed devices, particularly network cards. This includes not only IRQ, DMA, I/O address, and connector data, but also network protocol settings such as IP address, DNS location, router address, DHCP information, IPX card address, and so on.

Finally, follow a naming convention for your computers and workgroups that ensures uniqueness, recognizability, and ease of maintenance. If you are becoming a member of a domain, be sure that your computer already has a computer account in the domain you are joining (as well as a user account for you).

Occasionally, you may encounter unusual errors relating to your hard disk. If installation fails due to disk-related problems, here are a few areas to explore:

1. Is the hard disk supported (on the HCL)?
2. Do you have a valid boot sector available on the disk. Recall that, especially for RISC-based systems, NT requires a minimum 2M FAT system partition.
3. Are your SCSI drives being detected correctly by NT? You may need to check physical settings, such as termination.
4. Check for viruses in the Master Boot Record (MBR). If there is a virus that alters the MBR either before, during, or after installation, NT will not be able to boot successfully. A likely message you may receive is: `Bad or missing NTLDR.`
5. When NT reboots to start the GUI Setup Wizard, if it fails, usually with the message: `Bad or missing NTOSKRNL`, it could be due to a missed detection of the SCSI drive. Boot to DOS and use the DOS Editor to modify the BOOT.INI file. This read-only system file is

created by NT during installation and is used to display the boot menu. It is stored in the root directory of the system partition. Use the DOS ATTRIB command to turn off the Read Only (R) and System (S) attributes before editing the file. Change all references of SCSI for this installation to MULTI. Also, check that the partition numbers listed in the BOOT.INI file for Windows NT match the partition number of the NT system file directory. Be sure to save your changes and set the attributes back.

The syntax for using the DOS ATTRIB command to turn off attributes is as follows:

```
C:>ATTRIB -?R BOOT.INI
Set the attributes back by typing:
c:>ATTRIB +S +R BOOT.INI
```

NT counts partitions, starting with "0," as follows:

1. Hidden system partitions.
2. The first primary partition on each drive.
3. Additional primary partitions on each drive.
4. Logical partitions on each drive.

So, if the physical disk has a hidden system partition (like a COMPAQ BIOS partition), a C: drive primary partition, and a D: drive logical partition, and you are installing NT on drive D:, you are installing NT on partition 2 (hidden-0, C:-1, D:-2).

Using NTHQ to Troubleshoot

NT also supplies a troubleshooting utility that may be of use for both NT 4.0 Workstation and Server in discovering how NT is detecting your hardware configuration. This utility is called NTHQ and can be found in the \SUPPORT\HQTOOL directory on the installation CD-ROM.

To use this utility, boot to DOS, place a blank disk in the A: drive, switch to the directory on the CD-ROM, and run MAKEDISK.BAT. This creates a bootable disk that you can use to run NTHQ. Reboot the computer with this disk and follow the directions.

NTHQ creates an on-screen report that can be saved to a log file on disk and can be printed out. It performs a hardware detection on the computer, similar to that performed by NT during Setup, and can be used to determine your hardware settings and, specifically, which ones are causing Setup to fail. It includes data about the motherboard, such as I/O, DMA, and IRQ settings for CMOS, Memory Access Controller, Comm and Printer Ports, Plug and Play BIOS, data about the Network Card, Video, Storage Devices, and a Summary of all device configuration settings. It also shows what is questionable regarding the Hardware Compatibility List.

NTHQ Sample Report

Here is an example of the kinds of data that NTHQ captures and reports.

```
Hardware Detection Tool For Windows NT 4.0

Master Boot Sector Virus Protection Check
Hard Disk Boot Sector Protection: Off.
No problem to write to MBR

ISA Plug and Play Add-in cards detection Summary Report

No ISA Plug and Play cards found in the system
ISA PnP Detection: Complete

EISA Add-in card detection Summary Report
Scan Range: Slot 0 - 16
Slot 0: EISA System Board
EISA Bus Detected: No
EISA Detection: Complete

Legacy Detection Summary Report

System Information
Device: System board
Can't locate Computername
Machine Type: IBM PC/AT
Machine Model: fc
Machine Revision: 00
Microprocessor: Pentium
Conventional memory: 655360
Available memory: 32 MB
BIOS Name: Phoenix
BIOS Version:
BIOS Date: 06/12/96
Bus Type: ISA

Enumerate all IDE devices

IDE Devices Detection Summary Report
Primary Channel: master drive detected
Model Number: TOSHIBA MK2720FC
```

continues

continued

```
Firmware Revision: S1.16 J
Serial Number: 66D70208
Type of Drive: Fixed Drive
Disk Transfer Rate: >10Mbs
Number of Cylinders: 2633
Number of Heads: 16
Number of Sectors Per Track: 63
Number of unformatted bytes per sector Per Track: 639
LBA Support: Yes
DMA Support: Yes
PIO Transfer Cycle Time Mode 2
DMA Transfer Cycle Time Mode 2

IDE/ATAPI: Complete

=============End of Detection Report============
Adapter Description: Cirrus Logic VGA
Listed in Hardware Compatibility List: Yes

Adapter Description: Creative Labs Sound Blaster 16 or AWE-32
Adapter Device ID: *PNPB003
Listed in Hardware Compatibility List: Not found-check the
latest HCL

Adapter Description: Gameport Joystick
Adapter Device ID: *PNPB02F
Listed in Hardware Compatibility List: Not found-check the
latest HCL

Adapter Description: Unknown Cirrus Logic chipset, report!
Adapter Device ID: 12021013
Listed in Hardware Compatibility List: Not found-check the
latest HCL
```

Performing an Unattended Setup of Windows NT 4.0 Server

It is possible to automate the setup process to provide some or all of the information needed during setup and thus provide for little or no additional user input. This can be especially helpful when installing a large number of computers with similar configurations, such as having the same domain name, monitor settings, network card drivers and setting, and so on.

There are five basic steps involved in implementing an unattended setup of NT 4.0 Server:

- Create a distribution server by placing the Windows NT 4.0 Server installation files for the appropriate computer platform in a shared directory on a file server.
- Create an answer file that supplies information common to all the computers being installed.
- Create a uniqueness data file that supplies information specific to each computer's installation.
- Provide access to the installation files on the distribution server for the computers that are being installed.
- Run NT Setup, referencing the location of the Setup files, answer files, and uniqueness data files.

Each of these steps will now be discussed in more detail.

Create a Distribution Server

It is relatively simple to copy the installation files to a shared directory on a file server. Simply identify which Windows NT server you want to use. This should be a server that the target computers will be able to access easily, preferably a server on the same subnet, and one which is not already being used to capacity by other applications or processes. IT also should have its own CD-ROM, or be able to access a CD-ROM drive.

Next, create an installation folder on that server. Into that folder, copy the installation files for the target computers' hardware platform from the appropriate platform directory on the NT 4.0 Server installation CD-ROM (i386, MIPS, ALPHA, or PPC). You can use the MD-DOS xcopy command with the /S switch (to copy all subdirectories) from a command prompt, or use Windows Explorer.

Finally, share the newly created directory.

Create an Answer File

Answer files (unattend.txt) are used to supply setup information that is common to all the computers using that file. The kind of information that is common to the computers includes network settings, such as card driver, interrupts, DMA. Protocols to be installed, and services to be installed, which workgroup or domain the computers are joining, modem types, and the organization name. Here is a copy of the sample unattend.txt file for an Intel-based computer that can be found on the NT 4.0 Server CD-ROM. Each platform directory contains its own version of this file.

```
; Microsoft Windows NT Workstation Version 4.0 and
; Windows NT Server Version 4.0
; (c) 1994 - 1996 Microsoft Corporation. All rights reserved.
;
; Sample Unattended Setup Answer File
;
; This file contains information about how to automate the instal-
lation
; or upgrade of Windows NT Workstation and Windows NT Server so
the
; Setup program runs without requiring user input.
;
; For information on how to use this file, read the appropriate
sections
; of the Windows NT 4.0 Resource Kit.

[Unattended]
OemPreinstall = no
ConfirmHardware = no
NtUpgrade = no
Win31Upgrade = no
TargetPath = WINNT
OverwriteOemFilesOnUpgrade = no

[UserData]
FullName = "Your User Name"
OrgName = "Your Organization Name"
ComputerName = COMPUTER_NAME

[GuiUnattended]
TimeZone = "(GMT-08:00) Pacific Time (US & Canada); Tijuana"

[Display]
ConfigureAtLogon = 0
BitsPerPel = 16
XResolution = 640
YResolution = 480
VRefresh = 70
AutoConfirm = 1

[Network]
Attend = yes
DetectAdapters = ""
InstallProtocols = ProtocolsSection
JoinDomain = Domain_To_Join
```

```
[ProtocolsSection]
TC = TCParameters

[TCParameters]
DHCP = yes
```

As you can see, this text file looks very much like a Windows .INI file. It can be created simply by copying and modifying the sample file, creating your own file by using any text editor, or by running the Setup Manager utility, also found on the Windows NT 4.0 installation CD-ROM. While it usually is called unattend.txt, you can give it any legal file name, so long as you refer to it correctly when running Setup. The Setup Manager utility provides a graphical interface for creating and modifying the unattend.txt file(s). A complete treatment of the unattend.txt file and using Setup Manager can be found in Appendix A, "Answer Files and UDFs," of the *Windows NT Workstation Resource Kit Version 4.0* (a recommended companion to this exam guide).

After it is created, this file should be placed in the same location as the Windows NT 4.0 installation source files on the distribution server.

Create a Uniqueness Data File

The unattend.txt file creates a setup data file that contains information common to all the computers being installed. However, this will not completely automate the process when installing more than one computer. Recall that each computer's computer name, for example, must be unique. That sort of information can not be supplied in the unattend.txt file alone.

A uniqueness data file (UDF) can be created to supply the more detailed and machine-specific information required to more fully automate the setup process. The UDF file identifies specific sections that should be merged into the answer file. Here is a sample UDF file.

```
; This section lists all unique ids that are supported by this
database.
; The left hand side is a unique id, which can be any string but
; must not contain the asterisk (*), space, comma, or equals
character.
; The right hand side is a list of sections, each of which should
match the name
; of a section in unattend.txt. See below.
;
id1 = section1,section2
id2 = section1,section3,section4
```

```
[section1]
; This is a section whose name should match the name of a section
in unattend.txt.
; Each line in this section is written into the same section in
unattend.txt,
; via the profile APIs. A line here thus replaces a line in
unattend.txt with the
; same left hand side. (If a matching line does not exist in
unattend.txt, the line will
; be added.) A line that just has a left hand side and does not
have a value will delete
; the same line in unattend.txt.
;
; To make this section specific to a particular unique id, precede
its name with id:.
; This allows specification of different sections in this file
that map to the same
; section in unattend.txt. See below.
;
key1 = value
key2 = value

[id2:section2]
; This section is merged into [section2] in unattend.txt for
unique id2.
;
key5 = value
```

The sections contained in the UDF are the same sections used in the unattend.txt file. A section's entries in the UDF are merged into the corresponding section in the unattend.txt file. The unique id referred to in the sample represents an id that you assign for each computer you are installing. By assigning a unique id to each section, you can create copies of the same section, each of which modifies the installation slightly from computer to computer. For example, the [UserData] section can provide a different user name and computer name for each subsequent computer installation by creating multiple copies of the [UserData] section, modifying each accordingly, and assigning each a different unique id corresponding to that computer.

Suppose that you are installing three computers. Each should have a unique computer name: ComputerA, ComputerB, and ComputerC. You assign each computer a unique id: ID1, ID2, ID3. The attend.txt section that modifies the computer name is [UserData]. The UDF would then look like this:

```
ID1=[UserData]
ID2=[UserData]
ID3=[UserData]
[ID1:UserData]
Computername=ComputerA
[ID2:UserData]
Computername=ComputerB
[ID3:UserData]
Computername=ComputerC
```

A complete treatment of the UDF files can be found in Appendix A, "Answer Files and UDFs," of the Windows NT Workstation Resource Kit Version 4.0 (a recommended companion to this exam guide).

Connect to the Distribution Server

The computers on which NT 4.0 Server will be installed must be able to connect to and access the shared folder containing the installation, answer, and UDF files. This generally is accomplished by installing the DOS Network Client 3.0 software on the computer, if there is no other means of connecting to the distribution server, such as through Windows for Workgroups network connectivity options, Windows 95, or an existing installation of Windows NT Workstation.

After a network connection has been established, a simple *net* command can be used at a command prompt to access the installation source files by using the command syntax: `net use d: \\distribution_server\ shared_folder`. This net command maps a logical drive letter on your computer to the shared folder on the distribution server. Switching to that drive letter at a command prompt, or through File Manager or Windows Explorer, effectively points you to the files in the shared folder. For example, if the NT 4.0 installation files have been installed in a shared folder called INSTALL on a distribution server called SOURCE1, connect to the folder by typing the following command at a command prompt: **net use E: \\SOURCE1\INSTALL**. The E: drive is now mapped to the NT 4.0 source file directory on the distribution server.

Run Setup

The final step is to run NT Setup by referring to the source directory, answer files, and UDFs that you created. This is accomplished by using several of the boot switches that were outlined in Table 3.2, earlier in this chapter.

After you map a drive to the shared folder containing the NT 4.0 installation files on the distribution server, switch to that drive. At a command prompt, enter the following command syntax: **winnt / u:answer_filename /s:source_drive /UDF:ID[,UDF_filename]**.

For example, suppose you have created an answer file called unattend.txt that contains common setup information for your computers, as well as a uniqueness data file called unique.txt that contains specific setup instructions for each computer. Each computer is identified by a unique id, following the convention ID1, ID2, and so forth. At the first computer, corresponding to ID1, you map a drive (E:, for example) to the distribution server. At a command prompt, you enter the following command: **winnt /u:unattend.txt /s:e: /UDF:ID1[,unique.txt]**.

At the next computer, you would do the same thing, changing the ID reference to one appropriate to that computer, and so on until you have completed your installation.

Tip

The command to map the drive and the setup command can be placed together in a batch file, along with any other batch commands you may want to include, such as disconnecting from the mapped drive.

Uninstalling Windows NT 4.0 Server

You may encounter a need to uninstall Windows NT 4.0 Server from your computer. For example, if you were testing it and the evaluation period has completed, or if you want to install a different operating system entirely. The steps required to remove NT 4.0 Server from your computer depend on the file system your computer uses when booting.

Dual Boot Systems

If you dual boot between MS-DOS or Windows 95 and the Windows NT 4.0 Server, then your system partition is using the FAT file system. You can remove the NT 4.0 Server and restore the boot up operating system back to what it was before (MS-DOS or Windows 95) by following these steps:

1. Boot your computer to start either MS-DOS or Windows 95.

2. Create a boot disk, also called a system disk:
   a) Place an unformatted diskette in the A: drive of your computer.
   b) At a DOS prompt, enter the command: FORMAT A: /S. This command transfers the MS-DOS or Windows 95 system files used for booting to the diskette.
   c) Answer YES to the prompt and proceed.
3. Copy the SYS.COM file from the DOS directory on your computer to the diskette you just formatted.
4. Reboot your computer from the system disk you just created by leaving it in the A: drive and restarting your computer.
5. At the A: prompt, enter the command: **SYS C:**. This command will transfer the MS-DOS or Windows 95 system files from the system disk to the master boot record of the computer.
6. Remove the system diskette from the A: drive and restart the computer. The computer should now boot directly to MS-DOS or Windows 95 and no longer display the NT boot menu.
7. Remove the following NT-related files from the hard disk:
   a) C:\pagefile.sys (this file may be located on a different partition if NT was installed in a different partition)
   b) C:\boot.ini (marked with the attributes system and read-only)
   c) C:\nt*.* (marked with the attributes hidden, system, and read-only—these files include ntldr, ntdetect.com, and possibly ntbootdd.sys)
   d) C:\bootsect.dos (marked with the attributes hidden and system)
   e) \winnt system file folder (found on whichever partition you installed NT 4.0)
   f) \program files\Windows NT (found on whichever partition you installed NT 4.0)

NTFS Partition

If you chose to install NT in the system partition and formatted the partition to use the NTFS file system, you do not have a dual-boot system. Consequently, you cannot boot to either MS-DOS or Windows 95 because they require a FAT partition to boot. In this case, you essentially must remove the partition to remove NT 4.0 Server. You can use the MS-DOS

FDISK utility from MS-DOS versions 6.0 and higher to remove the partition and re-partition it for MS-DOS, or you can use the Windows NT Setup program to remove the NTFS partition.

Using FDISK

FDISK is a low-level disk utility that is used to create partitions. If you created a partition during an install, then you have already used FDISK.

Create a system disk from an MS-DOS or Windows 95-based computer:

1. Copy the file fdisk.exe from the DOS directory on that computer to the system disk.
2. Boot the NT 4.0 Server from the system disk by placing it in the A: drive and then restarting the computer.
3. At the A: prompt, enter the command: **FDISK**.
4. Choose option 3—Delete Partition or Logical DOS Drive from the FDISK menu.
5. Choose option 4—Delete Non-DOS Partition from the delete partition menu. A list of the partitions is displayed.
6. Select the partition number of the partition you want to delete. This likely will be partition number 1.
7. Confirm your intent to delete the partition.

Using Windows NT 4.0 Setup

1. Restart the computer with the NT startup disk in the A: drive. (Refer to the section titled "Executing the NT 4.0 Workstation Setup Process—Beginning Setup," as well as Table 3.2 for information about using and creating a startup disk.)
2. Proceed through Setup to the screen prompting you to choose or create a partition.
3. Select the NTFS partition that you want to delete.
4. Press D on the keyboard to delete the partition.
5. Press F3 to exit NT Setup and the partition will be deleted.

There are other utilities that also can be used to delete the NTFS partition. The NT and Windows Resource Kits include a utility called DELPART that can be used to remove partitions. Partition Magic, manufactured by Power Quest, and Norton Utilities for Windows NT, manufactured by Symantec, also provide partition-management utilities that give you options for deleting NTFS partitions.

Taking the Disc Test

If you have read and understood the material in this chapter, you are ready to test your knowledge. Insert the CD-ROM that comes with this book and run the self-test software, as described in Appendix K, "Using the Self-Test Software."

From Here...

This chapter discussed in detail the installation and setup process for the Windows NT 4.0 Server. Now that you have the server installed, you need to become familiar with the new Windows 95 Interface. Those of you who are already Windows 95 literate will have no trouble adjusting to the Windows NT 4.0 Server. Those of you coming from a Program Manager background will want to spend a little more time playing with the new interface to find all your favorite utilities, explore the enhancements that the new interface brings to the desktop, and perhaps play the new pinball game.

The next chapter, "Configuring Windows NT Server 4.0," is designed to help you become familiar with the new interface and explore how to modify the configuration.

Chapter Prerequisite

The only prerequisites that the reader should have for this chapter is a familiarity with Control Panel and other utilities that affect entries in the Windows NT Registry.

4

Configuring Windows NT Server 4.0

This chapter explores various means of configuring and customizing Windows NT 4.0 Server. Customization includes something as simple as changing the color of the desktop. Configuration includes tasks such as installing new device drivers. The Registry maintains the configuration information for NT and provides NT with the data it needs to boot successfully.

NT provides several utilities to help you configure and customize Windows NT. This chapter introduces you to these utilities and the Registry. Certain utilities, such as User Manager, Disk Administrator, and Network, while introduced here, are discussed in more detail in separate chapters.

Topics discussed in this chapter include:

- Personalizing the desktop environment through the display properties sheet

- Exploring the many Control Panel applets through which you make the majority of your configuration choices
- Reviewing the NT administrative tools
- Examining the NT 4.0 Registry to see how NT maintains the system configuration, and how and when you can modify that configuration
- Booting-up NT 4.0 and the way in which NT uses the Registry to start your system

Personalizing Your Desktop Environment

One of the first things most users want to do when they get Windows, Windows 95, or now, Windows NT 4.0, is to personalize the desktop. Usually, the first thing that is changed is the default color set, or the desktop background becomes a picture of the grandkids. Everyone likes to have control over their working space.

NT 4.0 Server offers several ways to customize your desktop environment. The first that is discussed here is the Display Properties sheet.

Display Properties

Access the Display Properties sheet by right-clicking anywhere on the desktop background, and then choose Properties, which will bring up a screen similar to that shown in Figure 4.1.

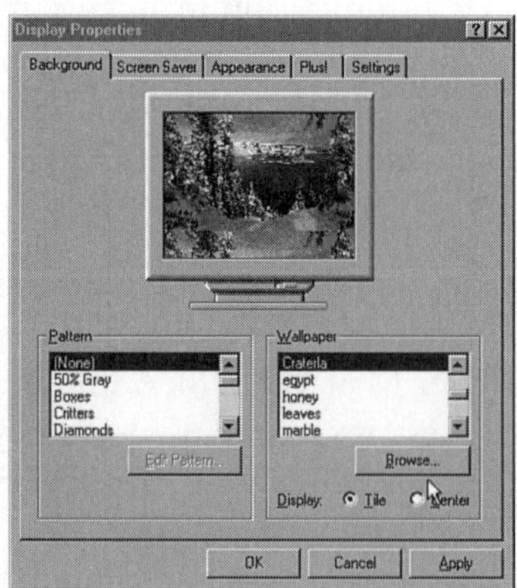

FIG. 4.1 ⇒ A new wallpaper bitmap has been chosen to replace the default background in this Display Properties sheet.

The Display Properties sheet has five tabs, each corresponding to one or more of the most popular changes users like to make to customize their computers: Background, Screen Saver, Appearance, Plus!, and Settings. A nice addition to this and many other properties sheets is the Apply button. This enables you to apply a change without closing the dialog box.

The Background tab lets you change the desktop wallpaper and pattern. These are the same types of changes you may have made in Windows when using the Desktop applet in Control Panel. A wallpaper display can be any bitmap image, and it can be stored anywhere on your computer. The Browse button helps you to easily find the bitmap you want to use as your wallpaper pattern.

Screen savers were first introduced to protect monitors from "burning in" an image of what's on the screen. Screen savers display a moving image on-screen after a designated time period of time of mouse and keyboard inactivity. Screen savers can also be fun to look at. Most new monitors today are designed to prevent burn-in.

Because it conforms to the OpenGL standard (direct draw to the screen, 3-D graphics support, and so on), Windows NT 4.0 supports some pretty cool screen savers. Among the new screen savers included in NT Server is the 3-D Maze, which displays a three-dimensional maze and then proceeds to maneuver you through it.

Most of the screen savers have additional customization options that can be accessed through the Settings button. You also can designate the time period of inactivity before the image kicks in, preview it in full-screen, and password-protect it, whereby you have to know the password before you can release the screen saver to display your regular screen. However, screen savers can use a lot of processor time, which can be wasteful because you won't be looking at the screen of the server very much anyway. Setting the screen saver option to the password box or a blank screen is the best option for serious servers (as opposed to test servers).

Having Fun with a Screen Saver!

Many software manufacturers build in little surprises or hidden features in their products. No, I'm not talking about bugs (which I like to call eccentricities). No, these hidden features are fun things and are usually referred to as *Easter eggs.* Here are a couple of Easter eggs that are built in to the NT screen savers.

continues

continued

Open the Display Properties sheet and select the 3-D Pipes screen saver. Change its settings so that the joint type is Ball. When the screen saver kicks in, look at the ball joints. Occasionally, one of them becomes a teapot. This is easier to spot on a 486 than on a Pentium.

Another Easter egg can be found by selecting the 3-D Text screen saver. In its settings, change the text to **i love nt**. The screen saver displays a surprise response. I leave it to you to determine whether it is "good!"

Through the Appearance tab, you can change color schemes and set the color, size, and, in some cases, the font settings for individual items, such as icons.

The Plus! tab gives you the option of using different icons for some of your desktop objects, as well as the choice of refining visual settings. For example, a visually impaired person might want to use large icons. If you have a high-resolution monitor, you can direct NT to smooth the edges of screen fonts and display icons using the full color range available.

Settings enables you to make changes to the monitor settings. From this tab, you can modify the display type, screen resolution, refresh frequency, color palette, and font size. Before applying a change, Microsoft suggests pressing the Test button and previewing the screen to be sure that it is viewable.

Exploring Control Panel

If you have worked with previous versions of Windows, you most likely have spent some time in Control Panel. Control Panel offers a variety of applets that modify your system configuration. Microsoft has reworked most of the Control Panel applets in NT 4.0 to provide a much greater degree of granularity when making your selections.

Control Panel, shown in Figure 4.2, can be opened in a variety of ways. You most commonly will open it from the Settings option on the Start menu. However, you can also access it through My Computer, Windows Explorer, or by creating a shortcut to it or any of its applets on your desktop. There are 25 applets in Control Panel.

FIG. 4.2 ⇒
NT 4.0 Server Control Panel is where many useful utilities can be found.

As you add applications or NT services to your computer, additional applets are likely added to the Control Panel.

Whenever you need to change a system parameter, your first stop should be Control Panel. The following is a list of the applets provided in Control Panel:

- Accessibility Options
- Add\Remove Programs
- DOS Console
- Date\Time
- Dial-Up Monitor (installed with RAS)
- Devices
- Display
- Fonts
- Internet
- Keyboard
- Licensing
- Mail and Fax
- Modems
- Mouse
- Multimedia
- Network
- ODBC (installed with any ODBC-compliant database)
- PC Card
- Ports
- Printers
- Regional Settings
- SCSI Adapters
- Server
- Services
- Sounds
- System
- Tape Devices
- Telephony
- UPS (uninterruptible power supply)

Your control panel will have additional utilities to help you manage the specific hardware and software installed on your system. Next, the functions each applet provides are explained briefly.

Accessibility Options is new to NT 4.0. It is designed for those individuals with visual, hearing, or movement challenges. It offers several modifications, including making the keyboard easier to use, visualizing computer sounds, and using the keyboard to control the mouse.

Add/Remove Programs lets you install and remove Windows NT components, such as games and accessories. It also provides a built-in procedure to automatically install or uninstall applications from disk or CD-ROM. If the application that is being installed is set up by using either a Setup.exe or Install.exe, Add/Remove Programs will record the setup process, display the application in its list of installed applications, and let you remove the application by using its Uninstall Wizard.

MS-DOS Console is often confused with the MS-DOS Prompt that is accessed through the Start menu. MS-DOS Console provides a means of modifying the way in which a DOS window appears on the desktop. You can alter screen colors, window size, font style and size, cursor size, and the command history buffer.

Date/Time, of course, modifies the computer's internal date and time values. There really is nothing remarkable here except that the screens are far more graphic and easy to use than ever before. It even shows you which part of the world your time zone covers.

Devices shows you all the device drivers detected and installed by NT, and which devices are currently running. It offers you the ability to start, stop, and configure startup types for device drivers.

Display produces exactly the same Display Properties sheet that was previously discussed. This is just another place to access it.

Fonts lets you view fonts installed on your system, add new fonts, and remove fonts that are no longer needed. You also have the option to display only TrueType fonts in applications.

Internet is installed in Control Panel if you have installed Internet Explorer. It lets you set the proxy server on your network through which you access the Internet. The proxy server is usually the firewall that is used to filter which users on your network can access the Internet and which users from the Internet can access your network.

Keyboard allows adjustment of the delay and repeat rates of your keyboard and enables you to change the keyboard type. It also enables you to specify alternative language keyboards if you want to include foreign language symbol sets.

Modems displays the properties of any modems installed on your computer. From here, you can add and remove modems and modify modem settings. Choosing Add starts the Install Modem Wizard. This Wizard walks you through the detection, selection, and connection of your system's modem.

Mouse lets you customize many characteristics of your mouse device. You can switch button usage for left-handed persons, modify the double-click speed (test it on the jack-in-the-box!), and change the pointer speed. There is also a tab for changing the various mouse pointers, where you'll find the more interesting visual representations for the select, wait, working, and other pointers (see Figure 4.3). Pressing Browse displays all the neat pointer files that NT supplies, including the infamous animated cursors. Look for the files with an .ANI extension. You can preview them before you apply them.

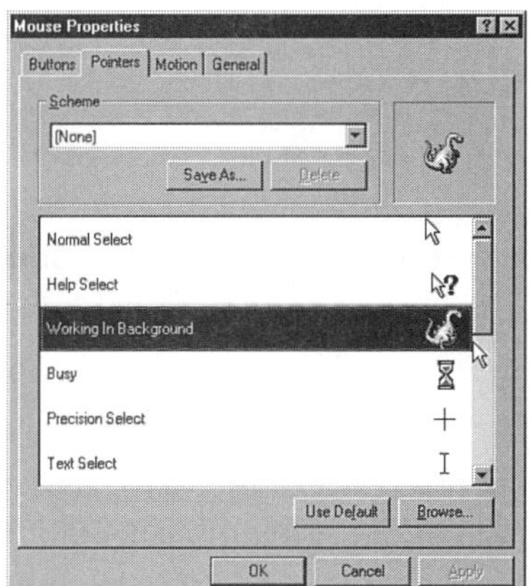

FIG. 4.3 ⇒
The Browse button displays a list of mouse pointer files that can be used to customize the pointers. Notice how the mouse pointer for Working has changed from the default hour-glass with an arrow to a dinosaur.

Multimedia provides configuration options for audio, video, MIDI, CD music, and any other multimedia-related devices.

Network identifies the computer, its relationship to the rest of the network, and all service, protocol, adapter, and bindings settings. This applet can also be accessed by selecting the properties for Network Neighborhood. This is where the majority of your network configuration takes place.

PC Card (PCMCIA) displays whether you have PC Card support on your computer, which cards are currently in use, and the resources they are using.

Ports lets you add, modify, and delete parameters for your computer's COM ports. For example, if you add a new com port adapter card to your computer, or connect a serial printer to an existing port, you may want to configure it for a certain speed and parity.

Printers replaces Print Manager and displays icons related to each printer installed on your computer or connected through the network. From these, you can manage the printing devices and print jobs. There is also an Add Printer Wizard that walks you through the process of installing, configuring, and sharing your printing device. This applet can also be accessed from the Task Bar by choosing Start, Settings, Printers.

Regional Settings displays current settings for number symbols, currency formats, date and time values, and input locales based on world regions. This used to be called International and has been greatly enhanced.

SCSI Adapters displays SCSI adapters and drivers that have been installed on your computer and their resource settings (I/O, interrupt, and so on).

Server opens a dialog box that offers statistics relating to the server-based activities of your computer. It shows which network users are currently connected, which shared resources are being used and by whom, and any replication settings that may have been configured. It also lets you set administrative alerts that deliver system message pop-ups to a specified user or computer.

Services displays a list of all the services that have been installed on your computer and their current running status. NT services are functions or applications that are loaded as part of the NT Executive. Thus, they run as part of the operating system instead of running as a background or resident program (TSR).

As Figure 4.4 demonstrates, this applet also gives you the ability to start and stop services, and to modify their startup configuration.

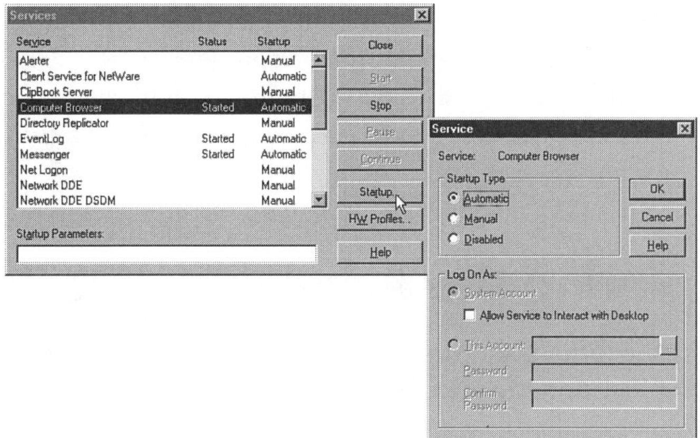

FIG. 4.4 ⇒
The Services dialog box shows the status of several NT services running on this computer, as well as the Startup Options box for one of the services, which is displayed by selecting Startup.

You can also set services based on hardware profiles so that only certain services run, depending on the specific hardware installation. For example, a laptop that is not connected remotely to a network while the user is on the road may have certain network-related services turned off. This makes additional resources available to other applications. When docked at the user's desk at a station that is wired to the network, those network services are then turned on again.

Sounds lets you assign different types of sounds to system and application events, such as warnings, opening a program, doing what you shouldn't, and so on.

System displays the System Properties sheet, in which you can define the default operating system at boot time, set recovery options for Stop errors, determine which hardware profiles to use during startup, view and delete user profiles stored on your computer, view and define environmental variables, modify application performance, and configure and customize pagefile parameters.

Tape Devices displays a dialog box to view, add, or delete tape devices and their driver settings that are installed on your computer.

Telephony opens the Dialing Properties dialog box that lets you view, add, or remove telephony drivers, and modify dialing parameters, such as pressing 9 to get an outside line or disabling call-waiting. You can create a different set of dialing parameters for different situations or locations. For example, dialing out through your modem at work may require no additional settings, whereas dialing out from a hotel room may require dialing one or more numbers in sequence to access a local or long distance line.

UPS lets you set configuration parameters for your uninterruptible power supply that is connected to the computer. Parameters include setting interface voltages for power failure and low battery signals, specifying a command file to be executed when the UPS is activated, and other UPS-specific characteristics, such as expected battery life.

Exploring the Administrative Tools

The Administrative Tools group contains utilities that are specific to your installation of either NT 4.0 Workstation or NT 4.0 Server.

The following 12 tools are installed on the Windows NT 4.0 Server:

- Backup
- UPS Disk Administrator
- Event Viewer
- UPS License Manager
- Migration Tool for NetWare
- Network Client Administrator
- Performance Monitor
- Remote Access Administrator
- Server Manager
- System Policy Editor
- User Manager
- UPS Windows NT Diagnostics

The *Backup* utility gives you considerable control over what data you want to back up and to where you want to back it up. It also controls the restore process. You can back up entire disks or directories, or specific files, including the Registry. It keeps summary logs indicating what was backed up or restored, when it was backed up or restored, and any files that it determined were corrupted.

The *Disk Administrator* can best be described as a much improved FDISK utility with a GUI interface. From the Disk Administrator, you can easily create and format disk partitions, create volume sets and extended volumes, and create stripe sets. On the Server version, you can also enable software fault tolerance (also known as RAID—Redundant Array of Inexpensive Disks), such as striping with parity and mirrored disk partitions.

The *Event Viewer* is a great troubleshooting utility. It records system events, such as services that failed to start or devices that could not be initialized. When various audit functions are enabled in NT, Event Viewer provides logs that record the audit information and display it for your review.

License Manager tracks software licenses throughout an enterprise. License information is collected from all primary domain controllers in your organization to a central database. You can view summaries of all per seat licenses and per server licenses in use. You can also view usage patterns.

The *Network Client Administrator* enables you to install or update client workstations. You can use the Client Administrator to install any of the client files contained on the NT Server 4.0 CD.

Performance Monitor is still receiving rave reviews from NT administrators for the sheer amount of system performance data that can be charted, saved, and reviewed. This utility is used to help determine performance bottlenecks on your system, processor utilization, server access, and so on. It is covered in more detail, along with Event Viewer, in Chapter 10, "Performance Monitor."

After *Remote Access Service* (RAS) has been installed and configured on your computer, the *Remote Access Admin* utility offers you management functions for your RAS client, such as defining which users can access your computer through a dial-in connection, who is currently connected, which ports are in use, and whether the service is running. This utility is reviewed again in Chapter 21, "Remote Access Support."

Server Manager can be used to administer both local and remote computers. You can view a list of users connected to another computer, view shared resources, enable/disable alerts, manage directory replication, and send messages to users. You can also add or remove computers from a domain, promote backup domain controllers, and synchronize servers in a domain with the primary domain controller.

System Policy Editor enables an administrator to control what users can do on client machines. You can restrict access to various portions of the machine. For example, you can prevent Windows 95 users from launching the DOS shell.

You create and manage user and group accounts through *User Manager*. Password policy information, location of user profiles and login scripts, users' functional rights, and user-access auditing are all configured through User Manager.

Windows NT Diagnostics is an enhanced and GUI version of Microsoft's MS-DOS-based MSD (Microsoft Diagnostics). This cool utility gives detailed information culled directly from the NT Registry relating to the system, display, disk drives, memory and pagefile usage, network statistics, environment variable values, resources in use and their settings, and services installed and their state. This version actually provides a far greater level of detail than previous NT versions. You can even print out the information screens.

Creating and Managing Hardware Profiles

Hardware Profiles offer a way for you to create and maintain different hardware configurations—including which services and devices are initialized—for different computing scenarios. The most common use for hardware profiles is with laptop computers that are sometimes placed in a docking station. While portable, the user can use the laptop's modem to dial in to the company network. When docked, that user can access the network through the network card installed in the docking station.

These are two different methods of connecting to the network, which are used in two different scenarios, and therefore require different hardware. You certainly can maintain the same profile for both scenarios. However, when the user is portable, they are likely to receive event or system messages relating to the "missing" network card. Likewise, if the docking station disables the laptop's modem, you can receive similar messages when the computer is docked. If you maintain two hardware profiles, you can customize which device is activated during which scenario.

Creating a Hardware Profile

To create a Hardware Profile, you first must access the System Properties dialog box, as displayed in Figure 4.5. The System Properties dialog box can be opened in one of two ways:

- Right-click My Computer on the desktop and then choose Properties.
- Open Control Panel and start the System applet.

FIG. 4.5 ⇒
The System Properties dialog box with the Hardware Profiles tab selected.

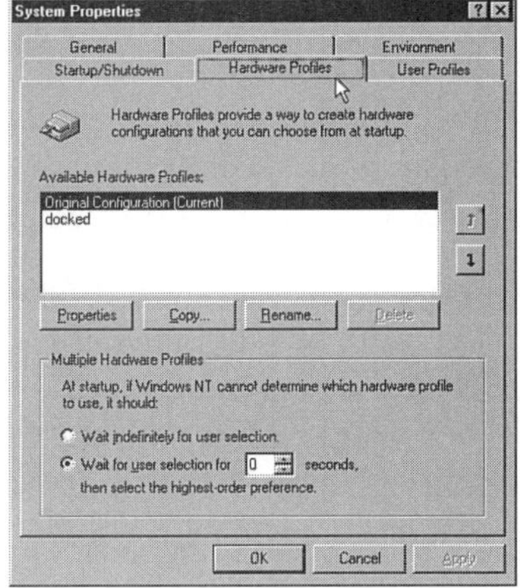

After the System Properties dialog box is displayed, follow these steps to create a new Hardware Profile:

1. Select the Hardware Profiles tab.
2. Choose an existing or original profile from the Available Hardware Profiles list box and choose Copy.
3. Enter the name of the new profile and choose OK.
4. Use the arrow buttons to the right of the profile list to determine the order preference of the profiles. This determines which order NT uses to load the profiles during system startup.
5. Use the Properties button to indicate whether the computer is a portable, its docking state, and whether this profile should disable all network functions (see Figure 4.6).

Ch 4

FIG. 4.6 ⇒
This Hardware Profile has been designated as a portable computer that is undocked.

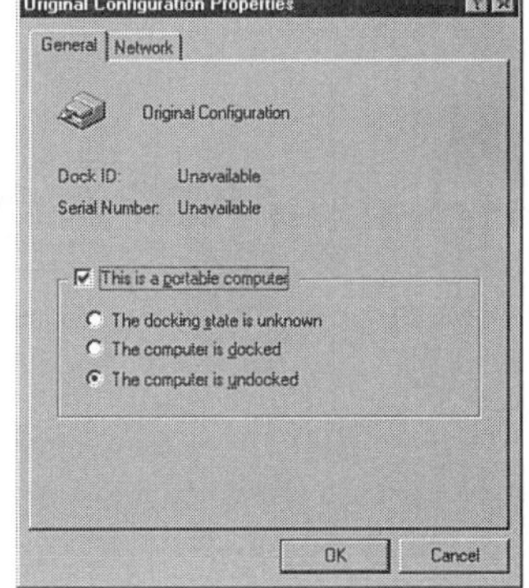

6. Specify what NT should do during startup. If you want NT to display a list of profiles at startup, choose Wait Indefinitely for Use Selection. NT does not continue with the startup operation until a profile selection is made. Profiles are displayed after you are prompted to press the spacebar for the Last Known Good Configuration.

   If you want to set a timeout value for selecting a profile before NT selects the first profile in the list, choose Wait for User Selection for xx Seconds, Then Select the Highest-Order Preference. If you set the timeout value to 0, NT simply boots with the highest order profile on startup. Pressing the spacebar when prompted for the Last Known Good Configuration redisplays the profile list.

Now that the Hardware Profile has been created, you need to identify which services and devices to enable and disable for each profile. This is accomplished through the Services and Devices applets, respectively, in Control Panel.

To define a specific Service or Device to the Hardware Profile, follow these steps:

1. Select the service or device from the list.
2. Press the HW Profiles button. This displays a new dialog box, as shown in Figure 4.7.
3. Select the profile that you are modifying from the list.
4. Choose Enable or Disable to turn the service or device on or off, respectively, for that profile.
5. Choose OK and close the Services or Devices applet.

When you start NT and choose your hardware profile, the services and devices start as you configured them.

Examining the Windows NT 4.0 Server Registry

The Windows NT 4.0 *Registry* is perhaps the single most important element of the NT operating system architecture. The Registry is an encrypted database of configuration and environment information relating to the successful booting of NT 4.0. Think of this file as being the DOS

AUTOEXEC.BAT and CONFIG.SYS files rolled into one—and then some.

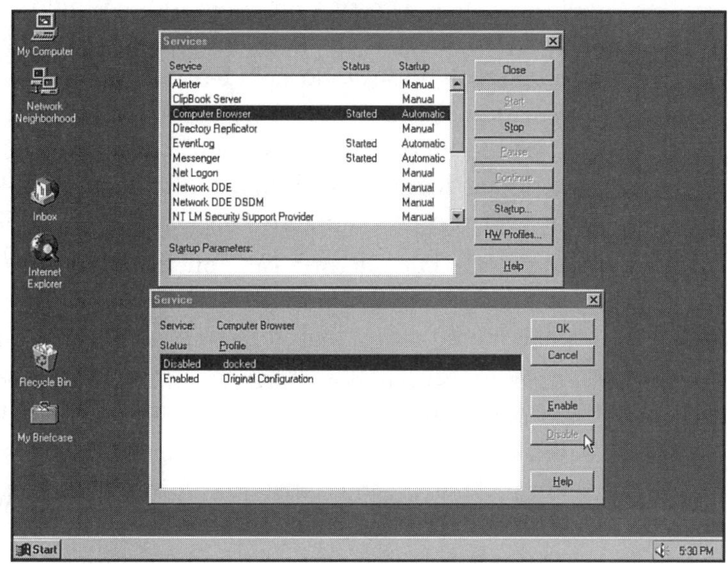

FIG. 4.7 ⇒
In this example, the Computer Browser service, while enabled normally, has been set to disabled for the profile called DOCKED.

Key Concept

The Registry is central to the operation of Windows NT 4.0. Driver information, services, hardware profile information, security objects and their permissions, and account information are all stored in the Registry. Microsoft considers the Registry so integral a part of Windows NT that they strongly discourage you from making changes to it.

In fact, the Control Panel, Administrative Tools group, and various properties sheets give you all the utilities you need to modify and customize your installation of Windows NT 4.0 for normal maintenance. All of these utilities modify one or more Registry entries. Therefore, there are only limited and very specific reasons for you to make changes to the Registry directly.

Caution

A good rule of thumb for modifying the Registry: If there is a utility that can do the modification, *use the utility*! If you make substantial changes to the Registry that result in problems during bootup or execution, Microsoft will *disallow* your support call.

The Registry has several advantages over the older system:

- *Centralized* Instead of a PROGMAN.INI, CPANEL.INI, and a host of other such files for your applications, Windows NT stores all its configuration data in the Registry. As a result, all Windows NT components and Windows NT-based applications can easily find information about any other aspect of the computer. In addition, the Registry supports remote administration: An administrator, sitting at his or her own workstation, can alter another computer's configuration by remotely editing its Registry.
- *Structured* The Registry can contain subsections within sections, something that was impossible with INI files. The end result is a much more orderly, logical record.
- *Flexible* INI files contained ASCII text. The Registry can contain text as well, but it also can hold binary and hexadecimal values. It can even hold executable code or entire text files. The Registry also contains preferences and restrictions for individual users, something that INI files never have done. This provides a configuration database that stores not only computer-specific information, but also user-specific information.
- *Secure* You can protect the Registry just like any object in Windows NT. An access control list can be defined for any Registry key, and a special set of permissions exists specifically for dealing with the Registry.

When viewed from this perspective, one wonders how users survived without the Registry. However, the Registry has its drawbacks:

- *Cryptic* Unlike INI files, the assumption with many parts of the Registry seems to be: "Humans just don't go here." It isn't always easy to determine why certain entries are present or how to effectively configure them.
- *Sprawling* Imagine all the INI files on an average Windows 3.x-based computer merged into a single file, with some additional hardware information as well. The Registry begins its life big, and it only gets bigger.
- *Dangerous* If you make a mistake when editing an INI file, or if you aren't sure about the potential effect of a change, you can always exit the text editor without saving the file. Even a fatal change to an INI

file can be fixed by booting to MS-DOS and using a text editor to alter the problematic file. Not so with the Registry: Direct changes to the Registry are often dynamic and potentially irreversible.

That said, there *are* specific instances when you have to modify the Registry directly. These usually have to do with the absence of a utility to make a necessary change, or for troubleshooting purposes. Some of the more common of these changes are discussed later in this chapter in the section, "Using the Registry to Configure NT 4.0 Server."

Navigating with the Registry Editor

The Registry can be accessed by starting the Registry Editor utility, which can be accessed in several ways, including the following two methods:

- Open the Windows Explorer and select the SYSTEM32 folder under the Windows NT system folder (usually called WINNT or WINNT40). Double-click the file REGEDT32.EXE.
- Choose RUN from the Start menu and type in **REGEDT32.EXE**. Then choose OK.

If you are going to access the Registry often, you can also create a shortcut to REGEDT32.EXE on your desktop.

Throughout the remainder of this book, the Windows NT system directory is referred to as WINNT40.

The Registry Editor displays the five main windows, called *subtrees*, of the Windows NT 4.0 Registry for the local computer, as shown in Figure 4.8. The following are the five subtrees:

- HKEY_LOCAL_MACHINE
- HKEY_CURRENT_CONFIG
- HKEY_USERS
- HKEY_CURRENT_USERS
- HKEY_CLASSES_ROOT

By default, only those users with Administrator access can make modifications to the Registry. Other users can only view the information contained there.

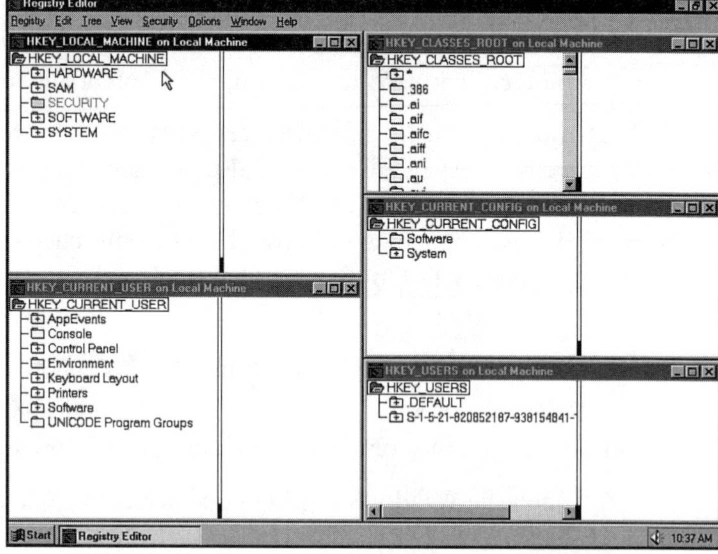

FIG. 4.8 ⇒
This screen shows the five subtrees of the Windows NT Registry, tiled for better viewing.

Tip

I recommend setting the View option to Read Only, even for administrators. This guards against any accidental modifications that can lead to serious boot and operation problems. Enable it by selecting Read Only Mode from the Options menu in Registry Editor.

From Options, choose Font to change the font style and size to facilitate viewing, and Confirm on Delete to guard against accidental deletions.

At first glance, these windows look a lot like File Manager or the Windows Explorer, and, in fact, you can navigate them in much the same way. The left pane of each subtree window displays the keys pertinent to that subtree. As each key is selected, the parameters and values assigned to that key are displayed in the right pane. You can think of a key as being a more sophisticated .INI file.

You may recall that an .INI file (see Figure 4.9) consists of section headings, each section containing one or more parameters unique to that section, and each parameter having an appropriate value or values assigned to it. The values can be text strings, file names, or simple `yes` or `no` or `1` or `0` values.

FIG. 4.9 ⇒
Here is an example of a Windows .INI file. Notice the section headings in square brackets. Each section has at least one parameter. The values assigned to each parameter represent what the parameter "expects."

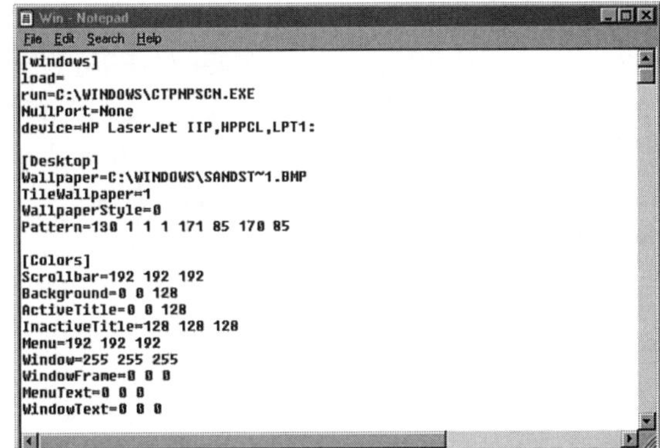

A registry key is quite similar. Think of it as a "nested" .INI file (see Figure 4.10). A key can consist of parameters with assigned values, or it can consist of one or more subkeys, each with its own parameters.

FIG. 4.10 ⇒
An NT Registry key can go several levels deep before finally displaying parameter values.

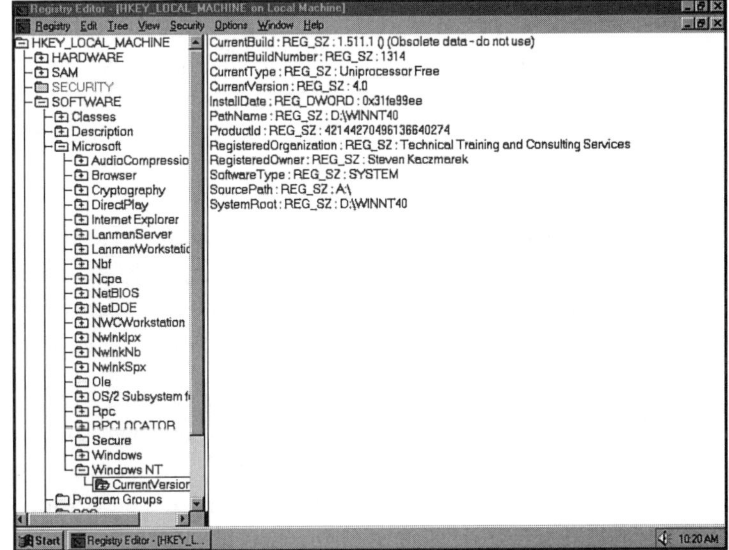

HKEY_LOCAL_MACHINE contains all the system configuration data needed to boot and run the operating system successfully. This data includes services that need to be run, device drivers, hardware profiles, including which hardware is currently loaded, login parameters, and so on.

It is composed of five primary keys called *hives*, each of which can contain subtrees that are several folders deep (refer to Figure 5.10). Each of the hives relates to a corresponding Registry file saved in the WINNT40 \SYSTEM32\CONFIG directory, except for the Hardware hive, which is built when the computer is booted. The Hardware hive is more properly referred to as a *key*. The five hives are as follows:

- Hardware (properly called a key)
- SOFTWARE
- System
- SAM
- Security

The *Hardware* hive, or key, contains data related to detected hardware devices installed on your computer.

Key Concept

The Hardware key is built during the startup process and, as such, is called a volatile key. This information is not written down anywhere or stored permanently on the system. Instead, NT "detects" this information each time it boots.

The Hardware key includes such information as the processor type and power, keyboard class, port information, SCSI adapter information, drive data, video, and memory. This information is primarily stored as binary data, and because it is built during startup, it is useless to modify. The Windows NT Diagnostics utility is the best tool to use to view this data.

The *SAM* and *Security* hives contain security-related information. SAM stands for *Security Account Manager* and, as you may suspect, contains user and group account information, as well as workgroup or domain membership information. The Security hive contains *Local Security Account* (LSA) policy information, such as specific user rights assigned to user and group accounts.

Neither of these hives or their subtrees are viewable. It is part of Microsoft's security policy to hide this information, even from the system administrator. Even if you could look at it, it probably would not make a lot of sense, nor give you any insight into violating account information.

Unlike the Hardware key, SAM and Security *are* written to files on the hard disk. Each has a registry and log file associated with it—SAM and SAM.LOG, and SECURITY and SECURITY.LOG, respectively. You can find them in the WINNT40\SYSTEM32\CONFIG subdirectory on the NT system partition.

The *SOFTWARE* hive consists of computer-specific software installed on your computer, as opposed to user-specific settings. This includes manufacturer and version; installed driver files; descriptive and default information for NT-specific services and functions, such as the Browser, NetDDE, and NT version information; and the WINLOGON service. This hive also has two files associated with it that can be found in the WINNT40\SYSTEM32\CONFIG subdirectory: SOFTWARE and SOFTWARE.LOG.

While the SOFTWARE hive contains more descriptive information regarding the installation of applications, drivers, and so forth, on your computer, the *SYSTEM* hive provides configuration and parameter settings necessary for NT to boot successfully and correctly maintain your computer's configuration. A quick look at the subtrees below SYSTEM shows at least three *control set* entries, as shown in Figure 4.11.

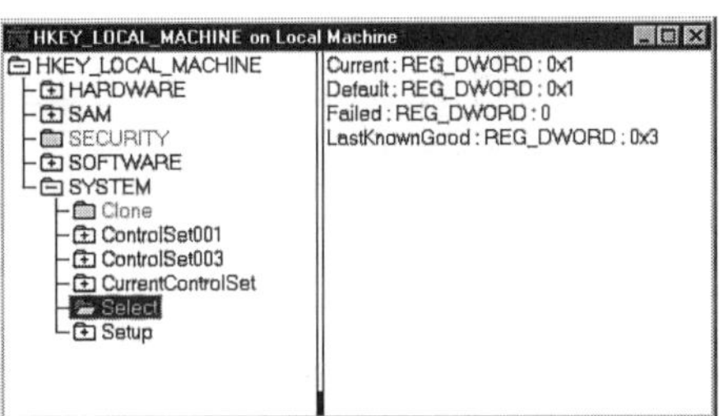

FIG. 4.11 ⇒ HKEY_LOCAL_MACHINE with the SYSTEM hive expanded to show the boot control sets.

These control set entries are used to control the startup process, indicating which services should load, which drivers to load and initialize, and so on. Any changes you make to existing driver settings, or any new drivers you install and configure, are added to a control set in the SYSTEM hive. Its corresponding files in the WINNT40\SYSTEM32\CONFIG subdirectory are SYSTEM and SYSTEM.ALT.

HKEY_CURRENT_CONFIG is a new subtree added to Windows NT 4.0. It is a subset of HKEY_LOCAL_MACHINE and reflects only the current software and system modifications made during the current session, as well as the current startup settings. This is useful for isolating data specific to a hardware profile from other data stored in the Registry.

HKEY_CLASSES_ROOT will look familiar to administrators of previous versions of Windows. It represents OLE and file association data that is specific to file extensions. This is information that was stored in Windows' REG.DAT file. This subtree is also a subset of HKEY_LOCAL_MACHINE and can be found there under the SOFTWARE hive.

HKEY_USERS consists of two subkeys relating to user settings. DEFAULT contains system default settings that are used when the LOGON screen is first displayed. The second entry represents the user who is currently logged on to the system. The long alphanumeric value you see is the user's *Security Identifier*, hereafter called the SID of the user.

Tip

All the entries you see under the SID subkey represent changes that can be made to the user's environment, primarily through Control Panel. If the user changes the color scheme, cursor pointers, wallpaper, and so on, the values can be found here in their respective keys. If you need to modify a user's entries, perhaps remotely, you can do so here as well. You will find two file entries in WINNT40\SYSTEM32\CONFIG that correspond to the users who have modified their profiles or whose profiles you have modified. For example, the environmental settings (profile) of user JONESB are represented by the files JONES000 and JONES000.LOG.

HKEY_CURRENT_USER represents a subset of HKEY_USERS, and points back to the settings of the current user (the SID entry in HKEY_USERS).

Using the Registry to Configure Windows NT 4.0 Server

This section is designed with two goals. The first is to introduce you to the method for looking up keys and making changes to them. The second is to point out some specific modifications that you can accomplish *only* by changing the Registry.

Let me begin by stating the not-so-obvious. As you navigate through the Registry and select various keys, you may or may not see parameter values displayed in the windows. If there are not any parameters displayed, it does not mean necessarily that there are *no values* present. It may simply mean that NT is using the *default* values for that entry.

For example, if you select the HKEY_CURRENT_USER\CONTROL PANEL\CURSORS subkey, and you have made no changes to your mouse pointers, you will see no entries here. However, it is obvious that you do, in fact, have default mouse pointers displayed on your screen. In this case, NT does use parameter values—the default values.

Tip

Here is the general rule of thumb: If the Registry does not display parameter values when you select a subkey, assume that NT is using the defaults for that subkey, and realize that the default for some parameters is to have *no* values loaded at all.

As an example of NT using the default values, consider the choice of the cursor pointer. A user has selected the peeling banana to replace the hourglass "wait" cursor, and wants to change it to the running horse. Also, this user wants to change the application-starting cursor (hourglass with an arrow) to the lumbering dinosaur. You can simply and easily do this through the Mouse applet in Control Panel, but you feel particularly bold today.

There are basically three areas of information that you need to know before modifying this particular entry, and in general, for changing any Registry entry:

- Which Registry entry you are going to change, what subkey or subkeys are involved (yes, there might be more than one!), and where they are located.
- Which parameter needs to be added, modified, or deleted to make your change effective.
- What value needs to be assigned to the parameter, and its type.

Now you will be told how to change the cursor pointer, step by step.

First, to determine what is the subkey and where it is located is not always easy. If the change you are making modifies the way the system operates (new device driver, changing the video display, adding a new hardware profile), the subkeys to make this change are most likely found under HKEY_LOCAL_MACHINE, in the SYSTEM hive, under one of the control-set entries. If the change you are making affects the working environment of a particular user (desktop wallpaper, cursors, colors, window properties), those subkeys most likely are found under HKEY_USERS in the current user's subkey, identified by the user's SID.

Sometimes the subkeys that need to be modified are easy to identify, such as "cursors." Sometimes they are not easily identifiable. Who could know intuitively that the HKEY_LOCAL_MACHINE\SYSTEM\CURRENTCONTROLSET\SERVICES\CE2NDIS31 entry refers to the driver settings for the Credit Card Ethernet Adapter installed in a particular laptop? So how do you find out? Sometimes your documentation tells you. Most times, however, you find the subkeys only by exploration, trial, and error. But remember, Microsoft recommends that you *not* make configuration changes through the Registry directly, especially when there is a utility that can do it for you. In the case of the example network adapter just mentioned, you don't really need to know where its configuration values are stored in the Registry because you can configure it through the Network applet in Control Panel or through the Properties sheet of the Network Neighborhood.

Finding Subkey Names in the Registry

If you are not sure of the subkey name for the subkey that you are looking for, but you know what it might be called, or a category that it might fall within, you can use the Registry's *FIND KEY* function to look it up. Follow these steps:

1. Place your cursor at the top (root) of the directory structure in the subtree in which you think the key is located.
2. Choose View, Find Key.
3. Type in your guess for the key name or category you are looking for.
4. Choose Match Whole Word Only or Match Case if you are relatively sure of the key entry; otherwise, deselect these options.
5. Choose Find Next.

FIND KEY places a box around the first subkey entry that matches the text string you entered. You can move the Find window out of the way if it blocks your view. Choose FIND NEXT again until you locate the appropriate subkey.

FIND KEY only works with key entries. It does not work for parameter entries.

Getting back to the example, because changing the cursor is a user environment change, you know you can find the subkey in the HKEY_USERS subtree, under the user's SID entry. You can also select the HKEY_CURRENT_USER subtree because it points to the same location in the Registry.

From there, because you are modifying cursors, you want to look for a subkey called Cursors. Because cursors are modified through the Control Panel, it is a pretty safe bet that you will find a Cursors subkey under the Control Panel subkey. You now know the location and the subkey to modify: HKEY_CURRENT_USER\CONTROL PANEL\CURSORS.

The second thing you should know is which parameter needs to be added, modified, or deleted to make your change effective.

Once again, finding out which parameter value to change is difficult, unless someone gives you the parameter and value to enter. In this example, the parameter corresponding to the working hourglass is called `WAIT`, and the parameter corresponding to the application-start hourglass with an arrow is called `APPSTARTING`.

Finally, you need to know what value needs to be assigned to the parameter, and its type.

By now, you probably get the idea. Again, in this example, the file names that correspond to the various cursors either have a .CUR or .ANI extension. You can find these listed in the WINNT40\SYSTEM32 subdirectory. Recall that the `WAIT` cursor needs to change from the banana (BANANA.ANI) to the running horse (HORSE.ANI), and that the `APPSTARTING` cursor needs to be the lumbering dinosaur (DINOSAUR.ANI).

There are five data types that can be applied to a parameter value. Again, you usually know which one to use, either because it is obvious or because someone has told you or because you took the time to read the manual. Table 4.1 lists the value types and a brief description of each.

Table 4.1 Parameter Value Data Types

Data Type	Description
`REG_SZ`	Expects one text string data value

continues

Table 4.1 Continued

Data Type	Description
REG_DWORD	Expects one hexadecimal string of one to eight digits
REG_BINARY	Expects one string of hexadecimal digits, each pair of which is considered a byte value
REG_EXPAND_SZ	Expects one text string value that contains a replaceable parameter, such as %USERNAME% or %SYSTEMROOT%
REG_MULTI_SZ	Expects multiple string values separated by a NULL character

In the cursor example, cursors can be associated with only one file name (a text string). Therefore, your parameter value will have a data type of REG_SZ and its value will be the file name. Now you can modify the Registry. Just follow these steps:

1. Open the Registry Editor. From Options, deselect READ ONLY MODE, if it is selected.
2. Maximize the HKEY_CURRENT_USER subtree window to make it easier to work with.
3. Expand the Control Panel key.
4. Highlight the Cursors key. In the right pane, because the WAIT cursor has been modified once already, there is an entry called WAIT, of data type REG_SZ, and value BANANA.ANI.
5. Double-click the parameter entry (WAIT) to display the String Editor (see Figure 4.12).
6. Enter the new parameter value (**D:\WINNT40\SYSTEM32\HORSE.ANI**).
7. To add a new parameter and value, choose Edit from the Registry Editor menu bar, then Add Value.
8. In the Add Value dialog box, enter the Value Name (APPSTARTING) and choose the appropriate Data Type (REG_SZ). Then choose OK (see Figure 4.13).
9. In the String Editor dialog box, enter the appropriate parameter value (**D:\WINNT40\SYSTEM32\DINOSAUR.ANI**), and click OK.

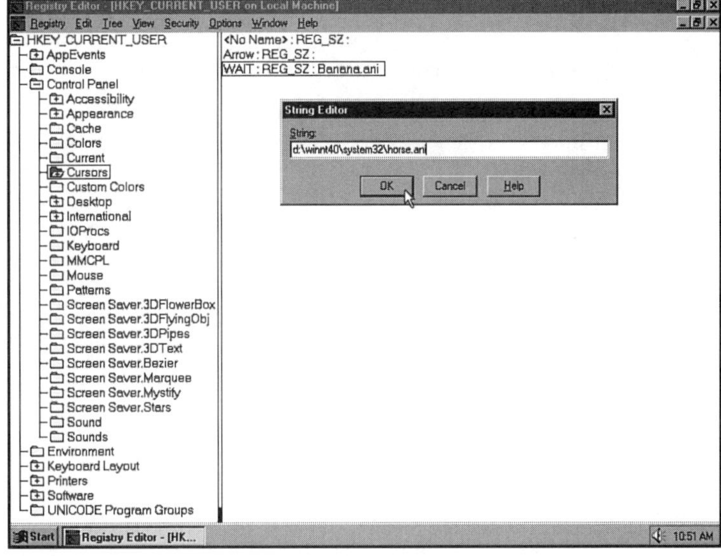

FIG. 4.12 ⇒
The `WAIT` cursor currently has the value BANANA.ANI. Double-click it to display the String Editor and change the value to HORSE.ANI.

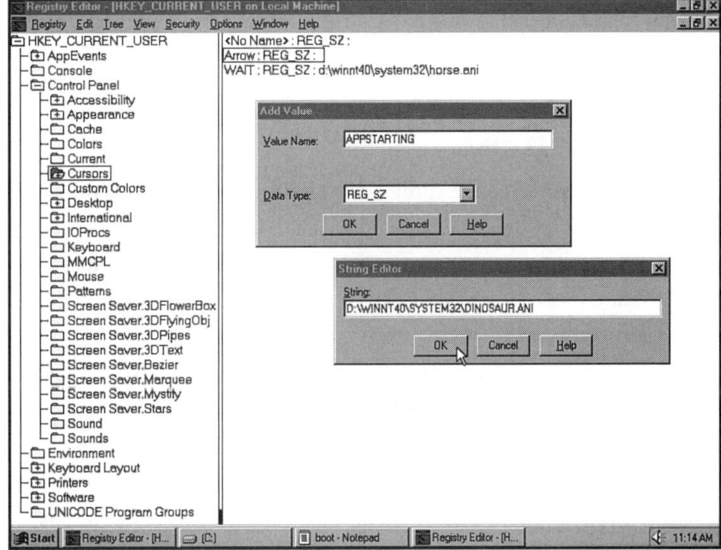

FIG. 4.13 ⇒
Choose Edit, Add Value to add the new cursor parameter APPSTARING, with a data type of REG_SZ, and click OK. In the String Editor, type in **DINOSAUR.ANI**.

10. Reselect Read Only Mode from the Options menu, then close the Registry Editor.

The change does not take effect immediately.

Tip

In general, if you make a user environment change, the user has to log off and log back on before the change takes effect. In general, if you make a system change, the computer has to be shut down and restarted before the change takes effect.

Caution

Parameter names are *not* case-sensitive. However, because they can be quite lengthy, Microsoft uses proper case (the first letter of each word is capitalized) when displaying these values to make them easier to read.

If you misspell a parameter name, the result may be that NT simply ignores it, or the misspelling may result in a service stopping altogether. This is also true with parameter values. If in doubt, look up the spelling in the Windows NT Resource Kit, or test it first. Before testing, back up your original Registry or, at the very least, save the original subkey.

The following sections cover some other modifications that you can make to the Registry for which a utility does not exist.

Legal Notices

Legal notices are dialog boxes that pop up before a user can log on, and usually indicate who is authorized to access that computer. You generally see these while logging into enterprise networks. You can change these dialog boxes in the Registry by modifying the following subkey and parameter values:

```
HKEY_LOCAL_MACHINE\SOFTWARE\MICROSOFT\WINDOWS NT\CURRENT
VERSION\WINLOGON\
LegalNoticeCaption and LegalNoticeText.
```

`LegalNoticeCaption` modifies the title bar of the dialog box that displays during logon, and `LegalNoticeText` is the text that is displayed in the dialog box.

For example, modify *LegalNoticeCaption* to display `Legal Notice for Computer SDK`. Modify *LegalNoticeText* to display `Unauthorized users will be shot on sight!`

To see this change, log off and log back on.

Logon User Names

By default, NT records in the Registry the name of the last user who logged on to a system (along with the workgroup or domain that the user logged into). You can view this information in the following entries:

```
HKEY_LOCAL_MACHINE\SOFTWARE\MICROSOFT\WINDOWS NT\CURRENT
VERSION\WINLOGON\
DefaultUserName and DefaultDomainName
```

For added security, you can hide the display of the last user who logged on so that no one can try guessing the password to get on to the system. As you know, users tend to use passwords that are easily guessed. If a potential hacker also must guess the username, it makes the computer less desirable to hack (kind of like putting the Club® on your steering wheel). If you would rather not display the last user who logged on to a computer, you need to *add* the following parameter name and value:

```
HKEY_LOCAL_MACHINE\SOFTWARE\MICROSOFT\WINDOWS NT\CURRENT
VERSION\WINLOGON\
DontDisplayLastUserName
```

`DontDisplayLastUserName` expects a data type of `REG_SZ` and a value of either `1` (Yes, *don't* display the last username) or `0` (No, *do* display the last username). This is an example of a parameter that does not display in the right pane, but whose default value is loaded by the Registry.

The System Policy Editor

Windows NT 4.0 Server includes a configuration-management utility called the *System Policy Editor.* It is intended to be used to manage server-based workstation and user policies—that is, configuration information that is stored on a login server (domain controller) and downloaded to the user's workstation when the user logs on to the network. Most of the Registry changes that have been discussed so far in this chapter can be made more safely through the System Policy Editor. Also, the configuration is assured to "follow" the user and, thus, be consistent and standard.

In Figure 4.14, for example, a system policy has been created for user SDKACZ. Note that, simply by pointing and clicking through a variety of intuitive screens, the user's access and environment can be fixed. In this example, the user's ability to modify the screen is reduced, a wallpaper has been selected, and the RUN and Settings Folders have been removed. This policy affects the user wherever SDKACZ logs on.

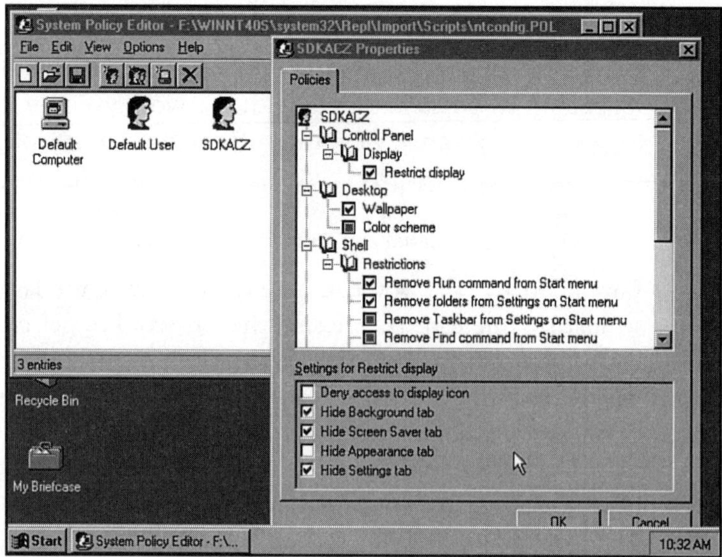

FIG. 4.14 ⇒
Sample System Policy Editor screen from NT 4.0 Server.

Similarly, a system policy can be established by workstation name, thus regulating a user's environment and access by workstation. For example, you can disable the last user name from displaying, or modify the legal notice dialog box, again, by simply pointing and clicking the appropriate check box. These settings then affect every user who logs on to this specific workstation.

The workstation and user policies are saved in a file called NTCONFIG.POL and stored in the WINNT40\SYSTEM32\REPL\IMPORT\SCRIPTS subdirectory of each domain controller. This directory is also known by the share name *NETLOGON*.

Changing the Default Startup Screen

The default startup screen is the Ctrl+Alt+Del screen that is displayed when you log off or boot NT. You can modify how this screen looks by modifying entries in the `DEFAULT` subkey of `HKEY_USERS`. For example, if you have created a company logo called XYZ.BMP that you want all your computers to display during startup, you need to modify the default desktop wallpaper. Access the following Registry entry:

```
HKEY_USERS\DEFAULT\DESKTOP\Wallpaper
```

Next, you would need to change the Wallpaper entry from (DEFAULT) to XYZ.BMP. The change takes effect when you log off, and displays the logo centered on the desktop.

If you want your bitmap to be tiled, change the `TileWallpaper` value in the same subkey from `0` to `1`.

Through a little experimentation, you will find other changes that can be made to the cursor using the Registry. For example, try changing the cursor pointers!

Accessing the Registry Remotely

A computer's Registry may have been modified, either through a utility or directly, and now the computer is not functioning quite as it should. The Registry Editor provides a facility for accessing the computer's Registry remotely. If you have an administrator account on your computer that matches one on the other machine (including password), you can access the other computer's Registry. Just follow these steps:

1. Open your Registry Editor.
2. From the Registry menu option, choose Select Computer.
3. In the Select Computer dialog box, enter the name of the computer, or select it from the browse list, and then click OK.
4. The Registry Editor now displays the HKEY_LOCAL_MACHINE and HKEY_USERS subtrees from that computer. The title bar of each window displays the remote computer's name.
5. When you have finished working with the remote Registry, choose Close from the Registry menu option, and be sure that the remote Registry window is highlighted.

If you do not close the remote Registry windows, they reappear on your computer the next time you start the Registry Editor.

Ch 4

Windows NT Core Services

A service is a built-in application that provides support for other applications or other components of the operating system. Windows NT inlcudes dozens of services, each performing a highly specialized function. Many of Windows NT's services support NT's networking capabilities.

Examples of Windows NT services include:

- Windows Internet Name Service (WINS), which maps IP addresses to NetBIOS names.

- UPS service, which interacts with an Uninterruptible Power Supply system to prevent your system from abruptly shutting down.
- Server service, which accepts I/O requests from the network and routes the requested resources back to the client.
- Workstation service, which accepts I/O requests from the local system and redirects the requests to the appropriate computer on the network.

Services are background processes that perform specific functions in Windows NT. Typically, services don't interact with the user interface in any way (including appearing in the Task List), so users shouldn't be aware of their existence. Think of a Windows NT service as the equivalent of UNIX daemon, or if you are more comfortable with NetWare, the equivalent of a NetWare Loadable Module (NLM).

This section will take a closer look at some important Windows NT services and how to configure them.

Key Concept

Microsoft lists the following objectives for the Windows NT Server exam:

Configure Windows NT Server core services. Services include: Directory Replicator, License Manager, other services.

The Services Application

The Control Pandel Services application manages the services on your system.

The Services application writes directly to the following key, where configuration data for Windows NT services is maintained:

```
HKEY_LOCAL_MACHINE\SYSTEM\CurrentControlSet\Control\Services
```

Double-click the Services icon in Control Panel to open the Services dialog box (see Figure 4.15). The Services dialog box lists the services on your system, as well as the Status (whether the service is started or not) and the Startup type. The Startup type setting describes whether the service will start automatically or manually, or whether it is disabled. Automatic services start at the very end of the boot process, after the "Welcome: Press Ctrl+Alt+Del to log on" window appears. (Because services are Win32 programs, they require a fully functional operating system before they can be opened.) Manual services start when you select the service in the Services dialog box and click the Start button.

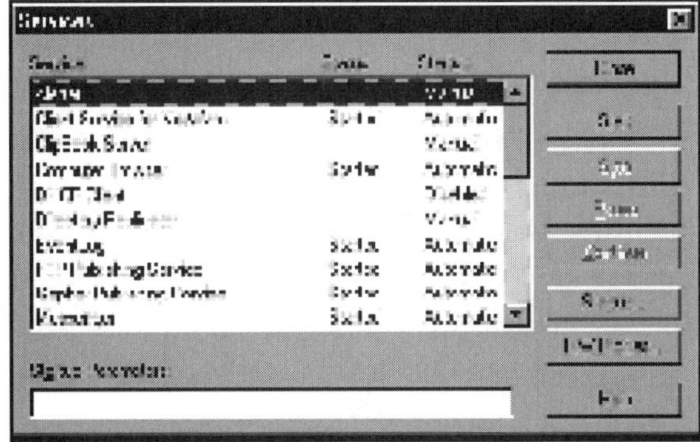

FIG. 4.15 ⇒
The Control Panel Services application.

Note that the Services dialog box also includes buttons that stop a service, pause a service, or continue a service that has been paused. Pausing a service causes the service to continue handling the processes it's currently serving but not take on any new clients. For example, the Server service is required to run on a server before it can accept connections from a client. Stopping the Server service causes all connections to be immediately dropped, but pausing the service preserves existing connections while rejecting new connection attempts.

To enable a service for a given hardware profile, click the HW Profiles button in the Services dialog, select a profile, and click OK.

Double-click a service to open a configuration dialog box—called the Service dialog (as opposed to the Services dialog)—that enables you to configure a startup type and define a logon account for the service.

The logon account defines a security context for the service. Because services are Win32 programs, they must run under the aegis of a user account. The problem is, services continue to execute even when nobody is logged on to the computer, so the administrator must configure the service to use a specific user account. Here are two options:

- *System Account.* An internal account, called SYSTEM, can be used either by the operating system or by the service. This method isn't recommended, however, because you can't fine-tune rights and permissions without possibly affecting the performance and stability of the operating system and other services that may use this account

- *This Account.* You may designate any user account from your account database here. You should create a separate account for each service for which you want to configure rights and permissions.

Network Services

The Services tab of the Control Panel Network application lets you add, configure, and remove services that support network functions. The Add button opens the Select Network Service dialog box, which provides a list of available Windows NT network services. Select a service and click OK to add the service to your configuration. Or, click the Have Disk button if you are attempting to install a new service from a disk.

Some of the services in the Network Services list are configurable through the Network application and some are not. Select a service and click the Properties button to open a configuration dialog box for the service (if there is one). Figure 4.16 shows the configuration dialog box for the Server service.

FIG. 4.16 ⇒
The Server dialog box.

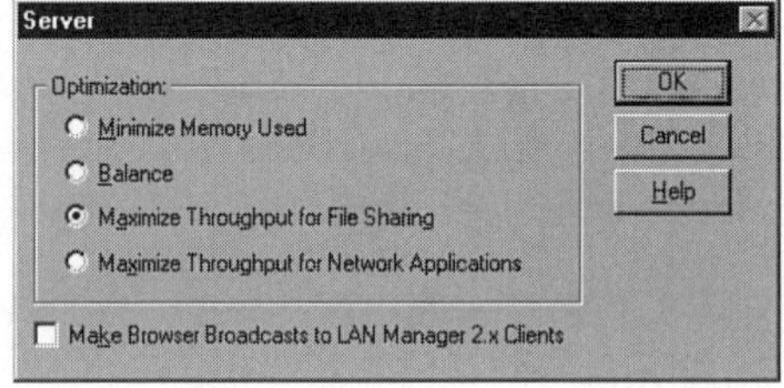

Many of the network components you'll read about elsewhere in this book (DHCP, WINS, DNS, RAS, and Gateway Services for NetWare) are actually services that, though often configured elsewhere, can still be added, started, stopped, and managed through the Network Services tab and the Control Panel Services application. For the most part, anything you do on the network occurs through some form of network service.

The following sections examine some important topics relating to Windows NT services, as follows:

- Directory replication
- Client license management
- The browser process

Directory Replication

Directory Replication is a facility that lets you configure Windows NT Servers to automatically transmit updated versions of important files and directories to other computers on the network.

The purpose of Directory Replication is to simplify the task of distributing updates for logon scripts, system policy files, Help files, phone lists, and other important files. The network administrator updates the file(s) on a single server (called the export server) and the export server automatically distributes the file(s) to other network servers or even to network workstations. The computer receiving the update is called the import computer. A Windows NT Server, a Windows NT Workstation, or a LAN Manager OS/2 server can act as an import computer.

Directory Replication is performed by the Directory Replicator service. You can start and stop the Directory Replicator service from the Control Panel Services application. The parameters for the Directory Replicator service are found in the Registry key:

```
HKEY_LOCAL_MACHINE\SYSTEM\CurrentControlSet\Services\Replicator\
Parameters
```


Note Most of the parameters in the Registry key HKEY_LOCAL_MACHINE\SYSTEM\CurrentControlSet\Services\Replicator\Parameters can be configured within Server Manager (described later in this chapter). Two important exceptions are:

Interval. A REG_WORD value that defines how often an export server checks for updates. The range is from 1 to 60 minutes and the default is 5 minutes.

GuardTime. A REG_WORD value that defines how long a directory must be stable before its files can be replicated. The range is 0 to one half of the Interval value. The default is 2 minutes. See the "Configuring the Export Computer" section later in this chapter for a discussion of the Wait Until Stabilized check box. ■

The export directory on the export server holds the files and directories are replicated across the network. The default export directory is

```
\<winnt_root>\System32\Repl\Export
```

For each group of files that set for replication, create a subdirectory in the export directory. When the Directory Replicator service starts, NT shares the export directory with the share name Repl$.

Each import computer has a directory called the import directory, and the default directory is

```
\<winnt_root>\System32\Repl\Import
```

The Directory Replicator service copies files from the export server's export directory to the import directories of the import computers. In addition to copying files, the Directory Replicator service automatically creates any necessary subdirectories in the import directory so that after each replication the directory structure of the import directory matches the export directory's directory structure.

The process occurs as follows:

1. The export server periodically checks the export directory for changes and, if changes have occurred, sends update notices to the import computers.
2. The import computer receives the update notices and calls the export computer.
3. The import computer reads the export directory on the export server and copies any new or changed files from the export directory to its own import directory.

The following sections describe how to set up the export and import computers for directory replications.

Configuring the Export Computer To set up the export server for directory replication:

1. Double-click the Control Panel Services application to start the Directory Replicator service.
2. Create a new account for the Directory Replicator service. The Directory Replicator account must be a member of the Backup Operator group or the Replicator group for the domain. When you set up the new account, be sure to enable the Password Never Expires option and disable the User Must Change Password at Next Logon option. Also, make sure the account has logon privileges for all hours.
3. Start the Server Manager application in the Administrative Tools program group (see Figure 4.17). Server Manager is a tool for managing network servers and workstations from a single location.
4. In the Server Manager, double-click the export server to open the Server Properties dialog box (see Figure 4.18).

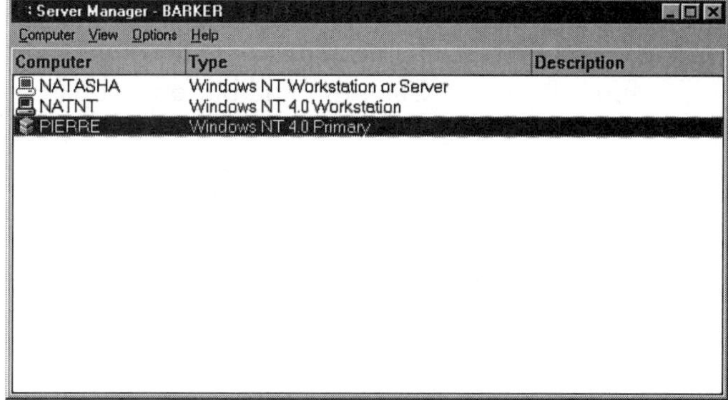

FIG. 4.17 ⇒ The Server Manager main screen.

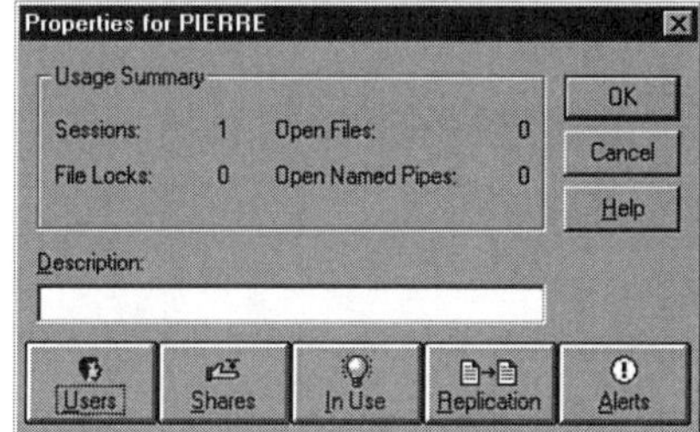

FIG. 4.18 ⇒ The Server Properties dialog box.

5. Click the Replication button to open the Directory Replication dialog box (see Figure 4.19).

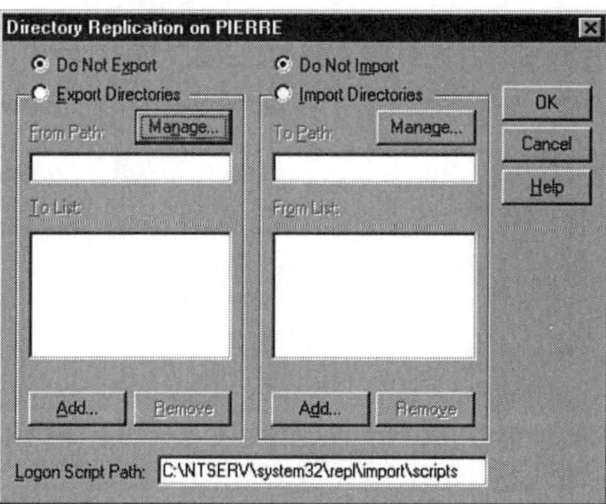

FIG. 4.19 ⇒ The Directory Replication dialog box.

Note A Windows NT server can serve as an export server, an import computer, or both. The left side of the Directory Replication dialog box defines export properties. The right side of the Directory Export dialog box defines import properties.

Ch 4

6. In the Directory Replication dialog box, select the Export Directories option button. The default path to the export directory appears in the From Path box. Click the Add button to open the Select Domain dialog box (see Figure 4.20). Click a domain to select it. Double-click a domain to display the computers within that domain (see Figure 4.21). If you select a whole domain, all import servers in the domain receive the replicated data. If you choose a specific computer, only that computer receives the replicated data. You can choose any combination of domains and specific computers.

FIG. 4.20 ⇒
The Select Domain dialog box.

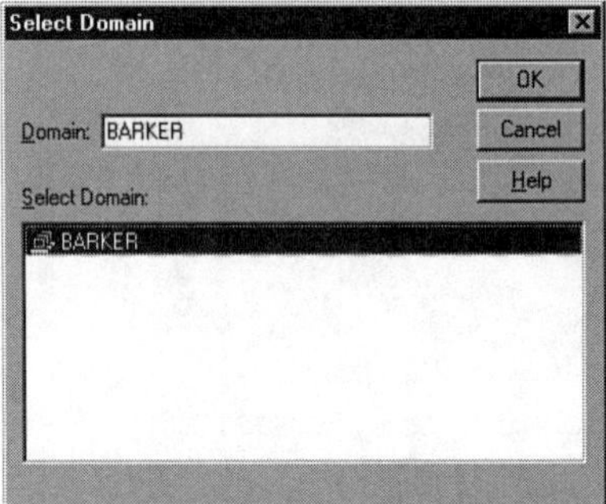

FIG. 4.21 ⇒
The Select Domain dialog box displaying specific computers within the domain.

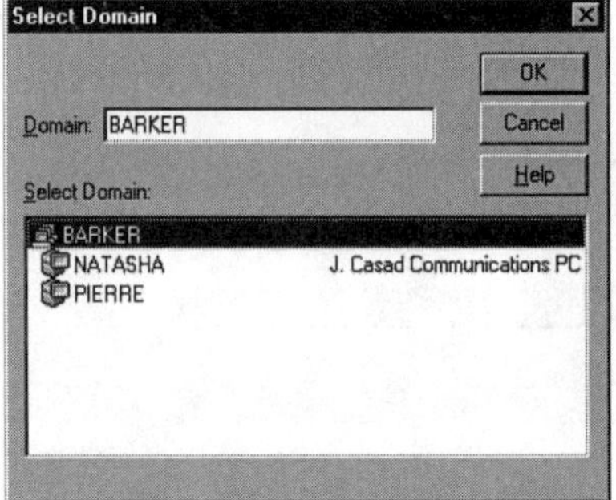

7. Click the Manage button to open the Manage Exported Directories dialog box (see Figure 4.22). Subdirectories within the export directory appear in the Sub-Directory list. You can add or remove subdirectories from the list by clicking the Add or Remove buttons. Note the check boxes at the bottom of the screen. Enabling the Wait Until Stabilized check box tells the Directory Replicator service to wait at least two minutes after any change to the selected subdirectory

tree before exporting. Enabling the Entire Subtree check box tells the Directory Replicator service to export all subdirectories beneath the selected subdirectory. The Add Lock button lets you lock the subdirectory so it can't be exported. More than one user can lock a subdirectory. (Consequently, a subdirectory can have more than one lock.) To remove a lock, click the Remove Lock button.

FIG. 4.22 ⇒
The Manage Exported Directories dialog box.

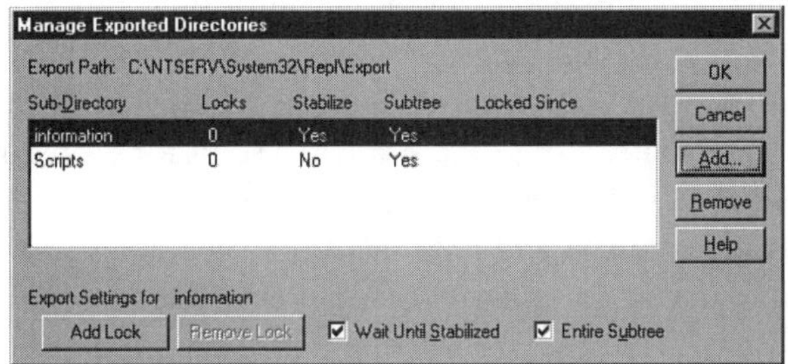

8. Click OK in the Manage Exported Directories dialog box, the Directory Replication dialog box, and the Server Properties dialog box.

Configuring the Import Computer To set up the import computer for directory replication:

1. Double-click the Services icon in the Control Panel. Select the Directory Replicator service and click the Startup button to open the Service dialog box (see Figure 4.23).

FIG. 4.23 ⇒
The Service dialog box.

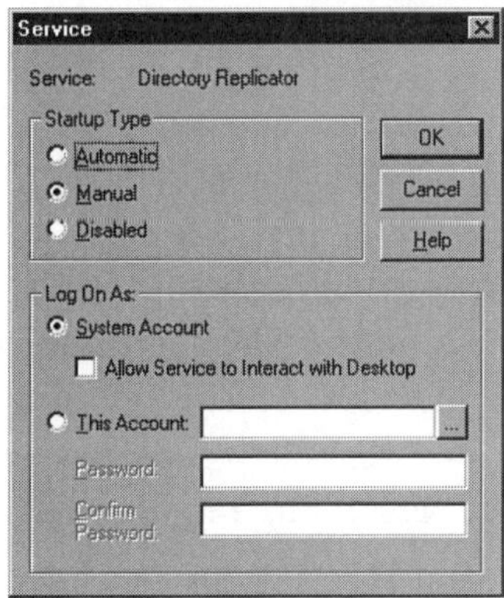

2. In the Startup Type frame, select the Automatic option button. Select the This Account option button and enter a username and password for the replicator account you created on the export server.

Note If the import computer and the export server aren't part of the same domain or a trusting domain, you must create a replication user account on the import computer and give that account permission to access the Repl$ share on the export server. Enter this account and password in the Service dialog box in Step 2.

3. Start Server Manager, select the computer you're now configuring, and click the Replication button in the Properties dialog box. The Directory Replication dialog box appears. This time, you're concerned with the import side (the right side) of the dialog box, but the configuration steps are similar to steps for configuring the export side. The default import directory appears in the To Path box. Click the Add button to add a domain or a specific export server (see Step 6 in the preceding section). Click the Manage button to open the Manage Imported Directories dialog box, which lets you manage the import directories (see Figure 4.24).

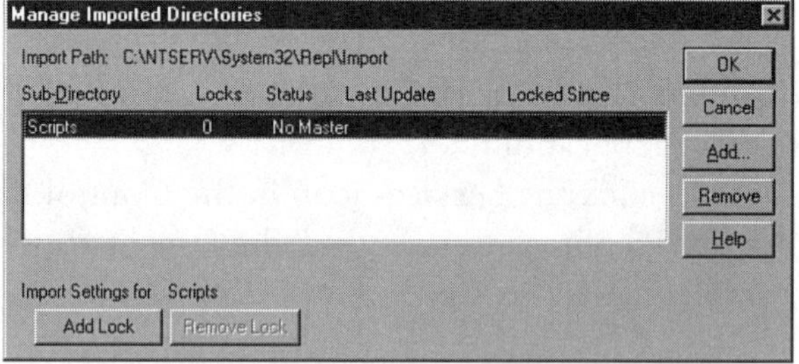

FIG. 4.24 ⇒
The Manage Imported Directories dialog box.

4. In the Manage Imported Directories dialog box, click Add or Remove to add or remove a subdirectory from the list. Click Add Lock to add a lock to the subdirectory (see preceding section).

Troubleshooting Directory Replication The Status parameter in the Manage Exported Directories and the Manage Imported Directories dialog boxes gives the status of the directory replication for a subdirectory. The possible values are as follows:

- *OK.* The export server is sending regular updates, and the import directory matches the export directory.
- *No Master.* The import computer isn't receiving updates, which means the export server may not be running, or the Directory Replicator service on the export server may not be running.

- *No Sync.* The import directory has received updates, but the data in the updates isn't what it should be, which means there could be an export server malfunction, a communication problem, open files on either the import of the export computer, or a problem with the import computer's access permissions.
- *(Blank).* Replication has never occurred. The cause could be improper configuration on either the import or the export computer.

When the Directory Replication service generates an error, check Event Viewer to learn what you can about the cause.

Microsoft recommends the following solutions for some common replication errors:

- *Access Denied.* The Directory Replicator service might not be configured to log on to a specific account. Check Event Viewer. Check the Startup dialog box in the Control Panel Services application to see if an account is specified, and use User Manager for Domains to check the permissions for the logon account.
- *Exporting to Specific Computers.* Designate specific export servers for each import server and specific import computers for each export server. If you just choose a domain in the dialog box opened by clicking the Add button in the Directory Replication dialog box, every domain computer receives replicated data and every import computer receives updates from every export server in the domain.
- *Replication over a WAN link.* When transmitting replication data across a WAN link, specify the computer name rather than just the domain name when you click the Add button in the Directory Replication dialog box.
- *Logon Scripts for Member Servers and Workstations.* NT Workstations and non-controller NT Servers must use the default logon script directory:

```
C:\<winnt_root>\System32\Repl\Import\Scripts
```


Windows NT Client Licenses

Microsoft requires that every client accessing a resource on a computer running Windows NT Server have a Client Access License (CAL). The Client Access License is separate from the license for the client's operating system. Your Windows 95 or Windows NT Workstation doesn't include implied permission to access resources on a Windows NT Server—to access NT Server resources, you must have a CAL.

Microsoft provides two options for purchasing Client Access Licenses, as follows:

- *Per Server mode.* Client Access Licenses are assigned to each server. A Windows NT Server might be licensed for, say, 10 simultaneous client connections. No more than 10 clients will be able to access the server at one time—additional clients will not be able to connect.
- *Per Seat mode.* Client Access Licenses are assigned to each client machine. You purchase a CAL for every client computer on the network. If the total number of simultaneous connections on all Windows NT Servers exceeds the number of per seat licenses, a client can still connect.

Microsoft allows a one-time switch from Per Server to Per Seat licensing mode. If you aren't sure which option to choose, you can choose Per Server mode and change later to Per Seat mode if you determine that Per Seat mode is more cost-effective.

If your network has only one server, Microsoft recommends that you choose Per Server licensing mode. If you have more than one server on your network, Microsoft suggests the following formulas:

A=number of servers

B=number of simultaneous connections to each server

C=total number of seats (clients) accessing computers

If A * B < C, use Per Server licensing. Number of CALs=A*B

If A * B > C, use Per Seat licensing. Number of CALs=C

Windows NT Server includes the following tools for managing client licenses:

- The Licensing Application
- License Manager

The following sections describe these Windows NT license-managing tools.

The Licensing Application The Control Panel Licensing application opens the Choose Licensing Mode dialog box (see Figure 4.25). The Choose Licensing Mode dialog box lets you add or remove client licenses or switch from Per Server to Per Seat licensing mode.

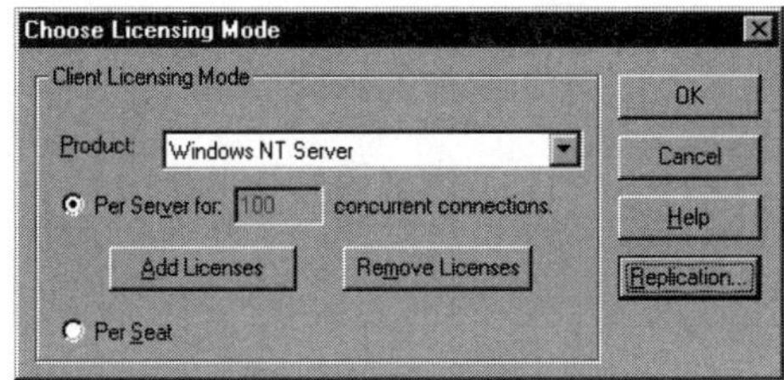

FIG. 4.25 ⇒ The Choose Licensing Mode dialog box.

The Replication button opens the Replication Configuration dialog box (see Figure 4.26). The Replication Configuration dialog box lets you configure license replication.

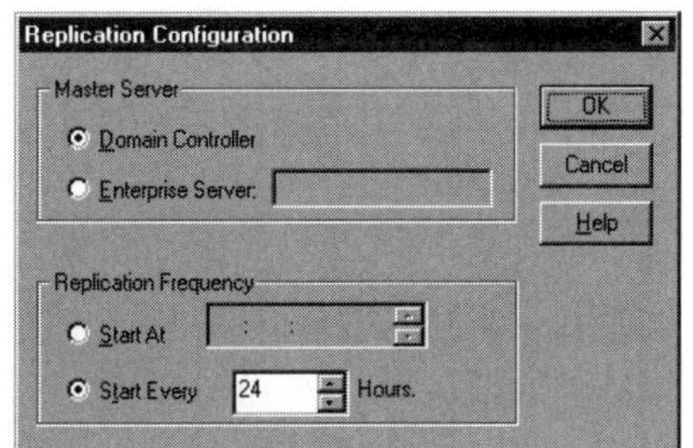

FIG. 4.26 ⇒ The Replication Configuration dialog box.

License replication is a convenient feature that lets individual servers send their licensing information to a master server. The master server creates and updates a database of licensing information for the entire network. This provides a single central location for licensing information.

License Manager License Manager, a tool in the Administrative Tools program group, displays licensing information for the network (see Figure 4.27). You can maintain a history of client licenses, examine your network's Per Server and Per Seat licenses by product, and browse for client license information on particular network clients. You also can monitor server usage by Per Seat clients, and even revoke a client's permission to access a server.

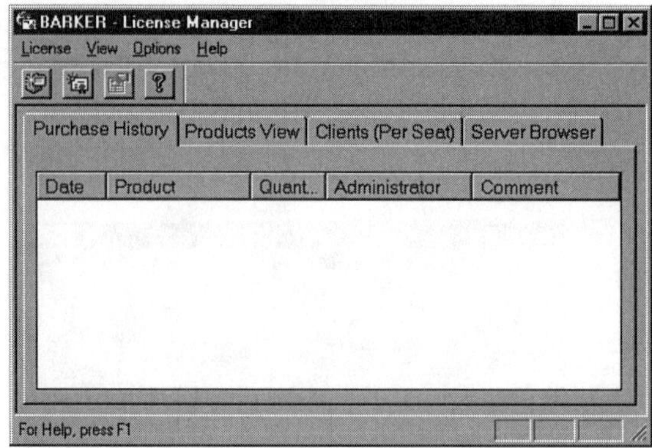

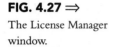

FIG. 4.27 ⇒
The License Manager window.

You also can use License Manager to add or edit license groups. A license group is a group of users mapped to a group of Per Seat licenses. License groups are a means of tracking per seat license usage in situations where an organization has more users than computers (or in some cases, more computers than users). For example, a retail outlet may have 10 employees sharing three Per-Seat-licensed computers.

Computer Browser Service

One of the most important network services is the Computer Browser service. The Computer Browser service oversees a hierarchy of computers that serve as browsers for the network. A browser is a computer that maintains a central list of network servers. (In this case, a server is any computer that makes resources available to the network.) That list then becomes available to clients who are "browsing" the network looking for remote computers, printers, and other resources. The list that appears when you open the Network Neighborhood application, for instance, comes from a network browser list.

The advantage of the browser process is that it allows a small number of network computers to maintain browse lists for the whole network, thereby minimizing network traffic and eliminating duplication of efforts. (The alternative would be for all computers to constantly poll the network in order to maintain their own lists.) Before the browser process can function efficiently, however, it must be highly organized so that clients know where to find a list and so that contingencies can take effect when a browser fails.

In a Windows NT domain, each computer assumes one of five browser roles:

- *Master browser.* Each workgroup or domain subnet must have a master browser. At startup, all computers running the Server service (regardless of whether they have resources available for the network) register themselves with the master browser. The master browser compiles a list of available servers on the workgroup or subnet and forwards the list to the Domain Master Browser. Master browsers then receive a complete browse list for the entire domain from the domain master browser.
- *Domain master browser.* The domain master browser requests subnet browse lists from the master browsers and merges the subnet browse lists into a master browse list for the entire domain. It also forwards the domain browse list back to the master browsers. The Primary Domain Controller (PDC) serves as the domain master browser for a Windows NT domain.
- *Backup browser.* The backup browser gets a copy of the browse list from the master browser (on the subnet) and distributes the browse list to subnet clients who request it. If the master browser fails, a backup browser can serve as the master browser for the subnet.
- *Potential browser.* A potential browser is a computer that isn't presently serving as a browser but can become a browser at the request of the master browser or as a result of a browser election (described later in this section).
- *Non-browser.* A non-browser is a computer that cannot serve as a browser.

The first time a client computer attempts to access the network, it obtains a list of backup browsers for the subnet or workgroup from the master browser. It then asks a backup browser for a copy of the browse list.

If a master browser fails, a new master browser is chosen automatically in what is known as a browser election. A browser election can occur if a client or backup browser cannot access the master browser. A browser election isn't exactly an election; it's really more of a contest. The browsers and potential browsers rank themselves according to a number of criteria, and the machine with the highest ranking becomes the new master browser.

Some of the criteria used in a browser election are as follows:

- *Operating system.* Windows NT Server gets a higher score than Windows NT Workstation, which gets a higher score than Windows 95.
- *Version.* Windows NT Server 4 gets a higher score than Windows NT Server 3.51, and so forth.
- *Present browser role.* A backup browser scores higher than a potential browser.

You can configure a Windows NT computer to always, never, or sometimes participate in browser elections, using the MaintainServerList parameter in the Registry key:

```
HKEY_Local_Machine\System\CurrentControlSet\Services\Browsr
\Parameters
```

The possible values are as follows:

- *Yes.* Always attempt to become a browser in browser elections (default for Windows NT Server domain controllers).
- *No.* Never attempt to become a browser in browser elections.
- *Auto.* The Auto setting classifies the computer as a potential browser (default for Windows NT Workstations and Windows NT Servers that aren't acting as domain controllers).

To make other domains available to the browser service, select the browser service in the Network application's Services tab and click the Properties button. The Browser configuration dialog box appears. Enter a domain name in the box on the left and click the Add button; then click OK.

Configuring Peripherals and Devices

Control Panel includes several applications that help you install and configure peripherals and devices. You should be familiar with how to use these applications to install drivers and configure peripherals and hardware. The following sections examine these applications:

- Devices
- Multimedia
- Ports
- UPS
- SCSI

- Tape Devices
- PC Card
- Modems
- Keyboard
- Mouse
- Display

You should be familiar with how to use these applications for installing and configuring peripherals and devices. Some of the following sections also appear in the full discussion of Control Panel applications in Appendix A.

Key Concept

Microsoft lists the following objectives for the Windows NT Server exam:

Configure peripherals and devices. Peripherals and devices include: communications devices, SCSI devices, tape device drivers, UPS and UPS service, mouse drivers, display drivers, and keyboard drivers.

Devices

The Devices application (SRVMGR.CPL) writes to HKEY_LOCAL_MACHINE\SYSTEM\CurrentControlSet\Services. You can start, stop, or disable device drivers in this Control Panel applet (see Figure 4.28).

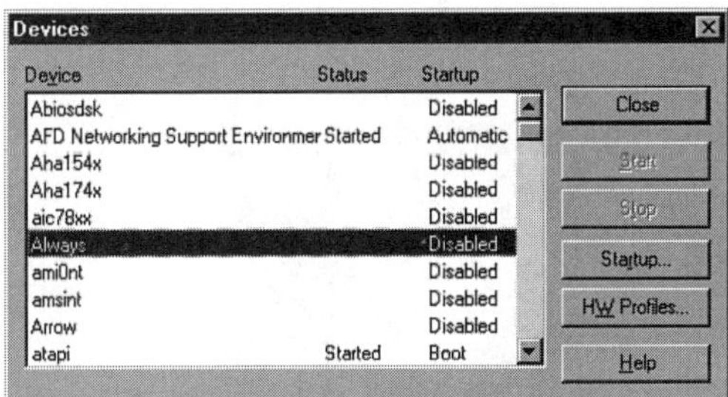

FIG. 4.28 ⇒ The Devices application.

The three columns in the Control Panel Devices main display area are labeled Device, Status, and Startup. The Device column identifies the name of the device driver as it appears in the Registry; the Status column reads "Started" if the driver is active, and otherwise appears blank; the Startup column denotes when each driver is configured to initialize.

To set the Startup value, select the device driver you want to modify and choose the Startup button. In the Device dialog box, shown in Figure 4.29, choose one of the following Startup Types:

- *Boot.* These devices start first, as soon as the kernel is loaded and initialized (see Chapter 13, "The Windows NT 4.0 Boot Sequence," for more details about the boot process). These devices have a Start value of 0 in the Registry. Atdisk, the hard disk driver, is an example of a boot device.
- *System.* These devices start after the boot devices and after the HKEY_LOCAL_MACHINE subtree has begun to be built. These devices have a start value of 1 in the Registry. The video driver is a system device.
- *Automatic.* These devices start late in the boot process, after the Registry is almost entirely built, just before the Winlogon screen appears. These devices have a start value of 2 in the Registry. Serial, the serial port driver, is an automatic device.
- *Manual.* These devices are never started without administrator intervention. They may be manually started through the Control Panel Devices menu. These devices have a start value of 3 in the Registry.
- *Disabled.* These devices cannot be started at all unless their startup Type is changed to something other than Disabled. These devices have a start value of 4 in the Registry. File system drivers are disabled by default (although file system recognizers are started with the system devices; if any file systems are "recognized," the Startup Type of the file system drivers is changed to System as well).

FIG. 4.29 ⇒
The Device dialog box.

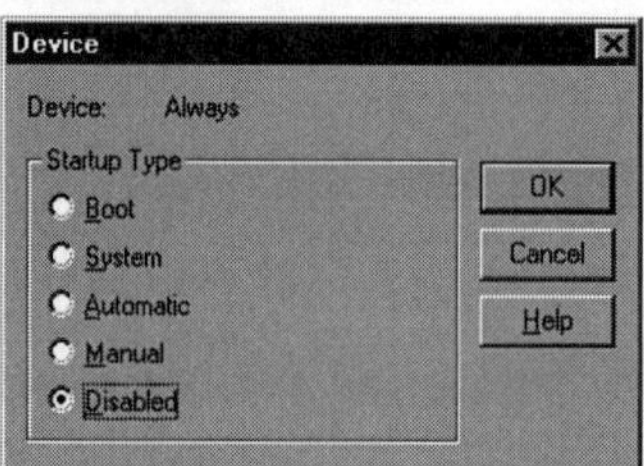

To start a device that isn't active, select the device and choose the Start button. If the Start button is grayed out, the device is already started or disabled.

To stop a device that's active, select the device and choose the Stop button.

A grayed-out stop button indicates that the device already is inactive.

To enable or disable a device for a given hardware profile, select the device, click HW Profiles, select enable or disable to change to the desired status, and click OK. You learn more about hardware profiles later in this chapter.

Multimedia

The Multimedia application (MMSYS.CPL) writes to HKEY_LOCAL_MACHINE\SYSTEM\CurrentControlSet\Services. Multimedia device drivers are added and configured from this Control Panel applet. The Multimedia application also provides settings for CD music, audio, video, and MIDI.

Ports

The Ports application (PORTS.CPL) writes directly to the following key:

```
HKEY_LOCAL_MACHINE\SYSTEM\CurrentControlSet\Services\Serial
```

This Control Panel interface lists only the serial ports that are available but not in use as serial ports. In other words, if a mouse is connected to your COM1 port, COM1 doesn't show up in the Control Panel Ports dialog box. All serial ports, regardless of whether they appear in Control Panel Ports, are logged in the Registry under the following key:

```
HKEY_LOCAL_MACHINE\HARDWARE\Description\System
\<multifunction_adapter>\ 0\åSerialController\<COM_port_number>
```


The Settings button displays values for the port's baud rate, data bits, parity, stop bits, and flow control.

If you need an additional port for use under Windows NT, choose the Add button. You may assign a different COM port number, base I/O port address or IRQ, or enable a First In-First Out (FIFO) buffer for that port (see Figure 4.30).

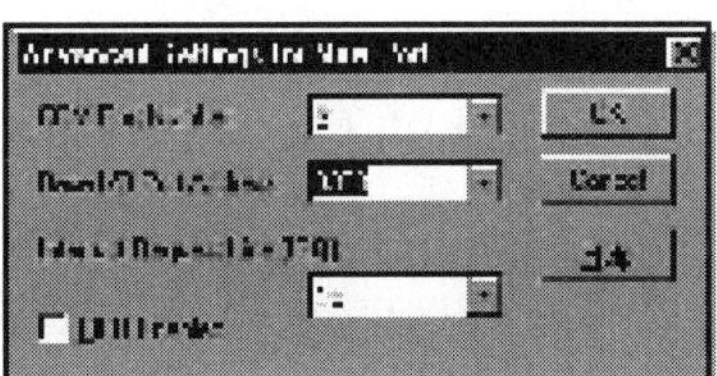

FIG. 4.30 ⇒ Adding a new port using the Ports application's Add button.

To remove a port, simply select it and click the Delete button.

UPS The UPS application (UPS.CPL) writes to the following key:

```
HKEY_LOCAL_MACHINE\SYSTEM\CurrentControlSet\Services\UPS
```

If your computer is equipped with an Uninterruptible Power Supply (UPS), Windows NT can be configured to communicate with it. The specific voltages requested in the UPS Configuration area depend on the UPS manufacturer and model. You may need to consult with your vendor to get these values. Armed with the correct information, Windows NT can recognize the following:

- *Power failure signal.* The point when an event is logged and the Server service paused. No new connections to this server can be made, but existing connections still function.
- *Low battery signal at least 2 minutes before shutdown.* As the name implies, Windows NT recognizes when the UPS battery is about to be exhausted.
- *Remote UPS Shutdown.* Signals Windows NT that the UPS is shutting down.

The Execute Command File option enables an administrator to specify a batch or executable file that runs immediately preceding a shutdown. The program has 30 seconds before the system shuts down. The program cannot open a dialog box because that would require an attendant user.

If no Low Battery Signal is configured, the administrator can enter the Expected Battery Life and the Battery Recharge Time Per Minute of Run Time in the lower left corner of the dialog box.

After the initial PowerOut alert is raised (the power failure signal has been received), Windows NT waits until the Time Between Power Failure and Initial Warning Message has elapsed, and then sends an alert to all interactive and connected users. Windows NT continues to send these alerts every time the Delay between Warning Messages elapses.

If the UPS is about to run out of steam, the system shuts down safely. If power is restored, users are notified, an event is logged, and the Server service resumes.

SCSI Adapters This application is one of the great misnomers in Windows NT. As it suggests, this application opens the SCSI Adapters dialog box, which is used to install SCSI adapter drivers. However, this dialog box also is used to install and remove IDE CD-ROM drivers as well as drivers for CD-ROM drives that use proprietary interfaces, such as Mitsumi or Panasonic drives. The dialog box should refer to both SCSI adapters and CD-ROM drives; currently the interface is completely counterintuitive.

To add a SCSI adapter or CD-ROM device driver, follow these procedures:

1. Double-click in the SCSI Adapters application in the Control Panel.
2. In the SCSI Adapters dialog box, choose the Drivers tab and click the Add button.
3. Select the driver from the list of available drivers in the Install Driver dialog box. If your driver isn't listed but you have a disk from the manufacturer with a Windows NT driver, click the Have Disk button.
4. Choose OK. You must point Windows NT toward the original installation files (or the disk that contains the driver) and restart the computer in order for the new driver to initialize.

To remove a SCSI adapter or CD-ROM device driver, perform these instructions:

1. Select the Drivers tab in the SCSI Adapters dialog box.
2. Select the driver you want to remove.
3. Choose the Remove button.

Tape Devices Almost identical to the SCSI Adapter Setup dialog box in both appearance and function, this dialog box allows the installation and removal of tape drives for use with a Windows NT Backup program.

To add a tape drive device driver, use these steps:

1. Double-click the Tape Devices icon in Control Panel.
2. Select the Drivers tab.
3. Click the Add button.
4. Select the driver from the list of available drivers. If your driver isn't listed but you have a disk from the manufacturer with a Windows NT Driver, click the Have Disk button.
5. Choose OK. You must point Windows NT toward the original installation files (or the disk that contains the driver) and restart the computer in order for the new driver to initialize.

To remove a tape drive device driver, do these steps:

1. Select the driver from the list of installed drivers in the Tape Devices dialog box of the Drivers tab.
2. Choose the Remove button.

PC Card (PCMCIA) The PC Card application helps you install and configure PCMCIA device drivers. Select a PC card and click Properties. Select the Drivers tab and then choose Add, Remove, or Configure as necessary.

A red X next to a device in the PC card list indicates that NT doesn't support the device.

Modems The Modems application enables you to add or remove a modem. You can ask NT to detect your modem, or you can select a modem from a list.

To add a modem:

1. Double-click the Modems application in the Control Panel.
2. Click Add in the Modem Properties dialog box (see Figure 4.31).

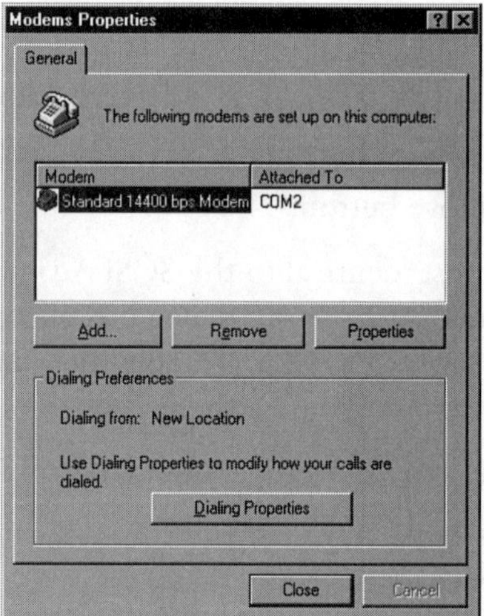

FIG. 4.31 ⇒ The Modem Properties dialog box.

3. In the Install New Modem dialog box, click Next if you want NT to try to detect your modem. If you want to select your modem from the list, or if you're providing software for a modem not listed, enable the check box and then click Next (see Figure 4.32).

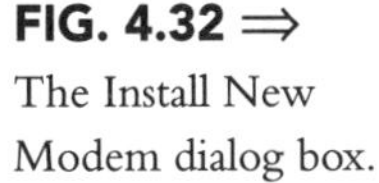

FIG. 4.32 ⇒
The Install New Modem dialog box.

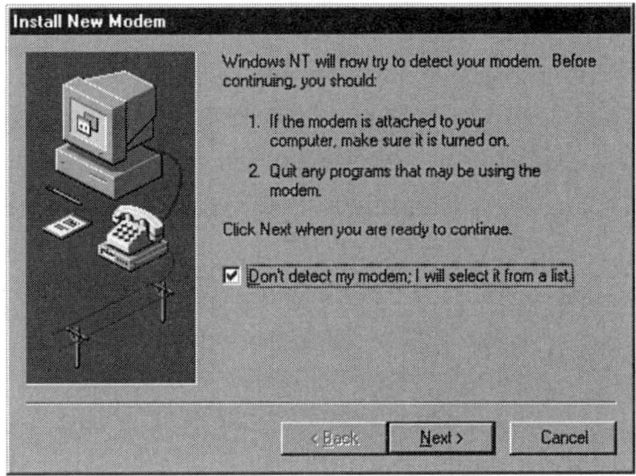

4. Select a manufacturer and a model, and click Next. Or click the Have Disk button if you're installing software for a modem not shown on the list.
5. Select a port for the modem, or select All ports. Click Next.

Select a modem in the Modems list and click Properties to change the parameters for that modem. A new dialog box opens, with two tabs, General and Connection. The General tab enables you to set the port number and the maximum speed. The Connection tab enables you to define some connection preferences, such as the Data bits, Stop bits, and Parity. Click Advanced for additional settings.

The Dialing Properties button in the Modem Properties dialog box calls up the My Location tab, which is also in the Telephony application. The My Locations tab enables you to set the dialing characteristics for the modem. If you have a portable computer, you can define additional locations and configure a complete set of dialing properties for each location. If you sometimes travel to a certain hotel in Paris, for instance, you can define a location called Paris and specify the dialing properties you want to use for the Paris hotel. The next time you're in Paris, you only have to change the location setting in the I Am Dialing from box at the top of the My Location tab. The other settings automatically change to the settings you defined for Paris.

To add a new location, follow these steps:

1. Click the New button at the top of the My Locations tab. (NT announces that a new location has been created.)

2. The new location has the name New Location (followed by a number if you already have a location called New Location). Click the name and change it if you want to give your location a different name. (NT might not let you erase the old name completely until you add your new name. Add the new name and then backspace over the old text if necessary.)
3. Change any dialing properties. The new properties will apply to your new location.

Keyboard The Keyboard application opens the Keyboard Properties dialog box, which enables the user to set the keyboard repeat rate, the repeat delay, the cursor blink rate, and the keyboard layout properties. The keyboard driver appears in the General tab in the Keyboard Type text box (see Figure 4.33). To select a new driver, click the Change button. The Select Device dialog box appears (see Figure 4.34). The Show All Devices option button will cause a list of available drivers to appear in the Models list. Choose the keyboard model that matches your hardware. If your keyboard comes with its own installation disk for a model that isn't in the list, click the Have Disk button.

FIG. 4.33 ⇒ The Keyboard Properties dialog box.

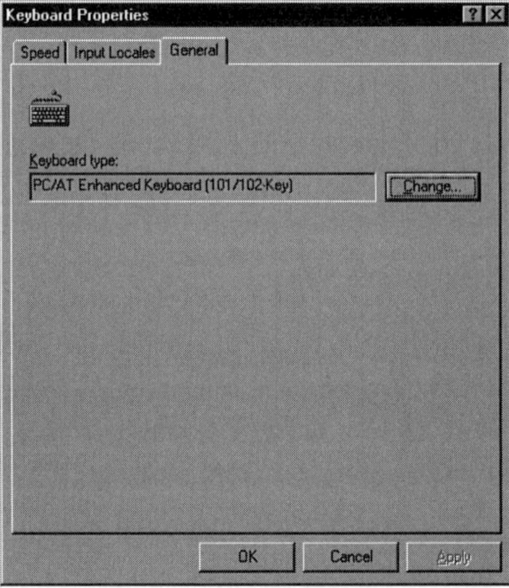

FIG. 4.34 ⇒
The Select Device dialog box.

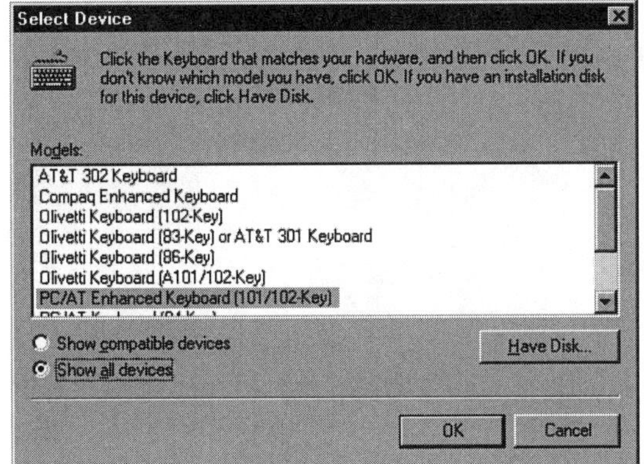

Mouse The values for this key control the mouse speed, sensitivity, and left- or right-handedness. The one new setting added to this dialog box's Win3.x predecessor is the Snap to Default option in the Motion tab, which instantly positions the pointer over the default button in the active dialog box. In the Pointers tab, you can select a pointer type. The General tab lets you install a new mouse driver. The procedure for selecting a mouse driver is similar to the procedure for selecting a keyboard driver (described in the preceding section).

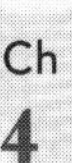

Display The Display application configures the values in the following key, including the video driver, screen resolution, color depth, and refresh rate:

```
HKEY_LOCAL_MACHINE\SYSTEM\CurrentControlSet\Services
\<video_driver>\Device0\
```

The five tabs of the Display Properties dialog box, shown in Figure 4.35, are as follows:

- *Background.* Defines the wallpaper for the Desktop.
- *Screen Saver.* Defines the screen saver for the Desktop.
- *Appearance.* Defines window properties.
- *Plus!.* The Visual Enhancements tab from the Microsoft Plus! package for Windows 95 lets you configure the desktop to use large icons or stretch the wallpaper to fit the screen.
- *Settings.* Defines desktop colors, refresh frequency, and other screen-related settings.

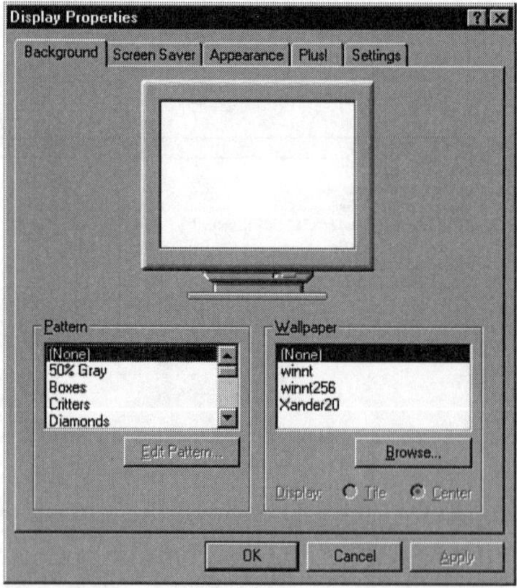

FIG. 4.35 ⇒
The Display Properties dialog box.

The Settings tab contains a Test button. You should always test new display settings before making changes permanent. Although Windows NT can detect the capabilities of your video card, it can't do the same with your monitor. Testing these settings before applying them ensures that both video card and monitor can support the new settings.

Unlike Windows 95, Windows NT doesn't let you change video resolution on-the-fly. The computer must be restarted for the changes to take effect.

Tip

All hardware breaks sooner or later, including monitors. When a monitor dies, you often can dig up an older model to use temporarily. Often, however, such a resurrected monitor isn't as advanced as the one that just died, and when you restart Windows NT, such video card settings as the resolution and refresh rate aren't supported. The typical result is that you no longer can view anything on-screen.

If this happens, reboot the computer by using the [VGA mode] option on the Boot Loader menu. Windows NT boots using the standard VGA driver at 640x480 resolution. When the system is fully loaded, log on and go to the Settings tab of the Control Panel Display application, so that you can choose optimal settings for your temporary monitor.

To change the video display adapter:

1. Start the Control Panel Display application and click the Settings tab (see Figure 4.36).

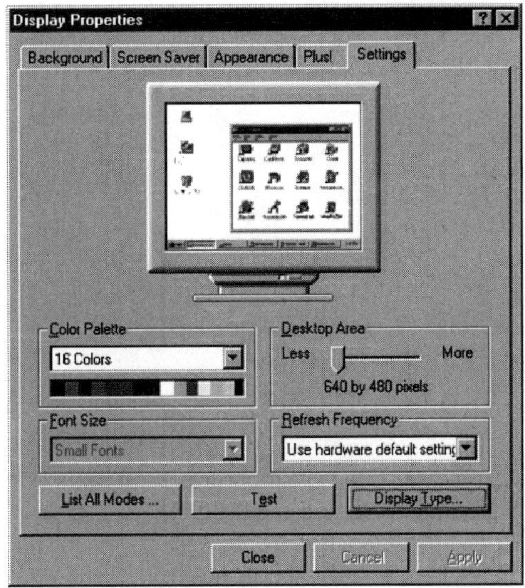

FIG. 4.36 ⇒ The Display Properties Settings tab.

2. Click the Display Type button. The Display Type dialog box appears (see Figure 4.37).

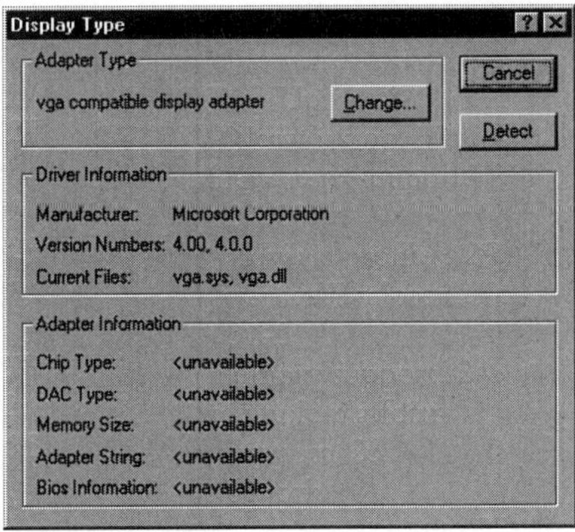

FIG. 4.37 ⇒ The Display Type dialog box.

3. Click the Change tab in the Adapter Type frame. The Change Display dialog box appears (see Figure 4.38). Select an adapter from the list and click OK. Or, if you have a manufacturer's installation disk, click Have Disk.

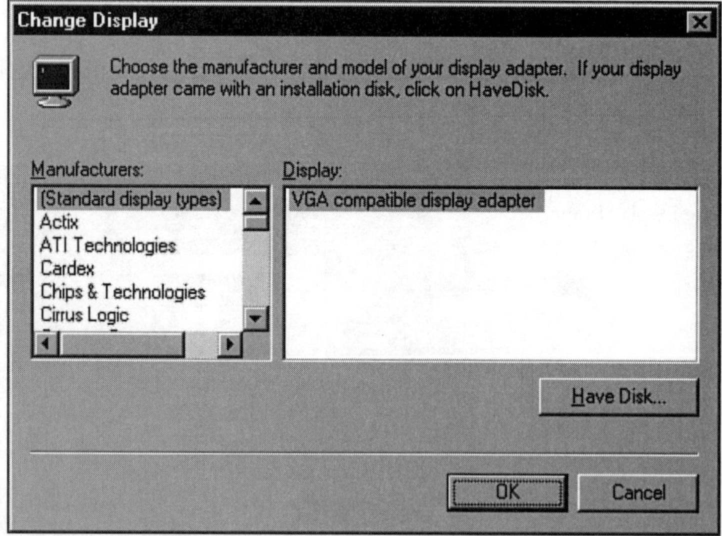

FIG. 4.38 ⇒
The Change Display dialog box.

Taking the Disc Test

If you have read and understood the material in this chapter, you are ready to test your knowledge. Insert the CD-ROM that comes with this book and run the self-test software. Information about the CD-ROM is found in Appendix K, "Using the Self-Test Software."

From Here...

This chapter explored how to configure your NT installation, reviewed the Control Panel applets, and examined the Registry. These all are configurations of the computer and environment settings. Another way to configure, or administer, your computer is to create and manage user accounts. Chapter 5, "Managing Users and Groups," covers the creation and management of user accounts in detail.

Chapter Prerequisite

Though this chapter reviews the basic concepts regarding the creation and management of user and group accounts, it is considered a prerequisite for this book that you have already performed this type of administrative function.

5

Managing Users and Groups

This chapter reviews the creation and management of accounts on Windows NT Server 4.0. This basic administrative function will be addressed primarily from the enterprise perspective, including a discussion of how to administer accounts remotely and across a trust relationship.

Topics covered in this chapter include the following:

- Discussing what user and group accounts are all about
- Creating user and group accounts in the domain
- Highlighting the uniqueness of account identification
- Managing users through global group accounts
- Exploring account policies and system rights
- Administering accounts through a trust relationship
- Troubleshooting account management issues

Understanding User and Group Accounts

The first screen you see after booting Windows NT and pressing Ctrl+Alt+Delete is the Logon Security dialog box. Here, you must enter your username and password to gain access to the domain through network authentication—for example, the NETLOGON process.

Key Concept

You should therefore consider the user account as the first and foremost security object for access to your local and network resources.

Each user and group account that is created in the domain is unique to that Windows NT domain and, as such, has a unique security identifier associated with it. This identifier is called the *Security Identifier*, more commonly referred to as the SID. All references that Windows NT makes to any account, especially those dealing with security access and permissions, are linked to the SID.

If you delete the user account and re-create it by using exactly the same information, Windows NT will create a new SID for that user, and all security access and permissions will have to be reestablished. The account information is stored in the *Security Accounts Manager* (SAM) database, which is part of the Windows NT 4.0 Registry—`HKEY_LOCAL_MACHINE\SAM`.

If the account is a *local account*—in other words, an account that a user uses to log on to a specific workstation —the account is included in the SAM database of that workstation's Registry. If the account is a *network account*—meaning an account that is used to log on to the enterprise network from any given workstation—the account is included in the SAM database of the primary domain controller (PDC) for the account domain of the enterprise.

Key Concept

A local account, in general, will have access to resources only on the local workstation. A network account will have access as provided to network resources such as shared printers, files, and folders.

Default User Accounts

When you first install Windows NT Server 4.0, two default accounts are created for you: the Guest and Administrator accounts. You cannot delete either of these accounts. For this reason, you must take care to preserve the integrity of these accounts.

The Guest account provides the least amount of access for the user and is, in fact, disabled by default on both Windows NT Workstation and Server to prevent inadvertent access to resources. It is strongly recommended that you assign a password to this account (preferably something other than **password**) and, for additional security, rename the account. This account is automatically made a member of the default domain global group Domain Guests.

The *Administrator account*, as you might expect, provides the greatest amount of access and complete functional rights to the domain. Because Windows NT creates this account by default, it also is the first account with which a user has to log on to the domain controller. In most organizations, this account is used to perform almost every administrative task in the domain. Therefore, it is strongly recommended that this account be password-protected (again, with a unique, though memorable, password), and, for additional security, it should also be renamed.

After all, if you were a hacker trying to break in with administrative access, the first account name you would try would be **administrator**, and then perhaps **supervisor** or **admin** or *XYZ***admin,** in which *XYZ* is your company name. If this has exhausted your choices for alternate administrator account names, good! With Internet access especially prevalent, enterprise security has become an extremely significant and sensitive issue.

Another suggestion that Microsoft makes is to create a separate user account for specific functional access. For example, Windows NT provides a default group that is local to the domain controllers called *Account Operators*. Members of this group are given just enough functional access to be able to successfully manage user and group accounts for the domain. The administrator might identify a user or users who have the responsibility of managing accounts or create a specific user account for that purpose and add them to the Account Operators group for the domain. The user would then use his or her account or the specific user account to access the domain and manage accounts. This security eliminates a potential security "hole"—for example, being logged in as administrator and leaving for lunch without locking the workstation or logging out. This situation may not be quite so significant when the intruder is logged on as a local administrator, but it becomes far more disconcerting when the intruder is logged on to a domain as a network administrator.

Default Group Accounts

When you first install Windows NT Server 4.0, eight default local groups are created for you:

- Administrators
- Users
- Guests
- Back-up Operators
- Server Operators
- Account Operators
- Print Operators
- Replicator

These groups are considered *local* groups in that they are used to provide a certain level of functional access for that domain. Because the domain controllers share the same account database, a local group created on the PDC is considered local to all the domain controllers.

Windows NT also creates three global default groups:

- Domain Administrators
- Domain Users
- Domain Guests

You can use a global group account, like a global user account, anywhere in the domain or through a trust relationship to a trusting domain to manage user access to network resources. As with local groups, global groups created on a PDC are considered global to all the domain controllers for that domain.

▶ **See** Chapter 15, "Windows NT 4.0 Trusts," for a complete treatment of local and global user and group accounts and their impact when managing resources.

Windows NT also creates and manages four groups to "place" a user for accessing resources, called *internal* or *system groups*:

- Everyone
- Interactive
- Network
- Creator Owner

Everyone, of course means just that. Every user who logs on to the workstation or accesses a resource on the workstation or a server locally or remotely becomes a member of the internal group Everyone. It is interesting to note that Windows NT's philosophy for securing resources is not to secure them at all. By default, the group Everyone has full access to resources. It is up to the administrator to restrict that access and *add* security.

Everyone, when applied to Directory Services, means everyone within and outside of the enterprise. A user from one domain could access a resource on another domain if that user has a valid account in the other domain and if no trust relationship exists. This happens through pass-through authentication between the domains. That user then becomes a member of the Everyone group on the other domain.

There is a subtle distinction between the Everyone group and the Domain Users global group. Though Everyone always means absolutely everyone who accesses that domain, Domain Users means only those users *from the domain*. If you recall that Windows NT's default permission for network resources is Everyone with Full Control, replacing Everyone with Domain Users now subtly changes the access from absolutely everyone to only users from the domain.

Interactive represents to Windows NT the user who has logged on at the computer itself and accesses resources on that computer. This is also referred to as *logging on locally*.

Network represents to Windows NT any user who has connected to a network resource from another computer remotely.

Creator Owner represents the user who is the owner or has taken ownership of a resource. For example, you can use this group to assign file access only to the owner of a file. Though Everyone may have read access to files in a directory, Creator Owner will have full access; thus, though other users can read a file, only the owner of the file can make changes to it.

The Windows NT operating system fixes the membership of these internal groups and they cannot be altered. For example, if you create a file, you are the owner of that file, and Windows NT places you in the Creator Owner group for that file.

Group Management in Domains

Microsoft's group strategy for domains recommends that domain users be grouped into as many global groups as is appropriate. Local resource managers should then create local groups to maintain access to the resources. The global groups are then used as members of the local groups. Whichever domain users are members of, the global group will get whatever level of access was given to the local group. Though this may at first seem to be a bit of over-management, in large networks with hundreds or thousands of users this strategy makes much sense and can actually facilitate user management and resource access.

Extending this concept to the trust relationship follows naturally. Because the trust gives a resource administrator access to the account database of a trusted domain, the resource administrators can use the global groups created in the trusted domain as members of the local groups they create to manage access to their resources. For example, if you wanted the administrators of the trusted domain to also administer the domain controllers or resource servers in the trusting domain, you would make the Domain Administrator global group from the trusted domain a member of the local Administrators groups of the PDC and resource servers for the trusting domain.

Planning for New User Accounts

Part of setting up new user accounts—or group accounts, for that matter, especially on a domain controller—involves some planning. Here are six basic areas to consider before creating new accounts:

- Account naming conventions
- How to deal with passwords
- Group membership

- Profile information
- Logon hours (when logon is possible)
- Which workstations from which the user can log on

Naming Conventions

The choice of username determines how the user will be identified on the network. In all lists of users and groups, the account names will be displayed alphabetically, so the choice of username can be significant. For example, if your naming convention is FirstnameLastinitial, your usernames for the following users would look like this:

User	User Name
Luke Smith	LukeS
Henry Sage	HenryS
Jerry T. Holmes	JerryTH

Now what if you had several LukeSs or HenrySs? In a large corporation, it would not be uncommon to have 20 or 30 persons with the same first name. Looking through a list of users with the same first name and only a couple of letters from the last name to go by could become not only confusing but irritating as well.

A more effective convention might be LastnameFirstInitial, like so:

User	User Name
Luke Smith	SmithL
Henry Sage	SageH
Jerry T. Holmes	HolmesJT

Finding the appropriate user in a list will be easier. Many organizations will already have a network ID naming convention in place and it may be perfectly acceptable to follow that.

Usernames must be unique with Windows NT's Directory Services. Therefore, your naming convention must plan for duplicate names. Henry Sage and Herbert Sage, for example, would both have the username SageH according to the second convention previously suggested. So perhaps the convention could be altered to include middle initials in the event of a tie—such as SageHA and SageHB—or include extra letters from the first name until uniqueness is achieved—such as SageHen and SageHer. User names are not case-sensitive and can contain up to 20 characters, including spaces, except the following characters:

“ / \ { } : ; [vb] = , + * ? < >

You might also consider creating user accounts based on function rather than the user's name. For example, if the role of administrative assistant is assigned from a pool of employees, it may make more sense to create an account called AdminAsst or FrontDesk. This will ensure that the assistant of the day will have access to everything to which that person should have access—as well as minimize your administrative setup for that person.

Considerations Regarding Passwords

Besides the obvious consideration that requiring a password provides the greater level of security, there are some other things to think about. One of these is who controls the password.

When you create a new user account, you have three password-related options to determine:

- User Must Change Password at Next Logon
- User Cannot Change Password
- Password Never Expires

Selecting User Must Change Password at Next Logon allows you to set a blank or *dummy* password for the user. When the user logs on for the first time, Windows NT will require the user to change the password.

Key Concept

It is important to set company policy and educate the user in the importance of protecting the integrity of their accounts by using unique and "unguessable" passwords. Among the most common choices for passwords include children's names, pets' names, favorite sports teams, or team players. Try to avoid the obvious association when choosing a password.

User Cannot Change Password provides the most control to the administrator. This option is particularly useful for temporary employees or the administrative assistant pool account.

Password Never Expires ensures that the user will not need to change the password, even if the overall password policy requires that users change their passwords after a set period of time has elapsed. This option is useful for the types of accounts just mentioned or for service accounts.

Passwords are case-sensitive and can be up to 14 characters in length. It is generally suggested among network administrators to require a minimum password length of eight characters, using alphanumeric characters and a combination of upper- and lowercase. For example, I might use as my password a combination of my initials and the last four digits of my Social Security number—two things I am not likely to forget, but not obvious to anyone else. Thus, my password might be SDK4532, or it might be sdk4532, SdK4532, 4532sdK, 45sdk32, and—oh well, you get the idea.

Group Membership

The easiest way to manage large numbers of users is to group them logically, functionally, departmentally, and so forth. Creating local groups for local resource access control is the most common use for creating groups on the resource computers. As already discussed, local group membership consists primarily of domain global groups, although in specific instances, it may include domain global users as well.

Determining User Profile Information

The reference to User Profiles on a Windows NT Server usually refers to a file of environment settings that is stored on a specific computer and downloaded to whatever Windows-NT-based computer from which the user is logging in. The location of the logon script and personal folder might also be located on a remote computer rather than on the local workstation, which is especially useful if the user moves around a lot (like a pool of administrative assistants).

It is helpful, though not necessary, to determine ahead of time where you will keep this information and how much of this information you will use. Will you need a user profile stored on a server for every user or only for administrative assistants? Does everyone need a logon script? Should personal files be stored on the local workstation or on a central computer? (Again, this setup is useful for users who move around.)

A more thorough discussion of user profile files, login scripts, and another related utility called the System Policy Editor will be undertaken in Chapter 7, "Policies and Profiles."

Home Directory

The *Home Directory* simply represents a place in which the user can routinely save data files. This place is usually a folder (directory) that has been created on a centrally located server in the domain, though in small workgroups, it may actually be found on the user's local workstation—or not identified at all.

The advantages of placing the home directory on a centrally located server somewhere in the domain is primarily that of security. By using NTFS permissions, you can secure the users' folders quite nicely, so that only they (and whomever they determine) can have access to them. In addition, you can then include these folders in regular server data backups, thus ensuring the availability of the files in the event of accidental deletion, corruption, or system crashes.

In the Home Directory section of the User Environment Profile dialog box (accessed by viewing the Properties of the user account and choosing Profile), you have two choices:

- Local Path
- Connect To

The first option represents the drive and path to an existing home directory folder, such as `C:\USERS`, in which you can create the user's own profile folder. The other represents a *Universal Naming Convention* (UNC) path that identifies the name of the server that contains an existing home directory share and a logical drive letter to assign to it that the user can use for saving files in applications, searching, exploring with the Windows Explorer, and so on.

Note A UNC name is very much like a DOS path in that it represents the path through the network to a network resource. In this case, the network resource is a directory that has been "shared" for the creation of the home directory folder for the user. UNC names take the following form:

*servername**sharename**path*

in which *servername* represents the name of the server computer that contains the folder, *sharename* represents the name of the directory that has been made available for use as a resource (shared), and *path* represents an optional path to a subdirectory or specific file. ■

When entering the Home Directory location, you can either specify the name of the folder explicitly or use an environmental parameter to create and name it for you. For example, by using the variable %USERNAME%, Windows NT will create a directory using the user name value as the directory name. This is particularly useful when you use a template for creating large numbers of users. Recall that when you create a new user account by copying an existing account, the User Environment Profile information is also copied. Using %USERNAME% will enable you to create individual user home folders by using each user's username as the directory name. Table 5.1 displays a list of the environment variables that Windows NT 4.0 can use.

Table 5.1 Additional Environment Variables for Home Directories and Logon Scripts

Variable	Description
%HOMEDIR%	Returns the logical mapping to the shared folder that contains the user's home directory
%HOMEDRIVE%	Returns the logical drive mapped to the home directory share
%HOMEPATH%	Returns the path name of the user's home directory folder
%HOMESHARE%	Returns the share name of the folder that contains the user's home directory folder
%OS%	Returns the operating system of the user's computer
%PROCESSOR_ARCHITECTURE%	Returns the processor's base architecture, such as Intel or MIPS, of the user's computer
%PROCESSOR_LEVEL%	Returns the processor type, such as 486, of the user's computer
%USERDOMAIN%	Returns the name of the enterprise account domain in which the user is validating
%USERNAME%	Returns the user's logon ID (username)

Logon Scripts

If you have had any dealings with networks before, you have encountered a logon script. *Logon scripts* are simply files that contain a set of network commands that must be executed in a particular order. Often, as is the case with Novell NetWare, logon scripts have a specific command language and structure that should be used. In the case of Windows NT, they are simply batch files and support all the Windows NT command-line commands, or in some cases, an executable file.

Here is an example of a Windows NT logon script called `LOGON.BAT`:

```
@echo Welcome to the NT Network!
@echo off
Pause
Net use p:\\server5\database
Net use r:\\server4\budget
Net time \\server1 /set /y
```

The two `net use` commands map drives to existing network resource shares. The `net time` command synchronizes the system time on the current computer with the system time of the server specified.

The name of the logon script is arbitrary. Windows NT does provide a place for storing logon scripts. In a domain setting, they are usually placed in the WINNT\SYSTEM32\REPL\IMPORT\SCRIPTS folder on a domain controller. The scripts are then copied to WINNT\SYSTEM32\REPL\EXPORT\SCRIPTS so that they are replicated to all other domain controllers. Because the user uses any available domain controller to gain access to the network, it makes sense that the logon scripts be stored on all the domain controllers in the domain.

The advantage of storing the logon scripts on a domain controller is that, through Directory Replication, the scripts can be distributed to *all* the domain controllers in the network. Because a user may authenticate at any one of the domain controllers, this provides a convenient way to ensure that the logon scripts are always available. Also, it provides the administrator with one central storage place for the scripts, making maintaining them easier.

Windows NT assumes that you will store the login script file in the WINNT\SYSTEM32\REPL\IMPORT\SCRIPTS folder on the domain controller server. Because of this assumption, it is not necessary to use a UNC name when specifying the location of the login script in the User

Properties Environment Profile dialog box. In fact, once you have distributed the login scripts to all the appropriate domain controllers, you need only enter the file name in the Logon Script Name text box. More Windows NT environment variables were shown previously in Table 5.1.

Understanding User Manager for Domains

Domain user and group accounts are created and managed through an Administrative Tool called *User Manager for Domains* (called just User Manager if you are not using domains). Account policies are also created and maintained through this utility, as well as the assignment of functional user rights, the enabling of security auditing, and the establishment of trust relationships. Functional rights define what functions a user can perform at a Windows NT computer. For example, shutting down the computer, changing the system time, formatting the hard disk, and installing device drivers are all functional rights.

User Manager for Domains acts as the database manager for user and group accounts stored in the SAM database, as shown in Figure 5.1. There are five menu options:

- *User.* Creates and modifies user and group accounts; copies, deletes, renames, and changes properties of user accounts; and enables you to change the domain focus for remote management of other domain databases
- *View.* Enables you to sort user account entries by Full Name or Username (the default)
- *Policies.* Sets account policies, assigns functional user rights, enables security auditing, and establishes trust relationships
- *Options.* Enables/disables confirmation and save settings, sets display fonts for User Manager, and allows a low-speed setting for use when administering a domain database across a slow connection, such as a 56K WAN line
- *Help.* Displays the Windows NT help files specific to User Manager

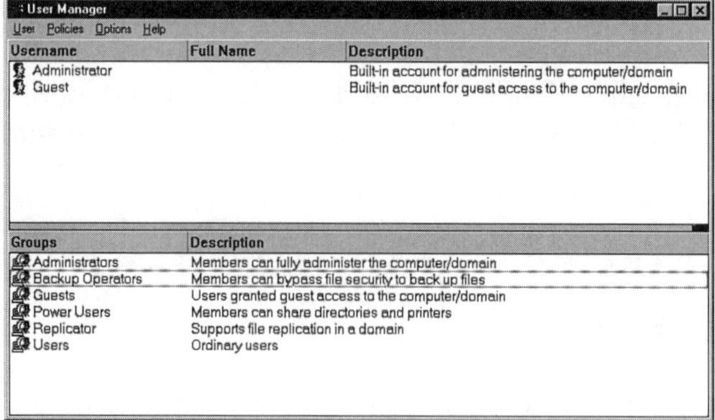

FIG. 5.1 ⇒ User Manager displays the account database showing all user and group accounts. Here you see the two default users and six default local groups.

Creating a New User

Selecting New <u>U</u>ser from the <u>U</u>ser menu displays the New User dialog box shown in Figure 5.2. This fairly intuitive screen is described in Table 5.2.

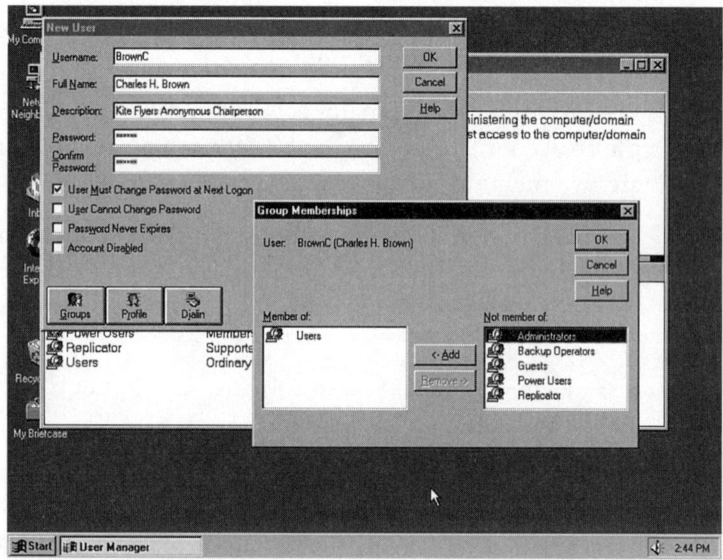

FIG. 5.2 ⇒ Options are selected in the New User dialog box and the Group Memberships window is showing the default membership in the Domain Users global group.

Table 5.2 New User Dialog Box Options

Option	Description
Username	The logon ID you have chosen for the user. Recall that this name must be unique in the database (or in the enterprise when creating the account on a domain controller) and can be up to 20 characters including spaces but excluding " / \ [ ] : ; [|] = , + * ? < >.
Full Name	The user's full name. As with usernames, it is recommended that you determine a convention for entering this name (such as "Luke Robert Smith") because Windows NT uses the full name as an alternative user account sort order.
Description	A simple description of the account or user, such as `Admin Assistant Account` or `Project Manager`.
Password	The password is case-sensitive and can be up to 14 characters long. Recall the discussion of password integrity earlier in the section "Considerations Regarding Passwords."
Confirm Password	You must confirm the password here before Windows NT can create the account.
User Must Change Password at Next Logon	This password option forces the user to change his or her password the next time he or she logs on.
User Cannot Change Password	This password option prevents the user from being able to change his or her password. As mentioned earlier, this setting is useful for accounts for which the password should remain the same, such as temporary employee accounts.
Password Never	This password option prevents the

continues

Ch 5

Table 5.2 Continued

Option	Description
	Expires password from expiring and overrides both the Maximum Password Age option set in the Account Policy, as well as the User Must Change Password at Next Logon option.
Account Disabled	Prevents the use of the account. This option is a useful setting for users who are on vacation, extended leave, or whose accounts otherwise should not be available for logging into the network. It is always more appropriate to disable an account if there is any possibility of the user returning. Remember that deleting a user account also deletes the user's SID, and thus removes all previous network resource access for that user.
Account Locked Out	Displays when the Account Lockout account policy is enabled. When a user exceeds the number of allowed incorrect logons, this option is checked by the operating system and can only be deselected by an administrator or account operator.
Groups	Displays the Group Memberships dialog box, which displays the user's group membership and from which you can modify group membership.
Profile	Displays the User Environment Profile dialog box from which you can reference a server-based profile, define a logon script, and identify a home folder (directory).
Hours	Displays the Logon Hours dialog box from which you can determine what times of the day the user can log onto the network. This option is useful for shift employees or for backup times.

Option	Description
Logon To	Displays the Logon Workstations dialog box and enables you to identify by computer name the computers at which this account can log on to the network. You can identify up to eight workstations.
Account	Displays the Account Information dialog box in which you can specify an expiration date for the account and identify whether the account is a global domain account (default) or one for a user from another untrusted domain who needs occasional access to your domain.
Dialin	Displays the Dial-in Information dialog box, with which you grant permission to use Dial-up Networking to the user account and set Call Back options.

As you can see, it is a fairly straightforward process to create user accounts. By double-clicking the account name in the User Manager window or highlighting the username and choosing Properties from the User menu, you can view these settings for each user and modify them as is appropriate.

Creating a New Local or Global Group

The process of creating a new local or global group is even more straightforward in the Local Group Properties dialog box. The options available in the Local Group and Global Group Properties dialog boxes are described in Table 5.3.

Table 5.3 Global Group Dialog Box Options

Option	Global or Local	Description
Group Name	Both	The name you have chosen for the local group. It can have up to 256 characters except the backslash (\), which, though descriptive, would be somewhat confusing in display lists of groups. Group names, unlike user names, *cannot* be renamed. You can copy a group name, however, and preserve its member list for the copied group.
Description	Both	A simple description of the group, such as Administrative Assistants or Project Managers.
Show Full Names	Local Only	Displays the full name associated with each user account displayed in the Members list box.
Members	Both	Displays all the current user accounts (or domain user and global group accounts) that are members of this local group.
Not Members	Global Only	Displays the users from the domain whom you can add to the group member list.
Add	Local Only	Displays the Add Users and Groups dialog box from which you can select user accounts from your domain's user and global group accounts database on the PDC or from the accounts database from a trusted domain. Select the trusted domain that has the desired accounts from the List Names From list user box,

Option	Global or Local	Description
		click the user you want to add to the group in the Names list box, and choose Add, then OK. Use the Search button to look for an account among all possible account databases. If you have selected a global group in the Names list box, use Members to display the members of that global group. You can select multiple accounts at one time by Ctrl+ clicking the additional accounts.
		In the New Global Group dialog box, this button will add the users you selected in the Not Members list to the Members list.
Remove	Both	Deletes the account selected in the Members list, thus removing it from group membership.

Tip

Here's a shortcut to populating a group. Before you create the group, select all the usernames you want in the group from the User Manager Username screen by Ctrl+ clicking the additional accounts. Then create the group. The Members list box will display any user account that has been highlighted before the group was created.

Key Concept

Remember that the primary membership difference between local and global groups is that though local groups can contain user accounts from the local account database, global user and global group accounts from the domain database of the domain of which the server is a member, and global user and global group accounts from the domain database of a trusted domain, global groups can only contain user accounts from their own domain database.

Renaming, Copying, and Deleting Accounts

Recall from the discussion of the default Administrator and Guest accounts that for a higher level of security, you can rename these accounts. Renaming an account does not affect the account's SID in any way: It makes it relatively easy to change a username without affecting any of that user's access—whether it be changing the Administrator account to enhance its security or reflecting a name change due to marriage or the Witness Protection Program. Simply highlight the username in User Manager for Domains, choose Rename from the User menu, and type the new username in the box provided. You *cannot* rename group names.

Key Concept

If you choose to delete an account, remember that the account's SID will also be deleted and all resource access and user rights will be lost. This means that if you re-create the account even *exactly* as it was before, the SAM database will generate a new SID for the account, and you will have to reestablish resource access and user rights for that account.

To delete the account, highlight it and press Delete on the keyboard or choose User, Delete. Windows NT will warn you that the SID will be lost. Choose OK, and the account will be deleted.

Note You cannot delete built-in user or group accounts, global or otherwise.

The User, Copy menu command is useful for duplicating user account information that is the same for a group of users. Because you cannot rename a group, copying a group to a new name also duplicates its membership list and is the next best thing to renaming. Copying user and group accounts results in new accounts being created. As such, each new account will have its own new SID assigned to it.

When you copy a user account, the following settings are maintained: the Description, the password options that have been checked off, and if Account Disabled has been selected, it will be unchecked for the copy. Also, group membership and profile information is maintained for the copied account, as are Logon Hours, Logon to Workstations, and Account Expiration and Type, which greatly simplifies the task of creating large numbers of similar users.

Creating and Managing Account Policies, System Rights, and Auditing

Account Policy information and User Rights are considered part of account management and, as such, are administered through User Manager for Domains. *Account Policy* information includes password-specific information such as password, age, minimum length, and account lockout options.

User rights represent the functional rights that a user acquires for a given server when logging in either at the console or remotely. Auditing for file and directory access, print access, and so forth is accomplished by specifying the users or groups whose access you want to audit and is performed at the file, directory, and print levels. You must first enable auditing for those security events for user and group accounts; however, you perform that through User Manager for Domains as well.

Account Policy

Figure 5.3 shows a typical domain account policy. The options presented in this dialog box should be very familiar to network administrators. The policies determined here apply to *all* domain users.

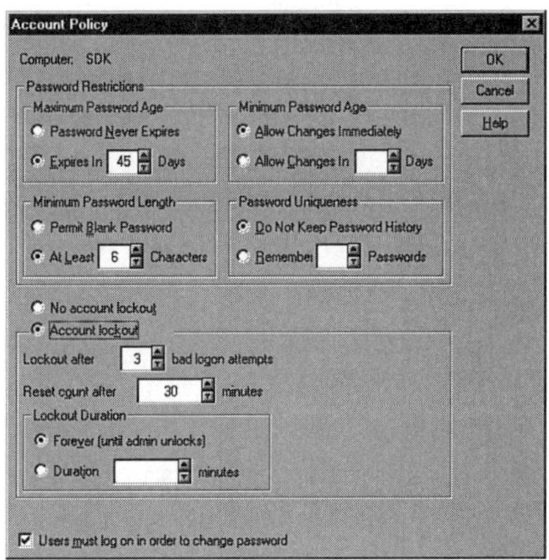

FIG. 5.3 ⇒
In this example of an account policy, the password must be at least six characters long and expires every 45 days. Also, if the user forgets the password in three consecutive tries within 30 minutes, the account will be locked out until an administrator releases it.

Table 5.4 describes the various entries you can make for an account policy.

Table 5.4 Account Policy Options

Option	Description
Maximum Password Age	You may set the password to never expire or you may select a set number of days after which the user will be prompted to change the password. The default is set to 42 days.
Minimum Password Age	The default here is to allow a user to change the password any time. Many organizations now prefer that passwords cannot be changed whenever the user wants. The user must wait a specified number of days before he or she can change the password, which helps to maintain password uniqueness. By forcing users to have a password for several days, organizations make it less likely that users will always change their password back to their kid's name.
Minimum Password Length	The default, oddly enough, is to allow blank passwords. As discussed earlier in the section "Considerations Regarding Passwords," you will probably want to define a minimum length for the password. Most network administrators use 8 as the minimum length. The maximum length can be 14.
Password Uniqueness	The default is to not maintain a history of past passwords, which allows a user to reuse passwords when they expire. Though being able to reuse a password is convenient for the user, it is not always the most secure way to deal with passwords. Many organizations require passwords to be unique, which is accomplished by specifying the number of passwords to be "remembered" by the system for each user (up to 24) and requir-

Option	Description
	ing a maximum password age and a minimum password age. For example, by setting the maximum and minimum password age to 30 days and uniqueness to 24, the user would not be able to reuse the first password for two years. This in effect accomplishes uniqueness simply because the user is not likely to be able to remember that far back.
Account Lockout	Lockout prevents an account from being used after several failed logon attempts. The default is to not enable account lockout. In the enterprise where security is essential, this option will probably be enabled and, in fact, it is recommended.
Lockout After	Specifies the number of bad logon attempts (incorrect passwords) that the system will accept before locking out that account. The default is 5 and can be set from 1 to 999.
Reset Count After	This number represents the number of minutes that the system will wait between bad logon attempts before resetting the bad logon count to 0. For example, if you misstype my password, the bad logon count is set to 1. If the reset count is 15 minutes and after 15 minutes you do not log on incorrectly again, the bad logon count is set back to 0. If you do log on incorrectly again within 15 minutes, the logon count is set to 2, and so on. The default is 30 minutes and can be set from 1 to 99,999 minutes (or roughly 70 days, for those of you who couldn't help wondering).
Lockout Duration	You can require an administrator to reset the account after lockout. You could also specify a length of time for the lockout to

continues

Table 5.4 Continued

Option	Description
	be in effect before letting the computer hacker try again. The default for this choice is 30 minutes and can be set from 1 to 99,999 minutes.
Users Must Log On…	This option requires that the user log on to the system before making password changes. Normally, when a password expires, the user is prompted during logon to change the password. With this option selected, the user will *not* be able to change the expired password, and the administrator will need to reset it. This option is useful for short-term employee accounts that expire in a specific amount of time to ensure that the employee cannot change the password on his or her own.
Forcibly Disconnect…	By default, logon hours settings merely stop a user from logging in during the specified time period. If the user is already logged in, the logon hours settings have no further effect on the user. This option causes the user to be logged off the system when the logon hours have expired. This option can be used to force users off a system before it is backed up or rebooted.

User Rights

As mentioned previously, user rights are *functional* rights and represent functions or tasks that a user or group can perform locally on a given workstation or server, or while remotely connected to a server. User rights include shutting down the computer, formatting a hard disk, backing up files and directories, and so forth. Contrast this with *permissions* such as read-only, write, and delete, which reflect resource access rights.

In the domain, user rights are granted primarily to local groups because they usually represent access at the server console itself. You can also grant user rights to global groups, however, especially when remote access and administration are involved.

For example, the user right Log on Locally defines which users can log on at the server console. Only members of the local Account Operators, Administrators, Backup Operators, Print Operators, and Server Operators are granted this access. Note that, unlike Windows NT Workstation, the group Everyone is not listed under User Manager on Windows NT Server installations by default.

Assume, for this discussion, that the server in question functions as a print server for a Multiple Master Domain model. You would like Print Operators from all domains to be able to manage this print server; that includes the ability to log on at the print server itself. Following Microsoft's group management strategy, you would create a global group in each trusted domain, perhaps called GlobalPrintOps, and then add it to the local Print Operators group on my print server. Those users have the ability to log on locally at the print server to manage the printers.

By virtue of the trust relationship, however, you could also have added the GlobalPrintOps global group directly to the Log On Locally user right as well to allow them the ability to log on at the print server. As with all security objects, user rights maintain *Access Control Lists* (ACLs). Groups and users represented by their SIDs are members of the ACL for each user right. Consequently, there is no way to select an account and see what user rights (or file permissions, for that matter) have been assigned to that account because the rights do not "stay" with the account.

Ch 5

Table 5.5 highlights the basic user rights on domain controllers and the default groups assigned to each.

Table 5.5 User Rights on Domain Controllers

User Right	Group(s) Assigned
Access This Computer from the Network	Administrators, Everyone
Add Workstations to Domain	No groups explicitly assigned; a default Administrator function

continues

Table 5.5 Continued

User Right	Group(s) Assigned
Back up Files and Directories	Administrators, Backup Operators, Server Operators
Change the System Time	Administrators, Server Operators
Force Shutdown from a Remote System	Administrators, Server Operators
Load and Unload Device Drivers	Administrators
Log on Locally	
Manage Auditing and Security Log	Administrators
Restore Files and Directories	Administrators, Backup Operators, Server Operators
Shut Down the System	Account Operators, Administrators, Backup Operators, Print Operators, Server Operators
Take Ownership of Files or Objects	Administrators

You can administer accounts assigned to the various user rights through the User Rights Policy dialog box, displayed by choosing User Rights from the Policy menu (see Figure 5.4). Select the user right from the Right drop-down list. The default groups assigned this user right will be displayed in the Grant To list box. Choose the Add button to display the Add Users and Groups dialog box (described in the section "Creating Groups") and add user and group accounts to the user right's Grant To list or choose Remove to delete members from the Grant To list.

You can also display advanced rights by checking the Show Advanced User Rights option at the bottom of the User Rights Policy dialog box. These rights are for use primarily by developers. There are two advanced user rights, however, which, as an administrator on a network, you may need to modify from time to time:

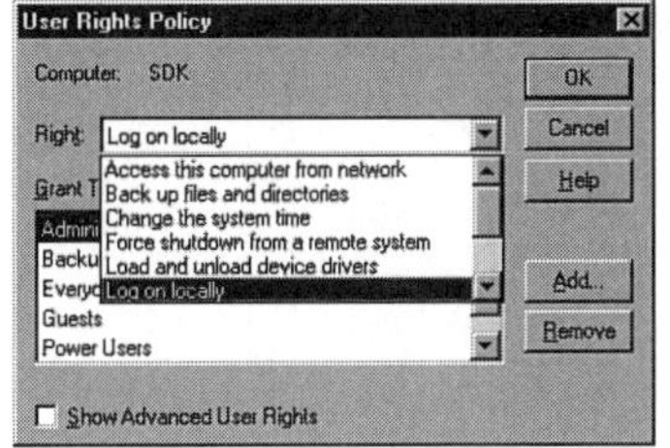

FIG. 5.4 ⇒ The User Rights Policy dialog box shows some of the user rights that you can select. Log on Locally has been selected, and in the Grant To box behind the drop-down list, you can see the groups assigned this user right.

- *Bypass Traverse Checking.* This advanced user right allows the specified user or group accounts to change between directories and navigate directory trees even if permission has been denied to various directories. This might be assigned to power users or resource managers.
- *Log On as a Service.* This advanced user right is intended for user accounts that are used by certain background application tasks or Windows NT system functions such as Directory Replication. This right allows the service or function to log in as the specified account for the express purpose of carrying out that specific task. No other user needs to be logged in for the task to be performed.

Audit Policy

To audit for events relating to file and directory access, print access, and so forth, specify the users or groups whose access you want to audit. You perform this audit at the file, directory, and print levels. You must first enable auditing for those security events for user and group accounts; however, you do this through User Manager by selecting Audit from the Policies menu. The Audit Policy box is displayed (see Figure 5.5).

By default, auditing is not enabled because of the additional resources required to monitor the system for related events. You can enable auditing for seven areas:

- *Logon and Logoff.* Monitors user logon and logoff of the server, the domain, and network connections.

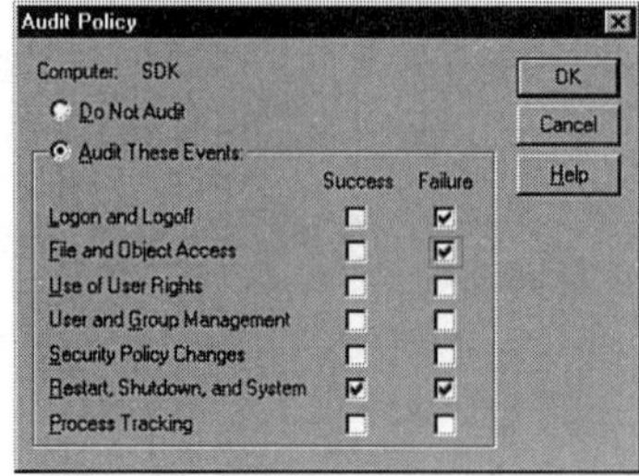

FIG. 5.5 ⇒
This audit policy has enabled auditing of failed logon and logoff attempts, unsuccessful file and object access, and any events relating to restart, shutdown, or system processes relating to this domain controller.

- *File and Object Access.* Monitors user access of files, directories, or printers. This access enables the auditing of those objects to take place. The users and groups that are audited are set up at the file, directory, and printer resource levels.
- *Use of User Rights.* Monitors when a user right is exercised by a user (such as formatting the hard disk).
- *User and Group Management.* Monitors events relating to user and group management, such as the creation of new users, the modification of group membership, or the change of a password.
- *Security Policy Changes.* Monitors changes made to User Rights or Account Policy information.
- *Restart, Shutdown, System.* Monitors events related to these activities.
- *Process Tracking.* Monitors events related to certain process activity such as starting a program, indirect object access, and so on.

You can log successful and unsuccessful events in the Security Log, which you can view through the *Event Viewer*, another useful Administrative Tools utility. It is generally not at all useful for you to monitor successful and unsuccessful events for all seven options on a server because of the resources involved and the volume of data that would be collected in the Security Log. Auditing can be very helpful in troubleshooting events, however, such as unsuccessful logins or unsuccessful file access.

Troubleshooting Account and Policy Management

If you have been reading carefully, you already have the necessary building blocks for understanding and troubleshooting account management. The best tool for learning is to practice.

Most of the problems you will encounter regarding user and group accounts will have to do with permissions to use resources rather than with the account setup itself. Nevertheless, here are some things to keep in mind.

User Cannot Be Logged On by System

When a user cannot log on, fortunately the message(s) that Windows NT displays to the screen are self-explanatory. Usually, the reason why a user cannot log on involves the user incorrectly typing the username or, more likely, the password. Usernames are not case-sensitive, but passwords are. Usernames and passwords can both have spaces but that tends to confuse users more than provide descriptive account names. Be sure to be consistent in your use of usernames. Educate your users in the importance of maintaining the integrity of their passwords, and expect a call every now and then from someone who has forgotten a password or has the Caps Lock on when the password is in lowercase.

If a user forgets a password, the easiest thing for the domain administrator to do is to use User Manager for Domains to give the user a new temporary password and check the User Must Change Password at Next Login properties option. If an account lockout policy has been established and the user exceeds the allowed number of incorrect passwords, the Account Locked Out properties option for that user will be checked. Only an Administrator or Account Operator can remove the lock, again, through User Manager for Domains.

Unable to Access Domain Controllers or Servers

Another possibility that can slow or inhibit a person's ability to log on successfully is the unavailability of a server. If the user is logging on locally, the user is being validated on the local computer for access to resources on that computer; unless the computer suddenly turns itself off, the user should be able to log on successfully.

When a Windows NT workstation or server is made a member of a domain, the From box on the Logon Security screen will display the local computer as well as the domain name. If one or more trusts are established, the From box will display all available trusted domains. So the first thing to check if a user cannot be authenticated is whether the user chose the correct domain from the list when logging on.

If the user is validating on a network domain controller, the domain controller must be accessible to the user or the user may not be able to log on. For example, if the PDC is down and there is no backup domain controller (BDC) identified to the network, the user will be unable to log on. If the user logged on successfully at the computer in a previous session, a message may display that the domain controller is unavailable and that the user will be logged on with cached information from the Registry.

Any changes that may have been made to a profile since the last session will probably not be available.

You troubleshoot this one, of course, by verifying that the domain controller is up and that the computer in question has a valid connection to the network. If you are using TCP/IP as your protocol, you will want to check that the computer has a valid IP address and subnet mask and, if routing is involved, a valid default router address. If a trust relationship is involved, verify that the trust is valid and working.

Sometimes the location of the BDC can cause user logon to be slow or to fail due to WAN traffic. Determine whether the location for the BDCs in your domain best meets the needs of your users and the logon traffic they generate. You can track network traffic and performance by using the Network Monitor service and utility that comes with Windows NT Server 4.0. This utility will be discussed in some detail in Chapter 23, "Network Monitor."

Sometimes you cannot track down network-based errors easily. For example, everything may seem to be functioning okay, but you just can't seem to access the network. Sometimes the network card can get confused, and the best thing to do is to shut down the computer and do a cold boot. A warm boot does not always reset the hardware—in this case, the network card.

Other Logon Problems

Other problems may be related to other settings made through User Manager for Domains. Recall that in this utility the administrator can additionally add logon hour and workstation restrictions for the user, as well as account expiration. Again, the messages that Windows NT displays are pretty obvious in this regard and will direct you to the appropriate account property to check and modify.

Remote Account Management Tips

You can perform most account management remotely by installing User Manager for Domains on a local Windows NT workstation. Versions also exist for Windows 95 and Windows for Workgroups.

Two options are available in User Manager for Domains that can facilitate the remote management of accounts across trust relationships and across slow network connections: Select Domain and Low Speed Connection.

The User menu in User Manager for Domains offers a Select Domain option. Selecting this option will display the Select Domain dialog box. Here, you can either choose the domain whose account database you want to administer from the Select Domain list (all trusted domains will be listed), or type it in the Domain text box. User Manager for Domains will display the account database for that domain, provided you have the appropriate level of access. For example, you must be made a member of the trusted domain's Administrators, Server Operators, or Account Operators local groups.

In the Select Domain dialog box, there is a check box option for Low Speed Connection. This option, also available from the Options menu, is useful for facilitating administration when the network connection is particularly busy or when administration takes place over a slower connection medium, such as a 56K line. Selecting this option will result in the following modification to User Manager for Domains.

- The list of user and group accounts will not appear and the User, Select User menu option is unavailable, though the administrator can administer accounts by using the other User menu commands.
- The capability to create and manage global group accounts is unavailable, although you can affect global group membership through the group membership of individual user accounts.
- The View menu options are unavailable.

Taking the Disc Test

If you have read and understood the material in the chapter, you are ready to test your knowledge. Insert the CD-ROM that comes with this book and run the self-test software as described in Appendix K, "Using the Self-Test Software."

From Here...

The next chapter will discuss an issue that is of paramount importance to any type of network, security in the domain. Chapter 7, "Policies and Profiles," and Chapter 8, "Remote Server Management," will discuss remote management of servers and clients and will finish up this discussion of basic Windows NT administration.

Chapter Prerequisite

The reader should be familiar with the concepts of Directory Services and Domains Models, discussed in Chapter 2, "Understanding Microsoft Windows NT 4.0," as well as the basics of user and group management, discussed in Chapter 5, "Managing Users and Groups."

Security and Permissions

Thus far, you have encountered two levels of access security: logon and user rights. Logon security is implemented through the use of user accounts and passwords. User rights, as you saw in the last chapter, are functional in nature and define what activities a user can engage in on a given computer.

This chapter discusses more thoroughly the Windows NT 4.0 security model. The security model itself applies both to Windows NT 4.0 Workstation and Server, as does the method of applying permissions and sharing resources. Specifically, this chapter covers specific security model topics by:

- Examining Windows NT 4.0 security
- Exploring the Windows NT logon process for the domain
- Examining access tokens and access control lists (ACLs)
- Determining access rights to a security object
- Determining resource access in the domain
- Reviewing shared resources and assigned permissions
- Troubleshooting security access

Examining the Windows NT 4.0 Security Model

All security provided by Windows NT 4.0 is handled through a kernel mode executive service known as the Security Reference Monitor. When a user logs on, tries to perform a function at the workstation—such as formatting a disk—or tries to access a resource, the Security Reference Monitor determines whether, and to what extent, a user should be granted access. The authentication process provides security through user account location and password protection. User rights are functional in nature, and define what actions a user can take at a given workstation, member server, or domain controller, such as shutting down the workstation or formatting a disk. These actions are discussed in Chapter 5, "Managing Users and Groups."

There are also *permissions*, which define a user's access to network resources. Permissions define what a user can do *to* or *with* a resource, such as delete a print job or modify a file. The terms *rights* and *permissions* are often used interchangeably, and usually refer to resource access. With Windows NT, the term *rights* invariably refers to those functional user rights that you can set through User Manager and User Manager for Domains; the term *permissions* refers to resource access. This is how these terms are used throughout this book.

There are two types of permissions that can be applied in Windows NT:

- *Share-level permissions* Define how a user can access a resource that has been made available (shared) on the network. This is a resource that resides some place other than the workstation at which the user is sitting and that the user accesses remotely. The owner or administrator of the resource makes it available as a network resource by sharing it. The owner or administrator of the resource also defines a list of users and groups who can access the resource through the share, and determines just how much access to give them.
- *Resource-level permissions* Also defines a user's access to a resource, but at the resource itself. The owner or administrator of the resource assigns a list of users and groups that can access the resource and the level of access to grant them. Combined with share-level permissions, the owner and administrator of a resource can provide a high degree of security.

The most common resource-level permissions you will encounter are those for files and folders. File and folder permissions are available only on NTFS-formatted partitions. If you do not have a partition formatted for NTFS, you will be able to use only the FAT-level properties—read-only, archive, system, and hidden. Under NTFS, you get a more robust set of properties, including read, write, delete, execute, and change permissions.

Shared devices, such as printers, also provide a means of assigning permissions to use the device—for example, printing to a print device, managing documents on the print device, and so on.

Key Concept

Any resource for which access can be designated is considered to be a security object. In other network operating systems, such as Novell NetWare, some permissions used to set access to resources are assigned directly to the user or group and stay with the user or group account. This is not true with Windows NT. In all cases, it is important to note that permissions are assigned to, and stay with, the security object and *not* the user. A user's access to a resource is determined at the time the user tries to access it, *not* when the user logs on.

When a user logs on to Windows NT, whether at the local workstation or through a domain controller, the user is granted an access token. Permissions ascribed to an object (resource) reside in an access control list (ACL) with the object. The Security Reference Monitor compares the user's access token information with that in the ACL and determines what level of access to grant the user. These concepts are explained further in the following section.

Exploring the Windows NT Logon Process

When a user logs on to Windows NT on a Windows NT-based computer, the user name, password, and point of authentication must be provided. This is part of the WIN32 Winlogon service that monitors the logon process. The Winlogon service passes this information to the Security Subsystem, which in turn passes it to the Security Reference Monitor (see Figure 6.1).

FIG. 6.1⇒
A diagram of the Windows NT 4.0 local logon process.

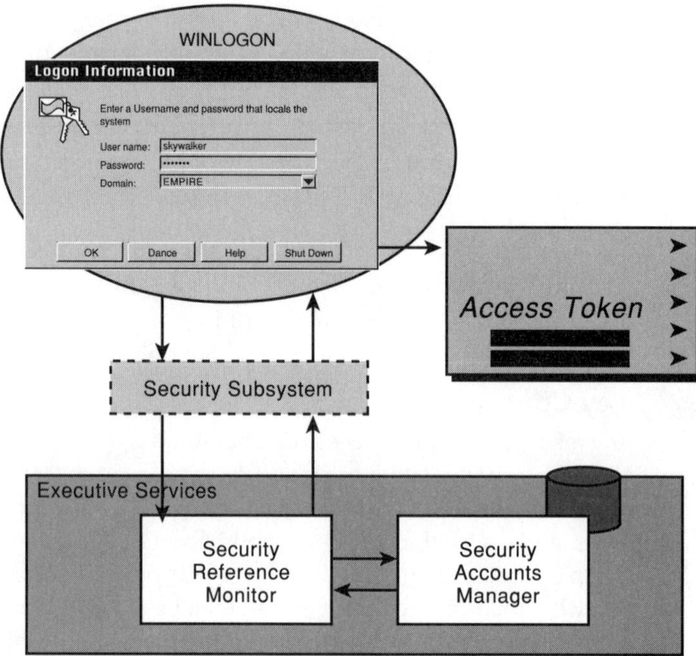

The Security Reference Monitor checks the information entered by comparing it against the Security Accounts Manager (SAM) and the account database. If the information is accurate, the Security Reference Monitor authenticates the user and returns a valid access token back to the Security Subsystem and the Winlogon process. With Directory Services, users are authenticated by a domain controller in the domain for which they are a member. This domain authentication is governed by another process, called *Net Logon*. Figure 6.2 demonstrates this process.

Net Logon is very similar to the local logon process. The difference is that the Security Subsystem passes the logon information to the Net Logon process on the user's Windows NT computer, which then establishes a secure network IPC (inter-process communication) connection with the Net Logon process on an available domain controller.

The Net Logon process of the domain controller then passes the logon information to the SAM and database on the domain controller, where the user is authenticated. The validation confirmation is sent back through the secure connection to the Security Subsystem on the user's Windows NT computer, where the access token is generated.

FIG. 6.2⇒
This example highlights how network authentication takes place in Windows NT 4.0 by using Net Logon.

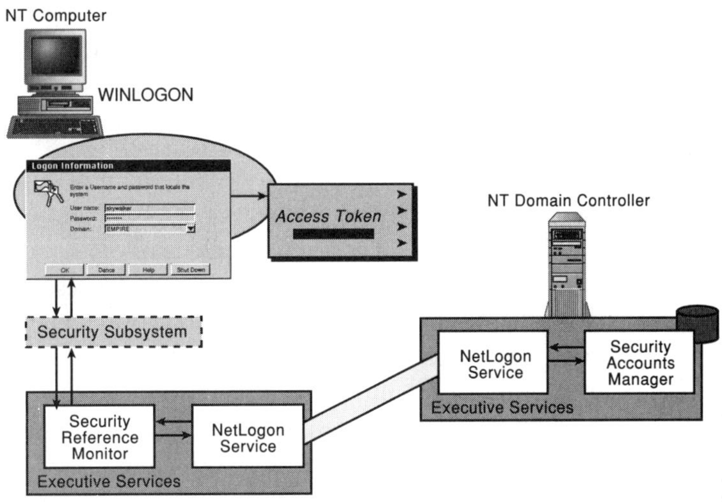

The Account Access Token

Many companies that have secure areas provide access to those areas through an electronic key card. A magnetic stripe on the back of the card contains the user's information, such as a Security ID. The card is read by a card reader at the point of entry. Often, the user also has to enter a security number or password on a keypad before the door is unlocked.

The *access token* is a lot like a key card. It contains important security information about the user. This information includes, most importantly, the user's SID. Recall from Chapter 5 that the *SID* is the unique security identifier that Windows NT assigns to the user's account when the account is created. All security-related requests made by the user are linked to, and matched first and foremost against, the user's SID. Other security information includes the username and password, group memberships by name and group SIDs, profile location, home directory information, logon hours, and so on.

The access token is used by Windows NT to determine whether a user can gain access to a resource, and how much access the user should be provided.

Local versus Domain Access Tokens

When a user logs on to a local Windows NT Workstation that is participating in a workgroup, the user's account resides in the local Windows NT

Workstation's Registry (SAM database). Hence, the user's access token is created on that local Windows NT Workstation and can be used to access only the resources on that Workstation.

As Figure 6.2 demonstrated, when a user logs on to a Windows NT computer that is a member of a domain, the user's account resides in the domain Security Accounts Manager's database on the domain controller. Recall that this type of account is called a *domain*, or *global*, account because the user can log on just once and gain access to any resource in the network that the account has permission to use. Hence, the user's access token is created on the domain controller for that domain and can be used (as it is a global account) to access any resource throughout the enterprise domain that the account has been given permission to use. This is a hallmark of Windows NT's Directory Services.

Because access to remote resources is determined by examining the Security IDs for each account in the access control list with the SIDs listed in the user's access token, the point of logon validation affects the user's ability to access a resource.

In a domain, the user and group accounts are global and can be used in the access control list of any resource in the domain. When the user logs on to the domain, the access token contains the user's Security ID (and group SIDs, per group membership) which is global to the network. Both the access tokens and the access control lists obtain their SIDs from the same Security Accounts Manager's database. Thus, the user can access any resource that has granted access permission to any one of the Security IDs that are contained in the user's access token (access to the extent the permission allows).

User access is controlled the same way where trust relationships exist between domains. A trust relationship enables users to log on and authenticate at a Windows NT computer that participates in either the trusting domain or the trusted domain. Also, the trust relationship enables resource managers to assign access to user and group accounts from any trusted domain (including their own).

Among domains where no trust relationships exist, a user's access token is good only in the validating domain. The ACLs for network resources in another domain consist of Security IDs from that domain's own account database. If the user has an account in that other domain, the user's SID in that domain is necessarily different (see Chapter 5, "Managing Users and Groups") from the SID the user uses when logging in to his or her own domain. When the user tries to access the other domain's resources, the two SIDs (access token and ACL) do not match, and the user cannot access the resources.

Regardless of whether a trust exists between two domains, Windows NT uses a process called *pass-through authentication* to validate the user on the other domain. When a trust does exist, the Net Logon process determines, as the user logs on, that the user's account does not reside within the trusting domain and therefore passes it through to the Net Logon service on a domain controller in the trusted domain, where it then is authenticated (refer to Figure 6.2).

When a trust does not exist, the user must log in to the user's own domain. Windows NT then takes the username and password from the user's access token on the user's domain, instead of the user's SID, and "passes it through" to the Net Logon service on a domain controller in the other domain. Once there, the user, in effect, is logged on to the other domain, and a new access token is created with the user's account and group Security IDs from the other domain's account database. The user then can access on that domain's computer the resources to which the access control list grants permission.

This all works great as long as the username and password match in both domains. The user can select the resources in the other domain by using Network Neighborhood or browse lists to point and click to those resources. However, the passwords, if not both the username and password, usually do not match. In this case, the user still may be able to access the resource through pass-through authentication, but, generally, the user has to connect to the resource by mapping a drive, entering a valid username from the other domain in the Connect As box, and supplying a valid password.

Consider the following example. If DOMAINA has account BrownC with password ABC, and BrownC wants to access a shared printer on Pserver2 in DOMAINB, the first thing the print administrator must do is add BrownC to the access control list for the printer. If DOMAINB trusts DOMAINA, the print administrator need only add the account to the printer's access list because it is available through the trust. However, without a trust between the domains, the administrator of DOMAINB can add members of DOMAINB's account database only to the printer's ACL. This means that an account for BrownC must be created in DOMAINB and added to the ACL for the printer.

Assume that BrownC's account in DOMAINB also expects password ABC. When BrownC uses the Add Printer Wizard to connect to the printer on Pserver2 in DOMAINB, Windows NT uses pass-through authentication and the Net Logon service to pass BrownC and ABC from BrownC's access token in DOMAINA to the Security Reference Monitor on a domain controller in DOMAINB to be authenticated. A new access token is created for BrownC in DOMAINB. This can be used successfully to access the printer, because now the Security ID for BrownC in DOMAINB matches the Security ID for BrownC in the ACL for the printer.

Unlike mapping to shared folders, there is no Connect As text box for shared printers, in which the user can supply a valid username and password for the printer. Thus, if the passwords don't match, BrownC can't access the printer at all. If BrownC attempts to access a folder under these same circumstances, BrownC can supply his or her username, or a valid username from DOMAINB in the Connect As text box that appears when mapping a drive through Network Neighborhood or Windows Explorer. BrownC then would be prompted for the appropriate password, and if correct, will gain access to the folder with the appropriate level of permissions.

Examining Access Control Lists

When a key card is read by the card reader, the information on the card generally is checked against a central database to see whether this user has the appropriate level of access to be permitted in the secured area. The database may indicate that the cardholder has full access and allow the door to open; or the database may indicate that the cardholder has minimum access and only allow a window in the door to open. If the access token is thought of as the key card for access to secured areas, an access control list (ACL) can be thought of as the card reader database.

An access control list is just that—a list of users and groups that have some level of access to the resource. It is created at the object (resource or share) level and stays with the security object. It consists of user and group account entries that reference the accounts' SIDs rather than the accounts' names. These entries are called *Access Control Entries*, or ACEs. Each entry has a particular level of permission associated with it, such as Read-Only, Full Control, or No Access.

When a user tries to access a resource, the request is passed once again to the Security Reference Monitor, which then acts as the card reader. It checks the SID entries in the access token against the SID entries in the ACL (see Figure 6.3).

FIG. 6.3⇒
A diagram of the security access process.

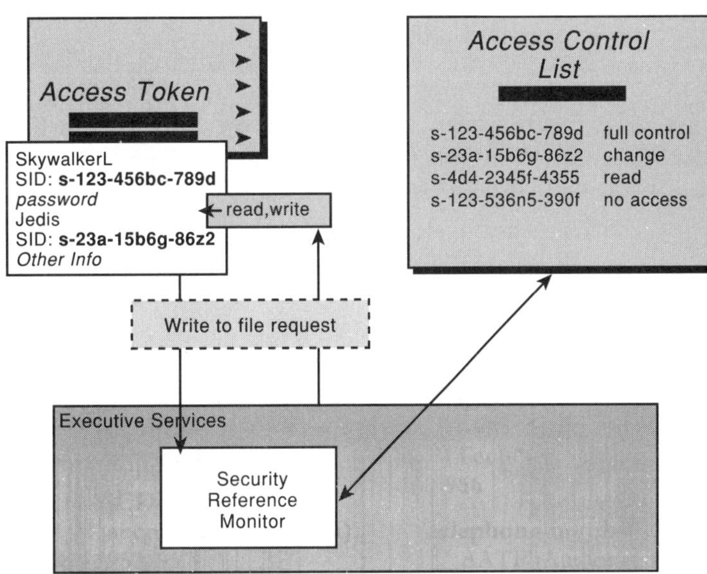

The Security Reference Monitor determines all matches, evaluates the permissions assigned to each matching entry, and calculates an overall permission level for the user, which becomes the user's effective access to the resource. It then returns that effective access as a security "handle" to the object—for example, read and write permissions for a file. The security handle becomes part of the access token for as long as the user accesses the object.

Key Concept

As long as the user maintains access to the object, the same security handle is in effect, even if the owner or administrator of the resource changes the user's access. The changed permissions do not take effect for the user until the user releases control of the object and tries to access it again. For example, if BrownC has full access to a file that he or she has opened, and the owner of the file decides to restrict BrownC to Read-Only access, BrownC continues to have full control until closing the file and trying to reopen it.

Sharing Resources and Determining Network Access

A resource, such as a folder or printer, is made available as a network resource by sharing the resource.

Only a user who is an Administrator, Server Operator, or Print Operator (or Power User on a member server) has the ability to share a resource on a workstation or server. In addition, the Server service must be running, and the network card must be operational. If you suspect a problem with the Server service or the network card, a good place to begin troubleshooting is the Event Viewer. Look for any devices or services that failed to start.

Sharing a folder is a relatively simple process. A folder is shared by selecting the file or folder through Windows Explorer or My Computer, right-clicking it, and choosing Sharing; or through the object's properties sheet. Figure 6.4 shows an example of a folder that has been shared.

FIG. 6.4⇒
Rebel Plans has been shared with the name Force. Notice the list of groups and the permissions assigned to each.

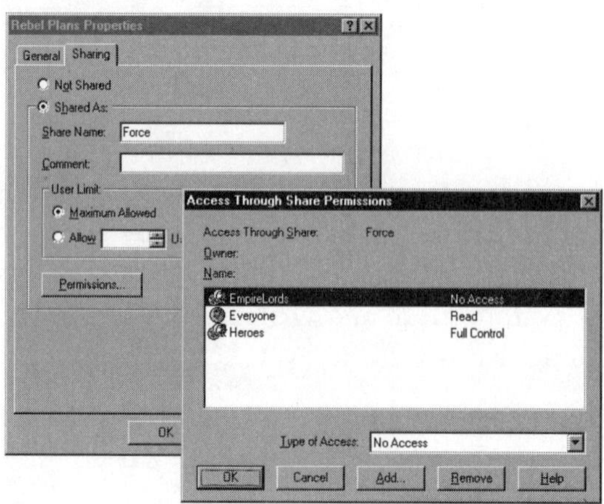

Sharing is enabled by clicking the Shared As option. When you share a folder, the share name defaults to the folder name, but can be changed to be more descriptive for its potential users. You can also indicate the number of users that are allowed to access the share at the same time, or accept the default of Maximum Allowed.

Note Recall that the maximum number of remote connections allowed on a Windows NT Workstation is 10. On a Server, the number of connections is effectively unlimited, except as defined by the license option chosen.

If you go no further, Windows NT shares this resource to any and all users. The default permission for every shared resource is Everyone with Full Control.

Key Concept

Windows NT's philosophy of sharing resources is to make information readily and easily available. Therefore, the default is to give every network user access to the resource. Hence, the default permission is always Everyone with Full Control. With printers, the default for Everyone is Print.

If you want to add a layer of security to the shared folder, you must choose Permissions and Add the appropriate group and user accounts, modifying the permissions as necessary. By doing this, you are creating and modifying the ACL for the folder.

Caution

It is recommended that you either remove the Everyone group and explicitly assign permissions to specific users and groups, or give Everyone the least level of access (Read) to provide a greater level of security. Do not give the Everyone group NO ACCESS. Because every network user is automatically a member of Everyone, giving it NO ACCESS results in locking every user—even the owner and administrator—out of that shared resource.

There are four share-level permissions that you can assign in your ACL. They are defined in Table 6.1.

Table 6.1 Permissions for Shared Folders

Permission	Effect
Read	Displays the folder and file names; allows files to be opened and programs to be run; allows similar access to subfolders.

continues

Table 6.1 Continued

Permission	Effect
Change	In addition to read permissions, allows changes to be made to files and folders, including creating and deleting files and folders.
Full Control	Allows complete access to the folder and its files and subfolders, including the ability to take ownership of files and change permissions of files and folders.
No Access	Denies access to the folder and its contents.

Caution

Share permissions take effect for users accessing the resource remotely over the network. If the user sits down at the computer that has the folder, and no other permissions have been assigned, the user still has complete access to the folder and its files.

Note If two or more users attempt to access the same file at the same time, the first user is able to modify the file, and the rest see the file in read-only mode. ■

Permissions assigned to a folder also apply to all files and folders within the shared folder. For example, if you give the group Sales read permissions for the folder DATA, the members of the Sales group also have read permissions for all files and subfolders within DATA.

Effective Permissions

The Security Reference Monitor checks the user's access token against the entries in the ACL, as you have seen already. When it identifies a match or matches, it then must determine the permissions to give the user. The effective share permissions are cumulative. The permissions explicitly assigned to a user, as well as permissions assigned to any groups in which the user is a member, are added together, and the highest level of permission is granted to the user. The only exception to this rule is that the No Access permission always denies access, regardless of any other permissions assigned.

For example, suppose BrownC is a member of Managers and Sales. BrownC has been given Change access, Managers has been given Full Control, and Sales has been given Read access to a shared folder. BrownC's effective permissions are Full Control by virtue of BrownC's membership in the Managers group.

The only exception to this rule is No Access. No Access always supersedes any other permission, even Full Control. Using the same example, if BrownC explicitly is given No Access, then BrownC can't access the shared folder, even though BrownC is a member of the Managers group that has Full Control.

It is important, therefore, that you take sufficient time to plan your shared folders and their permissions. For example, take a look at the home directory folders. Suppose that users' home directories are created under a share that is called Users. By default, Users are shared to Everyone with Full Control. This means that all files and folders within Users also give Everyone Full Control. Thus, all network users can see all other users' files in their home directories. This probably is not a good idea. This problem is best solved using NTFS file and directory permissions. NTFS permissions are covered later in this chapter in the section "Securing Folders and Files with NTFS Permissions." Briefly, you can set the permissions on the directory to only grant access to the user that owns the directory. Administrators are also denied access. Although administrators can still grant themselves access to a user's home directory at any time, this action would be recorded in the security log.

Administrative and Hidden Shares

When Windows NT is installed, it creates several shares, called administrative shares, all of which are hidden, except for Net Logon. Hidden shares are shares that exist, but cannot be seen by any user in the lists of available shared resources. Hidden shares are meant to be used by either the operating system for specific tasks and services, such as IPC$ and REPL$, or an administrator for security access or troubleshooting, such as the root drive shares.

Table 6.2 summarizes these hidden (and Net Logon) administrative shares.

Table 6.2 Administrative Shares

Share Name	Description
drive$	The root directory of every partition that is recognizable to Windows NT is assigned an administrative share name consisting of the drive letter, followed by $. Administrators, Server Operators, and Backup Operators have the ability to connect remotely to these shares. CD-ROMs do not count.
`Admin$`	Used by the operating system during remote administration of the computer, and represents the directory into which the Windows NT system files are installed (such as C:\WINNT40). Administrators, Server Operators, and Backup Operators have the ability to connect remotely to these shares.
IPC$	Represents the named pipes that are used for communication between programs and systems, and is used by the operating system during remote administration of a computer and when accessing another computer's shared resources.
`Netlogon`	Created and used on domain controllers only to authenticate users who are logging on to the enterprise domain. This share is not hidden.
`Print$`	Similar to `IPC$`, provides remote access support for shared printers.
`REPL$`	Created and used on a Windows NT Server computer when the Directory Replication service is configured and enabled. It identifies the location of the directories and files to be exported.

Hidden shares can be identified by the `$` after the share name. As an administrator, you can view all the administrative shares on a computer by starting the Server applet from Control Panel and viewing Shares (or by starting Server Manager on a Windows NT Server, viewing a computer's properties, and then its Shares).

Tip
You also can create hidden shares personally by adding $ to the end of the share name that you enter. This is a way to keep certain shares more secure. The only users that can connect to these shares are those who know the share name.

Accessing a Shared Folder

There are several ways a user can access a shared folder (assuming the user has been given permission to do so). Shares can be accessed by connecting directly to the resource through Network Neighborhood or the Find command, or by mapping a drive letter to a shared folder through My Computer or Windows Explorer.

All four utilities offer a point-and-click method of accessing the resource, which means that you do not necessarily have to know exactly where the resource is located. The Computer Browser service (see Chapter 17, "Windows NT Networking Services") provides the lists of domains, computers, and resources that you see. With Network Neighborhood and Find, you do not waste a drive letter on the resource. With My Computer and Windows Explorer, you use a drive letter for every mapping that you create—and the alphabet is not an unlimited list. Explorer, Network Neighborhood, and Find will not locate hidden shares.

Network Neighborhood

Perhaps the easiest way to connect to a shared folder is to use Network Neighborhood, especially if you need only occasional or short access to the folder and its contents (see Figure 6.5).

To connect to a shared folder by using Network Neighborhood, follow these steps:

1. Double-click Network Neighborhood.
2. All members of your domain are listed under Entire Network. To see members of other domains, double-click Entire Network, then The Microsoft Network, and select the domain from the list.
3. To display a list of the domain's shared folders, double-click the computer that has the shared folder.

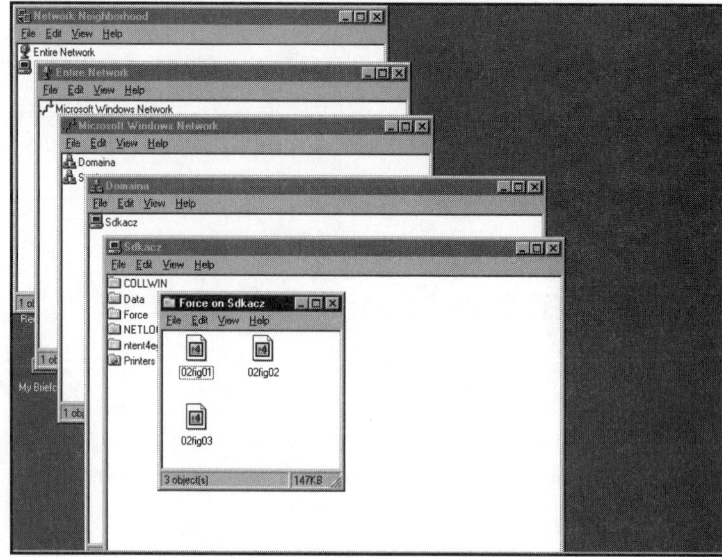

FIG. 6.5⇒
Network Neighborhood is used here to display the contents of the Force folder shared on the computer SDKACZ in DOMAINA.

4. Double-click the appropriate share name to see the contents of that folder.

Find Command

The Find command on the Start menu can be used effectively to search for computers that do not show up right away in a browse list, such as Network Neighborhood displays, or for a specific file or folder in a shared folder whose name you cannot recall.

To find a computer, follow these steps:

1. Choose Start, Find, and then Computer from the taskbar.
2. In the Computer Name box, enter the name of the computer that has the shared folder.
3. Choose Find Now. Find displays a window that shows the computer it finds.
4. Double-click the computer to display its shared folders.
5. Double-click the appropriate share name to display its contents.

To find a file or folder by name, follow these steps:

1. Choose Start, Find, and then Files or Folders from the taskbar.
2. In the Look In box, enter the name of the computer that contains the shared folder. Or, you can choose Browse to browse the Network Neighborhood entry to find the computer.
3. In the Named box, enter the name of the file or folder for which you are looking.
4. Choose Find Now. Find displays a window with its search results. Double-click the appropriate file or folder to work with it.

Note Several Find options are available to help narrow your search, such as Date Modified and Advanced. For example, if you are looking for a folder contained only in some particular share on a computer, use Advanced to narrow the search only to folders.

My Computer and Windows Explorer

My Computer can be used to map a network drive to a shared folder on a computer. This is similar to the way logical drives are assigned to Novell NetWare resources for those of you who are familiar with that network operating system (see Figure 6.6).

Using Windows Explorer probably is most similar to using File Manager in previous versions of Windows NT or Windows for Workgroups. Windows Explorer displays a Map Network Drive dialog box similar to that used with My Computer, and, in fact, it operates in much the same way.

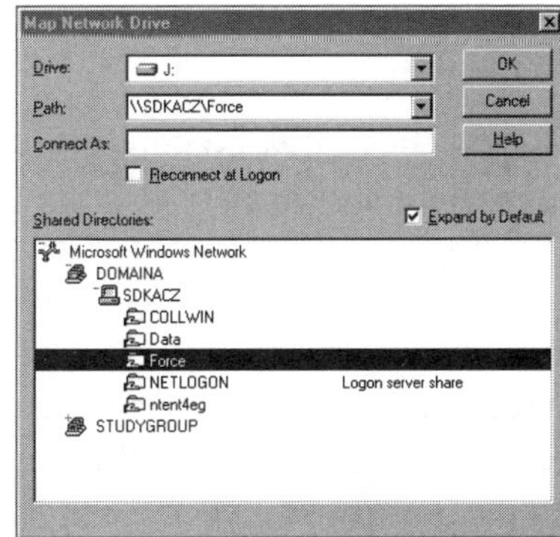

FIG. 6.6⇒ Making the same connection as in Figure 6.5 to Force on SDKACZ.

To map to a shared folder by using Network Neighborhood, follow these steps:

1. Right-click My Computer and choose Map Network Drive. Or, you can start Windows Explorer, choose Tools from the menu, and then Map Network Drive.
2. The next available drive letter is displayed in the Drive box. Select it, or make another choice of letter.
3. Double-click the appropriate network entry in the Shared Directories list box to display a browse list of Workgroups and Domains.
4. Double-click the Workgroup or Domain that contains the sharing computer to display a list of computers with shared resources.
5. Double-click the appropriate computer to display its list of shared resources.
6. Select the appropriate shared folder from the list.

Or, if you do not see the computer or folder in the browse list but know the name of the computer and share, follow these steps:

1. Right-click My Computer and choose Map Network Drive. Or, you can start Windows Explorer, choose Tools from the menu, and then Map Network Drive.
2. The next available drive letter is displayed in the Drive box. Select it, or make another choice of letter.
3. In the Path box, enter the UNC name to the shared folder by using the convention ***\\server\share***, where *server* represents the name of the computer that has the shared folder, and *share* represents the name of the shared folder.
4. Click OK.

Notice in Figure 6.6 that the check box Reconnect at Logon may be selected. This is known as a *persistent connection*. When a user maps a drive through Windows NT Workstation 4.0, this option is selected by default. If you select this box, drive J is reconnected to the share every time the user logs in. If this is a resource that the user accesses frequently, then this is a convenient tool. If the user does not access this resource frequently, then you just are taking up extra system resources to locate the shared folder, make the connection, and monitor for access.

Note When no longer needed, mapped drives can be disconnected by right-clicking My Computer and then choosing Disconnect Network Drive, or by choosing Disconnect Network Drive from the Windows Explorer's Tools menu. Select the drive from the list that you want to disconnect and choose OK. ■

Likewise, you may need to access a resource on a computer on which you do not have a valid user account. This situation is possible particularly in workgroup configurations, or in the case of administrative access to various workstations or servers. If you know the name and password of a valid user account on that computer (including Guest), you can enter the UNC name in the Path box (as described in Step 3 of the preceding list), and then enter the name of the valid account in the Connect As box. Windows NT asks you for the password, if it is required or different from your own, before connecting you to the resource.

Securing Folders and Files with NTFS Permissions

Up to this point, you have learned how to make resources available to other network users, how to secure those resources that you share on the network, and how you access those resources. There is another level of security that can be applied to files and folders stored on an NTFS partition. Among the many benefits of formatting a partition as NTFS (Windows NT's own file system) is the ability to assign permissions directly to the file and folder—that is, at the resource level.

Permissions are set for a file or folder by right-clicking the file or folder, displaying its Properties sheet, and selecting the Security tab. Choosing Permissions here displays the file or folders permissions dialog box, from which you can make your choices.

Effective File and Folder Permissions

When you assign permissions to a folder or file, you are creating an ACL for that folder or file, much like you did for the share. The Security Reference Monitor checks the user's access token against the entries in the ACL, as you previously have seen. When the Security Reference Monitor identifies a match or matches, it then must determine the permissions to give the user. The effective file or folder permissions are cumulative. The permissions explicitly assigned to a user, as well as permissions assigned to any groups in which the user is a member, are added together, and the highest level of permission is granted to the user at the file or folder level.

For example, suppose BrownC is a member of Managers and Sales. For a particular file, BrownC has been given Change access, Managers has been given Full Control, and Sales has been given Read access. BrownC's effective permission level for that file is Full Control, by virtue of his membership in the Managers group.

The only exception to this rule is No Access. No Access always supersedes any other permission, even Full Control. Using the same example, if BrownC explicitly is given No Access, he can't access the file, even though he is a member of the Managers group, which has Full Control.

Unlike share permissions, which are effective for all files and folders within the share, folder and file permissions are effective only for the immediate folder and its contents, or for an individual file, if applied to that file. The permissions for files in a folder, or for subfolders, *can* trickle down, but also can be applied individually. If permissions have been applied to an individual file, the file permission *always* supersedes the folder permission.

For example, if BrownC has been given Read permission for the folder DATA, and Change permission for the file budget.doc, BrownC's effective permission for the file budget.doc is Change because of his folder permission, even though he has only read access to all the other files in DATA.

As you can see, you have a great deal of discretion, flexibility, and control over the application of permissions to folders, subfolders, and files. It is important, therefore, that you take sufficient time to plan your folder and file permissions. For example, take another look at the home directory folders. Suppose that users' home directories are created under a share called Users. By default, Users are shared to Everyone with Full Control. If the home folders are on an NTFS partition, you can assign each user the NTFS permission Full Control to their own home folder only, while assigning the Everyone group List access to the directory. This effectively restricts access to each folder only to the owner of the folder.

Tip

If you create the users' home directories on an NTFS partition by using the %USERNAME% variable and NT's user manager utility (see Chapter 5, "Managing Users and Groups"), Windows NT automatically restricts access to the home directory so that only this specific user account can access the directory.

Assigning File and Folder Permissions

There are six individual permissions that can be applied to files and folders. Table 6.3 describes these permissions.

Table 6.3 NTFS File and Folder Permissions

Permission	Folder Level	File Level
Read (R)	Can display folders, attributes, owner, and permissions	Can display files and file data, attributes, owner, and permissions
Write (W)	Can add files and create subfolders, change folder attributes, and display folder owner and permissions	Can change file contents and attributes and display file owner and permissions
Execute (E)	Can make changes to subfolders, and display folder owner, attributes, and permissions	Can run executable files, and display file owner, attributes, and permissions
Delete (D)	Can delete a folder	Can delete a file
Change Permission (P)	Can change folder permissions	Can change file permissions
Take Ownership (O)	Can take ownership of a folder	Can take ownership of a file

Files and folders can be assigned these permissions individually or, more often, by using standard groupings provided by Windows NT security. There are nine standard folder permissions, which include two choices for setting your own custom choice of folder permissions and file permissions to apply to all files in a folder. There are five standard file permissions, which include an option for setting your own custom choice of file permissions per individual file. Tables 6.4 and 6.5 outline these permissions and what they allow the user to do.

Note that when viewing and setting permissions, Windows NT always displays the individual permissions in parentheses alongside the standard permission. For Folder permissions, the first set of parentheses represents the permissions on the folder, and the second set represents the permissions that apply to files globally, including any new file created in the folder.

Table 6.4 Standard Permissions for Folders

Permission	Access
No Access (None)(None)	Supersedes all other file permissions and prevents access to the file.
List (RX)(Not Specified)	Allows the user to view folders and subfolders, and file names within folders and subfolders. List is not available as a valid permission option for files.
Read (RX)(RX)	In addition to List access, the user can display file contents and subfolders, and run executable files.
Add (WX)(Not Specified)	The user can add files to the folder, but not list its contents. Add is not available as a valid permission option for files.
Add and Read (RWX)(RX)	In addition to Add, the user can display the contents of files and subfolders, and run executable files.
Change (RWXD)(RWXD)	Provides the user the capability to display and add files and folders, modify the contents of files and folders, and run executable files.
Full Control (All)(All)	In addition to Change, the user is given the capability to modify folder and file permissions, and to take ownership of folders and files.
Special Directory Access	Allows the selection of any combination of individual permissions (R, W, E, D, P, O) for folder access.
Special File Access	Allows the selection of any combination of individual permissions (R, W, E, D, P, O) for file access.

Table 6.5 Standard Permissions for Files

Permission	Access
No Access (None)	No access is allowed to the file.
Read (RX)	Allows the user to display file data and run executable files.
Change (RWXD)	In addition to Read, the user can modify the file contents, and delete the file entirely.
Full Control (All)	In addition to Change, the user can modify the file's permissions, and take ownership of the file.
Special Access	Allows the selection of any combination of individual permissions (R, W, E, D, P, O) for a file.

Caution

The Folder permission Full Control provides the user an inherent ability to delete files in a folder through the command prompt, even if the user is given No Access permission to a specific file. This is done to preserve Posix application support on UNIX systems, for which Write permission on a folder enables the user to delete files in the folder. This can be superseded by choosing the Special Directory Access standard permission and checking all the individual permissions.

Permissions are set for a file or folder by right-clicking the file or folder, displaying its Properties sheet, and selecting the Security tab. Choosing Permissions here displays the file or folder permissions dialog box, as shown in Figure 6.7, from which you can make your choices.

FIG. 6.7⇒
The Force folder's access control list (ACL) shows that Administrators have Full Control access, Everyone has Read access, and Heroes has Change access. The Type of Access list box displays the standard permission options.

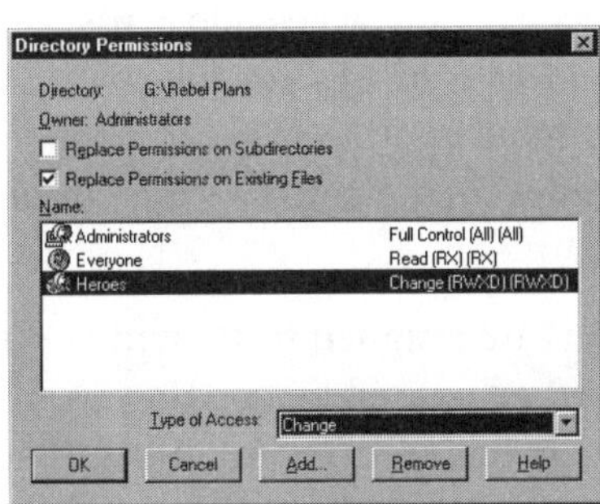

Notice in the Directory Permissions dialog box shown in Figure 6.7 that there are two Replace choices: Replace Permissions on Subdirectories and Replace Permissions on Existing Files (which is selected by default).

Caution

The effect of Replace Permissions on Existing Files is to change any and all permissions that you have set on individual files to the permissions that you have set at the folder level. Because this option is selected by default, it is easy to forget when setting permissions at the folder level, and you can accidentally change permissions on files that you do not want to change. Bottom line: Read all screens carefully.

Choosing Replace Permissions on Subdirectories causes Windows NT to apply the permissions set at this folder level to all subfolders. Any new files added to the folder will assume the folder's permissions. If Replace Permissions on Existing Files is also left selected, the permissions are applied not only to the subfolders, but also to their contents.

The Type of Access list box shows all the standard permissions that are available at the folder level, including the two special options, Special Directory Access and Special File Access, from which you can customize your choice of permissions.

As with share permissions, users and groups can be added or removed from the ACL through the Add and Remove buttons.

Determining Access When Using Share and NTFS Permissions

A folder (and its contents) is made accessible across the network by sharing it. As discussed, an ACL can be created for the share. This defines which users and group accounts can access the share, and the level of access permitted. You know that the effective permissions are cumulative at the share level.

When NTFS permissions are assigned to individual folders and files, the level of access can be further refined by creating an ACL at the file and folder level. You know that the effective permissions at the file and folder level also are cumulative.

When a user accesses a file or folder protected by NTFS permissions across the network through a share, the Security Reference Monitor determines the cumulative permissions at the share and the cumulative permissions at the file or folder. Whichever permission is most restrictive becomes the effective permission for the user.

For example, if BrownC, a member of the Managers group, has been given Read access individually and Change access through the Managers group to a share called Public, then BrownC's effective permission for the share Public is Change. If BrownC has been given Read access to a file budget.doc (contained in the folder that has been shared as Public) and Full Control through the Managers group, BrownC's effective permission at the file level is Full Control. However, BrownC's net effective permission to budget.doc, when accessing it through the network share, is Change, which is the more restrictive of the two permissions.

	Budget.doc Accessed Through the Public Share	**Budget.doc File Level**
BrownCRead	Read	Read
Managers	`+ Change`	`+ Full Control`
Effective Permissions	Change	Full Control Change (more restrictive than Full Control)

Through a shrewd use of share- and file\folder-level permissions, you can create a very effective security structure for resources stored on your Windows NT Workstations and Servers.

Understanding the Concept of Ownership

The user who creates a file or folder is considered by Windows NT to be the owner of that file or folder, and therefore is placed in the Creator Owner internal group for that file or folder. A user cannot give someone else ownership of their files or folders. However, a user can give someone the permission to take ownership of their files and folders.

The Take Ownership permission is implied through Full Control, but also can be assigned to a user or group through the Special Access permission options. A user that has this permission can take ownership of the file or folder. After ownership has been taken, the new owner can modify the file or folder's permissions, delete the file, and so on. Administrators always have the ability to take ownership of a file or folder. All ownership changes are logged in the security log.

A user who has the Take Ownership permission can take ownership of a folder or file by following these steps:

1. Right-click the folder or file and select Properties.
2. In the Properties sheet, select the Security tab.
3. On the Security tab, choose Ownership. The current owner is displayed.
4. Choose Take Ownership, and then choose OK.

If any member of the Administrators group takes ownership of a file or folder, or creates a file or folder, the owner becomes the Administrators group.

Taking ownership of files and folders can be useful, especially when users move around from department to department or position to position, or leave the organization permanently. Taking ownership provides a way to assign an appropriate replacement for the files and folders that are no longer being used by a user.

Copying and Moving Files...and Permissions

When you *copy* a file from one folder to another, the file assumes the permissions of the target folder. When you *move* a file from one folder to another, the file maintains its current permissions. This sounds simple enough, except that a move isn't always a move. When you move a file from a folder in one partition to a folder in another partition, you actually are copying the file to the target folder, and then deleting the original file. When permissions are involved, a move is considered a move only when you move a file from a folder in one partition to another folder in the *same* partition.

Managing Shares and Permissions Remotely

As an administrator, it is possible to create and manage shares and set permissions for folders and files remotely. If you are working on a Windows NT-based computer, simply map a drive to the hidden drive share—for example, D$—and then proceed as described in the previous section of this chapter, "Assigning File and Folder Permissions."

If you have installed the server tools on your computer (see Chapter 8, "Remote Server Management"), you can also use Server Manager to manage shares. Server Manager displays a list of the Windows NT-based domain controllers, member servers, and workstations in your domain. Manage shares by following these steps:

1. Select the computer on which you want to manage the share from the computer list.
2. Choose Computer, Shared Directories to display the Shared Directories dialog box (see Figure 6.8).
3. Choose New Share and enter a Share Name, folder Path (there is no Browse feature here), and set permissions in the New Share dialog box.

   Select an existing share from the Shared Directories list, and then choose Properties to modify its current properties, such as permissions.

   Select an existing share from the Shared Directories list and then choose Stop Sharing to remove the share.
4. Choose Close to save your changes.

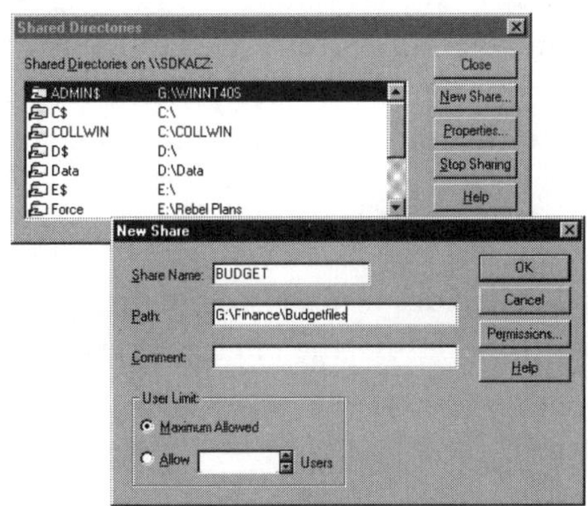

FIG. 6.8⇒
Server Manager enables an administrator to create and manage shares remotely on Windows NT computers in the domain.

If you have administrative access to other domains, through either a valid administrator's account or a trust relationship, you also can remotely administer shares on Windows NT computers in that domain. Follow these steps to switch to that domain:

1. Choose Computer, Select Domain to display the Select Domain dialog box.
2. Either select the appropriate domain from the Select Domain list, or enter the domain name in the Domain text box.
3. Choose OK. The Server Manager screen will refresh and list computers in the selected domain.
4. Manage shares as outlined in the steps at the beginning of this section.

Troubleshooting Security

The problem that you most likely will have with security is a user being unable to access a resource. You must attempt to isolate possible sources of error. To begin with, have the user logoff and then log back on. If this doesn't work, try login on as that user locally (on the machine providing the resource). If logging on locally works (the user has access) then you need to check the share level permissions. If logging on locally doesn't work, then the access control list for that resource is probably in error. You will need to carefully check all groups and users in the ACL. Remember, when comparing share permissions to file and folder permissions, Windows NT assigns the most restrictive permission to the user.

When changing permissions on a share, file, or folder, the user will not notice the effect of the change until the next time the resource is accessed. This is due to the way in which Windows NT assigns the permission to the user. Recall that, when the user's access token is compared to the ACL and the effective permission is established, the user's access token receives a permission handle to the resource. This handle remains effective until the user releases the resource.

For example, BrownC has effective permission Change to budget.doc. The owner of budget.doc decides to restrict BrownC to Read. While BrownC has budget.doc open and in use, the effective permission remains Change.

When BrownC closes budget.doc and opens it later, the effective permission changes to Read.

Suppose BrownC has established a logical drive mapping to the Data share and has effective permission Change to the share. The owner of the share changes BrownC's permission to Read. BrownC maintains Change permission to the share until either disconnecting and reconnecting to the share, or logging off and logging back on to the share.

In another case, suppose BrownC is currently a member of the Managers group. BrownC has Read permission to the Data folder but Full Control permission through BrownC's membership in the Managers group. You take BrownC out of the Managers group to ensure that he or she has Read access only to the folder. When BrownC accesses the folder, he or she still has Full Control access to the folder, because BrownC's access token still maintains that he or she has membership in the Managers group. Remember that the access token is created during *logon*. Thus, the group change is not effective until BrownC logs off and logs back on.

Taking the Disc Test

If you have read and understood the material in this chapter, you are ready to test your knowledge. Load the CD-ROM that comes with this book and run the self-test software, as described in Appendix K, "Using the Self-Test Software."

From Here...

In this chapter, you learned about security and the management of network resources. Chapter 7, "Policies and Profiles," focuses on a different aspect of computer and user management—managing users through the use of profiles. User profiles and system policies, and their effect within the domain, are discussed at length.

Chapter Prerequisite

It is important that the reader be comfortable with the concepts of user and group management that were covered in Chapter 5, "Managing Users and Groups," as well as the Directory Services concepts presented in Chapter 2, "Understanding Microsoft Windows NT 4.0."

7

Policies and Profiles

This chapter discusses how to manage the user's and computer's environments through the use of user and computer profiles. In particular, the following topics are covered:

- Understanding user and computer profiles
- Creating and managing server-based profiles
- Exploring the System Policy Editor
- Troubleshooting profiles

Understanding User and Computer Profiles

As discussed in Chapter 5, "Managing Users and Groups," when speaking of the User Profile in Windows NT 4.0, what really is being discussed is managing the user's working environment. In contrast, when speaking of the Computer Profile, you actually are talking about managing the computer's environment and configuration settings. Both types of profiles involve making modifications to the Windows NT Registry.

Through the User Environment Profile dialog box in User Manager for Domains, various elements of the user's environment can be defined. These include:

- The User Profile Path   Identifies the location of the Registry files and profile folders for the user.
- The Logon Script Name   Identifies the name and optional path of a set of commands that are executed when the user logs on.
- The Home Folder   Identifies the location of the user's personal data folder.

Each of these elements is discussed in Chapter 5.

Through the System Policy Editor, Registry settings can be modified for both the user's environment and the computer's configuration. These settings might include restricting the use of the File, Run command for the user, or configuring a legal notice to display on a Windows NT workstation when a user attempts to log on.

When the computer boots and the user logs on, the user's computing environment is configured automatically and according to predetermined settings.

User Profiles

The User Profile represents the user's environment settings, such as screen colors, wallpaper, persistent network and printer connections, mouse settings and cursors, shortcuts, personal groups, and Startup programs. These settings normally are saved as part of the Windows NT Registry on the user's computer, and then loaded when the user logs on to the system.

In Windows NT 3.51 and earlier versions, these settings were kept in the WINNT\SYSTEM32\CONFIG subdirectory with the other Registry files on the local computer, workstation, or server that the user logged into. The next time that the user logged on, the profile settings were made available and merged into the Registry for that session. If the user moved to another computer, whether the user logged on locally or to the network, a new profile was created on that computer and saved locally. The settings saved on that computer, in turn were merged into the local Windows NT Registry on that computer.

Under Windows NT 4.0, profiles still are saved on the local computer to which the user logs on. However, all information relating to the user's profile now is saved in a subdirectory structure created in the WINNT\PROFILES folder, which contains the Registry data file, as well as directory links to desktop items. An example of this structure is displayed in Figure 7.1.

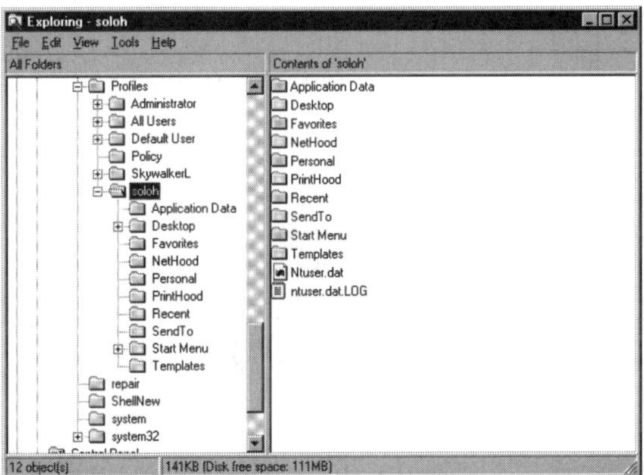

FIG. 7.1 ⇒
In this view of Windows Explorer, the WINNT\PROFILES folder with the profile subdirectory structure for SOLOH is expanded. Notice the Registry files NTUSER.DAT and NTUSER.DAT.LOG.

There are three default profile structures created during installation:

- Administrator This structure is created because the Administrator's account is a default account.
- Default User New user accounts can derive their initial environment settings from this structure.
- All Users This structure is used with the user's profile settings to assign settings that should be common to all users, such as startup items and common groups.

The directory structure of the user's profile directory is outlined in Table 7.1.

Table 7.1 Overview of the Profile Folder Directory Structure

Profile Folder	Description
Application	Contains references to application-specific data and usually is modified by the application during installation or when a user modifies a setting for the application
Desktop	Contains references to shortcuts created on the desktop and the Briefcase
Favorites	Contains references to shortcuts made to favorite programs and locations
NetHood	Contains references to shortcuts made to Network Neighborhood items, such as shared folders
Personal	Contains references to shortcuts made to personal group programs
PrintHood	Contains references to shortcuts made to print folder items
Recent	Contains references to items most recently accessed by the user
SendTo	Contains shortcuts to the last items that documents were "sent to" or copied such as the A: drive or My Briefcase
Start Menu	Contains references to program items contained on the start menu, including the Startup group
Templates	Contains references to shortcuts made to template items

When the user first logs on, the settings contained in Default User are used to create that user's own profile folders. In addition, the Registry data file, called NTUSER.DAT, is created and stored in the root of the user's profile folder (refer to Figure 7.1). Windows NT also creates and maintains a corresponding transaction log file, called NTUSER.DAT.LOG. Changes to the profile actually are recorded in the log file and applied to the NTUSER.DAT file when the user logs off. In the event of a problem, the changes are kept in the log file and can be applied the next time the user logs on. So, as the user modifies the environment by changing settings, creating shortcuts, installing applications, and adding programs to the Start menu, Windows NT adds and modifies entries in the appropriate profile folder and updates the Registry log file.

For example, if SoloH (the profile folders shown in Figure 7.1) adds a shortcut to his or her desktop for Word 97, Windows NT adds an entry representing the shortcut to Word 97 in the Desktop folder, under WINNT\PROFILES\SOLOH. If SoloH modifies the desktop wallpaper, the change is recorded in SoloH's NTUSER.DAT.LOG file and applied to the NTUSER.DAT file when SoloH logs off.

The Registry subtree HKEY_CURRENT_USER is actually a cached copy of the Registry data file, NTUSER.DAT, and, as discussed in Chapter 4, "Configuring Windows NT Server 4.0," it contains information relating to the user's environment settings, such as color schemes, cursors, wallpaper, and so on.

Note By default, the NetHood, PrintHood, Recent, and Templates folders are hidden from display in Windows Explorer. To view these folders, choose View, Options, select the View tab, and then choose Show All Files. ■

Server-Based User Profiles

As you have seen, user profile information is stored in the computer(s) on which the user logs on. If a user routinely logs on to any one of several computers, it might be inconvenient for that user to create or modify preferred settings on each computer before using it. It is far more efficient for the user's work-environment settings to follow the user to whichever computer the user logs on. This type of user is known as the *roaming user*, and their profiles are known as *server-based*, or *roaming* profiles. This type of profile is used more often to provide a level of consistency among an organization's users' desktops than to accommodate roaming users.

Windows NT 4.0 Workstation and Server computers support two types of server-based profiles: Roaming User Profiles and Mandatory User Profiles. They are both user profile settings that have been copied to a centrally located server for access by the user when logging on. The location and name of the profile is identified in the user's User Environment Profile information through User Manager for Domains.

When the user logs on to a computer, either a mandatory or a roaming profile is copied to that local computer to provide the best performance (local rather than over-the-network access). Changes made to the roaming profile are updated on both the local computer and the server. The next time that the user logs on, the server copy is compared to the local copy. If the server copy is more recent, then it is copied to the local computer. If the local copy has the same time and date stamp as the server copy, the local copy is used again to facilitate the logon process. If the local copy is more recent, as might happen if the user uses a laptop that is infrequently connected to the network, then the user is notified and asked which copy to use.

The primary difference between mandatory and roaming profiles is that the *mandatory* profile is created by an administrator for the user and *cannot* be modified by the user. The roaming profile can be, and is meant to be, modified by the user, and it follows the user, as a convenience.

Key Concept

The user may change environment settings while in a particular session, but those settings are *not* saved back to the mandatory profile. Also, a mandatory profile can be configured so that, if the profile is unavailable when the user attempts to log on, the user will be prevented from logging on.

Server Profiles over Slow WAN Links

Logging in over a slower WAN connection, such as a dial-up line or a 56K link, can result in slowed response time for the logon process. This can be particularly painful for the user when a server-based profile must be copied across the slow link. If you have told Windows NT to monitor for slow WAN connections (User Manager for Domains), when Windows NT detects a slow link (more than two minutes to respond to a request for the profile), it displays a dialog box that asks the user to select either a locally cached profile or the server-based profile. If the user selects the local profile, all changes are saved to the local version.

The user also can make the choice to switch to the local profile during his session. Through the User Profiles tab, located in the System applet in the Control Panel, users can change their profile from roaming to local, or from local to roaming. Again, if the user selects local, all changes are saved to the local profile until the user switches back to the server profile.

If the user requires a mandatory profile, the user is unable to log on, unless he or she opts to install the user-based profile over the slow connection.

Creating the Server-Based Profile

Windows NT 4.0 Server no longer provides the User Profile utility that some users are familiar with from using Windows NT Server 3.51.

Windows NT Server 4.0 has, however, implemented support for server-based profiles in a couple of interesting ways.

A server-based profile is always identified to the user's account by the account administrator, who provides the UNC path and file name of the profile file in the user account's User Environment Profile dialog box, as shown in Figure 7.2. This path identifies the server on which the profile will be maintained, as well as the shared folder in which it will be stored. If the file specified does not exist, Windows NT creates an empty profile for the user. When the user first logs on and modifies the settings, the server-based profile is updated.

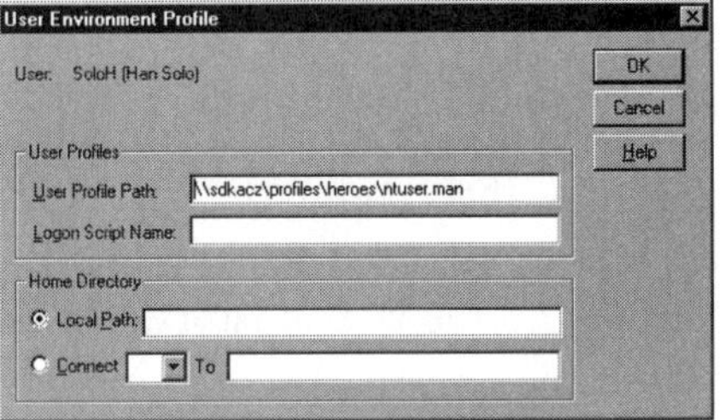

FIG. 7.2 ⇒ The server-based profile file for user SoloH is stored in the Heroes subfolder, in the Profiles shared folder, on the server SDKACZ. The .MAN extension on the profile file indicates that this is a mandatory profile.

In some cases, the administrator may want, or need, to predetermine the users' profiles. Windows NT provides management for this type of user profile through the User Profiles tab of the System applet in the Control Panel.

The User Profiles tab of the System Properties dialog box displays the profiles that have been created and stored on that computer. Remember that a profile is created each time a user logs on. If you plan to delete a user, you first should delete the user's profile through this tab. If you first delete the user, you will see an entry `Account Deleted`, as shown in Figure 7.3. This really is not such a big deal if only one or two accounts are involved; if the account is deleted anyway, it is a pretty safe bet that you can delete its profile information. With large numbers of users, deleting the appropriate profiles after the accounts have already been deleted can be confusing. Recall that all settings relating to a user account are linked to the user's security ID. Deleting the account deletes the SID and renders all previous settings obsolete, including profile information.

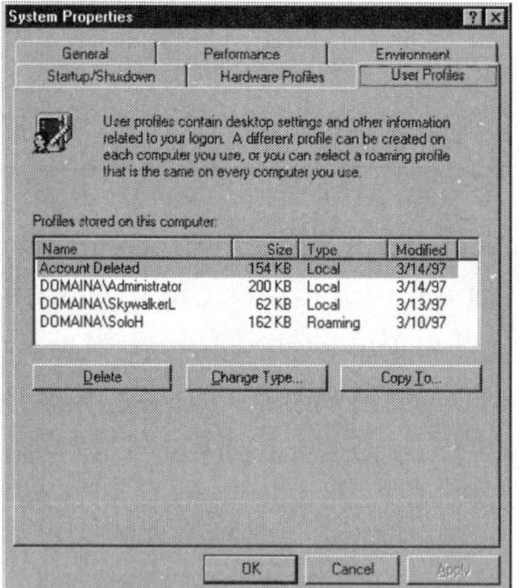

FIG. 7.3 ⇒
There are four user profiles contained on this computer. One of them is for an account that has since been deleted. It should be removed to clean up the Profiles directory on the hard disk.

The first step necessary to create a roaming or mandatory profile is to identify the users or groups that require this type of profile. The Registry file name NTUSER.DAT cannot be changed, and it is this file that determines whether or not the profile is mandatory. The next step is to identify the central computer on which you plan to store the users' profiles. This should be a computer that is readily accessible by the users on that network or subnet, particularly if the profiles are mandatory. The directory then should be shared on the network. Within this directory, create subdirectories for the different users or groups that will use various profiles you create.

Caution

If you permit several users or a group of users to use the same roaming profile, remember that the profile *can be modified* by the user. It is possible that multiple users may make multiple changes to the profile. It is better to use mandatory profiles for groups of users. Individual roaming users each should have their own roaming, changeable profile.

Roaming and mandatory profiles are then configured in the following manner:

1. Identify a server and shared folder location on which you will save the profile.
2. Identify or create a user account, and make the appropriate changes to that account's environment settings.

3. Select that account's profile through the User Profiles tab, located in the System applet in the Control Panel, and choose Copy To.
4. In the Copy Profile To box, enter the UNC name to the share and directory that will contain the profiles, or choose Browse to look for the location.
5. Select Change, and from the Choose User dialog box that is displayed, and then select the user or groups that you are permitting to use this profile by choosing Show Users.
6. Choose OK to save the profile, and then exit the System applet.

Next, you must identify the profile file to the user(s) you are configuring through the User Manager utility.

1. Open User Manager for Domains.
2. From the User Properties of the user being configured, choose Profile to display the User Environment Profile dialog box.
3. In the User Profile Path text box, enter the UNC path to the profile file. For example, if the profile NTUSER.DAT is located in the BROWNC directory, in the share PROFILES on the server KITESERVER, then you enter **\\KITESERVER\PROFILES\BROWNC\NTUSER.DAT**.
4. Choose OK and exit User Manager for Domains.
5. Test the profile by logging on as that user.

Mandatory Profiles

As stated earlier, a mandatory profile is one that does not accept user changes. It always provides the same settings for every user who has been identified as using that profile. For this reason, it is the best choice when maintaining the same configuration settings for large groups of users, or for users who should not be allowed to make configuration changes.

The steps for creating a mandatory profile are the same as those for a roaming profile. If you require the profile to become mandatory, you must use Windows Explorer to select the NTUSER.DAT file, and then change the extension to NTUSER.MAN. This effectively makes the profile mandatory, and any changes that users may make to their desktops will not be saved back to the profile.

Key Concept

Furthermore, if the administrator specifies this file by name in the user's User Environment Profile settings dialog box, the user will be prevented from logging on if the profile is, for any reason, unavailable.

If the administrator does not specify the file by name, the user is still able to log on with default user settings.

Default User Profiles

It is possible for an administrator to create a default profile that all users can receive when they first log in. For example, perhaps all users should have the same screen colors, or the company logo as their desktop wallpaper. Again, this profile is created as a regular roaming profile. However, this profile must be copied to the NETLOGON share (WINNT\SYSTEM32\REPL\IMPORT\SCRIPTS) for every domain controller in the user's account domain. The user accounts also must be configured, as outlined earlier in the chapter, to use a personal profile.

When the user logs on, Windows NT checks the user account's specified profile path for the existence of a profile file. If none exist, and there are none stored locally on the computer from which the user is logging in, Windows NT checks the NETLOGON share for a folder named Default User, and loads the profile stored there. When the user logs off, these settings, and any changes the user makes, are saved to the user's own profile folder.

Caution

When copying a profile to a server, you must use the Server applet in the Control Panel. Using Windows Explorer will not make the necessary modifications to the Windows NT Registry to record the location of the profile. Only the Server applet makes the appropriate Registry changes. Profile entries are found in the following Registry subkey: HKEY_LOCAL_MACHINE\Software\Microsoft\Windows NT\CurrentVersion\ProfileList.

Supporting Windows 95 Profiles

Windows 95 administrators can also create and maintain profiles for Windows 95 users. Both Windows 95 and Windows NT 4.0 profiles operate similarly, although Windows 95 profiles are created differently and have some functional differences. Windows 95, for example, does not support the concept of common groups or a centrally stored default profile. For that matter, Windows 95 profiles can be copied only from the user's home folder, as opposed to a specific profile path. In addition, the Registry files created by Windows 95 to support profiles are different than the files of Windows NT 4.0—USER.DAT, USER.DA0, and USER.MAN in Windows 95, as opposed to NTUSER.DAT, NTUSER.DAT.LOG, and NTUSER.MAN for Windows NT 4.0.

Nevertheless, Windows 95 users can obtain their profiles when logging in as a member of a Windows NT domain by creating their profiles as they normally do in Windows 95, which includes storing the profiles in the users' home folders and referencing the locations of the home folders in each user account's User Environment Profile dialog box in Windows NT.

Managing Profiles with the System Policy Editor

The System Policy Editor can be used, alternatively—and perhaps more effectively, to control user profile settings. It is available only on Windows NT 4.0 servers. Through the System Policy Editor, you can modify the default settings for all users, or copy the settings and then modify them by individual users or groups. The policy file then is saved as NTCONFIG.POL in the WINNT\SYSTEM32\REPL\IMPORT\SCRIPTS subdirectory on all validating domain controllers. This concept will seem quite familiar to Windows 95 administrators as it is similar to the system-policy file that can be created for Windows 95 clients (CONFIG.POL). However, Windows 95 system policies are not compatible with Windows NT 4.0 system policies, due, in part, to differences in their registries.

System Policy Editor allows the administrator to affect both the computer configurations and settings, such as those saved in the HKEY_LOCAL_MACHINE subtree of the Registry, as well as user-environment settings, such as those saved in the HKEY_USERS subtree. Settings can affect all computers and users as default or general settings, or they can be created to affect only specific computers or users.

For example, through the System Policy Editor, you can restrict user activity in the Display applet in the Control Panel; specify desktop settings, such as wallpaper and color schemes; customize desktop folders; create custom folders and Start menu options; restrict use of Run, Find, and Shutdown;

and disable editing of the Registry. Combined with computer-system policies applied to the computer at which a user logs on, the administrator can achieve a finer level of control over the user's work environment.

Working with the System Policy Editor

There are two types of policy modes that are provided by the System Policy Editor—Registry mode and Policy mode. The Registry mode enables an administrator to administer local or remote registries, without using the Registry Editor. The System Policy Editor provides a point-and-click method of implementing Registry changes. Thus, the administrator has a safe and relatively intuitive utility to use to modify a local or remote Registry. Additionally, changes made through the Registry mode of the System Policy Editor take effect immediately, in contrast to those made through the Registry Editor.

You initiate Registry mode by selecting File, Open Registry from the menu. The Local Computer icon displays options to implement the changes to the HKEY_LOCAL_MACHINE subtree of the local Registry. The Local User icon displays options to implement changes to the HKEY_Users subtree. Access the Registry on a remote Windows NT computer by selecting File, Connect from the System Policy Editor menu, and then enter the name of the Windows NT computer you want to manage.

You must have administrator privileges on the Windows NT computer whose Registry you want to manage.

The Policy mode provides an administrator with a method of implementing configuration changes for all users or computers, or for selected users and computers. This is done by creating a single policy file that contains references to various computers or users, each with a distinct set of configuration requirements. The policy file then can be saved on a specified server, accessed during user logon, and downloaded to the logon workstation.

Initiate Policy mode by selecting File, New Policy from the main menu to create a new policy file; or select File, Open Policy to modify an existing policy file. The Default Computer icon displays options that affect all computers connecting to the domain, and the Default User icon displays options that similarly affect all users logging on to the domain. Specific users and computers can also be added to the policy file, each with its own set of configuration options selected.

In both modes, when the user logs on, the settings contained in the system policy are merged with the current Registry settings to provide a specific environment for the computer and the user. The options displayed for both modes are the same, so they will not be separated by mode as this section continues.

Policy Templates

The policy options that are displayed when you modify computer or user settings in either mode are determined by a set of template files provided by Widows NT 4.0. These templates provide options for the most common configuration settings that administrators modify. The templates are text files with a specific structure and, as such, can be modified or customized for specific usage by the administrator.

Two policies are loaded by default when System Policy Editor is started. COMMON.ADM offers options that are common to both Windows NT 4.0 and Windows 95, such as Network, Desktop, Control Panel, System, Shell, and System settings. These options primarily effectuate changes to HKEY_Users in the Windows NT 4.0 and Windows 95 Registries. WINNT.ADM offers Windows NT 4.0-specific options, such as Windows NT Network, Windows NT Printers, Windows NT User Profiles, Windows NT System, Windows NT Remote Access, and Windows NT Shell. These options primarily effectuate changes to HKEY_LOCAL_MACHINE in the Windows NT Registry.

A third policy is also available, called WINDOWS.ADM, which offers options that are specific to Windows 95 computers, such as Windows 95 Control Panel, Windows 95 System, Windows 95 Shell, and Windows 95 Network.

Through a combination of these templates, system policies can be created from the same policy file to govern the working environments of all your Windows NT 4.0 and Windows 95 clients.

Setting System Policy Options

When the administrator modifies a system policy by selecting the computer or user icons, a list of option categories is displayed in a manner similar to the Windows Explorer folder screen. The administrator drills down through each option category and makes a selection by checking off the option desired. In many cases, as an option is checked, the bottom half of the screen displays additional settings that can be made, or text that can be entered, as demonstrated in Figure 7.4.

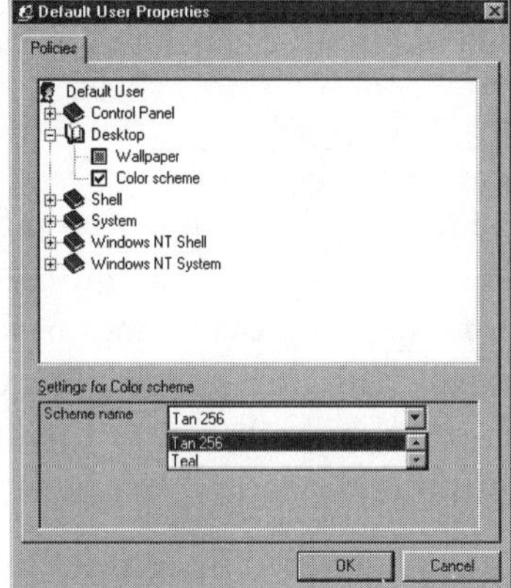

FIG. 7.4 ⇒
The Desktop category for the Default User is selected. With the selection of Color Scheme, the administrator can choose from a list of available color schemes in the Scheme Name list box.

There are three selection possibilities for each policy option:

- Checking an option indicates that the option should be merged with the current Registry and override any existing settings.
- Clearing a check box indicates that the option should be merged with the Registry, if there is no current Registry setting for that option. If there is a current setting, then the policy setting is ignored.
- Leaving the check box gray, the default, means that the policy setting is not modified at all.

In fact, only the options that are checked or cleared are saved to the policy file, so as to keep the file to a manageable size when downloading it across network connections.

Default and Specific User and Computer Settings

Changes made to policy settings under Default User or Default Computer are applied to all computers and users affected by this policy file. When a user logs on, the policy file is checked first for the default settings that should be applied to all computers and users, then the Registry is modified accordingly.

However, policy options also can be set for individual computers and users within a domain. For example, suppose that computer WOOKI5 needs to have a specific network setting configured when a given user logs on. A policy setting can be configured specifically for WOOKI5. When a user logs on at WOOKI5, the policy file is checked for any specific options set for that computer, and then for default settings. It finds WOOKI5 and implements those settings, in addition to, or overriding, the default settings. Similarly, specific settings can be provided for individual user accounts. When the user logs on, any specific settings meant for that particular user are implemented, in addition to, or overriding, the default settings.

Furthermore, policy settings can be implemented by group membership. Options for specific groups can be set, along with a group priority to determine which settings take precedence when a user belongs to several groups for which policies have been set. If a user has a specific policy, however, any group policy that might otherwise have been set for the user will be ignored. The specific order for implementing system policy settings is outlined in Figure 7.5.

FIG. 7.5 ⇒
A flow chart for applying system policy settings.

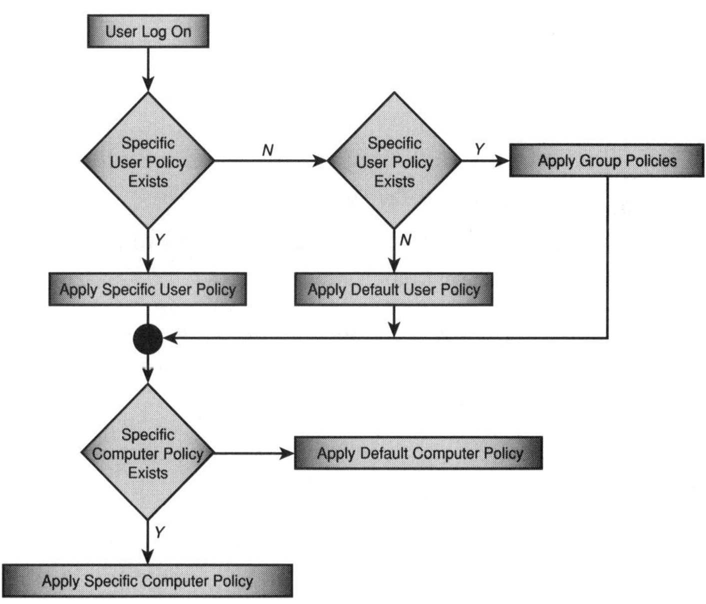

Follow these steps to create a specific policy for an individual user:

1. Start System Policy Editor.
2. Choose Edit, Add User.
3. Enter the username of the user you are adding, or select the Browse button to display the domain database.
4. Double-click the new user's icon in the System Profile Editor dialog box and make your choices.

Follow these steps to create a specific policy for an individual computer:

1. Start System Policy Editor.
2. Choose Edit, Add Computer.
3. Enter the name of the computer you are adding, or select the Browse button to display the list of computers in the Network Neighborhood.
4. Double-click the new computer's icon in the System Profile Editor dialog box and make your choices.

Follow these steps to create a specific policy for an individual group:

1. Start System Policy Editor.
2. Choose Edit, Add Group.
3. Enter the name of the group you are adding, or select the Browse button to display the domain database.
4. Double-click the new group's icon in the System Profile Editor dialog box and make your choices.

When two or more groups are added to the policy file, you can specify the priority order in which group policy settings are applied to users by following these steps:

1. Highlight a group in the System Policy Editor dialog box.
2. Choose Options, Group Priority.
3. Select a group from the Group Order list and choose Move Up or Move Down, as appropriate, to create the desired priority order for your groups.

Windows NT 4.0 makes use of a predefined policy file name to automatically implement system policies across the domain. The file is called NTCONFIG.POL and must be saved in the NETLOGON share

(WINNT\SYSTEM32\REPL\IMPORT\SCRIPTS). When the user logs on, Windows NT automatically looks for the existence of this file in the NETLOGON share on all domain controllers for the domain. If the file exists, it is checked for default and specific policy settings (refer to Figure 7.5).

Key Concept

If you are using NTCONFIG.POL to implement system policies automatically, be sure to place a copy of the file on every domain controller in the domain. Recall that, when a user logs on to the domain, the NETLOGON service locates an available domain controller to authenticate the user. If the user authenticates on a domain controller that does not have the NTCONFIG.POL file on it, then the policy settings will not be implemented. You can use Directory Replication to distribute the NTCONFIG.POL file to all the domain controllers.

However, the administrator can choose to create individual policy files for specific users, groups, or computers and save them in an accessible, shared directory on a server. These files can have any file name, but they must have the extension .POL. Also, these policy files must be specified by a UNC path in the user account's Profile settings dialog box.

Caution

Windows NT applies system profiles that it finds on the domain from which the user logs in. In a trusted domain environment, this can be confusing because computers may belong to a different domain than that from which the user is logging in. A default computer policy for a computer in a trusting domain, maintained in a NTCONFIG.POL file in the trusting domain, for example, is not implemented when a user from the trusted domain logs on at that computer. Windows NT looks for the NTCONFIG.POL file on the trusted domain and implements whatever policy settings it finds there.

Taking the Disc Test

If you have read and understood the material in this chapter, you are ready to test your knowledge. Insert the CD-ROM that comes with this book and run the self-test software, as described in Appendix K, "Using the Self-Test Software."

From Here...

This chapter deals with utilities, concepts, and techniques for managing resources in the enterprise. Chapter 8, "Remote Server Management," continues the discussion of resource management by exploring remote server-management tools.

Chapter Prerequisite

Readers should have a basic knowledge of User Manager for Domains and Server Manager; both are covered in Chapter 5, "Managing Users and Groups."

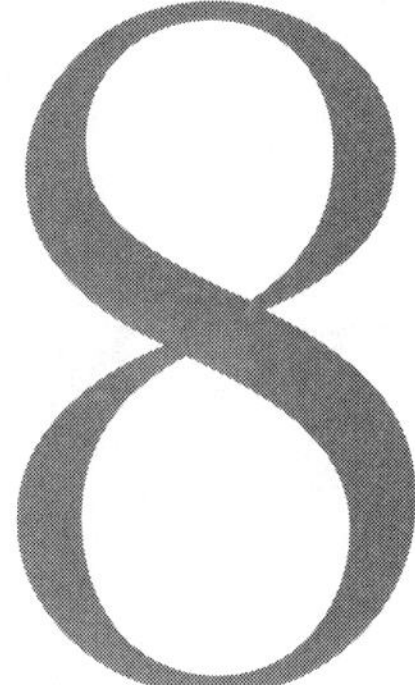

Remote Server Management

The first subject presented in this chapter is the purpose of server tools in the Windows NT environment. Then the chapter explains the server tools available for a number of Windows NT 4.0 clients and what tools are available for each client.

This chapter also provides server-tool installation procedures for all clients, including Windows NT 4.0 Workstation and Windows 95. Installation procedures also are provided for older clients, such as Windows for Workgroups 3.11 and Windows 3.1.

Topics in this chapter include:

- Server tools introduction
- Server tools system requirements
- Server tools for Windows NT 4.0 Workstation
- Server-tool installation for Windows NT 4.0 Workstation
- Server tools for Windows 95

- Server-tool installation for Windows 95 Workstation
- Server tools for Windows for Workgroups 3.11/Windows 3.1
- Server-tool installation for Windows for Workgroups 3.11/ Windows 3.1

The Purpose of Server Tools

Administrators use server tools to administer domain controllers from remote locations. It is quite possible for a domain to be spread out among a number of buildings, towns, cities, or even countries. User and group account changes and additions, password changes, and other administrative duties all are included in the domain administrative functions.

From previous chapters, you may recall that, to make any change in a directory services database in a domain, an administrator must be located at a domain controller. Even if the administrator is sitting at a Backup Domain Controller (BDC), the change is physically made in the database on the Primary Domain Controller (PDC). It is possible that all locations of the domain do not have a domain controller present. Depending on the location of PDCs and BDCs, it is almost impossible for an administrator to always be at a domain location where a domain controller is located, or to always be in one place and make all database changes from one location.

With server tools, an administrator can be physically located at any client computer and still be able to perform a number of domain administrative duties. Server tools also eliminate the need for a domain controller at each and every remote domain location, thereby lowering the overall cost of required software in the domain.

The reason server tools originally were made available for a number of Microsoft clients was to alleviate the problem of the administrator always having to be located at a domain controller in order to administer a domain.

System Requirements

As with any software or utilities, server tools do require system resources to be installed and function correctly. The following sections summarize the system requirements for the various client platforms.

Required Resources for Windows NT 4.0 Workstation

The following resources are required to install server tools on a Windows NT 4.0 Workstation:

- Microsoft Windows NT 4.0 Workstation software installed
- 486DX/33 or higher CPU
- 12M of memory
- 2.5M of free hard disk space
- Workstation and Server services installed

Required Resources for Windows 95

The following resources are required to install server tools on a Windows 95 computer:

- Microsoft Windows 95 installed
- 486/33 or higher CPU
- 8M of memory
- 3M of free hard disk space
- Client for Microsoft Networks installed

Required Resources for Windows 3.1 or Windows for Workgroups 3.11

The following resources are required to install server tools on a Windows 3.1 or Windows for Workgroups 3.11:

- Microsoft Windows 3.1 or Windows for Workgroups 3.11 installed. Both must be running in 386-enhanced mode and have paging (virtual memory, either a permanent or temporary swap file) enabled.
- 8M of memory
- 5M of free hard disk space
- The Microsoft redirector installed

In addition to the above requirements, the `FILES` statement in config.sys must be set to at least 50.

Windows NT 4.0 Workstation Server Tools

The following 32-bit server tools are available for Windows NT 4.0 Workstation:

- User Manager for Domains
- Server Manager
- System Policy Editor
- Remote Access Administrator
- Services for Macintosh
- DHCP Manager
- WINS Manager
- Remoteboot Manager

After these tools are installed on a Windows NT 4.0 Workstation, they function exactly the same as they do on a Windows NT 4.0 server installation.

Tip

Server tools installed on a Windows NT 3.5/3.51 Workstation are the same as for Windows NT 4.0 Workstation, with the exception of System Policy Editor. User Profile Editor is installed on Windows NT 3.5/3.51 instead.

Installation of Workstation Server Tools

Installation of server tools on a Windows NT 4.0 Workstation is relatively easy and can be accomplished in a number of ways. All the required files for any platform for Windows NT 4.0 Workstation are located on the Windows NT 4.0 Server CD-ROM in the CLIENTS\SRVTOOLS\WINNT folder.

Installation from the CD-ROM

Installation can be accomplished simply by accessing the Windows NT 4.0 Server CD-ROM and running the Setup.bat file in the

CLIENTS\SRVTOOLS\WINNT folder. The Setup.bat file determines the architecture of the client computer and copies all the server tools files and supporting files to the <winntroot>\System32 folder. The Setup file will *not* make an Administrative Tools Program Group on the Workstation platform. If you want a specific program group, it must be created manually.

Figure 8.1 illustrates what events take place when the Setup.bat file is executed. Notice that it does display the .exe files that can be included manually in a program group. It does not, however, display the support files loaded with the executables.

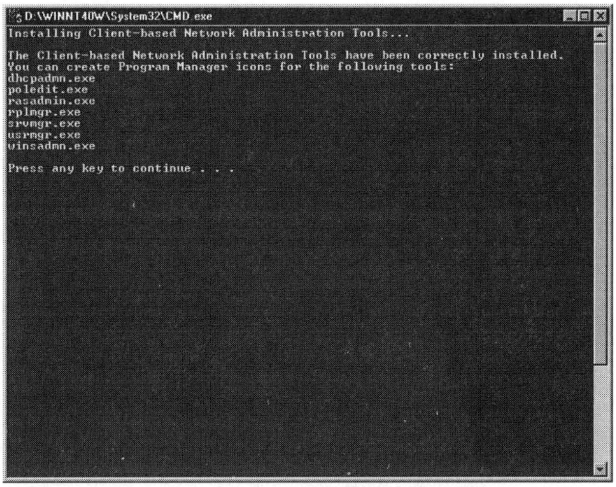

FIG. 8.1 ⇒
The Windows NT 4.0 Workstation Server tools files.

Creating a Server Tools Share Using Network Client Administrator

The Network Client Administrator application, found on Windows NT 4.0 Server, is a tool that is used to perform four functions. One of these functions is related to Windows NT 4.0 server tools. The Copy Client-based Network Administration Tools option simply copies the CLIENT\SRVTOOLS folder to a specified location on a network and creates a share for that location. The default location is <*diskdrive*>\CLIENTS\SRVTOOLS, and the default share name of the srvtools folder is SetupAdm. From this share, the tools can be installed on any Windows NT 4.0 client workstation computer that can map to or access the share.

The Network Client Administrator is invoked by accessing the administrative tools program group on a server and clicking the Network Client Administrator selection. Once started, the Network Client Administrator dialog box appears, displaying the four options available. By selecting the third option, Copy Client-based Network Administration Tools, and then clicking Continue, the Share Client-based Administration Tools dialog box appears (see Figure 8.2). Enter the path where the server tools files are located, such as a CD-ROM location (***<CD-ROM drive>*\clients**) or a network location (***<computername>**<rauth2sharename>*\clients**). Select Copy Files to a New Directory, and then the Share option. After you click OK, the files will be copied to the specified location.

Upon completion of the file copy, a Network Client Administrator information box appears stating how many directories and files were copied; click OK to continue. Next, the srvtools folder is shared, and another Network Client Administrator information box appears, stating that the network administration tools are now available in a shared directory; click OK to continue.

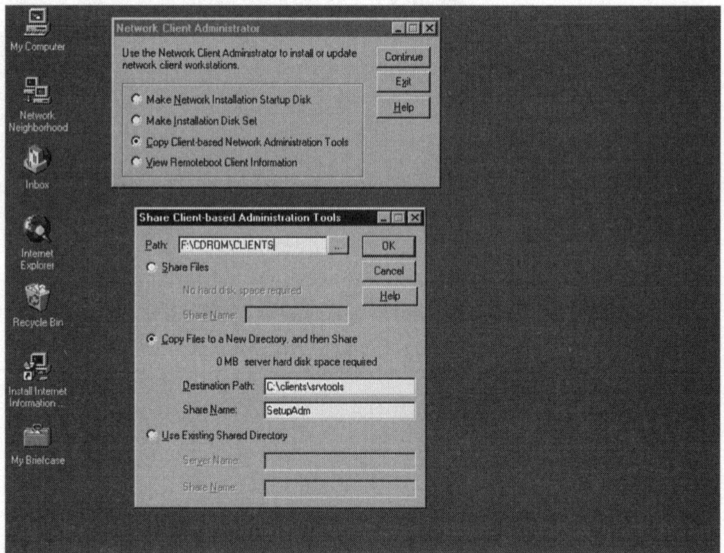

FIG. 8.2 ⇒
The Network Client Administrator and Share Client-based Administration Tools dialog boxes.

Installing the Server Tools from a Network Share

When a network share is created with the Network Client Administration application, simply map a client computer to that share. For example, secondary-click My Computer or Network Neighborhood, select Map Network Drive, and either type the path or select the path from the shared directories window (**<*computername*>\SetupAdm**).

From the mapped drive, either in Explorer or My Computer, select the WINNT folder and execute the Setup.bat file. Refer to Figure 8.2 for an illustration of the events that take place.

Windows 95 Server Tools

The following 32-bit server tools are available for Windows 95:

- User Manager for Domains
- Server Manager
- Event Viewer
- User Manager Extensions for Services for NetWare
- File and Print Services for NetWare (FPNW)

Key Concept

User Manager Extensions for Services for NetWare will be installed only if FPNW or DSNW is installed.

File and Print Services for NetWare will be installed only if FPNW is installed.

In addition, a File Security tab and a Print Security tab are available to establish file, folder, and print permissions.

When these tools are installed on a Windows 95 computer, they function exactly the same as they do on a Windows NT 4.0 server installation.

Installation of Windows 95 Server Tools

Installing the Windows NT server tools on a Windows 95 platform requires a few more steps than the Windows NT Workstation version. First of all, the source files must be made available; either the Windows NT 4.0 Server CD-ROM or a network share can be used.

Next, on the Windows 95 computer, access the Control Panel and select the Add/Remove Programs icon. When the Add/Remove Programs

Properties dialog box appears, select the Windows Setup tab, and then click the Have Disk button. When the Install from Disk dialog box appears, supply the path to the source files such as ***<computername>*\SetupAdm\Win95** if the files are on the network, or ***<CdromDriveLetter>*\clients\Srvtools\Win95** if the Windows NT 4.0 Server CD-ROM is being used. Click OK.

Next, a Have Disk dialog box appears, asking you to select the check box next to the Windows NT Server Tools item in the Components window if you want to install the server tools (see Figure 8.3).

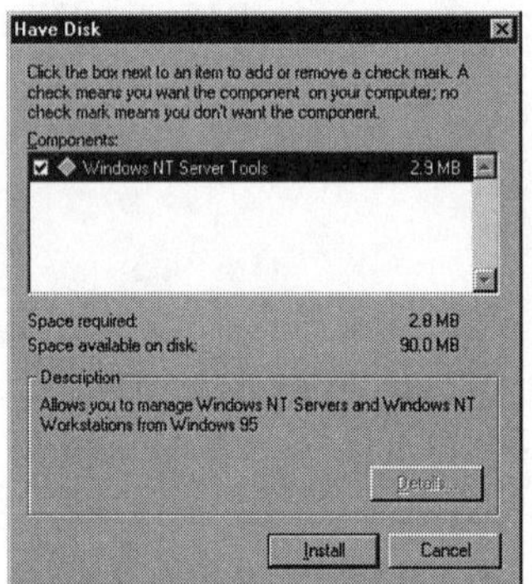

FIG. 8.3 ⇒
The Have Disk dialog box is part of the Windows 95 Server tools-installation procedure illustration, Part 2.

After the check box is selected, click the Install button and the Windows NT 4.0 server tools will be installed. After the tools are installed, a new selection appears in the Start, Programs group.

Figure 8.4 displays the Add/Remove Programs Properties dialog box with the Windows Setup tab selected, after the server tools are installed (note the added selection in the components window as shown).

Windows 3.1 and Windows for Workgroups 3.11 Server Tools

The following 16-bit server tools are available for Windows 3.1 and Windows for Workgroups 3.11 installations:

- User Manager for Domains
- Server Manager
- Event Viewer

- Print Manager for Windows NT Server
- File Manager Security menu

FIG. 8.4 ⇒ The Windows Setup tab is selected in the Add/Remove Programs Properties dialog box.

Installation of Windows 3.1 and Windows for Workgroups 3.11 Server Tools

To install Windows NT server tools on a Windows 3.1 or Windows for Workgroups 3.11 platform, the source files must be made available, as mentioned previously in the section "Installation of Windows 95 Server Tools." The server tools for these two platforms can be found on the Windows NT 3.5/3.51 Server CD-ROM in the Clients\Srvtools directory. The Srvtools directory on this CD-ROM has two subdirectories; one is the Windows directory, the other is the WINNT directory. The Setup.exe program in the Windows directory is used for the Windows or Windows for Workgroups server tools installation. After Setup is run, the server tools are available in the Windows NT Server Tools program group.

When Setup.exe is run, a Windows NT Server Tools Setup screen appears, with a Welcome dialog box that gives you the choices to Continue, Exit, or get Help. It also informs you that both the Microsoft Win32s and RPC components and the Windows NT Server tools will be installed. Selecting Continue displays an Installation Options dialog box where you decide to do either a Custom Install or Install All Files. The default installation path of C:\SRVTOOLS can also be changed from this window. Choosing Continue proceeds with the server tool installation.

The next window that appears is the Time Zone Setup window. Select the correct time zone and choose Continue.

The Microsoft Win32s Setup Target Directory is the next window that appears. This window informs you where various components will be installed. Choose Continue.

From this point, the files are copied; when the copying is complete, a Windows NT Server Tools Setup information dialog box appears, informing you that some system changes will take effect when the system reboots. Choosing OK displays the final dialog box, informing you the installation was successful and that you should reboot your system. Choose Continue to reboot.

Key Concept

Two files of importance are located in the <default>\SRVTOOLS directory: new-conf.sys and new-vars.bat. The statements in these two files must be added to the existing config.sys and autoexec.bat, respectively, and then the system must be rebooted.

New-conf.sys includes FILES=50

New-vars.bat includes PATH=<default>\SRVTOOLS and SET TZ=UTC+0DST.

Without these changes, File Manager will not contain a Security drop-down menu.

Taking the Disc Test

If you have read and understood the material in this chapter, you are ready to test your knowledge. Insert the CD-ROM that comes with this book and run the self-test software as described in Appendix K, "Using the Self-Test Software."

From Here...

The next chapter, "Managing Disk Resources," covers the various options for setting up disks and partitions. Disk utilities are discussed in detail.

Chapter Prerequisite

You should already be familiar with the basic workings of your computer system, especially the basics of working with files and directories.

9

Managing Disk Resources

The first third of this book examines installation issues, configuration methods and concerns, the NT registry, account management, and managing and securing network resources. The next three chapters cover information specific to disk and printing resources.

The goal of this chapter is to teach you how to optimize your management of disk resources. Toward that goal, this chapter will:

- Discuss partition support and management
- Review the Disk Administrator utility
- Discuss NT file system support
- Consider the effect of long file names
- Explore stripe sets and volume sets
- Examine Microsoft's Backup and Restore utility

Understanding Partitions

Before a computer can be used effectively, an operating system must be installed. Before an operating system can be installed, the computer's hard disk(s) must be partitioned into the storage space required by the operating system *and* the user, and formatted with a file system supported by the operating system, such as File Allocation Table (FAT).

There are many types of partitions supported by NT 4.0 Workstation and Server. The most common partitions you will encounter are primary and extended. Others include volume sets and stripe sets. NT 4.0 Server adds fault-tolerant partition options, such as stripe sets with parity and disk mirroring.

In MS-DOS, the *primary partition* contains the boot files needed to start MS-DOS and initialize the system. It is also called the *active partition*, and it cannot be subdivided any further. Under NT 4.0, a primary partition usually holds the operating system files for NT or an alternate operating system, but also can designate simply another data or application storage place. Up to four primary partitions are supported per physical disk device under NT 4.0. MS-DOS recognizes only one primary partition per physical disk device. To boot to MS-DOS (or Windows 95), the primary partition also must be marked as the active partition.

An *extended partition* offers a way to get beyond the four-drive per physical disk limit and subdivide a partition into more than four logical drives. Consequently, an extended partition usually comprises the remaining free space on a disk after the primary partition is created. Because MS-DOS recognizes only one primary (active) partition per physical disk, logical drives in an extended partition provide a way to support a larger number of "drives" under MS-DOS. A *logical drive* is virtually the same as a partition, except that, from the point of view of MS-DOS and NT, it is a division *within* a partition. That's logical isn't it? (A little partition humor.) The use of logical drives provides the disk administrator greater control and flexibility over the storage of applications and data on the physical disk.

There is also the matter of simple arithmetic in the way that NT counts partitions. This becomes more of a concern for NT when the partition scheme changes frequently, or when troubleshooting with a boot disk among a variety of NT computers, because it involves the ARC path to the NT system files.

The *ARC path*, as you may recall from Chapter 3, "Windows NT Server 4.0 Setup," specifies the physical location of the partition that contains the NT operating system files (the WINNT40 installation directory). Here is an example of an ARC path used by the BOOT.INI file:

```
multi(0)disk(0)rdisk(0)partition(2).
```

According to this path, the WINNT40 directory can be found on the second partition (`partition(2)`) of the first physical drive (`disk(0)rdisk(0)`) attached to the first physical controller card (`multi(0)`). Because the ARC path involves the *physical path*, which includes the controller, disk device, and *partition number*, if partition schemes change frequently, it is possible that the partition number of the NT system partition could also change.

NT always counts the active primary partition first, or the first primary partition on each additional physical disk, then other primary partitions from the first to the last physical disk, then the logical drives from the first physical disk to the last (see Figure 9.1).

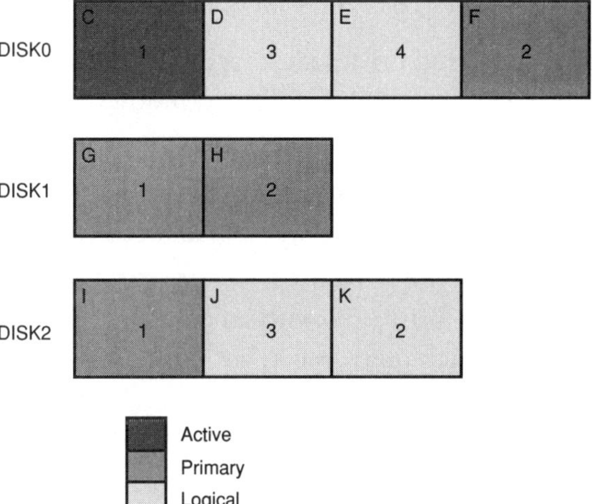

FIG. 9.1 ⇒
In this partition scheme, you see primary, extended, and logical partitions. They are numbered as NT would number them when it boots. Notice that primary partitions are counted before logical drives in an extended partition.

Key Concept

NT refers to the partition from which the computer system boots as the *system partition*. This is the partition that, for NT, contains the files that NT uses to boot (NTLDR, NTDETECT.COM, BOOT.INI, NTBOOTDD.SYS, and BOOTSECT.DOS). The partition that contains the NT system files, such as NTOSKRNL.EXE (the WINNT40 installation directory), is called the *boot partition*. In other words, the system partition contains the operating system boot files, and the boot partition is the partition that contains the NT directory. I use this terminology for the remainder of this chapter.

Exploring File System Support in NT 4.0

After the partition scheme has been decided and applied to the physical disk(s), the disk(s) must then be formatted with a file system that the operating system can understand. MS-DOS and Windows 95 support the FAT file system. NT supports FAT and its own NTFS (New Technology File System). All three support the CD-ROM file system (CDFS). NT 4.0 does not support Windows 95 FAT32.

Previous versions of NT provided support for IBM OS/2's HPFS (High Performance File System). This support is no longer available under Windows NT 4.0. ■

An Overview of FAT

FAT support under NT is somewhat expanded from that offered under MS-DOS. For example, FAT under NT supports long file names. Here are some characteristics of FAT as supported under NT 4.0:

- FAT is required on at least one partition if you intend to dual boot between NT and MS-DOS or Windows 95.
- FAT supports file names of up to 255 characters.
- The file name can have multiple sections, separated by periods and, as such, can be considered multi-qualified. The last section is treated as the file extension.
- File names must begin with an alphanumeric and can contain any characters, including spaces, but excluding the following: " / \ [ ] : ; | = , ^ * ?
- FAT offers only the traditional file attributes: Read, Archive, System, and Hidden, and, as such, does not provide the range of security that NTFS permissions provide.
- Folders in a FAT partition can be shared.
- FAT supports a maximum partition (file) size of 4G.
- FAT is considered most efficient for file access on partitions of less than 400M in size.

- Formatting a partition as FAT requires less than 1M of overhead for the file system.
- The system partition of RISC-based systems must be at least 2M, formatted as FAT.

An Overview of NTFS

NTFS provides the most features and benefits for securing your data. However, it is recognized only by NT computers. Also, your old MS-DOS-based disk utilities most likely do not recognize NTFS-formatted partitions, nor do your MS-DOS or Windows 95-based applications. NTFS is used extensively on NT 4.0 server computers to provide a high level of security and fault tolerance.

The following are some characteristics of NTFS:

- NTFS supports long file and folder names of up to 255 characters including the extensions.
- File names preserve case, but are not case-sensitive, except when using POSIX-based applications for which case-sensitivity is supported.
- File and folder names can contain any characters, including spaces, but excluding the following: " / \ < > : | * ?
- NTFS supports a theoretical partition (file) size of up to 16 exabytes. However, on most hardware, this translates to file size limits of 4G to 64G, and to a functional partition size of up to 2TB, due to industry-standard limitations of disk sectors.
- NTFS is more efficient on partitions larger than 250M.
- Formatting a partition as NTFS requires between 4M and 5M of system overhead, making it impossible to format a diskette with NTFS.
- NTFS provides support for built-in file level-file compression (NT can compress individual files rather than whole partitions). File compression is treated as an attribute of a file and is enabled through the properties of the file or folder.
- NTFS offers automatic Transaction Tracking, which logs all disk activity and provides a means of recovery in the event of a power failure or system crash.
- NTFS offers automatic Sector Sparing, also called hot fixing, in which so-called bad clusters are determined and marked, and the data contained therein is moved to a new good cluster.

- Through the Services for Macintosh feature on NT 4.0 Server, NTFS provides support for Macintosh files.
- NTFS provides the highest level of security for files and folders through its permission set (see Chapter 6 "Security and Permissions").
- NTFS maintains a separate Recycle Bin for each user.

As you can see, NTFS is quite a robust file system.

Converting a FAT Partition to NTFS

It certainly is not necessary to format a partition as NTFS right away, or during installation. One of the nicest things about NTFS is its capability to be applied to an existing FAT partition.

NT provides a conversion tool that you can use to apply NTFS to an existing FAT partition. It is called CONVERT.EXE and can be found in the WINNT40\SYSTEM32 subdirectory. No data is lost during the conversion process as this is not a reformatting operation. The syntax of the command is as follows; at an MS-DOS prompt, type:

```
CONVERT D: /FS:NTFS
```

where `D:` represents the drive letter of the partition to be converted.

If NT is currently accessing the drive in some way—for example, the pagefile is located on it—or you have the drive window open through My Computer or Windows Explorer, NT displays a message to that effect and offers to schedule the conversion for the next boot. If you choose to accept the offer, when NT boots, it detects that the partition is marked for conversion. It reboots and performs the conversion, then it reboots again to start the operating system and lets the user log in.

Considering Long File Names

Both FAT and NTFS under Windows NT 4.0 support long file names for files and folders. However, not all Microsoft Network clients support or recognize long file names. For example, MS-DOS and Windows 3.x-based computers and their applications do not recognize long file names. NT has allowed for this variety in operating systems. When you create a file or folder by using a long file name to identify it, NT automatically assigns an 8.3 format version of the name. This allows DOS and Windows-based systems to be able to "see" the files and folders. There are, however, several considerations to keep in mind as you work with long file names.

How 8.3 Names Are Created

The internal algorithm that NT uses to auto-generate an 8.3 name from a long file name is really quite simple within the first four iterations. NT takes the first six characters of the name, minus spaces, and adds a ~ followed by a number increment. Notice the convention followed in this example:

1995 Budget Summary Spreadsheet.XLS	1995Bu~1.xls
1995 Budget Detail Spreadsheet.XLS	1995Bu~2.xls
Budget Overages.DOC	Budget~1.doc

As you can see, the short file name does not give anywhere near the level of description that the long file name does. Do you see another consideration? You probably notice that if several long file names start with the same characters within the first six, the 8.3 versions are identifiable only by the number increment. After the fifth iteration, NT's algorithm performs a name hash, retaining the first two characters of the long file name, and generating the remaining characters randomly, as shown in this next example:

KiteFlyers Corp Budget—January.XLS	KiteFl~1.XLS
KiteFlyers Corp Budget—February.XLS	KiteFl~2.XLS
KiteFlyers Corp Budget— March.XLS	KiteFl~3.XLS
KiteFlyers Corp Budget—April.XLS	KiteFl~4.XLS
KiteFlyers Corp Budget—May.XLS	Kia45s~1.XLS
KiteFlyers Corp Budget—June.XLS	Ki823x~1.XLS

On a network with a variety of clients that include NT, MS-DOS, and Windows 95, the short names can become a source of confusion for users who are using those clients and applications that only support and display the short name. Consequently, in a mixed environment, try to keep the long file names unique within the first six characters.

Additional Thoughts on Long Names

Here are some additional considerations to ponder:

- When referring to long names at a DOS prompt, most DOS commands require that the name be placed in quotes. For example, if copying the file MY BUDGET SPREADSHEET.XLS from C:\Apps to the D:\Data directory, you would need to type it as:

  ```
  COPY "C:\Apps\MY BUDGET SPREADSHEET.XLS" D:\Data.
  ```

- Some DOS and Windows 16-bit applications save files by creating a temporary file, deleting the original file, and renaming the temporary file to the original name. This deletes not only the long file name, but also any NTFS permissions associated with the file.
- Third-party DOS-based disk utilities that manipulate the FAT can also destroy long file names contained in FAT because they do not recognize those entries as valid DOS files. Most of these utilities do not run under NT in any case.
- The 8.3 version of the long file name can be displayed at a DOS prompt by typing `DIR /X` at the prompt.
- Every long file name utilizes one FAT directory entry for the 8.3 name (called the alias) and a hidden secondary entry for up to every 13 characters of the long file name. MY BUDGET SPREADSHEET.XLS, for example, uses 1 FAT directory entry for the 8.3 name—MYBUDG~1.XLS—plus 2 secondary entries for the long file name (25 characters divided by 13), for a total of three FAT directory entries. The FAT root directory has a hard-coded limit of 512 directory entries. It is, therefore, possible to run out of directory entries if using very long file names consistently.

As you can see, if you are supporting a variety of clients in an NT network enterprise, the use of long file names must be duly considered, and if widely used, explained thoroughly to the end-users who will encounter them.

Chapter 4, "Configuring Windows NT Server 4.0," makes a concerted effort to dissuade you from ever modifying the registry if a utility is available to you. That having been said, there are occasions in which you can only accomplish a change by modifying the registry. Preventing the support of long file names is an example of this for your NT 4.0 server.

You can prevent altogether the support of long file names on FAT partitions by modifying a registry entry. Use the Registry Editor to expand the HKEY_LOCAL_MACHINE subtree to the following subkey:

```
HKEY_LOCAL_MACHINE\SYSTEM\CurrentControlSet\Control\FileSystem\
```

Change the parameter setting for Win31FileSystem from 0 to 1. This is particularly useful when several clients are accessing files stored on a central server and there is any chance of confusion amongst them. Clients are only able to name files and folders following the 8.3 convention on the FAT partitions.

Exploring File Compression Under NTFS

When a partition is formatted as NTFS, among the features provided is the capability to compress files and folders. Compression is treated as another attribute of the file and folder, and is, in fact, enabled through the General Properties for the file or folder. This compression is handled on-the-fly and, like all compression algorithms, while resulting in greater disk capacity, can result in a performance decrease especially across heavy traffic networks.

NTFS compression follows a roughly 2:1 ratio, with slightly more compression for data files and slightly less compression for executables. In general, compression can be most effective for those files that are not accessed on a regular basis, but that cannot be archived because ready access is required. Good file candidates also are going to be those fairly large in size and located on disk partitions whose storage space is at a premium.

Note NTFS does not support compression on NTFS-formatted partitions whose cluster size is greater than 4K. You can determine cluster size by starting the Windows NT Diagnostics utility in the Administrative Tools group and then viewing the specific partition's Properties on the Drives tab. Multiply the bytes per sector by the number of sectors per cluster. ■

How to Enable Compression

As stated earlier, compression is considered an attribute of the file or folder on an NTFS partition. To enable compression for either a file or a folder, right-click the file or folder and display its Properties sheet. On the General tab, select Compress.

If a folder's compress attribute is set, then any new files placed in the folder also have their compress attribute set. Also, for folders, you can choose to apply the compress attribute down through that folder's subfolders. Disable compression for folders and files by deselecting the compress attribute.

Windows Explorer can be configured to display compressed files and folders in blue on the screen. You can do this by choosing View, Options and selecting Display compressed files and folders with alternate color.

The WINNT40 installation folder and all its files and subfolders can be compressed if disk space is an issue. However, as NT is accessing these folders and files rather frequently, compressing them almost certainly results in a noticeable decrease in performance on that computer. This is especially unwise on an NT 4.0 Server computer or domain controller. NTLDR and the current pagefile can never be compressed.

Managing Compression from the Command Prompt

NT provides a command prompt utility called COMPACT.EXE, described in Table 9.1, that you can use to enable and disable file and folder compression on NTFS partitions. The basic syntax is either one of the following:

```
COMPACT /C d:\path\filename
COMPACT /C d:\foldername
```

```
COMPACT /?.
```

Table 9.1 COMPACT.EXE Switches

Switch	Description
/C	Enables compression of specified files and folders.
/U	Disables compression of specified files and folders.
/S	Applies the command to files in the specified folder and to all subfolders.
/A	Displays hidden and system files (omitted by default).
/I	Continues the operation even if errors are encountered. By default, Compact stops when it encounters an error.
/F	Forces compression on all specified files, even if previously marked as compressed. If a file is being compressed when power is lost, the file may be marked as compressed without actually being compressed.
/Q	Displays summary information about the operation.

Note Like NTFS permissions, when you *copy* a file from one folder to another, it assumes the compression attribute of the target folder. Similarly, if the file is *moved* from one folder to another, it retains its compression attribute. Of course, a move is considered a move only when the operation takes place between folders on the same partition. (A rose is a rose…)

Managing Disks with Disk Administrator

Now that you have explored partitions and file systems, you'll next take a look at another utility in the Administrative Tools group called *Disk Administrator.*

Disk Administrator is essentially a GUI "FDISK." You should remember the MS-DOS FDISK utility that you used to create the primary and extended partition and logical drives. Disk Administrator does the same for your NT workstation and server, plus a whole lot more. Its capabilities are discussed in this section.

Creating and Managing Partitions

You'll begin with the simplest task: creating a new partition. Recall that you can create up to four primary partitions per physical disk, and one extended partition that can contain many logical drives. Refer to Figure 9.2 as this discussion continues.

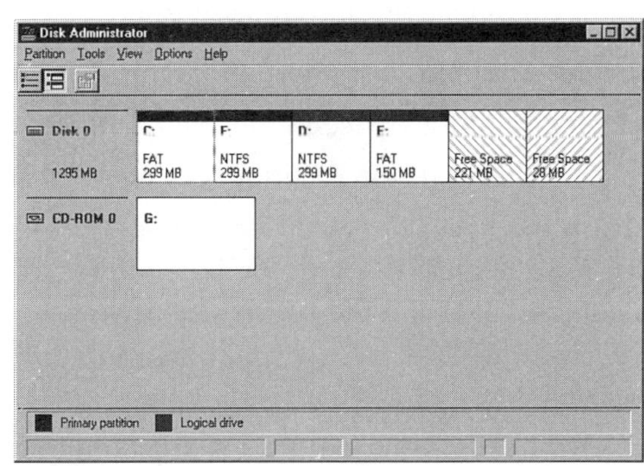

FIG. 9.2 ⇒
This shows a sample Disk Administrator screen.

To create a partition, follow these steps:

1. Start Disk Administrator (Start, Programs, Administrative Tools).
2. Click an area of free space on a physical disk.
3. From the menu, choose Partition, Create to create a new primary partition. Or, from the menu, choose Partition, Create Extended to create an extended partition.
4. The Create Primary or Create Extended Partition dialog box is displayed, showing you the smallest size (2M) and the largest size partition you can create. In the Create Partition of Size text box, enter the size partition you want to create.
5. Press OK. The new primary partition is displayed in Disk Administrator as Unformatted. The new extended partition is set apart from any additional free space with an opposing cross hatch.

Note If a primary partition already exists, when you create the next 2-4 primary partitions, NT displays a message to the effect that the partition scheme may not be compatible with MS-DOS. This is because MS-DOS cannot recognize more than one primary partition on the same physical disk. If you dual boot between DOS and Windows NT on the same computer, DOS can see only the primary active partition. Users connecting to your computer through and sharing drives will be able to see all your partitions. ■

After you have created an extended partition, you need to create logical drives within it to store data and other files. You can create a logical drive following the same basic set of steps used to create a partition:

1. Start Disk Administrator (Start, Programs, Administrative Tools).
2. Click an area of free space in the extended partition.
3. From the menu, choose Partition, Create to create a new logical drive.
4. The Create Logical Drive dialog box is displayed, showing you the smallest size (2M) and the largest size drive you can create. In the Create Logical Drive of Size spin box, enter the size drive you want to create.
5. Press OK. The new logical drive is displayed in Disk Administrator as Unformatted.

The Format Process

The next step, of course, is to format the new primary partition or logical drive. Before you can do that, you must confirm your partition changes to NT. Do this by choosing Partition, Commit Changes Now. Disk Administrator asks that you confirm your changes, and then reminds you to update the Emergency Repair Disk with this new configuration information by using the RDISK.EXE command-line utility.

To format the new primary partition or logical drive, follow these steps:

1. Select the partition or drive.
2. Choose Tools, Format from the menu. The Format drive dialog box is displayed. If you are formatting a drive or partition that has already been formatted, the Capacity text box displays its size. Otherwise, it simply says Unknown Capacity.
3. In the File System list box, select either FAT or NTFS.
4. Specify an Allocation Unit Size. Unless you know something different, stick with Default.
5. Enter a Volume Label if you want. The label displays in Disk Administrator and Windows Explorer and helps to make the drive and/or its contents more descriptive.
6. Select Quick Format if the disk has been previously formatted and you know it is not damaged. Quick Format removes all files and does not perform a scan for base sectors before formatting. It is faster, but potentially more risky.
7. Select Enable Compression if you are formatting as NTFS and want to turn on the compression attribute for the entire drive or partition.
8. Choose Start. The dialog box charts the progress of the format operation. Click OK when the formatting is complete, and then choose Close.

Deleting Partitions and Drives

Deleting a partition is as simple as choosing Partition, Delete from the menu. Disk Administrator warns you that deleting the partition or drive irrevocably loses any data stored on the partition. But you already know that, don't you? Always check the contents of a drive or partition before you delete it to ensure that you will not inadvertently lose something valuable—something that you don't have backed up!

Ch 9

Disk Management Extras—Drive Letters, Properties, and Display Options

Besides the format option, the Tools menu gives you the capability to assign a specific drive letter to a logical drive or primary partition. By default, NT assigns the next available drive letter to your primary partition or logical drive. Some programs require that a particular drive letter be used for the partition that holds the application files. Or, you can choose to assign drive letters for consistency. Sometimes, a persistent connection to a mapped drive takes up a drive letter that you would prefer to assign to a logical drive or primary partition after you have disconnected.

To assign a drive letter, follow these steps:

1. Select the drive or partition in Disk Administrator.
2. Choose Tools, Assign Drive Letter.
3. In the Assign Drive Letter text box, select the desired drive letter. Only the available drive letters are shown. If there is a drive letter that you want to use that is currently in use by a persistent connection, disconnect that mapping first to release the drive letter.

You have the option of not assigning a drive letter at all. Because there are a limited number of letters in the alphabet, and some are reserved up front, this option allows you to create additional drives and partitions now, and assign drive letters to them as you need to access them.

You can quickly display the Properties sheet of any partition or logical drive by selecting that drive and choosing Tools, Properties. From here, you can see usage statistics, change the volume label, run volume scan and defragmentation tools, and view sharing information for the drive.

As you create primary partitions, logical drives, volume sets, and so forth by using Disk Administrator, it uses various color codes and cross hatching to facilitate your interpretation of the disks' partition and formatting schemes. The Options menu choice includes options for changing Colors and Patterns used in the legend, whether to show partition and drive sizes to scale through Disk Display, and whether and how to show a specific physical disk only through Region Display. Through Customize Toolbar, you can even create and customize your own icon toolbar to facilitate your most frequent activities.

System, Boot, and Active Partitions

As mentioned earlier, NT refers to the partition that contains the NT boot files (NTLDR, NTDETECT.COM, NTBOOTDD.SYS, BOOT.INI, BOOTSECT.DOS) as the system partition, and the partition that contains the WINNT40 installation directory as the boot partition. Only one partition can be marked as active. On MS-DOS computers, this usually refers to the C: drive. In NT, on dual boot computers (booting between both NT 4.0 and MS-DOS or Windows 95), this probably is still the C: drive. However, it *must* be the partition that contains the NT boot files. There may be multiple operating systems on your computer, such as NT 4.0 and UNIX or NT 4.0 and OS/2. Each expects its boot files to be on the partition marked active. You are most likely to find this type of configuration on test servers.

You use the boot manager utility that comes with the other operating system to mark the NT system partition as the active partition when you want to restart your workstation and boot into NT. When you are in NT and ready to restart your system and boot into another operating system, you use Disk Administrator as your boot manager.

To change the active partition marker, follow these steps:

1. Start Disk Administrator.
2. Select the partition to be marked active (primary partitions only).
3. Choose Partition, Mark Active from the menu. Disk Administrator displays a confirmation message stating that the partition has been marked active and will boot with whatever operating system is on the partition the next time you restart your system.

The active partition can be spotted if you look very closely in the color bar above the drive letter. The active partition is marked with a star. You can see this better if you choose Options, Colors and Patterns and change the color bar to something other than dark blue.

Creating and Managing Volume Sets

A volume can be thought of as any partition or logical drive on any physical disk that can be accessed as a single unit. In NT, a volume can be a single contiguous area of disk space or a collection of non-contiguous areas of disk space. The latter is called a *volume set*.

A volume set can consist of from 2 to 32 areas of free disk space on one or more physical disk drives. They are combined and treated by NT as though they are one large volume, and can be formatted as either FAT or NTFS. After these areas have been combined, they cannot be split apart. Consequently, deleting any part of a volume set deletes the entire volume set.

You can use volume sets to "clean" up areas of free space that, by themselves, may not be large enough to be useful, or to create storage areas larger than any one physical disk can provide.

Here are some more fun facts about volume sets:

- Volume sets can contain areas of free space from different drive types, such as SCSI, ESDI, and IDE.
- NT system and boot partitions may not participate in a volume set.
- Like NTFS, on workstations that dual boot between NT and MS-DOS or Windows 95, volume sets are not accessible by MS-DOS or Windows 95.
- If any member of a volume set fails, or the disk on which a member resides fails, the entire volume set is corrupted.

Note When you choose areas of free space of very disparate sizes, Disk Administrator sizes each member of the volume set proportionate to the amount of free disk space selected. For example, if you choose to create a 50M volume set out of a 10M and 200M area of free space, you might expect Disk Administrator to use all of the 10M space for the first member of the volume set, and then 40M from the remaining 200M free space for the second member of the volume set. However, Disk Administrator determines, as you see in Figure 9.3, that *proportionate to the size of the free areas selected*, the first member is 4M and the remaining is 47M. This same note applies to extended volume sets.

Creating and Formatting a Volume Set

To create a volume set, follow these steps:

1. Start Disk Administrator.
2. Select from 2 to 32 areas of free disk space by clicking the on the first free space area, and then Ctrl-clicking the rest.
3. Choose Partition, Create Volume Set. The Create Volume Set dialog box is displayed showing the smallest size (2M) and largest size volume set you can create from your selections.

4. In the Create Volume Set of Total Size text box, enter the *total* size you want for the volume set.
5. Choose OK. Disk Administrator displays the new volume set, similar to the example shown in Figure 9.3.
6. Format the new volume set as FAT or NTFS.

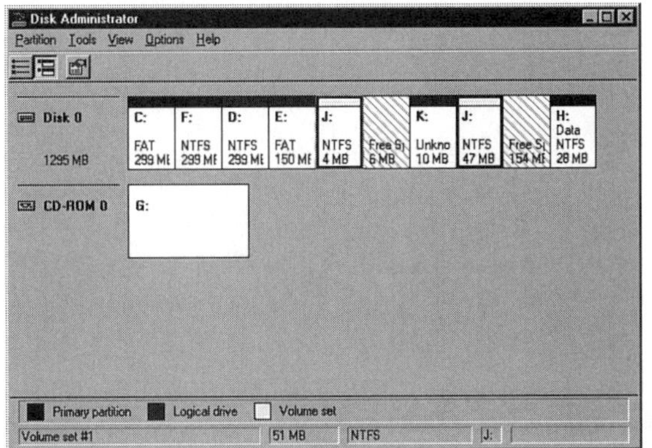

FIG. 9.3 ⇒ In this example, note that the volume set J: consists of two non-contiguous areas of disk space and has been formatted as NTFS.

Extending a Volume Set

If you have formatted a partition, logical drive, or volume set as NTFS, and you are running out of space on it, never fear—NTFS-formatted space can be extended into free space without any loss of data and without having to reformat the space. This process is called *extending* the volume set.

This can be particularly helpful in adding extra print spool space to a partition, or allowing for the growth of a database.

To extend a volume set, follow these steps:

1. From Disk Administrator, select the NTFS partition, drive, or volume set.
2. Ctrl+click an area of free space that will be added to the existing partition.
3. Choose Partition, Extend Volume Set to display the Extend Volume Set dialog box. The minimum and maximum *total* size for the extended volume is shown.
4. In the Create Volume Set of Total Size text box, enter in the total size you want the volume set to be.

5. Choose OK. Disk Administrator creates what appears to be a volume set and applies NTFS to the new volume set member (see Figure 9.4).

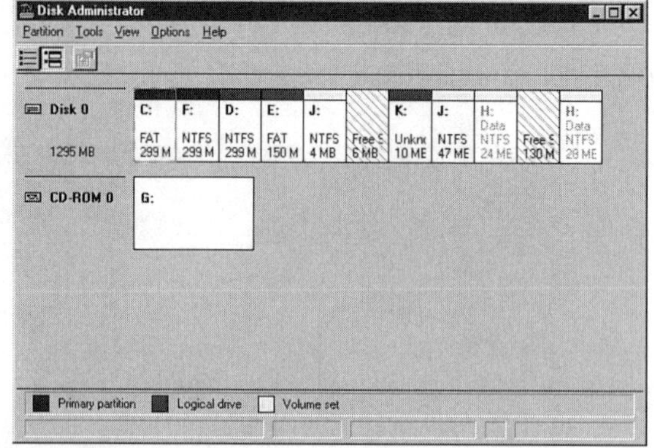

FIG. 9.4 ⇒ Note how drive H has been extended from 28M to a total of 52M. Because it was formatted as NTFS, NTFS is automatically applied to the extended volume.

Creating and Managing Stripe Sets

A stripe set in NT is quite similar to a volume set in that both involve combining areas of free disk space into a single large volume. The similarities end there, however.

Key Concept

There are two common confusions regarding stripe sets, also known as RAID 0:

1) Data is written to each member of a volume set in turn. In other words, when one member is filled, the next member is written to, and so on. Therefore, a volume set really does not improve disk I/O performance.

2) A stripe set consists of free space from at least 2, and up to 32, different *physical* drives. The area of free space chosen on each disk must be the same size on each disk. For example, if you have three disks with 100, 200, and 300M of free space each, and you want to combine all three to create a stripe set, the largest any member can be is the smallest of the areas of free space, or 100M, providing a total stripe set across all three disks of 300M (100M×3 disks). Or, you can combine two 200M areas from the second and third disks to create a total stripe set size of 400M. It's all just simple(?!) arithmetic.

Unlike volume sets, in which the first member gets filled up before the second member is written, in stripe sets, data is written uniformly in 64K blocks across all members of the stripe set (see Figure 9.5). Because data can be written concurrently across the physical disks, a stripe set will normally result in an overall disk I/O performance increase.

Here are some more fun facts about stripe sets:

- NT system and boot partitions can not participate in a stripe set.
- Like NTFS, on workstations that dual boot between NT and MS-DOS or Windows 95, stripe sets are not accessible by MS-DOS or Windows 95.
- If any member of a stripe set fails, or the disk on which a member resides fails, the entire stripe set is corrupted.

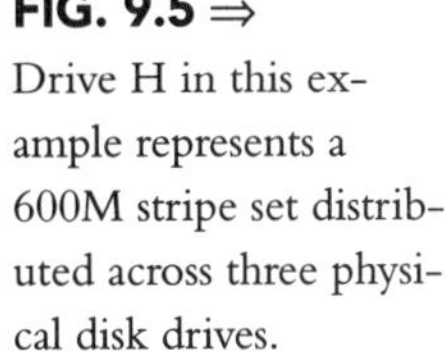

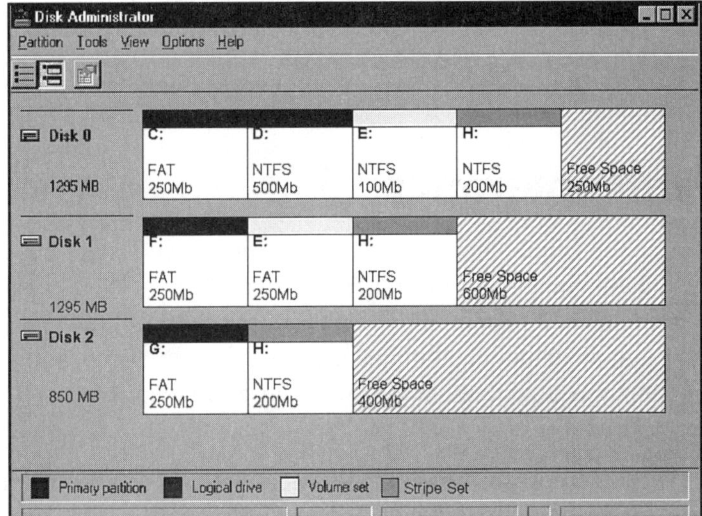

FIG. 9.5 ⇒
Drive H in this example represents a 600M stripe set distributed across three physical disk drives.

To create a stripe set, follow these steps:

1. From Disk Administrator, select from 2 to 32 areas of free disk space on different physical disks. Click the first area and Ctrl-click the remaining areas. The areas should be of approximately the same size. If not, Disk Administrator sizes the stripe set based on the smallest area of disk space selected.
2. Choose Partition, Create Stripe Set to display the Create Stripe Set dialog box. The minimum and maximum total sizes for the stripe set are shown.
3. In the Create Stripe Set of Size text box, enter the total size stripe set you want.

4. Choose OK. Disk Administrator displays the equal-sized members of the stripe set distributed across the physical disks selected.
5. Format the stripe set.
6. Quit Disk Administrator or choose Partition, Commit Changes Now to save your changes in the registry.

The System Partition and RISC

The system partition on a RISC-based computer must be formatted as FAT because these computers can only boot from FAT. There is no way to protect the system partition in this environment with local security. However, Disk Administrator provides an additional menu choice called Secure System Partition. When this option is selected, only administrators on that computer are able to access the system partition.

Fault Tolerance

In addition to the partition, volume set, and stripe set options that you have seen, Disk Administrator on an NT 4.0 Server provides additional disk-fault tolerant options. From the menu option Fault Tolerance, you can create stripe sets with parity, also called RAID 5, and disk mirroring, as well as regenerate data lost because of failed stripe sets with parity or mirrored disks.

This is software-based fault tolerance that is built into the NT operating system. When enabled, it places additional stress on the processor for resource management and disk I/O. Also, when a member of a stripe set fails, or a disk mirror fails, NT must be shut down, the drive replaced, and the data regenerated. Hardware-based fault-tolerant systems generally allow for hot-swapping failed disks without shutting down NT. However, NT's software-based fault tolerance is less expensive than its hardware counterparts. If you are just getting started and need to secure your servers with fault tolerance, this is a good way to go.

Backing Up and Restoring Data

By now, if you have spent any length of time working with microcomputers, especially within a network environment, you have heard the words "backup and restore" at least once. Perhaps you have heard yourself utter them, as in, "Why didn't I...?"

Backing up data and having the capability to recover it is perhaps the most important part of disk management, especially within an enterprise network environment. As companies move faster and closer toward electronic media for conveying information—and in spite of rhetoric to the contrary, believe that it is happening—the backup process has taken on a much more prominent and integral role in securing data.

There are several strategies that one might follow in implementing a backup procedure, and just about as many hardware and software options to choose from. This section is not intended to drive home the importance of developing and implementing a sound backup\restore policy. If you haven't yet been convinced, you will be the first (and last) time that you lose $20,000,000 dollars worth of financial records because the incremental daily backup failed to occur and no one monitored it.

The purpose of this section is to introduce you to the backup\restore utility included with your installation of NT 4.0 server, explain some terms that Microsoft uses (and that you are apt to encounter on the server exam), and to posit a couple backup and restore strategies.

Requirements, Terms, and Strategy

The Windows NT Backup utility is designed for use with an NT-compatible tape-backup device. To determine whether your tape-backup device is compatible, as with any new piece of hardware, consult the NT 4.0 Hardware Compatibility List (HCL).

The Windows NT Backup utility is meant primarily as a file and folder backup product and does not back up data at the sector level. Consequently, NT's backup utility cannot be used to perform volume recovery—restoring an entire partition. If you need this kind of functionality, or want built-in scheduled backups, and so on, you should review the many third-party backup programs available now for NT. Nevertheless, the Windows NT Backup utility is a fine product, and does allow the backup of the registry.

The following persons can perform the backup and restore function:

- Administrator
- Members of the local Backup Operators group

- Members of the local Server Operators group
- Users granted the user right Backup(Restore) Files and Directories
- Users who have read permission to files and folders

As for strategy, Microsoft promotes the following three areas of consideration when planning your backup procedure:

- *What do you need to backup?* Significance of the data
- *Where are you backing up from?* Centrally stored data or locally distributed
- *How often do you need to backup?* Frequency with which the data should be backed up to provide recovery

The significance of the data is always subjective. For purposes of your strategy, you need to determine how much data is significant in order to plan for the appropriate number of backup devices, the right-sized media, the location of devices, and so on.

Data stored centrally tends to be easier to maintain than data stored at local computers. For one thing, while you can back up users' data remotely with NT's backup utility or various third-party products, you rely more heavily on the users to either back up their own data or make their computer available for the remote backup, sharing folders, closing files, and exiting applications. The backup of centrally-stored data is usually the responsibility of one or two persons who can monitor network usage and ensure that important files are closed and can be backed up regularly.

Key Concept

The obvious recommendation, then, is to store critical files in a central location and always back them up. Files that you cannot live without—including the registry, especially on the domain controller (SAM and Security databases)—should be backed up regularly, perhaps daily. Files that change infrequently or are of less importance might also be backed up on a regular basis, perhaps weekly. Temporary files and files that are used once and forgotten probably never need to be backed up.

Table 9.2 lists some backup terms that NT uses and with which you already may be familiar.

Table 9.2 Tape Backup Categories

Term	Effect
Normal	Backs up all selected files and folders and sets their archive attribute.
Copy	Backs up all selected files and folders but does not set the archive attribute. This option is generally used for creating tape copies outside the regular backup routine.
Incremental	Backs up only selected files and folders that have changed since the last backup, and sets their archive attribute.
Differential	Backs up only selected files and folders that have changed since the last time they were backed up, but does not set their archive attribute.
Daily	Backs up only files and folders that changed that day without setting their archive attribute.

The use of the archive attribute is significant for any backup strategy. The archive attribute indicates whether the file has been previously backed up. The difference between a differential and incremental backup is examined next as an example.

According to Table 9.2, differential and incremental backups do precisely the same thing, except for setting the archive attribute: The incremental sets it and the differential does not.

Suppose that you have a data folder in which users make frequent contributions and modifications. If you employ an incremental backup each day of the week, starting with a normal backup on Monday, the backup would proceed like this:

Monday	Back up all files and set their archive attribute
Tuesday	Back up all files that are new or have changed since Monday and set their archive attribute
Wednesday	Back up all files that are new or have changed since Tuesday and set their archive attribute
Thursday	Back up all files that are new or have changed since Wednesday and set their archive attribute
Friday	Back up all files that are new or have changed since Thursday and set their archive attribute

By the end of the week, you have created five backup tapes, each containing data that changed since the previous day. If data is lost in the folder on Friday, all tapes can be employed to recover the data that is lost because you would not know necessarily which day's data is lost. The backup process is faster, but the restore can take longer.

Now back up the same folder by using a normal backup on Monday and a differential backup the rest of the week:

Monday	Back up all files and set their archive attribute
Tuesday	Back up all files that are new or have changed since Monday, but do not set their archive attribute
Wednesday	Back up all files that are new or have changed since Monday, but do not set their archive attribute
Thursday	Back up all files that are new or have changed since Monday, but do not set their archive attribute
Friday	Back up all files that are new or have changed since Monday, but do not set their archive attribute

Notice that each day's tape contains files that are new or have changed since the beginning of the week. This backup process takes a little longer, but if data is lost from the folder on Friday, only the Monday and Thursday tapes need be restored because Monday contains all the original data, and Thursday contains everything that has changed since Monday.

Another twist on these strategies is to perform a complete normal or copy backup once every week or every month, and archive that tape off site. By designating a series of tapes in rotation, you can cycle your off-site archive tapes into the regular routine and always maintain a valid and timely recovery system that includes off-site data storage.

Table 9.3 lists some additional terms that Microsoft uses regarding the backup process.

Table 9.3 Backup Terms

Term	Description
Backup Set	The group of files and folders backed up during a backup session. A tape may contain one or more backup sets.
Family Set	The group of tapes that contains files and folders backed up during a single backup session.

Term	Description
Backup Log	The backup text file that the backup utility creates that records details relating to the session, such as the date, type of backup, which files and folders were backed up, and so on.
Catalog	A listing of the files stored on the backup tape that are loaded during the restore process and displays the backup sets on a tape, and the files and folders contained in a backup set.

Initiating Backup

The first step in initiating a backup is to determine what you will be backing up (see Figure 9.6). It helps to know ahead of time what files and folders you want to back up, and where they are located. For example, if you are planning on backing up files located in a remote server or a user's workstation, the folder containing the files must first be shared, and then you must connect to that share from the computer that is doing the backup. Unfortunately, you cannot back up the registry from a remote computer. All files, of course, must be closed because backup cannot operate on open files. After you have made these preparations, you can start the backup utility.

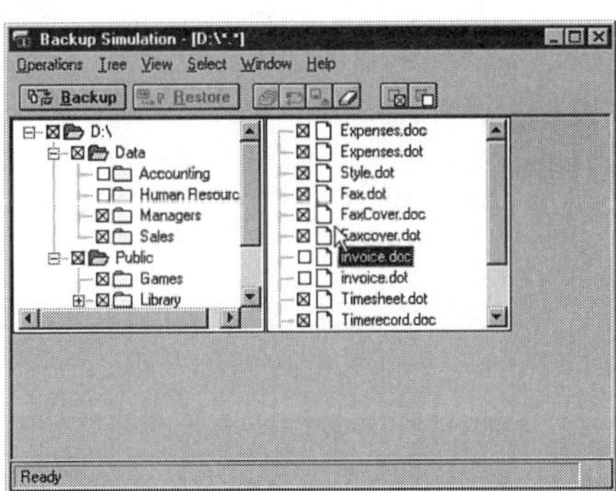

FIG. 9.6 ⇒ Notice in this backup example that files and folders on drive D: are selected by a simple point-and-click.

To back up files and folders, follow these steps:

1. Start the Windows NT Backup utility (Start, Programs, Administrative Tools, Backup).

2. In the Backup dialog box, select the drives, folders, and/or files to be backed up by pointing and clicking the appropriate check boxes. Your selections are hierarchical in that if you select a drive or folder, you automatically select its contents and subfolders (see Figure 9.6).
3. Next, choose Operations, Backup, or just click the Backup button to display the Backup Information dialog box, shown in Figure 9.7.
4. In the Tape Name text box, enter in a name for the tape, which can be up to 32 characters. If you are appending to an existing tape, the Tape Name box is not available.
5. Choose the appropriate tape options. See Table 9.4 for a description of the tape options.
6. Enter a Description for the backup set you are creating.
7. Choose a Backup Type.
8. In the Log File text box, enter the name and path for the text file you want to use to record details about the backup operation, and select whether you want to capture all backup information (Full Detail), only major operations such as starting, stopping, and failing to open files (Summary Only), or Don't Log at all.
9. Choose OK. Backup displays the status of the operation as it takes place and a summary when it is complete. This is shown in Figure 9.8.
10. Choose OK to complete the operation. Store your tape in a safe place.

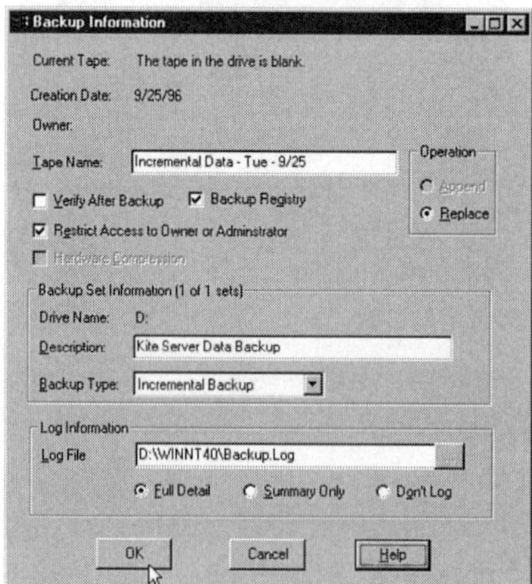

FIG. 9.7 ⇒
This tape for the files selected on Kite Server includes an incremental backup of the registry and is restricted to the user that performed the backup.

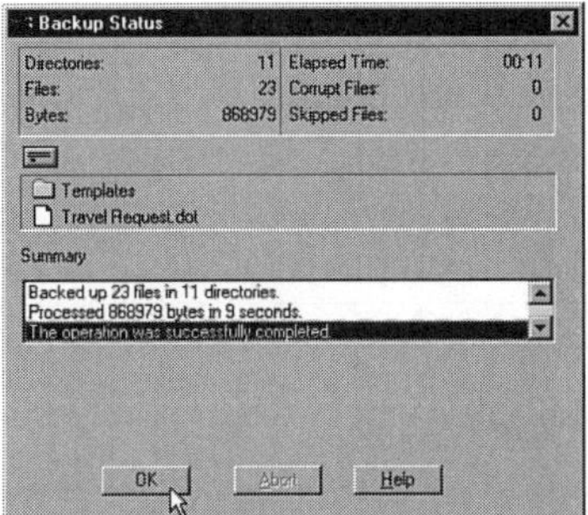

FIG. 9.8 ⇒
The statistics compiled for a successful backup of the files and folders selected in Figure 9.6.

Ch 9

Table 9.4 Tape Options

Option	Description
Append	Adds a new backup set to an existing tape.
Replace	Overwrites the data on an existing tape.
Verify after backup	Compares files selected with files backed up and confirms that they are backed up accurately.
Backup Registry	In addition to the files selected, copies the registry to the backup set. (At least one file in the volume containing the registry must have been selected for the registry to be backed up successfully.)
Restrict Access	Only Administrators, Backup Operators, or the user that performed the backup is allowed access to the backup set for purposes of recovery.
Hardware Compression	If the tape drive supports data compression, select this option to enable it.

Initiating a Restore

The restore process is much the same as the backup process, but in reverse. The same rules apply regarding who can perform the operation, and your restore strategy pretty much depends on what type of backup strategy you implemented. Refer back to the two backup examples outlined earlier in the section titled, "Requirements, Terms, and Strategy."

Also, as with backup, the first step in initiating a restore is to determine what you will be restoring. You will make good use of the backup logs created during the backup process to determine which files and folders you want to restore, on what backup set they are located, and to where you need to restore them. For example, if you are planning to restore files to a remote server or a user's workstation, you must connect to the appropriate drive on that computer.

Key Concept

Unfortunately, the registry cannot be backed up from or restored to a remote computer.

To restore files and folders, follow these steps:

1. Start the Windows NT Backup utility.
2. The Tapes window displays the name of the tape in the device and information regarding the first backup set on the tape.
3. To see additional backup sets, load the tape catalog by choosing Operations, Catalog. The Catalog Status dialog box is displayed.
4. Choose OK when the process is complete. A new window with the tapes name is displayed.
5. In this window, select the appropriate backup set to load its catalog.
6. Next, select the drives, folders, and/or files to be restored by pointing and clicking the appropriate check boxes. Your selections are hierarchical in that, if you select a drive or folder, you automatically select its contents and subfolders.
7. Next, choose Operations, Restore, or just click the Restore button to display the Restore Information dialog box, shown in Figure 9.9.
8. In the Restore to Drive text box, the original drive and path are displayed. You can accept this default or select an Alternate Path.
9. Select the appropriate restore option. See Table 9.5 for a description of the three options.
10. Enter the name and path for the text file you want to use to record details about the restore operation in the Log File text box, and select whether you want to capture all restore information (Full Detail), only major operations, such as starting, stopping, and failing to restore files (Summary Only), or Don't Log at all.
11. Choose OK. Restore displays the status of the operation as it takes place and a summary when it is complete, as shown in Figure 9.10.
12. Choose OK to complete the operation.

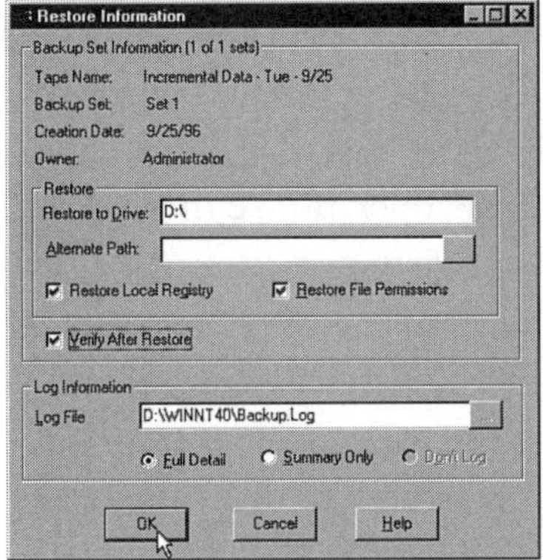

FIG. 9.9 ⇒
This operation restores the selected files and folders to the original D: drive, as well as the registry, and maintains the original permission settings.

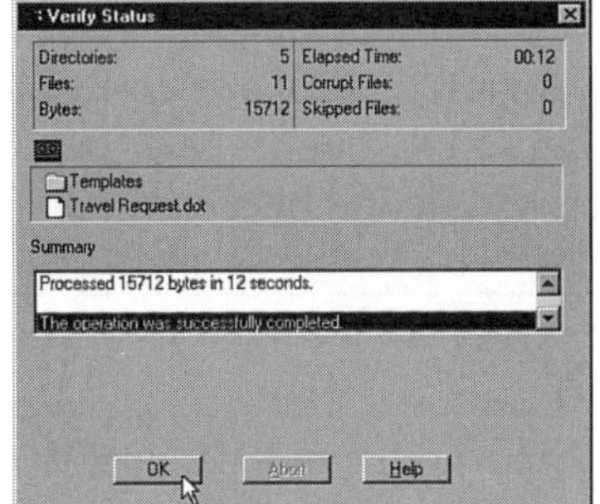

FIG. 9.10 ⇒
Here are the summary statistics for the restore operation you began in Figure 9.9.

Table 9.5 Tape Restore Options

Option	Description
Restore Registry	Restores the local registry to the target computer.
Restore Permissions	Restores the NTFS permissions to the files as they are recovered. If this option is not selected, files assume the permissions of the target folder. If you restore to a different computer, be sure that you have valid user and group accounts or your permissions may be inaccurate.
Verify After Restore	Compares files selected with files restored and confirms that they are restored accurately.

Troubleshooting Backup and Restore

You are not likely to encounter any problems with the Backup utility, provided you are using a supported tape device and have the appropriate level of permission to perform the operation, either by virtue of membership in the Administrators, Backup Operators, or Server Operators group, by assignment of the Backup (Restore) Files and Directories user right, or through Read permission to the files and folders.

If you have chosen to log the backup and restore operations, any exceptions to the process, such as open files that couldn't be backed up, are duly recorded there. You can use that file to troubleshoot what did and did not get backed up, from where it was backed up from, in which backup set it can be found in, and so on.

Also, you should review the catalog for the selected backup set before restoring files. Corrupted files and folders are highlighted with a red X. Obviously, you should probably should not restore these files and folders.

Scheduling a Tape Backup

NT provides a command-line backup utility that you can use in combination with NT's AT command to schedule a tape-backup operation. To accomplish this scheduling, you need to create a batch file that contains the backup command syntax, and then use the AT command to schedule the batch file to run. The schedule service must be running for the AT command to work.

The basic backup command syntax is as follows:

```
NTBACKUP BACKUP path\filenames options
```

where `path\filenames` indicates the location of any selected files, and `options` is any of the items listed in Table 9.6.

Table 9.6 NTBACKUP Options

Option	Description
`/A`	Adds (appends) the backup set to the existing tape.
`/b`	Backs up the local registry.
`/d` "text"	Adds a description for the backup set.
`/e`	Creates a summary log rather than a detail log.
`/l` *`filename`*	Assigns a file name to the backup log other than the default.
`/r`	Restricts access to only the Administrators, Backup Operators, Server Operators, or users who perform the backup.

Option	Description
`/t type`	Indicates the *type* of backup (*Copy, Incremental, Differential, Daily*) other than the default *Normal*.
`/v`	Verifies that files were backed up accurately.
`/hc:on/off`	Turns on or off hardware compression for tape devices that support the option.

If you need to connect to a remote share to back up files, begin the batch file with a connection to that remote share by using the following syntax:

```
CMD /C net use d: \\server\share
```

where `d:` represents the logical drive mapping, and `\\server\share` the UNC path to the remote share. At the end of the batch file, include the same line with a `/d` at the end to disconnect from the share.

The following is an example of a batch file called DATABACK.BAT; it connects to a share called DATA on server ACCT1, does an incremental backup of the files in that share including the registry, restricts access, and verifies the backup:

```
CMD /C NET USE M: \\ACCT1\DATA
NTBACKUP M: /a /t Incremental /b /r /v
CMD /C NET USE M: /D
```

To use the AT command to schedule this batch file, the Scheduler Service must be running. Use the Services applet in the Control Panel to enable and configure this service.

The AT command uses the following syntax:

```
AT \\computer time options batchfilename
```

where `computer` represents a remote computer (otherwise the local computer is assumed), `time` indicates the 24-hour time hour:minute (00:00) notation for the operation to take place, `options` are as described in Table 9.7, and `batchfilename` indicates the command or batch file that you want to execute.

For example, if you want to schedule your ACCT1 backup to occur at 11:00 P.M. every weekday, the AT command would look like this:

```
AT 23:00 /every:M,T,W,Th,F DATABACK.BAT
```

Table 9.7 AT Command Options

Option	Description
`/delete`	Cancels a scheduled command by the ID number assigned to it.
`/interactive`	Lets the job interact with the currently logged-on user.

continues

Table 9.7 Continued

Option	Description
`/every:date`	Runs the command on the specified day(s) of the week (M,T,W,Th,F,S,Su) or on one or more days of the month by using numbers (1-31). Default is the current day.
`/next:date`	Runs the command on the next occurrence of the day(s) specified or one or more days of the month.

Troubleshooting Disk Management

As with all the troubleshooting sections so far in this book, if you have read the material and understand it, and have taken the opportunity to experiment with the utilities discussed, you already have the basic tools you need to troubleshoot most problems. Here are a few more considerations.

Saving Disk Configurations

When you have made changes to the partition and format scheme on your computer, it is important to update that information. Of course, the current registry settings are updated. However, if you are using the Emergency Repair Disk as a recovery tool, then you must remember to update it. You can do so by running the RDISK command at the command line. This updates the Emergency Repair information with any registry changes, including the disk configuration.

You can also choose Partition, Configuration, Save from the Disk Administrator menu to save assigned drive letters, volume sets, stripe sets, stripe sets with parity, and mirror sets to a blank diskette or the Emergency Repair Disk. This can be particularly useful when planning migrations, software upgrades, and so on.

Other Considerations

If NT fails to recognize a drive, it is most likely an incompatibility problem or driver problem. Always check the HCL before upgrading any hardware on your NT 4.0 computer. Detected hardware errors are listed in the registry in the key: `HKEY_LOCAL_MACHINE\Hardware`.

Corrupted files and folders generally should be deleted and good versions restored from your most recent backup. The worst cases require that you reformat the disk and then restore from backup.

When dual booting to MS-DOS, running some third-party MS-DOS-based utilities that modify the FAT entries can result in corruption or loss of data in NT, especially if long file names are in use. To avoid file corruption or loss, don't use these utilities and don't disable long file name support for FAT partitions.

1G IDE disk drives that follow the EIDE standard have a BIOS limit of 1024 cylinders, which restricts NT's capability to access all of the available storage space on these disks. Either the BIOS needs to be able to get around the limit through sector translation or relative cluster addressing, or NT needs to be able to communicate with the disk's controller. NT currently supports Western Digital 1003-compatible controllers.

Taking the Disc Test

If you have read and understood the material in this chapter, you are ready to test your knowledge. Insert the CD-ROM that comes with this book and run the self-test software, as described in Appendix K, "Using the Self-Test Software."

From Here...

Next up on your agenda is a trip through the wonderful world of monitoring and printing—still an adventure after all these years. Before you journey on, be sure to try the review questions and lab for this chapter.

Chapter Prerequisite

Because this chapter discusses a monitoring utility used to chart Windows NT's system and network performance, it is important that the reader have a working knowledge of networking and computer systems. It is also advantageous for the reader to have an understanding of the basic concepts of Windows NT Server 4.0, outlined in Chapters 1 through 9 of this book.

Performance Monitor

This chapter explores Windows NT 4.0's Performance Monitor utility. This utility provides an administrator with the capability to chart a Windows NT-based computer's performance in a given situation. Specific topics that will be discussed include:

- Exploring the benefits of Performance Monitor
- Creating a baseline of performance
- Examining specific objects and counters

Monitoring System Performance with Performance Monitor

Windows NT Server 4.0 contains a performance-tracking tool called Performance Monitor, which collects data about system resources and presents them in a graphical chart-based format. It can be used to:

- Create a baseline of normal system performance
- Monitor use of system resources for given periods of time
- Identify periods of abnormal system activity
- Predict system resource usage given specific parameters
- Justify upgrades to hardware and resources

The Performance Monitor treats system resources as *objects* with characteristics, or *counters* that can be tracked (see Figure 10.1). Multiple occurrences of an object and counter, or variations on them, are called *instances*. For example, the processor is an object that can be monitored. It has counters that can be charted, such as the total percentage of processor usage, the percentage of the processor used by the kernel mode, and so on. Recall that Windows NT Server 4.0-based computers can support up to 32 processors. If there are multiple processors on a given system, each is considered an instance. You can then track each processor's total percentage of usage, total percentage of kernel mode usage, and so on for each instance of the processor.

Most counter instances include a *Total* selection that provides the activity generated by all of the instances. For example, each of four processors installed in a computer would have a Processor>%Processor Time instance. You can monitor data for each processor. However, if you want a total value for processor usage by all four processors, you can select the Total instance.

With Performance Monitor, you can also create and view log files, view summary statistics, and create system alerts based on monitored values. Performance Monitor is used primarily for two purposes: creating baselines of performance, and monitoring aberrations from the baseline—in other words, troubleshooting.

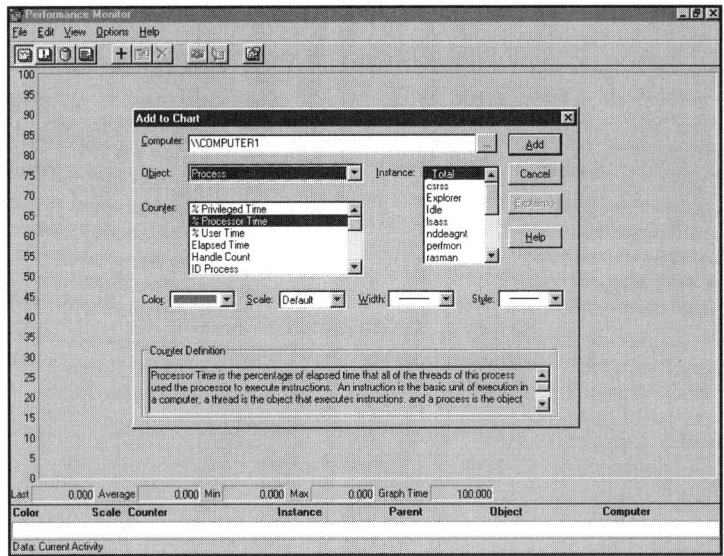

FIG. 10.1 ⇒ The Add to Chart dialog box displays some of the objects and instances that can be tracked through the Performance Monitor.

Key Concept

It does you no good as an analyst to turn on Performance Monitor to monitor system activity once a problem has been detected if you have no normal baseline of activity against which to measure the problem. A baseline represents the normal level of activity for a system. The certification tests assume that having a baseline for each system is desirable.

There are eleven core objects that can always be selected in Performance Monitor. These are described in Table 10.1. However, there are numerous other objects that appear only when certain services and devices are installed. Each object has numerous counters, also available by default. Every additional protocol, service, driver, and in some cases application you install on your Windows NT workstation or server will likely add additional objects and counters to the list. The number of instances varies greatly with each object.

Note In this chapter, Performance Monitor counters will be referred to by using the following notation: *Objectname>countername* where *objectname* represents the object to select, and *countername* the corresponding counter for that object.

There are two types of counters that are described in the following list.

- **Averaging**—Averaging counters measure a counter's value over a period of time and show the averaged value of the last two measurements.
- **Difference**—These counters are sometimes included with other applications that are installed on your system. Difference counters subtract a measurement from the previous measurement and display the difference if the value is positive. Otherwise, a zero is displayed.

Tip
The Add to Chart dialog box contains an Explain button. This button expands the dialog box to display a full explanation of the counter and the resource that it monitors (refer to Figure 10.1). This is very useful, especially for those counters that you might use infrequently.

Table 10.1 Core Objects in Performance Monitor

Object	Description
Cache	Monitors the effectiveness of physical memory used for caching disk operations
Logical Disk	Monitors disk activity by logical partitions and drives
Memory	Monitors the utilization of physical and logical/virtual memory
Objects	Monitors synchronization objects
Paging File	Monitors page file activity
Physical Disk	Monitors disk activity for each physical disk installed in the system
Process	Monitors activity of programs that are currently running on the system
Processor	Monitors activity of the CPU or CPUs installed on the system
Redirector	Monitors the activity of network requests generated by this system
Server	Monitors the activity of network requests to which this system responds
Thread	Monitors activity of process threads

Of the objects listed in Table 10.1, there are five specific objects that are of particular concern when troubleshooting your system, and will be the focus of concentration in this chapter: processor, memory, disk, process, and network.

This is not to say other objects aren't important to monitor. These are simply the objects most often looked at first to determine aberrations from the baseline and bottlenecks in the system. After all, if the system is running with poor performance, the most likely problem spots are the processor (too many programs and processes running), memory (not enough RAM for the number of processes that are running), disk (too many disk requests), or with the process itself (an application that overuses resources).

Configuring Performance Monitor

Performance Monitor can be found with the other Administrative Tools. There are four types of views that you can configure with Performance Monitor: Chart, Report, Log, and Alert.

Creating a Performance Monitor Chart

The most frequently used view is the Chart view. Chart view plots a real-time graph of the system activity being generated by the objects and counters selected (see Figure 10.2). Here are the basic steps to follow when configuring a Performance Monitor chart:

1. From the taskbar, select Start, Programs, Administrative Tools, Performance Monitor.
2. Choose Edit, Add to Chart to display the Add to Chart dialog box.
3. In the Computer text box, type or browse for the computer you want to monitor.

Tip

If you have a valid administrator's account, or participate in a domain in which you are a domain administrator, you can monitor other Windows NT computers remotely by selecting them from the browse list. While Performance Monitor is designed to utilize minimal system resources, nevertheless, depending on what resources you are charting on a system, you can skew performance results somewhat because Performance Monitor itself will be using resources. In such situations, Microsoft recommends monitoring resources on those systems remotely.

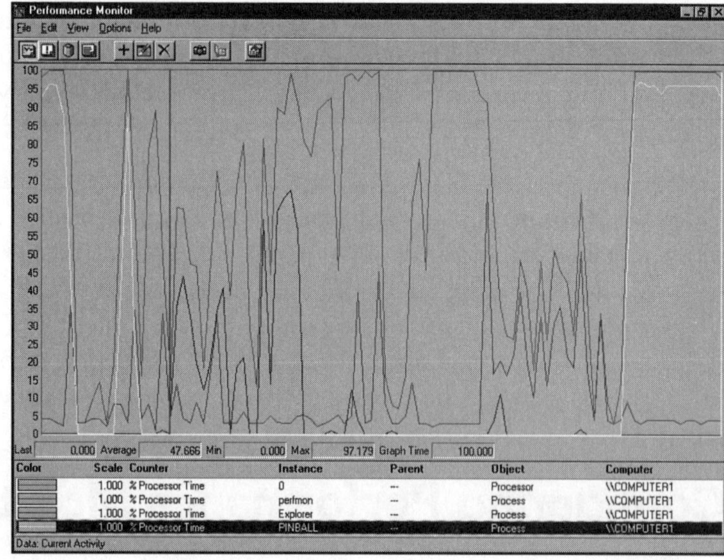

FIG. 10.2 ⇒
Here is a sample chart created in Performance Monitor. This chart tracks Processor>% Processor Time for the total system, as well as for three individual processes.

4. Select the Object that you want to monitor.
5. As you select an object, the Counter list displays counters associated with the chosen object that you can chart. Select the counter that you want to track. Select multiple counters by clicking the first counter, then holding down the Ctrl button while clicking the others.
6. If you are unsure about what a counter measures, select Explain to display descriptive text about the counter.
7. If appropriate, choose an Instance for each object counter. Again select multiple instances for each counter by selecting the first instance and then CTRL-clicking the rest.
8. Modify the legend characteristics as you want (Color, Scale, Width, and Line Style).
9. Choose Add to add the counter(s) to the chart window.
10. Repeat steps 3-9 for any additional objects that you want to monitor.
11. Choose Done when you are finished.

Tip

Performance Monitor, by default, displays a line chart that charts activity for every second in time. These defaults can be modified by selecting Options, Chart to display the Chart Options dialog box.

Most of the options in the Chart Options dialog box are self-explanatory. However, note the Update Time section. The Periodic Interval is set to 1 second, the default. If you want to capture information in smaller or larger time intervals, modify the value accordingly. The value you enter will affect the Graph Time value on the Statistics bar at the bottom of the graph itself. At a setting of 1 second, it will take 100 seconds to complete one chart pass in the window. A setting of 2 seconds will take 200 seconds to make a complete pass. A setting of .6 seconds will take 60 seconds, or one minute, to complete a pass, and so on.

Tip

To save chart settings for future use, such as creating a chart to compare against baseline activity, choose File, Save Chart Settings. The chart settings can then be loaded later to monitor system activity as designed.

Creating a Performance Monitor Log

As was mentioned before, charting values really is ineffective unless you have some baseline values against which you can compare activity. Log files are designed to collect this kind of information for viewing later. Object and counter values can be collected and saved in a log file, as well as values from multiple computers (see Figure 10.3).

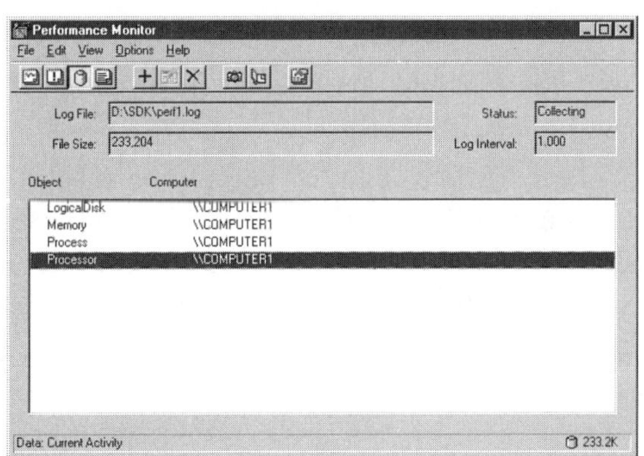

FIG. 10.3 ⇒ This example shows the log file as it is recording data for specific objects.

While the log file is collecting data, you cannot view its contents. If you want to monitor what kinds of data the log view is recording, you must start another copy of Performance Monitor and configure the Options, Data From option so that it will view chart data from the running log.

To create a log file, use these steps:

1. Start Performance Monitor.
2. Choose View, Log to display the log window.
3. Choose Edit, Add to Log. Select all the objects whose data you want to capture and choose Add. This will cause the log to record activity for every counter associated with each object. Choose Done when you are finished.
4. Choose Options, Log.
5. Enter a name for the log file and a directory to save it in, and set the Periodic Update interval if you want.
6. Choose Start Log to begin recording system activity.
7. Monitor the file size counter (shown in bytes) until the file grows as large as you like, or simply use your watch to collect data over a specific period of time.
8. When you have collected the desired amount of data, choose Options, Log, Stop Log.
9. Choose Options, Log, Save to save the log file.

To view the contents of a log file, use these steps:

1. Start Performance Monitor.
2. Choose View, Chart to display the chart window.
3. Choose Options, Data From to display the Data From dialog box.
4. Choose Log File and enter the path and file name of the log file, or browse for it. Choose OK.
5. Choose Edit, Add to Chart. The only objects listed will be those you captured in the log file. Select the object and each appropriate counter for which you want to view chart values. Choose Add to add them to the chart. A static chart view will be created.
6. Adjust the time view of the chart by choosing Edit, Time Window and then make your adjustment.

Note There is no facility in Performance Monitor to print charts. However, you can press Print Screen to copy a chart window to the Clipboard, then paste it into a word processing document and print it that way. You could also export the data to an Excel spreadsheet and use its utilities to create graphs and analyze the data. ■

You can make the log file even more useful by placing bookmarks at various points while you are recording data to the log. For example, perhaps you are performing a series of benchmark tests for which you are creating a log file.

Tip

Before each benchmark test, choose Options, Bookmark. Enter a bookmark name and choose Add. Later, when you are viewing the log, you can more accurately perceive the effects of each benchmark test by the bookmarks placed in the log.

Creating a Performance Monitor Report

The Report View enables you to see a summary window of the object and counter values recorded in a given log file, or collected dynamically for specified values from a current chart (see Figure 10.4). Each object and its counters and instances are summarized in this view.

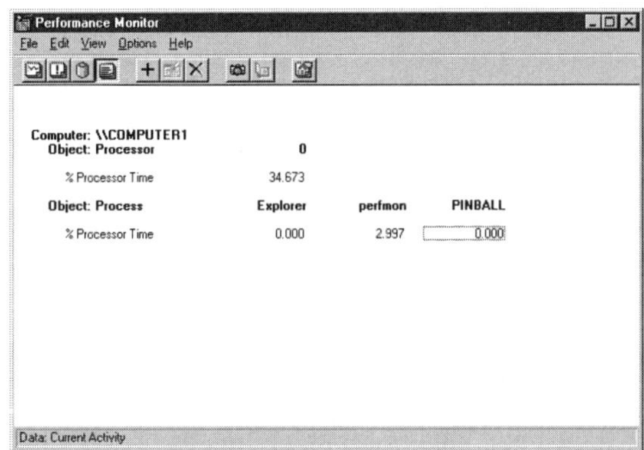

FIG. 10.4 ⇒ This sample report is based on and summarizes the same values charted in Figure 10.2.

To create a report, use these steps:

1. Choose View, Report from the menu.
2. Choose Edit, Add to Report. The Add to Report dialog box displays, which is similar to the Add to Chart dialog box.
3. Add the desired objects, counters, and instances as you did when creating a chart. This is described earlier, in the section "Creating a Performance Monitor Chart."

Creating a Performance Monitor Alert

The Alert View enables the administrator to monitor a system, and record and receive alerts when a specified threshold is reached for given counters and instances. Alert settings are configured through the Add to Alert dialog box (see Figure 10.5). This enables an administrator to continue to work, perhaps remotely, until notified of an alert.

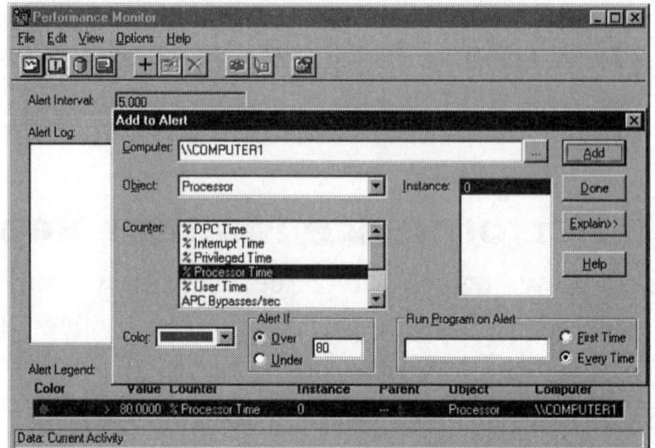

FIG. 10.5 ⇒
An alert is generated when the Processor>% Processor Time counter exceeds 80 percent for a period of five seconds.

Many counters can be measured concurrently in Alert View, and up to 1,000 alerts can be recorded before the oldest are overwritten with new information. As with charts, logs, and reports, alerts can be saved for future reference. For example, you might use alerts as documentation of increases in resource usage when specific applications are run, or when services are started. The saved files can then be used for troubleshooting or as growth-prediction tools.

To create an alert, use these steps:

1. Choose View, Alert.
2. Choose Edit, Add to Alert to display the Add to Alert dialog box (surprisingly similar to the Add to Chart and Add to Report dialog boxes).
3. Add the desired objects, counters, and instances as you did when creating a chart. This is described earlier, in the section "Creating a Performance Monitor Chart."
4. Enter an alert threshold appropriate to the counter selected in the Alert If text box. For example, select Over and 90 for the Processor>% Processor Time counter if you want to generate an alert when the

counter exceeds 80 percent over a default period of time. (The default is five seconds.)

5. Optionally, enter the name of a program or command prompt command to execute when the threshold is reached in the Run Program on Alert text box. The program or command can be configured to execute the first time the alert is generated, or every time the alert is generated. For example, you might enter the command: **NET SEND COMPUTER1 Processor Limit Exceeded** to send a system message to COMPUTER1, where the administrator is currently working, to notify the administrator of the alert.

Considering Specific Objects to Monitor

There are five useful objects to monitor, especially when creating a baseline of normal system activity. They are: processor, process, disk, memory, and network. The following sections outline specific counters that can be useful to monitor for each object.

Monitoring the Processor

The Processor object monitors processor usage by the system. There are four counters that you may want to chart.

Processor>%Processor Time (refer to Figure 10.2) tracks the total processor usage and gives a picture of just how busy the processor is. This counter, in and of itself, is not enough to tell you what is driving the processor to a particular level of usage, but it does help to indicate whether the problem or bottleneck is related in any way to the processor.

Processor>%User Time and Processor>%Privileged Time define processor usage by displaying what percentage of the total processor usage pertains to the user mode (application) or the kernel mode (executive services) components of the Windows NT 4.0 operating system activities. Again, these do not indicate what specific activities are driving the percentages. Microsoft recommends that these three counters (%Processor Time, %User Time and %Privileged Time) should, in general, remain below 75-80 percent, depending on computer use. For example, you would expect these values to be lower on a desktop computer, but consistently higher on a server running a client/server or system management application—for example, Microsoft Systems Management Server.

Processor>Interrupts/Sec tracks the number of device interrupt requests made from hardware devices, such as network cards or disk controllers, which are serviced by the processor. The optimum number of requests will vary from processor to processor. For example, you would expect a Pentium-based processor to handle perhaps three times as many requests as a 486 processor. In general, the higher the number (greater than 1,000 suggested for 486), the more likely the problem is related to the hardware rather than the processor.

If this is true, one might next monitor queue lengths for the suspected hardware devices, such as the disk controller or network card. Optimally, there should be only one request waiting in queue for each device. Queue lengths greater than two indicate which device is the likely culprit causing the bottleneck and that may need to be replaced or upgraded.

Caution

Processor object counters, as with all object counters, should never be monitored alone. As pointed out previously, the mere indication of activity beyond the norm does not in itself point to the processor as the focus of the problem. Use these and the other object counters recommended to draw attention to a problem. Then add additional object counters to help pinpoint and troubleshoot the problem.

There are two additional counters other than Processor object counters that can be used to identify the processor as a potential bottleneck. The first is the System>Processor Queue Length. This counter tracks the number of requests currently waiting for processing. At least one process thread must also be monitored for any data to be collected for this counter. Microsoft suggests that the queue length value should not be greater than two. Even if it is greater than two, it may not mean necessarily that the processor is the bottleneck. A particular application or process may be generating excessive requests. Your next step would be to monitor %Processor usage for individual suspected processes to obtain further results.

The other counter is the Server Work Queues>Queue Length counter. Similar to the System>Processor Queue Length counter, this one indicates the number of requests for network resources currently in queue. Again, this value should not exceed two on average.

Monitoring Processes

For every service that is loaded and every application that is run, a process is created by Windows NT—a process that can be monitored by Performance Monitor. Each process is considered an instance in this case, and each Process object instance has several counters that can be charted.

Notice that the %Processor Time can be tracked for each process instance (see Figure 10.6). This is how you can determine which specific process is driving the processor to higher-than-normal usage.

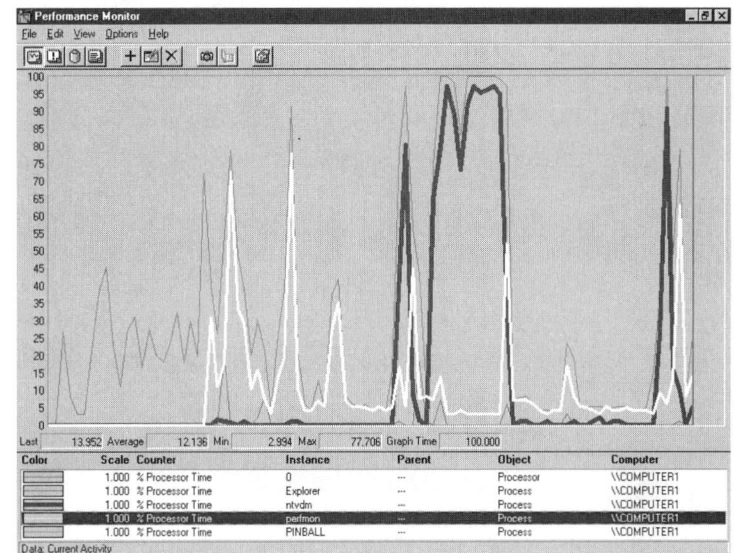

FIG. 10.6 ⇒ The Performance Monitor is driving the total percentage of processor usage.

Another useful process counter is the Process>Working Set. This counter actually tracks the amount of RAM required by the process and can be used to help determine when additional RAM is necessary. For example, if paging appears to be excessive, you might monitor the Working Sets of the processes suspected of causing the increased paging. The Memory>Pages/Sec example in the next section, "Monitoring Memory," gives a complete scenario for combining counters to determine a need for additional RAM.

Monitoring Memory

Perhaps the most common problem encountered on heavily used computers is inadequate RAM for the processes to perform at their optimum rates.

There are several Memory object counters that can be of particular service to you. Some of these are displayed in Figure 10.7. In this chart, the Memory>Pages/Sec counter (thick dark line) is somewhat high, with the Memory>Committed Bytes counter (highlighted in white) at about 22M larger than available RAM (16M on this computer). This indicates that the computer may need to add more RAM to improve performance and reduce paging.

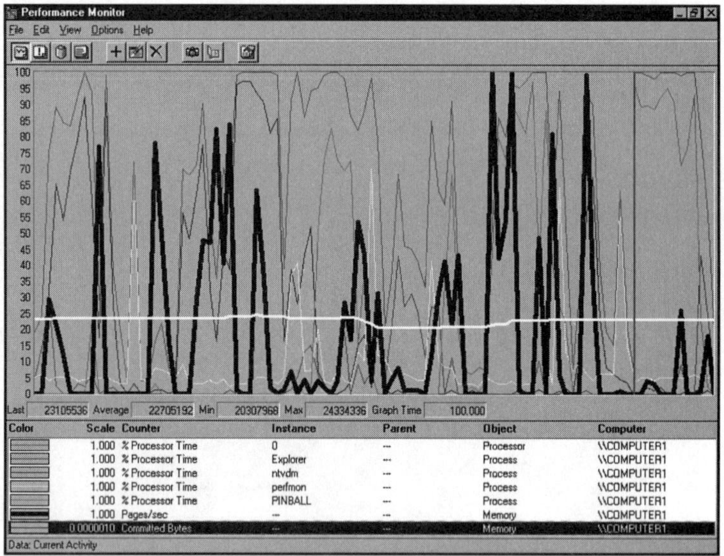

FIG. 10.7 ⇒
Some useful memory object counters.

Memory>Committed Bytes indicates the amount of virtual memory that is currently stored in either physical RAM or the pagefile. If this value is consistently larger than the total RAM installed on the computer, you may need to install additional RAM to accommodate the system's memory requirements and reduce paging.

Memory>Commit Limit indicates the number of bytes that can be written (committed) to the pagefile without extending or growing it. As this number falls, the pagefile is more likely to grow. Whenever the page file needs to expand or grow, it must allocate additional disk storage space. This allocation requires extra disk I/O. Any time additional disk I/O is generated, your system will experience a performance hit. Use this counter to help you determine whether you need to right-size your pagefile.

For example, if you are running several large applications simultaneously, which is quite probable on a Windows NT server, it is likely that the initial size of your pagefile may be inadequate. If, as you load and run each application, the Memory>Commit Limit quickly expands and the pagefile expands, you can assume that the initial size is inadequate. You first need to determine the expanded size of the pagefile, which you can do by using Windows Explorer. Then, modify the pagefile size so that the initial size matches the expanded size, which enables you to start with the right size pagefile and eliminate the disk I/O involved with growing the pagefile.

Note While you can use Windows Explorer to monitor the size of the pagefile, the size shown for the pagefile stored on an NTFS volume probably will be inaccurate. This is because in NTFS, file size is not updated while the file is open. It is updated only when it is closed. Of course, the pagefile always opens to its initial size when Windows NT boots.

There is a way around this phenomenon. Try to delete the pagefile through Windows Explorer. You will get a message that the file is in use by another process (of course, Windows NT). Now refresh Windows Explorer, or type **DIR** at a command prompt to display the correct pagefile size.

Memory>Pages/Sec (refer to Figure 10.7) indicates the number of pages requested by a process that were not in RAM and had to be read from disk, or had to be written to disk to make room available in RAM for another process. In itself, this value should remain rather low—between 0 and 20 pages per second is suggested by Microsoft.

Multiply this counter's average value by that of the Logical Disk object's Avg. Disk sec/Transfer counter. This counter indicates the average number of seconds for each disk I/O. The resulting value shows the percentage of disk I/O used by paging. Microsoft suggests that if this value consistently exceeds 10 percent, then paging is excessive and you probably need more RAM. The actual threshold is based on the function of the particular computer. You might expect more paging to occur on a SQL server than on a desktop, for example. When combined with the Process>Working Set counter, described in the section "Monitoring Processes," you can determine approximately how much additional RAM you may need to install in the computer.

Suppose you have determined that paging is excessive by multiplying the Memory object's Pages/Sec counter by the Logical Disk>Avg. Disk sec/ Transfer counter and got a value of 20 percent. You presume that you need additional RAM. But how much?

You also have been tracking the Processor>%Processor Time for the processor as a whole, and for several suspect processes. You note three processes that really push the processor.

For each process, also monitor that process' Process>Working Set counter. Recall that this is the amount of RAM required by the process. Make note of the amount of RAM used by each process. Now, terminate one of the processes. Check the percent of disk I/O used by paging. Has it dropped below the acceptable threshold (10 percent as recommended by Microsoft)? If so, then the amount of RAM required by that application is the minimum amount of additional RAM to add to your computer. If not, terminate another application and check the results again. Keep doing this until the pagefile I/O drops to an acceptable level, and add up the working set values for the terminated processes. The total represents the minimum amount of RAM to add to your computer. Administrators often round this value up to the nearest multiple of four.

Monitoring Disk Activity

There actually are two objects related to disk activity: the physical disk object and the logical disk object. The physical disk object counters (see Figure 10.8) track activity related to the disk drive as a whole, and can be used to determine whether one disk drive is being used more than another for load-balancing purposes. For example, if the activity of a disk is particularly high due to operating system requests and pagefile I/O, then you might want to move the pagefile to a disk that is being under-utilized, especially if the disk controller can write to each disk concurrently. The number of instances will be the number of physical drives installed on the computer.

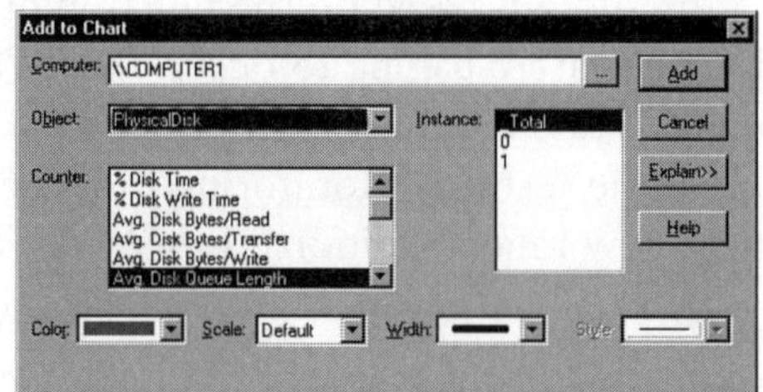

FIG. 10.8 ⇒
Here you can see some of the counters available for tracking activity on the Physical Disk. Note that there is an instance for each of two disk drives, as well as a Total option that measures both drives together.

The Logical Disk object counters track activity related to specific partitions on each disk and can be used to locate the source of activity on the disk; for example, on what partition the pagefile is located. The number of instances will be the number of partitions created by drive letter.

Both objects pretty much have the same group of counters for tracking activity. The following five counters, in particular, can be useful:

- **Avg. Disk sec/Transfer**—You saw this counter when reviewing Memory object counters in the "Monitoring Memory" section of this chapter. It shows the average amount of time for disk I/O to complete and can be used with the Memory object's Pages/sec counter to determine whether paging is excessive.
- **Current Disk Queue Length**—This counter represents the number of requests for disk I/O waiting to be serviced. This number generally should be less than two. Consistently high numbers indicate that the disk is being over-utilized, or should be upgraded to a faster access disk.
- **Disk Bytes/sec**—This counter indicates the rate at which data is transferred during disk I/O. The higher the value, the more efficient the performance.
- **Avg. Disk Bytes/Transfer**—This counter is the average number of bytes of data that are transferred during disk I/O. As with Disk Bytes/sec, the larger the value, the more efficient the disk transfer.
- **%Disk Time**—This counter represents the amount of time spent servicing disk I/O requests. A consistently high number indicates that the disk is being heavily used. You may choose to determine which processes are driving this usage and partition or move the applications to a less heavily used disk to load-balance disk activity.

These counter values, when used with the others previously discussed, can help you determine bottlenecks and possible courses of action to alleviate disk-related problems (see Figure 10.9). In this sample chart, the %Disk Time, Avg. Disk sec/Transfer and Current Disk Queue Length values are consistently high, indicating that the disk is being heavily used. Additional analysis can determine what is being accessed (files, applications, and so on) and whether anything can be done to improve disk performance.

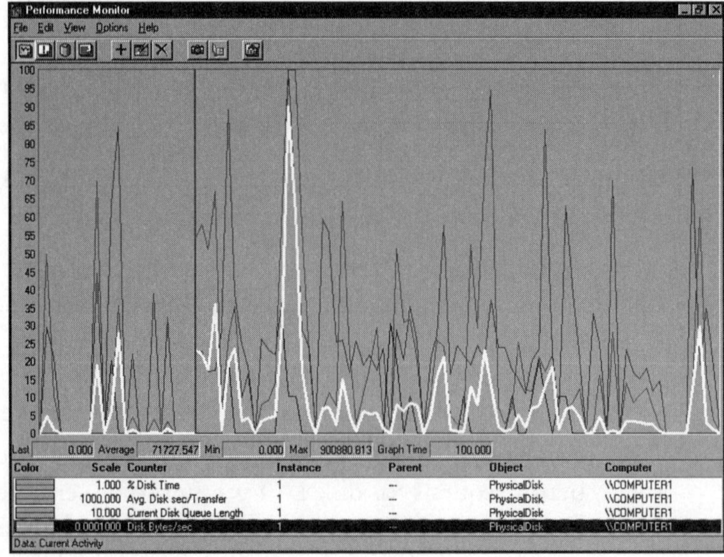

FIG. 10.9 ⇒
Counters that can help determine bottlenecks in a system.

Key Concept

Disk object counters, while they are visible in the Add to Chart dialog box, are not enabled by default. This is because the resource required to monitor disk activity is, itself, rather demanding. Disk object monitoring must be enabled before any charting can take place; otherwise, your chart will always display a flat-line graph.

Enable disk monitoring by typing the following command at a DOS command prompt:

DISKPERF -Y *computername*, where ***computername*** optionally references a remote computer whose disk activity you want to monitor.

When you are finished capturing your data, type **DISKPERF -N *computername*** to disable disk monitoring.

Disk bottlenecks generally are resolved by upgrading the disk or its controller, increasing the amount of controller caching that can take place, if possible, implementing striping on a server and load balancing applications across physical disks, or even by moving heavily used applications to their own servers.

Monitoring Network-Related Objects

Perhaps one of the more difficult components of system activity to monitor and analyze is the network activity. Windows NT Server 4.0 provides a rather thorough network-analysis tool called Network Monitor. This is a frame analysis tool that helps isolate and identify network traffic related to different types of network activity generated between two or more computers. This tool is explored in detail in Chapter 23, "Network Monitor."

However, there are also some network-related objects and counters that can be used to determine the performance of network-related processes on the computer itself. These include Server, Redirector, and entries for the protocols installed on the computer, such as TCP/IP, NWLINK, and NetBEUI. As additional network services are installed—RAS, DHCP, WINS—objects and counters relating to those services are added to Performance Monitor. If you have multiple network adapter cards installed on your computer, each of them will be considered an instance making it possible to chart network objects and counters for each network adapter.

Protocol counters include Bytes Total/sec, Datagrams/sec, and Frames/sec. A high value, in general, is desired because this indicates a high rate of throughput for network activity. However, high values can also indicate excessive generation of traffic, such as excessive frames due to browser broadcasts.

Note TCP/IP counters are enabled only if the SNMP (Simple Network Management Protocol) service agent is installed on the computer. When the SNMP service is installed, it also adds some TCP/IP-related counters to the Performance Monitor. For example, SNMP>TCP Segments/sec indicates the number of TCP/IP-specific frames that are being generated or received by the computer. SNMP>UDP Datagrams/sec identifies the number of broadcast, or UDP (User Datagram Protocol), frames that are generated.

The workstation service on a computer can be monitored by charting *Redirector object counters*. One counter of interest is Redirector>Network Errors/sec. This counter indicates the number of errors detected by the workstation service as it attempted to direct frames onto the network. The higher this number goes, the more serious the problem may be. Use Network Monitor to observe and detect network traffic as a whole, especially to and from this computer.

Two more Redirector counters are Redirector>Reads Denied/sec and Redirector>Writes Denied/sec. If either of these numbers rises significantly, it may indicate that the server with which this computer is communicating may be having difficulty handling the number of network requests for resources it is receiving. You would want to monitor activity on that server to pinpoint the problem and posit a solution, perhaps by using one or more of the following Server object counters:

- The Server>Bytes Total/sec counter indicates the number of bytes sent and received by the computer responding to network resource requests. This gives an idea of how busy the server service is on the computer.
- The Server>Logon/sec counter indicates how many logon attempts took place during the last second on the computer, either locally, over the network, or by a service account.
- The Server>Logon Total counter indicates the total number of logon attempts that took place during the current computer session. This counter, together with Server>Logon/sec and the protocol counters, is particularly beneficial when used with Network Monitor to achieve a complete view of network activity relating to a domain controller.
- The Server>Pool Nonpaged Failures counter indicates how frequently the server tried to allocate memory for server-based request handling but was unable due to a lack of physical RAM. Similarly, Server>Pool Paged Failures indicates how frequently the server tried to allocate paged memory but was unable to because either physical RAM was inadequate, or the paging file was full. In either case, it may be appropriate to reconfigure memory usage by the server. This can be done by accessing the server service properties through the Network Properties dialog box. There are four memory options that can be selected:
    - Minimize Memory Used allocates the smallest amount of memory to handle server-based requests for network resources. This value is adequate for workgroups where the number of users accessing the server is small—no more than 10—or where the server functions primarily as a workstation.
    - Balanced allocates enough memory to handle up to 64 network connections to the server. This might be a member server in a moderately used network environment.
    - Maximize Throughput for File Sharing is an optimal choice for file and print servers as it allocates enough memory for heavier user access.

- Maximize Throughput for Network Applications allocates the greatest amount of memory for network connections to the server while minimizing the memory cache. This setting is most appropriate for servers running client/server applications as it also takes into account that the applications will need to perform some functions in RAM on that computer. It also is recommended for domain controllers with large numbers of users configured in a master or multiple-master domain model.

Summarizing Performance Monitoring and Optimization

Here are some suggestions for collecting meaningful performance data, analyzing it, and using it effectively for problem solving and planning.

First, establish a performance baseline for the computer. If you do not understand what normal performance is like, you will not be able to accurately identify, resolve, or predict abnormal performance. For example, Microsoft recommends that processor usage should not consistently exceed 80 percent. However, some Back Office applications normally exceed 80 percent processor utilization or more when performing their regular functions and service cycles. Your baseline should include counters from each of the objects discussed in this chapter.

Tip

You will notice that as you select an object, one counter will be highlighted already by default. This is the counter that Microsoft considers to be most commonly included in a measurement baseline.

Next, analyze performance for specific functions and during specific periods. For example, if you are analyzing a file and print server, you might monitor the Server>Pool Nonpaged Failures and Pool Paged Failures to determine whether the server memory is configured appropriately. You also might want to keep track of the number of users connected to the server concurrently, as well as the number of files open by monitoring Server>Server Sessions and Server>Files Open, respectively. Because a high level of disk activity on a file and print server is expected (for example, file reads and writes, and print spooling), it is beneficial to track Physical Disk>Avg. Disk Bytes/Transfer, %Disk Time, %Disk Read Time, and %Disk Write Time. These can help you determine, among other things, whether one disk is enough, whether additional disks should be added and the files load-balanced, or even whether disk striping might be considered as a viable optimizing solution.

On a domain controller, you might monitor the number of simultaneous logons the server is receiving and the number that it can handle at peak logon periods throughout the day by using Server>Logon/sec and Server>Logon Total. Other useful counters include Memory>Available bytes and Committed bytes to identify how RAM and the pagefile are being utilized.

On servers functioning as WINS, DHCP, and DNS servers, it is advantageous to monitor the object counters associated with those services to see how they affect performance on a given computer, in conjunction with the Network Monitor utility as it tracks network traffic associated with that service. For example, WINS servers perform NetBIOS name registration and resolution. The WINS Server>Total Number of Registrations/sec and Queries/sec counters can provide data relating to those functions as they take place on this computer and affect resources. Network Monitor can identify how many frames are generated for each function, how large the frames are, how long it took to send them, and where the requests for registration and name resolution originated.

Remember that you can monitor performance on computers remotely. This is suggested particularly so as not to skew data collected with the activities of Performance Monitor itself. Remotely monitoring a computer can be especially useful when trying to pinpoint network bottlenecks. For example, if you suspect that a particular server may be the source of a network bottleneck, you might consider remotely monitoring the Server object counters described in the previous section, "Monitoring Network-Related Objects." A consistently high Server>Pool Paged Failures counter indicates that the server is trying to allocate paged memory, but cannot, perhaps because it doesn't have enough RAM, or the page file is full or inadequately sized. This causes server performance to denigrate, resulting in a potential bottleneck of network requests.

Document your performance measurements and convey the information appropriately. If the system as it is currently configured—hardware purchased, software installed, network traffic generated—can perform only at a particular level, document that fact. If a higher level of performance is required, use your data to justify to management upgrading in hardware, load-balancing heavily used applications by purchasing additional servers and moving applications to them, upgrading WAN links, and so on.

Extrapolating data collected for the current system can give a rough estimate of future performance. This is more commonly referred to as *trend analysis*. Performance Monitor can help facilitate the identification of potential resource requirements, hardware and software upgrades, and budget needs.

Taking the Disc Test

If you have read and understood the material in this chapter, you are ready to test your knowledge. Insert the CD-ROM that comes with this book and run the self-test software, as described in Appendix K, "Using the Self-Test Software."

From Here...

The next chapter completes the discussion of managing resources. Printer management issues are covered in detail. Topics from the next chapter include adding printers, creating printer pools, and an overview of the components of the printing process.

Chapter Prerequisite

There are no prerequisites for this chapter.

11

Printing

This chapter provides a short discussion of the Windows NT 4.0 print process, followed by discussions on adding and configuring printing devices and working with printer pools and printer priorities. Lastly, a discussion on troubleshooting printing problems is presented. The concepts and procedures discussed in this chapter apply to both workstation and server installations.

The following topics are covered in this chapter:

- Examining the Windows NT 4.0 print process
- Adding and configuring printers
- Working with printer properties
- Troubleshooting printing

Examining the Windows NT 4.0 Print Process

In the past, configuring a printer has been somewhat of a problem not only from a local desktop, but also across the network. Microsoft has expended great effort in designing the Windows NT 4.0 operating system to streamline and simplify management of the printing process, particularly on the network.

Microsoft has been aware of the problems associated with local and network printing and has, throughout its history, successfully enhanced the process. For example, each MS-DOS application generally requires its own print driver to be loaded to successfully print to a given printing device. With Windows, Microsoft introduced a single set of print drivers that can be used with all applications. In other words, Windows required the installation of only one printer driver, which all its applications could use, instead of a driver for each application.

Windows NT follows this same concept by using a generic set of drivers, along with a specific printer mini-driver that is used by all applications running under Windows NT. Windows NT 4.0 also takes this concept a step further by requiring a set of drivers to be installed only on the printer server and not on every installation using the printing device.

Before you begin, terminology used in the Windows NT 4.0 print process must be defined. A *printer* in Windows NT 4.0 is the software interface between the application and the physical printing device, which consists of the print driver and the print queue. The physical hardware that does the printing is referred to as the *print device*. A print request or print job can be sent to either a *local print device* connected directly to the user's local computer, or a *remote print device*, which is attached to and managed by another computer or print server on the network. Requests can also be sent to a *network interface print device*, which is controlled and managed by a print server on the network, but is connected directly to the network and not to a print server.

The printer, or software interface, interacts with the print device to ensure the print device receives a print job that has been formatted appropriately for that device. The printer also provides the print management interface from which print jobs can be viewed and manipulated.

Once a print device has been made available to users on the network, any valid Microsoft network client (Windows NT, DOS, Windows 95, Windows for Workgroups, Windows 3.1, LAN Manager 2.x, NetWare, Macintosh), and even OS/2 and UNIX clients, are able to directly print jobs to that device.

When a print device is made available on the network as a remote printer, you are not actually sharing the print device itself. The actual printer, or the *management interface*, is being shared. A given print device might have several printers associated with it, each with a different set of characteristics, priorities, or permissions. This concept is discussed further in Chapter 20, "Network Printing."

Print Process Components

There are four basic components of the print process: print driver, print spooler, print processor, and print monitor. Each is discussed in the following paragraphs.

Print Driver

As stated earlier, the print driver interacts with the print device to allow applications to generate printed output. The print driver also provides the graphic interface through which the print device and queue can be managed. The print driver consists of three pieces—two DLLs and a characterization data file:

- The *printer graphics driver DLL* converts the print job output from an application into a print device ready format.
- The *printer interface driver DLL* provides the interactive management screen through which the print jobs and the print device can be manipulated.
- The *characterization data file* provides information concerning device-specific characteristics of the print device, such as the amount of memory, internal cartridges, additional form trays, and so on.

Examples of the three print driver files for an HP LaserJet 4 printing device are as follows:

- Rasdd.dll—Printer graphics driver DLL
- Rasddui.dll—Printer interface driver DLL
- Pcl5ems.dll—Characterization data file

Print Spooler

The print spooler actually refers to the spooler service running in Windows NT 4.0. The spooler is responsible for making a connection to the spooler on a remote print server. It also tracks print jobs, sends print jobs to the appropriate ports, and assigns jobs an appropriate print priority.

The spooler can be considered the print queue for the Windows NT print process. Because the spooler is a Windows NT service, it can be controlled through the Services applet in the Control Panel. If a print job gets stuck or hangs, simply select the spooler service from the list, choose Stop, and then choose Start. This effectively cancels the stuck print job waiting in the spooler. If a print job hangs, or the spooler does not seem to be responding, you can also purge the spooler. If the spooler is purged, all jobs in the spooler are also purged.

Key Concept

It is always preferable to use the printer interface to try to pause or delete a problem job instead of stopping and starting the spooler service, so as not to lose any other jobs in queue. However, if the spooler is not responding and jobs cannot be deleted, the spooler service must be stopped and then started again.

By default, print job files are spooled to the `<winntroot>\SYSTEM32\SPOOL\PRINTERS` directory. Depending on the size of the partition, as well as the number and size of the print jobs spooled, it is possible to run out of disk space.

Tip

The folder compression attribute, available through the properties dialog box for files and folders on an NTFS partition, can be used to compress the spool files and conserve disk space. However, keep in mind that compression does add additional overhead to your system and can, with large print files, possibly result in a performance decrease.

If the spool folder is located on an NTFS partition, the Disk Administrator can be used to *extend* the partition into a volume set to increase the space available for the spooler folder. Windows NT also provides a Registry entry through which you can modify the location of the spooler folder globally for all printers, as well as for individual printers.

Use the Registry Editor to select the HKEY_LOCAL_MACHINE subtree and expand through to find the following key:

```
SYSTEM\CurrentControlSet\Control\Print\Printers
```

Look for a parameter entry called `DefaultSpoolDirectory` and modify its value to correspond to the new spool location. This change affects *all* printers installed on the computer.

On the next level below the Printer key, you will find an entry for each printer you created on the computer. Each of these printers also has a `SpoolDirectory` entry that, if modified, will change the spool location just for that printer. Figure 11.1 displays these two Registry locations.

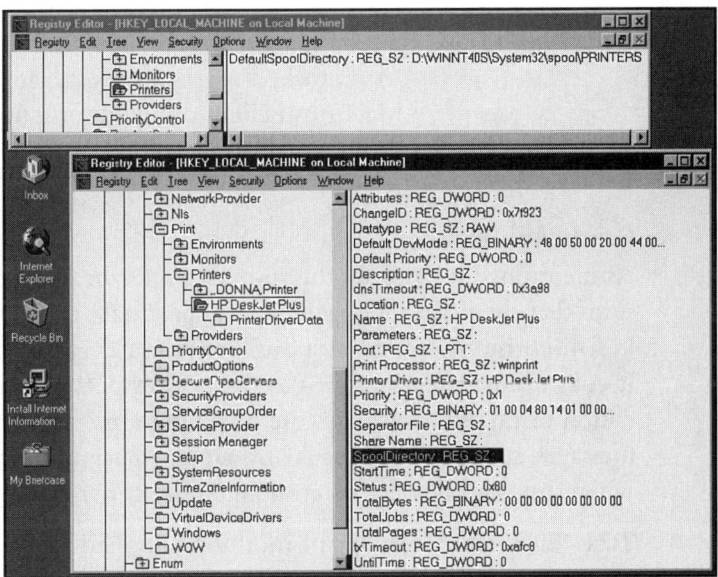

FIG. 11.1 ⇒
Here are two Print Spooler locations in the Registry.

When planning an installation of Windows NT 4.0, especially if the installation will be a print server, allow for enough print spooler disk space.

Print Processor

The print processor is responsible for carrying out any further formatting or rendering of the print job required for the specific printer to understand it. The default print processor for Windows NT 4.0 is WINPRINT.DLL. It recognizes and renders the print job types listed in Table 11.1.

Table 11.1 WINPRINT.DLL—Print Job Types

Type	Description
Raw Data	The most common print job type. It represents a print job that has been fully rendered and ready for the specific print device, such as PostScript.
Enhanced Metafile (EMF)	A portable format that can be used with any print device.
Text	Represents a print job rendered with raw, unformatted ASCII text and minimal control codes (linefeeds, carriage returns).
PSCRIPT1	Used on Windows NT servers running Services for Macintosh, it represents Postscript code from a Macintosh client destined for a non-Postscript print device on a Windows NT print server.

Print Monitor

As mentioned previously, the spooler tracks the location of the job and ensures that the print job reaches the appropriate destination. The Windows NT 4.0 print monitor is responsible for tracking the status of the print job. It controls the stream of jobs to the printer ports, sends the job to its destination print device, releases the port when finished, returns print device messages, such as `out of paper` or `out of toner`, and notifies the spooler when the print device has completed the generation of print output.

Table 11.2 outlines the print monitors supplied by Windows NT 4.0. The print monitor installed depends on the print driver that you are using, the print device type, such as Postscript, HPPCL, or DEC, as well as the network protocol used to direct print traffic.

Print Monitor	Description
LOCALMON.DLL	Monitors print jobs targeted for print devices connected to local ports.
HPMON.DLL	Monitors print jobs targeted for Hewlett-Packard network print devices. The DLC protocol must be installed on the print server, and the printer port must be identified by supplying the print device's hardware address.
SFMMON.DLL	Monitors Macintosh print jobs routed by using the AppleTalk protocol to network print devices.
LPRMON.DLL	Monitors print jobs targeted for print devices that are communicating through the TCP/IP protocol, such as UNIX print devices and print spooler services.
DECPSMON.DLL	Monitors print jobs targeted for DEC's Digital PrintServer and other DEC print devices. Either the DECnet protocol or TCP/IP may be used to communicate with these print devices. Obtain the DECnet protocol from DEC (Digital Equipment Corporation).
LEXMON.DLL	Monitors print jobs targeted for Lexmark Mark Vision print devices that use DLC, TCP/IP, or IPX to communicate.
PJLMON.DLL	Monitors print jobs targeted for any bidirectional print device that uses the PJL (Printer Job Language) standard, such as the HP LaserJet 5Si.

Table 11.2 Windows NT 4.0 Print Monitors

Ch 11

Adding a Printer

Recall the definition of a printer. When speaking of a *printer* in Windows NT 4.0, you are referring to the *print driver* and the interface through which you interact with the print device and from which you can monitor and manipulate print jobs.

The first step in creating a printer is to ensure that the print device is compatible with Windows NT 4.0. This information can be verified from the Hardware Compatibility List (HCL).

Only certain users have the ability to create printers and share them on the network. Administrators, of course, have this ability by default. However, members of the Print Operators and Server Operators groups on domain controllers, and Power Users group members on any other Windows NT workstation or server, can also perform this task.

Printers are added and connected to by using the Add Printer Wizard, which is accessible through the Printers folder in My Computer or by choosing Start, Settings, Printers. The following paragraphs and figures will step through the process of adding a new printer that is physically connected to a local computer. The local computer (either workstation or server platform) will act as a print server for users on a network (either a workgroup or a domain).

To create a new printer, follow these steps:

1. From the Printers folder in My Computer, start the Add Printer Wizard by double-clicking Add Printer (see Figure 11.2).

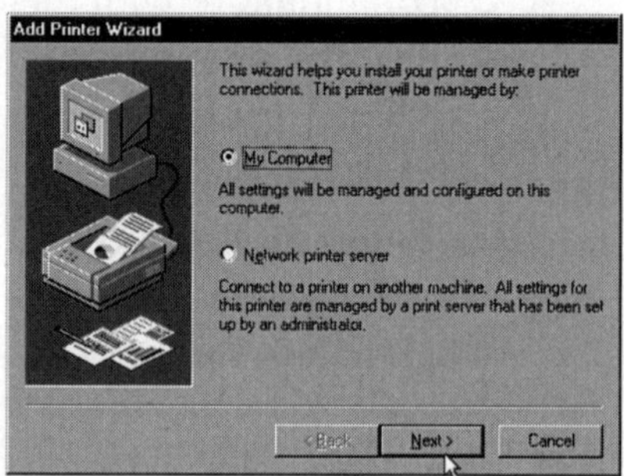

FIG. 11.2 ⇒ The Add Printer Wizard dialog box.

2. If the printer is directly connected to the computer you are currently sitting at, keep the default setting My Computer. Network Printer Server will be used to connect to a remote printer. Choose Next.
3. Select the port to which the printer is physically attached, such as LPT1: or COM1: (see Figure 11.3). Use Configure Port to modify transmission retry of an LPT port or the baud rate settings of the designated COM port. Choose Next.

If the print device is a network printer or is identified through a hardware or IP address, choose Add Port to provide new port information, or select or add the appropriate print monitor. This information is covered later in this chapter. You also have the option of enabling a printer pool. Printer pools and their benefits are discussed later in this chapter in the section, "Print Pools."

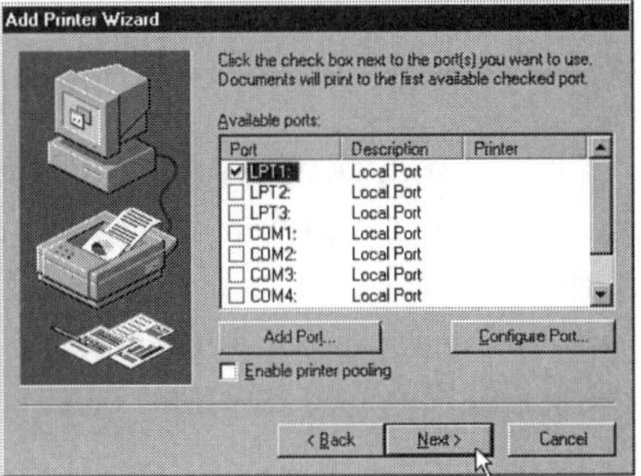

FIG. 11.3 ⇒ In this example, the Available Ports window in the Add Printer Wizard dialog box indicates that the print device is physically attached to LPT1.

4. The list of supported print driver options has grown tremendously (see Figure 11.4). The driver selection menu has been divided into a Manufacturers list and a Printers list. If the device you are installing is not represented in the list, and you have an OEM disk with a Windows NT-compatible driver on it, choose Have Disk to install it. Choose Next.

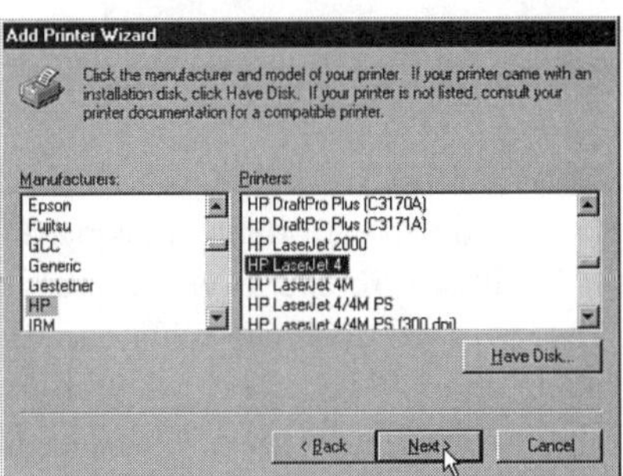

FIG. 11.4 ⇒ In the Add Printer Wizard Dialog Box, you can see the selection of a print driver for the HP LaserJet 4.

5. Enter a printer name that is descriptive of the print device (see Figure 11.5). This is the name that print administrators will use to identify the printer. Also, if the printer is being installed for local use, identify it as the default printer for use by applications, if you want. The first installed printer is always designated as the default. Choose Next.

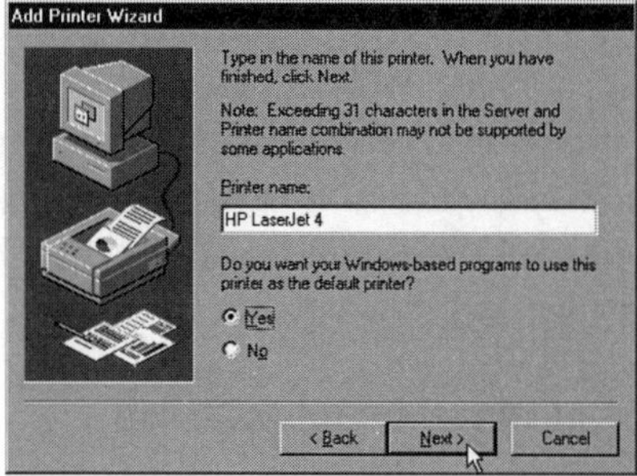

FIG. 11.5 ⇒
In this example, the printer name remains the default name of the print device and will be the default print device for applications run on this computer.

6. If the printer is to be shared, you can do so by selecting the Shared option button and then by supplying a share name; otherwise, by default, the Not Shared option button is selected. The printer can always be shared later. When sharing a printer, enter a Share Name that is descriptive for the users that will connect to this printer (see Figure 11.6). Choose Next.

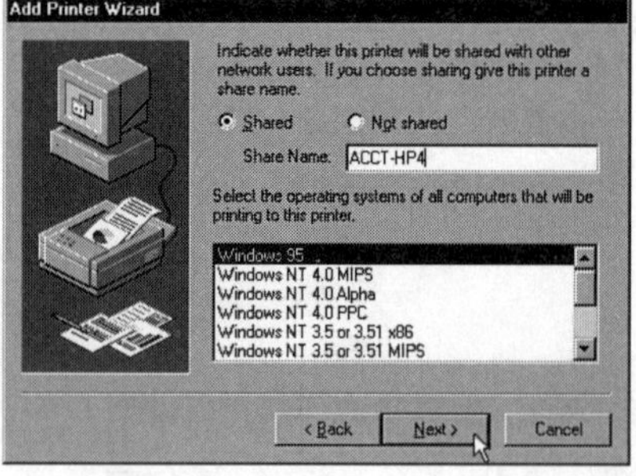

FIG. 11.6 ⇒
This printer has been shared by using the user-friendly name of ACCT-HP4.

Note Also, in the list box on the lower portion of this dialog box, a list of drivers for alternative platforms appears, allowing all required drivers to be installed. For example, if Windows 95 clients will be accessing this printer, and you want to download the driver to each client instead of installing it separately on every Windows 95 client, then select Windows 95 from the list. The Printer Wizard will prompt you later for the Windows 95 source files. Any required drivers always can be added at a later time.

Note that in this example, the Windows 95 drivers are selected to be installed.

7. The Printer Wizard then asks if you want to print a test page to the print device. This usually is a good idea, especially if you are identifying a network print device through a hardware or IP address. Choose Finish.

8. As Windows NT installs the print driver, note the various driver files, DLLs, monitor files, and so forth being loaded. If asked, supply the path to the location of the Windows NT 4.0 source files.
9. As the installation completes, the Printer Wizard adds an icon to represent the printer in the Printer folder (see Figure 11.7), and asks whether the test page printed successfully. If it did, the installation is complete. If it did not, you have the opportunity to go back and modify your settings. The new printer icon is your access to the print manager for that printer, its jobs, and its print device(s).

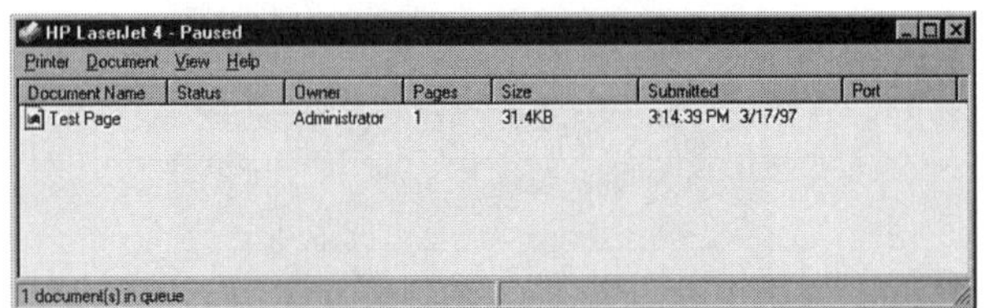

FIG. 11.7 ⇒ Notice the new HP LaserJet 4 icon created in the Printers dialog box. By double-clicking the HP LaserJet 4 icon, the print manager window for that printer is displayed.

Working with Printer Properties

This part of the chapter explores the printer properties tabs, except for the Sharing tab and the Securities tab, which are covered in Chapter 20, "Network Printing."

General Tab

The General tab gives you the option of entering a descriptive comment about the printer, such as who can use it, what options it provides, and so on (see Figure 11.8). A descriptive location of the printer can also be entered here. This is useful when users are browsing for printers, viewing print manager screens, or receiving device-specific messages.

The General tab also enables you to identify a Separator Page, to select an alternate Print Processor, or to choose to Print Test Page. Separator Pages, sometimes called *banner pages*, identify and separate print output by printing a page before the document, which indicates who submitted the document, as well as the date and time it was printed. Separator pages also have the function of switching a printer between modes. Windows NT provides three separator pages, located in <winntroot>\SYSTEM32, as shown in Table 11.3. Separator pages can be selected by choosing the Separator Page button.

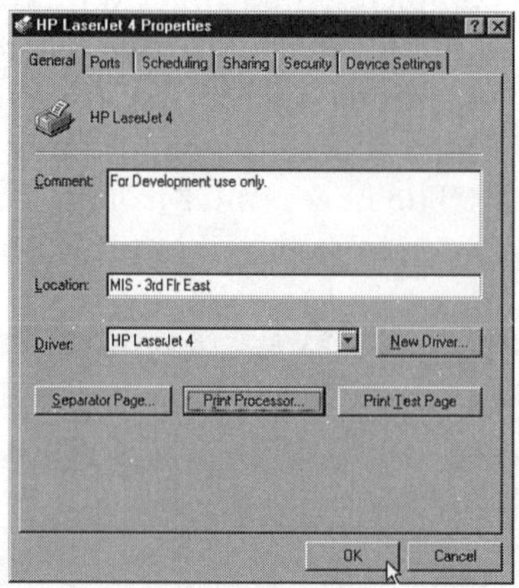

FIG. 11.8 ⇒ In this printers Properties sheet, a comment and descriptive location have been added. When users view the printers or receive device-specific messages, they will see the location as well.

Table 11.3 Windows NT 4.0 Separator Pages

Separator File	Description
SYSPRINT.SEP	Causes a separator page to print before each document and is compatible with PostScript print devices
PCL.SEP	Causes the device to switch to PCL mode for HP devices and prints a separator page before each document
PSCRIPT.SEP	Causes the device to switch to PostScript mode for HP devices and does not print a separator page before each document

Separator pages are text files that can be created and saved with a .SEP extension in the <winnt root>\SYSTEM32 directory by using any text editor. Control characters that you can use to customize a separator page include:

- `\N`—Returns the name of the user who sent the document.
- `\D`—Returns the date the document was printed.
- `\T`—Returns the time the document was printed.
- `\H`*nn*—Sets a printer-specific control sequence based on a specified hexadecimal ASCII code.

Note More information about creating custom separator pages can be found in the online help and in the Books folder on the Windows NT Server CD-ROM. Simply choose Find and search for "separator."

The Print Processor button enables you to specify an alternate print processor for the print device and port, and to modify the job types it creates to accommodate your applications. For example, WINPRINT.DLL offers five default print-job types, including RAW (the default), RAW (FF appended), RAW (FF auto), NT EMF 1.003, and TEXT.

If an application is not adding a form feed to the end of the document when the application sends a print job to a particular printer, the last page might remain stuck in the printer. You can choose RAW (FF appended) to force a form feed on the end of any document sent to the printer, or RAW (FF auto) to let the print processor decide.

Note The Print Test Page button can be used at any time to test a change in printer configuration.

Ports Tab

The Ports tab is used for a number of different activities. First, you can use it to view the port with which the printer and print device are associated and what kind of print device it is.

From this tab, you can also change the port associated with a given printer. For example, if the LPT1 port fails and you move the print device to the LPT2 port, you only need to change the port designation; you don't have to create a new printer.

The port associations listed here can also be used to redirect print output from one printer to another. For example, if the printer stalls for some reason—perhaps because of a failed port, broken printer, or problem print job—the output of the printer can be redirected from the current printer to another printer, such as a remote printer (see Figure 11.9).

Note It would be good idea to test this type of redirection before implementing it. If the spooling has been done in extended metafile format (EMF), the print job will print correctly. If not, the remote print device needs to be identical to the printer you are redirecting from.

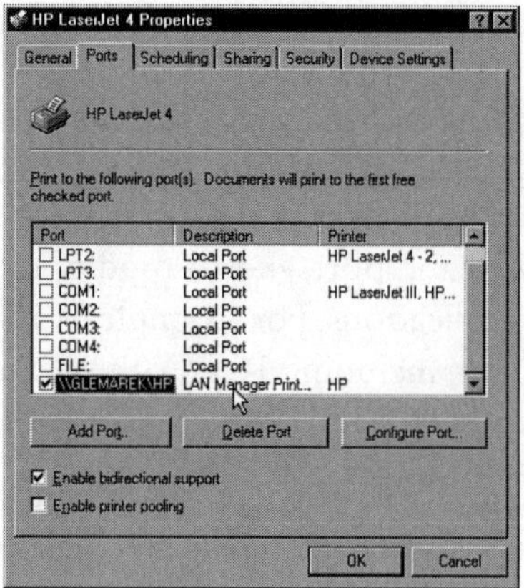

FIG. 11.9 ⇒
Here, the HP LaserJet 4 has been redirected from LPT1 to a remote printer HP on a server named Glemarek.

Use the Add Port button to add additional ports, such as a network port IP address for an LPD-enabled print device. For example, if you need to redirect print jobs from an existing printer to a network printer, use Add Port to add the remote printer to the list of ports, then select it from the list on the Ports tab. Use the Delete Port button to delete ports that you no longer need. Use the Configure Port button to modify the LPT transmission retry value, COM port settings, and so on.

Bidirectional Support

When the print device associated with the printer you installed supports the sending of setting and status information back to the printer, it is said to provide *bidirectional support.* Any extra information about the print process that you can get will be helpful in troubleshooting. If the print device supports this feature, select Enable Bidirectional Support.

Print Pools

One of the most useful configuration activities you can perform from the Ports tab is the creation of a *printer pool.* A printer pool represents one printer (queue or software interface) associated with two or more print devices. In other words, the same printer driver and management window is used to interact with two or more print devices that are compatible with that printer driver. This type of arrangement is particularly efficient on a network with a high volume of printing. Print jobs sent to the pool will print on the next available print device, thus reducing the time that jobs stay in queue. In addition, you need to manage only one printer rather than several.

As shown in Figure 11.10, three print devices are available for use on a print server computer. An HP LaserJet 4 is connected to LPT1, another HP LaserJet 4 is connected to LPT2, and an HP LaserJet III is connected to COM1. Three separate printers—one for each print device—could have been created; however, this does not stop users from favoring one printer over another. For example, users may decide not to use the HPIII printer because of its slower performance. Consequently, print jobs may get stacked up on the other two printers.

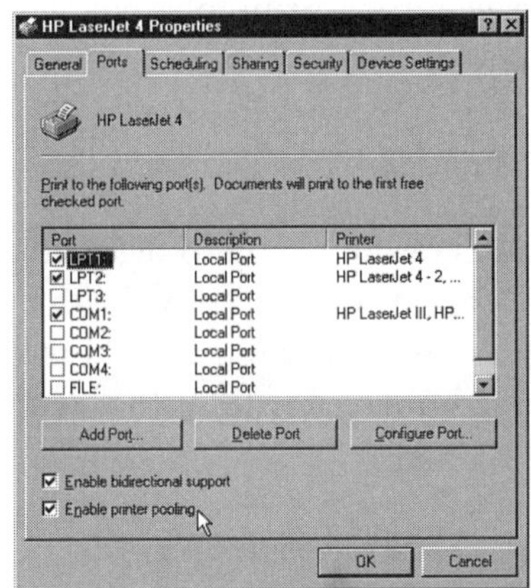

FIG. 11.10 ⇒ Three printers have been configured as a printer pool in this example.

By associating one printer with all three devices, users have only one shared printer choice to make and their print jobs will be serviced by any of the configured print devices. However, the user will not know to which printing device the job will be printed. For this reason, you should physically position all printing devices in the printer pool in the same location.

To set up a print pool, use these steps:

1. Choose Enable Printer Pooling on the Ports tab.
2. Check the ports connected to the print devices that you want as part of the pool.
3. Click OK.

Caution
Make sure that the print device you associate with the printer in the printer pool supports that print driver. If it does not, print output may be unintelligible.

Printer pools can be combined with other printers to produce a variety of output control options for the print manager. For example, three shared printers are created: one for Developers, one for Accountants, and one for Managers. Permissions are configured so that members of each group can print only to their specified printer; however, it is imperative that any of the Manager's print jobs get printed as quickly as possible.

The Manager's printer is configured into a print pool by associating it with the other two print devices. Now, Developers and Accountants each have one print device that services their print jobs, but all of the Manager's print jobs can be printed on any of three printers.

Scheduling Tab

The Scheduling tab, besides enabling you to define the time when the printer can service jobs, lets you set a priority for the printer and define additional spool settings, as shown in Figure 11.11. All three of these option settings assist a print administrator to further refine how and when print jobs are serviced.

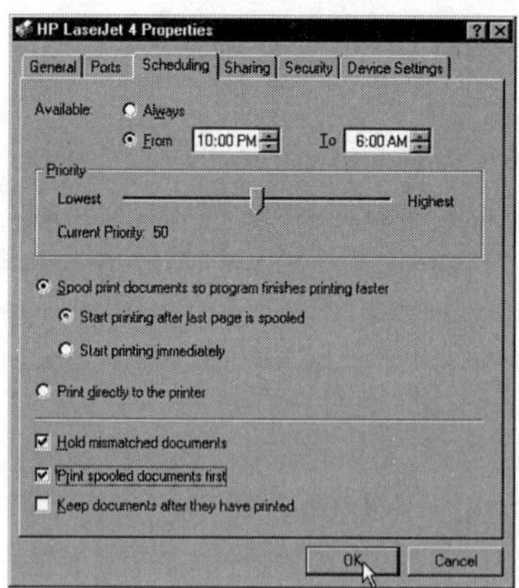

FIG. 11.11 ⇒
This printer begins sending print jobs to the print device after 10 P.M. It also waits until the entire job is spooled before it sends it, and prints jobs that have finished spooling ahead of jobs that are still spooling.

Available Time

Defining the time the printer can service jobs is fairly straightforward. Select the Available: From option button and select the time range you want. Print jobs sent to this printer will still be spooled, but will not print until the designated time.

For example, suppose that you have a color LaserJet print device to which several different groups of users send print jobs. One group, Graphics, tends to send very large graphics files that cause the other group's print jobs to wait in the spooler. You could create a separate printer for that print device and assign only the Graphics group print access. Then, you could set the printing time to print at off-peak hours. The Graphics group's print jobs will then wait in queue until the print time for their printer is reached.

Priority

When a priority is configured for a printer, the priority really is being set for all print jobs received by that printer. The printer priority can be set from 1 (lowest) to 99 (highest).

Setting a priority on a printer really only makes sense when you want documents that are sent to the *same* print device to have different priorities to that device. The key to making a priority effective is to associate two or more printers with the *same* print device. This is the exact opposite of creating a printer pool in which only *one* printer is associated with *two or more* print devices.

After you have created and associated a number of printers with one print device, the priority for each printer is configured from the Scheduling tab by using the sliding bar under Priority.

The priority theory can be illustrated as follows. Three groups, Managers, Developers, and Accountants, all use the same HP LaserJet 5Si network print device. Accountants send large spreadsheets to the printer, while Developers send small to medium source files. Managers, on the other hand, always want their documents to print as soon as possible.

To solve this printing scenario, create three *printers* and associate each with the *same* HP LaserJet 5Si print device. Set permissions so that each group can print only to their respective printer and then set the priority for each printer, as follows:

99 (highest) for the printer used by Managers

50 (medium) for the printer used by Accountants

1 (lowest) for the printer used by Developers

Because the Managers' printer has been given the highest priority, their print jobs will print ahead of the Accountants' and Developers' print jobs. Likewise, because the Accountants' printer has been given a medium priority, their print jobs will print ahead of Developers' print jobs. Because the Developers' printer has the lowest priority, their print jobs will always wait until Managers' and Accountants' print jobs finish printing.

Key Concept

Priorities will not affect a job that has begun printing. If a Developer's print job has begun printing, a Manager's print job will wait until it is finished. However, any subsequent Developers' print jobs will wait until Managers' and Accountants' print jobs have completed.

Other Spool Options

There are several other options that can be used to determine how jobs are spooled. These options, in combination with print pools and priorities, give the print administrator many choices for affecting how, when, and where print jobs are printed.

The first option is Spool Print Documents So Program Finishes Printing Faster. This option is set by default, and simply means that print requests will be spooled in the Printers folder instead of being sent directly to the printer, resulting in a faster return to the application for the user.

If you choose Spool Print Documents So Program Finishes Printing Faster, two secondary options are available. Start Printing Immediately—set by default—indicates that the print job will be sent to the print device for printing as soon as enough information has been spooled. Printing, of course, will be faster overall. The other option, Start Printing After Last Page is Spooled, indicates that the print job will not be sent to the print device for printing until the entire job has been spooled. When used with printers of different priorities, this option can be effectively used to prevent large documents from "hogging" the print device. Smaller documents will be printed first, because they will be spooled first.

The other option is to Print Directly to the Printer. In this case, the print job is not spooled. It decreases printing time because the rendered print job is sent directly to the print device. However, the user will wait until the print job is complete before control is returned to the application.

Did you ever experience the problem of sending a legal size print job to a print device that only had a letter size tray? The print job will hang the print device. The Hold Mismatched Documents option is designed to prevent that from happening by comparing the format of the print job with the configuration of the printer. If they do not match, the print job will be held in queue and will not be allowed to print while other print jobs in the queue proceed.

The Print Spooled Documents First option allows print jobs that have completed spooling to print ahead of those that are still spooling, even if their priority is lower. When used with the option Start Printing After Last Page is Spooled, it virtually assures that smaller print jobs will print ahead of larger print jobs. If no print jobs have finished spooling, larger jobs will print ahead of smaller jobs.

When a print job finishes printing, the spooler deletes the print job from the queue (the printers folder), which deletes it from the printer management window. If you want to keep the document in queue to see its complete status, to keep open the option of resubmitting the job, or to redirect it to another printer if it prints incorrectly, choose the option Keep Documents After They Have Printed. After the print job is complete, it is held in the spooler rather than being deleted, and its status is displayed. For example, if you have an end-of-month report that is difficult to reproduce and you want to resubmit it, use this option to keep the job in the spooler. On the other hand, the jobs do remain in the spooler folder, taking up space, and it becomes the responsibility of the print administrator to remove these jobs when they are no longer needed.

Device Settings Tab

The Device Settings tab is used to assign forms to paper trays, indicate the amount of memory installed in the print device, specify font cartridges, and configure other device-specific settings, such as soft font or halftone settings.

Configuring these options is as easy as selecting the option you want to configure and choosing a setting from the list box displayed in the lower portion of the dialog box. The options available, and their settings, depend on the print device (or the printer) you installed. For example, while an HP LaserJet 4 has only one paper tray, an HP LaserJet 5Si may have several, including an envelope feed. The Device Settings tab will reflect these device features.

Note Some printers offer page protection as a feature, and this option will be displayed on the Device Settings tab. Page protection ensures that the print device prints each page in memory before creating the output page. If you regularly send print jobs whose pages are composed of complex text and graphics, enabling this option helps ensure that the print device prints the page successfully instead of possibly breaking the page up as it prints it.

Managing the Printer and Its Documents

Double-clicking a printer icon in the Printers dialog box displays its Print Management window. There are four menu options from which to choose: Printer, Document, View, and Help. View and Help are fairly self-explanatory. Most of your time will be spent using the Printer and Document options.

Printers Drop-Down Menu

From the Printer drop-down menu, you can pause the printer, change the default printer for the computer, manage sharing and permissions, purge all documents from the spooler, and manage printer properties. In addition, you can set document defaults that apply to all print jobs sent to the printer. Among the options that can be set are the paper size, paper tray, number of copies, orientation, and resolution settings.

Document Drop-Down Menu

From the Document drop-down menu, you can pause, resume, restart, and cancel print jobs. Each print job also has individual properties that can be set much like the properties for the printer itself.

Individual print jobs can have their properties set just like printers. However, the most important options, such as scheduling a time and priority for the job, are available (see Figure 11.12). Only users who have Full Control or Manage Documents permissions, or the owner of the document, can modify the print job's properties.

Display a print job's properties by highlighting the document in the Printer Management window and then by selecting Document, Properties or by double-clicking the print job.

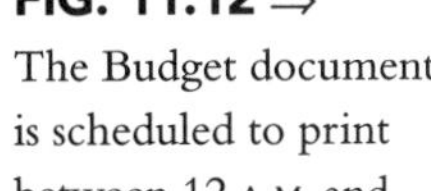

FIG. 11.12 ⇒

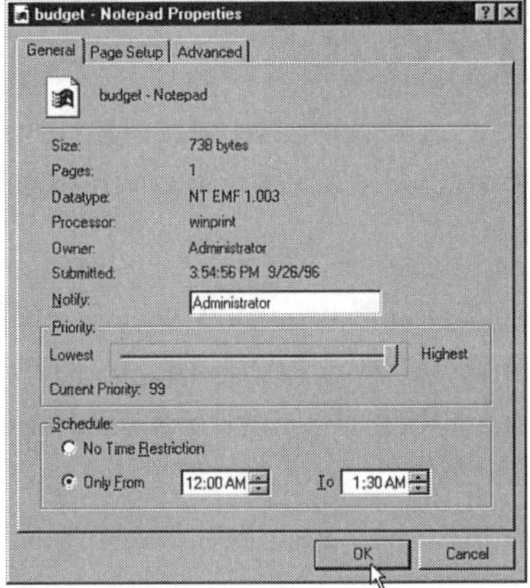

The Budget document is scheduled to print between 12 A.M. and 1:30 A.M. with the highest priority.

The General tab displays statistics about the print job, such as its size, number of pages, data type, print processor, its owner, and when it was submitted. In addition, you can specify a user account to send a message to when the print job is complete.

You can set an individual priority for the job here like you did for the printer; however, the priority selected overrides the printer priority. If there is one particular large print job that has been sent to a low priority printer that needs to be printed as soon as possible, you can set its priority higher from this tab. The priority change only affects the specific print job, other jobs will use the priority setting of the printer (print queue).

Finally, time restrictions can be set for the individual print jobs. Using Figure 11.12 as an example, suppose the Budget document is a large job that has been sent to the low priority Developers' printer. Other jobs undoubtedly have been sent to the Managers and Accountants printers, which have higher priorities. Budget's individual property settings are being set from this document properties sheet to ensure that it will print with the highest priority between 12 A.M. and 1:30 A.M.

The Page Setup and Advanced tabs let you set additional options for the particular document, such as the paper size, paper tray, number of copies, orientation, and resolution settings.

Troubleshooting Printing

This troubleshooting discussion contains some extremely basic steps to follow when the printing process fails. The following bullets outline this troubleshooting checklist:

- Check to see if the print device is turned on and online.
- Check to see whether the physical print device connection is good. Swap out cables, and check the network card and IP address. Also verify the configured MAC address.
- Verify that the printer driver installed is compatible with the print device. Verify that the correct version of print driver is installed (3.1, 3.5/3.51, 4.0, or 95). Also verify that the print driver for the correct platform is installed (I386, Alpha, MIPS, or PowerPC).
- Confirm that the printer is available and has been selected. Verify that sharing has been enabled and that the permissions allow printing to take place for the users affected.
- Verify that the appropriate print port has been selected and configured by printing a test page.
- Monitor network traffic in the case of remote printing to verify that print jobs are being routed correctly and not being dropped.
- Check the amount of disk space available for spooling. Recall that the default spool directory is <winnt root>\SYSTEM32\Spool \Printers. The installation partition often contains only the Windows NT files and is kept purposely small. If there is not enough space for the spooled files, printing will fail. Either add more disk space (extend the partition if it is NTFS), or move the spool folder to a disk with adequate space by editing the Registry. Disk compression can also be enabled for the spool directory; however, this can have a negative effect on printing performance for large print jobs. Recall that the Registry location to change the default spool folder is HKEY_LOCAL_MACHINE\System\CurrentControlSet\Control\Print\Printers.
- Determine whether the printing problem is due to a specific application error, or occurs within all applications. Some MS-DOS and Windows 16-bit applications may require their own print drivers installed to successfully print their documents.

- Determine whether the printing problem is due to a non-updated print driver installed on a Windows 95 client. Recall that there is not a version checking done between a Windows NT print server and a Windows 95 client; the update must be done manually on the Windows 95 client.
- Resubmit the print job to print to a file and then copy the file to a printer port. If the job prints successfully, the problem may be related to the spooler or transmission process. If not, the problem is probably related to the application or printer driver.

Another source of help for troubleshooting printing problems is the built-in Windows NT Help program. It also provides a set of troubleshooting steps and tips to help resolve printing-related problems. Access help for printing problems by following these steps:

1. Select Help, Help Topics from the menu of any window opened through My Computer or Network Neighborhood; or select the Start button and choose Help from the Start Menu.
2. Choose the Contents tab in the Help dialog box.
3. Double-click the contents entry titled Troubleshooting.
4. Select the topic If You Have Trouble Printing.
5. Find the problem you are having and click it.
6. Help will guide you through a series of questions and suggestions to help resolve the problem.
7. Exit Help when you are finished by closing the Help window.

Additional Considerations

As noted earlier, most printing problems stem from an improper print driver, inadequate disk space, incorrect port or address settings, or restrictive permissions. Also, recall that most older MS-DOS-based applications, and some Windows-based applications, require that their own printer driver be installed. Be sure to consider these possibilities as well when troubleshooting.

Windows-based applications will print just like they did under Windows. Settings saved in WIN.INI or CONFIG.SYS are copied into the Windows NT Registry and will be used for these applications printing under Windows NT. Applications that produce PostScript-specific graphics will probably print incorrectly or not at all. If no default printer has been selected, these applications produce an out-of-memory error message when loading or will not allow selection of fonts.

If print jobs stall in a printer, or no one is able to print to it any longer, the spooler probably has stalled. The spooler can be purged of its documents by starting the Print Manager for that printer, selecting the Print drop-down menu, and choosing Purge Print Documents. The spooler service can also be stopped and restarted through the Services applet in the Control Panel to purge the specific job that is stalled.

If your print server and clients happen to be of different or mixed platforms, and you want the print server to download the appropriate driver to all the Windows NT Workstations, you need to install the appropriate platform drivers on the print server. A given print server may have multiple platform drivers installed for just this purpose.

For example, suppose that your print server is a RISC-based DEC Alpha computer. The Windows NT clients connecting to shared printers on the print server are Intel-based computers. You must install the Windows NT 4.0 Alpha printer driver for the print server to interact successfully with the print device. In addition, the Windows NT 4.0 Intel print driver must be installed on the print server for it to automatically download the Intel print driver to Intel clients. When an Intel client accesses the shared printer, the Intel driver is downloaded to them. The Alpha print server, in turn, uses the Alpha driver to manage the print job on the print device.

Table 11.4 lists the folders in which the drivers will be located for Windows 95 and the different Windows NT versions. The printer driver location starts with <Winnt root>\System32\Spool\Drivers\.

Table 11.4 Windows NT Printer Driver Locations

Location	Description
Win40	Windows 95 Drivers
w32x86\0	Windows NT 3.1 Intel Drivers
w32x86\1	Windows NT 3.5/3.51 Intel Drivers
w32x86\2	Windows NT 4.0 Intel Drivers
Alpha\0	Windows NT 3.1 Alpha Drivers
Alpha\1	Windows NT 3.5/3.51 Alpha Drivers

Location	Description
Alpha\2	Windows NT 4.0 Alpha Drivers
MIPS\0	Windows NT 3.1 MIPS Drivers
MIPS\1	Windows NT 3.1 5/3.51 MIPS Drivers
MIPS\2	Windows NT 4.0 MIPS Drivers
PPC\0	Windows NT 3.1 PPC Drivers
PPC\1	Windows NT 3.5/3.51 PPC Drivers
PPC\2	Windows NT 4.0 PPC Drivers

Taking the Disc Test

If you have read and understood the material in this chapter, you are ready to test your knowledge. Insert the CD-ROM that comes with this book and run the self-test software, as described in Appendix K, "Using the Self-Test Software."

From Here...

The next chapter discusses the disk-management utilities that are included with Windows NT.

Chapter Prerequisite

You should be familiar with Windows NT basic capabilities as outlined in Chapter 2, "Understanding Microsoft Windows NT 4.0." You should already have a cursory knowledge of device drivers, threads, interrupts, and swap files.

Windows NT 4.0 Architecture

An integral part of understanding Windows NT is a discussion of the internal architecture of the NT operating system. Several resources are available to you for an in-depth coverage of this topic, including the Windows NT Resource Kit. The Windows NT Resource Kit's basic overview will add to your knowledge of NT security, service support, and other topics covered in this book.

The topics covered in this chapter include the following:

- User and kernel application modes
- Executive services
- Hardware abstraction layer
- Memory management
- Cache management

Understanding Modes

The Windows NT 4.0 architecture consists of two primary processing areas: User or Application Mode and Kernel or Privileged Processor Mode. The User mode, as it implies, provides operating system support primarily for user applications and the environment. Figure 12.1 shows this basic architecture.

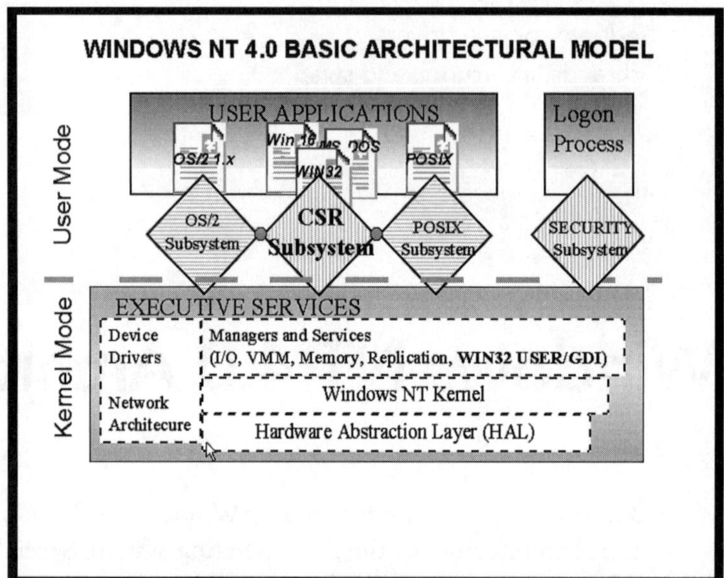

FIG. 12.1⇒
The User mode basic architectural model is for user applications.

The kernel mode provides operating system support services for just about everything else, including kernel processing, memory management, hardware access, and so forth. These kernel mode services are referred to as the *Executive Services.*

Understanding User (Application) Mode

The User mode of the operating system provides application processing support. Applications in Windows NT run in one of three subsystems—the WIN32, OS/2, and POSIX subsystems—provided by the operating system. The primary subsystem, which is loaded at boot time, is WIN32. WIN32 supports both 32-bit Windows and Win95 applications as well as 16-bit DOS and Windows applications.

Note IBM designed and implemented OS/2 to support 32-bit applications in an object-oriented environment. POSIX stands for "Portable Operating System Interface for UNIX" and was originally an IEEE effort to standardize the portability of applications across UNIX-based environments.

The OS/2 subsystem provides support for 1.x character-based OS/2 applications. POSIX provides support for POSIX-based applications. Any application program calls from these two subsystems that read/write to the display are forwarded to the WIN32 subsystem. Any other calls to drivers or other executive services are communicated directly to the kernel mode.

In NT version 3.51, the USER and Graphics Device Interface (GDI) portions of the operating system were included in the WIN32 subsystem, thus, in User mode. The USER is the window manager and responds to user input on-screen. The GDI processes graphics primitives such as pixels, lines, fills, and so on. The GDI also performs graphics rendering for print files.

If an application needed either the user or GDI for processing, it would have to create an *InterProcess Communication* (IPC) to it. This process would involve a context switch from user mode to kernel mode (ring 0 to ring 3 of the processor) as well as 64K buffering. Then, another context switch would take place back to user mode. This, obviously, involves some time and decreases overall performance.

NT version 4.0 moves the USER and GDI into the kernel mode. This move significantly improves application performance by eliminating the 64K buffer and leaving only a kernel transition. You can see the benefit particularly in those applications that involve direct draw to the screen such as Pinball as well as in multimedia applications such as QuickTime.

Understanding Kernel (Privileged Processor) Mode

Kernel mode provides support for all major operating system functions. The kernel controls access to memory and the execution of privileged instructions. All kernel mode processes run in the protected mode of the processor—ring 0. As such, the applications running in User mode are effectively buffered from direct access to hardware. Thus, 16-bit applications that are designed to access hardware directly will not run successfully under Windows NT. You must rewrite these to "talk" to the NT kernel mode services before you can run them under Windows NT.

The kernel mode consists of three parts:

- Executive Services
- Windows NT kernel
- Hardware Abstraction Layer (HAL)

Executive Services

Executive Services make up most of the kernel mode functionality. Executive Services provides support for processes, threads, memory management, I/O, IPC, and security. It is here that most NT services and process managers execute. This layer provides device driver support, including NT's network architecture support drivers and protocols. This layer is written in C code to help make NT portable across platforms. It is this C code that is recompiled for each of platforms that NT supports such as Dec Alpha, PowerPC, and MIPS.

Windows NT Kernel

The NT kernel provides support for thread management and context switching, synchronization among services and processes in the Executive Services layer, multiprocessor load balancing, and exception and interrupt handling.

Hardware Abstraction Layer (HAL)

The HAL provides hardware platform support. It isolates specific platform details from the Executive and the NT kernel. It is largely due to the HAL that those 16-bit applications that like to talk directly to hardware are unable to run. It can be said, therefore, that users' applications are effectively isolated from base hardware interaction under Windows NT.

Understanding Windows NT Virtual Memory Management

One Executive Services manager is the Virtual Memory Manager (see Figure 12.2). The memory architecture of Windows NT is a 32-bit, demand-based flat model. This model allows the Virtual Memory Manager to access up to 4G of RAM—far more than the amount of physical RAM installed in most computers.

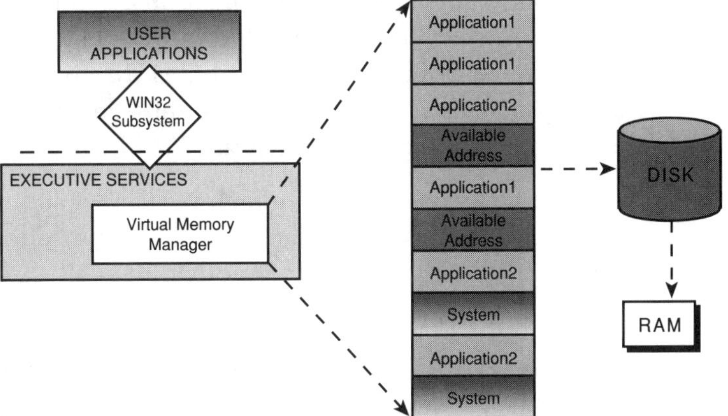

FIG. 12.2 ⇒
Virtual Memory Manager manages up to 4G of memory.

Those readers who recall Windows' swap file model will recall that there were two types of swap files: permanent and temporary. Both swap files managed available RAM in 4K pieces by using an internal Windows algorithm called the LRU (Least Recently Used). Essentially, the LRU assumes that the piece of code in memory that was least recently accessed by a process is the best choice of memory to be swapped to disk when more RAM is needed. On computers with the minimal required RAM for Windows, a considerable amount of swapping takes place when several applications are open.

The main difference between permanent and temporary swap files is that a permanent swap file has a preallocated amount of space reserved on the disk. Temporary swap files begin at 2M and then "grow" as needed to a predetermined amount. Thus, though a permanent swap file actually provided better swap performance because the space was always there and available, it also reduced the amount of available disk storage. Similarly, though temporary swap files did not reduce the amount of disk storage available up front, more resource was expended in finding additional storage space when the swap file needed to "grow."

Windows NT combines the "best" of these swap files. The NT pagefile (`PAGEFILE.SYS`) is created when NT is installed and generally defaults to an initial, preallocated size (à la permanent swap files) of 12 plus physical RAM and a maximum size of three times physical RAM (depending on the amount of disk space available). So, on a computer with 16M of physical RAM, the default initial pagefile size would be 28M (12+16M) and the maximum size would be about 48M (3*16M). NT will boot with the initial size pagefile available. The pagefile subsequently grows as applications are loaded and demands for physical RAM increase.

It is important to realize that though NT allows addressing of up to 4G of physical RAM, the virtual memory manager can allocate up to 2G of *virtual* storage for *each* application. Another 2G is allocated for all system (kernel mode) processing.

The Virtual Memory Manager addresses application memory as follows:

1. When an application is loaded, the Virtual Memory Manager assigns it virtual memory addresses in physical RAM.
2. The data is then moved in pages out of physical RAM and into the pagefile.
3. As the application needs the data, it calls for the virtual memory addresses.
4. The Virtual Memory Manager moves those pages on demand into available locations in physical RAM.

This process of assigning virtual addresses to the application effectively hides the organization of physical RAM from the application. The various pages of the application may wind up in noncontiguous space in physical RAM (that is, in sectors that may be distributed at different locations on the disk rather than next to each other). But, because the virtual memory manager is providing the application with its addresses, it really doesn't care. This allows NT to use available physical RAM most efficiently and provide an overall performance increase for application processing.

Windows NT Cache Manager

The final aspect of the NT Architecture that you will examine is the NT Cache Manager. As you might expect by now, the tried-and-true Windows and DOS SMARTDrive disk cache manager is no more. It has been replaced by an operating-system-driven Cache Manager that runs as part of the Executive Services and, thus, in kernel mode. Its actual physical size depends on the amount of physical RAM installed. NT's cache competes for RAM with other applications and processes and thus is automatically sized by the Cache Manager working in sync with the Memory Manager.

The Cache Manager provides an intelligent read-ahead/write-back operation. It predicts the next read location based on the locations of the last three reads. It also performs lazy writes—that is, using the processor when it is not being accessed by any other process to update the file on disk while maintaining data in memory for quick access.

Taking the Disc Test

If you have read and understood the material in the chapter, you are ready to test your knowledge. Insert the CD-ROM that comes with this book and run the self-test software as described in Appendix K, "Using the Self-Test Software."

From Here...

The next chapter covers the Windows NT boot sequence. An understanding of the boot sequence is critical in solving many types of problems.

Chapter Prerequisite

You should read Chapter 3, "Windows NT Server 4.0 Setup," and Chapter 4, "Configuring Windows NT Server 4.0," before reading this chapter. Also, it is very useful to have actually installed Windows NT Server 4.0.

13

The Windows NT 4.0 Boot Sequence

Recovering from serious errors often entails changing the way Windows NT boots. Understanding the sequence of events and knowing from where input information is being gathered are critical pieces of knowledge. This chapter explains the boot process in detail.

Understanding the NT Boot Process

The Windows NT 4.0 boot process, while a bit more complicated during the operating system load phase, is still pretty much like booting most any other operating system. There are five basic steps:

1. Power On SelfTest (POST). This occurs with every computer when you first power it on. This is the BIOS check of installed hardware, interrupts, I/O, memory, and so forth.
2. The Master Boot Record (MBR) is read to determine which operating system (OS) governs the boot process.
3. The OS system file recorded in the MBR is loaded, and the operating system is initialized, hardware is initialized, and drivers and configuration files are loaded.
4. The OS kernel is loaded.
5. Environment settings are initialized.

Windows NT 4.0 follows these same basic steps with some variation for Steps 3, 4, and 5.

The Windows NT boot process has two primary phases: Boot and Load.

The *boot phase* consists of the pre-boot sequence, during which the operating system is initialized, hardware is detected, and the Executive Services is loaded. When Windows NT is installed, it replaces the MS-DOS entries in the Master Boot Record with its own system file NTLDR. Along with NTLDR, the following boot files are read during the boot phase: BOOT.INI, NTDETECT.COM, NTOSKRNL.EXE, and NTBOOTDD.SYS (all files with any of the hidden, read-only or system file attributes are stored in the root directory of the boot partition), NTOSKRNL.EXE and HAL.DLL (stored in the NT system directory), and the HKEY_LOCAL_MACHINE\SYSTEM hive.

The entire boot sequence is:

1. NTLDR loads a mini-OS and changes memory to a flat 32-bit model.
2. NTLDR next reads the BOOT.INI file to display the Operating System Menu on the screen.
3. If the user chooses NT, or that is the default, NTLDR loads NTDETECT.COM, which determines what hardware is installed in

the computer and then uses this information to build the HKEY_LOCAL_MACHINE\HARDWARE hive.

If the system boots NT from a SCSI drive whose SCSI adapter BIOS is disabled, NTLDR will load NTBOOTDD.SYS to initialize and access that device.

If the user chooses MS-DOS or Microsoft Windows (for Windows 95), NTLDR loads BOOTSECT.DOS, which records the boot sector location of the alternate OS system files and loads them. OS initialization then proceeds as normal for that OS.

4. NTLDR next loads NTOSKRNL.EXE, which initializes the Executive Services of the operating system. Think of this as NT's COMMAND.COM.
5. NTLDR then loads the HAL.DLL and the SYSTEM hive and any drivers that need to initialize at boot time to continue the building of the Executive Services.
6. At this point, the screen displays progress dots across the top indicating the loading and initialization of drivers. The user is also prompted to press the spacebar to invoke the Last Known Good boot configuration. Control is passed to NTOSKRNL.EXE and the load phase begins.

   During the *load phase*, the rest of the kernel and user modes of the operating system are set up. The kernel is initialized, control set information is initialized, NT services are loaded, and the WIN32 subsystem starts.
7. The blue screen is displayed, indicating that the kernel is initializing, drivers are initialized, and the CurrentControlSet is created and copied to the CLONE control set.
8. The Services load phase begins with the starting of SMSS.EXE, the session manager. The session manager runs the programs listed in HKEY_LOCAL_MACHINE\SYSTEM\CURRENTCONTROLSET\CONTROL\ SESSION MANAGER\BootExecute, usually containing at least AUTOCHK.EXE (which performs a CHKDSK of each partition). If a drive has been flagged to be converted to NTFS, then the drive is added to BootExecute and conversion takes place at this time. Next, the pagefile is configured, as defined in HKEY_LOCAL_MACHINE\SYSTEM\CURRENTCONTROLSET\CONTROL\ SESSION MANAGER\MEMORY MANAGEMENT parameters.

Finally, the required subsystem, defined in HKEY_LOCAL_MACHINE\SYSTEM\CURRENTCONTROLSET\CONTROL\ SESSION MANAGER\SUBSYSTEMS\Required, is loaded. The only required subsystem at this time is WIN32.

9. With the loading of the WIN32 subsystem, WINLOGON.EXE, the service that governs the logon process, is loaded and started. WINLOGON, in turn, starts the Local Security Authority (LSASS.EXE), which displays the CTRL-ALT-DEL screen, and the Service Controller (SCREG.EXE), which starts services that are configured to start automatically, such as the Computer Browser, Workstation, and Server.
10. Finally, the user enters in the username and password and logs in to the computer or domain. If the logon is successful, the CLONE control set is copied to Last Known Good. If the boot is not successful, the user can power off or shut down and choose Last Known Good to load the last values that resulted in a successful logon.

The Boot Process for RISC-based Computers.

The boot process for RISC-based computers is essentially the same as for Intel machines. During the boot phase, the resident ROM firmware of the system selects the boot device from a preference table stored in RAM, and then controls the selection of the boot partition and the appropriate OS file. In this case, the firmware finds and loads OSLOADER.EXE, which is NT's operating system file for RISC-based computers.

OSLOADER, in turn, finds and loads NTOSKRNL.EXE and then the load phase continues as usual.

Note that, because the computer's firmware controls the initialization of hardware and the selection of the boot partition, there is no need for the NTLDR, NTDETECT.COM, BOOT.INI, or BOOTSECT.DOS files on a RISC-based computer.

BOOT.INI

The BOOT.INI file is a read-only system, ASCII text file that is created by NT during installation. BOOT.INI is stored in the root directory of the primary boot partition of the computer. It contains the information that NT uses to display the Boot Menu when the computer is booted (refer to Step 2). It is divided into two sections: Boot Loader and Operating System.

The *Boot Loader* section contains the default operating system and timeout values, and the *Operating System* section displays operating system choices and the location of the system files. It can be modified using any ASCII text editor, after first turning off the system and read-only properties.

Note You can locate the BOOT.INI file, using Windows Explorer, Windows Find, or My Computer. To change its properties, right-click the file and choose Properties. Deselect Read-only and System. Be sure to re-select these attributes when you finish modifying the file.

In the following example, the default timeout value is 30 seconds. If the user does not make a selection during that time, the default operating system will be loaded. Notice that the unusual-looking path to the WINNT40 directory matches a line under the Operating Systems section:

```
[Boot Loader]
Timeout=30
Default=multi(0)disk(0)rdisk(0)partition(4)\WINNT40
[Operating Systems]
multi(0)disk(0)rdisk(0)partition(4)\WINNT40="Windows NT
➥Workstation Version 4.00"
multi(0)disk(0)rdisk(0)partition(4)\WINNT40="Windows NT
➥Workstation Version 4.00 [VGA mode]"
   /basevideo /sos
C:\="Microsoft Windows"
```

That unusual-looking path is called an *ARC path* (Advanced RISC Computer). The best way to describe an ARC path is as a hardware path. By now, everyone has used a DOS path. It indicates the drive and directory location of a specific file. An ARC path indicates the *physical* disk location of the NT system files—the specific partition on a specific physical disk connected to a specific physical controller.

Referring back to the preceding example, the ARC path `multi(0)disk(0)rdisk(0)partition(4)\WINNT40` can be interpreted as described next.

The first value can be either *multi* or *scsi*. This really has no direct relation as to whether the controller is a SCSI controller. NT chooses SCSI if the controller does *not* have its card BIOS enabled. Otherwise, the choice is MULTI. The number that appears in parentheses is the ordinal number of the controller.

The next two values are disk and rdisk. If the first value choice was SCSI, then the *disk* number represents the SCSI bus number and is incremented accordingly (the physical disk attached to the card), and the *rdisk* value is ignored. If the first value is *multi*, then the disk value is ignored and the rdisk value representing the physical disk on the adapter is incremented accordingly.

Next, the *partition value* indicates on which disk partition the directory *\WINNT40* can be found. Recall that this is the NT system directory that you selected during installation.

To tie it all together for this example, during boot, if the user lets the timeout value expire, or specifically selects NT from the menu, NT can find the Windows NT system files (specifically, the location of the NTOSKRNL.EXE file) in the WINNT40 directory, on the fourth partition of the first disk, attached to the first controller in this computer. If the user selects "Microsoft Windows" from the menu, then NTLDR loads BOOTSECT.DOS and proceeds to boot (in this case) Windows 95.

The Boot Menu

The Operating System's section values are what build the boot menu that you see during startup. Each ARC path has a text-menu selection associated with it that is enclosed in quotes. By default, there are always two entries for NT and one for the other operating system, usually MS-DOS (C:\=M MS-DOS")or Windows 95 (C:\="Microsoft Windows"). The second entry for NT represents a fall-back entry that loads NT with a generic VGA driver. If you make changes to the display settings that make it difficult or impossible to read the screen, selecting this choice during startup ignores those settings and loads a generic VGA driver so that you can see the screen and rectify the problem. This is accomplished through the /basevideo switch.

Tip

NT provides a variety of switches that can be added to these or additional NT boot entries to modify the way NT boots. For example, you might want to create another entry in your boot menu that displays all the driver files that are loaded during boot. You can copy the first line in the Operating Systems section to a new line, modify the text to read **Windows NT Workstation 4.0 Driver Load**, and add the /SOS switch to the end of the line. Thus, if you are having trouble booting, or aren't sure whether a particular driver is being located, you can select this choice and these items will be displayed during the load phase (refer to Step 6, earlier in this chapter).

Table 13.1 contains a description of the more practical boot switches that can be used in the Boot.ini file. An exhaustive list can be found in the Windows NT Resource Kit.

Table 1z3.1 NT Boot Switches for BOOT.INI

Switch	Description
/Basevideo	Boots NT with the standard VGA display driver in 640 by 480 resolution.
/SOS	Displays driver file names instead of progress dots during the load phase.
/Crashdebug	Used for troubleshooting, it enables Automatic Recovery and Restart mode for the NT boot process, and displays a system memory dump during the blue screen portion of the load phase.
/Maxmem:n	Specifies the maximum amount of RAM, in megabytes, that NT will recognize and work with. This is helpful when you suspect a bad SIMM or memory chip and you are trying to pinpoint its location.

Understanding Control Sets and the Last Known Good Option

In the HKEY_LOCAL_MACHINE\System hive, there are several control set subkeys. These subkeys are used by NT to boot the system, keep track of configuration changes, and to provide an audit trail of failed boot attempts. In general, there are four control sets: Clone, ControlSet001, ControlSet002, and CurrentControlSet. There is also a subkey called Select, whose parameter values point out which control set is being used for the current settings, default settings, failed settings, and Last Known Good settings. For example, if the value for Current is 0x1, then 1 indicates that CurrentControlSet is being derived from, or mapped to, ControlSet001.

Clone is used by NT during the boot process (refer to Step 7, earlier in the chapter) as a temporary storage area for the boot configuration. Settings from CurrentControlSet are copied into Clone during the load phase. When a user logon results in a successful boot, the configuration settings in

Clone are copied to another control set, such as ControlSet002, and is referred to as the Last Known Good. If the boot attempt is unsuccessful, these values are copied to a different control set number.

ControlSet001 generally is the default control set and produces the CurrentControlSet. As such, by default, it also contains the NT boot configuration.

ControlSet00x represents other control sets. The control set with the highest number increment usually is pointed to in the Select subkey as the Last Known Good configuration. Other control set numbers invariably refer to failed boot configurations.

CurrentControlSet is mapped back to ControlSet001. These settings are copied to Clone during the load phase of the boot process. Whenever an administrator makes a change to the configuration of the computer, such as modifying the virtual memory parameters, adding a new driver, or creating a hardware profile, those changes are saved to CurrentControlSet (and thus to ControlSet001, if that control set is set as the Default in the Select subkey).

Key Concept

During the load phase, the settings in CurrentControlSet (derived from ControlSet001) are copied to Clone and used to determine service order, the driver files to load, startup configurations, hardware profiles, and so forth. If the boot is successful, in other words, it logs in to NT successfully, Clone is copied to the control set designated as the Last Known Good, for example, ControlSet002. If changes made by the administrator result in a failed boot attempt, the failed configuration in Clone is copied to ControlSet002, what used to be the Last Known Good control set becomes ControlSet003, and the user has the option of selecting to boot with the Last Known Good control set.

The Last Known Good control set contains the last boot configuration that resulted in a successful logon to the computer. The user is given the option to use Last Known Good when the load phase begins and the progress dots are displayed on-screen. The user has five seconds within which to press the SPACEBAR to invoke the Last Known Good.

Caution

If the system itself detects a severe or critical device initialization or load error, it will display a message recommending that the user choose Last Known Good as the boot option. Users can choose to bypass this message, but do so at their own risk.

Tip

The Last Known Good enables the server to boot after a failed boot. But remember that a failed boot is one in which a user cannot successfully log on to NT. The user *may be able to* log on successfully, but still have a system that fails to run correctly due to a configuration error. The Last Known Good is not helpful in this situation because it is created as soon as the boot is successful; in other words, as soon as you log on successfully.

Troubleshooting the Boot Process

The most common errors that you are likely to encounter during the boot process are due to corrupt or missing boot files. Recall the boot files needed by NT:

```
NTLDR
BOOT.INI
BOOTSECT.DOS
NTDETECT.COM
NTOSKRNL.EXE
```

If the *NTLDR* file is missing or corrupt, the following message is displayed after the POST:

```
BOOT: Couldn't find NTLDR
Please insert another disk.
```

While there are various reasons for this file to become missing or corrupt, the most common reason is a virus attacking the MBR (Master Boot Record), and a user inadvertently reinstalling MS-DOS onto the computer. If the problem involves a virus, use a virus-protection program to restore the MBR. If this is unsuccessful, you can use the Emergency Repair Disk to reestablish NTLDR in the MBR. The worst case scenario is that you will have to reinstall NT from scratch—which you should try to avoid.

If the problem involves a user reinstalling MS-DOS you need, again, to use the Emergency Repair Disk to reestablish the NTLDR. As previously stated, in the worst case scenario, you will have to reinstall NT.

If *BOOT.INI* is missing or corrupt, NT will look for the default NT system-directory name (usually WINNT) on the boot partition. If NT is installed in a directory other than the default name, or if NT cannot otherwise locate it, the following message is displayed after the prompt for Last Known Good:

```
Windows NT could not start because the following file is missing
➥or corrupt:
\winnt root\system32\ntoskrnl.exe
Please reinstall a copy of the above file.
```

If the ARC path to the NT system file directory is incorrect in the Boot.INI file, NTLDR may display this message:

```
Windows NT could not start because of a computer disk hardware
➥configuration
problem. Could not read from the selected boot disk. Check boot
➥path and
disk hardware. Please check Windows NT ™ documentation about
➥hardware
disk configuration and your hardware reference manuals for
➥additional information.
```

Incorrect paths are relatively easy to fix. Because BOOT.INI is a text file, turn off its System and Read-Only attributes and edit the ARC path by using your favorite text editor.

Caution

The ARC path indicated in the Default parameter in the Boot Loader section of the BOOT.INI *must match* an ARC path for a parameter under the Operating Systems section. If it does not match, the menu displays a phantom selection option called "NT (default)," which may result in the same error message that was discussed for a missing Boot.ini file.

If BOOTSECT.DOS is missing, NTLDR displays the following error message when the user tries to select the other operating system from the boot menu:

```
I/O Error accessing boot sector file
multi(0)disk(0)rdisk(0)partition(1):\bootsect.dos
```

Because this file is unique to each computer, the best way to recover it is to restore the file from the backup you create regularly (!), or to use the Emergency Repair Disk.

If NTDETECT.COM is missing or corrupt, expect the following message after the user selects NT from the boot menu, or the menu times out to NT:

```
NTDETECT v1.0 Checking Hardware...
NTDETECT v1.0 Checking Hardware...
```

Again, recover by using the Emergency Repair Disk, or from a backup.

If NTOSKRNL.EXE is missing or corrupt, NTLDR displays this message after the prompt for Last Known Good:

```
Windows NT could not start because the following file is missing
➥or corrupt:
\winnt root\system32\ntoskrnl.exe
Please reinstall a copy of the above file.
```

As before, this file can be recovered by using the Emergency Repair Disk, or from a file backup.

The Emergency Repair Disk

The Emergency Repair Disk usually is created during the NT installation process (see Chapter 3, "Windows NT Server 4.0 Setup"). However, it can be created (and updated) at any time by running the NT command RDISK.EXE at an NT DOS prompt.

To use the Emergency Repair disk, you first must boot the computer by using a Windows NT Startup disk.

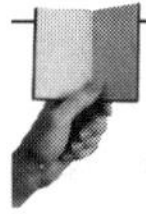

Tip

If you do not have a Windows NT Startup disk, but have access to the original installation files, you can create a Startup disk by typing the command: **WINNT /OX**. Be sure to have three diskettes available.

From the Startup menu, choose Repair. The repair process offers four options:

- Inspect Registry Files   This option prompts the user for replacement of each registry file, including System and SAM.

Caution
The files on the Emergency Repair Disk overwrite the files in the registry. For this reason, this is *not* the best way to recover damaged security or account information. A backup is much more useful for maintaining the integrity of existing account entries.

- Inspect Startup Environment This option checks the BOOT.INI file for an entry for Windows NT. If it doesn't find an entry, it adds one for the next boot attempt.
- Verify Windows NT System Files This option verifies whether the NT system files match those of the original installation files. For this option, you need to have access to the original installation files. This option also looks for and verifies the integrity of the boot files.

Tip
If you updated Windows NT with a service pack, you need to reinstall the service pack after initiating a repair.

- Inspect Boot Sector This option checks the MBR for NTLDR. If it is missing or corrupt, it restores the boot sector.

If you know specifically which file is missing or corrupt, you can replace the file directly from the source files by using the NT EXPAND utility. At an NT prompt, type **EXPAND -R**, followed by the compressed filename. If NT is inoperable on your system, use another NT system to expand the file and then copy it to your computer.

NT Boot Disk

Another useful tool to have in your toolkit is an NT boot disk. This is not a diskette formatted with NTFS. Rather, it is a disk that has been formatted under NT that has copies of the boot files on it.

Tip
You can format a diskette from My Computer. Right-click the A: Drive icon and select Format. Make the appropriate selections and choose OK.

When you format a diskette under NT, NT creates a boot sector on that disk that references NTLDR. Simply copy the five boot files to this disk and voilá, you have an NT boot disk. This disk can be used in a variety of NT computers because it is not unique to each installation. The only file you may need to modify for each computer is the BOOT.INI file. This makes it much easier to replace missing or corrupt boot files.

Taking the Disc Test

If you have read and understood the material in this chapter, you are ready to test your knowledge. Insert the CD-ROM that comes with this book and run the self-test software, as described in the Appendix K, "Using the Self-Test Software."

From Here...

The next few chapters discuss basic networking architectures and Microsoft's implementation of these architectures and protocols. The two most popular networks, TCP/IP and Novell NetWare, are discussed in detail.

Chapter Prerequisite

This chapter has no prerequisites.

14

Networking Essentials

This chapter covers Networking Essentials. Concepts and skills covered include:

- An understanding of networking in general, including protocols, layers, topologies, architectures, and interface specifications.

Understanding Networking

Networks provide a method for computers to communicate with each other and to share resources. In the early days of computing, prior to the availability of networks, when someone wanted to share the information stored in a file with someone else, he or she had to copy the file to some form of media, such as a disk or tape, and physically carry that media to the other person. This process eventually became known as a *Sneaker-Net.*

Sneaker-Net worked for awhile, but eventually, people were spending more of their day walking around than actually working.

The next development was the use of asynchronous communication equipment to transfer files directly from one computer to another. This had several drawbacks, the most significant being speed, with a second drawback being that a communication utility had to be running, to the exclusion of any actual work-related application, while the file was being transferred.

The first true networks were proprietary networks connecting minicomputers and mainframes.

Examining the ISO OSI Model

In 1983, the *International Standards Organization* (ISO) defined a model for networking, called the *Open Systems Interconnection* (OSI) reference model. This model describes the flow of information between the physical network and applications. Networking vendors use the OSI model as a guideline to develop real-world systems.

The OSI reference model defines the communication between the computers in a network as a series of *layers* (see Figure 14.1). Each layer implements a particular functionality, such as routing (network layer) or frame construction (data-link layer). Layers logically communicate with their counterpart on other computers, but in actuality, each layer provides services to the layer above it, and uses the services of the layer below it. The lower layer shields the layers above it from having to know, or deal with, the details handled by the lower layers.

The OSI reference model, like other models, is a set of abstract guidelines only. Actual network implementations may implement a single functional layer in several software layers, or implement many functional layers in a single software component. No actual networking products implement all seven layers of the OSI model.

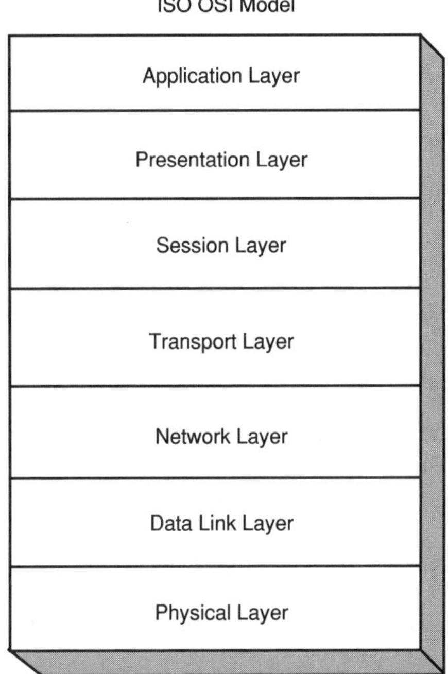

FIG. 14.1 ⇒ The layers of the OSI reference model.

The OSI reference model defines seven layers. The layers are usually pictured with the Physical layer at the bottom, and the Application layer at the top.

The Seven ISO OSI Layers

Each of the layers communicates with its adjacent layers through an *interface*. The sets of rules that the layers use to communicate logically with their counterpart on the other computer in a conversation are called *protocols*.

As data passes through each of the layers, from the Application Layer down to the Physical Layer, it is wrapped with layer-specific information, and is passed to the next lower layer, which wraps its own information around the outside of the data, and so on.

On the recipient computer, each layer removes its layer-specific information before passing the data up to the next layer.

There are seven layers, from bottom to top, as discussed in the following sections:

- Physical
- Data Link
- Network
- Transport
- Session
- Presentation
- Application

Physical Layer

The Physical layer defines the methods used to transfer the bitstream that makes up the data across a physical network. It defines the interfaces (electrical, optical, and so forth) to the network cable. The Physical layer carries the signals generated by all of the higher layers directly to its counterpart on the remote computer.

The Physical layer defines the complete configuration of all of the physical parts of the network, including cabling type, pin configurations, signal encoding, and so on. It deals with bits only, and does not impose any meaning on the bit stream. Transmission speed, modulation, and encoding are all defined by this layer.

Data-Link Layer

The Data-Link layer converts the bit stream received from the Physical Layer into data *frames*, or *packets*. A packet is an organized structure that can contain data. The packet contains error-correction information in the form of a CRC to ensure that the frame is received properly. The upper layers are guaranteed error-free transmission through this layer.

Usually, the Data-Link layer relies on acknowledgments from its counterpart to ensure that a frame was received. If a frame is not acknowledged, the Data-Link layer normally retransmits the frame. The frame also contains the sender ID and destination ID for the frame.

The Data-Link layer establishes the logical link between two network nodes, and handles frame sequencing and frame traffic control.

Network Layer

The Network layer addresses messages and translates logical addresses and names into physical addresses. It is also responsible for routing packets from the source computer to the destination computer. It determines the route based on a number of criteria, including network conditions and service priorities.

The Network layer also is responsible for dealing with problems on the network, including network congestion. If the destination computers cannot handle packets as large as the sending computer, the Network layer on the sending computer will break the packets up into smaller packets. The packets are reassembled by the Network layer on the receiving computer.

Transport Layer

The primary function of the Transport layer is to ensure that messages are delivered to the higher layers without errors, in the proper sequence, and with no losses. This layer also packages messages for efficient transfer—short messages will be combined into larger ones, and large messages may be split into smaller messages. The Transport layer on the receiving computer unpacks the messages into their original form.

The Transport layer also provides session multiplexing—it can multiplex several message streams into a single logical link, and separate them on the receiving node. (Multiplexing refers to any technique that allows multiple message streams to share a logical link).

Session Layer

The Session layer allows applications on two computers to talk to each other by establishing a conversation called a *session*. This layer handles name recognition and other functions that permit two applications to communicate with each other over the network.

The Session layer places checkpoints in the data stream. Checkpoints provide a means of synchronizing the data stream on both computers. In the event of a network failure, only the data after the last received checkpoint needs to be resent. This layer also controls which side of a conversation is permitted to transmit, and for how long it may transmit.

Presentation Layer

The primary responsibility of the Presentation layer is to translate applications data into a commonly recognized intermediate format for transmission across the network. On the receiving side, the Presentation layer translates the intermediate format back into the original format.

The network redirector operates at this layer. A *redirector* redirects reads and writes to a server on the network.

Other services of the Presentation layer can include data compression, data encryption, character-set translation, and other conversions.

Application Layer

The Application layer allows application processes to access network services. Application layer services directly support user applications, such as file transfer, messaging, or database access.

Tip

You can remember the order of the OSI layers by using the mnemonic device: **P**lease **D**o **N**ot **T**rust **S**ales **P**eople **A**lways.

IEEE 802 Model

The *Institute of Electrical and Electronic Engineers* (IEEE) developed another network model to address the proliferation of LAN products that was beginning to take place in early 1980. This project, named 802, was in development at roughly the same time that the ISO was working on the OSI reference model, resulting in a compatible model.

One key difference between the IEEE committee and the ISO committee is that the IEEE committee was made up of networking vendor representatives from companies who had products to sell. In some instances, the IEEE standard was driven by *products* rather than the other way around.

Most of today's networks comply with the IEEE 802 standards. The IEEE 802 standards, including 802.2 (LLC), 802.3 (Ethernet), and 802.5 (Token Ring) are standards that actually can be implemented, whereas the OSI reference model is a more general, abstract set of guidelines.

The key difference between the OSI reference model and the IEEE 802 standard lies in the Data-Link layer. The IEEE felt that more detail was needed at this layer, and decided to further divide the layer into two sublayers, the *Media Access Control* (MAC) layer and the *Logical Link Control* (LLC) layer (see Figure 14.2).

Media Access Control (MAC) Sublayer

The MAC sublayer is the lower of the two sublayers defined by the IEEE. It provides shared access to the computer's network adapter cards. It talks to the network adapter card directly, and is responsible for error-free delivery of packets across the network.

FIG. 14.2 ⇒
The IEEE 802 standard divides the Data-Link layer into two sublayers.

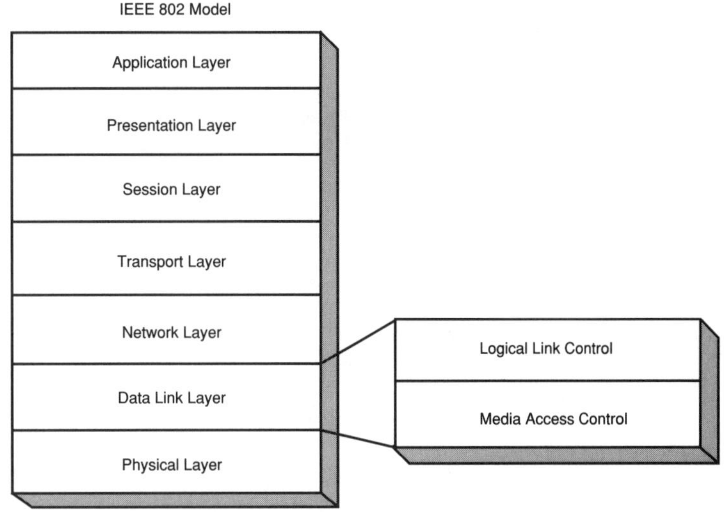

Logical Link Control (LLC) Sublayer

The upper sublayer of the Data-Link layer is the Logical Link Control layer. It is responsible for link establishment and control, frame sequencing and acknowledgment, and provides Service Access Points (SAPs) that are used to transfer information to higher layers.

Understanding Network Topologies

The *topology* of a LAN describes the way it is arranged. There are three topologies in current use—ring, bus, and star. Topology usually is used to refer to the logical arrangement, rather than the physical one. For example, the IBM Token Ring network is logically and electrically a ring, but wired physically in a star shape. It's also common for large networks to be hybrids of two or more topologies.

Ring

Nodes in a ring topology (see Figure 14.3) are connected, one to the other, in a closed loop. Although usually physically wired in a star shape, the ring is electrically a complete circuit. Messages may pass though one or more other computers before reaching their destination.

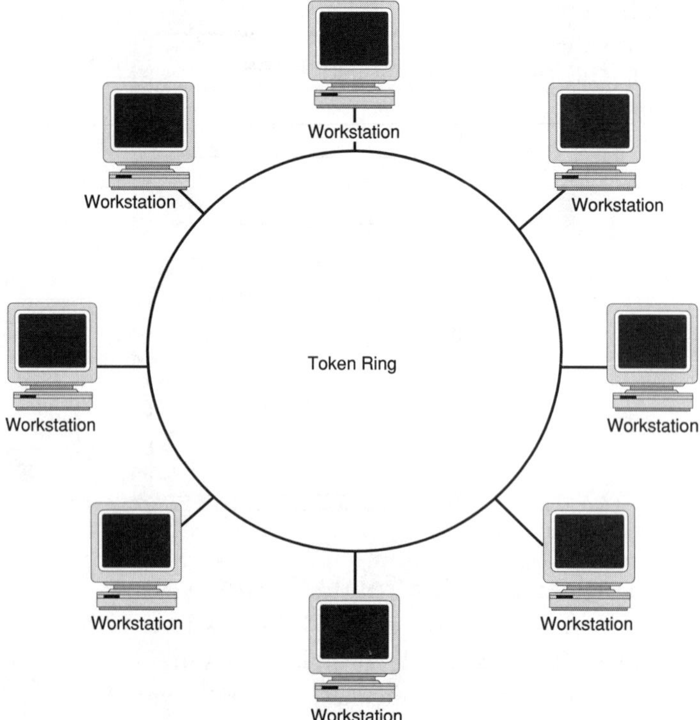

FIG. 14.3 ⇒
Ring network topology.

A token-passing access method is used with ring topologies. The only example of an IEEE 802-compliant ring topology is a token-ring network.

Bus

Nodes in a bus topology (see Figure 14.4) are connected to a central cable, known as a trunk, or bus. The ends of the cable are each connected to a terminator, which is a resistor that typically matches the characteristic impedance of the cable.

There are two methods commonly used to connect the nodes to the bus. The first, used more often with Thin Ethernet networks, uses T-shaped BNC connectors. One side of the T is connected to the node's network adapter card, and the other two are connected to two cables (or one cable and a terminator) that make up the bus.

The second method, more commonly used with Thick Ethernet networks, places a transceiver on the trunk cable, which is connected to the AUI port on the node's network adapter card with a drop-down cable.

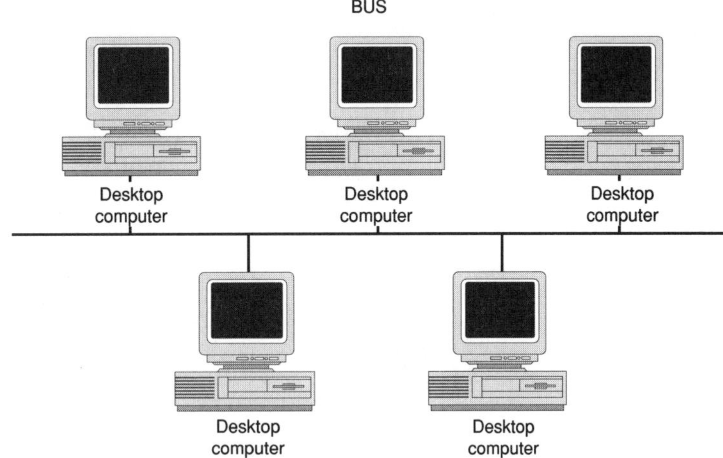

FIG. 14.4 ⇒
Bus network topology.

Examples of networks with a bus topology are 10Base2, 10Base5, and Arcnet.

Star

Nodes in a star topology (see Figure 14.5) are connected to a central wiring concentrator, or *hub*. A hub usually acts as an electrical *repeater*, regenerating the signals received from transmitting nodes and sending them to all of the other nodes.

10BaseT is the best example of a star topology network.

Understanding Architectures

The architecture of a network is determined by its topology, media access method, and transmission media.

Token Ring

IEEE standard 802.5 defines the token-ring network access method. It uses the ring topology, although it is physically shaped like a star.

Token-ring networks use a token-passing access method. A token is a special bit pattern that is passed around the ring from computer to computer. When a computer possesses the token, it has the right to transmit on the network. After it transmits its data, the computer places the token back on the ring so that the next computer has a chance to transmit.

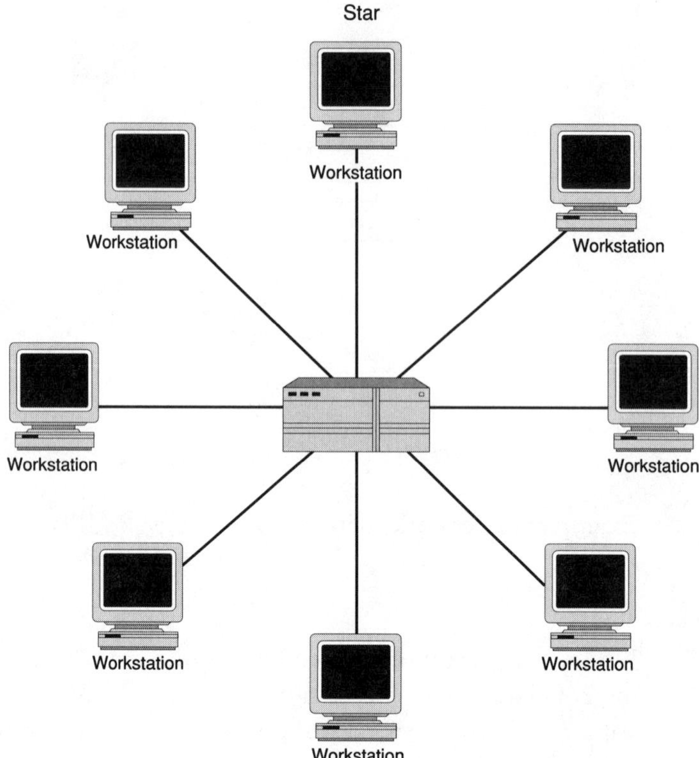

FIGURE 14.5 ⇒
Star network topology.

The token-ring access method is non-competitive, meaning that computers do not have to compete for access to the cable; they merely have to wait their turn. The token-ring standard does impose a maximum limit on how much data a computer may transmit at one time, to ensure that the token is passed on fairly. In fact, a computer that holds the token for too long will be partitioned out of the network by the central Multi-station Access Unit (MAU). Because a token ring is non-competitive, performance degrades slowly as more computers are added to a network.

The first token-ring network was designed by E. E. Newhall in 1969. The first commercial support for a token-ring network began with an IBM presentation to the IEEE 802 project in March 1982.

IBM announced the IBM Token Ring Network in 1984, and its design was approved as ANSI/IEEE 802.5 in 1985. Key to the design was the IBM Cabling System, which was based on shielded twisted-pair (a later design allowed the use of unshielded twisted-pair) cable that connected from the network adapter card to a wall socket, with a Multi-station Access Unit (MAU) located in a centralized location.

The token-ring network cabling is distinguished by a unique genderless connector. (A genderless connector can connect to any replica of itself, rather than having a corresponding part, as a plug and socket do). The self-shorting design of the connector, coupled with the redundant data path available in the cable, ensure that the ring can remain electrically complete, even if a wire breaks, or a computer is turned off. In the former case, the redundant path is automatically switched in by the MAU; in the latter, the cabling to the computer is removed from the ring by the MAU, and reinserted when the computer is turned on. You can recognize a token-ring connector because it is the largest of the connectors used in networking, a roughly cubical shape, that is about 1.25 inches on a side.

The original token-ring network used a transmission speed of 4M/sec; it was later adapted to 16M/sec. All network cards on the ring must be configured at the same speed.

Each computer can be up to 100 meters from the MAU when using shielded twisted-pair cable, or 45 meters when using unshielded cable. Cables must be at least 2.5 meters in length.

There can be up to 33 MAUs on a ring, each supporting a maximum of 260 computers with shielded twisted-pair cable.

Token rings are most efficient on heavily loaded networks that have a lot of traffic. On lightly loaded networks, the difference between Ethernet and token ring is not significant.

Ethernet

The precursor of the Ethernet network was a wide area network (WAN), called ALOHA, that was developed at the University of Hawaii in the late 1960s. It was the first network to use the Carrier-Sense Multiple Access with Collision Detection (CSMA/CD) access method.

Unlike the token-passing method, which is non-competitive, computers using the CSMA/CD access method compete for a chance to transmit on the cable. A computer that wants to transmit follows several steps:

1. The computer checks the cable to see if a carrier (a transmission signal) is already present. If one is present, it waits until no carrier is

detected plus some random amount of time and tries again (Carrier-Sense).

2. If there is no carrier present, the computer assumes that the cable is available to it. Other computers may be testing to see if the cable is available at the same time (Multiple Access).
3. The computer transmits its data, and listens for a double carrier. If a double carrier is found, then a collision has occurred. A collision is caused by another computer starting to transmit at the same time (Collision Detection).
4. If a collision is detected, both computers wait a random amount of time, and begin with step 1 again.

Xerox Corporation started experimenting with CSMA/CD networks in 1972, and by 1975, introduced its first Ethernet product, a 2.94M/sec system that could connect over 100 computers on a 1 kilometer-long cable.

The success of the first Ethernet led to Xerox, Intel, and Digital Equipment drawing up a standard for the 10M/sec Ethernet, which was used as the basis of the IEEE 802.3 specification. The product complies with most, but not all, of the 802.3 specification.

There are three different types of cable supported by Ethernet networks—thick coaxial cable (ThickNet, or 10Base5), thin coaxial cable (ThinNet or 10Base2), and unshielded twisted-pair (10BaseT).

The 10Base5 specification is for baseband communications over thick cabling. The maximum physical segment length is 500 meters. Baseband communications refers to communications where the cable is dedicated to a particular type of signal. The alternative, broadband communications, refers to communications in which multiple signals are multiplexed over a single cable. An example of broadband communications is cable television.

The 10Base2 specification is for baseband communications over thin (RG-58) coaxial cabling. The maximum physical segment length is 185 meters.

The 10BaseT specification uses baseband communications over unshielded twisted-pair cable. The maximum physical segment length is 100 meters between the workstation and a wiring concentrator, or hub.

ThickNet (10Base5)

Thick, or Standard Ethernet, uses a thick cable. The IEEE designation is 10Base5 because it is a 10M/sec, baseband network with a maximum segment length of 500 meters.

10Base5 uses a bus topology to support up to 100 nodes per trunk segment. A node is a workstation, repeater, or bridge. (A *bridge* is a device that connects two different network segments, passing only traffic destined for another segment. A *repeater* electrically connects two or more segments, regenerating the signals to each of them.)

Each trunk segment is terminated by resistors at each end. Transceivers are placed along the trunk, and a drop cable attaches to the AUI port on the workstation network adapter cards. Drop cable length is not considered in calculating the length of the trunk cable. As many as five backbone segments can be connected by using repeaters.

ThickNet requires a minimum of 2.5 meters between connections on the trunk segment. Drop cables usually are made from shielded-pair cable, and have a maximum length of 50 meters.

ThickNet is typically used to support the network backbone for a building because of its greater resistance to electrical interference and longer segment length.

ThinNet (10Base2)

The 10Base2 network runs over thin, relatively inexpensive coaxial cable (RG-58). The IEEE designation is 10Base2 because it transmits at 10M/sec over a baseband cable for a maximum distance of approximately 200 meters (actually 185 meters).

10Base2 uses a bus topology to support up to 30 nodes per segment.

Each segment is terminated by resistors at each end. Instead of using external transceivers, 10Base2 transceivers are contained on the network adapter card, and a T connector is used to connect the cable to the card. There must be at least 0.5 meters of cable between adapters.

As many as five cable segments can be combined by using repeaters, giving 10Base2 a maximum of 150 computers per logical segment.

10Base2 was designed to be economical and easy to set up. Many small networks use 10Base2; in fact, Microsoft used to bundle Windows for Workgroups with 10Base2 adapters and cable.

Twisted-Pair (10BaseT)

The most popular form of Ethernet in use today is best know by its IEEE designation, 10BaseT.

10BaseT runs over unshielded twisted-pair cable, similar to that used by ordinary telephone systems. It is designated 10BaseT by the IEEE because it transmits at 10M/sec over a baseband cable for a maximum distance of 100 meters from the wiring hub. Cables must be at least 2.5 meters in length.

10BaseT is wired in a star topology, but it uses a bus system between the adapter card and the hub, which acts as a repeater.

ArcNet

ArcNet (Attached Resource Computer Network) is a proprietary token-passing bus network developed by Datapoint Corporation. It transmits at 2.5M/sec, although later versions support rates of up to 20M/sec.

ArcNet is a proprietary network, predating the IEEE 802 project. It bears some resemblance to 802.4, but 802.4 describes a broadband network, while ArcNet is a baseband network. ArcNet can use either a bus or star topology over coaxial cable. Star configurations use active or passive hubs. Active hubs regenerate the signals, while passive hubs simply divide up the signals.

Understanding Transport Protocols

Transport protocols enable you to route information and network requests over LANs and WANs. (A LAN is a *Local Area Network*, intended to interconnect nodes in the same building or campus, while a WAN, or *Wide Area Network*, can be world-wide.)

NetBEUI

The NetBEUI protocol stack (a stack is a particular implementation of a protocol) was designed by Microsoft and IBM for use with IBM's PC Network product, which was introduced in 1985. At that time, most people expected LANs to consist of small departmental workgroups that would be connected to mainframes via gateways. In fact, the PC Network hardware could support only a maximum of 72 workstations.

NetBEUI was optimized for use in this environment. One consequence of this optimization is the fact that NetBEUI is not routable (NetBEUI packets cannot pass through a router).

NetBEUI uses the NetBIOS interface at the top and NDIS at the bottom (see Figure 14.6).

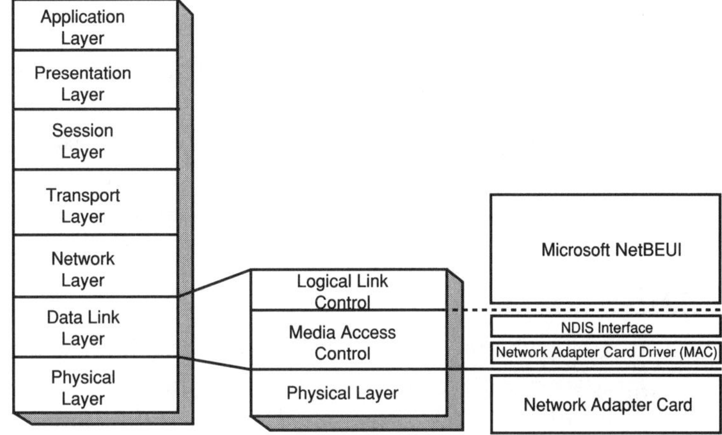

FIGURE 14.6 ⇒ How NetBEUI fits into the OSI/IEEE networking models.

IPX/SPX

IPX was designed by Novell as a routable transport protocol, based on Xerox XNS. The Microsoft version, IPX/SPX-compatible protocol, is completely compatible with Novell's version, but is a fully 32-bit implementation. The Microsoft implementation includes an optional NetBIOS interface that is required to utilize resource sharing with Microsoft networks.

TCP/IP

The *Transmission Control Protocol/Internet Protocol* (TCP/IP) is a suite of protocols designed specifically for wide-area networks. It was first developed in 1969 as part of an experiment called the ARPANET, the purpose of which was to interconnect the networks that were used by the contractors and universities doing research for the U.S. Department of Defense.

Understanding MAC Drivers

A *MAC driver* is a driver located at the MAC sub-layer. It provides support for data transmission to and from the network adapter, and manages the adapter itself. MAC drivers are also known as network adapter card drivers.

Understanding Interface Specifications

Device drivers at the MAC and LLC sub-layers move data received by the Physical layer up to the other OSI layers.

Until the development of the NDIS standard in 1989, most transport protocol implementations were tied to a proprietary MAC-level interface. Supporting these proprietary interfaces meant that network adapter card manufacturers had to write drivers for each proprietary interface in order to support a variety of network operating systems.

NDIS

In 1989, Microsoft and 3Com developed a joint standard that defined an interface for communicating between the MAC sublayer and transport protocol drivers on layers 3 and 4 of the OSI model. This standard, the *Network Device Interface Specification* (NDIS), is designed to create an environment where any transport protocol can talk to any network adapter-card driver without either one knowing anything about the other.

The initial communication channel between the protocol driver and the MAC driver is established through a process called *binding*, in which the *Protocol Manager* establishes the connection between the MAC and transport protocol drivers.

NDIS also permits a single network adapter to support multiple protocol drivers, as well as supporting multiple network adapters. The Protocol Manager is responsible for routing network requests to the appropriate driver.

ODI

Novell's version of an architecture that allows the use of multiple LAN drivers and protocols is called the *Open Data-Link Interface* (ODI) specification.

There are two parts to an ODI stack. The first, the *Multiple Link Interface Driver* (MLID), is a network adapter-specific driver, and the second, the *Link Support Layer* (LSL) provides the interface to the transport protocols.

Taking the Disc Test

If you have read and understood the material in this chapter, you are ready to test your knowledge. Insert the CD-ROM that comes with this book and run the self-test software, as described in Appendix K, "Using the Self-Test Software."

From Here...

The next few chapters discuss Microsoft's implementation of the architectures and protocols reviewed in this chapter. The two most popular networks, TCP/IP and Novell NetWare, are discussed in detail.

Chapter Prerequisite

You should complete Chapter 2, "Understanding Microsoft Windows NT 4.0," especially the introduction to domains and workgroups, before reading this chapter. You should already be familiar with Windows NT 4.0's features, interface, and basic concepts, such as setting security permissions, network architecture, and basic networking.

Windows NT 4.0 Trusts

This chapter is designed to introduce you to Windows NT 4.0's fundamental concept of directory services, or what Microsoft calls the *enterprise challenge*. One of the security relationships that enables Directory Services to accomplish its objectives is the trust relationship.

This chapter focuses on the following topics relating to trusts:

- The nature of trust relationships
- How and when to implement trusts
- Managing accounts across trusts
- Managing resources across trusts
- Authenticating user requests for logging on in the domain and across the trust

Understanding the Nature of a Trust Relationship

As you read in Chapter 2 ("Understanding Microsoft Windows NT 4.0"), the primary objectives of the enterprise challenge are to provide network users a single logon account, easy access to resources, regardless of the location of the user or the resource in the enterprise, and centralized administration of accounts and resources.

For example, hypothesize that you have two domains in your enterprise. Domain A has network resources that the users of Domain B want, or need, to access. Each domain is established by the creation of its *primary domain controller* (PDC). Each domain, therefore, is considered completely separate from any other domain. The users from Domain B can't access the resources on Domain A unless they have access to a valid user account in Domain A, which is included in the *Access Control Lists* (ACLs) for the resources on Domain B (see Figure 15.1). Even then, the user effectively has to log on again to Domain A to access the resource, and this violates one of the goals of Directory Services.

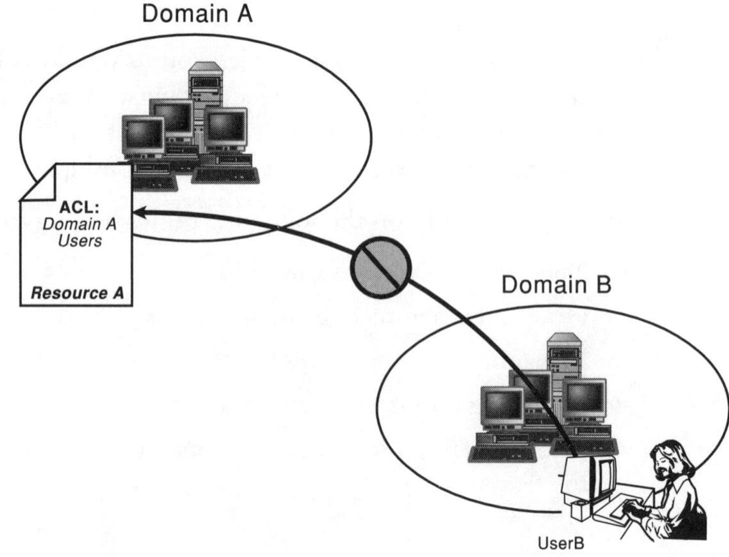

FIG. 15.1 ⇒ UserB logging on to a computer in Domain B cannot access a resource in Domain A without a valid user account in Domain A. The two domains, as is, are completely separate security objects in the enterprise.

A *trust relationship* establishes a security relationship, or secure connection, between the two domains. It allows secure user authentication and resource access to occur between the two domains. After the trust has been established, users from one domain can access resources in another domain to which they have been given access. Thus, the user needs to log on only once, and can have easy access to resources elsewhere in the enterprise—two of your Directory Services goals. Also, account management can be centralized in one of the domains in the trust, thus satisfying yet another Directory Service goal: centralized account management.

Trusts can be established only between two Windows NT Server domains. In fact, trusts are created between the PDC servers for each domain.

Key Concept

The domain that has the resources needed by users in another domain is referred to as the *trusting domain* because it trusts the users to use the resources responsibly. The domain that contains the users who need access to the resources in the trusting domain is referred to as the *trusted domain* because the users are trusted to use the resources responsibly. The trusting domain has the resources; the trusted domain has the accounts.

Once the trust has been established, resource managers in the trusting domain can create ACLs for their resources by adding accounts from their own domain, as well as from the account database on the trusted domain. So, if UserB from Domain B needs access to a resource in Domain A, Domain A's resource manager can add UserB to the ACL for the Domain A resource by virtue of the trust. When UserB logs on in to Domain B, UserB has access to all her usual resources in Domain B and any resource she is given permission to use in Domain A, again by virtue of the trust. In addition, the trust gives UserB the capability to log on to a computer that is a member of Domain A and still access the same set of network resources (see Figure 15.2).

The type of trust relationship just described is known as a *one-way trust.* In fact, trust relationships are, by nature, unidirectional. They are always directed from the domain that contains the resources toward the domain that contains the users and groups that require access. The relationships generally are represented by Microsoft as an arrow drawn from the resource (trusting) domain to the account (trusted) domain. This book follows that convention as well.

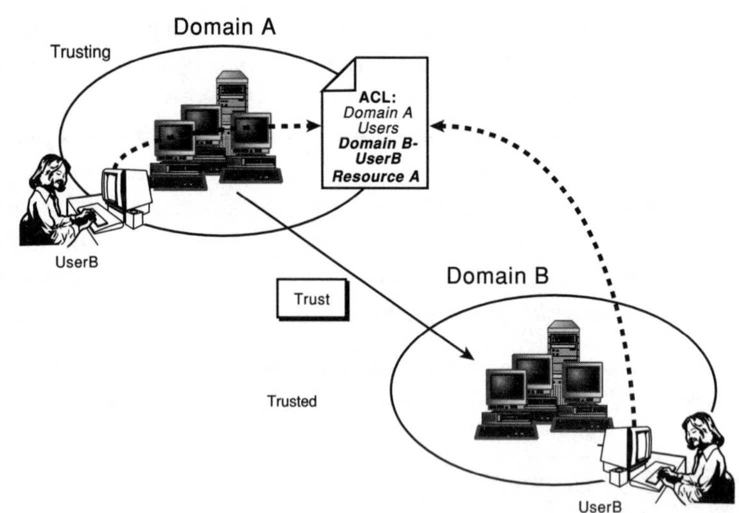

FIG. 15.2 ⇒
When the trust is established between Domain B and Domain A, UserB can access any resource in Domain A or Domain B to which she has been given access, and from any computer in Domain A or Domain B.

Chapter 2, "Understanding Microsoft Windows NT 4.0," discusses a scenario in which an organization decides to centralize management of accounts for XYZ Corporation in the MIS department, while providing all departments the ability to manage their own resources. To expand this scenario further in this chapter, suppose each department—Human Resources, Finance, Accounting, and so on—is given its own resource domain. MIS is given the master account domain for the organization—read: enterprise (see Figure 15.3). Here, MIS manages the account domain as all users and groups are managed by this department. Finance, Accounting, and Human Resources each manage their own resources and therefore are given their own resource domains.

One way that trusts granted from the resource domains to the master account domain enable the resource managers for each resource domain to create and manage ACLs for their resources is by selecting users and groups from the master account domain through the trust. They also allow a user to log on at a computer belonging to any of the domains in the enterprise and still have access to the same set of network resources.

As we have seen, a one-way trust allows users from the trusted domain to access resources in the trusting domain by logging in to a computer belonging to either domain. However, users in the trusting domain do not have the ability to access resources in the trusted domain, nor to log on and authenticate through computers belonging to the trusted domain.

FIG. 15.3 ⇒
Each department manages its own resources, but accounts are centrally managed.

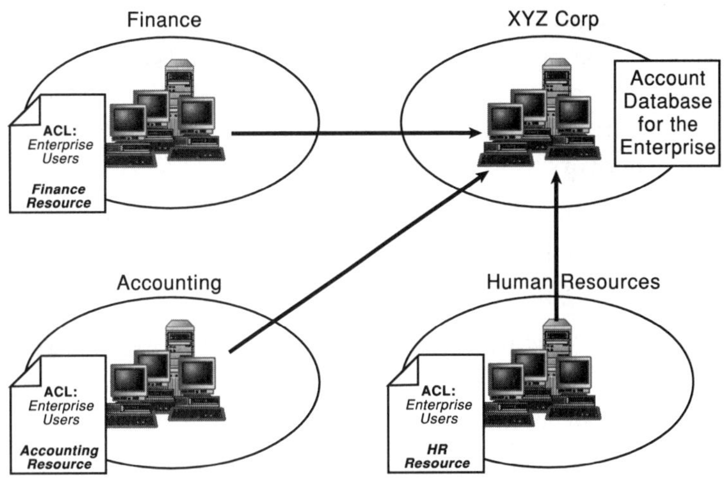

Key Concept

A one-way trust is directed from the resource domain to the account domain (trusting to trusted). This allows users from the account domain to access resources in the resource domain, and even to log on and authenticate at computers belonging to the resource domain. Users in the resource domain can access only their own domain's resources, and log on and authenticate only on computers belonging to their domain.

If both domains have users and resources, and users from both need to access resources in the other domain, then a trust can be established each way between the two domains. These two *one-way trusts* establish a two-way trust between the two domains. This effectively allows users from both domains to access any resources in either domain to which they have been given access, as well as the ability to log on and authenticate at computers belonging to either domain.

Key Concept

Trust relationships are not transitive. A trust is established between two domains. If Domain A trusts Domain B, and Domain B trusts Domain C, it does not automatically follow that Domain A trusts Domain C. For Domain A to also trust Domain C, a separate trust relationship must be established between Domain A and Domain C.

Like domains, trusts are logical communication channels. The physical location of the domains is not important. Neither, as we have seen, is the physical location (where they log on) of the users important. What is important for you, as an administrator, is to make the administration of your network as streamlined as possible. This means you need to identify:

- Where the resources and accounts are located—for example, resource domains and account domains
- Which domains require trusts
- Whether the trust needs to be one-way or two-way
- What is the minimum number of trusts to establish to satisfy the Directory Services goals of your enterprise

Setting Up a Trust Relationship

This discussion begins by reviewing the elements necessary to successfully set up a trust between two domains:

- A trust is established between two domains. A domain is identified by its PDC and retains its own *Security IDentifier* (SID). Therefore, the PDCs for both domains must be up and accessible.
- Be sure to disconnect any currently established sessions between the PDCs of the two domains involved in the trust.
- After the trust is established, users authenticating through the trust will authenticate on either the PDC or the *backup domain controllers* (BDCs) for their domain. Therefore, the BDCs for the trusted domains must be set up properly and regularly synchronized with the PDC.
- Administrators can establish the trust relationship. Be sure that you have access to an administrator account in both domains.
- User Manager for Domains is the tool used to set up trust relationships. You must have access to a computer in both domains on which the server tools have been installed. This probably is a Windows NT 4.0 Workstation or Server computer, but also can be a Windows 95 or Windows for Workgroups client on which remote server tools have been installed. Remote server tools are discussed in Chapter 8, "Remote Server Management."

After you have determined that these prerequisites have been met, you can begin to set up the trust.

As explained previously, the domain that has the users and groups who want access to another domain's resources is referred to as the trusted, or account, domain. The domain that has the network resources to which users from another domain want access is referred to as the trusting, or resource, domain. These terms, *trusted*, *trusting*, *account*, and *resource*, are used throughout this discussion to help you become familiar with the terminology and the concepts.

Establishing a trust relationship is a two-step process. The trusted domain must identify which domain will do the trusting (has the resources that the trusted users want to use). The trusting domain must identify which domain is to be trusted (has the accounts that want to use the resources). While it doesn't matter too much which domain goes first, generally it is recommended that the trusted domain first permit the trusting domain to trust it. Then the trusting domain can complete the relationship.

Caution

When the trusted domain goes first, the trust generally is established immediately after the trusting domain completes the trust. However, if the trusting domain goes first (before the trusted domain permits it to trust), the trust can take up to 15 minutes to complete.

Follow these steps to permit a trusting domain to trust you:

1. At a computer on which the server tools have been installed, log on as an administrator to the domain that will be the trusting domain.
2. Start User Manager for Domains.
3. Choose Policies, Trust Relationships. The Trust Relationship dialog box appears (see Figure 15.4).
4. Choose the Add button alongside the Trusting Domains list box.
5. Enter the name of the trusting domain in the Trusting Domain text box.
6. Optionally, enter a password in the Initial Password text box and confirm it in the Confirm Password text box. This password must be provided by the trusting domain when it completes the trust. It is used only once—at the time the trust is established—and is designed as an

optional level of security because only an administrator who knows the password can complete the trust from the trusting domain.

7. Choose OK. The trusting domain name will appear in the Trusting Domains list box.
8. Complete Steps 4 through 7 for any additional trusting domains.
9. Choose Close.

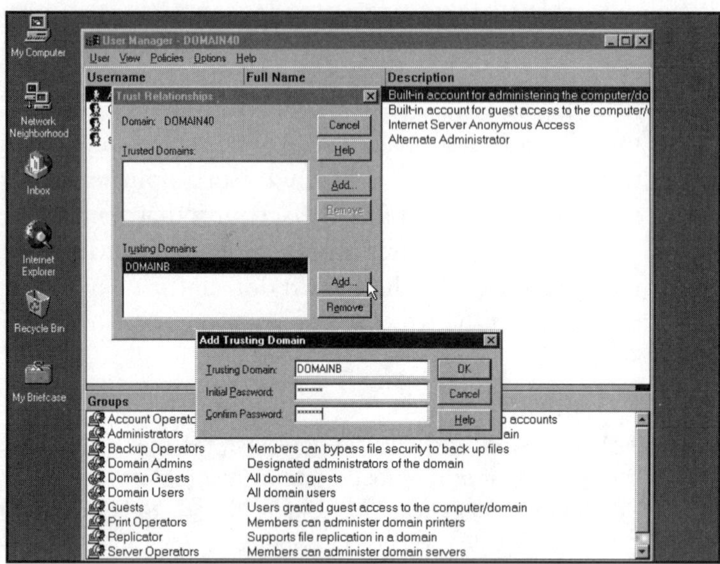

FIG. 15.4 ⇒ In this example, the domain DOMAINB has the resources your domain users want to access and therefore is added as the Trusting Domain.

Follow these steps to identify which domains will be trusted to use your resources:

1. At a computer on which the server tools have been installed, log on as an administrator to the domain that will be the trusting domain.
2. Start User Manager for Domains.
3. Choose Policies, Trust Relationships. The Trust Relationship dialog box will appear (see Figure 15.5).
4. Choose the Add button alongside the Trusted Domains list box.
5. Enter the name of the trusted domain in the Domain text box.
6. If a password is required to complete the trust, enter the password in the Password text box.

7. Choose OK. If the trusted domain permits your domain to trust it, and the passwords match, then a message will appear within a few moments indicating that the trust has been successfully established. If the trusted domain has not yet permitted your domain to trust it, a message to that effect is displayed.
8. Repeat Steps 4 through 7 for any additional trusted domains.
9. Choose Close.

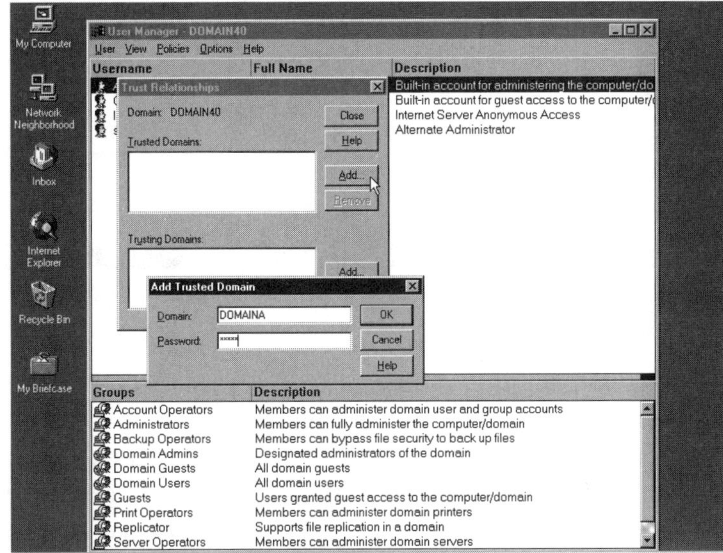

FIG. 15.5 ⇒ In this example, DOMAINA has the accounts that want access to your resources. Therefore, it is added as your Trusted Domain.

The Trust Relationship dialog box can be confusing. An easy way to remember which list box is which is to ask yourself the following questions:

- *I have network resources; whom do I trust?* Fill in the Trusted Domains list box.
- *I have users that want to access network resources; who trusts me?* Fill in the Trusting Domains list box.

If a two-way trust is necessary—that is, if the users from both domains want to access the resources from each other's domain—you must create two one-way trusts. Simply perform the process twice, reversing the roles of the domains for each time through the steps. The Trust Relationship dialog box looks similar to that in Figure 15.6.

FIG. 15.6 ⇒
Here, both Domain A and Domain B have resources that each other's accounts want to access. Each domain indicates the other as both the domain they trust and the domain that trusts them.

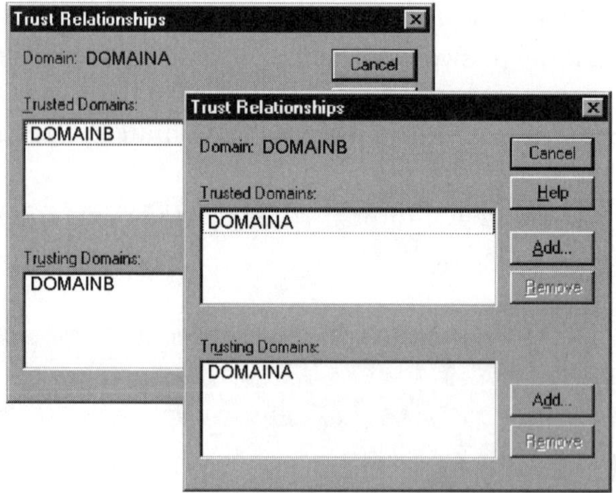

Managing Users and Groups Across Trusts

Now that the trust relationship is established, communication can take place between the two domains. Users from the trusted domain have the ability to log on at a computer belonging to either their own domain or the trusting domain. The ACLs for the resources in the trusting domain can now include accounts from the trusted domain. This section discusses account management and authentication across trust relationships.

The NetLogon Service and Pass-Through Authentication

The *NetLogon Service* is a Windows NT Server service that is started by default every time you boot your computer. Within a domain, it is responsible for locating a domain controller for the domain and validating a user when the user logs on. It also keeps the domain account database synchronized between the PDC and its BDCs.

More pertinent to this discussion, however, is *pass-through authentication*. This NetLogon function allows a user from a trusted domain to log on and validate at a computer belonging to the trusting domain. When the user logs on at a computer belonging to the trusting domain, the From box on the NT Welcome screen displays not only the trusting domain as a valid domain option, but also any trusted domains that have been set up.

Suppose that Domain A trusts Domain B. Domain A, therefore, is the trusting domain, and Domain B is the trusted domain. UserB is a member of Domain B. When UserB tries to log on to an NT computer that belongs to Domain A, he will see a choice for both Domain A *and* Domain B when he selects the From box on the NT Welcome screen. By selecting Domain B, the NetLogon service determines that this account cannot be validated by a domain controller for Domain A. Therefore, the request is *passed through* the trust to Domain B where it can be validated by a domain controller for that domain. Once UserB is validated, the user's access token information is returned to the computer at which he is logging on.

Local versus Global Accounts

When a user or group account is created on a Windows NT Workstation or member server, that account is considered to be *local* in that it can only be used to access resources on that computer. A user or group account created on a Windows NT PDC is, by default, a *global* account. This means that it can be used to access resources anywhere it has been used within a domain—for example, in the ACL of any resource on any member computer in the domain. It also can be used across trusts to access resources in other domains. By virtue of the trust relationship, the ACLs for resources in the trusting domains can include global accounts from the trusted domain. Whenever and wherever a user with a global account logs on, that user can access any resource to which that global account has been given permission.

A local account also can be created for the domain, but it does not share the same benefits for the global account. A local account in a domain has two very specific purposes:

- It allows a user in an untrusted domain to access a resource in another domain. This can be thought of as peer-to-peer networking between domains because a user must have a valid account in the other domain to access a resource there.
- It allows a user in a network that does not support trust relationships, such as Microsoft LAN Manager, to access a resource in a Windows NT domain.

Group Management in the Domain

Similar in concept to a local user account, global groups provide a means of managing users within a domain environment, as well as across trusts. Local groups reside on the computer at which they are created and are used to more effectively manage user access to resources on that computer. Local groups may include local users from the local account database, as well as global users and global groups from the domain account database. With the trust in place, a local group on a computer in the trusting domain can, additionally, include global users and groups from the trusted domain.

Key Concept

Microsoft's recommended strategy for managing resources effectively is to create local groups to manage the local resource, and populate it with global groups from its own domain and from the trusted domain. More simply stated, create user accounts and make them members of global groups. Then add the global groups to local groups of resource domains, or servers, for more effective resource management.

Table 15.1 describes the local groups that are created by default when installing Windows NT Server 4.0 as a domain controller.

Table 15.1 Built-In Domain Local Groups

Group	Default Members	Description
Administrators	Administrator; Domain Admins global group	Members of this group can fully administer the computer, or the domain. Only administrators can modify this group.
Users	Domain Users global group	Members of this group have the necessary level of access to operate the computer for daily tasks such as word processing, database access, and so forth. Only administrators and Account Operators can modify this group.
Guests	Domain Guests global group	Members of this group have the least level of access to resources.

Group	Default Members	Description
		Only administrators and Account Operators can modify this group.
Backup Operators	None	Members of this group have only enough access to files and folders as is needed to back them up or restore them on this server. Only administrators can modify this group.
Replicator	None	When Directory Replication is configured, this group is used to identify the specific user account, often called a service account that NT uses to perform the replication function. Only administrators can modify this group.
Server Operator	None	Members of this group can log on at the server, manage shared resources on the server, lock or override the lock of a server, format server hard disks, back up and restore the server, and shut down the server. Only administrators can modify this group.
Account Operator	None	Members of this group can log on at the server, create and manage accounts (except those groups as identified in this table), and shut down the server. Only administrators can modify this group.
Print Operators	None	Members of this group can log on at the server, create and manage printers, and shut down the server. Only administrators can modify this group.

Key Concept

A group that is local to the PDC is also local to all the BDCs for that domain because they share the same database.

This means that, if a user is made a member of the Backup Operators group on the PDC, that user will be able to back up and restore files on the PDC and all the BDCs as well because all the domain controllers for a domain share the same account database.

Three global groups are created by default, as well. These groups are described in Table 15.2. A *global group account*, like a global user account, can be used anywhere within the domain, or through a trust, to facilitate the management of user access to network resources. In other words, you don't have to create individual local groups of domain users on individual computers. You can use the same global groups of domain users that are available to all resource managers in the network. Global groups can be created and maintained only on domain controllers and can contain only global users from their domain as members.

Table 15.2 Domain Global and Local Groups

Group	Default Members	Description
Domain Admins	Administrator	Members of this group enjoy all the benefits of the local Administrators group. This group also is used to assign its members administrative privileges on local computers by making it a member of that local Administrators group. It automatically becomes a member of the Administrators local group on the domain controller. Only administrators can modify this group.
Domain Users	Administrator	This group contains all domain user accounts that are created, and is itself a member of the Users local group on the domain

Group	Default Members	Description
		controller. If made a member of a workstation's local Users group, its members will assume the user privileges that the local Users group has on that workstation. Only administrators and Account Operators can modify this group.
Domain Guests	Guest	This group contains the domain Guest account, which is disabled by default. Its members enjoy only the level of access that has been assigned to it. If made a member of a workstation's local Guests group, the domain guest account will also have guest access to the workstation resources. Only administrators and Account Operators can modify this group.

Members of local groups can include any local users, as well as global users and groups from the domain in which that computer participates. It can also contain global users and groups from trusted domains. However, it cannot have another local group as a member.

Key Concept

Global groups can only have users from their own domain as valid members.

As stated earlier in this section, Microsoft's group strategy for domains recommends that domain users be grouped into as many global groups as needed to manage the network. Local resource managers should then create local groups for maintaining access to the resources. The members of the local groups become the global groups of domain users. While this may, at first, seem to be a bit of over-management, in large networks with hundreds or thousands of users, this strategy makes much sense and can facilitate user management and resource access.

This strategy is actually implemented by default through Directory Services. When a new user account is created on the PDC, it is made a member of the Domain Users group, which is itself a member of the Users (local) group for the domain. When a Windows NT Workstation or Server computer joins a domain, the Domain Users and Domain Admins groups automatically become members of the computer's local Users and Administrators groups, again to facilitate administration and management of all the Windows NT-based computers in the domain, and to preserve the goals of Directory Services—for example, a single logon account to provide the same level of access throughout the domain.

Extending this concept to the trust relationship follows naturally. Because the trust gives a resource administrator access to the account database of a trusted domain, the resource administrator can use the global groups created in the trusted domain as members of the local groups the administrator creates to manage access to resources. For example, if you want the administrators of the trusted domain also to have the ability to administer your trusting domain's domain controllers, you make the Domain Admins group from the trusted domain a member of the Administrator's local group for the trusting domain. Or, if you have a database to which certain users from the trusted domain need access, you can have an Administrator or Account Operator for the trusted domain create a global group for those users. You then make that global group a member of your local group that manages access to the database.

Resource Management Across Trusts

You already should be familiar with Windows NT's share level, file level, and folder level permission structure, as well as how to assign permissions, as those are prerequisites for this chapter. Next, the steps involved in sharing a folder are covered to demonstrate how the trust expands your ability to manage resource access.

You already have seen that, when the trust relationship is established, the user from the trusted domain can log on from either a computer that participates in the trusted domain or the trusting domain. The trusted domain becomes a valid domain logon option for computers that are members of the trusting domain. Trusted domains appear in the From box on the NT logon screens for Windows NT-based computers.

Similarly, the permissions dialog boxes for shares, files, folders, printers, and any other network resources—as well as local group management through User Manager and User Manager for Domains—are also modified to display a choice of domain account databases from which to select users and groups.

For this example, suppose once again that Domain A trusts Domain B. This makes Domain A the trusting domain and Domain B the trusted domain. You have a folder called Data on a Windows NT-based server in Domain A that you want to share to the Global Finance group in Domain B, with Read permission. How do you do that? You proceed just as you always do when sharing the folder:

1. Select the folder that you want to share (through Windows Explorer or My Computer, for example).
2. Right-click the folder and choose Sharing.
3. On the Sharing tab of the Data Properties dialog box, choose Shared As.
4. Leave the default share name (the same as the folder name) or change the share name in the Share Name text box.
5. Modify the User Limit, if appropriate.
6. Select Permissions.
7. Use the Add and Remove buttons to make changes to the existing permission list—the ACL for this resource. The Add button displays the Add Users and Groups dialog box. The Remove button merely removes the selected account from the list.
8. In the Add Users and Groups dialog box, select List Names From. Scroll up and down to see the list of valid domains, including the trusted domains, from which you can select accounts (see Figure 15.7).
9. Choose Domain B from the list. Available global groups from Domain B will be displayed in the Names list box (and users, if you select Show Users).
10. Choose the Global Finance group from the list, select Add, modify the Type of Access, if necessary (Read is the default), and then select OK.

Wherever you have a choice to select users or groups, the trusting and trusted domains appear as valid domain selections.

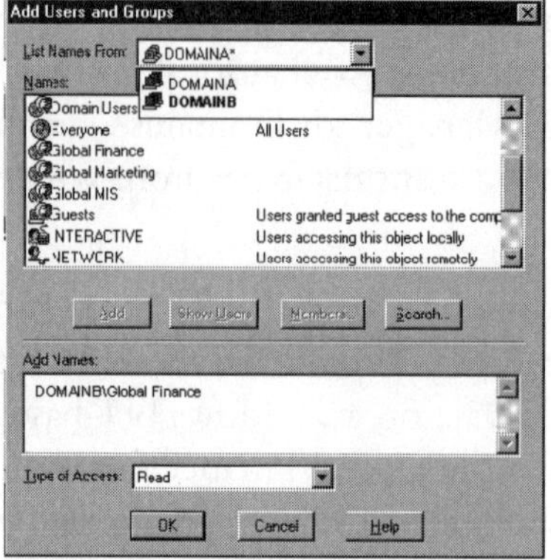

FIG. 15.7 ⇒
Once the trust has been established, accounts can be added from both the trusting and trusted domains. Notice how both domains are listed in the List Names From box.

Troubleshooting Trust Relationships

There are generally two main categories into which trust-related problems might fall: Either the trust isn't working, or access does not take place as expected.

Failure to Establish a Trust

Recall that, for a trust relationship to be successfully established, the following conditions must be met:

- Because a trust is established between two domains, and a domain is identified by its PDC, the PDCs for both domains must be up and must be accessible or else the trust will fail to be established.
- Be sure to disconnect any currently established sessions between the PDCs of the two domains involved in the trust. If a session does exist, the trust will fail to be established.
- After the trust is established, users authenticating through the trust authenticate on either the PDC or the BDCs for their domain. Therefore, the BDCs for the trusted domains must be set up properly and regularly synchronized with the PDC. If the BDCs are not regularly or properly synchronized, a user from a trusted domain may not be able to log on successfully from a computer participating in the trusting domain.
- Administrators can establish the trust relationship. Be sure that you have access to an administrator account in both domains, or you will not be able to set up the trust.

- The User Manager for Domains tool is used to set up trust relationships. You must have access to a computer in both domains on which the server tools have been installed. This probably is a Windows NT 4.0 Workstation or Server computer, but also can be a Windows 95 or Windows for Workgroups client.
- Establishing the trust is a two-step process: The account domain must permit the resource domain to trust it, and the resource domain must complete the trust. If either the account or resource domain fails to do their part, the trust will not be established.
- If a password is used to permit the resource domain to complete the trust, be sure that you know what it is, keeping in mind that it is case-sensitive. If the passwords do not match, the trust cannot be completed.
- The resource domain is considered to be the trusting domain, and the account domain is considered to be the trusted domain. If you are unable to add users from a domain to the ACLs for resources in your domain, check the direction of the trust. Be sure that your domain is actually trusting the other domain.

Broken Trusts

No, this has nothing to do with soap-opera plot lines. It refers to what happens when one side of the trust fails for some reason. A trust can be broken when one of the domains in the trust is renamed, the NetLogon service stops, or an administrator purposely removes the trust. Once the trust has been broken, it must be re-established by following the steps outlined in the previous section, "Establishing a Trust."

A trust relationship has a SID associated with it, just like user and group accounts do when they are created. As such, when an administrator chooses to break the trust, it must be broken on both sides and then re-established to create a new SID. A trust can be broken by following the steps.

At the trusted domain:

1. At a computer on which the server tools have been installed, log on as an administrator to the trusted domain.
2. Start User Manager for Domains.
3. Choose Policies, Trust Relationships. The Trust Relationship dialog box will appear.

4. In the Trusting Domains list box, highlight the trusting domain whose trust you want to break and then choose the Remove button alongside the list box.
5. Choose OK and confirm that you want to break the trust.
6. Choose Close.

At the trusting domain:

1. At a computer on which the server tools have been installed, log on as an administrator to the trusting domain.
2. Start User Manager for Domains.
3. Choose Policies, Trust Relationships. The Trust Relationship dialog box will appear.
4. In the Trusted Domains list box, highlight the trusted domain whose trust you want to break and then choose the Remove button alongside the list box.
5. Choose OK and confirm that you want to break the trust.
6. Choose Close.

Resource Access Anomalies

Anomalies refers to two specific situations that might occur:

- Access to a resource fails or is denied when logged on as a trusted account.
- A user *can* access a resource in a remote domain that they should not be able to access.

Of course, the first thing to check when a user cannot access a resource, whether you are using a trusted account or not, is whether that account actually has been given appropriate levels of access. Recall that a user's effective permissions are determined by adding up all the accesses the user has, either explicitly, or implicitly through group membership at the file/folder level and at the share level. When both share-level and file- or folder-level security is in use, the effective access is whichever of the two (share or file/folder) is more restrictive. So, of course, check the user's permissions and effective access.

However, if the same account exists in both the trusting domain and the trusted domain, the user can be denied access as well because the account SIDs will not match.

> **Caution**
> When a trust relationship exists, the user account should exist only in one domain—not both.

Conversely, a user who is logged in to one domain might find that she has access to a resource in another domain that she should not have. This also can occur when an account exists in both domains. Look at Figure 15.8. Domain A is trusted by both Domain B and Domain C. UserB has an account in both Domain A and Domain B. Through the trust, a resource in Domain C gives access to the UserB account from Domain A. Suppose UserB logs onto Domain B by using Domain B's account rather than the UserB account that is available from the trusted domain, Domain A. It is possible that UserB can access the resource on Domain C, even though he is not logged in as that account.

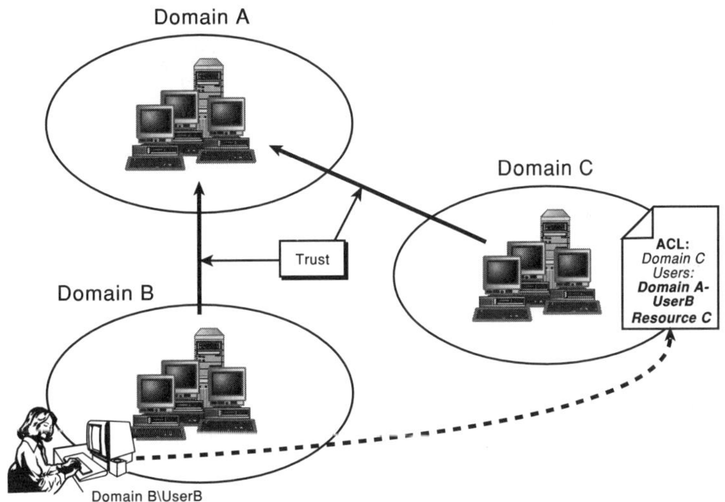

FIG. 15.8 ⇒ Domains B and C both trust Domain A. However, a duplicate user account exists in both Domain A and Domain B, thus making it possible for a user logging in as one account to gain resource access intended for the other account.

Here is how this occurs: When UserB attempts to access the resource in Domain C, the request is passed to Domain C, which cannot validate it. As a result, the request is passed through the trust (pass-through authentication) to Domain A to be validated. Pass-through authentication just passes the user name and password to the validating domain—not the SID. Consequently, Domain A successfully validates the account, and gives UserB access to the resource.

Caution
When a trust relationship exists, the user account should exist only in one domain—not both.

Taking the Disc Test

If you have read and understood the material in this chapter, you are ready to test your knowledge. Insert the CD-ROM that comes with this book and run the self-test software, as described in Appendix K, "Using the Self-Test Software."

From Here...

Now that you have learned the concept of trust relationships and the implications of account and resource management, you can apply them to your enterprise. Chapter 16, "Domain Models," explores the four basic domain models, how trusts are used to implement each model, and how to determine which model is appropriate for the enterprise.

Chapter Prerequisite

You should have read Chapters 2 and 15 in this book, have completed the labs associated with those chapters, and have received some hands-on experience to reinforce those concepts. Additionally, you should have a knowledge of basic NT concepts, such as SIDs, domain controllers, and so forth.

16

Domain Models

This chapter explores the significance of the domain for Microsoft's Directory Services and discusses four domain models that can be used as the basis for implementing Directory Services within a networked organization. Specific topics include:

- Domains and Directory Services
- Single Domain Model
- Master Domain Model
- Multiple Master Domain Model
- Complete Trust Domain Model
- Group management considerations

Understanding the Role of the Domain for Directory Services

As discussed in the last two chapters, a Windows NT 4.0 domain is characterized by a centralized database of user and group account information. When users log onto the domain, their user account is passed on to an available authenticating server called a *domain controller*. Because each user's account is centralized at the domain level rather than the local level, the user can log on to the domain from any workstation participating in the domain.

Likewise, resource access is provided by adding users from the domain database to resource *Access Control Lists* (ACLs). Thus, only one account database is necessary to manage any resource available within the domain. Recall that in the workgroup model, each computer maintains its own account database, which is used for managing resource access at that computer. Resources may actually reside on various server and workstation computers within the domain. By virtue of their participation in the domain, the resources use the same central account database for managing user access. These are, of course, two of the primary goals of Directory Services and why the domain plays a significant role in implementing Directory Services.

A *domain* is best thought of as a logical grouping of computers for the purpose of authenticating users and sharing resources.

Key Concept

While the physical layout of the network may affect the type of domain model you choose to implement—as well as the number and location of domain controllers and servers—nevertheless, the domain does not depend on the physical layout of the network, nor does it depend on the physical location of the computers or the users.

This doesn't mean that you can just throw together a domain without some thought and planning. Quite to the contrary, it is important that you carefully consider what the domain structure should look like and how it will best meet the needs of your enterprise. Perhaps one large domain will more than adequately serve the networking needs of your organization.

Often, there are multiple domains within an organization joined by trust relationships, each with its own resources and, in some cases, with its own account database.

The following are the four domain models that Microsoft posits as the foundations for any network enterprise:

- Single Domain Model
- Master Domain Model
- Multiple Master Domain Model
- Complete Trust Model

These domain models are discussed in more detail in the upcoming sections of this chapter.

The considerations discussed in the next sections ultimately may affect which type of model or models you decide will best meet the networking needs of your enterprise.

User and Group Accounts

The number of users and groups that participate in the network will influence your decision-making somewhat. In brief, there is an upper limit to the number of accounts a domain can support, which is 40,000 or a 40M account database consisting of user, group, and computer accounts. Once you reach the database limit, you must create another account domain for additional accounts.

However, you probably have already decided to split your account database into two or more domains, just for ease of administration. If you are the administrator for a network resource and you are creating an ACL for that resource, do you really want to scroll through 40,000 user and group accounts to find the ones that you want? Would you want to go through 10,000? It is not enough to think about how many accounts you have to manage; you must also consider how, where, and by whom those accounts will be used.

Another consideration is the location of the users and groups. If the company is located within one campus location, it may be easily managed by one centralized account domain. However, if the users are localized by region (such as West, Midwest, and East), it might be more effective to manage them by account domains located in those regions.

However your decision may be impacted by the number or location of users, keep in mind that the goal of Directory Services is to keep account management centralized.

Resource Management

Your choice of domain model will be dependent on the management of network resources. You must know where the network resources are located and who will manage them. This affects both the kind of model you choose and, as demonstrated in Chapter 15, the number of trust relationships that need to be established. For example, an organization that is relatively localized and whose resources are in that same general location may be best served by a single domain model. With a single domain, all resource servers participate in the same domain. Perhaps the same people who administer the users also administer the resources. No trust relationships are necessary in this scenario.

However, suppose the company is multinational, and resources are regionally or departmentally located. Perhaps each region wants, or needs, to administer its own resources. Indeed, perhaps each region needs to administer its own accounts. A single domain model will not suffice in this scenario. This environment may be best suited for a Master or Multiple Master Domain Model.

Organizational Culture

The preceding considerations lead directly to yet another important consideration—the *cultural factor*. The makeup of the organization necessarily drives decisions related to the domain structure and implementation. Is your organization built around departments, regions, or hierarchies? Is the management philosophy territorial or team-oriented? Are there politics that must be employed when organizing corporate-wide resources? Remember that domains are logical groupings of computers. As such, they can span locations such as cities, regions, or countries.

For example, perhaps the Finance department for Global Enterprises has offices in six major cities around the world. It also has several SQL databases on which it maintains the company's financial history, and it must administer these databases internally.

In one scenario, each office maintains its own databases for that location. Here, you might give each office its own domain for managing its database resources. In another scenario, all the offices use the same databases. You might then create one Finance domain that all the offices participate in.

The domain doesn't care that the offices are in different physical locations. Remember that a domain is identified by its *primary domain controller* (PDC) and has its own *Security ID* (SID). The workstations and servers need only identify that they are members of the domain. Windows NT-based computers do this by creating a computer account for themselves in the domain's account database. Other Windows NT network clients do this by identifying in their network properties which domain they belong to.

Understanding the Single Domain Model

In the *Single Domain Model*, shown in Figure 16.1, all accounts and all resources are contained within one enterprise-wide domain. Thus, trust relationships are not necessary. Account management is centralized to the PDC, and resources are maintained on resource servers that are members of the domain.

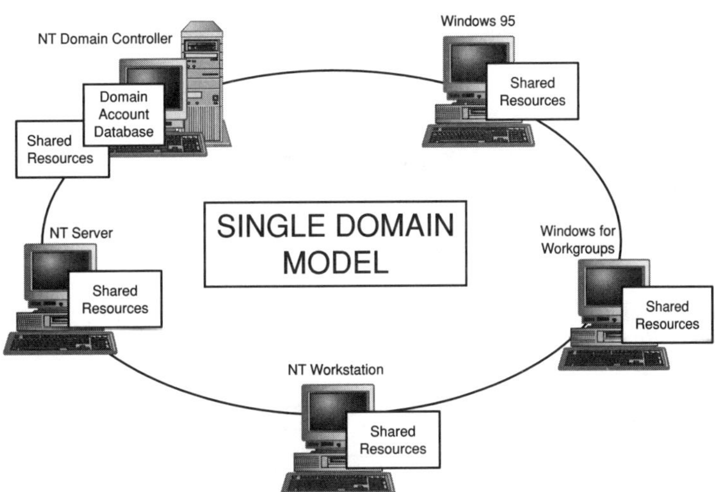

FIG. 16.1 ⇒ In the Single Domain Model, all accounts and resources are maintained in the same domain structure, so trust relationships are unnecessary.

This model scales well for small businesses, or where the computers do not participate in a larger WAN environment. A single domain model can accommodate up to 40,000 accounts. However, if the domain controller hardware is unable to handle the number of accounts, it will certainly experience performance problems. Also, as the number of resource servers increases in this model, the browsing of shared resources becomes slower.

Understanding the Master Domain Model

In the *Master Domain Model*, demonstrated in Figure 16.2, there is one domain that maintains the account database, and one or more other domains that administer resources. The resource domains trust the account domain. This is the type of domain model referred to in Chapter 15, "Windows NT 4.0 Trusts," when trust relationships were first introduced. This is also the type of model that you create when you complete the one-way trust in the Trust Relationship Lab for Chapter 15. The resource domains are the trusting domains, and the account domain is the trusted domain.

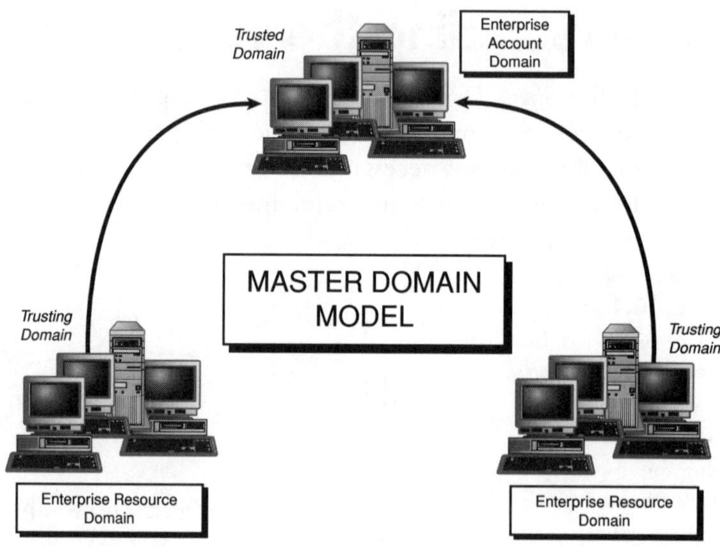

FIG. 16.2 ⇒ The Master Domain Model using two resource domains and one central account database.

This model is common in organizations where resources belong to various departments, and those departments want or need to maintain authority over access to their resources, because it allows resources to be grouped according to the needs, or culture, of the organization. Recall from Chapter 15 that Microsoft's recommended group strategy is to create global groups for managing domain users, and local groups for managing local resources, and then populate the local groups with the global groups.

The resource domains, therefore, do not need to maintain user accounts. In fact, resource managers only need to create local groups on the resource servers to manage access to their resources. Because a trust relationship exists with the account domain in this model, the resource managers simply add the appropriate global groups—and in some cases, global users—to their local groups. Any changes to group membership take place on the PDC. The resource manager needs to be concerned only with the ACL permissions granted to the local groups.

The model is transparent to the users. Because the trust relationship exists, users can log on any computer that is a member of any of the domains and still access any network resource that the user has been given permission to use. Thus, your Directory Services goals are once again preserved.

Understanding the Multiple Master Domain Model

The *Multiple Master Domain Model* is similar to the Master Domain Model in that the accounts are managed centrally, the resources are grouped logically and managed where they need to be managed, and trust relationships exist between the resource and account domains. The main difference in this model is that the account database may be distributed between two or more account domains. This may be a result of the way users are distributed through a WAN, their physical location, the size of the account database(s), the hardware of the domain controller, or the organizational culture or structure.

This model scales well for large organizations, with users located in several different areas, that still want to centralize account management within a particular administrative group, such as MIS. The biggest disadvantage is that there are more trust relationships to create and manage.

In this model, each resource domain trusts each account domain. In other words, each resource domain will have one trust relationship for every account domain, and each account domain will trust each other. As shown in Figure 16.3, if there are two account domains, each resource domain will have two trust relationships—one for each account domain. The formula for calculating the number of trusts in the master domain model is M*(M-1)+(R*M) where M represents the number of master account domains and R represents the number of resource domains. Thus, if your master domain model has two account domains and three resource domains, you will need 2*(2-1)+(3*2) or 8 total trusts.

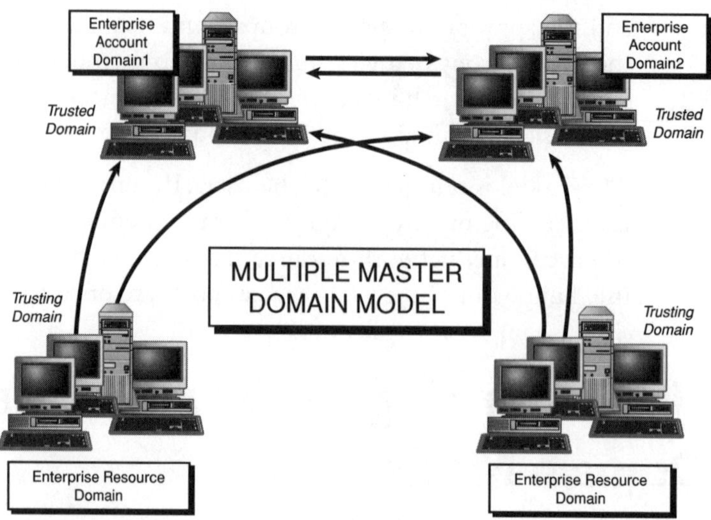

FIG. 16.3 ⇒ In this example of a Multiple Master Domain Model, there are two account domains that are trusted by each resource domain. Each account domain also trusts the other to facilitate account management.

Account and resource management takes place just as in the Master Domain Model. Domain users are created once in the appropriate account domain, and then grouped into global groups in their respective domains. Resource managers manage access to their resources by assigning permissions to local groups, and by making global groups—and in some cases, global users—members of the local groups.

The account domains also trust each other—that is to say, there are two one-way trusts established between the account domains. This facilitates the administration of accounts from either account domain. It also ensures that a user can log on any computer that is a member of any of the domains and still be able to access any network resource that the user has been given permission to use. Thus, your Directory Services goals are once again preserved.

Understanding the Complete Trust Domain Model

The *Complete Trust Model*, shown in Figure 16.4, is the simplest model to describe, though it also provides the least amount of security. In this model, every domain trusts every other domain. Account administration as well as resource management is distributed throughout the enterprise. Every domain maintains a copy of its own account database. Resource administrators can provide resource access to users from any other domain. The number of trust relationships required for the Complete Trust Model can be obtained by using the following formula, which is supplied by Microsoft: $n*(n-1)$, where n represents the number of domains to be included in the model.

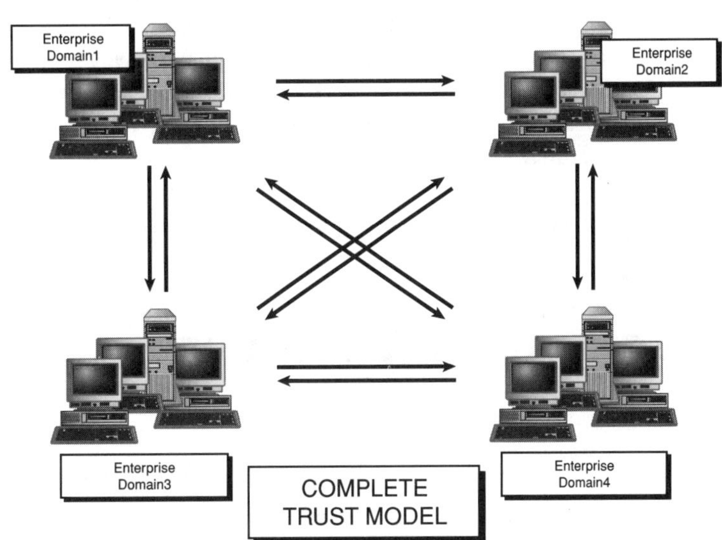

FIG. 16.4 ⇒ In this example of a Complete Trust Model, all four domains contain both accounts and resources. All domains trust each other in this model. Note that there are 4*(4-1) or 12 trusts in all to create and manage.

> **Caution**
> Resource access and security in this model is only as secure as the *worst* administrator in the enterprise.

Because there is no one person or group overseeing the administration of user accounts and resource access, duplicate users can be created, and inappropriate access can be granted to secure network resources. It is difficult to ensure the overall integrity of your network. Because of this, this model is sometimes called the *chaos model*. Even with these difficulties, this model has been successfully implemented in several large organizations, especially those that do not have a central or corporate MIS group. It does, however, require a greater degree of controls to remain secure.

This model also happens to be more common than you might expect. In companies for which there is no high-level strategy for implementing a

Domain Model, departmental or regional Windows NT networks are introduced independently. Over time, these departments find the need to communicate with each other and share resources. To accommodate that need, trust relationships are established among the domains and—voilà!—you have a Complete Trust Model.

Note The domain models presented here represent the purest form of the model. For example, the ideal Multiple Master Model has each resource domain trust every account domain. However, given your organization's structure, culture, and networking needs, not every resource domain may need to trust every account domain, and every user may not need the capability to log on anywhere in the enterprise. Microsoft recommends creating all the trusts for the chosen model to preserve the Directory Services goals of one logon account, centralized administration, and universal resource access.

Managing Global Groups in the Domain Models

This section reviews Microsoft's strategy for managing users through group accounts. Recall that Microsoft recommends that users be managed at the PDC by being grouped into one or more global groups. Global groups are global to the domain and, as such, can be used to manage local resources on that computer by any computer that is a member of the domain. Microsoft recommends that local resources be managed by creating local groups and by assigning permissions to these local groups. Local group membership then should consist of global groups from the domain (and when appropriate, global users from the domain). This provides a rather flexible and easy method of managing local resources, without having to deal with the user accounts directly.

As stated in Chapter 15, "Windows NT 4.0 Trusts," the establishment of a trust relationship between the resource (trusting) domain and the account (trusted) domain makes it possible for resources to be grouped into their own domains (by department, region, or function, for example) without sacrificing the Directory Services' goal of centralized account management. Local resource managers in each resource domain still manage their resources by creating local groups, assigning them access to their resources, and then by making global groups (and users) members of the local groups.

However, the global groups now can come from the trusted domain by virtue of the trust relationship.

Three of the domain models discussed in this chapter rely on trusts for their foundation: Master Domain, Multiple Master, and Complete Trust models.

Master Domain Model

The Master Domain Model is precisely what was just described in the second-to-last paragraph of the last section: The user and group accounts are centralized into one master account domain and are perhaps managed by an MIS group. Resources are localized in the hands of those users, departments, regions, and so on, that want or need to manage them. The local resource managers create ACLs for their resources, which consist of local groups. Those local groups' members consist of global groups (and users) from the trusted domain.

This concept is easy enough to comprehend. However, the next question to consider, from a planning point of view, is how many global groups need to be created? If the same logical grouping of users in a global group can be used in all resource domains, then the one global group is sufficient. If each resource domain requires a variation of the users in a global group, then ideally, a separate global group should be created in the trusted domain for each resource domain.

Here's an example. Suppose that the Finance department has three database files that contain the company's financial records. These database files are distributed across three regional resource domains—West, East, and Midwest. There are nine managers in the Finance department, with each region having three managers. All company users and groups are managed by MIS in the CORP account domain, and each resource domain trusts the CORP domain.

In the first scenario, all the managers need access to the database files in all regions. Access to the file in each region has been given to a local group called FINMGR on the resource server in each resource domain. The Finance managers have been grouped into a logical global group in the CORP domain called FINMANAGERS. To give all the Finance managers access to each database file in each region, the resource manager in each region adds the FINMANAGER global group to the local FINMGR group. Now all nine managers have access to all the database files.

In another scenario, suppose that only the three managers for each region should be able to access the database file in their respective regions. The global group FINMANAGER will not suffice here because it contains *all* the managers.

In this scenario, you need to create three global groups in the CORP domain. Call them FINMGR-EAST, FINMGR-WEST, and FINMGR-MID. Each of these groups contain the three managers for their respective regions. The FINMGR-EAST global group is added to the FINMGR local group in the EAST resource domain; the FINMGR-WEST global group is added to the FINMGR local group in the WEST domain; and the FINMGR-MID global group is added to the FINMGR local group in the MIDWEST domain. Now, only the appropriate managers have access to the database file in each region.

Multiple Master Domain Model

The Multiple Master Domain Model is much the same as the Master Model, except that the user and group accounts themselves have been grouped into two or more account domains, perhaps again by region or country, for example. Resources are still localized in the hands of those users, departments, regions, and so on, that want or need to manage them. Trust relationships exist from each resource (trusting) domain to *each* account (trusted) domain. The local resource managers create ACLs for their resources, which consist of local groups. Those local groups' members consist of global groups (and users) from one or more of the trusted domains.

Now return to the Finance department example introduced in the last section.

In the first scenario, all the managers need access to the database files in all the regions. Access to the file in each region has been given to a local group called FINMGR on the resource server in each resource domain. The Finance managers have been grouped into logical global groups in each account domain, called FINMANAGERS, such as CORPEAST\FINMANAGERS, CORPWEST\FINMANAGERS, and CORPMID\FINMANAGERS.

To give all the Finance managers access to each database file in each region, the resource manager in each region adds the FINMANAGER global group *from each* account domain to their local FINMGR group. Now all nine managers have access to all the database files.

In another scenario, suppose that only the three managers for each region should be able to access the database file in their respective regions. Because the managers for each domain are already grouped into a global FINMANAGERS group in their region's account domain, the resource manager for each domain should add the FINMANAGERS global group from their respective account domains to their local FINMGR local group.

However, this solution does not offer the greatest flexibility. Suppose that the management changes and one of the new managers for the EAST region has her account in the CORPWEST domain, and a manager for the MIDWEST region has an account in the CORPEAST domain. Clearly, the global groups that have been created will not provide the level of access required.

Microsoft suggests that, when creating global groups in a Multiple Master Domain Model, you can achieve the greatest flexibility by creating the same set of global groups *in each account domain* and then by adding the global group from each domain to the local group in the resource domain.

In this scenario, you need to create three global groups in each account domain—FINMGR-EAST, FINMGR-WEST, and FINMGR-MID. This means you have created nine global groups in total. Each of these groups contains the three managers for their respective regions. The FINMGR-EAST global groups from CORPEAST, CORPWEST, and CORPMID are added to the FINMGR local group in the EAST resource domain; the FINMGR-WEST global groups from CORPEAST, CORPWEST, and CORPMID are added to the FINMGR local group in the WEST domain; and the FINMGR-MID global groups from CORPEAST, CORPWEST, and CORPMID are added to the FINMGR local group in the MIDWEST domain. Now it does not matter where the manager's account resides. As long as the account is a member of the appropriate global group in that account domain, the appropriate managers have access to the database file in each region.

At this point, it is worth reiterating that global groups can have user accounts only from their own domain as valid group members.

Complete Trust Model

In the Complete Trust Model, all domains manage resources and all domains manage users and groups. Every domain trusts every other domain.

The local resource managers in each domain create ACLs for their resources, which consist of local groups. Those local groups' members consist of global groups (and users) from their own domain, and one or more of the trusted domains.

Returning one more time to the Finance department example, the Finance department still has three database files that contain the company's financial records. These database files are distributed across three regional domains—WEST, EAST, and MIDWEST. There are nine managers in the Finance department, with each region having three managers. All company users and groups are managed in each regional domain as well, and each domain trusts the other for a total of 3*(3-1) or six trust relationships. The Finance managers for each region have accounts in their respective regional domain.

In the first scenario, all the managers need access to the database files in all regions. Access to the file in each region has been given to a local group called FINMGR on the resource server in each regional domain. The Finance managers have been grouped into logical global groups in each regional domain called FINMANAGERS, such as EAST\FINMANAGERS, WEST\FINMANAGERS, and MIDWEST\FINMANAGERS. To give all the Finance managers access to each database file in each region, the resource manager in each region adds the FINMANAGER global group from its own domain, as well as from each regional domain to their local FINMGR group. Now all nine managers have access to all the database files.

In another scenario, suppose that only the three managers for each region should be able to access the database file in their respective regions. This is easy. Because the managers for each domain are already grouped into a global FINMANAGERS group in his/her region's domain, the resource manager for each domain should add the FINMANAGERS global group from his/her respective domains to their FINMGR local group.

You know what's coming next. This solution does not offer the greatest flexibility. Suppose that management changes and that one of new the managers for the EAST region has her account in the WEST domain, and a manager for the MIDWEST region has an account in the EAST domain. Clearly, the global groups that have been created will not provide the level of access required.

Once again, Microsoft suggests that you can achieve the greatest flexibility by creating the same set of global groups in each regional domain and then by adding the global group from each domain to the local group in the resource domain. This is applied to the Complete Trust Model next.

In this scenario, you need to create three global groups in each regional domain—FINMGR-EAST, FINMGR-WEST, and FINMGR-MID. This means you have created nine global groups in total. Each of these contains the three managers for their respective regions. The FINMGR-EAST global groups from EAST, WEST, and MIDWEST are added to the FINMGR local group in the EAST resource domain; the FINMGR-WEST global groups from EAST, WEST, and MIDWEST are added to the FINMGR local group in the WEST domain; and the FINMGR-MID global groups from EAST, WEST, and MIDWEST are added to the FINMGR local group in the MIDWEST domain. Now it does not matter where the manager's account resides. As long as the account is a member of the appropriate global group in that account domain, the appropriate managers have access to the database file in each region.

You can see that, as the number of domains in a Complete Trust Model increases, the number of global groups that must be created and maintained increases exponentially. You can also see that the security of resource access relies heavily on the integrity of the resource managers in each domain. This model can require a great deal of monitoring and planning.

Taking the Disc Test

If you have read and understood the material in this chapter, you are ready to test your knowledge. Insert the CD-ROM that comes with this book and run the self-test software as described in Appendix K, "Using the Self-Test Software."

From Here...

Chapter 17, "Windows NT Networking Services," presents the protocol choices available for Windows NT. Some NT-specific network services, such as the browser, are also discussed. Chapters 18, "TCP/IP and Windows NT," 19, "Novell NetWare and Windows NT," and 20, "Network Printing," discuss TCP/IP and Novell NetWare compatibility.

Chapter Prerequisite

You should have read Chapter 16, "Domain Models," in this book and have an understanding of the concepts presented therein. Ideally, you also have completed the labs associated with the chapter.

Windows NT Networking Services

This chapter reviews the Windows NT 4.0 network architecture, including the protocols supported by NT 4.0, and the newest advantages of this release. This chapter also reviews the function of services related to network activity. This is not meant to be an exhaustive discussion. This chapter is meant as a primer for the TCP/IP and Novell chapters that follow.

Topics to be covered include:

- Exploring the Windows NT 4.0 networking model
- Reviewing Workstation and Server services
- Introducing the browser service
- Configuring and installing network options
- Becoming a member of a domain
- Understanding dial-up networking and remote access service

Exploring the NT 4.0 Networking Model

Networking capabilities are fully integrated into Windows NT 4.0 workstation and server. Network support is supplied for Microsoft network clients, such as Windows 95 and Windows for Workgroups, and also for Apple Macintosh clients (through Services for Macintosh on the NT Server), NetWare clients and servers (through a variety of NetWare connectivity products for both NT 4.0 workstation and server, but primarily for the server), and TCP/IP systems, such as Internet connectivity and UNIX hosts. In addition, dial-in capabilities are supported and fully integrated.

The NT 4.0 network architecture is positioned as part of the executive services running in kernel mode. In fact, the NT 4.0 network architecture is itself a three-tiered model that is an integrated part of the NT executive service called the I/O Manager (see Figure 17.1). The I/O Manager is primarily responsible for determining whether a request for resource access is locally or remotely directed. If it is remotely directed, the request enters the layers of the network model.

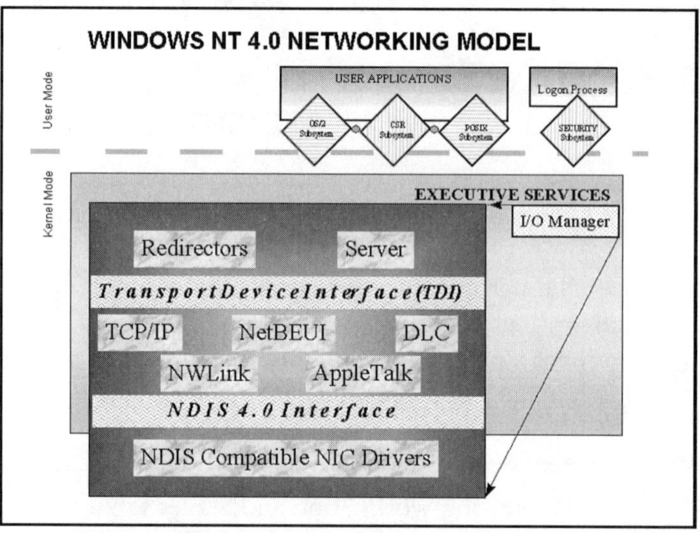

FIG. 17.1 ⇒
Windows NT 4.0 Networking model.

The three layers are the *File System* or *Redirector* Layer, the *Protocol* Layer and the *NIC* or *Adapter* Layer. Each layer communicates by using a *boundary* or *transmission* interface.

Comparing the OSI Model to NT's Network Model

Some of you may be familiar with the Open Systems Interconnection (OSI) network model created by the International Organization for Standards (ISO) (covered in detail in Chapter 14, "Networking Essentials"). This is a seven-layer model that begins with the Application layer and concludes at the Physical layer. The seven layers of the OSI model are Application, Presentation, and Session, corresponding to the File System layer in NT's model; Transport and Network, corresponding to the Protocol layer in NT's model; and Data Link and Physical, corresponding to the NIC layer in NT's model.

Microsoft decided to simplify the model and path that the requests took through the layers by synthesizing it into three layers connected by two boundary interfaces.

After the request is made, a path to the location of the resource is established by finding the most appropriate "path" through the layers of the client computer, through the network connection, and then up through the layers of the server computer—the computer that has the resource. These paths through the layers are known as the *bindings* for that computer. The established connection between a client and server computer is called the *interprocess communication* or *IPC* mechanism, which enables data to flow between the computers. This type of interaction is often referred to as *Distributed Processing*. A computer may have several bindings to various protocols to enable the establishment of various IPC mechanisms for different networking platforms, such as NetWare IPX or UNIX TCP/IP. Some of these mechanisms are outlined in Table 17.1.

Table 17.1 IPC Connections

Type of Connection	Description
Named Pipes	A two-way connection channel that guarantees data is sent, received, and acknowledged by both computers.
Mailslots	A one-way connection channel in which data is sent with no acknowledgment of receipt. NetBIOS broadcasts are examples of a mailslot IPC connection.

continues

Table 17.1 Continued

Type of Connection	Description
Windows Sockets	A Windows application-based programming interface (API) that enables two-way acknowledged data transfer between the computers.
NetBIOS	Another application-based programming interface (API) that enables two-way acknowledged data transfer between the computers.
Distributed Component Object Model	A new IPC model in Windows NT 4.0 that enables the distribution of processes across multiple servers in the NT network for the purpose of optimizing access and performance of network-based programs.

Now take a look at the various components of the NT 4.0 network architecture.

File System Layer

The *File System* layer is also known as the *Redirector* layer because the NT I/O Manager determines where to "redirect" the request for the resource in this layer. If the request is for a local resource, a file on an NTFS partition, the request is kept local and directed to the appropriate file system; in this case, to NTFS on the partition.

If the request is for a resource on another computer in the network, the request must be "redirected" to that *remote* location. As you learned, the remote location might be on another NT workstation or server. Therefore, the I/O Manager will redirect the request to NT's own built-in network redirector, RDR.SYS, also known as the workstation service. Every NT computer, whether workstation or server, has a workstation service configured to load and run automatically upon booting NT. Every NT computer has the capability of making, and does make, requests for resources on other computers.

However, the request may be for a resource on a NetWare server or a UNIX host; therefore, the request must be "redirected" accordingly. In the case of NetWare, this involves loading another redirector that can interpret requests meant for a NetWare server and finding the appropriate binding and IPC connection to which to send the message. On an NT Server, this additional redirector is the Gateway Services for NetWare service (CSNW) that comes with NT 4.0 server as an installable service. Other network redirectors may need to be obtained from the network manufacturer.

Protocol Layer

Protocols are responsible for creating the packets of information sent from one computer to another across the network connection. Various networks support or require specific protocols when communicating with a computer in that network. UNIX hosts generally require TCP/IP, for example, while NetWare networks prefer IPX/SPX.

Windows NT 4.0 supports five protocols:

- *TCP/IP* is a routable protocol supporting enterprise networking and NetBIOS connections, and is used to connect to the Internet and UNIX hosts.
- *NWLink IPX/SPX* is Microsoft's 32-bit implementation of IPX/SPX. It also is routable and supports enterprise networking among NT network clients, as well as connection to Novell servers.
- *NetBEUI* is a fast, efficient, but non-routable protocol used within smaller networks and thus is not well-suited for enterprise networking.
- *Data Link Control* (DLC) protocol is used to provide connection support to SNA mainframe computers and network-connected printers.
- *AppleTalk* protocol is used primarily on NT 4.0 server computers that provide remote access support for Apple Macintosh computers through Services for Macintosh.

TCP/IP, NWLink, and NetBEUI are examined in more detail in the next section. Windows NT 4.0 supports the installation of any number of protocols in each NT computer.

Network Adapter (NIC) Layer

The *Network Adapter* layer is the hardware layer that consists of the NDIS 4.0-compatible network interface card (NIC) drivers that initialize and manage communications through the hardware device connected to the network. NT 4.0 supports the installation of one or more network interface cards in each NT computer, provided that the card is compatible with NT and has an NDIS 4.0-compatible driver available to support it. All cards that are supported by Microsoft for use with NT will be on the Hardware-Compatibility List, available from Microsoft.

Transport Device Interface

The *Transport Device Interface* (TDI) is a boundary interface between the Redirector layer and protocols. It provides a common programming interface that any redirector can use to build a path (bind) to any and all appropriate installed protocols. This enables the redirectors to remain independent of the protocols installed and makes it extremely easy (and attractive) for network manufacturers to write redirectors for NT. The TDI provides the translation necessary to enable the redirector to "talk" successfully with the protocol. This is called *binding* the redirector to a protocol.

NDIS 4.0 Interface

The NDIS 4.0 boundary interface does for network cards what the TDI does for redirectors. It provides a common programming interface between the protocols and the NICs. Protocols are written to communicate with the NDIS 4.0 interface. NIC drivers also are written to communicate with the NDIS 4.0 interface. Consequently, only one set of drivers needs to be written for either a protocol or an NIC. In other models, each protocol requires drivers to communicate with every NIC installed in a computer. This is no longer necessary in NT 4.0. As with the TDI interface, this makes it attractive and easy to write protocol and card drivers to work with NT.

Benefits of TDI and NDIS 4.0

The ultimate benefit from this model is that the TDI and NDIS 4.0 interfaces do all the work of finding the appropriate path for a resource request out on the network. They provide the "bindings" between the layers. As a result, you can install any number of compatible protocols, redirectors, and NICs in a given NT computer. TDI and NDIS 4.0 will neatly manage communications among them.

Furthermore, each network card can have multiple protocols bound to it. Thus, your NT workstation can "talk" with any computer on the network that is running any of your installed protocols. For example, it is possible for your computer to have two NICs installed on your NT 4.0 Workstation. One NIC can use the NetBEUI protocol to communicate with computers on one subnet, while the other NIC can use TCP/IP to communicate with computers on another subnet. You can access resources on computers in either subnet with this arrangement.

As the administrator, you have the capability to fine-tune these bindings, even turn them off if they're not being used. You will explore this capability in a later section of this chapter.

Examining NetBEUI

Of the five communication protocols supported by NT 4.0, three are most likely to be used for computer-to-computer communications: NetBEUI, NWLink, and TCP/IP. The last section briefly reviewed each. This section covers NETBEUI, a protocol typically found only in small Microsoft-only networks. The next two chapters cover TCP/IP and NWLink in detail.

NetBEUI is a fast, efficient networking protocol used mostly for small, single-subnet LANs rather than large, multiple-subnet WANs because NetBEUI is not a routable protocol.

This protocol heavily relies on network broadcast messages to provide communications between computers. Consequently, NetBEUI LANs have a relatively high level of broadcast traffic. Think of a broadcast as a computer sending a message to every computer on the network, even if the message is intended for a specific computer.

NetBEUI has no configuration parameters that can be changed through the user interface in NT 4.0.

Configuring and Installing Network Options

Network-based options are installed, configured, and maintained through the Network applet in the Control Panel, also accessible through the Network Neighborhood properties (see Figure 17.2). There are five tabs included with the network applet, three of which are of particular interest to the current discussion. Those three tabs are Protocols, Adapters, and Bindings. The other two tabs are Identification and Services tabs.

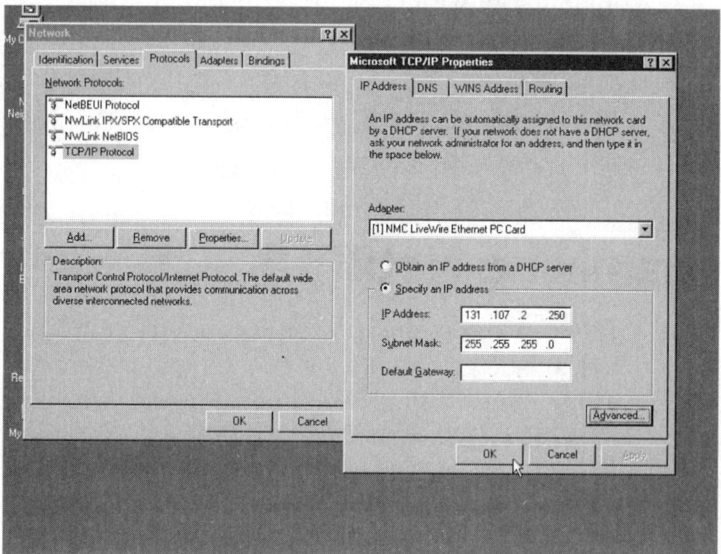

FIG. 17.2 ⇒ The Network applet showing the Protocols tab and the properties window for the TCP/IP protocol.

The *Protocols* tab displays a list of the currently installed network protocols. Choosing Add displays a list of all the protocols that are available for installation through NT, or through an OEM disk. You can Remove protocols from the computer and Update a protocol driver. Protocols are configured during installation of the protocol, or by selecting the protocol from the list and then choosing Properties. For example, notice the TCP/IP configuration parameters displayed in Figure 17.2.

The *Adapters* tab, shown in Figure 17.3, displays the installed network-adapter cards. Again, by choosing Add, NT displays a list of all supported adapter cards for which NT supplies an NDIS-compatible driver. You also can install a card by using a manufacturer-supplied driver, provided it is NDIS-compatible. You can Remove and Update drivers as well. Network adapter-card drivers are configured during installation of the card, or by selecting the card from the list and choosing Properties. Settings associated with the card are displayed in a dialog box similar to that displayed in Figure 17.3. Settings such as IRQ level, DMA base, I/O base, and transceiver type can be viewed and modified here.

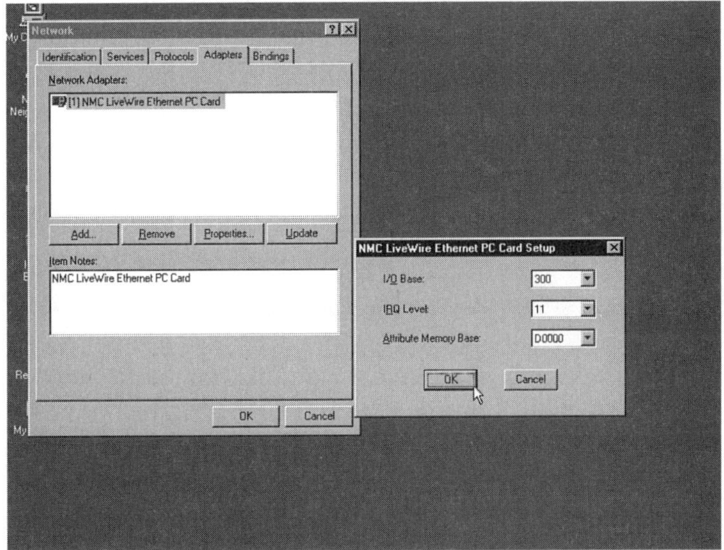

FIG. 17.3 ⇒ Through the Adapters tab, you can see and configure adapter card settings.

The *Bindings* tab displays, in a graphic format, the "paths" that network-bound communications may take to complete their tasks. Arranged like Windows Explorer, you can easily expand through a protocol or service to see what that protocol or service is bound to. For example, Figure 17.4 shows that an application using NetBIOS communicates with the network either through NWLink NetBIOS bound to NWLink IPX/SPX , or through NetBEUI to other computers running NWLink and/or NetBEUI.

As you also can see by looking at the available buttons on the Bindings tab, you can enable or disable bindings and change their order. If you think of network bindings as being a path that a communications request can take, all enabled bindings are possibilities, and NT will check each one to find the best path to take. Furthermore, it will search the paths in the order in which it encounters them. Therefore, you can improve network performance somewhat either by moving up in the list the "paths" most likely to be taken so that they are encountered and chosen ahead of the other paths, or by disabling paths that are infrequently used.

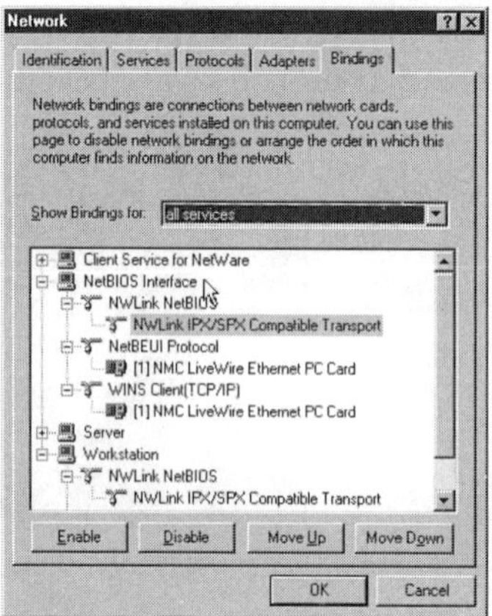

FIG. 17.4 ⇒
Here are some of the bindings for NetBIOS and workstation.

For example, suppose that you can communicate with several computers throughout your network by using TCP/IP and NWLink. Some of the computers have only NWLink, but most use TCP/IP or both. You most frequently communicate with the computers by using TCP/IP. If NWLink appears ahead of TCP/IP in the bindings list, NT will have to check the NWLink binding first before choosing TCP/IP (which it usually winds up choosing anyway because you most frequently talk with the TCP/IP computers). If you move the bindings for TCP/IP ahead of NWLink, then for those computers that you most frequently talk with by using TCP/IP, NT has to check only the first binding for TCP/IP and never go any further.

As another example, suppose that you maintain an archive computer on your subnet that you use to back up data once a month by using NetBEUI. There is no particular reason, then, to leave the binding for NetBEUI active because you use it only once a month. It is taking up resources, and very likely is sending out many broadcast messages that can affect network traffic. In this case, you can disable the binding for NetBEUI and enable it only when you need to use the protocol to communicate with the archive computer.

The *Identification* tab displays the current computer (NetBIOS) name and workgroup or domain in which the computer participates. You can change either setting through the Change button. This is explored in more detail later in this chapter.

The *Services* tab displays NT services that are currently installed on the computer. Recall that services are programs and processes that perform specific tasks, which are added to the Executive Services portion of the NT operating system. For example, if you want your Windows NT 4.0 workstation to be able to log in to a NetWare server, you need to install Client Services for NetWare on your computer. You can add that service through the Services tab by selecting Add and then by choosing the service from the list of available services.

Three of these services are discussed in particular in the next section—Workstation, Server, and Computer Browser.

Reviewing Workstation and Server Services

The *Workstation* and *Server* services are both integral to your ability to share and access resources on the network. Recall the earlier reference to the redirector that determines for which network and binding a resource request is intended. The NT 4.0 redirector file is RDR.SYS, which is more commonly called the *Workstation service*. In addition to accessing network resources, the Workstation service provides the capability to log on to a domain, connect to shared folders and printers, and access distributed applications. It is your "outgoing" pipe to the NT network.

The "incoming" pipe is the Server service. The Server service enables the creation and sharing of network resources, such as printers and folders. The Server service also accepts incoming requests for resource access, directs the request to the appropriate resource (or file system, such as NTFS), and forwards resources back to the source computer.

Now try to put the whole process together. A request for an NT network resource is made and sent to the I/O manager on a computer. The I/O manager determines that the request is not for a local resource and sends it to the appropriate network redirector, in this case the Workstation service. Through the redirector and the bindings, the appropriate protocol is chosen and a packet is created and sent through the network interface card out onto the network.

The request is received by the target computer (determined by the NetBIOS name, IP address, or NWLink hardware address or frame type, and so forth). It is serviced by the Server service on the target computer that determines which resource is required, where it is located (local printer, NTFS folder, and so forth), and then directs it there. After the access control list for the resource determines the effective access to the resource, the appropriate resource response (printer driver, file, and so forth) is forwarded back through the now-established IPC connection to the client computer.

Two additional components play a part in determining the name and redirector resolution for network requests. The *Multiple Universal Naming Provider* (MUP) enables the client computer to browse for and request network resources by their UNC name. Recall this is the syntax in which a resource path is established by naming the server and share name for the resource. For example, a folder shared as DATA on server ACCT1 can be accessed by mapping a network drive in Windows Explorer to \\ACCT1\DATA, its UNC name. Along with the MUP, the *Multiple Provider Router* (MPR) ensures that, on computers with multiple redirectors to multiple networks, requests for network resources are routed to the appropriate network redirector. Once a connection has been established to a network, it is cached for that session and the MPR again provides the "route" for additional requests for that network.

Introducing the Computer Browser Service

The *Computer Browser* service is an interesting NT service over which you have some control, unlike NetBEUI, which has no settings, short of editing the Registry. Figure 17.5 illustrates the browser.

Computer Browser's primary mission in life is to provide lists of network servers and their resources to waiting clients (see Figure 17.5). For example, when you choose Tools, Map Network Drive in Windows Explorer, the bottom of the dialog box displays a list of networks detected, domains and workgroups, computers in each domain or workgroup that have shared resources, and finally, the resources shared on each computer. This list is collected, maintained, and provided by the Computer Browser service.

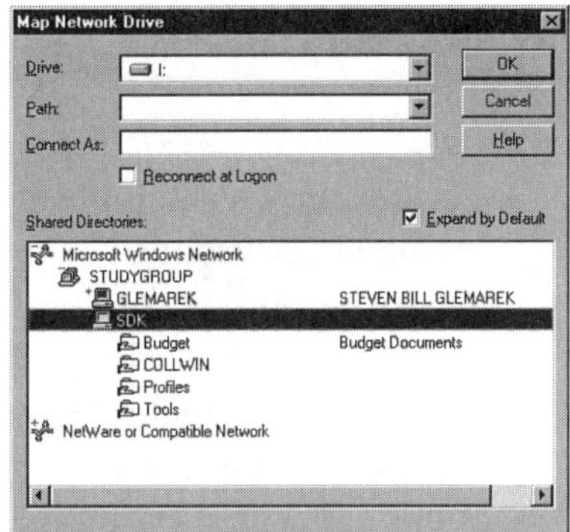

FIG. 17.5 ⇒ The Computer Browser Service creates and maintains the list of computers and shared resources that is displayed when mapping a network drive.

Browser lists are maintained on specific computers called *browsers*. There are various types of browsers, each with a specific role to play in the process. These are described in Table 17.2.

Table 17.2 Browser Computer Types and Roles

Type	Role
Master Browser	This browser computer compiles and maintains the master list of computers and their shared resources. Every subnet has its own master browser. It distributes copies of its list to backup browsers, or to a domain master browser, if applicable, on a periodic basis.
Domain Master Browser	This browser computer is always the primary domain controller in a domain-based enterprise network. It compiles and maintains an enterprise-wide list of network resources collected from all the master browsers in the domain, as well as from other domain master browsers for other domains in the enterprise. It distributes copies of its list to the master browsers in the domain, as well as to other domain master browsers on a periodic basis.

continues

Table 17.2 Continued

Type	Role
Backup Browser	This browser computer gets a copy of the master list from a master browser in its workgroup or domain subnet, and then distributes the list to client computers on request (as when mapping a network drive through Windows Explorer).
Potential Browser	These are all the computers that have not yet assumed a browser role, but have the potential of becoming a backup or master browser.
Non-Browser	These are computers that have been configured to never become a browser computer of any role, or are incapable of becoming a browser.

It is important to realize that there is a finite number of computers that assume a particular browser role. Every domain has one domain master browser. Every workgroup or domain subnet has one master browser and at least one backup browser. For every 32 computers in a workgroup or domain, an additional backup browser is configured. It is equally important to remember that these browser roles are determined with virtually *no* input from you.

Browser Elections

Computers assume their browser roles through an election process. If you check your Event Viewer's system log as the first thing after booting, you will notice several entries relating to the Browser. Closer inspection shows that these actually are browser-election events.

Examine first the presidential election process—simplified a great deal. Several people want to be elected president. They each publish their own criteria that they feel makes them appropriate for the office. These candidates are whittled down in primaries, and a winner is decided in a general election. After the president is elected, he or she names members to the

Cabinet, based on their qualifications. These members often are chosen from among those who ran for president.

The browser election process is quite similar. When computers boot up, they announce their criteria to become a browser computer. Of course, they'd like to be a master browser. The master browser is determined by the computer with the highest criteria—the best credentials for the job. For example, a primary domain controller will *always* become a domain master browser, because a PDC is supposed to be the most stable computer in a domain.

Criteria that decide browser roles include the operating system type and version, its current browser role (master browser, backup browser, or potential browser), the server type (primary domain controller, backup domain controller or member server), and the length of time it has been a browser. For example, a master browser is not likely to resign that role unless a truly more appropriate computer comes along.

So these election packets are broadcast on the network and received by a browser. Their criteria are compared, and those with lower criteria are discarded and the process continues until a master browser is elected. The master browser then assigns the role of backup browser to one or more computers, again based on election criteria.

If the master browser becomes unavailable, the backup browser detects that and forces another election to determine the new master browser.

Configuring Browsers

As previously stated, you have little control over the election process. In fact, the most you can do is make some determinations for your NT computer as to whether or not it should participate in the election process. There is no utility provided in NT—for example, in Control Panel—to affect these modifications. This being the case, the configuration must be done in the Registry.

You need to look for the Registry key HKEY_LOCAL_MACHINE\System\CurrentControlSet\Services\Browser\Parameters. Look for a parameter entry called `MaintainServerList`. By default, this entry is set to Auto. This means that the computer will participate in the election process and can become a master or backup browser. You can set this value to No to have it never become a browser. This is convenient for laptop computers or computers that are shut down frequently and then restarted. You also can set this value to Yes, which indicates that it always should try to become at least a backup browser.

Another parameter that you can add to the Registry key is `PreferredMasterBrowser`. This can be set to either 1 (Yes) or 0 (No). If set to Yes, then this computer is given an election boost to become master browser, among computers where the criteria are essentially the same. If set to No, the computer will never become a master browser.

How Does Browsing Work?

The Browser Process really is quite simple, and on a certain level, elegant. When computers boot, or share a resource, they announce themselves to the master browser. Computers announce themselves once a minute for the first five minutes after booting, then every 12 minutes thereafter. The master browser compiles a list of computers and their available resources and sends a copy of the list to the backup browser(s) approximately one time every 15 minutes.

When a client computer requests a list of resources, it actually begins by asking the master browser for a list of backup browsers in the computer's workgroup or domain subnet. Then the client asks the first available browser for a list of network computers and, subsequently, for a list of shared resources.

If a computer that is sharing resources is shut down normally, it announces that fact to the master browser, which then takes it off the list. At the next announcement interval, the updated list is distributed to the backup browser(s) (and the domain master browser). However, if the computer crashes, loses power, or is powered off without shutting down, the master browser is not notified. The master browser will wait for three announcement periods (12x3=36 minutes) until it revises its list. At the next announcement interval, it then updates the list.

This means that you can wait for a half-hour or longer before the browse list is updated. In the meantime, the computer still remains on the list, and you won't know it is down until you try to double-click it and the system seems to take forever to respond with a message, such as `path to computer not found`.

Similarly, backup browsers contact the master every 15 minutes and announce that they are still running. However, if they crash, lose power, and so forth, the master browser again won't know for three announcement periods, or in this case, up to 45 minutes. This can pose a performance problem for your users, who rely on browse lists to make connections. Because clients get the list from the backup browser, if there are two browsers and one crashes, the master browser won't select another browser for up to 45 minutes. All browse-list requests are now being serviced by just one backup browser, and it can get backed up with requests.

What can you do about this? Nothing. This process is strictly internal. But be aware of the timing issues involved both when computers become unavailable and when they first become available, or make additional resources available.

When a computer is booted, or you share a new resource on a computer, that computer or resource may not be listed right away in the browse list, because the browse list is cached and not updated right away by the master browser (remember, up to 15 minutes). This does not mean, however, that the computer or its resources are not available.

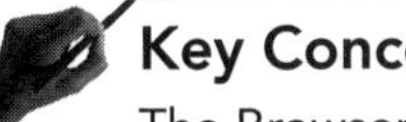

Key Concept

The Browser service is only a list provider and does not affect the availability or unavailability of network resources. A computer and its resources can always be accessed by using its UNC name, either through a `net use` command at a command prompt, or through the *Path* box when mapping a network drive.

Browsing and browser elections sometimes can adversely affect network traffic with the amount of announcements made. Under certain circumstances, it may be advisable to disable the Computer Browser service altogether. For example, if your user's network resource access is predetermined through System Profiles or login scripts and they never map their own connections, then disable the service. You will eliminate the traffic associated with the service and improve network response. Remember, the Computer Browser service is only a list provider. It does not affect access to a resource.

Becoming a Member of a Domain

Chapter 2, "Understanding Microsoft Windows NT 4.0," covered the various models of network computing available with NT, and compared workgroup computing with domain computing. When you participate in a workgroup, you are part of a logical grouping of computers that may or may not share resources with one another, and for which there is no single point of logon or authentication. Recall that every computer in the workgroup (workstation or server) maintains its own account database. When a user logs on at a computer, that user is authenticated on that local workstation and receives an access token for resources used on that local workstation.

As your network grows and as workgroups merge together, it may become appropriate to migrate to a domain model. Recall that a domain centralizes account information in one or more domain controllers. Thus, users have a single point of logon. They can log on to the domain from any computer that participates in the domain, be authenticated by a domain controller for the domain, and receive an access token that can be used to access any resources available within the domain.

You can switch your computer's participation from workgroup computing to a domain through the Identification tab in the Network applet, which is accessible through the Control Panel (or through the properties of Network Neighborhood). In order for your NT computer to join a domain, it must have a computer account created for it on the domain controller. This can be done ahead of time by a domain administrator, or during the change process by providing the name and password of a valid administrator's account. A stand-alone server can become a member of a domain, but a member server cannot be promoted to either a backup domain controller or primary domain controller.

Note Only NT workstation and member server computers require a computer account in an NT domain. Other network clients do not. However, Windows 95 workstations will appear in the list of computers in the domain if their workgroup setting matches the name of the domain.

> **Caution**
> Be sure that the computer name you are using is unique in the domain you are joining. If it is not, you can run into some serious connection problems in the domain. If you need to change your computer name to make it unique, modify the entry in the *Computer Name* text box in the change dialog box.

As Figure 17.6 demonstrates, choosing the *Change* button on the Identification tab displays a change dialog box. Select the *Domain* option and enter the name of the domain your computer is joining. If the computer account for your computer has already been created, choose OK and wait for NT to confirm that you have successfully joined the domain.

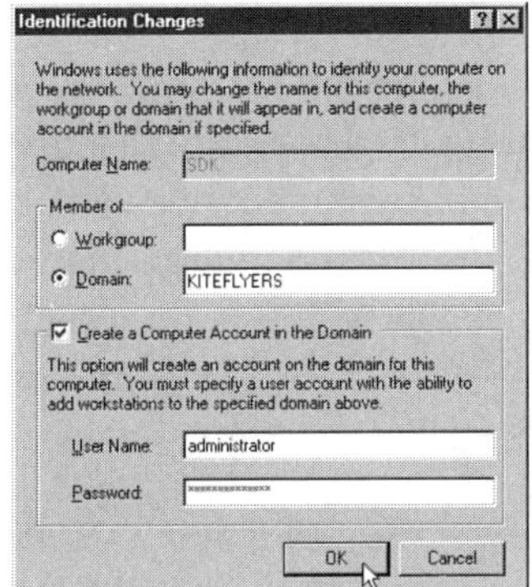

FIG. 17.6 ⇒ This computer is about to join the Kiteflyers domain by using the administrator's account from that domain to create a computer account for it there.

If you do not have a computer account already created, but know the name and password of a valid administrator account for the domain, select the option Create a Computer Account in the Domain. Enter the administrator account name in the User Name text box, and the valid password in Password. Then choose OK.

Once the computer account has been created for your computer, you can move back and forth between a workgroup and a domain. However, you cannot be a member of both simultaneously.

Troubleshooting Networking

If you encounter network-related difficulties, they are more likely due to traffic problems, protocol incompatibilities, or hardware failures than anything else. Troubleshoot your NT network as you would troubleshoot any other network. A good network-traffic analysis tool is beneficial for the network administrator, such as the NT Network Monitor utility that comes with NT 4.0 Server.

If you experience a network problem after the first installation of NT, or after installing an adapter card, double-check the adapter settings. Recall from Chapter 3, "Windows NT Server 4.0 Setup," that NT uses the default factory settings for most network interface cards. As a result, if you did not change the settings, your card might not be properly configured for the network.

Performance Monitor (also discussed in Chapter 10, "Performance Monitor") also provides objects and counters relating to the protocols installed, as well as to the Workstation and Server services. For example, for each protocol installed on an NT 4.0 server, you can chart total bytes/sec, session timeouts and retries, frame bytes sent and received, packets sent and received, and adapter failures. TCP/IP object counters become available when the SNMP service is installed.

Other tips include double-checking all protocol configuration options. For example, be sure that the TCP/IP address and subnet mask are correct, and that the IP address is unique (described further in Chapter 18, "TCP/IP and Windows NT"). If you are using WINS, be sure that the correct address to these servers has been configured for the workstation. Recall that NWLink auto-detects the network frame type. If multiple frame-types are detected, it simply defaults to 802.2, which may restrict access to certain resource servers. If necessary, determine what frame types are in use on the network, and manually configure NWLink to recognize them.

Check the Services applet in the Control Panel and the Event Viewer to see if any network-related services failed to start, and why. If the Workstation service is not running, you cannot connect to network resources. Similarly, if the Server service is not running, you cannot share resources or service network requests.

Table 17.3 describes which network protocols and which TCP/IP services each of the client systems supports.

Table 17.3 Network Protocol and TCP/IP Service Support for Various Windows NT Client Systems

Network Protocol	TCP/IP DNS Service	IPX-Compatible	IPX/SPX Compatible	NetBEUI	TCP/IP	DLC	DHCP	WINS
Network Client for MS-DOS	X	X		X	X	X		
LAN MAN 2.2c for MS-DOS	X			X	X	X		
LAN MAN 2.2c for OS/2	X			X				
Windows 95	X		X	X		X	X	X
Windows NT Work-Station	X		X	X	X	X	X	X

Taking the Disc Test

If you have read and understood the material in the chapter, you are ready to test your knowledge. Insert the CD-ROM that comes with this book and run the self-test software as described in Appendix K, "Using the Self-Test Software."

From Here...

The next two chapters discuss the TCP/IP (Chapter 18, "TCP/IP and Windows NT") and NWLink protocols (Chapter 19, "Novell NetWare and Windows NT") in detail.

Chapter Prerequisite

Before reading this chapter, you should have a basic understanding of LAN and WAN concepts, network adapter cards, transport protocols, the Windows NT 4.0 interface, and initial installation concepts. You should also be comfortable with the concepts of directory services, trusts, and domain models.

18

TCP/IP and Windows NT

This chapter expands on the information previewed in Chapter 17, "Windows NT Networking Services," relative to protocol choices by focusing on the TCP/IP protocol.

TCP/IP is the default protocol selected at installation time for Windows NT 4.0 for both the Workstation and Server platforms. At this point in time, TCP/IP is the protocol of choice because of its capability to connect to many types of computing equipment and to the Internet.

Numerous installation options are available pertaining to TCP/IP. This section will address the most common TCP/IP installation issues and options.

Topics for this chapter include:

- IP addressing formats
- WINS configuration
- DNS configuration
- IP routing

TCP/IP Addressing

To install TCP/IP, access the Network property sheet, select the Protocol tab, and click the Add button. During the installation process, an IP address and subnet mask must be configured for at least one network interface card in the machine (a unique IP address is required for every network adapter card using TCP/IP). This IP address and subnet mask can be obtained from a Dynamic Host Configuration Protocol (DHCP) server, or entered manually if no DHCP server exists on the network. Installation of DHCP is covered later in this section.

An IP address consists of 32 bits of address information and is denoted in a dotted decimal notation, such as 131.107.2.200. Each octet of the address is made up of 8 bits of information, with each bit assigned a binary weight. Each byte (8 bits) can contain any value from 0 to 255.

An IP address of 131.107.2.200 would have the corresponding bits (bolded) in each octet, as shown in Table 18.1.

Table 18.1 An Example IP Address

First Octet		Second Octet		Third Octet		Fourth Octet	
131		107		2		200	
128	8	128	**8**	128	8	**128**	**8**
64	4	**64**	4	64	4	**64**	4
32	**2**	**32**	**2**	32	**2**	32	2
16	**1**	16	**1**	16	1	16	1

An IP address consists of two parts: the network address and the workstation address. IP addresses are also divided into classes: class A through class C; each class, by default, denotes a number of networks and workstations available. The class of an address is resolved by the value in the first octet of the address. Table 18.2 illustrates the three classes of addresses, and the number of networks and workstations available by default in each class.

Table 18.2 IP Address Class Definitions

Class	Value in First Octet	Available Networks	Available Workstations
A	1-126	254	16,777,214
B	128-191	65,534	65,534
C	192-255	16,777,214	254

Note Address 127 is reserved for loop-back testing.

If the address is a class A address, the first octet (leftmost octet) of the address is the network address, and octets 2, 3, and 4 are the workstation address. If the address is a class B address, the first and second octets are the network address and octets 3 and 4 are the workstation address. If the address is a class C address, the first, second, and third octets are the network address and octet 4 is the workstation address.

A subnet mask is used to divide the address octets, as mentioned in the previous paragraph. If all bits are on (value 255) in the subnet mask for a specific octet, the bits are considered masked out when determining the address of a specific machine on a subnet. If no bits are on in the subnet mask for a specific octet, they are not masked out. For example, a class C address of 192.123.234.xxx will, by default, have a subnet mask of 255.255.255.0. The values in octets 1, 2, and 3 (192.123.234) are the network number. All workstations on this subnet will be on network 192.123.234 and will have a unique value from 1 to 254. In an IP address, the network number remains constant, while the workstation addresses change.

The default subnet mask parameter for each class of addresses is listed here:

- Class A 255.0.0.0
- Class B 255.255.0.0
- Class C 255.255.255.0

Note It should be noted that the above subnet mask parameter values are default values. Each class of addresses has a corresponding minimum value for the subnet mask. For example, a class B address can have a class C subnet mask (131.107.2.200 and 255.255.255.0), but cannot have a subnet mask below 255.0.0.0.

A subnet mask can be any value from 0 to 255. A subnet mask of 255.255.240.0 allows 1,048,575 network addresses and 4,096 workstations on each network. A subnet mask cannot have any zeroes to the left of any ones (binary).

Another parameter that may need to be configured is a Default Gateway or router parameter. Gateways and routers enable this computer to communicate with another computer on another TCP/IP network in or outside the enterprise. If your computer is going to be used to communicate with another computer on another TCP/IP network, in or outside the enterprise, a Default Gateway or router parameter needs to be configured.

Figure 18.1 illustrates the IP address, subnet mask, and default gateway parameters.

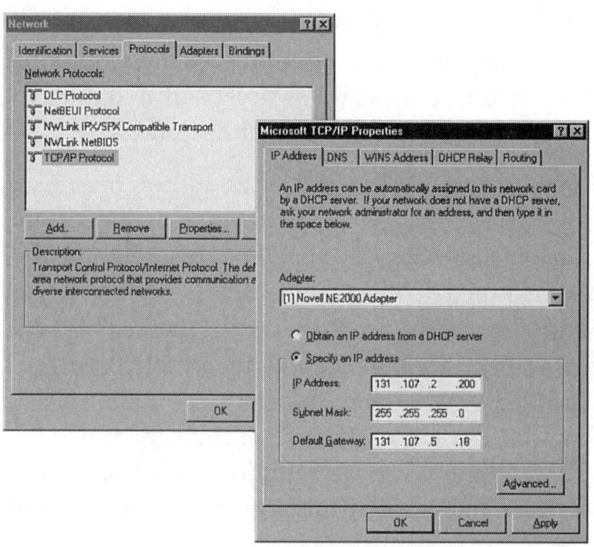

FIG. 18.1⇒
The Microsoft TCP/IP Properties dialog box.

The Advanced button on the Microsoft TCP/IP Properties dialog box presents the opportunity to add up to five additional IP addresses, and up to five additional default gateway (router) addresses. Machines that have more than one TCP/IP address are typically computers that are connected to more than one network.

Figure 18.2 shows an additional default gateway address being added to the already-configured default gateway address of 131.107.5.18.

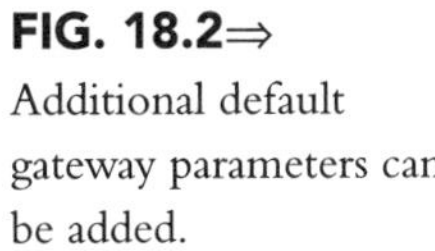

FIG. 18.2⇒
Additional default gateway parameters can be added.

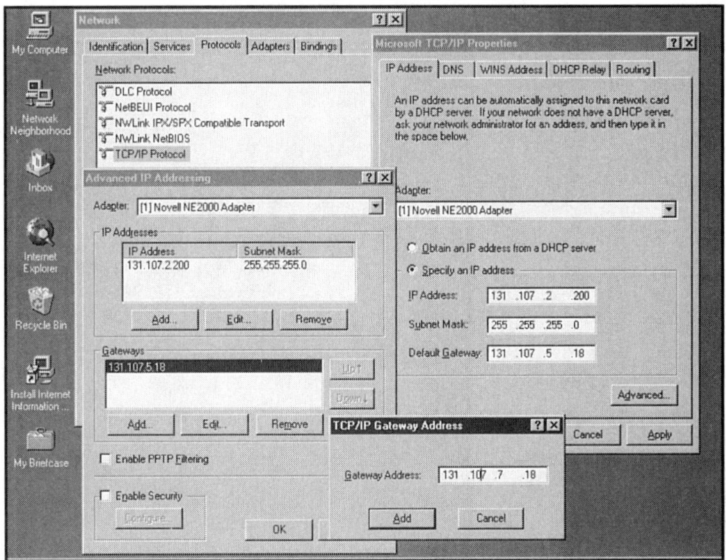

PPTP Filtering and Enable Security Options

In addition to the parameters previously mentioned, other protocols and security options including Point to Point Tunneling Protocol (PPTP), Filtering, and Enable Security for TCP Ports, UDP Ports, and IP Protocols can be configured from the Advanced button. Figure 18.3 shows PPTP Filtering enabled and shows the TCP/IP Security dialog box with TCP Port 23 (telnet), UDP Port 137 (nbname), and all IP Protocols or Ports enabled.

> **Caution**
> Enabling PPTP Filtering effectively disables all other TCP/IP packets from passing through the selected network adapter card. Only PPTP packets are allowed through.

FIG. 18.3⇒
The advanced button displays PPTP Filtering and TCP/IP security options.

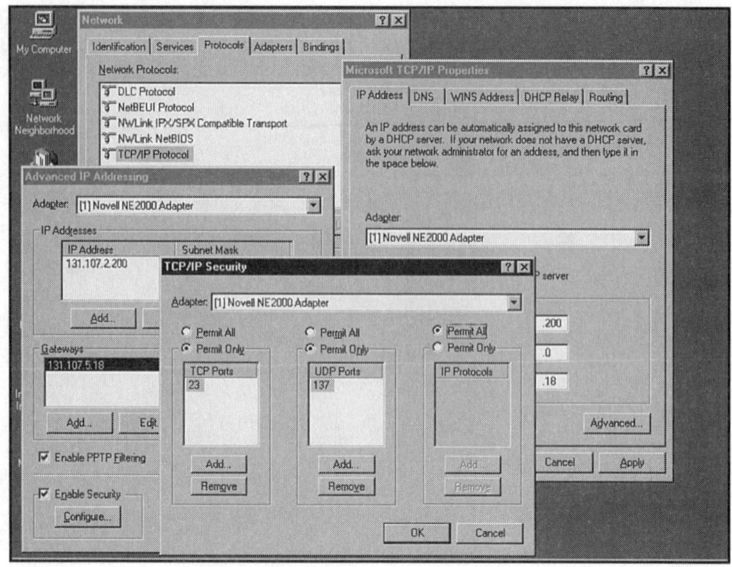

Dynamic Host Configuration Protocol (DHCP)

As mentioned previously, each network card installed in a computer requires an IP address to communicate in a TCP/IP network. Also mentioned was the fact that IP addresses can be configured manually, or obtained dynamically from a Dynamic Host Configuration Protocol (DHCP) server. Windows NT 4.0 Server is capable of being configured as a DHCP server. A DHCP server dynamically allocates IP addresses to DHCP-enabled clients in lieu of manual IP address configuration.

To configure a Windows NT 4.0 Server to become a DHCP server, the specific computer must be given a static IP address and subnet mask manually; then the DHCP service can be added. In fact, the following message dialog box is displayed when the DHCP service is loaded:

```
If any adapters are using DHCP to obtain an IP address, they are
now required to use a static IP address. Press Close on the
Network Control Panel and the TCP/IP Property Sheet will be
displayed, allowing you to enter an address.
```

After the service is added, configuration of the DHCP server is performed by using the DHCP manager tool in the administrative tools program group. DHCP manager is used to add and remove DHCP servers, create, configure, and manage scopes and reservations, and to configure and manage DHCP options. Figure 18.4 shows the DHCP Manager and the Scope Properties dialog boxes, with a scope configured and a range of excluded IP addresses. The figure also shows a default lease duration of three days.

FIG. 18.4⇒
Here you can configure a DHCP scope.

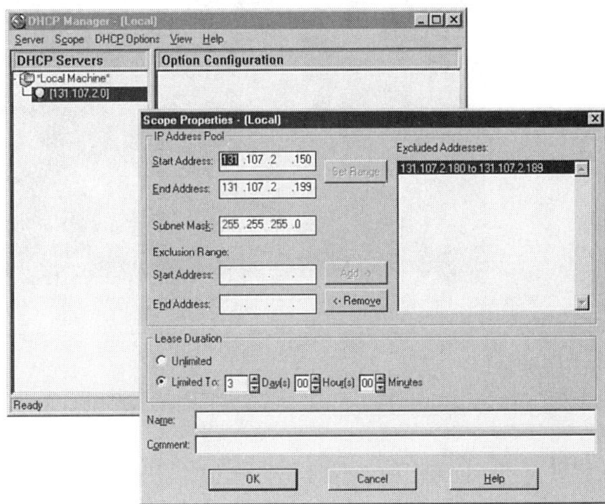

Caution

If more than one DHCP server is configured on a network or an enterprise, it is extremely important to note that each DHCP server must be configured with a unique scope of IP addresses. Failure to comply with this warning will result in duplicate IP addresses on the network.

DHCP options that a DHCP server assigns to clients are configured by using the DHCP options drop-down menu on the DHCP manager dialog box. Options can be set for a single scope (scope selection) or for all scopes (global selection). If the default choice is selected, default values for the default options can be changed, and default options can be deleted or additional options can be added. Active global options apply unless overridden by scope or client options. Refer to Windows NT 4.0 online help for a description of all default options.

If you want to assign a specific IP address to a network card, you can configure a reservation by using DHCP manager. You can make a reservation by associating an IP address to a unique 12-digit Mac address of a network card on the network. The 12-digit Mac address is found by activating a command prompt and typing **ipconfig /all**. The resulting display includes a line that indicates the physical address of the network card or cards in the computer. An example of the ipconfig command is shown in Figure 18.5.

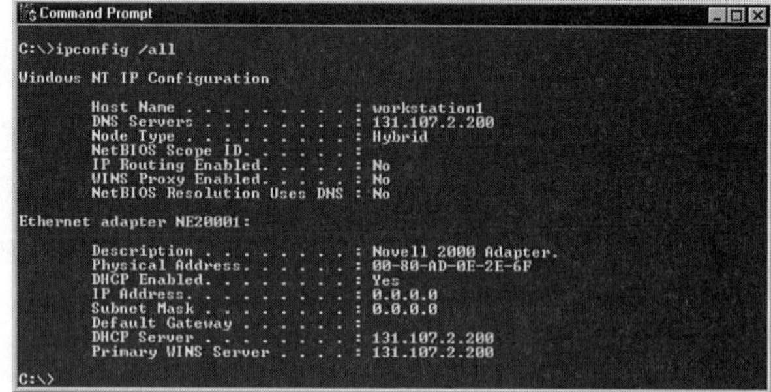

FIG. 18.5⇒
An example of the command prompt ipconfig /ALL command.

Key Concept

The TCP/IP protocol must be running for the ipconfig command to function.

Figure 18.6 displays the Add Reserved Clients dialog box that is used to specify an IP reservation. A reserved IP address of 131.107.2.180 is being assigned to a client computer named workstation1.

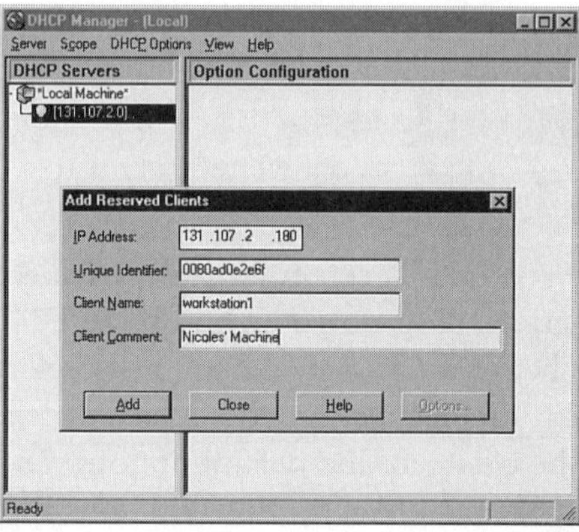

FIG. 18.6⇒
The DHCP Manager and the Add Reserved Clients dialog boxes.

If the routers that connect the IP subnets in an enterprise can function as a DHCP/BOOTP-relay agent (specified in RFC 1542), a DHCP server can lease IP addresses to clients in multiple subnets on the network. If the routers are not RFC 1542-compliant, a DHCP server must be configured on each subnet. The DHCP relay option is configured on one or two computers on each network that act as proxies for all DHCP traffic.

The DHCP Relay tab is found in the TCP/IP properties sheet, as shown in Figure 18.7.

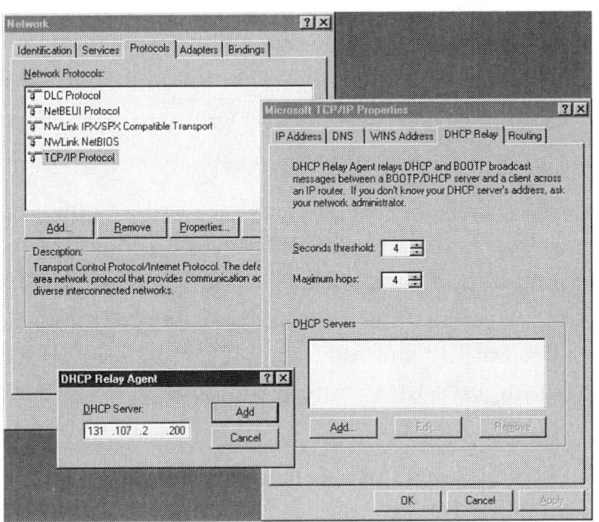

FIG. 18.7⇒
Configuring a DHCP relay agent.

Note A maximum of 16 hops can be configured in the DHCP Relay tab of the TCP/IP Properties dialog box.

Windows Internet Name Service (WINS)

The TCP/IP protocol communicates with other network devices by using an IP address. For an application to communicate with another computer through the NetBIOS session-level interface by using a computer name, the computer name must be mapped or resolved to an IP address. Methods used to map or resolve NetBIOS computer names to IP addresses are shown in Table 18.3.

Table 18.3 NetBIOS Name-to IP Address-Resolution Methods

Mapping Method	Configured
IP Broadcasts	NetBIOS Name Queries
Host Files	Manually Configured
LMHOST Files	Manually Configured
DNS Configuration	Manually Configured
WINS Configuration	Dynamically Configured

Windows NT 4.0 Server is capable of being configured as a Windows Internet Name Service (WINS) server, and multiple WINS servers can be configured in one network or enterprise. Multiple WINS servers help divide the load of handling computer-name registrations and queries, as well as database backup and redundancy. Unlike DHCP servers, WINS servers can be configured to communicate with one another, and to replicate their databases with one another to ensure a current database structure.

WINS is designed to lessen the use of IP broadcast messages on the network to establish IP addresses of specific network devices. Because WINS maintains a dynamic database that maps NetBIOS names to IP addresses, the administrative task of maintaining a Host or LMHost file is eliminated.

WINS is installed and configured as a service in the same way that the DHCP service is installed and configured.

Once installed, WINS is managed from WINS Manager in the administrative tools program group. Figure 18.8 illustrates the WINS Manager dialog box.

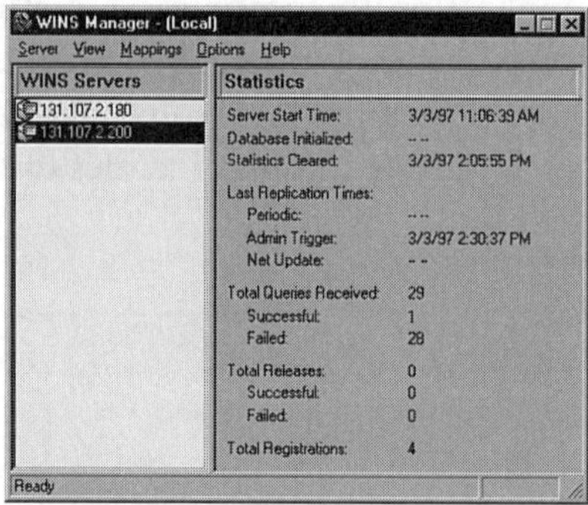

FIG. 18.8⇒
Manage WINS from the WINS Manager dialog box.

The WINS Manager dialog box displays the configured WINS servers and a Statistics window. The five drop-down menu choices are Server, View, Mappings, Options, and Help.

WINS Manager Server Menu

The Server menu provides options to add or delete WINS servers, display detailed information about a WINS server, display a WINS server-configuration dialog box, display a replication partner-configuration dialog box, and exit. Figure 18.9 shows the default settings for the WINS Server Configuration dialog box. In addition, Figure 18.9 shows the Advanced button selected, displaying information under the Advanced WINS Server Configuration section at the bottom of the screen.

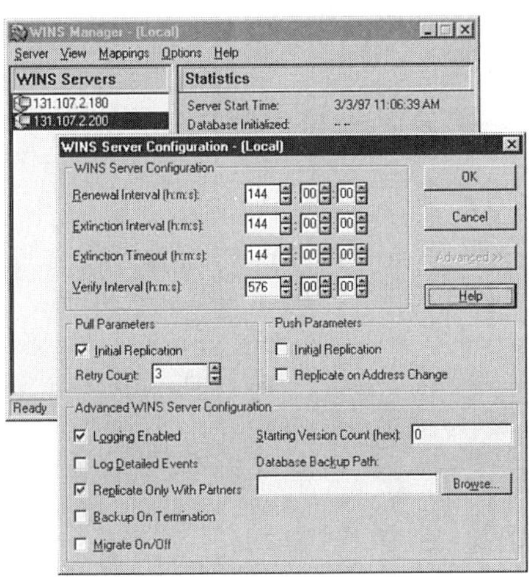

FIG. 18.9⇒ The WINS Server Configuration dialog box.

The WINS Server Configuration dialog box is used to configure parameters that are used to manage the WINS database and replication partner relationships. Figure 18.10 displays the Replication Partners dialog box.

The Replication Partners dialog box is used to add or delete WINS replication partners and to display the status of each WINS server on the network. The display shows whether a WINS server is a push partner, a pull partner, or both. The Replication Options area of the dialog box is used to configure the update count for push partners and the time interval for pull partners. If the Configure button is selected adjacent to Push Partner, an update-count parameter for push partners specifies how many changes or additions can be made in the WINS database before a replication is triggered. (The minimum value is 20.) If the Configure button is selected adjacent to Pull Partner, a time-interval parameter for pull partners specifies when replication of the WINS database should begin and how often replication should occur.

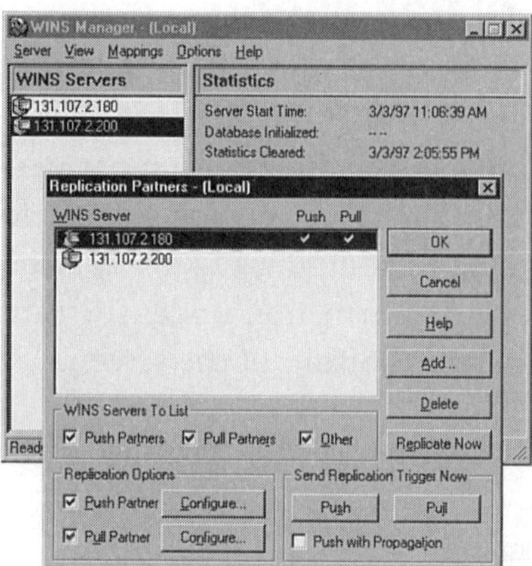

FIG. 18.10⇒ The WINS Replication Partners dialog box.

Other options that can be selected from this dialog box include the Send Replication Trigger Now for both push and pull partners to replicate the WINS database immediately, without waiting for the time interval to time out for the pull partners or the update count to be exceeded for the push partners. Another available choice is the Replicate Now button to initiate replication immediately in both directions.

WINS Manager View Menu

The WINS Manager View menu is used simply to select/deselect two options: One option is to clear the statistics window on the right pane of the WINS manager dialog box; the other option is to refresh the statistics window.

WINS Manager Mappings Menu

The WINS Manager Mappings menu is used to display the WINS database, initiate scavenging, add static mappings, and back up and restore the WINS database. Figure 18.11 shows an example of a WINS database.

The Show Database dialog box displays the WINS servers and the actual database mappings—either all mappings or individual WINS server mappings.

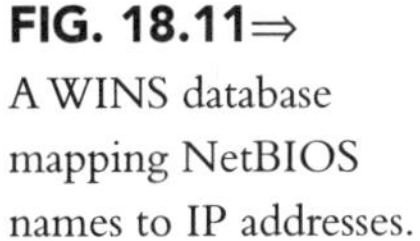

FIG. 18.11⇒
A WINS database mapping NetBIOS names to IP addresses.

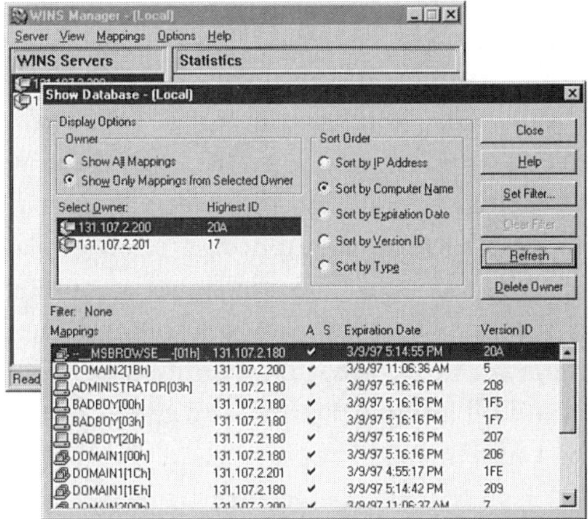

Scavenging can be initiated from the mappings menu; however, by default, it is performed automatically. Scavenging is the process of cleaning out the database of old released mappings and old mappings from other WINS servers that did not get deleted. Scavenging is done automatically, based on the renewal interval time and extinction interval time defined on the WINS Server Configuration dialog box.

Static mapping and importing mapping files, such as LMHost files, can also be accomplished from the Mappings drop-down menu. Figure 18.12 shows an example of adding a static mapping for a computer named Michelle, configured with an IP address of 131.107.2.182.

Ch 18

FIG. 18.12⇒
An Add Static Mappings example.

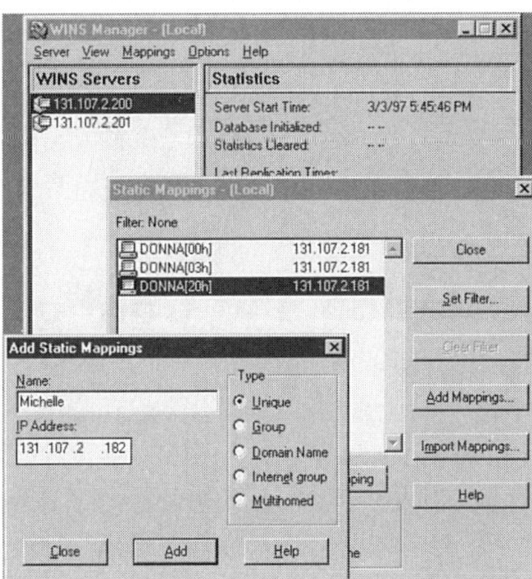

WINS Manager Options Menu

The one important option in this drop-down menu is the Preferences option, which allows the configuration of a default setting for two parameters (clear the statistics window on the right pane of the WINS manager dialog box, refresh the statistics window) that were discussed earlier. As can be seen in Figure 8.13, most of the options are self-explanatory; however, by selecting the partners button, two additional parameters become available: the New Pull Partner Default Configuration and the New Push Partner Default Configuration options. Values entered here are configured automatically for the pull and push partners if the Set Default Value option is selected in the Pull Partners Properties and the Push Partner Properties dialog boxes. Recall that these two properties sheets are accessed from the Replication Partners dialog box, selected from the Server drop-down menu. Figure 18.13 displays the Preferences dialog box with the Partners button selected.

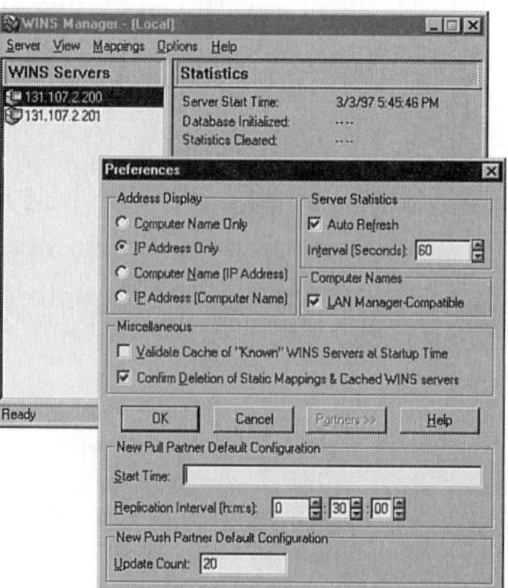

FIG. 18.13⇒
The Preferences dialog box.

WINS Client Installation and Configuration

When the TCP/IP protocol is installed on a WINS-compliant client—such as a Windows NT domain controller or member server, a Windows NT Workstation, or a Windows 95 computer—WINS can be installed and configured. WINS is configured from the WINS Address tab in the TCP/IP Properties sheet (Figure 18.14). The only thing that has to be configured is the IP address of a primary or secondary WINS server. From that point, any time the WINS client is started, it will register its name, IP address, and user with a designated WINS server. When WINS client computers are shut down properly, the clients send a WINS server a name-release request, and then the computer name/IP mapping is released from the WINS database.

The TCP/IP properties sheet also has options to Enable DNS for Workstation Resolution and Enable LMHOST Lookup (which is selected by default). An LMHOST file can be imported from this screen and a Scope ID can also be configured.

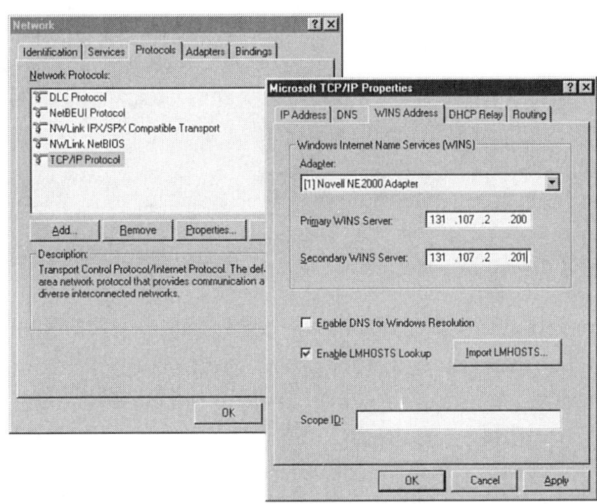

FIG. 18.14⇒
A WINS client configuration example.

Domain Name System Server

Windows NT 4.0 Server is also capable of being configured as a Domain Name System (DNS) server. DNS is installed from the Select Network Service dialog box by selecting Microsoft DNS Server.

In a DNS or Internet/intranet environment, clients (resolvers) query DNS servers and their databases for computer name resolution. DNS servers map DNS domain names to IP addresses.

DNS Server Configuration

After the DNS service is installed, open the TCP/IP protocol property sheet from the Network dialog box and select the DNS tab. The first thing that must be defined is a domain name, as well as the IP addresses of the

DNS servers in the DNS Service Search Order window, as illustrated in Figure 18.15.

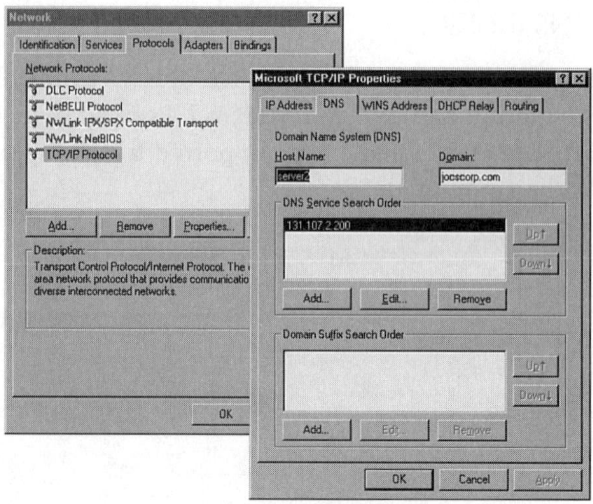

FIG. 18.15⇒
A DNS domain and server configuration example.

The next step in the process of configuring a DNS server is to start DNS Manager from the Administrative Tools program group, and then define a new server or group of servers in the Server List that is going to be managed from this computer's DNS Manager.

The drop-down menu options in DNS Manager include DNS, View, Options, and Help. Except for configuring Preferences in the Options menu, all other DNS configuration is performed from the DNS menu. The Preferences selection under the Options menu allows for Auto Refresh Statistics, Show Automatically Created Zones, and Expose TTL (TimeToLive). Either right-click the Server List icon and choose New Server, or, from the DNS drop-down menu, select New Server (see Figure 18.16). Figure 18.17 displays the result of entering a server name or IP address and then clicking OK.

When a DNS server has been created successfully and, if required, forwarded information is defined in the Servers properties sheet, a zone is created by right-clicking the server and selecting a new zone. In the Creating New Zone for Server dialog box, enter the required information by typing the zone name in the Zone Name window, then press the Tab key. A zone file name will appear automatically. Select the Next button to produce an information screen that states that all the information for the new zone has been entered. To create the new zone, click the Finish button. Figure 18.18 illustrates the creation of a new zone.

FIG. 18.16⇒
The Add DNS Server dialog box.

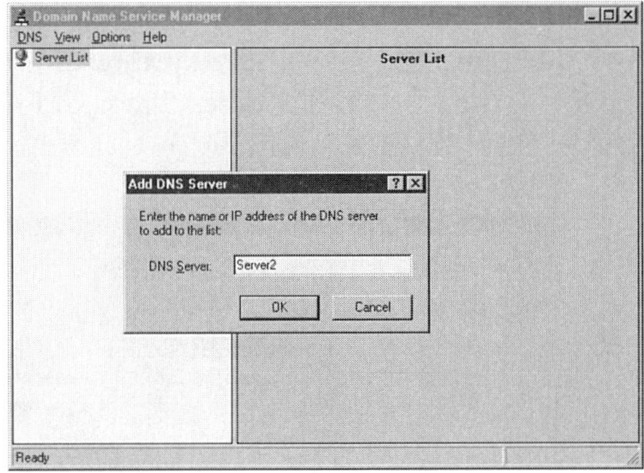

FIG. 18.17⇒
The results of adding a DNS server.

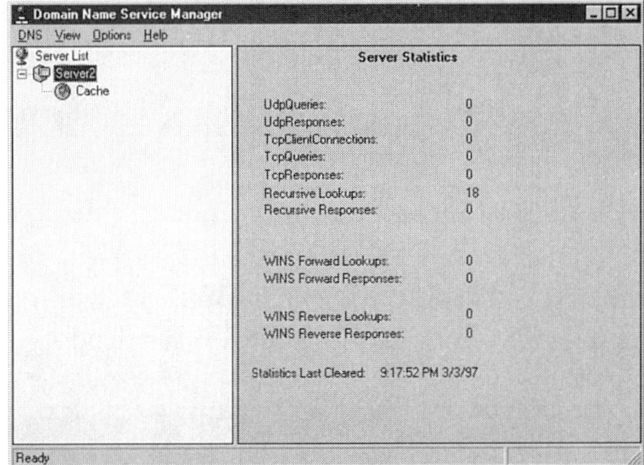

FIG. 18.18⇒
The creation of a new DNS zone.

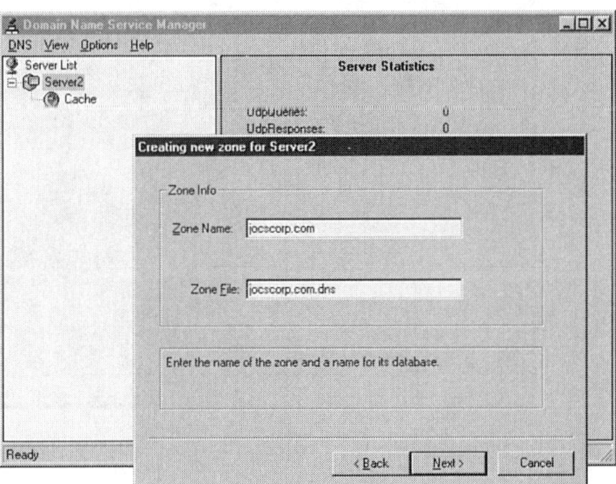

Ch 18

When a new zone is created, the DNS Manager is displayed as shown in Figure 18.19 (in Figure 18.19, two additional records have already been added). The first is the A Record (Address Record) for server2; the second is the CNAME Record (Canonical or Alias Record).

FIG. 18.19⇒
An example of the newly created DNS zone and DNS record associations.

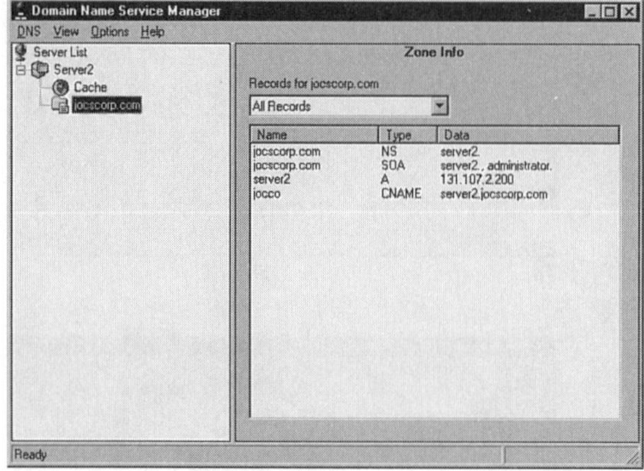

Figure 18.20 illustrates the Ping utility being utilized to ping both server2's address of 131.107.2.200 and the alias or CNAME of server2. Pinging the alias was successful because of the CNAME record (refer to Figure 18.19). The alias computer name to IP address is resolved by the DNS database.

FIG. 18.20⇒
This is an example of pinging an IP address and alias name.

```
Command Prompt

D:\users>ping 131.107.2.200

Pinging 131.107.2.200 with 32 bytes of data:

Reply from 131.107.2.200: bytes=32 time<10ms TTL=128
Reply from 131.107.2.200: bytes=32 time<10ms TTL=128
Reply from 131.107.2.200: bytes=32 time<10ms TTL=128
Reply from 131.107.2.200: bytes=32 time<10ms TTL=128

D:\users>ping jocco

Pinging Server2.jocscorp.com [131.107.2.200] with 32 bytes of data:

Reply from 131.107.2.200: bytes=32 time<10ms TTL=128
Reply from 131.107.2.200: bytes=32 time<10ms TTL=128
Reply from 131.107.2.200: bytes=32 time<10ms TTL=128
Reply from 131.107.2.200: bytes=32 time<10ms TTL=128

D:\users>
```

IP Routing

The Routing Information Protocol (RIP) for Internet protocol is another service available in Windows NT 4.0. After it is installed, a Windows NT 4.0 system can act as an IP router in a TCP/IP network. The service is installed from the Services tab in the network application.

When RIP for IP is installed, the Routing tab in the TCP/IP Properties sheet displays an Enable IP Forwarding check box, which is selected by default. The Routing tab also states that `IP Forwarding (IP Routing) allows packets to be forwarded on a multi-homed system.` A *multi-homed system* is a system with more than one network card installed, each of which is connected to a unique subnet. Windows NT 4.0 can forward TCP/IP packets between subnets. Figure 18.21 displays the IP Routing tab.

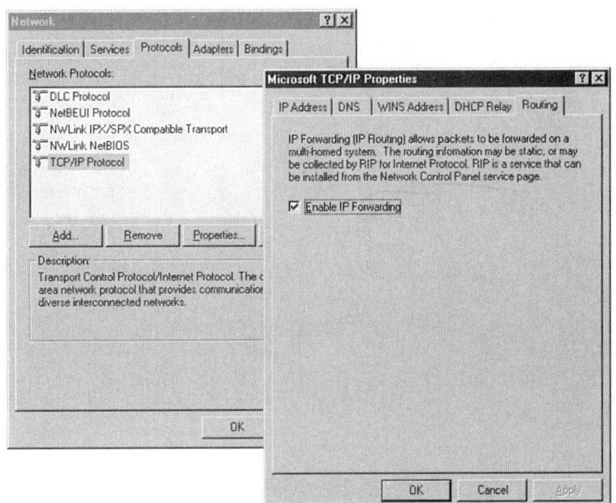

FIG. 18.21⇒
The IP Routing tab is used to configure NT as a network router.

TCP/IP and the Registry

Registry keys and values for the TCP/IP protocol and all of its additional services are found in many different locations in the Registry. To display all locations would be virtually impossible, as well as impractical; however, a number of default keys and values are shown in the following figures. Figure 18.22 displays the default TCP parameters.

FIG. 18.22⇒
The default TCP Registry parameter values.

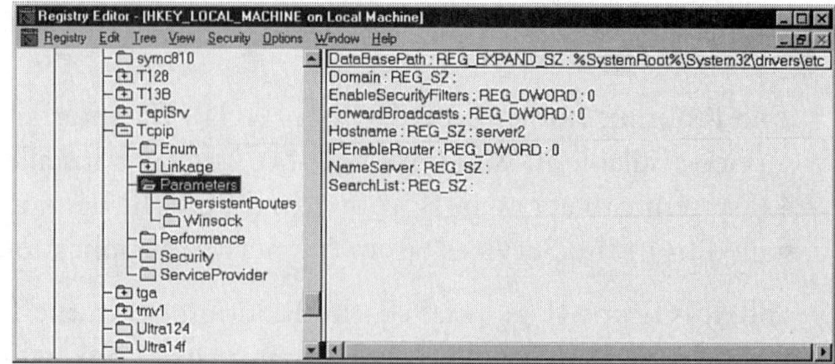

Figure 18.23 shows the default NE20001 network adapter card parameters for TCP/IP. Values can change depending on the network adapter card used.

FIG. 18.23⇒
The default TCP NE20001-compatible network adapter card parameters.

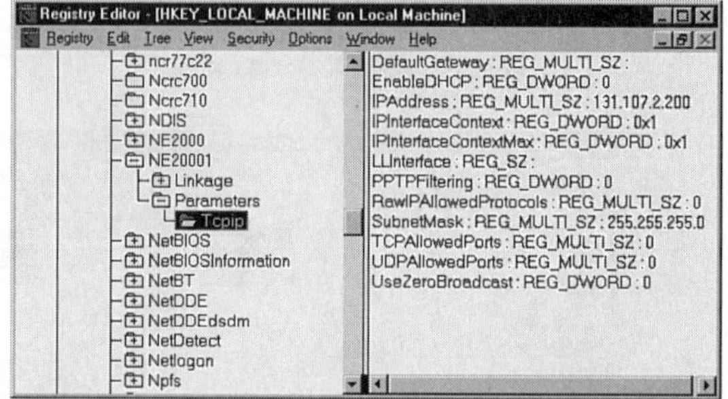

Default NetBIOS over TCP/IP parameters are established in the Registry when TCP/IP is installed. Figure 18.24 displays the NetBT over TCP/IP default Registry values.

FIG. 18.24⇒
The default NetBT over TCP/IP Registry parameters.

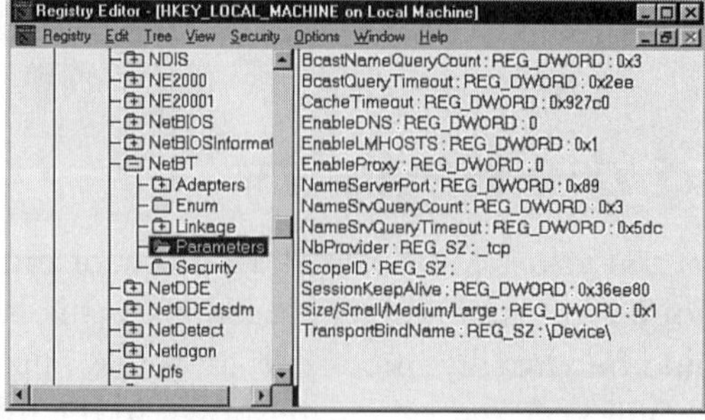

The default Windows sockets Registry entries are shown in Figures 18.25 and 18.26.

FIG. 18.25⇒
The default Winsock Registry parameters.

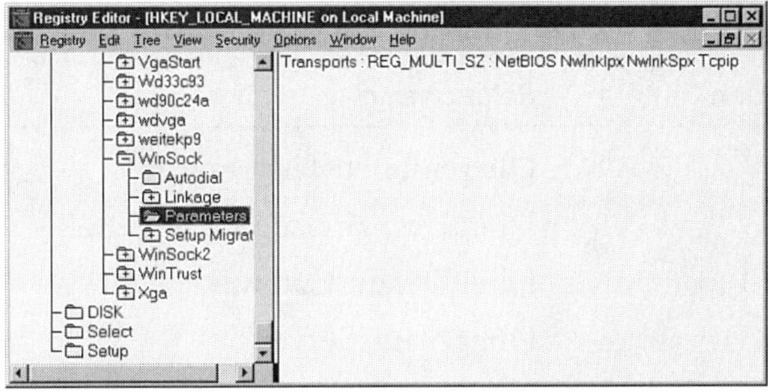

FIG. 18.26⇒
The default TCP/IP Winsock Registry parameters.

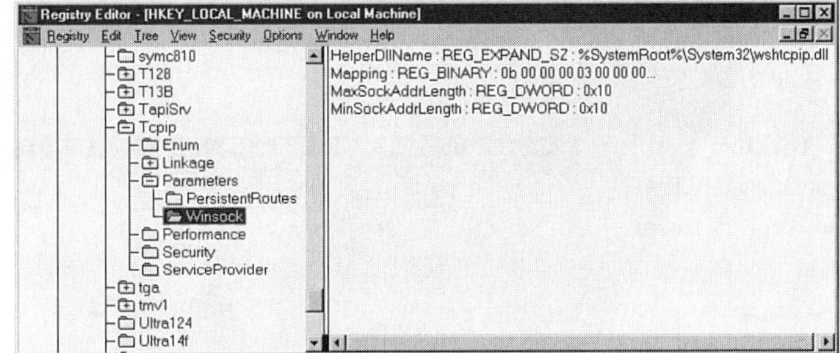

Default DHCPServer Registry parameters are displayed in Figure 18.27.

FIG. 18.27⇒
The default DHCP Server Registry parameters.

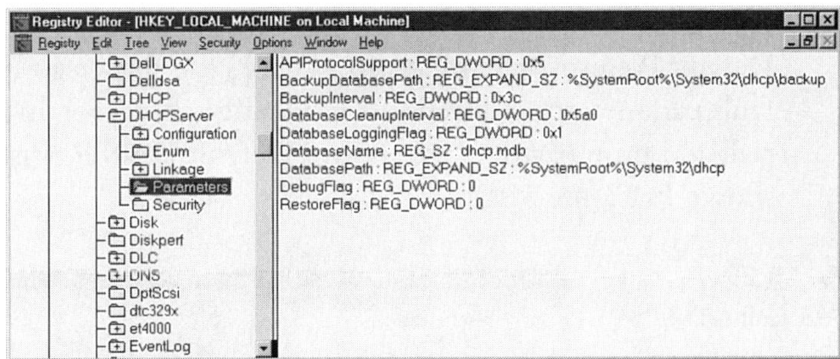

Figure 18.28 shows parameter information relating to the DHCP client portion of DHCP. Many parameter options are available in this location; however, only one option, 15, is shown in Figure 18.28. All of the default options and their relation to DHCP are listed in Table 18.4.

Table 18.4 DHCP Client Registry Options

Option	Relationship
1	DhcpSubnetMaskOption
15	DhcpDomain (see Figure 18.29)
3	DhcpDefaultGateway
44	DhcpNameServer
46	DhcpNodeType
47	DhcpScopeID
6	DhcpNameServer

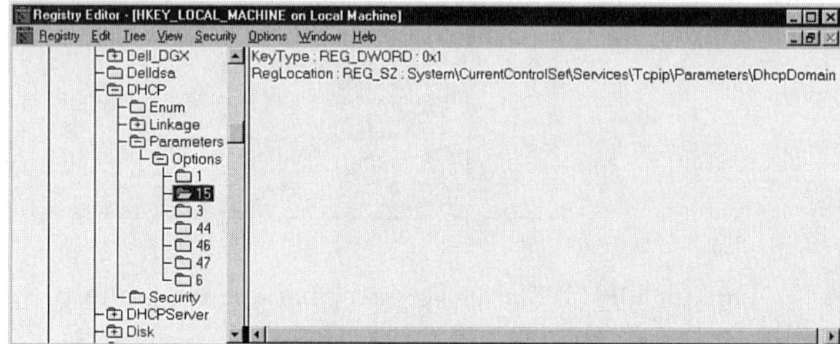

FIG. 18.28⇒
The default DHCP Client Registry parameters.

Default Registry parameters for WINS are shown in Figure 18.29. No default parameters are listed in this location; however, in this example, the pull and push partners are shown. Default DNS Registry parameters are shown in Figure 18.30.

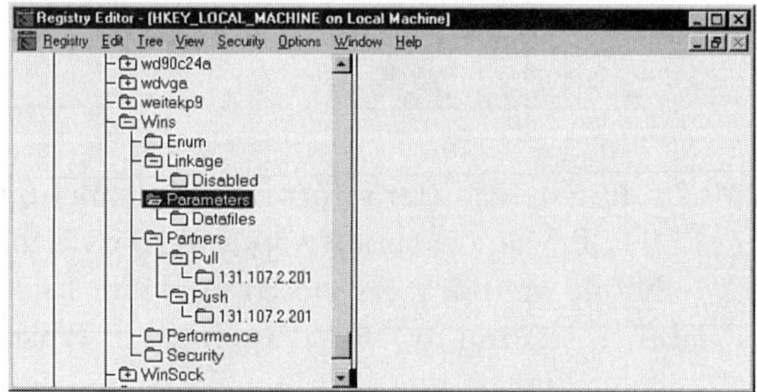

FIG. 18.29⇒
The default WINS Registry parameters.

FIG. 18.30⇒
The default DNS Registry parameters.

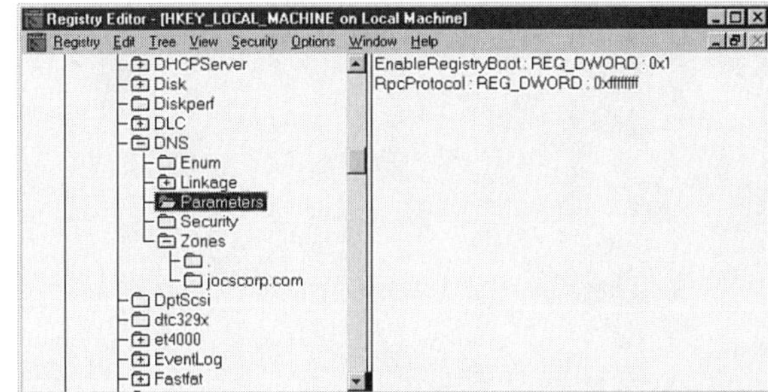

For additional information on the TCP/IP protocol, options, and Registry parameters, refer to the online help files in Windows NT 4.0 and the Windows NT 4.0 Resource Kit.

Taking the Disc Test

If you have read and understood the material in this chapter, you are ready to test your knowledge. Insert the CD-ROM that comes with this book and run the self-test software, as described in Appendix K, "Using the Self-Test Software."

From Here...

The next two chapters explore IPX/SPX and Novell NetWare networks.

Chapter Prerequisite

Before reading this chapter, you should be familiar with fundamental networking concepts and protocols. You should have read Chapter 14, "Networking Essentials," and generally be familiar with Novell NetWare.

19

Novell NetWare and Windows NT

Corporations and businesses today are faced with the challenge of a complex computing environment. Most of the issues associated with the management of this environment are related to integration of components within that architecture. In recognition of that fact, Microsoft has intensified its efforts to develop Windows NT connectivity tools. The efforts have included the development of NWLink, File and Print Services for NetWare (FPNW), Directory Service Manager for NetWare (DSMN), Gateway Services for NetWare (GSNW), Client Services for NetWare (CSNW), and the Migration Tool for NetWare.

This chapter covers the following topics:

- The Windows NT connectivity tools for NetWare
- FPNW—File and Print Sharing for NetWare
- DSMN—Directory Service Manager for NetWare

- GSNW—Gateway Services for NetWare
- Migration Tool for NetWare

NWLink IPX/SPX-Compatible Transport

The NWLink protocol is the foundation of NT/Novell integration. This protocol is an IPX/SPX-compatible protocol that is also compatible with SPX II. IPX/SPX stands for Internetwork Packet Exchange/Sequenced Packet Exchange and is the group of transport protocols used in Novell NetWare networks. Because NWLink is a Microsoft product, NWLink follows the Network Driver Interface Specification (NDIS) and is fully NDIS-compliant.

NWLink provides support for both Windows Sockets APIs (Application Programming Interfaces), Remote Procedure Calls (RPCs), Novell NetBIOS, and the NWLink NetBIOS. NWLink ships with both Windows NT Server and Windows NT Workstation. NWLink is the transport protocol necessary to implement any of the integration tools, and it can be loaded with any other transport protocol that might be needed. The protocol can be added, as well as other protocols, from the Network icon in the Control Panel, or from the Properties selection from the Network Neighborhood context menu. The access screen is shown in Figure 19.1

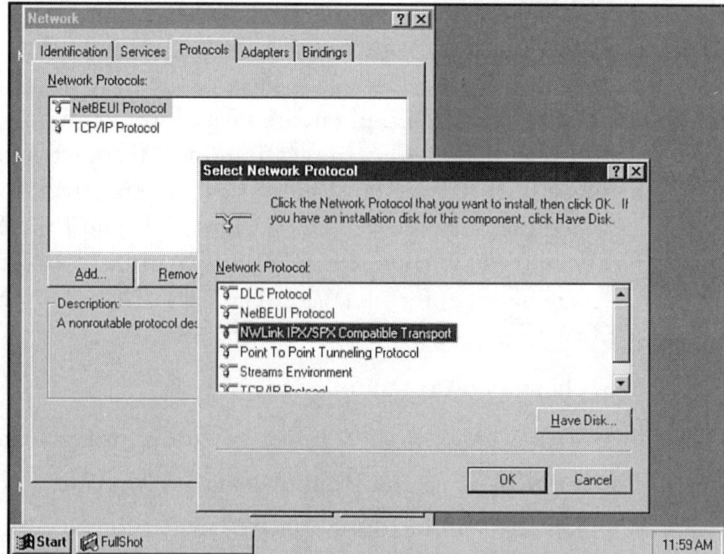

FIG. 19.1⇒
Protocols can be added from the access screen.

The configuration parameters for NWLink are straightforward. Most of the parameters needed will be provided by the NetWare LAN administrator. The NetWare Internal Network Number is the number that NetWare routers use to determine if the packet belongs on that LAN segment or another network. Further information regarding these parameters can be found in the Novell manuals. If NWLink does not detect that number, it will default to some random value.

Frame Type relates to the decision concerning frame types for Ethernet. You can specify a specific frame type or let NT automatically select a frame type. Frame Type is typically set to Autodetect when using Ethernet. When Frame Type is set to Autodetect, Windows NT will go through the list of frame types, as they are listed in the frame type selection box, and test each one until Windows NT gets a response. NT will select the default frame type when using Autodetect mode if there is no response. To set the frame type manually, you need to know which frame type to choose. Usually a NetWare 2.x or 3.11 server uses 802.3, whereas a NetWare 3.12 or 4.x server will typically use an 802.2 frame type.

Tip

When using NWLink, a fast way to determine the frame type is to use the IPXROUTE CONFIG command. The results of this command include the frame type.

Token Ring networks have their own set of parameters. These configuration parameters concern the Token Ring Source Routing Table, which is kept on each computer in a token ring environment. The Source Routing Table is used to determine the route the packet will take. If there is a packet that is received without a corresponding Mac address in the Source Routing Table, there is a slight problem. When this happens, the packet is passed on as a Single Route Broadcast. The IPXROUTE also is useful in this situation because it will indicate if a Single Route Broadcast packet is being sent.

Services for NetWare

The latest release of Windows NT combines two NetWare products—File and Print Services for NetWare and Directory Services for NetWare—into one product called Services for NetWare. The following sections cover the capabilities of this new product.

File and Print Services

File and Print Services for NetWare (FPNW) emulates a NetWare 3.x server, *not* a NetWare 4.x server. NetWare clients can connect to a Windows NT server running FPNW as if they were accessing a NetWare server. FPNW is supported on all Windows NT platforms, including MIPS, Intel, Alpha, and PowerPC machines. It actually is a service that runs on the Windows NT Server. Included with FPNW are the Administration Tools and the FPNW product. Generally, the complete package is installed on the Primary Domain Controller, and the Administrative Tools are installed on each Backup Domain Controller. When FPNW is running, the Windows NT Server can be a server for any NetWare client—without modifying the client workstation. The file and print services are supported by using either Netx, the NetWare shell, or VLM, the DOS requester.

FPNW is added as other Windows NT services are added, from the Network properties Protocol tab. Because FPNW is a separate add-on, the Have Disk option is used to install the service.

FPNW should be installed on an NTFS partition (see Chapter 9, "Managing Disk Resources," for details on NTFS). This enables NT to duplicate the security found on the NetWare volume. After the installation process, the directory structure has the required NetWare directories: MAIL, LOGIN, PUBLIC, and SYSTEM. FPNW provides NetWare-compatible commands in the PUBLIC directory, such as SLIST, USERLIST, MAP, CAPTURE, and so on.

The FPNW installation process also requests a server name. The server name is the Windows NT computer account that the NetWare clients are using. Windows NT defaults to the server's computer name, followed by FPNW.

The installation process creates a Supervisor account, which is added to the Administrators group. A system restart is done at this point and then the process is continued by adding new users. The new users are added from the FPNW icon in the Control Panel. When accessing the New User dialog box from User Manager for Domains, notice the additional selection at the bottom (see Figure 19.2). This is a check box to Maintain NetWare Compatible Logon. Checking this box enables the user-login for FPNW.

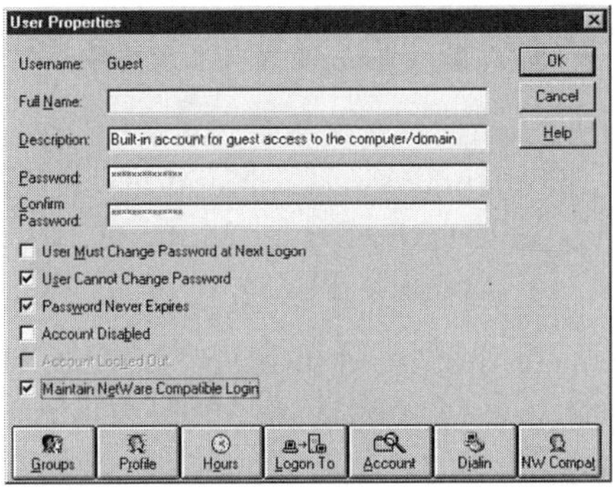

FIG. 19.2⇒
NetWare-compatible logons can be configured for individual users by checking the box at the bottom of the New User dialog box.

Directory Service Manager

Directory Service Manager for NetWare (DSMN), like FPNW, has to be purchased separately. DSMN is useful when your network has multiple NetWare 3.x file servers. In the NetWare environment, if a user needs access to files on various servers, then that user needs to be defined in the appropriate servers' accounts database (bindery). For example, if a user needs access to three NetWare 3.x servers, an account has to be created on each server for that user. While at first glance this may not seem to be a problem, it is. The requirement for multiple definitions of users has been an extra administrative task, with associated problems such as password synchronization and directory mappings.

DSMN is a time-saver because it brings the administrative tasks into one location, the Windows NT server. A user only has to be created in one location, the Windows NT server. DSMN updates the NetWare 3.x servers. DSMN is installed on the Primary Domain Controller, and the account information is replicated in the ordinary manner. Essentially, DSMN does not require any changes on the clients' workstation. Instead, core files are replaced in the SYS:PUBLIC directory.

DSMN requires Gateway Service for NetWare (GSNW) to be installed, which is covered in a later section "Gateway Services for NetWare." DSMN is installed, as are other services, from the Network icon.

> **Caution**
> Notice that if FPNW is installed before DSMN, the users defined for FPNW will not be synchronized to the NetWare server automatically.

Gateway Services for NetWare

Gateway Services for NetWare (GSNW), which is included with Windows NT, enables Microsoft clients to access NetWare servers. From the bit/byte perspective, GSNW converts the Server Message Block (SMB) packet to Novell's NetWare Core Protocol (NCP).

The Microsoft clients do not need to have NetWare client software or Microsoft's Client Service for NetWare (CSNW) installed. The Windows NT Server shares the NetWare resources and presents these resources to the Microsoft clients for use. The clients attach to the Windows NT Server share, which is actually a NetWare resource.

The Netware server sees only one attachment and access rights are assigned to that account. The Windows NT Server can permit multiple attachments to the share, and, as a consequence, there actually may be many people using the NetWare resource. This can be slow due to speed considerations for the translation between SMB and NCP. Also, because access rights are assigned to that account, all users from the Windows NT side that are accessing the resource have the same rights.

One of the ideal uses for GSNW is to allow access to NetWare print queues. To accomplish this, you have to add a *logical* printer to the NT Server and direct it to a NetWare print queue (printing device from Windows NT's perspective). Then, you add the driver from the Windows NT installation disk, and the printer appears in the printer folder as if it were a local printer. The Windows NT administrator must then share the printer before it will be available to all users. GSNW allows the creation of a gateway for resources on the NetWare Directory Service (NDS) tree, in addition to the resources available on any NetWare server with bindery security.

The installation process for GSNW follows the same process as installing other services. However, there are a few pre-installation tasks.

- From the NetWare server, create a group called NTGATEWAY. From this group, assign the access rights to the resource.
- From the NetWare server, create a user and put that user into the group NTGATEWAY.
- Log on to NT as a member of the Administrators group.

Use the Network icon to access the network configuration options. This also can be accessed by secondary clicking the Network Neighborhood icon and then selecting Properties from the Context menu. After the configuration screen is displayed, select the Services tab. Highlight the Service and Click Add to install the Gateway (and Client) Services for NetWare.

If NWLink has not been installed already, it will be installed automatically when this service is selected.

After the selection of the service, the Gateway Service for NetWare dialog box is displayed, as shown in Figure 19.3.

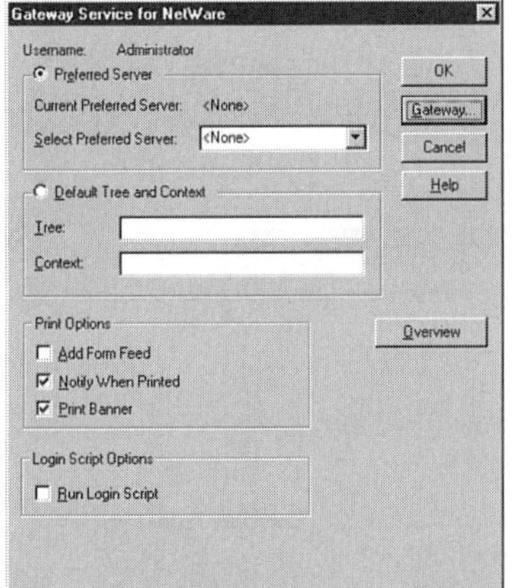

FIG. 19.3⇒
The Gateway Service for NetWare dialog box is the screen that allows the entry of configuration information.

In the Preferred Server box, enter the name of the NetWare server to which the Windows NT Server is attaching. If the NetWare server is using NDS, enter the name of the tree where the resource is located in the Tree box. Enter the position of the object in the Context text box. Next, enter any additional print commands to the Print Options text box. The Login Script Options control whether the login script should be executed at login time.

Selecting the Gateway button shown in Figure 19.3 displays the Configure Gateway screen, as shown in Figure 19.4.

Enter the gateway user name in the Gateway Account text box; in Figure 19.4 it is Gateway_User. Note that any name can be used, but it is wise to use names that remind you of the original intentions in creating the account. The NetWare configuration would have a group named

NTGATEWAY, with a user in it named Gateway_User. The creation of the group and user was done in the pre-installation steps.

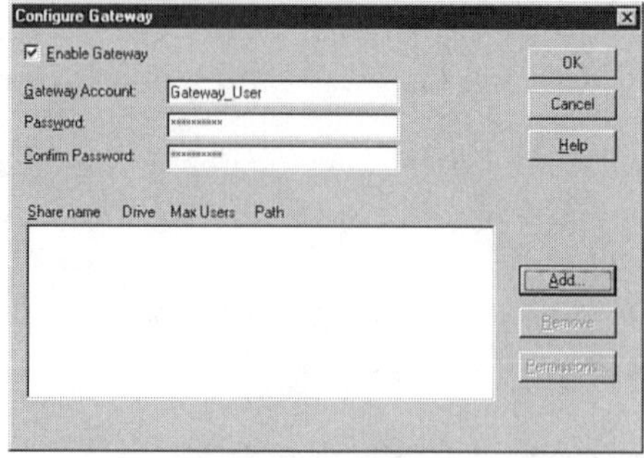

FIG. 19.4⇒ The Configure Gateway Screen allows the input of configuration information.

Use the Add button to add new shares that are going to be accessed, as shown in Figure 19.5.

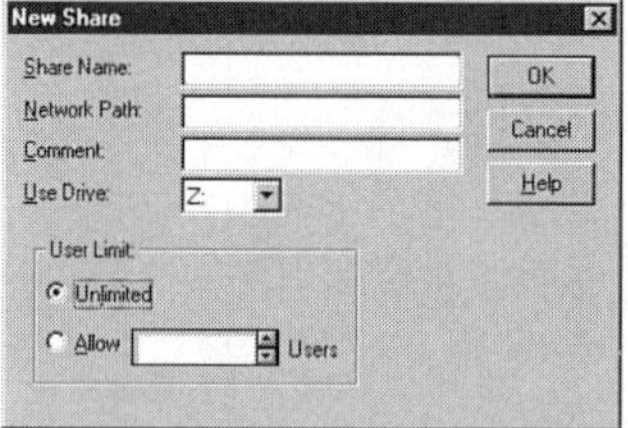

FIG. 19.5⇒ The share administration screen allows the entry of specific information related to new shares.

Enter the name of the share in the Share Name text box. The share name should be named as any other NT share is named. The share name will appear in the browse list. In the Network Path text box, enter the volume that is being shared, which is the NetWare volume and path name. In the Use Drive text box, enter the drive letter that is to be used to establish the gateway share. The User Limit area is used to control the number of users accessing the share.

After the share is configured as indicated in Figure 19.5, the screen returns to that shown in Figure 19.4 with the share information entered. From this screen, the permissions can be set. As with other Windows NT shares, the default is Full Control for the group Everyone. The trustee rights that are set in NetWare override the Windows NT share-level permissions.

After the gateway configurations are made and permissions set, the process is finished. The GSNW icon appears in the Control Panel for future use, as shown in Figure 19.6.

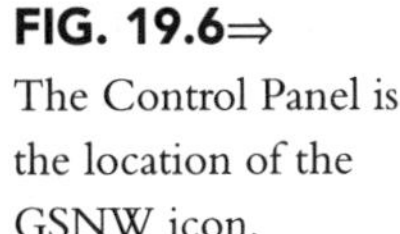

FIG. 19.6⇒
The Control Panel is the location of the GSNW icon.

Client Services for NetWare

The Client Services for NetWare (CSNW) are packaged with Windows NT. This software is also a service; however, it runs on the client Windows NT Workstation. The purpose of this service is to allow the users to access NetWare resources. CSNW supports NetWare 2.x servers, 3.x servers, and 4.x servers.

CSNW is installed on Windows NT Workstation the same way that a service is installed on Windows NT Server. Refer to Figure 19.3 to see the screen that demonstrates the configuration information that is needed of the service. It is significant to note that when the Client Services for NetWare are installed, they are installed on the NT Workstation machine. When that occurs, the Control Panel of the NT Workstation machine has a CSNW icon that brings up a screen titled Client Services for NetWare and asks for the same information. Of course, the CSNW screen does not have a button for Gateway configuration, which would apply only to Gateway Services.

Migration Tool for NetWare

Windows NT ships with a Migration Tool for NetWare. The purpose of this tool is to seamlessly move the users from NetWare to Windows NT. It works in conjunction with FPNW for the migration of the logon scripts; if FPNW is not running, the logon scripts won't be migrated. Essentially, the Migration Tool reads the NetWare bindery and creates the users and groups on the Windows NT Server. File and directory permissions can also be migrated if the receiving Windows NT volume is NTFS. Additionally, the Migration Tool has the added capability of migrating more than one NetWare server to the Windows NT primary domain controller (or BDC). The receiving Windows NT Server must have NWLink and GSNW already installed before using this utility. Working with this utility requires both Supervisor (for NetWare) and Administrator (for Windows NT) rights.

When using the Migration Tool, the screen looks similar to that shown in Figure 19.7. When you select the Add button, another screen is displayed to indicate the selection for the target and destination server. The boxes with the ellipses enable the administrator to select the server from a screen similar to Network Neighborhood, as shown in Figure 19.8.

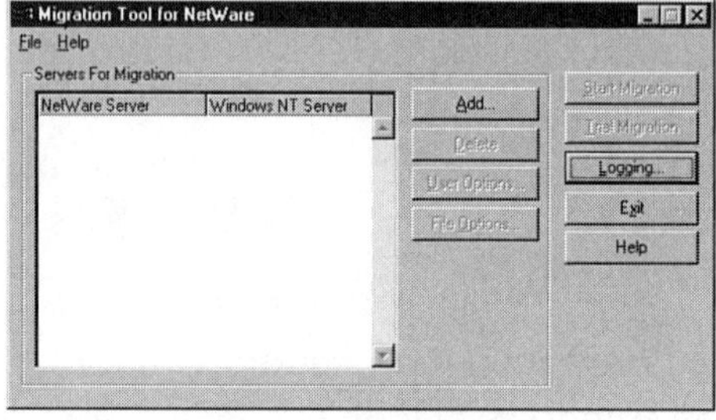

FIG. 19.7⇒ The first Migration Tool screen displays the list of the servers being migrated, and allows the setting of user and file options, as well as the actual migration options.

FIG. 19.8⇒ Enter the names of the NetWare and Windows NT Servers involved. The ellipses give access to a screen that allows the selection of the servers from the available servers.

The Users option box, which appears in the Migration Tool for NetWare dialog box (refer to Figure 19.7), allows control over the user accounts and groups. The default of this transfer is that all of the users and groups are migrated to the Windows NT domain, unless there is a name conflict. The administrator can choose to create a mapping file with a listing for each user, and specific information for each user's account.

Novell NetWare uses an encryption scheme for password storage; therefore, the passwords from a NetWare server cannot be migrated. In order to assign some type of password, an administrator can use a mapping file to include the password information. If the administrator chooses to use a mapping file, the password information can also be included with the group and user options. Possible options for password information include assigning all accounts a null password, setting the new password to the user's name, indicating a single password for all migrated accounts, and specifying that the password must be changed at the next logon.

The File Options button gives the administrator greater control over the transfer of folders and files. The preferred option is to have folders and files migrated to an NTFS partition so that the effective rights are retained.

The most helpful option is the option to run a trial migration. When the trial migration runs, it creates various log files (shown in Table 19.1).

Table 19.1 Trial Migration Log Files

Log File Name	Content
Logfile.log	User and group information
Error.log	Failures and error messages
Summary.log	Summary of trial migration, names of server, users, groups, and files

The Migration Tool for NetWare also has a convenient feature that enables the administrator to save the configuration. All of the configuration information entered for Users and Files can be saved by selecting File, Save Configuration, as shown in Figure 19.9.

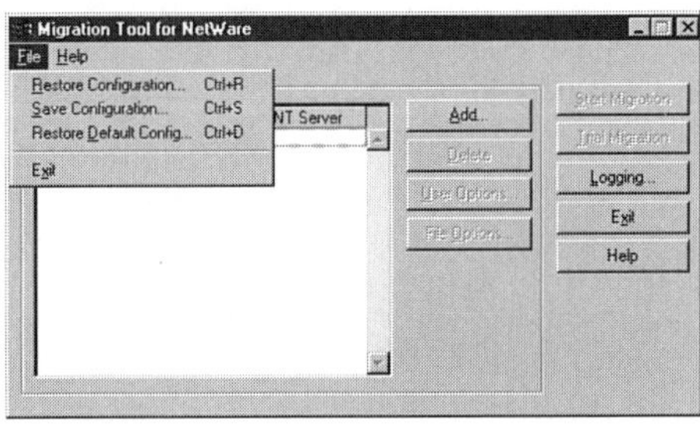

FIG. 19.9⇒ The Migration Tool for Netware offers three options under the File command.

Taking the Disc Test

If you have read and understood the material in this chapter, you are ready to test your knowledge. Insert the CD-ROM that comes with this book and run the self-test software, as described in Appendix K, "Using the Self-Test Software."

From Here...

The next chapter, Chapter 20, "Network Printing," discusses network printing. Topics of discussion include planning, sharing, and securing network printers.

Chapter Prerequisite

Readers should have read Chapter 11, "Printing," and also should have a general concept of Windows NT share-level security.

Network Printing

This chapter provides discussions on adding and configuring network printing devices, working with printer pools and printer priorities, and troubleshooting network printing. The concepts and procedures discussed in this chapter apply to both Workstation and Server installations.

The following topics will be covered in this chapter:

- Adding and configuring network printing
- Exploring DLC, TCP/IP, and Macintosh installation options

To get started, a brief review is presented of some of the printer terminology that is used in the Windows NT 4.0 print process. A *printer* in Windows NT 4.0 is the software interface between the application and the physical printing device, which consists of the print driver and the print queue. The physical hardware that does the printing is referred to as the *print device*. A print request or print job can be sent to either a *local print device*, connected directly to the user's local computer, or a *remote print device*, which is attached to, and managed by, another computer or print server on the network. Requests can also be sent to a *network interface print device*, which is controlled and managed by a print server on the network, but is connected directly to the network, not to a print server.

Windows NT 4.0 Print Process

The print process starts when an application makes a print request. As mentioned previously, print drivers do not have to be manually installed on each Windows NT installation—one of Microsoft's innovative designs found in the Windows NT 4.0 print process is automatic downloading of the required print drivers for Windows NT clients (all versions) and Windows 95 clients. While these clients do need a print driver to process print requests, these clients *do not require* that a print driver be manually installed locally. When any Windows NT or Windows 95 client connects to a network printer server through the Print Wizard application, the Windows NT print server automatically downloads the required print driver to the client.

After the print driver is downloaded, anytime a Windows NT client prints to the network printer, a version check is done to make sure the latest print driver exists on the client. If the latest version does not exist on the client, the print server automatically downloads a copy of the newer print driver to the client computer.

Key Concept

At this point in time, no version checking is done between Windows NT 4.0 print servers and Windows 95 clients. If a new print driver is installed on the Windows NT 4.0 print server, each Windows 95 client will require the newer print driver to be installed manually.

The automatic downloading of print drivers to Windows NT and Windows 95 clients provides network administrators the capability to easily provide a greater number and variety of print devices to their clients. Print drivers do not have to be manually installed on every client computer. Figure 20.1 shows a graphic representation of the print process, including the six specific print-process steps, which are explained next.

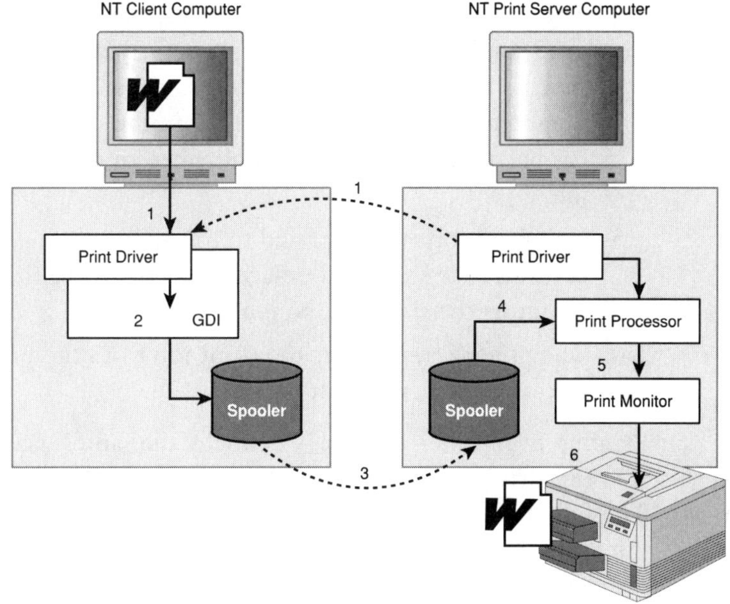

FIG. 20.1⇒
The Windows NT 4.0 print process for Windows NT and Windows 95 clients.

The following list presents the six print-process steps:

1. When a Windows NT client makes a request to print on a print device that is attached to a print server, the client computer checks its local print driver. If the client does not have one installed, or if the local copy is older than the copy on the print server, the print server automatically downloads a copy of the print driver to the client. (If a Windows 95 client's print driver is older than the print server, the newer print driver must be manually loaded on the Windows 95 client.)
2. By default, the Graphics Device Interface (GDI) component of a Windows NT 4.0 client operating system creates a print job in enhanced metafile format. This is sometimes called a *journal* file, and it represents the print job formatted to print on most any print device type, such as HPPCL or PostScript. The print job is then sent to the local spooler.
3. The local *Spooler* service makes a *Remote Procedure Call* (RPC) connection to the corresponding service on the print server and copies the print job to the print server spooler directory. The bulk of the print process now continues on the print server.

4. The print job is routed to the appropriate *print processor*, where the print job is further rendered into a format that is compatible for the specific print device. This usually is referred to as a *RAW* file (refer to the section "Print Processor" later in the chapter). If a *separator page* has been requested, then it is attached to the beginning of the print job.
5. The print job is then passed to the appropriate *print monitor*, which controls access to print devices, directs jobs to the correct port, and monitors the status of the job.
6. The *print device* receives the print job from the print monitor and generates the final print product.

Printing from other clients is essentially the same, except that the appropriate print driver must be installed on the respective local client computer. The fully formatted RAW print job file is generated locally and routed to the print server spooler. Because no further rendering is needed, a separator page is added, if required, and the print monitor sends the print job to the print device.

Windows NT 4.0 supports MS-DOS-based applications and Windows-based applications. In general, these applications take advantage of the Windows NT print driver and print successfully. Some MS-DOS applications that produce graphic print output, however, probably will require that the print driver native to that application be installed for that application. It is safe to say that if the print output from MS-DOS or Windows-based applications is not correct, you will need to install an application-specific driver.

Adding and Configuring Network Printing

This section explains how to create and share printers, set their characteristics and properties, assign security, and manage print jobs.

Sharing a Printer

If a printer is not shared during installation, it can be shared at a later time and permissions can be configured, too. The default permission for shared printers enables Everyone to print permissions.

To share a printer, use these steps:

1. Display the printer's property sheet by secondary-clicking the Printer's icon in the Printers dialog box and then choose Properties. Or, double-click the Printer's icon in the Printers dialog box, choose the Printer drop-down menu, and choose Properties.
2. Select the Sharing tab.
3. Enter a user-friendly share name. This is the name that users see when they are deciding to which printer they want to connect. Make the share name descriptive and informative.

Note Printer share names, as is true with all share names, must remain within the eight-character range for non-Windows NT/Windows 95 clients to be able to see the share name. If the share name is longer than eight characters, MS-DOS and Windows 3.1/3.11 network clients may not be able to connect to the printer.

4. Optionally, choose to install an alternate platform printer driver, if needed.
5. Choose OK. The printer now will be shared.

Setting Permissions for the Shared Printer

There are no permissions that you can set directly on a printer share. Instead, permissions are set on the printer itself. There are four permissions that can be used to secure a printer in Windows NT 4.0:

- *No Access* means just that. Regardless of the permission you have been assigned through group membership, if you get No Access explicitly or through a group, you will not be able to access the printer to print *or* view the print jobs.
- *Print* permission is the default permission for the Everyone group. It allows users to connect to the printer, send print jobs to the printer, and manage their own print jobs. Users can delete, pause, resume, or restart print jobs owned by the user.
- *Manage Documents* allows all the permissions of Print and extends job management to *all* print jobs.
- *Full Control*, in addition to the permissions allowed for Manage Documents, lets the user modify printer settings, enable or disable sharing, delete printers, and modify permissions.

Like file and folder permissions, the permission list is actually the Access Control List (ACL) for the printer. By default, Administrators and Power Users are given Full Control on Windows NT Workstations and Member Servers; Administrators, Print Operators, and Server Operators have Full Control on Windows NT domain controllers. On all Windows NT computers, Everyone has Print permission and Creator Owner has Manage Documents permissions. The *Creator Owner* group is a special internal group that Windows NT uses to identify the owner of a file, folder, or, in this case, a print job. By assigning it the Manage Documents permission, you basically are saying that only the owner of any given print job has the ability to pause, resume, delete, resend, or cancel it.

To secure a printer, use these steps:

1. Display the printer's property sheet by secondary-clicking the Printer's icon in the Printers dialog box, and then choose Properties. Or, double-click the Printer's icon in the Printers dialog box, choose the Printer drop-down menu, and choose Properties.
2. Select the Security tab.
3. Choose Permissions to display the Printer Permissions dialog box. The current ACL for the printer is displayed in the Name list box (see Figure 20.2).

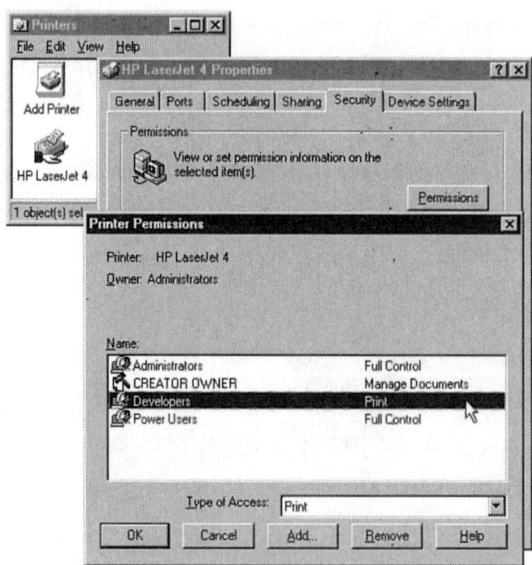

FIG. 20.2⇒ In the Printer Permissions dialog box for the HP LaserJet 4, the Everyone group has been removed and the Developers group has been added with Print permission.

4. Modify the access of the current ACL entries by selecting the entry and choosing a Type of Access; or choose Remove to remove entries

from the list (like Everyone, Print); or choose Add to add user and group accounts from the local or domain SAM database.

5. Choose OK to save the permissions.

Auditing the Printer

As with files and folders, access to a printer can be audited, provided auditing has been enabled in User Manager (see Figure 20.3). The audit events are saved as part of the Security log after auditing is enabled through User Manager or User Manager for Domains from the Policies drop-down menu. The Security log can be viewed through the Event Viewer utility. File and Object Access must be selected after auditing is enabled.

Auditing for the printer can be configured by selecting Auditing from the Security tab on the printer's property sheet. Recall that you audit the activities of specific users and groups regarding the printer, instead of auditing general access to the printer.

In the Printer Auditing dialog box, select Add to display the account database. Select the users and groups for whom you want to record printer activity. In the Printer Auditing dialog box, select the activities you want to audit.

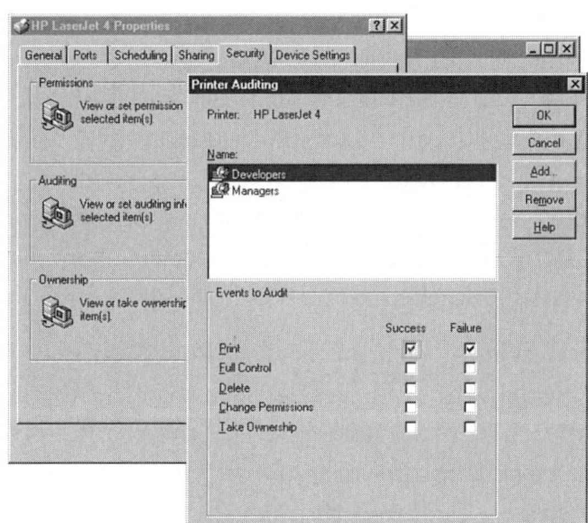

FIG. 20.3⇒ In this example, users who are members of the Developers and Managers groups that print to this printer will be recorded in the Security log of the Event Viewer.

> **Caution**
> Auditing causes additional overhead on resources and the processor. It is designed as a troubleshooting technique rather than a reporting tool.

Ch 20

Taking Ownership of a Printer

The user who creates the printer becomes the owner of the printer (usually an administrator). If, for some reason, that user is no longer able to manage a printer, another user must take ownership of the printer.

Members of the Administrators, Print Operators, Server Operators, and Power Users groups have the ability to take ownership of a printer. Also, any other user or group that has been given Full Control permission for the printer can take ownership of that printer.

To take ownership of the printer, navigate to the printer's property sheet, select the Security tab, and choose Ownership. Then choose Take Ownership.

Exploring DLC, TCP/IP, and Macintosh Installation Options

This section explains the installation and configuration options for network print devices using the DLC, TCP/IP, and AppleTalk protocols.

DLC Printing

The first thing you must do when configuring a print server to communicate with a network-interfaced print device using DLC is to install the DLC protocol on the print server. Installing the DLC protocol is covered in Chapter 17, "Windows NT Networking Services." This must be done in order to select any of the available network-interfaced print devices. After the DLC protocol is installed, the Hewlett-Packard Network Port choice becomes available in the Printer Ports dialog box, as shown in Figure 20.4.

When the Hewlett-Packard Network Port is chosen and the New Port button is selected, the Add Hewlett-Packard Network Peripheral Port dialog box appears. In this window, where the pointer is shown (refer to Figure 20.4), all available network-interfaced, print-device MAC addresses are displayed. Simply select the print device for this port by its MAC address, give the device a name, and choose OK. After a port is created for each available network-interface print device, each port can be configured as shared on the print server. Printer pools also can be configured, using any number of the DLC ports.

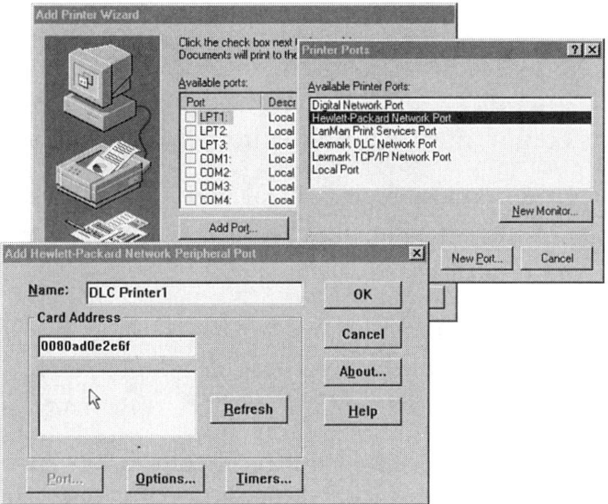

FIG. 20.4⇒ This figure is an example of adding a Hewlett-Packard Network DLC Printer Port.

Additional DLC configuration options include selecting the Options and Timers buttons from the Add Hewlett-Packard Network Peripheral Port dialog box. The Advanced Options for the All HP Network Ports dialog box, shown in Figure 20.5, is accessed by selecting the Options button. The HP Network Peripheral Port Timers dialog box, shown in Figure 20.6, is accessed by selecting the Timers button.

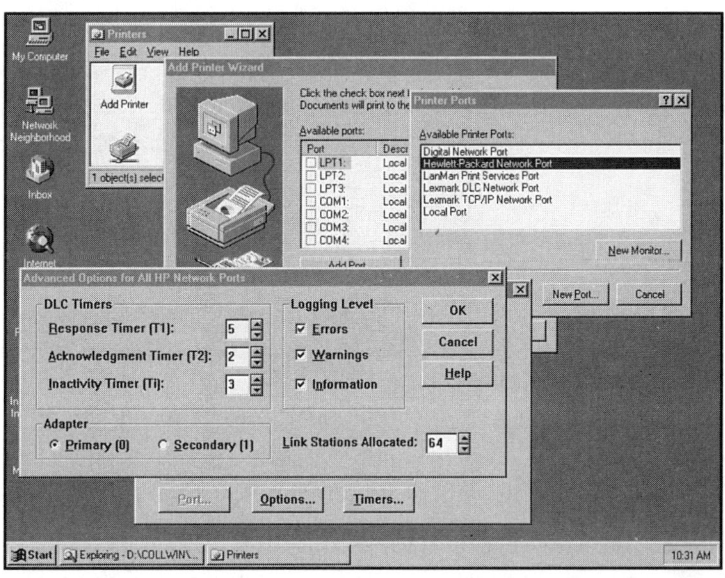

FIG. 20.5⇒ An example of setting advanced options for All HP Network Ports.

The DLC Timers options, which include the Response Timer (T1), the Acknowledgment Timer (T2), and the Inactivity Timer (Ti), control the network timing parameters. These parameters should be changed only if timeouts consistently occur on extremely busy networks.

The Logging Level options control how much information is placed in the event log. By default, all errors, warnings, and information events are entered in the event log.

The Adapter Primary (0) or Secondary (1) option allows the HPMON software to use one of the two possible adapter cards installed in the computer. The default, shown in Figure 20.5, is Primary (0).

The Link Stations Allocated option specifies how many network peripherals can be configured on this print server. The default is 64, with a range of 1 to 255. One link station is required for each print device configured.

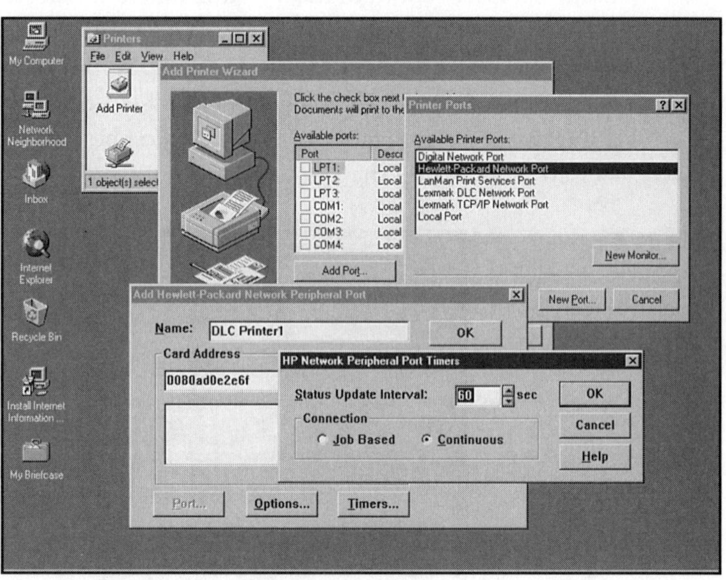

FIG. 20.6⇒ An example of configuring the HP Network Peripheral Port Timers dialog box.

In the HP Network Peripheral Port Timers dialog box, the Status Update Interval is simply the interval in which the status of print devices will be updated. The default is 60 seconds, with a range of 1 to 32,767 seconds.

The Connection option controls how the print server communicates with the network interface print device. If Continuous (the default) is selected, the server maintains a connection with the print device until either the server or the peripheral is turned off. This allows a single server to monopolize the network-interface print device. If Job Based is selected, the workstation establishes a connection with the print device during each print job. No connection is maintained between jobs. This allows other print servers to use the network-interface print device when this specific print server is not using it.

Figure 20.7 displays the Add Printer Wizard dialog box with a DLC Printer1 port configured.

FIG. 20.7⇒
Select a DLC configured print device by using the Add Printer Wizard dialog box.

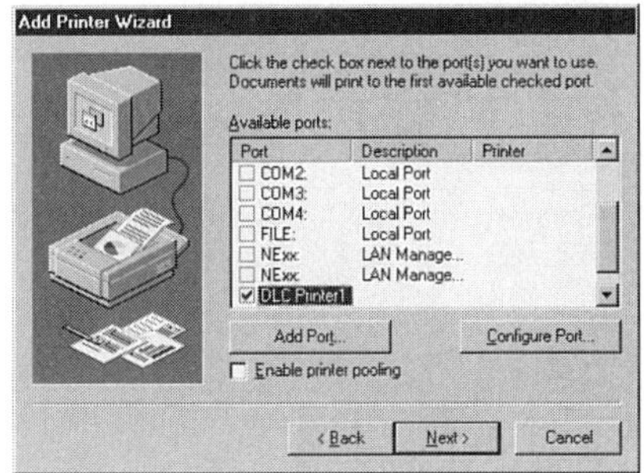

TCP/IP Printing

Printing to TCP/IP network-interface print devices also requires a specific installation configuration. The requirements for this configuration are outlined next.

The TCP/IP installation configuration requires that the TCP/IP protocol be installed on the print server, and that the Microsoft TCP/IP Printing service be installed. Recall that both the TCP/IP protocol and the Microsoft TCP/IP Printing service are installed from the Network icon in the Control Panel. Figure 20.8 displays how to install the Microsoft TCP/IP Printing service.

After the Microsoft TCP/IP Printing service is installed, the LPR Port option is available for adding and configuring LPR ports in the Printer Ports dialog box, as shown in Figure 20.9.

From the Printer Ports dialog box, the New Port button is selected, and the Add LPR compatible printer dialog box appears. Two options in this dialog box must be configured: the Name or Address of Server Providing lpd, and Name of Printer or Print Queue on that Server. These configuration options can be extremely misleading. The first option, Name or

Address of Server Providing lpd, requires the name or address of the MAC installed in the network-interface print device, or the address of the MAC installed in a special electronic controller attached to the print device. This can be a UNIX computer that controls a print device, or a Fiery PC controlling a Savin color-laser print device.

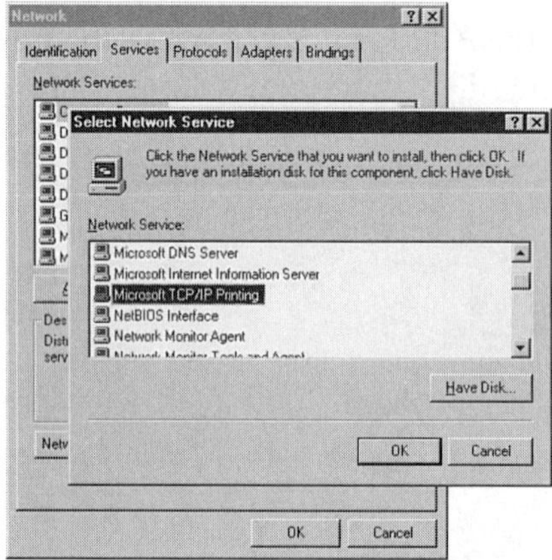

FIG. 20.8⇒ The installation procedure for the Microsoft TCP/IP Printing service.

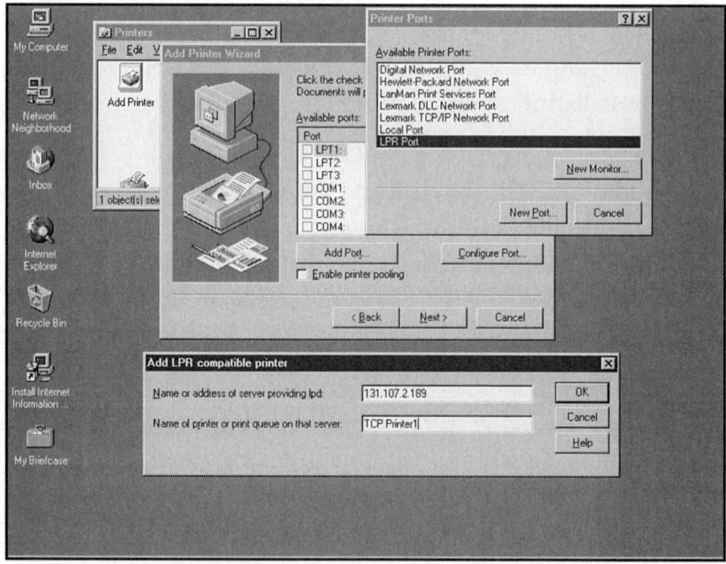

FIG. 20.9⇒ Adding and configuring an LPR Printer Port.

Key Concept

The address required in the Name or Address of Server Providing lpd text box is *not* the IP address of the print server.

After the port is added, it is accessible in the Available Ports window, where it can be selected and configured with the specific type of print device, as shown in Figure 20.10.

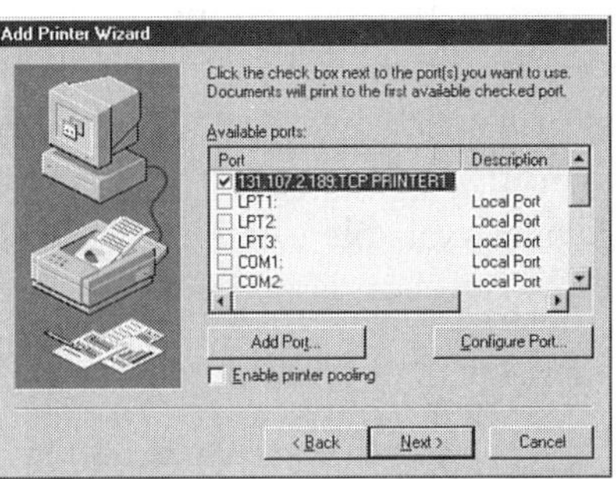

FIG. 20.10⇒ Select a TCP/IP-configured print device by using the Add Printer Wizard dialog box.

Printing to UNIX-Connected Printers

The Line Printer Port print monitor (LPRMON.DLL) is loaded when the TCP/IP Printing Support service is installed on the print server. It is designed to facilitate the routing and tracking of print jobs that are destined for network-ready print devices that communicate by using the TCP/IP protocol, or print devices that are connected to UNIX-based computers.

Windows NT provides two command-line utilities, LPR.EXE and LPQ.EXE, for directing and monitoring print jobs targeted for UNIX host printers. If you are familiar with the UNIX environment, you probably have used these commands before.

To direct a print job to a UNIX host print device, open a command prompt window and enter the command

```
LPR -S <IP address of UNIX host> -P <Printer Name> <filename>
```

where *IP address of UNIX host* is the TCP/IP address of the printer or host computer to which the printer is attached, *printer name* is the shared name of the printer, and *filename* is the name of the print job that you are directing.

To receive queue information on the print server, enter the command:

```
LPQ -S <IP address of UNIX host> -P <Printer Name> -l
```

Key Concept

Note that the LPR and LPQ command switches (such as `-S` and `-P`) are case-sensitive.

Macintosh Printing

After the AppleTalk protocol is installed on the Windows NT workstation platform, or the Services for Macintosh service is installed on a Windows NT server platform, either platform can function as a print server for AppleTalk print devices. Simply highlight the AppleTalk Printing Devices option in the Printer Ports dialog box and select the Add Port button. The Available AppleTalk Printing Devices selection window will appear, listing the AppleTalk print devices available (see Figure 20.11).

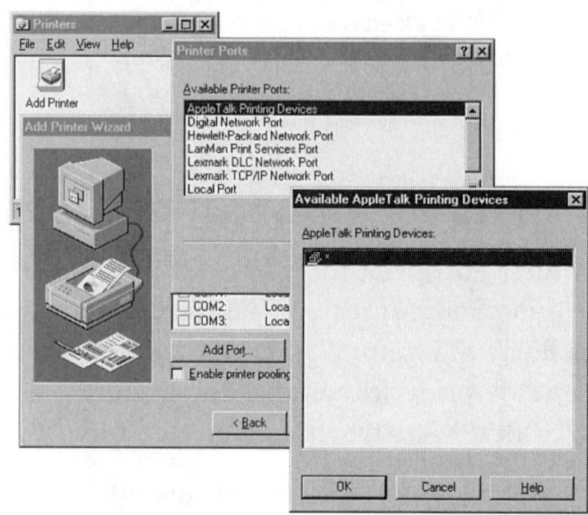

FIG. 20.11⇒ Select one of the print devices for each port and configure each port in the print server.

Note Print devices attached to and configured on the Windows NT print server will be available for selection on the Macintosh computers in Chooser.

Taking the Disc Test

If you have read and understood the material in this chapter, you are ready to test your knowledge. Insert the CD-ROM that comes with this book and run the self-test software, as described in Appendix K, "Using the Self-Test Software."

From Here...

The next chapter, Chapter 21, "Remote Access Support," discusses connecting NT Server to clients using modems. This process is managed by using NT's Remote Access Support (RAS).

Chapter Prerequisite

You should have completed Chapters 17 through 19 before continuing with this chapter. You should be familiar with LAN concepts and the TCP/IP and NWLink protocols.

Remote Access Support

This chapter will review remote access support, commonly referred to as RAS.

Topics to be covered include the following:

- Understanding dial-up networking and remote access service
- Introducing point-to-point tunneling protocol
- Understanding RAS security
- Installing and configuring RAS
- Troubleshooting Remote Access

Understanding Dial-Up Networking and Remote Access Services

What is commonly referred to as Remote Access Services (RAS) in NT 4.0 actually consists of two basic components that share some common elements: Dial-up Networking services and Remote Access Service services. Remote Access Services on an NT 4.0 workstation supports one inbound dial-in connection. RAS on an NT 4.0 server supports up to 256 inbound dial-in connections.

RAS provides the NT network with standardized WAN-based remote access support. *Dial-up Networking* is the service a client computer uses to connect to remote network resources through a RAS server. Through RAS, clients using Dial-up Networking can access network resources through regular telephone lines (public switched telephone networks, or PSTN) by using a modem through X.25 connections by using a packet-switching protocol (X.25 PAD) and an X.25 adapter, or through digital ISDN connections with an ISDN adapter installed at both the client and server computers.

You can use both Serial Line Internet Protocol (SLIP) and Point-to-Point Protocol (PPP) to establish connections to RAS servers, although for dial-up connections, you must use PPP. PPP and SLIP are the WAN equivalents of Ethernet and Token Ring. PPP and SLIP provide a media access layer for higher level protocols to use, such as TCP/IP.

SLIP is an older standard for establishing remote connections that provides little security. Though it supports TCP/IP, it cannot take advantage of DHCP, thereby requiring a static IP address assigned to the client. Also, SLIP does not support IPX/SPX or NetBEUI.

PPP, on the other hand, does support several protocols in addition to TCP/IP, can use DHCP and WINS to assign IP addresses and resolve names, and takes advantage of NT's security features. Besides IPX/SPX (which gives remote NT clients using Client Services for NetWare [CSNW] the ability to dial into NetWare servers) and NetBEUI, PPP supports Point-to-Point Tunneling Protocol (PPTP), AppleTalk, DECnet, and Open Systems Interconnection (OSI).

PPP support on RAS servers enables remote clients to dial in using any PPP-compliant dial-in software with a matching protocol enabled on the server side. Dial-in software must provide at least the level of security that the RAS service is configured to require.

In addition to PPP, Windows NT 4.0 has introduced the PPP Multilink Protocol based on the IETF standard RFC 1717. You can only use Multilink when both the client and server are NT computers. On computers that have multiple modems, X.25, or ISDN adapters each with its own analog or digital communications line installed, PPP Multilink Protocol enables them to be combined into logical groups that increase the bandwidth for transmissions. For example, an NT 4.0 workstation with two 14.4 modems and two phone lines can use PPP Multilink Protocol to create one 28.8 logical connection to a RAS server also using PPP Multilink.

For this to be effective, the workstation and the server must both have the same number of communications lines and connections available.

The RAS Server can act as a de facto router for the network. When RAS is installed on an NT 4.0 server, it automatically integrates whatever protocols have been installed on the server. The RAS administrator can enable gateway services for any or all of the network protocols installed on the server. For example, if NetBEUI, NWLink, and TCP/IP have been installed, you can enable the RAS gateway for any or all of these. Doing so effectively enables a remote client using any one of these protocols to not only access the RAS server but to access network resources located anywhere in the domain using any of the three protocols installed on the RAS server to get there. RAS on the server can also act as IP and IPX routers to link LANs and WANs together. Indeed, just about every function that a client computer enjoys while directly connected to an Ethernet or Token Ring network, it will also enjoy, though in decreased line speed, through dial-in networking to a RAS server.

Installing RAS

On the server side of things, RAS is configured as an NT service. As such, you select and install it through the Services tab of the Network applet, which is accessible through the Control Panel or the Network

Neighborhood properties. Recall that you install an NT service like any other protocol or adapter. Choose Add, select the service from the list of available services, and choose OK. You will be prompted for modem selection and configuration as well as RAS setting configuration.

You must shut down and restart NT to update the Registry, put the bindings into effect, and start the new service.

Follow these same steps to configure RAS services on an NT 4.0 server if you intend to use it as a dial-in server.

Configuring RAS on the Server

Once you have installed RAS, you can select it from the list of services on the Services tab and configure its *Properties*. You have the option of configuring the RAS server to act as a dial-out or dial-in server only or to accept both. Depending on the dialing option you choose, you can specify which protocol to use for dial-out or to accept through dial-in. You must install a protocol on the server before RAS will support it.

As you can see in Figure 21.1, clients dialing in using TCP/IP will be able to access the entire network and will receive their IP addresses from a DHCP server as well. Notice, too, that Microsoft authentication has been selected. Only clients whose dial-up networking has been configured to use Microsoft authentication will be able to access this server.

Encryption settings are also set for dial-in clients.

Key Concept

The encryption setting you select for dial-in clients (see Figure 21.1) represents the level of encryption that the *client* is configured to use rather than what the server uses. For example, if the NT workstation client's Dial-up Networking is configured to use Microsoft authentication, that client can access any RAS server configured to accept *any authentication*, *encrypted authentication*, or *Microsoft-encrypted authentication*. Conversely, if the client is configured to use clear text but the RAS server is configured to accept only Microsoft authentication, that client will *not* be able to establish a connection with the RAS server.

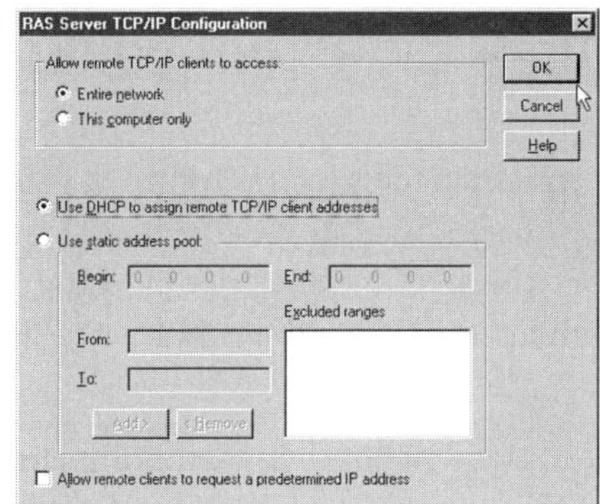

FIG. 21.1 ⇒
This server has been configured for both dial-out and dial-in. All protocols have been enabled for both.

Configuring RAS Protocols

You can configure each network protocol option similarly to the way you would configure them for the computer itself. For example, the IPX option enables you specify a range of network numbers to assign to the clients as they dial in. TCP/IP options include a range of IP addresses assigned by the RAS server or IP addresses assigned by a DHCP server. All three protocols include the option (selected by default) to enable gateway access to the entire network. If you want to restrict dial-up access to the RAS server only, you must disable gateway access for each protocol.

TCP/IP and RAS

When using the TCP/IP protocol, you can allow clients access to the entire network or limit them to the dial-in server. You can assign IP addresses using DHCP (covered in the TCP/IP chapter) or from a static address pool set aside for use with dial-in clients.

NWLink and RAS

As with TCP/IP, you can grant access to the entire network to clients dialing in using NWLink over a RAS connection. RAS can automatically assign network numbers to clients, or you can force RAS to start at a predetermined number. You can even have RAS assign the same network number to all IPX clients.

NetBEUI and RAS

There isn't much you can do with NetBEUI. The only option is to allow network access or limit clients to the dial-in server.

Introducing Point-to-Point Tunneling Protocol (PPTP)

If an organization maintains access to the Internet either directly or through an Internet provider, its users can gain access to their organization's network through the Internet by using a new network technology supplied by Microsoft in Windows NT 4.0—*Point-to-Point Tunneling Protocol (*PPTP*)*.

Clients using PPTP on their NT 4.0 workstations can connect securely to a RAS server in their company network either directly through the Internet—if they are themselves directly connected—or through their local Internet provider. This connection is known as Virtual Private Networking, or VPN. A VPN provides the ability to "tunnel" through the Internet or other public network to connect to a remote corporate network without sacrificing security. VPN's transmissions are encrypted and secure and usually less costly than modem, X.25, or ISDN connections. Because the RAS server can act as a gateway to the company network, you need only have one RAS server connected to the Internet.

Key Concept

PPTP supports multiprotocol encapsulation, which means that dial-up networking clients can use any protocol for their PPP connections. PPTP encapsulates the PPP packet within IP packets and sends it across the Internet using TCP/IP, making it possible to use the Internet as a NetBEUI or IPX/SPX backbone. The client and RAS server must be using TCP/IP only to access the Internet.

When the user's Internet provider provides PPTP, the Virtual Private Network support is completely transparent to the user. VPN is enabled when the user connects to his or her provider.

When PPTP is configured on the user's workstation through the Network Properties dialog box, the user can connect to any Internet provider, even those that do not provide PPTP in their points of presence. In addition to installing PPTP, the user creates a phone book entry for the VPN including the IP address of the PPTP server in the corporate network to which they are connecting in place of the phone number entry.

The Virtual Private Network uses RAS security. When the user connects through PPTP, the user account is validated in the NT domain database just as though he or she were directly connected to the network. In addition, through RAS, the username, password, and data can all be encrypted. On the PPTP server side, you can enable PPTP filtering to allow only PPTP-enabled users to connect to the PPTP server through the Internet. It also supports the use of firewalls to screen access to the network.

Configuring RAS Security

RAS actually implements several additional security features above and beyond what NT offers, including callback, encrypted passwords, and PPTP (covered in the previous section). RAS, of course, supports NT's domain security, requiring a dial-in user to authenticate using the domain account database before resource access can take place. The RAS server also maintains an ACL that identifies which domain users have permission to dial in.

Authentication is accomplished by using one of three authentication protocols supported by RAS:

- Password Authentication Protocol (PAP)
- Challenge Handshake Authentication Protocol (CHAP)
- Microsoft extensions to CHAP (MS_CHAP)

CHAP is the default authentication protocol. When you select this option, only Microsoft clients can connect to the RAS server.

When you use CHAP or MS_CHAP, RAS encrypts all logon information and data transmitted. You can enable auditing to track remote connection processes, such as logging on and dialing back users.

You can configure RAS servers to use callbacks to provide an extra layer of security. When a client calls in, you can configure the RAS server to call back the client at a predefined number, such as to a particular office location or at a user-defined number, perhaps a hotel room or client site.

Note Callback to hotel rooms may be tricky given that most hotel phones are routed through a hotel operator, making callback unusable. Some hotels are now providing data access lines with separate phone numbers, however.

RAS servers support the addition of third-party security hosts and firewalls. Firewalls screen incoming and outgoing access to network computers through the use of passwords or security codes.

When connecting through PPTP, the RAS server must have a connection to the Internet either directly or through a firewall, allowing connections to the PPTP port. This connection can become a security issue because the computer is left relatively open to packets other than PPTP. Fortunately, PPTP provides a security feature called "filtering," which, when enabled, *disables* all other protocols from using the network adapter that provides PPTP connection to the Internet.

Installing and Configuring Dial-Up Networking

This section will cover the installation and configuration of dial-up networking on an NT workstation as an example of setting up a client to access a RAS server. Don't infer from this that NT workstation is not the only possible client for RAS servers. RAS supports any operating system that supports PPP, at least one RAS protocol (TCP/IP, NetBEUI, IPX/SPX), and at least one authentication protocol (PAP, CHAP, MS-CHAP). All these client operating systems are supported (this is not an exhaustive list):

- Windows for Workgroups
- Windows 95
- Windows NT Workstation 3.1 and later
- Windows NT Server 3.1 and later
- PPP-based TCP/IP clients

In addition to the various Microsoft client operating systems, RAS can support any computer using TCP/IP dialing in via Point-to-Point Protocol (PPP). If the client computer wants to access resources on the network, it must support the protocol required for that resource such as NetBIOS for file access and HTTP for Web access.

Understanding and Configuring TAPI

Dial-up Networking is a TAPI-compliant application in Windows NT 4.0. TAPI stands for *Telephony Application Programming Interface* and provides a set of standards for communications programs to manage and control data, voice, and fax dial-up functions, such as establishing calls, answering and hanging up, transferring calls, holding, conferencing, and other common phone system functions.

Among the dialing properties configurable for TAPI-compliant applications are phonebook entries, area and country codes, outside line access, calling card data (encrypted, of course), and line control codes, such as disabling call waiting.

You configure these TAPI properties through the Telephony applet in Control Panel on the My Locations tab. The options here are fairly self-explanatory, as you can see in Figure 21.2.

FIG. 21.2 ⇒
These are some typical TAPI location settings.

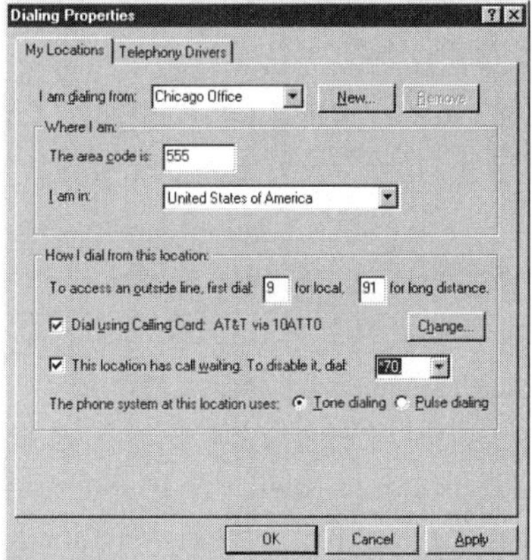

Dial-Up Networking

Choose or enter a descriptive name for your calling location in I Am Dialing From. Choose New to add additional locations. In the Where I Am section of the dialog box, enter your area code and country. In the How I Dial From This Location section, specify the number you must dial (if any) to reach an outside local line or to place a long distance call. Select the Calling Card option if you are using a calling card to charge the call and Change to specify the calling card, the call number, and any rules applicable for the card. If you need to disable call-waiting, you can choose to disable it here by specifying the line code to do so. Finally, indicate whether the phone uses Tone or Pulse dialing.

You use TAPI properties to configure the location from which you are dialing. The Dial-up Networking program enables you to configure the phonebook entry of the location to which you are dialing, establishes the connection, and monitors the call.

You access the Dial-up Networking program through the Accessories group. The first time you access it, a dial-up wizard will prompt you for the first phonebook entry. You need to provide a descriptive name for the entry whether you are calling the Internet or a non-Windows NT server and how to deal with that, the country code, area code, and phone number of the target location. Subsequent access will display the Dial-up Networking dialog box that you see in Figure 21.3.

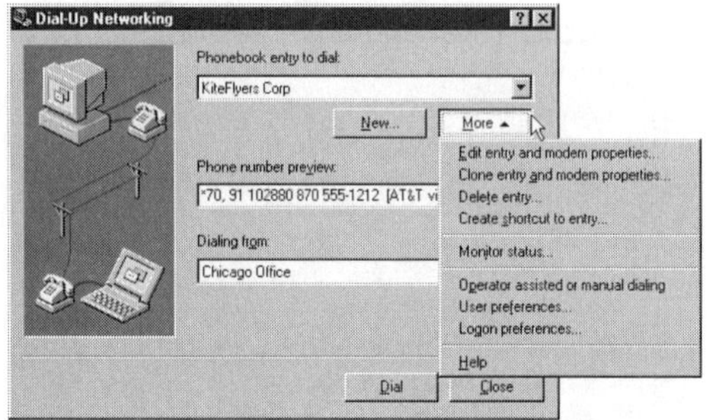

FIG. 21.3 ⇒ Dial-up Networking dialog box showing modification options available.

You can select a phonebook entry from the Phonebook Entry list or create a New entry. The phone number for the entry is displayed by using any TAPI location properties you specified for the Dialing From location.

The More button displays a list of additional options for modifying the dial-up data. For example, the Edit Phonebook Entry option lets you not only modify the basic entries but also specify the dial-up access type (SLIP, PPP, PPTP) and protocols of the target server, dial-up scripts that you want executed, and the level of security you want to use for this connection (see Figure 21.4).

You can specify parameters relating to redial attempts and callback options through the More, Logon Preferences option. Through More, User Preferences, you can enable the autodial feature, which automatically associates the phonebook entry used to map to a network resource. When the resource mapping is reestablished at the next logon, the appropriate RAS server is called automatically.

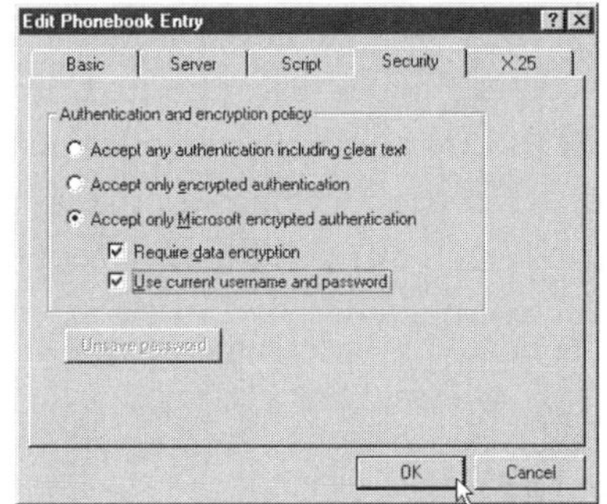

FIG. 21.4 ⇒
For this dial-up entry, the highest level of security possible is chosen. You are using Microsoft authentication with the current user's account and password and additionally encrypting data transmitted during this session.

Choose Dial, finally, to dial out and establish the connection with the target location. Once the connection has been made and any authentication has taken place, in the case of NT RAS servers, you now have access to network resources to which you have been given permission.

Troubleshooting Considerations

Troubleshooting either RAS or Dial-up Networking is largely a matter of checking settings, phone numbers, dial access codes, and so on. In addition, always check the Event Viewer for events related to Remote Access Service or Dial-up Networking because the descriptions of the events usually is quite good for pointing you to the root of the problem.

You can use the authentication options as a troubleshooting mechanism. If a client is having difficulty establishing a connection, you can set the server option to the lowest security setting, that is, allow *any* authentication. If the client can establish a connection with that setting, try again with the next highest security option and so forth until the connection fails. This process indicates at what level of security the client is configured and at what level of security they must be set.

Finally, you can enable a log file that tracks PPP connections through the NT Registry. Look for the key `HKEY_LOCAL_MACHINE\System\CurrentControlSet\Services\Rasman\PPP`. Here, look for the parameter Logging and change its value to "1." Setting this value to "2" initiates a "verbose" mode and will cause NT to record even more detailed information. NT will create the text file `PPP.LOG`, record PPP session information in it, and store it in the `WINNT40\SYSTEM32\RAS` directory. The information contained in the log includes the time the PPP packet was sent, the protocol used, such as LCP, the packet type, length and ID, and the port to which it's connected.

Taking the Disc Test

If you have read and understood the material in the chapter, you are ready to test your knowledge. Insert the CD-ROM that comes with this book and run the self-test software as described in Appendix K, "Using the Self-Test Software."

From Here...

The next chapter, which focuses on network monitoring, completes your tour of NT networking concepts.

Chapter Prerequisite

Readers should have a concept of LAN/WAN topology with regard to the purpose of routers and different subnets or networks. They should also be familiar with protocol characteristics for TCP/IP and NWLink and the DHCP service as discussed in Chapter 18, "TCP/IP and Windows NT," and Chapter 19, "Novell NetWare and Windows NT."

Multiprotocol Routing

This chapter adds to the discussion of multiprotocol routing that was presented in Chapter 17, "Windows NT Networking Services." The information presented in that chapter dealt with the installation of the multiprotocol routing services for both TCP/IP and NWLink. Discussions in this chapter will include the purpose of the Windows NT 4.0 addition of multiprotocol routing. Also presented will be how multiprotocol routing integrates with Dynamic Host Configuration Protocol (DHCP).

Topics in this chapter include the following:

- Networks, network segments, and the purpose of routers
- Windows NT 4.0 and multiprotocol routing
- RIP for Internet protocol routing
- DHCP relay
- RIP for NWLink IPX/SPX compatible transport routing
- AppleTalk routing

Networks, Network Segments, and the Purpose of Routers

NWLink and TCP/IP are considered routable protocols, whereas NetBEUI is considered a non-routable protocol. This means that if a number of computers are configured to communicate with each other using NetBEUI, they have to all be on the same network or physical piece of wire. They cannot be on different network segments connected physically by routing devices. Protocols such as NWLink and TCP/IP, on the other hand, are routable protocols that can communicate with computers on different physical networks through routers.

Routers are devices that pass information from one network segment to another. Routers work up to the Network layer of the Open Systems Interconnection (OSI) model and forward information based on both a network and a device address. Routing devices maintain a table of both network addresses and device addresses to which they are connected. When they receive a packet of information, they can analyze the packet header and determine which network or device to which they should route or forward the packet of information. Routers can also determine the best path to route information from one computer to another, therefore optimizing network performance.

Routers pass information packets from one network segment to another without regard to media type. For example, routers can pass information packets between an Ethernet network segment and a Token Ring network segment or between a x.25 network segment and an ARCnet network segment.

Routers are protocol dependent, however, meaning that they must understand the protocol inclusive of up to the OSI network layer. The same protocol must be used on each side of the router.

Routing Information Protocol (RIP) routers, in addition to forwarding information packets from one network segment to another, also dynamically exchange routing tables by broadcasting their route information with other routers on the network. This type of communication ensures that all routers on the network contain synchronized routing information.

Windows NT 4.0 and Multiprotocol Routing

After you install and enable Multiprotocol Routing on Windows NT 4.0, the computer will be able to function as a router and forward information packets from one network segment to another, provided you've install and configure more than one network card. You can enable either *Internet Protocol* (IP) routing or *Internetwork Packet Exchange* (IPX) routing, or both, provided that you've install the required protocol.

You can also use a Windows NT 4.0 server to function as a DHCP Relay Agent by installing the DHCP Relay Agent service, which allows DHCP messages to be relayed across routers in an IP network.

TCP/IP Routing

Windows NT 4.0 provides for both *Static* and *Routing Information Protocol* (RIP) IP routing. Fixed or manually maintained routing tables are used in Static routing, whereas routing tables are maintained dynamically when using RIP.

Static IP Routing

To enable Static Routing, simply install TCP/IP and, from the TCP/IP property sheet, choose the Routing tab. Select the Enable IP Forwarding check box.

Once you enable Static Routing, the Route utility maintains a static routing table. Simply start a command prompt and type **Route** to display all the route utility options. Figure 22.1 displays the route options.

Figure 22.2 displays a route print command. The route print command displays the static route table on the specific computer. This command was done on a computer configured with only one network adapter card, a static IP address of 131.107.2.200, and no default gateway assigned.

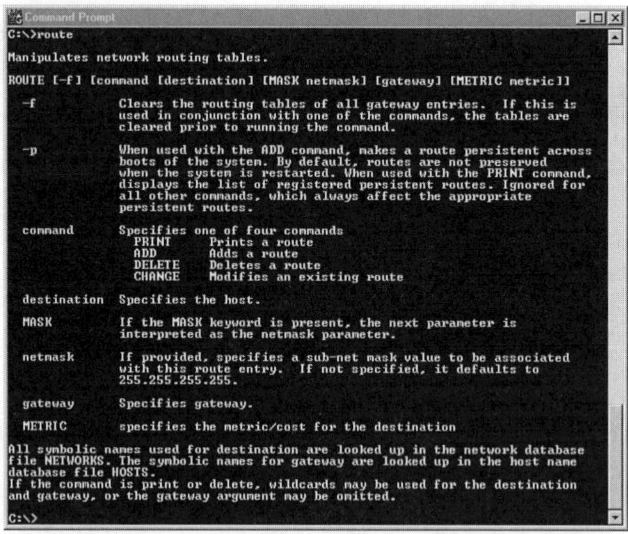

FIG. 22.1 ⇒ The Route utility syntax and options list.

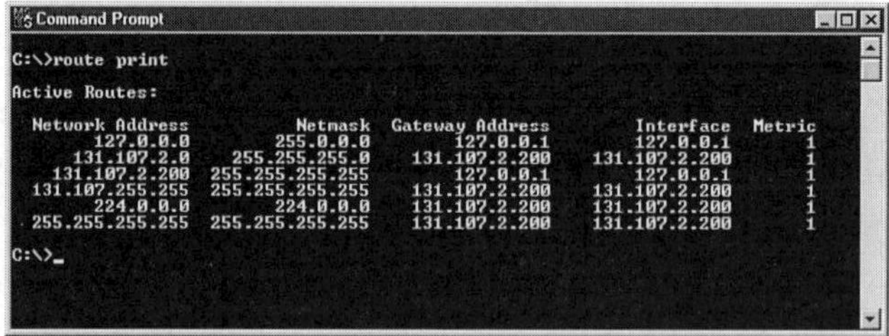

FIG. 22.2 ⇒ These are the results of the Route utility, Print command.

To add an entry or route to the static route table, use the Route Add command. The route add syntax and the results of an add route are shown in Figure 22.3. The addition establishes a route from computer 131.107.2.200 to a gateway subnet of 131.107.3.0 using a subnet mask of 255.255.255.0 that is configured on computer 131.107.2.180. The Metric value in this case indicates that subnet 131.107.3.0 is one hop or router away from computer 131.107.2.200.

Key Concept

Keep in mind that if a route is added to forward information to another computer or router, the route back to the first computer must also be added to the second computer to establish a path back to the first computer.

FIG. 22.3 ⇒
These are the results of adding a route to the static route table.

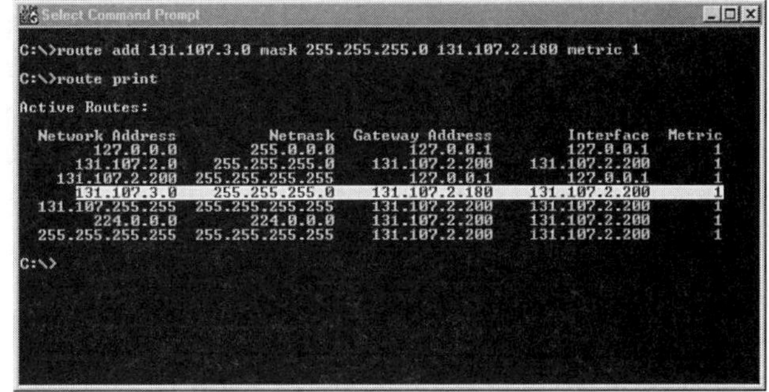

The Route utility can also use entries in the Networks file to convert destination names to addresses. Figure 22.4 displays an example of the default Networks file.

FIG. 22.4 ⇒
An example of the default Networks file.

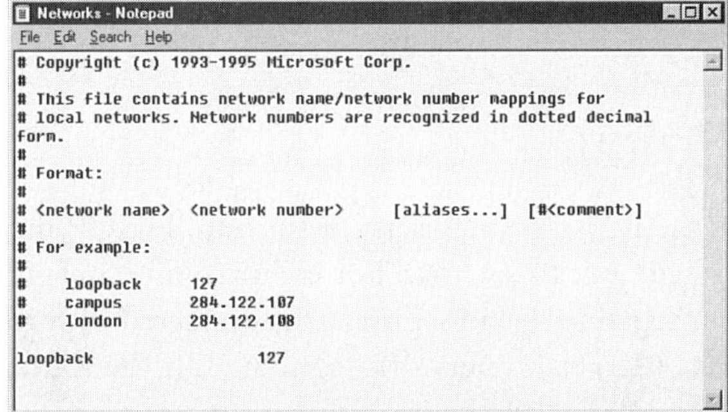

RIP for Internet Protocol Routing

Windows NT 4.0 server supports RIP for Internet Protocol (IP). RIP for IP will dynamically maintain IP routing tables; therefore, you do not have to maintain static IP routing tables manually.

After you install it, RIP for IP service is configured to start automatically when you start the computer. It also requires that you already have installed TCP, IP, and UDP (these protocols are all installed together at one time). TCP provides connection-oriented packet delivery, IP provides address and routing functions, and UDP provides for connectionless-oriented packet delivery.

As mentioned before, routing can take place between two or more network adapter cards installed in a computer. With RIP for IP installed, a

Windows NT 4.0 server can forward information from one IP network segment to another IP network segment; that is the purpose of RIP for IP. What if RIP is installed on a computer with only one network adapter card installed, however? If this is the case, the specific Windows NT 4.0 server will be placed in Silent Mode, meaning that the computer will update its own router table from RIP broadcast from other routers on the network, but, because it is connected to only one network segment, it does not broadcast its route.

Caution
If, at a later date, you install one or more network adapter cards, you must change the Registry entry for `SilentRip` from 1 to 0. The `SilentRip` Registry location is `HKEY_LOCAL_MACHINE\System\CurrentControlSet\Services\IpRip\Parameters`. Its value type is `REG_DWORD`.

DHCP Relay

You use the DHCP Relay service to route DHCP messages from one IP network segment to another. For example, an enterprise has two network segments, segment 1 and segment 2, connected by a router but has only one DHCP server on network segment 1. If the router is not capable of forwarding DHCP and `bootp` broadcast messages between the DHCP server on segment 1 and a DHCP client on segment 2, a DHCP server would have to be configured on each network segment. If the DHCP Relay service is installed on a server computer on segment 2, however, it will forward DHCP requests through the router to the DHCP server on network segment 1. You can configure the DHCP Relay service to route information up to 16 hops away (see Chapter 11, "Printing," for details).

RIP for NWLink IPX Routing

RIP for NWLink IPX, when enabled and configured correctly, allows a Windows NT 4.0 system to function as an IPX router to forward information from one IPX network segment to another. RIP for NWLink IPX, once installed, must be enabled manually, unlike RIP for IP, which is enabled automatically when installed. RIP for NWLink IPX is enabled or disabled from the Routing tab on the NWLink IPX/SPX Properties sheet. For the IPX router service to work properly, you must enable NetBIOS Broadcast Propagation (type 20 broadcast packets), which allows the computer to use NetBIOS over IPX for browsing and name resolution. If NetBIOS Broadcast Propagation is disabled, client computers will only be able to communicate with systems on the local IPX subnet.

Note RIP for NWLink IPX can only propagate up to eight hops, unlike RIP for IP and DHCP Relay, which can propagate up to 16 hops.

When RIP for NWLink IPX is installed, the Service Advertising Protocol (SAP), is automatically installed also. Pertaining to the Windows NT environment, SAP is a service that broadcasts shared files, directories, and printers by the domain or workgroup name first and then by the server name. In the IPX protocol and routing environment, servers use SAP to advertise their services and addresses on a network, and then clients use SAP to determine what network resources are available.

RIP for NWLink IPX also contains a utility to display information and statistics about the IPX route tables. The utility is called IPXRoute. Figures 22.5 and 22.6 display the IPXRoute options.

FIG. 22.5 ⇒ The IPXRoute and the IPX routing syntax and options list.

```
Command Prompt

C:\>ipxroute /?

NWLink IPX Routing and Source Routing Control Program v2.00

Display and modify information about the routing tables
used by IPX.

IPX Routing Options
-------------------

IPXROUTE servers [/type=xxxx]
IPXROUTE stats   [/show] [/clear]
IPXROUTE table

  servers       Displays the SAP table for the specified
                server type. Server type is an integer value.
                For example use IPXROUTE servers /type=4 to display
                all file servers. If no type is specified,
                servers of all types are shown. The displayed
                list is sorted by server name.

  stats         Displays or clears IPX router interface statistics.
                If no option is specified, statistics are shown.
                To clear the statistics specify /clear.

  table         Displays the IPX routing table. The displayed
                list is sorted by network number.
```

Figure 22.7 displays the results of the IPXRoute servers, IPXRoute statistics, and IPXRoute table commands. The type 1600 computers were Windows NT 4.0 installations; one is a Windows NT 4.0 workstation installation, the other is a Windows NT 4.0 server installation. The type 4 computer was a Novell 3.12 file server.

FIG. 22.6 ⇒
Here is the IPXRoute source routing syntax and options list.

```
Command Prompt

Source Routing Options
----------------------

IPXROUTE board=n clear def gbr mbr remove=xxxxxxxxxxxx
IPXROUTE config

  board=n       Specify the board number to check.
  clear         Clear the source routing table.
  def           Send packets that are destined for an
                unknown address to the ALL ROUTES broadcast
                (Default is SINGLE ROUTE broadcast).
  gbr           Send packets that are destined for the
                broadcast address (FFFF FFFF FFFF) to the
                ALL ROUTES broadcast
                (Default is SINGLE ROUTE broadcast).
  mbr           Send packets that are destined for a
                multicast address (C000 xxxx xxxx) to the
                ALL ROUTES broadcast
                (Default is SINGLE ROUTE broadcast).
  remove=xxxx   Remove the given mac address from the
                source routing table.

  config        Displays information on all the bindings
                that IPX is configured for.

All parameters should be separated by spaces.

C:\>_
```

FIG. 22.7 ⇒
This figure shows examples of three IPXRoute commands.

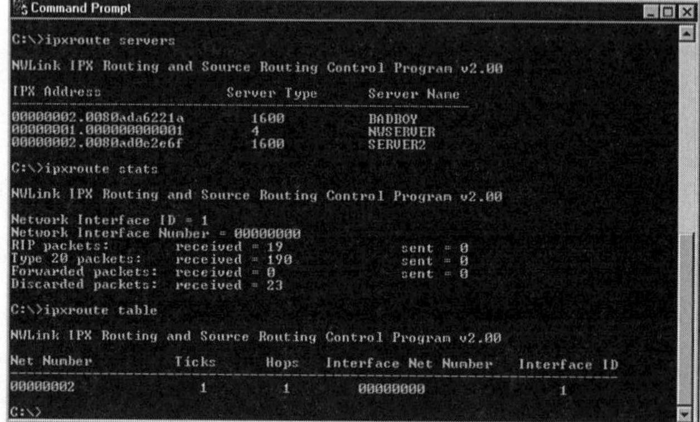

AppleTalk Routing

Windows NT 4.0 Server, with Services for Macintosh (SFM) installed, can function also as an AppleTalk router. Once you enable AppleTalk routing, all Macintosh clients can see the Windows NT 4.0 Server on all bound networks.

Windows NT 4.0 can function as a seed router or as a nonseed router in a Macintosh environment. Seed routers initialize and send routing information to other routers in the enterprise. Each physical network must have at least one seed router configured, and that system must be started first to pass routing information to other routers.

An AppleTalk routing table contains network numbers and ranges, zone names and lists, and the default zone on the network. Each network number must be unique as it identifies a specific AppleTalk network. Network numbers can range from 1 to 65,279.

Key Concept

LocalTalk networks can only have a single network number; EtherTalk, TokenTalk, and FDDI networks can support network ranges, however.

Taking the Disc Test

If you have read and understood the material in the chapter, you are ready to test your knowledge. Insert the CD-ROM that comes with this book and run the self-test software as described in Appendix K, "Using the Self-Test Software."

From Here...

The next chapter, "Network Monitor," will show you how to keep tabs on your network. You will learn how to track and analyze network traffic, solve typical network problems, and avoid network problems with careful planning.

Chapter Prerequisite

The reader should have a firm understanding of basic networking terminology and concepts before studying this chapter. Additionally, the reader should understand DHCP, WINS, and the Computer Browser service. These topics are covered in Chapter 17, "Windows NT Networking Services," and Chapter 18, "TCP/IP and Windows NT."

Network Monitor

This chapter concentrates on one particular monitoring and troubleshooting tool provided in Windows NT Server 4.0 called the Network Monitor. Those of you who have used or observed network monitoring tools, such as hardware-based sniffer products, will understand the concept and practical use of Windows NT's Network Monitor utility immediately.

This chapter discusses the following topics:

- Review the concept and use of the Network Monitor
- Analyze specific types of network traffic including the domain logon process, connecting to resources, and obtaining IP addresses
- Discuss techniques for identifying and planning for network traffic problems and usage

Understanding Network Monitor

The Network Monitor utility is a Windows NT Server 4.0 tool that provides a mechanism for monitoring and analyzing network traffic between clients and servers in your Windows NT domain. You can use it to identify heavily used subnets, routers, and WAN connections; help spot and troubleshoot network bottlenecks; and optimize network traffic patterns and plan for future growth in network traffic, bandwidth needs, transmission speed, and so on.

The Network Monitor utility was actually first introduced as part of Microsoft's Back Office server management application System Management Server (SMS). This full-featured software implementation of a network monitoring program provides a relatively low-cost alternative to the more expensive (and expansive) hardware-based network sniffer products available on the market today—roughly $900 compared to $10,000 or more.

Windows NT Server 4.0's version of Network Monitor has most of the functionality of the SMS product. The SMS version of Network Monitor enables you to monitor network activity directly for a specific computer or remotely for all devices on the subnet, such as determining which protocol consumed the most bandwidth and which devices are routers and editing and retransmitting network packets. By contrast, Windows NT Server 4.0's version provides local capturing only, to and from the computer running the utility.

Key Concept

Because Network Monitor is used primarily to analyze network traffic with an eye toward identifying and troubleshooting potential problems, you can consider this entire chapter a performance troubleshooting chapter for the network.

As you also saw with Performance Monitor, however, network troubleshooting is always facilitated when you can identify how far off the normal activity your network performance seems to be. Thus, it is important to understand what normal network activity is like on your subnets and across your domains. Only then can you accurately posit how well or how badly your network is performing at a given point in time and predict how it may perform under a given set of conditions.

Exploring Network Frames

Network Monitor is a packet or frame-analyzer tool. It provides the capability not only to capture network traffic but also to filter what is captured and displayed. The full version of Network Monitor, which is part of SMS, also allows for the editing and retransmission of network frames, as well as the capture of frames from a remote network device.

The frames that are captured represent segments of network traffic related to a particular type of network communication. A frame could be related to a request from a computer for an IP address from a DHCP server or a user's request to logon and validate at a domain controller. It could represent part of the transfer of data from a client/server application server. In all cases, the frames themselves consist of various parts that will be described shortly.

There are three general categories of frames. *Broadcast* frames are sent to all hosts on the network and use the unique destination address FFFFFFFF. All computers on the network accept the broadcast frame and pass it through their protocol stack to determine whether it is destined for that computer. If it is, it is processed appropriately. If it is not, it is discarded. The NWLink protocol bases much of its traffic on broadcasts, and TCP/IP uses broadcasts for some of its network communications.

A request for an IP address from a DHCP server is an example of a TCP/IP broadcast frame. The request for the IP address is sent to all computers in the network. The first DHCP server that receives the request responds to it with a directed frame.

A *directed* frame, as the name implies, is directed or sent to a specific computer on the network. All other computers discard it because it is not destined for those computers. TCP/IP relies primarily on directed frames to communicate between computers, which helps to minimize both the number of broadcasts that must take place as well as the amount of bandwidth used by TCP/IP.

Finally, a *multicast* frame is sent to a subset of the computers on the network depending on how that computer has registered itself on the network as opposed to its MAC (media access control) address. The NetBEUI protocol uses multicast frames to communicate on the network.

As mentioned earlier, a frame is itself composed of different pieces that identify what it is, where it came from, where it is going, and what it is carrying. It's kind of like public transportation but usually more reliable. The components of a frame vary according to the frame type but, generally, they consist of the same pieces.

An Ethernet 802.3 frame consists of the following components:

- Preamble This portion of the frame signals the receiving transceiver that the frame has arrived. It is 8 bytes, and is not captured by Network Monitor.
- Destination Address This portion identifies the MAC address of the target computer. If this address is FFFFFFFF, then all computers must accept the frame and determine whether it is meant for them. It is 6 bytes long.
- Source Address This portion identifies the MAC address of the computer at which the frame originated and is 6 bytes long.
- Type or Length This portion specifies the protocol that originated the frame, or the amount of data that it contains. It is 2 bytes long.
- Data This portion may be up to 1,500 bytes long and may contain the actual data or more specific information, about the protocol, such as headers and descriptions.
- CRC This 4-byte portion contains a checksum value that is used to determine whether the data arrived intact. CRC stands for Cyclic Redundancy Check.

As you can see in Figure 23.1, the data portion of the frame may not necessarily contain only data. Often, especially when the TCP/IP protocol is used as the network protocol of choice, the data portion of the frame contains additional protocol-specific data. With TCP/IP, for example, the data component consists of an IP datagram that contains IP header and data information such as the IP source address and destination address. The IP data component itself contains TCP header and data information, such as the source and destination port for NetBIOS or Windows Sockets.

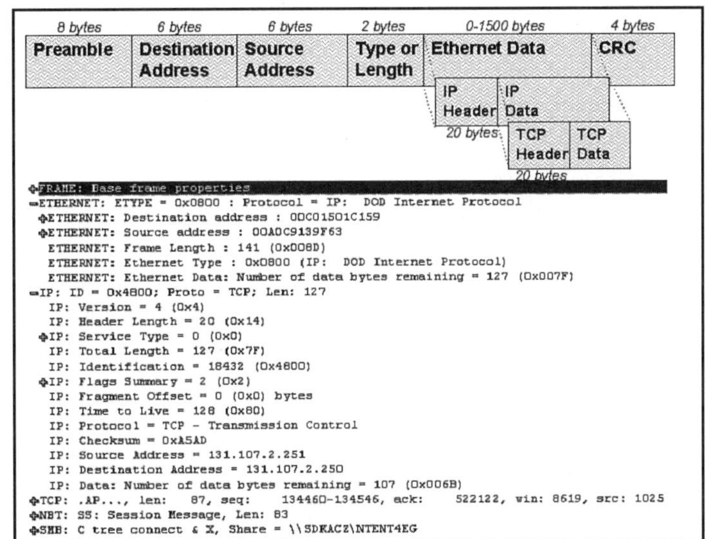

FIG. 23.1 ⇒ Here are the components of a typical frame along with the size of each. You can also see an example of a captured frame showing each component and its value. Notice that the Ethernet Data portion of the frame in this example consists of an IP piece and a TCP piece.

Ch 23

Implementing Network Monitor

The version of Network Monitor that comes with Windows NT Server 4.0 is a subset of the full product that is part of Microsoft SMS. It is meant to be installed on a Windows NT Server 4.0 computer and monitors network traffic sent and received by that computer.

You can install the full product version on any Windows NT Workstation or Server-based computer as well as computers running Windows 95.

The Network Monitor utility consists of two parts: the application itself and the Network Monitor agent. The agent allows a computer to capture network traffic and report it to the Network Monitor application. When using the full version of the product (SMS), install the agent on a Windows NT or Windows 95-based computer to allow remote monitoring of those computers. Remote monitoring is not a feature of the Windows NT Server 4.0 version. Therefore, it is not necessary to install the Network Monitor agent on your Windows-NT- or Windows-95-based computers. If you would like to use Performance Monitor's Network Segment object to track network performance on a given Windows NT computer, however, you must install TNetwork Monitor to activate the Network Segment object.

Tip

The more services you install on a Windows NT computer, the more overhead that computer will require to manage those services. In general, it is recommended that you only load those services that are necessary to facilitate optimal system performance.

For example, you may load the Network Monitor agent on a Windows NT Workstation to activate the Network Segment object to establish a Performance Monitor baseline for normal system performance on that computer. After you have done that, stop or remove the agent to release the resources needed to manage it. Turn it back on when you need to troubleshoot suspected network-related problems.

When you install the Windows NT Server 4.0 version of Network Monitor, both the application and the agent are installed on the server computer. Network traffic to and from the server will be monitored and recorded.

The full version of Network Monitor requires a compatible network card that can run in *promiscuous* mode. (It's not what you think.) Promiscuous mode indicates that the adapter is capable of accepting all frames on the network regardless of their true destinations. Though this does allow for remote monitoring of network traffic, it also places a greater processing load on that computer.

By contrast, Windows NT Server 4.0's version of Network Monitor, though it requires a supported network adapter card, does not require that the card run in promiscuous mode. This enhancement is part of NDIS 4.0 that allows a local capture mode for Network Monitor. As always, check the Windows NT 4.0 compatibility list for those network cards that Network Monitor supports.

Because this book deals with Windows NT Server 4.0, you will concentrate on its version of Network Monitor in this chapter. You install it as you would any other service through the Network Properties of the Windows NT Server 4.0 computer. To install Network Monitor, follow these steps.

1. Open the Network Properties dialog box and select the Services tab.
2. Choose the Add button and select Network Monitor Tools and Agent from the Network Service list. Choose OK.
3. When prompted for the location of the Windows NT Server 4.0 source files, enter the appropriate path.

4. After the service has been installed, choose Close to save your configuration and update the bindings. You will need to restart the computer when you are finished.

Once Network Monitor has been installed on a Windows NT server, a new program icon will be added to the Administrative Tools group on that computer. Choose the Network Monitor icon to start the utility. Figure 23.2 shows an example of a Network Monitor screen.

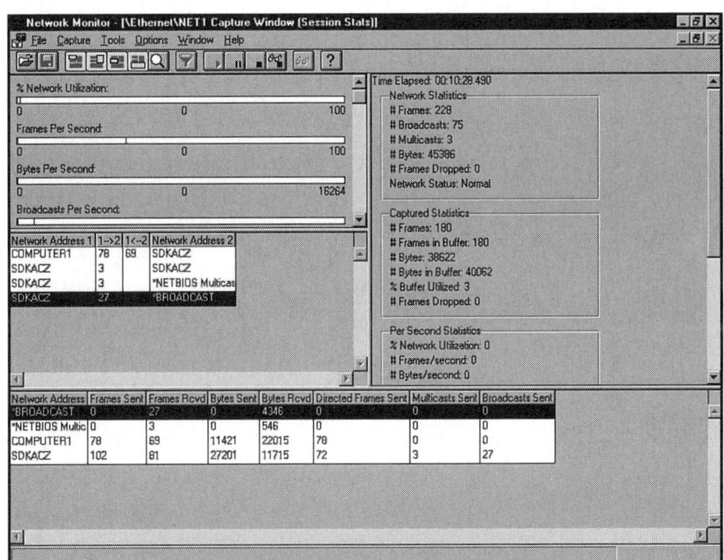

FIG. 23.2 ⇒ This example of a Network Monitor capture screen shows the four default windows that are displayed. Going counterclockwise from the upper-left window, the default windows are the Graph pane, Session Statistics pane, Station Statistics pane (bottom window), and the Total statistics pane. Network Monitor is running on SDKACZ.

The interface itself is fairly intuitive to use, especially if you are familiar with other network-sniffer products. As shown in Figure 23.2, you have five menu choices: File, Capture, Tools, Options, Window, and Help.

- **File** — Allows you to open an existing file of captured frames for viewing or to save the existing captured data as a file.
- **Capture** — Allows you to start, stop, view, and otherwise manage the capture session. You can identify what and how much in formation is collected, set filters, and trigger events based on captured information.
- **Tools** — Provides the most functionality when the full version of the product is used (SMS). In the Windows NT Server 4.0 version, you can identify Network Monitor users and start the local version of Performance Monitor.

- Options — Allows you to decide how to configure your viewing screen, for example, how much information is displayed. By default, all options are selected.
- Window — Presents options for the usual window management functions, such as tile and cascade. Also allows you to decide which statistics window to display on-screen.
- Help — Provides online help for Network Monitor.

To start capturing data with Network Monitor, simply choose Capture, Start. You could also click the Start Capture button (it looks like the forward button on a VCR) or press the F10 key.

The capture window begins to record and visually display statistical information regarding the network traffic sent and received by the computer. The capture window features four default panes (refer to Figure 23.2):

- Graph — This pane displays current network traffic as a set of five bar charts:% Network Utilization, Frames per Second, Bytes per Second, Broadcasts per Second, and Multicasts per Second.
- Session Statistics — This pane displays a summary of the frames that were communicated between this computer and other computers. Notice in Figure 23.2 that Computer1 sent 78 frames to SDKACZ and SDKACZ sent 69 to Computer1.
- Station Statistics — This pane provides specific frame data on a computer-by-computer basis, such as the number of frames sent and received, total bytes sent and received, directed frames sent, multicasts sent, and broadcasts sent. Note that computer SDKACZ, which is running Network Monitor, originated 102 frames and received 81, 78 of which came from Computer1.
- Total Statistics — This pane displays statistics for network traffic detected as a whole, as well as for frames that were captured, per second statistics, and Network Card statistics.

When you are finished capturing data, select Capture, Stop, click the Stop Capture button on the toolbar, or press F11 on the keyboard. To view captured data immediately, choose Capture, Stop and View. To save captured data to a file with a `.CAP` extension to view it later, choose File, Open.

Note In this version of Network Monitor, you can set a limited capture filter that identifies what type of frames you want to collect. Network Monitor provides no remote monitoring, so you will only capture frames relating to the computer running the utility. You can specify the capturing of frames from other specific computers, however, or identify and capture frames containing a specific pattern of hexadecimal or ASCII data.

To set a capture filter, follow these steps.

1. Select Capture, Filter from the menu.
2. Modify the existing address from the default setting Any to a specific computer by selecting an entry under Address Pairs and clicking the Address button. Enter the appropriate information in the Address Pairs dialog box.
3. Create or modify a pattern to match by selecting Pattern Matches (or an entry below it) and clicking the Pattern button. Enter the appropriate data in the Pattern Match dialog box.

Viewing Captured Data

You can view data that have been captured immediately by selecting Capture, Stop and View. To display data that have been captured and saved, select File, Open from the menu and choose the appropriate capture file. The capture file displayed in Figure 23.3 was created by having a Windows NT Workstation 4.0 computer (Computer1) log into a Windows NT Server 4.0 computer (SDKACZ), acting as a primary domain controller and DHCP server. Computer1 requests and obtains its IP address from SDKACZ, logs a user onto the domain from Computer1, connects a network drive to a share on SDKACZ, and downloads a file. The capture file represents all the frames relating to this network activity that were recorded by the Network Monitor running on SDKACZ.

By default, the capture file is displayed in a three-pane window format. The top pane, the Summary pane, displays all the frames that were captured, along with summary details about each frame. The middle frame, called the Detail pane, displays data specific to each frame selected in the Summary pane. In Figure 23.3, frame 100 has been selected in the Summary pane, and its detail is displayed in the Detail pane. The bottom pane, called the *Hex* pane, displays the content of the frame selected in the Summary pane in hexadecimal format. It also provides an ASCII view column that is used to see data more easily.

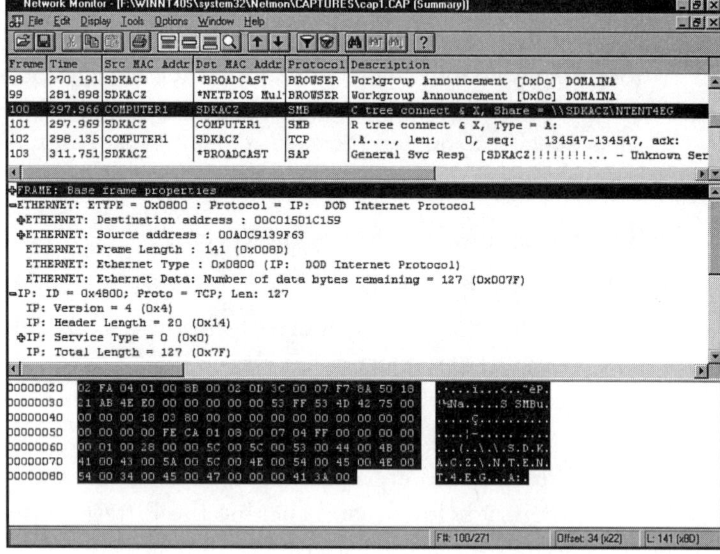

FIG. 23.3 ⇒
This example of the capture file data is displayed in a default, three-pane format: Summary (top), Detail (middle), and Hex (bottom).

Tip

You can view each pane alone by choosing Window and then selecting or deselecting Summary, Detail, and Hex as desired, by highlighting a pane and clicking the Zoom button (magnifying glass) on the toolbar, or by pressing F4. Viewing individual panes is most useful for viewing the Summary or Details pane. Because the Hex pane displays the hexadecimal version of the contents of a frame, it is best viewed in the default window by selecting a frame from the Summary pane. Nevertheless, you have the option to configure your display to best meet your needs.

Summary Viewing Captured DataPane

As stated earlier, the Summary pane lists all the frames that were captured and summary information about each. Nine columns of information are actually displayed for each frame. These columns are described in Table 23.1. Each column can be resized, moved by dragging and dropping it, or resorted by double-clicking the column header.

Table 23.1 Summary Pane Columns

Column Heading	Description
Frame	Displays the frames by number in the order in which they were captured
Time	Displays the time relative to the beginning of the capture in seconds. You can display this value alternately as the time of day or the number of seconds from that last frame
Src MAC Addr	Displays the media access control (MAC) address of the computer that sent the frame
Dst MAC Addr	Displays the media access control (MAC) address of the computer receiving the frame
Protocol	Identifies the protocol used to transmit the frame
Description	Summarizes the frame's contents
Src Other Addr	Displays an address other than the MAC address for the source computer, such as an IP address
Dst Other Addr	Displays an address other than the MAC address for the computer receiving the frame, such as an IP address
Type Other Addr	Identifies the type of "other" address, such as IP or IPX address

In Figure 23.3, frame 100 occurred 297.966 seconds into the capture period. Because the next frame occurred at 297.969, you know that frame 100 took 0.003 seconds to complete. It was sent by Computer1 to SDKACZ using SMB and was a request to connect to a share called NTENT4EG on SDKACZ. Though you cannot see it in the figure, the Src Other and Dst Other Addresses were the computers' NetBIOS names as resolved by IP—Computer1 and SDKACZ, respectively.

Tip

You can configure the frames displayed in the Summary pane to show only those frames relating to a particular protocol, address, function, or property. To do so, select Display, Filter from the menu to open the Display Filter dialog box (see Figure 23.4).

FIG. 23.4 ⇒

Here an expression for the property DHCP Request Exists is being added to the filter for this capture file.

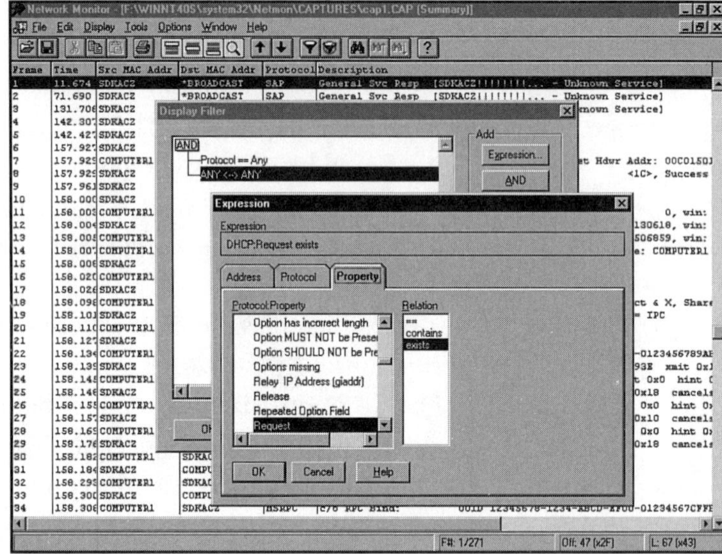

The Display Filter dialog box functions as a filter script writer. You will notice buttons to add, modify, and delete expressions and to create logical filtering using AND, OR, and NOT. You can use the Display Filter dialog box effectively to reduce a long capture file down to those frames that are of interest to you. For example, if you only want to see those frames dealing with the request for and assignment of an IP address from a DHCP server, you would edit the `Protocol == Any` line to read `Protocol == DHCP`.

Detail Pane

The detail pane displays frame-specific data for the frame selected in the Summary pane. To display this pane in full screen, highlight the pane and click the Zoom button on the toolbar. The details for frame 100 are shown in Figure 23.5.

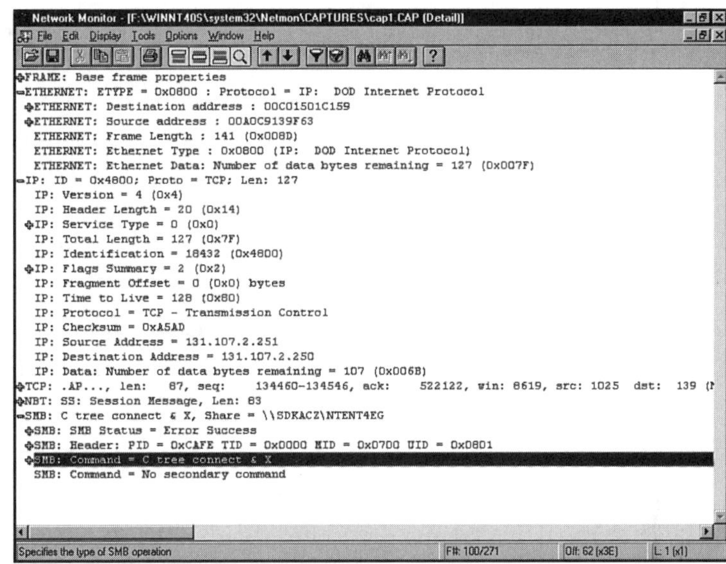

FIG. 23.5 ⇒
In this example, you see the detail data for frame 100 as selected in the Summary pane of Figure 23.3.

As you can see, a detail entry corresponds to each component of the frame (refer to Figure 23.1). If a particular entry has subentries or more data, a plus sign displays before the entry. Double-clicking the entry will expand it to show its additional information.

In Figure 23.5, you can see the source and destination MAC addresses (00C01501C159 for Computer1 and 00A0C9139F63 for SDKACZ). You see that the length of the frame is 141 bytes and that the data length is 127 bytes. The IP section displays Time to Live (TTL) data, Protocol type (TCP), and the IP addresses of the source and destination computers (131.107.2.251 and 131.107.2.250, respectively). Among the TCP data not shown in the figure is that the frame is using the NetBIOS service to make its request. The SMP entry shows us that the request is to connect to a share called NTENT4EG on SDKACZ.

Hex Pane

As you can see back in Figure 23.3, the Hex pane is relatively useless unless you can read hexadecimal notation. Notice that in the third column of data, however, you can see the UNC request for the NTENT4EG share on SDKACZ (`\\SDKACZ\NTENT4EG`). This column can be help you identify more specific information about the frame. For example, if the frame was a request for creating new users on the PDC, you would see the new user information listed in this column.

Interpreting Frames in a Capture File

In this section, you will begin to dissect the frames you have captured. You will identify which frames are part of various processes and services and how they impact the network performance as a whole. This discussion is by no means exhaustive and may prove tedious in its examination of minutiae. Nevertheless, it will provide you with the basic understanding needed to successfully interpret frames captured within your own network.

First, look at the communication that takes place between a client computer and a server. The following functions represent those communications most frequently associated with network traffic generated between a client and a server:

- IP address requests from DHCP server
- NetBIOS name registration with a WINS server
- Logon validation of a user at a domain controller
- Network browsing for resources
- Establishing file sessions

DHCP Frames

DHCP provides a service whereby IP address information is maintained on a DHCP server. When a client boots up, it obtains its IP address information from the DHCP server, which reduces the amount of IP administration that needs to take place at each client computer.

The DHCP process involves four frames (see Figure 23.6). The *DHCP Discover* frame is the client's broadcast attempt to find an available DHCP server on its subnet. The DHCP server that receives the DHCP Discover frame responds with an IP address that the client can lease contained in a *DHCP Offer* frame. The client responds that it accepts the IP address with the *DHCP Request* frame, which the DHCP acknowledges with the *DHCP ACK* frame. This last frame also contains any additional IP address information the client needs, such as the lease duration, router address, and WINS address.

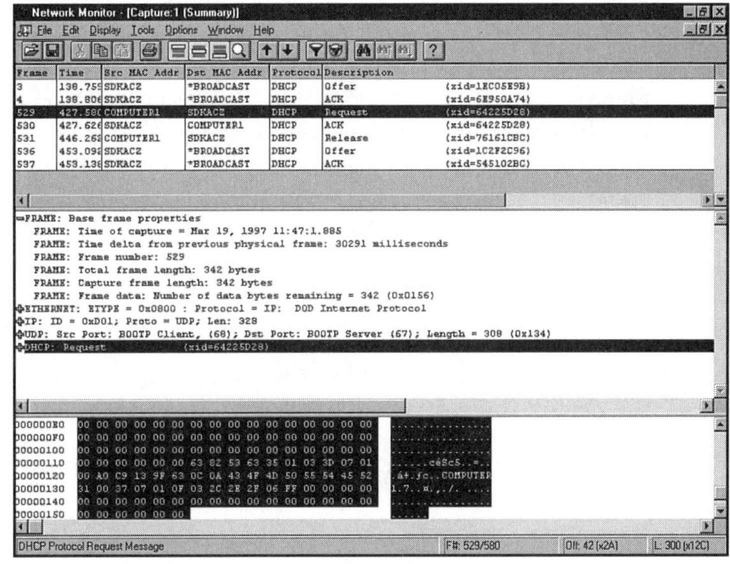

FIG. 23.6 ⇒ In this filtered capture display, you see only the frames relating to the DHCP protocol. You can see three of the four types of DHCP frames.

Each frame, as you can see from Figure 23.6, is 342 bytes long and together take about one-fourth of a second to complete. Figure 23.6 does not show a DHCP Discover frame. The two computers used to generate this capture file are the only two on the subnet, thus, this frame is not generated. You can see the other frame types clearly, however. Frame 529 represents a DHCP Request frame generated by a release renewal request by the client (IPCONFIG /renew). Frame 531, 536, and 537 represent frames generated first by a lease release by the client (IPCONFIG /release) followed by a release renewal.

The DHCP process usually takes place once a day, when the computer boots up. After that, additional DHCP traffic is generated by the lease renewal process. When a DHCP server assigns an IP address to the client, it does so in a lease arrangement. The default lease is three days. At the halfway point of the lease, the client automatically requests a lease renewal (DHCP Request) for an additional three days, or whatever the lease period happens to be, to which the DHCP server responds with an acknowledgment (DHCP ACK). The lease renewal process only requires two 342-byte frames and takes about half as long as the original DHCP process.

Key Concept

As you can see from the size and frequency of these frames, DHCP-related traffic is relatively minor and generally takes up less than one percent of the total bandwidth. Though the number of DHCP-related frames on a given subnet will certainly be influenced by the number of clients requesting IP addresses, as well as by the length of the lease period established, because the size and duration of the frames is so small, it should still not significantly effect the overall network traffic.

For example, a lease duration of one day will generate lease renewal requests every half-day (half of the lease period), whereas a lease duration of the default three days will generate lease renewal requests every day and a half. But the total length and duration of the two renewal frames is 684 bytes and less than 200 milliseconds.

If a network contains routers that can support BOOTP-relay agents and RFC 1542, those routers have the ability to forward DHCP Discover frames to other subnets with DHCP servers. These routers are usually employed via a time-out parameter to resolve IP address requests when a local DHCP server is busy or otherwise unavailable.

Caution

It is possible that a particular subnet can receive an unusually high number of DHCP-related frames in this configuration. If this occurs, it can begin to affect network traffic on that subnet. The full version of Network Monitor can help to identify those routers and monitor remote DHCP traffic as well as the local traffic.

WINS Frames

WINS (Windows Internet Name Service) provides a means of resolving IP addresses to NetBIOS names. You access most network resources by name rather than by address. For example, when you connect to a shared folder on a remote server, you generally map a drive to that resource by using its UNC (universal naming convention) name. The Public shared folder on the server ABCCorp would be addressed as `\\ABCCorp\Public`. When using IP addresses, this name must map back, or be resolved, to an IP address. You can effect name resolution in a variety of ways, and at least as many books explain the process. Briefly, here is how a NetBIOS name is resolved to an IP address.

1. As you make connections to network resources and resolve NetBIOS names to IP addresses, the names are stored in a local NetBIOS name cache. This cache is checked first. If the name can be resolved, it is. Resolved names stay in the cache for 10 minutes by default.
2. If the NetBIOS name cache does not contain the name and a NetBIOS Name Server, in this case a WINS server, has been implemented, the name is sent to the WINS server to be resolved.
3. If after three attempts the WINS server cannot resolve the address, a b-node broadcast is generated on the local subnet. A b-node broadcast is essentially a name request that is sent to every computer on the subnet. The computer whose name matches responds using ARP (address resolution protocol) and the source computer's hardware address.
4. If after three b-node broadcasts the name is still not resolved, the local LMHOSTS or HOST file is checked. Think of these files as IP address books, sort of like your company directory.
5. Finally, if there is still no resolution, the name request may be sent to a DNS (domain name server). If the name still cannot be resolved, an error message is returned to the originating computer.

You are concerned with the WINS portion of this process for this discussion because Microsoft recommends using WINS for name resolution in an IP network.

Note This section is not intended as a primer for WINS but, rather, as how to monitor WINS traffic on the network using Network Monitor.

Six frames are associated with WINS traffic: Name Registration, Name Response, Query Request, Query Response, Release Request, and Release Response. You can filter these frames by viewing NBT protocol frames.

Key Concept

Think of WINS as being a dynamic host file. When a computer boots up and receives its IP address from a DHCP server, it then broadcasts its name and IP address to the subnet. When a WINS server is implemented and identified to the client computer (either manually or through DHCP), the name and IP address are registered on the WINS server. Registration involves not only the NetBIOS name of the computer, however. NetBIOS names must also be registered for every server or application that supports the NetBIOS API (Application Programming Interface).

Network Monitor supports NetBIOS and, as such, the NetBIOS name of the computer acting as the Network Monitor "server" needs to be registered. PDCs and BDCs need to be registered for logon validation and database synchronization. It is not unusual for a client computer to register two or more names.

A NetBIOS Name Registration frame is sent to the WINS server for each name that needs to be registered. As you can see in Figure 23.7, in which frame 7 is highlighted, each name registration frame is 110 bytes long and contains the computer name of the client and its IP address. Frame 8 (see Figure 23.8) shows the WINS server's name response.

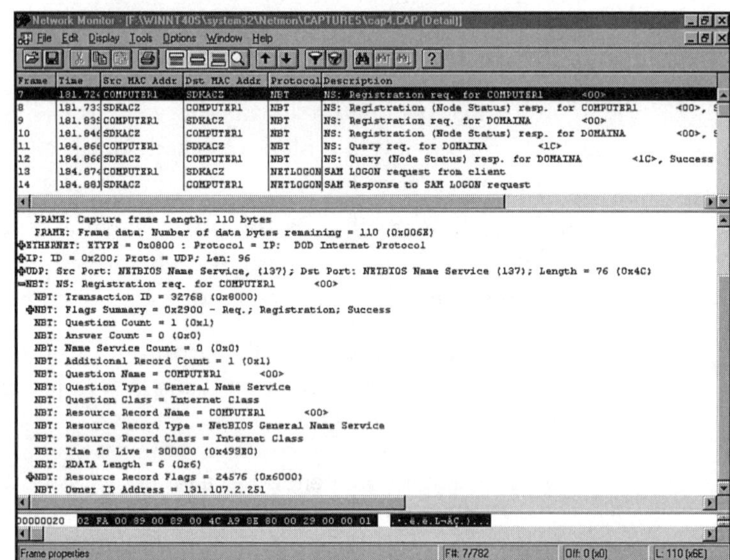

FIG. 23.7 ⇒
This example shows the name registration requests for COMPUTER1 to the WINS server SDKACZ.

Notice that the name response frame is 104 bytes and note in the NBT: Flags Summary line that the registration was a success. As with DHCP leases, the registration is good for a specific period of time—six days, by default. This length of time is indicated in the NBT:Time to Live line as 518,400 seconds. And as with DHCP leases, the client will automatically renew the registration at the halfway point with another name registration request.

Note in the Summary pane for every registration request the hex code in brackets: <00>. This code represents the type of name registration that is being requested. In this case, the <00> refers to computer name registered by the workstation service of the client computer. Table 23.2 outlines the more common registration codes used.

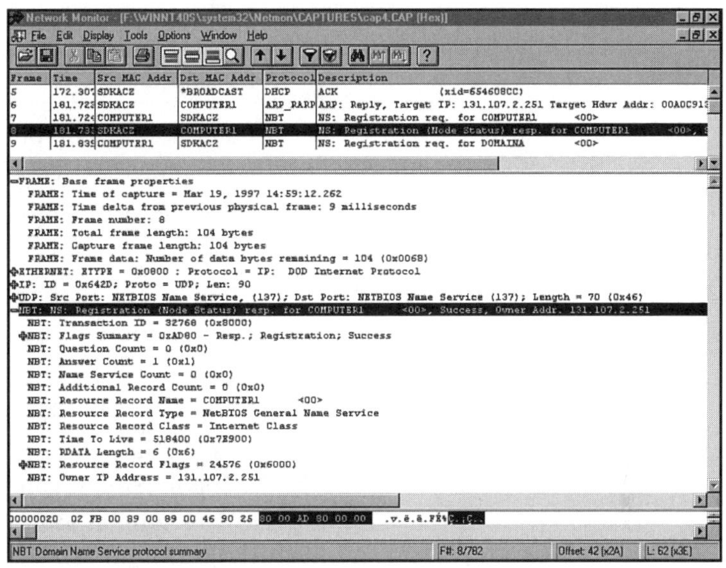

FIG. 23.8 ⇒ This example shows the WINS server's response to the first name registration request for COMPUTER1.

Table 23.2 WINS Registration Codes

Code	Description
Computername <00>	NetBIOS name registered by the client's workstation service
Computername <03>	NetBIOS name registered by the client's messenger service to receive network messages
Username <03>	User's logon name registered by the client's messenger service to receive network messages
Computername <20>	NetBIOS name registered by the client's server service
Workgroup or Domainname <00>	Identifies the user as a member of the workgroup or domain
Workgroup or Domainname <1E>	Identifies the user as a member of the workgroup or domain for browser elections
Workgroup or Domainname <1D>	Identifies the computer as being the subnet Master Browser for that domain

continues

Table 23.2 Continued

Code	Description
Domainname <1B>	Identifies the computer as being the Domain Master Browser for that domain
Domainname <1C>	Identifies the computer as a domain controller for that domain

Every name resolution request also generates WINS frames. For example, when the user logs on, a request is made to find a domain controller to do the authentication and resolve the domain controller name to an IP address. In Figure 23.9, frame 11 shows the 92 byte request for name resolution for DOMAINA to handle the logon request generated in frame 13. Frame 12 shows the WINS server's 104 byte response. Note the IP address of the domain controller contained on the last line of the Detail pane.

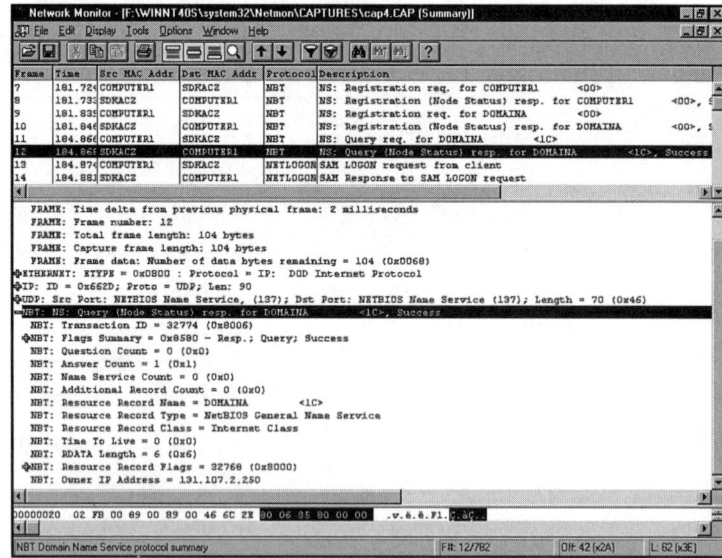

FIG. 23.9 ⇒ This example shows the two frames involved in resolving a name request for a domain controller.

Finally, when the computer stops a service or shuts down, it generates a 110 byte release request frame notifying the WINS server that the name is no longer needed and could be used to register another computer. The WINS server responds, as with registration, with a 104 byte release response with a Time To Live value of 0. Frames 780 and 781 in Figure 23.10 show the two release frames with the Time To Live value of 0.

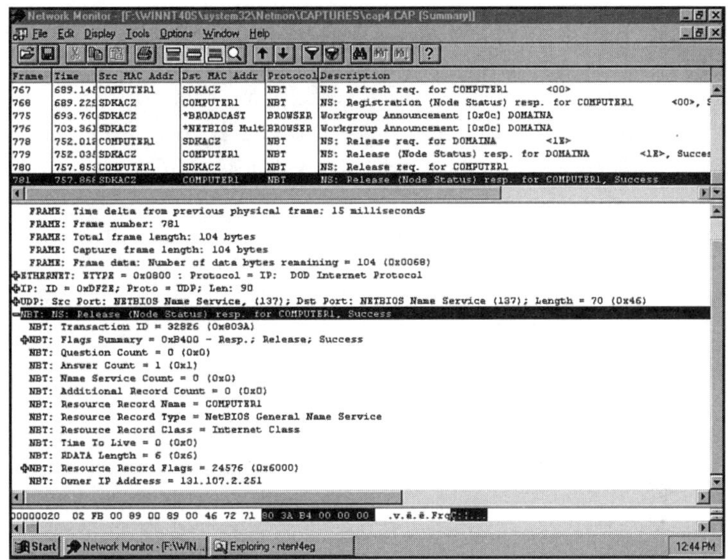

FIG. 23.10 ⇒
The two release frames generated when COMPUTER1 shuts down.

Ch 23

As with DHCP frames, WINS frames generate less than one percent of total network traffic on average. The size is never larger than 204 bytes. As a rule of thumb, recall that:

- Each name registration takes two frames (214 bytes) when the client boots, and every service, NetBIOS application, and so on must be registered.
- The client renews its name registration at the halfway point of the Time To Live value or, by default, every three days. Two frames (214 bytes) are generated.
- Every attempt to access a computer through the network, such as with a net use command, generates two frames (196 bytes).
- When the client stops a service or shuts down, a registered name is released, generating two frames (214 bytes).

Considerations for Optimizing WINS Traffic

If you do need to reduce WINS traffic on the network, recall the order in which name resolution takes place. The first place that the client checks is the NetBIOS name cache on the local computer. By default, resolve names stay in the cache for 10 minutes. You can increase this default by modifying the following Registry entry:

```
HKEY_LOCAL_MACHINE\System\CurrentControlSet\Services\NetBT\
➥Parameters\CacheTimeout
```

Because the resolved name entries will stay in cache longer, presumably fewer WINS frames will be generated in the attempt to resolve names. You could also create an LMHOSTS file that contains the addresses most frequently accessed and place it on each computer. You can configure these addresses to be preloaded into the NetBIOS cache, thus reducing WINS name resolution traffic.

Another consideration would be to disable unnecessary services on the computer. Recall that every service, application, and so on that supports or uses NetBIOS must register itself. Each name registration will generate two additional frames. If you disable unnecessary services, you will generate fewer registration frames. For example, if the computer doesn't use NetDDE, disable the service. Or, if the computer is not sharing any network resources to the network, disable its server service.

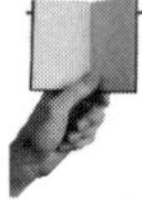

Tip

Disabling unnecessary services also has the added benefit of releasing unused resources on the computer, resulting in an overall performance gain.

File Session Frames

Before you can access a network resource, the client and server computers must establish a session between them. This session generates on average 11 frames and totals a little more than 1K. After a session is established to a resource server, the only additional frames that are generated will be for every additional resource connection that is made during that session. These connection frames tend to average 360 bytes.

Users who establish multiple sessions in a day by connecting and disconnecting drives, connecting to multiple servers, and so on, and the number of users on the network can have an impact on your overall network traffic. Unfortunately, usually you can do little to avoid this type of traffic because it is primarily user-generated. Keeping resource servers close to the users who need access, especially on the same subnet, certainly facilitates overall network traffic within the enterprise. Also, connection requests are sent over all protocols that are installed on the client or server simultaneously. Removing protocols that are not needed will reduce the number of session frames that are generated.

In general, six steps establish a file session.

1. As you saw with WINS, the NetBIOS name must be resolved to an IP address, and two frames are generated for this step.
2. Next, the IP address must be resolved to the hardware or MAC address of the computer. ARP (address resolution protocol), part of the IP protocol stack, is used to accomplish this step. Two frames are generated for this step: *ARP Request* and *ARP Reply*, both 60 bytes long. Because this address resolution is also cached for 10 minutes (like the NetBIOS name cache), these frames will be regenerated every time the two computers need to communicate beyond 10 minutes.
3. Now a TCP session must be established to allow two-way communications to take place between the client and the server computers. This session is commonly known as the three-way TCP handshake, and, as you might have guessed, generates three frames:
   - *TCP S* from the client to the server requesting a NetBIOS session
   - *TCP A S* from the server to the client acknowledging the request
   - *TCP A* from the client to the server establishing the session

   Figure 23.11 shows the three TCP frames (a total of 180 bytes) generated. Once this TCP session is established, the user can make any number of file connections to the same server.

Ch 23

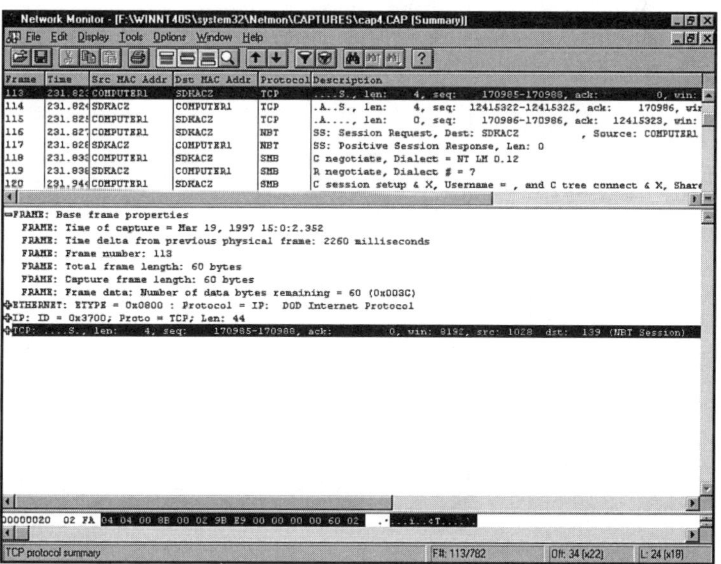

FIG. 23.11 ⇒
This example shows the three TCP handshake frames (113, 114, 115) with the final frame detailed, as well as the two NetBIOS session frames (116, 117).

4. A NetBIOS session is then established generating two frames of 126 bytes and 58 bytes each, respectively: *NBT Session Request* and *NBT Positive Session Response*. Like the TCP frames, these only need to be generated once per session between the client and server.
5. The two computers next negotiate their server message block protocols (SMB). The client sends a list of the protocols it understands (called dialects) through an *SMB C negotiate* frame (see Figure 23.12). The server finds the highest common SMB protocol understood by both the client and the server and notifies the client through an *SMB R negotiate* frame. The two frames average 360 bytes total. As with TCP and NetBIOS session frames, these only need be generated once per session.

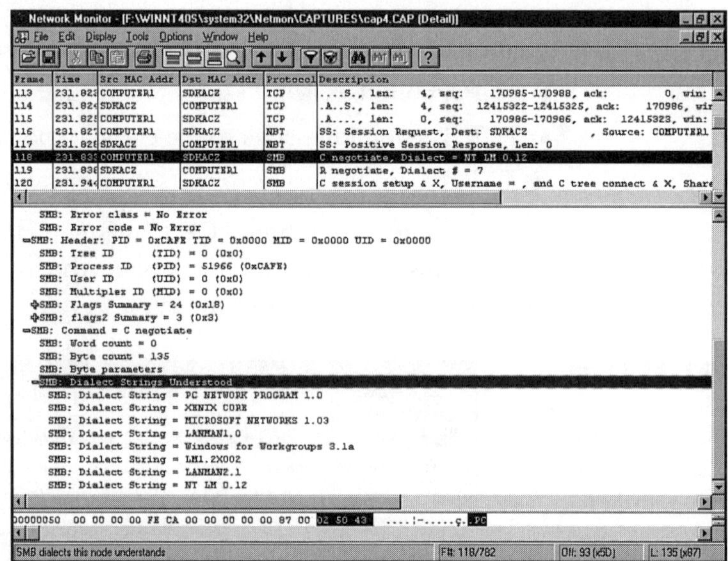

FIG. 23.12 ⇒ This example shows the two SMB negotiation frames (118 and 119) with the dialect list sent from the client in the Detail pane.

6. At last the connection to the resource can be made. This connection involves three more SMB frames. The *SMB C session setup* frame sent by the client indicates the name of the share and the user name and password of the user requesting access (pass-through authentication). The server validates the user and establishes the connection responding with an *SMB R session setup* frame. The total size of these frames depends largely on the type of command issued and can be anywhere from 360 bytes to more than 500 bytes, on average.

In Figure 23.13, you can see all the SMB frames involved in establishing a connecting from COMPUTER1 to the NTENT4EG share on server SDKACZ. Beginning with frames 120 and 121, the session is established. Two additional sets of background connections are made for remote API support (frames 130 and 131) before the connection to the share is finally established.

FIG. 23.13 ⇒
This example shows the frames generated between COMPUTER1 and SDKACZ that establish a connection to the NTENT4EG share of SDKACZ.

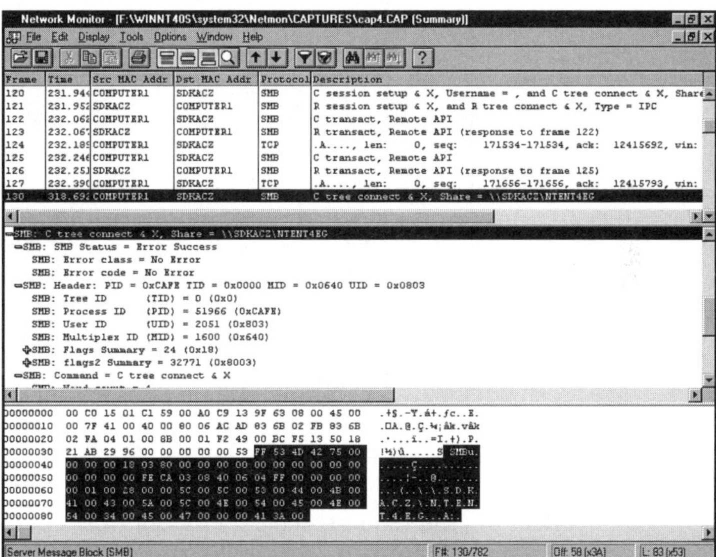

The number of frames that may be generated by the transfer of a file from the shared folder to the client disk varies greatly because it is generated by the size of the file, the frequency with which the file is accessed (saving changes, for example), the overall traffic burden already on the network, and so on. Figure 23.14 shows the frames generated by an application remotely accessing a file on a server. The file is `08FIG46.PCX` (frame 424). From start to finish, about 50 frames were generated, totaling nearly 40K.

When a connection is disconnected, the client initiates the request with an *SMB C tree disconnect* request frame that identifies which connection is to be terminated, to which the server responds with an *SMB R tree disconnect* request frame. The two frames total about 186 bytes, and two additional frames would be generated for every connection that is disconnected.

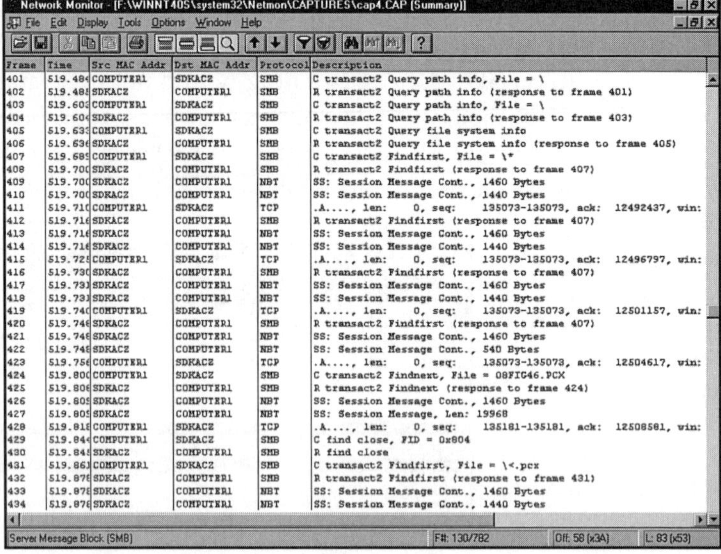

FIG. 23.14 ⇒
Shown are some of the frames generated when a file is accessed on a remote server from the client.

Finally, when the last file connection between the client and the server is disconnected, the TCP session is closed. As when you established the TCP session, three frames are generated for a total of 180 bytes: *TCP A F* from the client requesting termination of the session, *TCP A F* from the server acknowledging the request, and *TCP A* from the client terminating the session.

Logon Validation Frames

The logon process is one of the first network functions generated by a user. A user logs on by supplying the user name, password, and the authenticating domain. The Net Logon service then looks for an available domain controller for the requested domain and passes the logon information to it for validation where the authentication process completes. This, of course, generates some network traffic. The amount of traffic varies from network to network and depends on whether logon scripts must be executed, profiles must be loaded, or any other network task must be run. The ultimate impact that logon traffic has on the network as a whole also depends on when and how frequently users log on, which is determined easily enough using Network Monitor to establish baselines for your network. Being user-based, however, it is also difficult to control.

The first step in the process as previously stated is finding an appropriate and available domain controller. Doing so could take the form of a broadcast request to the Net Logon mailslot (UDP Port 138) or by sending a query request to a WINS server for a registered domain controller.

Broadcasting for the Domain Controller

The broadcast request generates a *NETLOGON Logon Request* frame that contains the NetBIOS name of the authenticating domain. This frame can be anywhere from 260 bytes for Windows 95 to 300 bytes for Windows NT. Each logon server responds with a *NETLOGON Response to Logon Request* frame that is directed back to the originating computer. Again, this frame can be anywhere from 230 bytes for Windows 95 to 270 bytes for Windows NT.

Using WINS to Find the Domain Controller

If the client is configured to use WINS for name resolution, an *NBT NS: Query request* frame (92 bytes) for the authenticating domain is generated and sent to the WINS server.

The WINS server responds with an NBT NS: Query response frame that contains a list of the first 25 domain controllers in the WINS database for that domain. The size will vary according to the number of domain controllers in the list. For example, two domain controllers generates a 116-byte frame.

The client sends a *NETLOGON SAM LOGON Request* frame directed to each domain controller in the list, ignoring any responses until it has completed sending the requests. Each frame is 328 bytes long.

Each domain controller responds in kind with a *NETLOGON SAM Response* frame similar to that generated for Net Logon broadcast.

Validating the Logon Request

The client establishes a session with the first domain controller that responds to its NETLOGON SAM LOGON Request in a manner similar to that outlined in the "File Session Frames" section earlier in this chapter.

- The NetBIOS name of the domain controller is resolved.
- The IP address is resolved to the MAC address of the domain controller.
- A TCP session is established between the client and the domain controller.
- A NetBIOS session is also established.
- SMB protocol negotiation takes place and a dialect is identified.
- An SMB connection to the IPC$ administrative share on the domain controller is established.

This process takes about 11 frames for a total of about 1.4K, depending on whether the client is Windows 95 or Windows NT. Figure 23.15 clearly shows the frames discussed from frame 11, the query request for the list of domain controllers from the WINS server (SDKACZ) to the IPC connection established in frame 25.

FIG. 23.15 ⇒ This example shows all the frames involved in connecting to a domain controller for user validation.

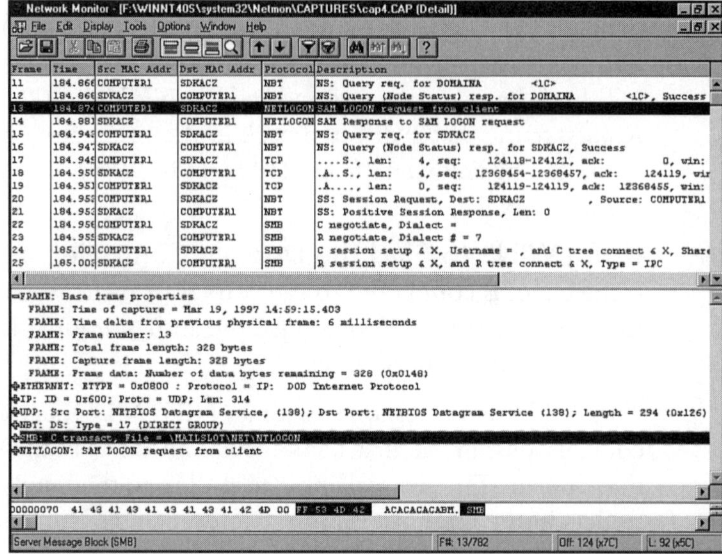

On Windows NT-based computers, the validation process consists of three steps.

1. Through a series of 12 frames and about 2,000 bytes of traffic, a list of trusted domains is returned if any exist.
2. Next, a secure channel is established between the client and the domain controller generating another eight frames and about 1,400 bytes of traffic.
3. Finally, an *RPC client call* frame is generated that contains the user name, password, and domain and is sent to the domain controller. The server responds with a successful *RPC server response* frame. Any additional named pipes that are necessary to the Net Logon share (for logon scripts, system policies, and so on) are also established.

The IPC$ connection is closed and the NetBIOS and TCP sessions are terminated as discussed in the section "File Session Frames."

Optimizing Logon Validation

The amount of traffic generated by logon validation depends on several factors. To minimize validation traffic and optimize the authentication process for the user, you need to have enough domain controllers to service those needs.

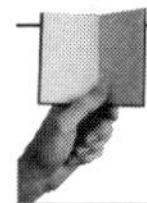

Tip

Microsoft recommends one domain controller for every 2,000 users.

The number and placement of domain controllers will itself depend largely on the type of domain model you have chosen, however, the location of users and the resources they need to access, the type of WAN connections you have in place, and so on.

In general, you will want to place a domain controller near the users who need to log on. For example, in a worldwide organization with users located in Chicago, London, and Tokyo, you would want at least one domain controller in each of those locations so that users validate locally rather than across WAN connections. The kind of hardware you use for the domain controller may itself determine how large an account database it can support and how long validation requests may take to process.

Another possibility for increasing throughput on a domain controller would be to increase the number of simultaneous logons that it can process. By default, domain controllers have their Server service memory management buffer configured as Maximize Throughput for File Sharing, which allows for about six or seven simultaneous logons per second. By changing this setting to Maximize Throughput for Network Applications, this number can increase to about 20. Modify this setting as follows.

1. Open the Network Properties dialog box and select the Services tab.
2. In the Network Services list box, select Server, then choose Properties.
3. In the Server dialog box, choose Maximize Throughput for Network Applications, then choose OK.
4. Choose OK to update the Registry and bindings. Shut down and restart the computer as directed.

Exploring Browser Traffic

The most common, and perhaps the easiest, way for users to access resources is to browse for them. When users open Network Neighborhood, for example, a list of computers and their resources in their workgroup or domain is presented as well as a list of other domains and their computers and resources. Users browse through the lists of domains and computers using a point-and-click method to find and connect to resources. The Windows NT service that furnishes this list is the Computer Browser. The Computer Browser service is responsible for creating, maintaining, and distributing lists of computers and their resources. You will briefly review the basic concepts of browsing here.

A domain master browser is selected for a domain and master browsers are selected for subnets within a domain by means of a predefined election process. Master browsers select one or more backup browsers for their subnets, depending on the number of computers in the workgroup or domain on that subnet. When a computer boots up, it announces itself to the master browser once every minute for the first five minutes and then every 12 minutes thereafter.

The master browsers create a list of the computers and their shared resources from their subnets and announces it to the domain master browser. The domain master browser creates and maintains a master list of all its own domain resources. It also receives lists of resources from other domain master browsers. It then distributes this list back to the master browsers. The master browsers in turn distribute the list to their backup browsers. Eventually, all the browsers in the domain maintain a copy of the same list of domains, workgroups, computers, and their shared resources.

Key Concept

A PDC will always become a domain master browser. BDCs will become master browsers, if on their own subnet, as well as backup browsers. Master browsers announce themselves to the domain master browser every 15 minutes and update their browse list from the domain master browser every 12 minutes. The domain master browser contacts the WINS server for a list of all domains every 12 minutes. Every backup browser contacts its master browser every 12 minutes to update its browse list.

When a user requests a list of resources, for example, by opening Network Neighborhood, the Computer Browser service contacts the master browser and obtains from it a list of backup browsers. The client computer then contacts a backup browser from the list to obtain a list of computers. When a computer is selected from the list, it responds with a list of its shared resources.

Not surprisingly, this entire process generates some network traffic. Given average usage, Microsoft estimates that 30 percent or more of total network traffic can consist of browser-related traffic.

Browser Elections and Announcements

Begin with the election process. There must always be a master browser to maintain the browse list for the subnet or domain. If it is determined that a master browser is needed, for example, a client is looking for a list of backup browsers to contact and cannot find a master browser to provide that list, and then an election for a new master browser is initiated. Chapter 17, "Windows NT Networking Services" discusses the election process. Now look at the frames generated.

It all begins with a host announcement. All computers that have the ability to share resources are de facto servers and can be included in browse lists. This includes Windows NT-based computers, of course, as well as Windows 95 and Windows for Workgroups-based computers. These computers announce themselves to the master browser every 12 minutes with a *Browser Host Announcement* frame. This broadcast frame is sent out to all computers in the subnet rather than a directed frame and is about 250 bytes long. It contains a list of its browser criteria.

If the computer making this announcement has the potential to become a master browser, it must first determine whether it should be, which means finding out who the master browser is and checking that computer's qualifications against its own. The computer generates a 220-byte *Browser Announcement Request* frame to find the master browser. The master browser responds with a 220-byte *Browser Local Master Announcement* frame that includes its qualifications (see Figure 23.16).

If there is no master browser or if the originating computer thinks its qualifications are better than the master browser, it generates a *Browser Election [Force]* frame of about 225 bytes, which is again broadcast to all other host computers. A host with higher browser criteria will respond with a

Browser Election response frame of about the same size. These frames continue to be generated until the host with the highest criteria wins the election and generates a Browser Local Master Announcement frame to celebrate the victory and let all the other computers know.

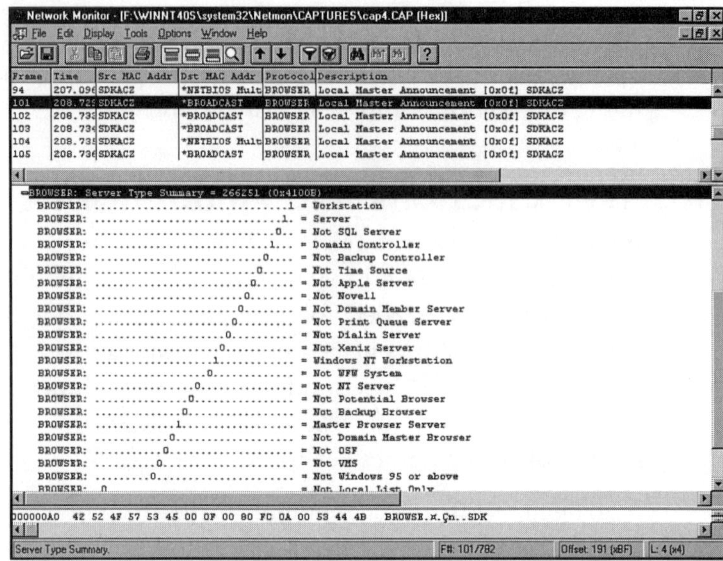

FIG. 23.16 ⇒ Frame 101 represents a Local Master Announcement from the master browser. Note the criteria listed in the Detail pane that make this a master browser.

Finally, the master browser will determine whether any of the potential browsers need to become backup browsers for the subnet. It will do so by generating a *Browser Become Backup Browser* frame (again, about 220 bytes) naming that computer as the backup browser (see Figure 23.17).

Every 15 minutes every master browser announces itself to other master browsers and the domain master browser with a 250-byte Browser Workgroup Announcement frame. You can see two of these in the Summary pane of Figure 23.17.

Every 12 minutes, the domain master browser contacts the WINS server for a list of registered domains with an *RPC Client call winsif:R_WinsGetBrowserNames* frame to which the WINS server responds with an *RPC Server response winsif:R_WinsGetBrowserNames* frame. As a benchmark, for a list of four domains, the entire process generates 22 frames and about 2.1K of traffic, including establishing the session with the WINS server, resolving names, and so on, as discussed earlier.

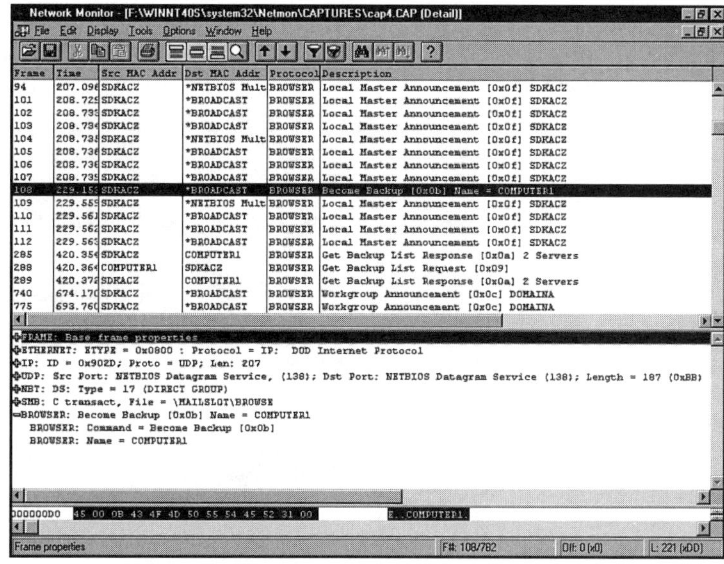

FIG. 23.17 ⇒
Frame 108 announces that Computer1 will become the backup browser for the subnet.

Master browsers, in turn, contact the domain master browser to retrieve the master browse list in a similar fashion every 12 minutes. Backup browsers, in their turn, retrieve an updated browse list from the master browser every 12 minutes. Frames are generated to establish the session, resolve the computer name and address, request the list, and retrieve it. Using four domains with four servers for a benchmark, the process of updating the backup browser list could generate up to 15 frames and 2,000+ bytes of traffic on average every 12 minutes.

What happens, then, when a user innocently requests a browse list by browsing through Network Neighborhood? The client computer begins by broadcasting a *Browser Get Backup List Request* frame to the master browser. The master browser responds with a *Browser Get Backup List Response* frame, which contains a list of browser computers from which the client can choose. Frame 289 in Figure 23.18 shows the response to a client's request. The Detail pane shows that the response frame was 233 bytes long, it took about 8 milliseconds to complete, and returned two browser computer names.

Next, the client computer connects to one of the backup browsers in the list and retrieves the browse list. This process can generate up to 19 frames and 2,150 bytes. Finally, the user selects a server from the browse list and obtains its list of available resources. The number and size of the frames generated depends on the number of shared resources on the server, its location, which domain is being browsed, and whether there is a trust.

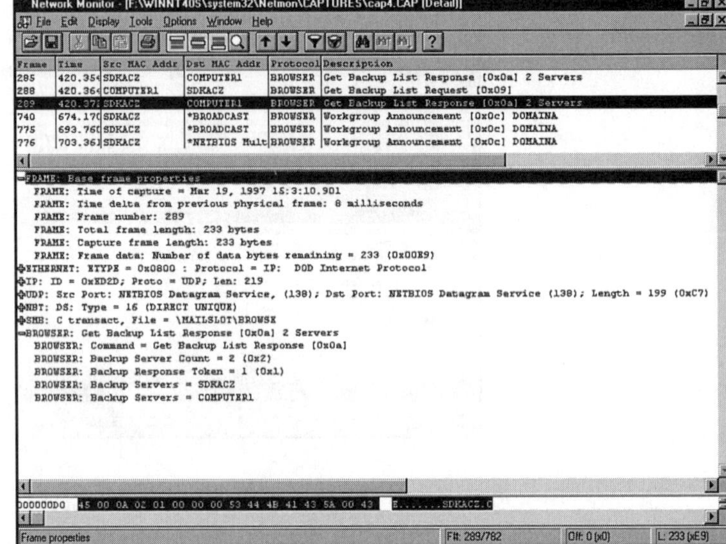

FIG. 23.18 ⇒
This figure shows the request and response for a backup browser list.

Suggestions for Optimizing Browse Traffic

Needless to say, browsing, though it provides an easy and intuitive way for users to locate and connect to shared network resources, also generates a fair amount of network traffic. Unfortunately, you can do little to optimize this type of traffic.

One way to reduce browser host server announcements would be to disable the Server service on any computers that will not share resources, thereby eliminating the host announcements that these computers will make. They will also never become members of a browse list. You can also effect the number of browsers by modifying the Registry entries for potential browsers and preferred master browsers.

In addition to those Registry entries, here are two more that you can add to `HKEY_LOCAL_MACHINE\System\CurrentControlSet\Services\Browser\Parameters`: `MasterPeriodicity` and `BackupPeriodicity`. Like many Registry parameters, these will not show up in the list of parameters when you look at this subkey. You will need to add them to the subkey parameters with a data type of `REG_DWORD`.

As you recall, the master browser contacts the domain master browser every 12 minutes to update its browse list. This amount of time is its `MasterPeriodicity`, and the default value is 720 seconds, or 12 minutes. You can modify this value to be anywhere from 300 seconds (five minutes) to 0x418937 (4,294,967 seconds, or about 50 days). The computer will not need to be restarted after making this change.

Each backup browser also contacts its master browser every 12 minutes to update its browse list. This amount of time is its `BackupPeriodicity`, and the default is also 720 seconds, or 5 minutes. You can configure it as you did the `MasterPeriodicity`, but if you modify this value, you will have to restart the computer. Increasing the value for either of these parameters reduces the frequency of browse list updates and the associated network traffic.

Note If you don't want a Windows-NT-based computer to become a browser, set the `HKEY_LOCAL_MACHINE\System\CurrentControlSet\Services\Browser\Parameters\ MaintainServerList` value to No. For Windows 95 computers, disable the File and Printer Sharing Properties Browse Master parameter in the Network Properties dialog box. For Windows for Workgroups computers, set the `MaintainServerList` parameter in the Network section of the `System.ini` file to `No`.

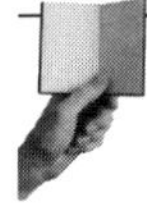

Tip

One last tip. Browsing is protocol dependent. Browser announcements and elections are generated for every protocol that is installed on a computer. For a server with all three protocols installed (TCP/IP, NWLink, and NetBEUI), this means that browser traffics are, effectively, tripled. If you can disable or remove unused protocols, this can help to reduce browser-related traffic.

Analyzing Traffic Between Domain Controllers

In the previous section, you dealt primarily with the traffic that is generated between the client computer and a server. In this section, you will examine some common traffic generated between servers. In particular, you will examine traffic associated with account database synchronization, trust relationships, and directory replication.

Account Database Synchronization

You will recall from Chapter 15, "Windows NT 4.0 Trusts," that when a user logs on to the domain, a domain controller performs the authentication process. You saw the network traffic that the logon process generates earlier in this chapter in the section titled "Logon Validation Frames." Though either a PDC or a BDC may authenticate a user, it is usually the BDC that performs this service. Any changes made to the account database are always made on the PDC, however. The BDCs obtain copies of the master account database from the PDC during a process called account synchronization. Because BDCs are primarily responsible for validating user requests for logon, it is of critical importance that their copies of the account database remain consistent with the master copy maintained on the PDC.

Actually, three databases maintain the accounts and are involved in the synchronization process.

- The SAM Accounts database (0) contains user and group accounts, built-in global groups, and computer accounts. SAM stands for Security Accounts Manager.
- The SAM Built-in database (1) contains built-in local groups and their members.
- The LSA database (2) contains the Local Security Account Secrets used for trust relationships, account policy settings, and domain controller computer account passwords.

Account synchronization takes place automatically, according to default parameters that you can modify in the Registry.

Key Concept

Account synchronization also occurs when the BDC is first installed, whenever the BDC is restarted, and when forced to take place by the administrator using either the Server Manager utility or a net accounts /sync command issued from the BDC.

Every five minutes by default, the PDC checks its master account database to see whether any changes have been made. This process is called its pulse interval. If the PDC finds that the master account database has been modified, it notifies the backup domain controllers that need the changes that they need to retrieve the changes. The PDC knows which BDCs need the changes by maintaining a record of the version ID that each BDC has. If the version ID is current, that BDC does not receive the notification. For example, if there are five BDCs and the administrator has already forced synchronization to take place with one of the BDCs, that one has a more current version ID than the others. At the next pulse interval, the other four BDCs will be notified of the changes.

The PDC generates a *NETLOGON Announce Change to UAS or SAM* frame that is sent to each BDC (see Figure 23.19, frames 363 and 365). This frame contains an encrypted date and time, the version IDs or serial numbers of the three databases, the domain's name and SID, the PDC name, and the `Pulse` and `Random` parameter values stored in the Registry.

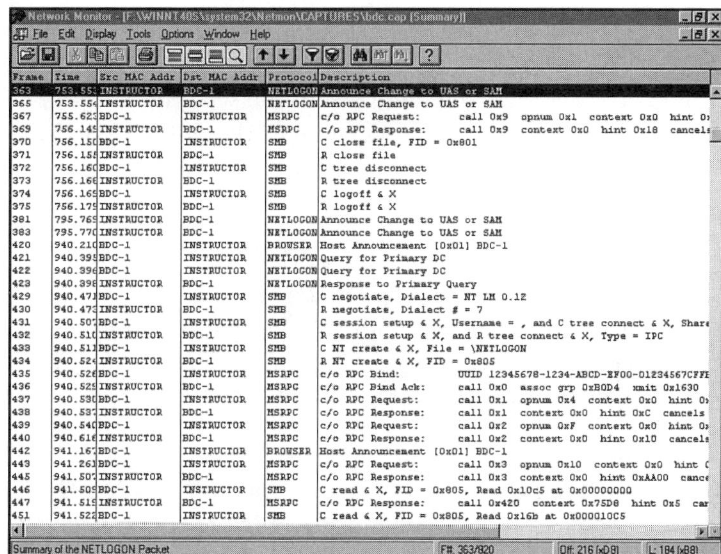

FIG. 23.19 ⇒
This figure shows some of the network traffic generated when the account database is synchronized between the PDC and the BDC.

The BDC checks the version IDs in the Announce Change frame. If they are more current than the BDC's version, the BDC connects to the IPC$ administrative share of the PDC and establishes a secure channel to the PDC if none already exists. It will also establish a TCP session if any previous TCP session connections have timed out. The frames that are generated are similar to those already discussed earlier in the sections "File Session Frames," and "Validating the Logon Request," and may take up to 15 frames.

Next, the BDC verifies the account database by making a named pipe request for the Net Logon service on the PDC through a series of four frames sent to the PDC, generating a total of 719 bytes: *SMB C NT Create*, *SMB R NT Create*, *MSRPC c/o RPC Bind*, and *MSRPC c/o RPC Bind Ack*. The BDC then retrieves the data using either SMB or RPC calls and the NetrDatabaseDeltas API (that only a developer can appreciate): *R_LOGON RPC Client call logon:NetrDatabaseDeltas* and *R_LOGON RPC Server response logon:NetrDatabaseDeltas* or *SMB C read & X* and *SMB R Read & X*. A set of these two frames is generated for each database with changes. The number of response frames will depend on how much data needs to be transferred. Adding two new users generally averages 12 frames, about 3,300 bytes and completes in about one second.

When the BDC is first installed or when an account synchronization is forced, a full transfer of the database takes place. The process begins, as always, with the discovery of the PDC. The BDC uses a standard name query of the type discussed in the section "WINS Frames" to the WINS server for the registered name of the domain. Because this name is only registered by the PDC, the WINS server responds with the PDC name and address.

The BDC then generates a 270-byte *NETLOGON Query for Primary DC* frame sent to the PDC. (Refer to Figure 23.19 beginning with frame 422.) The PDC responds with a *NETLOGON Response to Primary Query* frame of about the same size. A session is established between the BDC and the PDC as described in the section "File Session Frames."

Next, a secure channel is created between the PDC and the BDC. First an *SMB C NT Create & X* frame and an *SMB R NT Create & X* frame are generated to establish a named pipe to the Net Logon service on the PDC. Then an RPC connection is made between the BDC and the PDC through a *MSRPC c/0 RPC Bind* and *MSRPC c/o RPC Bind Ack* frame.

The secure channel is then established. The BDC verifies that its account name exists at the PDC by generating two NetrServerReqChallenge frames: R_LOGON RPC Client call logon:NetrServerReqChallenge and R_LOGON RPC Server Response logon:NetrServerReqChallenge. The BDC generates two similar frames (NetrServerAuthenticate2) to verify its account password.

Altogether, eight frames are generated to establish the secure channel for a total of about 1,550 bytes. After the secure channel is in place, the BDC can verify the accounts databases. An RPC Client Call and Response is generated for each account database. The frames that are generated are the same as those described previously when the automatic update of database changes was discussed. The number and size of the frames that are generated in response to these calls depend on the size of the databases.

Optimizing Account Synchronization Traffic

Truly, the only way to optimize synchronization traffic is to modify the Registry defaults that govern the synchronization process. You can find all these in the `HKEY_LOCAL_MACHINE\System\CurrentControlSet\Services\NetLogon\Parameters Registry` subkey. Some of them are briefly discussed here.

The `ReplicationGovernor` parameter can be modified on the BDC and provides a way to control how much bandwidth is consumed by the Net Logon service for synchronizing the databases. The default is, of course, 100 percent, which means that Net Logon will use 100 percent of the available bandwidth while the PDC buffers 128K of synchronization data. Across slow WAN links or on networks where traffic is already peaking, use of available bandwidth can be a concern. Modifying the value to, say, 50 percent would result in a 50 percent use of bandwidth, while the PDC buffers only half as much data, or 64K. Also, synchronization frames will be generated and sent with half the frequency.

Caution
Setting this value too low may result in the databases never fully synchronizing. Microsoft recommends testing synchronization after changing the value to ensure that the account databases do in fact become synchronized within an acceptable time period.

On the PDC, you can modify the `Pulse` value so that the PDC checks its master accounts database less frequently. Recall that the default is five minutes; you can set it from one minute to 48 hours.

Caution
Similar to the `ReplicationGovernor` caution, setting this value too high could result in the BDC not being updated in a timely fashion, and possibly forcing a full synchronization (and therefore generating much more network traffic) to occur.

The `PulseConcurrency` governs the number of BDCs that the PDC contacts when it has changes. The default value is 10, which means that in a network with 15 BDCs, 10 will be contacted when the PDC has changes. When one of those completes its update, the eleventh BDC will be contacted; when another BDC completes, the twelfth will be contacted, and so on. If you need to be sure that all domain controllers are updated within a shorter period of time, consider increasing this value. In our example, increasing the value to 15 results in all the BDCs being contacted when the PDC has changes. On the other hand, more synchronization traffic is also generated concurrently, and you will need to evaluate this effect against the benefit of having all BDCs updated at the same time.

Another PDC parameter that you can modify is the `ChangeLogSize` parameter. By default, the PDC maintains a 64K change log of database modifications, about 2,000 changes of an average 32 bytes each. If the change log fills up before synchronization takes place—many users with a large number of changes, setting the `Pulse` value to high—older entries in the log may be overwritten and a full synchronization may occur to ensure that the BDCs have the most current information. Increase this value to increase the size of the change log and reduce the possibility of forcing a full synchronization.

Analyzing Trust Traffic

Another process that generates a certain amount of network traffic is the trust relationship. Chapter 15, "Windows NT 4.0 Trusts," provides a thorough discussion of trusts and how they are created and used. What follows is a look at the traffic they generate.

Trust relationships allow you to maintain accounts in a centralized domain and to focus resources in the domains in which you need to manage them. They allow you to grant user accounts from the trusted domain access to resources located in the trusting domain, usually through global and local group management. Three basic events are related to trust relationships that generate network traffic:

- Establishing the trust
- Using accounts across the trust
- Pass-through authentication

Traffic Generated when Establishing a Trust

A trust is established between two primary domain controllers (PDCs). The PDC that has the accounts to be used across the trust is called the *trusted domain* and must permit the resource domain to trust it. The domain that has the resources that the user accounts want to access is called the *trusting domain* and must complete the trust relationship. The traffic associated with these two steps occurs only once, when the trust is established and generates about 110 frames for a total of about 16K (see Figure 23.20).

FIG. 23.20 ⇒
This example displays the network traffic generated during the establishment of a trust relationship.

Network Monitor - [F:\WINNT40S\system32\Netmon\CAPTURES\sam1.cap (Summary)]

File Edit Display Tools Options Window Help

Frame	Time	Src MAC Addr	Dst MAC Addr	Protocol	Description
219	118.467	SAM1	INSTRUCTOR	NETLOGON	SAM LOGON request from client
220	118.468	SAM1	INSTRUCTOR	NETLOGON	SAM LOGON request from client
221	118.469	INSTRUCTOR	SAM1	MSRPC	c/o RPC Response: call 0x3 context 0x0 hint 0x18 cancels
222	118.470	SAM1	INSTRUCTOR	SMB	C close file, FID = 0x800
223	118.473	INSTRUCTOR	SAM1	NETLOGON	SAM Response to SAM LOGON request
224	118.475	INSTRUCTOR	SAM1	SMB	R close file
225	118.480	SAM1	INSTRUCTOR	SMB	C tree disconnect
226	118.483	INSTRUCTOR	SAM1	SMB	R tree disconnect
227	118.484	SAM1	INSTRUCTOR	SMB	C logoff & X
228	118.497	INSTRUCTOR	SAM1	SMB	R logoff & X
229	118.498	SAM1	INSTRUCTOR	TCP	.A...F, len: 0, seq: 2947523-2947523, ack: 16721959, win:
230	118.499	INSTRUCTOR	SAM1	TCP	.A...F, len: 0, seq: 16721959-16721959, ack: 2947524, wir
231	118.499	SAM1	INSTRUCTOR	TCP	.A...., len: 0, seq: 2947524-2947524, ack: 16721960, win:
236	121.385	INSTRUCTOR	*NETBIOS Mult	BROWSER	Local Master Announcement [0x0f] INSTRUCTOR
246	123.019	INSTRUCTOR	*BROADCAST	BROWSER	Local Master Announcement [0x0f] INSTRUCTOR
247	123.026	INSTRUCTOR	*BROADCAST	BROWSER	Local Master Announcement [0x0f] INSTRUCTOR
248	123.028	INSTRUCTOR	*BROADCAST	BROWSER	Local Master Announcement [0x0f] INSTRUCTOR
256	149.979	BDC-1	INSTRUCTOR	BROWSER	Host Announcement [0x01] BDC-1
261	152.894	BDC-1	INSTRUCTOR	SMB	C transact, Remote API
262	152.896	INSTRUCTOR	BDC-1	SMB	R transact, Remote API (response to frame 261)
263	152.900	BDC-1	INSTRUCTOR	SMB	C transact, Remote API
264	152.904	INSTRUCTOR	BDC-1	SMB	R transact, Remote API (response to frame 263)
266	166.097	SAM1	INSTRUCTOR	TCP	....S., len: 4, seq: 2995627-2995630, ack: 0, win:
267	166.098	INSTRUCTOR	SAM1	TCP	.A..S., len: 4, seq: 16770454-16770457, ack: 2995628, wir
268	166.098	SAM1	INSTRUCTOR	TCP	.A...., len: 0, seq: 2995628-2995628, ack: 16770455, win:
269	166.100	SAM1	INSTRUCTOR	MSRPC	c/o RPC Bind: UUID E1AF8308-5D1F-11C9-91A4-08002B14A0F
270	166.106	INSTRUCTOR	SAM1	MSRPC	c/o RPC Bind Ack: call 0x0 assoc grp 0x18D52 xmit 0x16D0
271	166.107	SAM1	INSTRUCTOR	MSRPC	c/o RPC Request: call 0x1 opnum 0x3 context 0x0 hint 0x
272	166.121	INSTRUCTOR	SAM1	MSRPC	c/o RPC Response: call 0x1 context 0x0 hint 0x80 cancels
273	166.122	SAM1	INSTRUCTOR	TCP	.A...F, len: 0, seq: 2995856-2995856, ack: 16770667, win:
274	166.123	INSTRUCTOR	SAM1	TCP	.A...., len: 0, seq: 16770667-16770667, ack: 2995857, wir
275	166.126	INSTRUCTOR	SAM1	TCP	.A...F, len: 0, seq: 16770667-16770667, ack: 2995857, wir
276	166.126	SAM1	INSTRUCTOR	TCP	.A...., len: 0, seq: 2995857-2995857, ack: 16770668, win:
277	166.130	SAM1	INSTRUCTOR	TCP	....S., len: 4, seq: 2995667-2995670, ack: 0, win:

F#: 40/371 Off: 153 (x99) L: 66 (x42)

When a PDC permits a resource domain to trust it, no trust traffic actually is generated as such. The process of permitting the resource domain is just a change to the SAM database on the PDC. So, the network traffic that is generated would be the normal traffic that occurs when the PDC announces a change to the accounts database and the BDCs update their copies. This traffic is already described in the section titled "Analyzing Traffic Between Domain Controllers."

The PDC of the resource domain completes the trust by adding the account domain as a trusted domain. The first traffic that is generated when the domain is added relates to the name and address resolution that needs to take place, the establishment of TCP and NetBIOS sessions with the PDC of the trusted domain, and the negotiation of SMB protocols. These frames are discussed earlier in sections titled "WINS Frames" and "File Session Frames."

The PDC of the trusting domain attempts to connect to the IPC$ administrative share on the trusted domain's PDC as a regular user from the trusting domain with an *SMB C Session setup & X, Username =* frame. This attempt will fail because this account cannot make normal file session connections, and it generates an *SMB R Session setup & X - NT error* frame. The point of this process is to verify that the account used to create the trust was created in the trusted domain.

The session is then terminated generating three frames totaling about 180 bytes. The PDC of the trusting domain then retrieves a list of the BDCs in the trusted domain generating about 15 frames (2,400 bytes) as described in the section titled "Logon Validation Frames." It then connects to one of the domain controllers in the trusted domain and retrieves the domain name of the trusted domain, which it will use for allowing logon validation and pass-through authentication through the trust. The trusting domain's PDC also will initiate the synchronization process with its own BDCs.

Lastly, the PDC of the trusting domain attempts to log in to a domain controller in the trusted domain using the special Interdomain Trust User Account. Three frames are generated:

- *NETLOGON SAM LOGON Request from Client* broadcast to the trusted domain controllers (see Figure 23.20, Frame 219)
- *NETLOGON SAM LOGON Request from Client* to a specific trusted domain controller or the trusted PDC (see Figure 23.20, Frame 220)
- *NETLOGON SAM Response to SAM LOGON Request* from the trusted domain controller to the trusting PDC (see Figure 23.20, Frame 223).

If the logon attempt is successful, the trust has been successfully established. Along with these frames include, of course, the appropriate traffic associated with establishing and ending the session—altogether about 17 frames totaling 2,300 bytes. Whenever the PDC is restarted, it must verify the trust again by logging in using the Interdomain Trust User Account and regenerating these last 17 or so frames.

Traffic Generated When Using Trusted Accounts

More trust traffic centers around the use of trusted accounts. Traffic is generated whenever a trusted account is added to a local group in the trusting domain or to an access control list (ACL) directly. Also, displaying the list of trusted accounts on a computer in the trusting domain generates network traffic. This traffic involves frames that you have already seen. For example, a connection needs to be made to the IPC$ administrative share on a trusted domain controller. This involves, as you have seen numerous times in this chapter, resolving names and addresses, establishing TCP and NetBIOS sessions if necessary, and disconnecting the sessions when you are finished.

Tip

As a benchmark, Microsoft notes that retrieving a list of 12 trusted accounts generated a total of about 53 frames and 9.5K. One frame contained the list of global groups in the trusted domain and another frame contained the list of users. These frames are generated for every list request made by a server in the trusting domain.

Traffic is also generated when you view the membership of local groups in the trusting domain that have trusted domain members. This should make sense because lists of users are actually enumerated by their SIDs. The SIDs for trusted users are kept in the trusted domain, so traffic will necessarily be generated by the trusting domain that has to look up the SIDs for the trusted users in the trusted domain. Again, only two frames are needed to actually look up the SID and return the account name, but up to 43 frames will be needed—you guessed it—to resolve names and addresses, establish sessions, and so on.

Traffic Generated When Using Pass-Through Authentication

When a user from a trusted domain accesses a resource in the trusting domain, its account information must be verified or validated. Because the account does not exist in the trusting domain, pass-through authentication is used to validate the user account in the trusted domain. Pass-through authentication is also used to validate a user when the user tries to log on to or access a resource in a domain other than the domain of which the user's computer is a member. This is kind of like peer-to-peer networking among domains. Again, please refer to Chapter 15, "Windows NT 4.0 Trusts," for a more complete discussion. In any event, pass-through authentication is probably among the more common types of user and trust processes to generate network traffic.

The process begins with the user's request to see a browse list of resources available among the trusting domain's servers. Frames are generated, as described in the section titled "Exploring Browser Traffic" earlier in this chapter. Of course, names and addresses may need to be resolved and sessions may need to be established.

The user selects a resource from the list and attempts to connect to it. The user may also have simply entered the UNC path to the resource in the Path box of a connect dialog or at the command prompt using a NET USE statement. However the user connects, it is at this point that pass-through authentication occurs. The domain controller in the trusting domain contacts a domain controller in the trusted domain establishing TCP and NetBIOS sessions, negotiating SMB protocols, and connecting to IPC$.

A named pipe connection is created between the domain controllers to implement a secure channel between them—a process similar to that that takes place when the user logs on. Two frames generate and complete the validation request, which is really a logon request, sort of like an "attach" command in Novell's NetWare. The frames are *R_LOGON RPC Client call logon:NetrLogonSamLogon* and *R_LOGON RPC Server Response logon:NetrLogonSamLogon*. Altogether, including all the ancillary frames needed to resolve names and addresses and establish sessions, a pass-through authentication request across a trust generates about 20 frames totaling anywhere from 3,200 to 4,200 bytes.

Optimizing Trust Traffic

There are really two considerations you must keep in mind when trying to optimize trust traffic. The first is quite obvious, though not always practical or even possible within some organizations: Minimize the number of trusts you must maintain. In other words, only create the trusts you need to have. Chapter 16, "Domain Models," outlines how trusts are used to build various models of enterprise computing. These models represent the basic building blocks of domain models. All the trusts described may not be necessary, however. Eliminate those you don't really need. If you have to reestablish a trust between two domains, remember that the amount of traffic that will be generated to establish the trust is relatively small (110 frames and about 16K) and takes place once.

The other consideration involves Microsoft's recommended strategy for dealing with user accounts across trusts. This strategy was thoroughly outlined in both Chapter 15, "Windows NT 4.0 Trusts," and Chapter 5, "Managing Users and Groups." In brief, Microsoft recommends that you maintain trusted users in global groups and that you use the global groups used as members of local groups on resource servers in the trusting domain. Doing so will reduce the traffic generated when you display local group membership lists and add accounts to local groups across the trust because you only will need to validate the SIDs of global groups, as opposed to the SIDs of each individual user.

Key Concept

If you compare the amount of data transferred from a global group lookup as opposed to that generated with one or two users, the difference is only a few bytes. When large numbers of users are involved, however, the difference can quickly add up to a significant reduction in network traffic.

Traffic Generated Through Directory Replication

The Directory Replication service, described in Chapter 17, "Windows NT Networking Services," provides an automatic means of duplicating a directory tree among multiple computers. The administrator identifies a Windows NT server to act as an export server; identifies other Windows NT servers, Windows NT workstations, or LanMan servers to be the import computers; and creates the directory tree structure including any files and subfolders that need to be replicated from the export to the import computers.

This service is most often used to copy logon scripts and system policy files to all the domain controllers in the domain, thus ensuring that no matter which domain controller validates the user, the appropriate logon script and policy file are implemented. Because these types of files generally do not change frequently, Directory Replication should not generate an inordinate amount of traffic. If Directory Replication is used to send other files as well or if the files tend to be large or change frequently, however, then a great deal more traffic may be generated by this service.

Every five minutes, by default, the export server generates a notification to all the import servers that it is an export server and either has or doesn't have changes to its export directory tree. If there are no changes, that is the extent of the process. If there are changes, then the Directory Replication process kicks in.

The export server notifies the import servers in its list that it has changes in its directory tree through an *SMB C Transact, File=\Mailslot\Net\Repl_cli* broadcast frame sent to the NetBIOS UDP Port 138. The size of this frame will vary with the size of the export directory tree. From this point on, the import computers generate most of the traffic.

In response, the import computers make an SMB connection to the REPL$ administrative share on the export server. Again, they resolve names and addresses and establish a session, as you have seen many times through out this chapter. About nine frames are generated, totaling about 1,300 bytes.

Next, the import computer needs to check its system time against that of the export server. If the two times are not within 10 minutes of each other, Directory Replication will fail to complete. The import computer generates an *R_SRVSVC RPC Client call srvsvc:NetrRemoteTOD* frame directed to the export server which responds back with an *R_SRVSVC RPC Server response srvsvc:NetrRemoteTOD* frame.

The import computer checks the export server's replication parameters to determine what it needs to replicate (for example, all files, changed files), whether it has to wait for a specific time, whether any directories are locked, and so on. To do so, it must establish a named pipe session and a file open to \Winreg on the export server. Altogether, 18 frames are generated, totaling about 3,500 bytes of data. The four frames specific to making the named pipe connection and checking the Registry are *SMB C NT create & X, File=\Winreg, SMB R NT create & X, FID=0x809, MSRPC c/o RPC Bind*, and *MSRPC c/o RPC Bind Ack*.

Through another 30 frames and 5,000 bytes, the import computer verifies the parameters and the export directory tree. If all the files must be copied, the import computer queries the export server to find all the files in the directory tree. If an update of a file or files is necessary, the updated file or files are copied from the export server to the import computer.

Tip

As a benchmark, Microsoft tells us that replicating 16 files totaling about 426K of data can generate 1,425 frames and take about 42 seconds to replicate.

Optimizing Directory Replication Traffic

When the Directory Replicator detects that a file in its top level directory has changed, it will copy the entire directory during the replication process. Consequently, large, deep directory structures can generate a lot of replication traffic because, among large numbers of files, it is more likely that at least one file will change.

Key Concept

Microsoft therefore recommends that you keep the export directory tree flat and very shallow. Fewer files in a directory reduces the possibility that any one file may have a change; and if a file does change, a smaller directory is replicated, generating less network traffic overall.

You configure Directory Replication parameters through each computer's properties as accessed through Server Manager. Two options are frequently overlooked that can help to control what and how much is replicated. One option is the Add Lock option. The administrator can choose to lock one or more directories, effectively removing it from consideration for being replicated. This can be an effective way to keep large directories from replicating during busy times of the day, for example.

Also, each directory has a Wait Until Stabilized Option that is enabled by default. With this option enabled, the import computer will wait for activity in the directory to cease for a period of two minutes (by default) or more before replicating all the files in the directory. Disabling this option will cause the import computer to check the time, date, attributes, name, and size of each file individually and just copy the changed files.

Implement these two options through these steps.

1. Start Server Manager.
2. Open the computer properties of the export server.
3. Click the Replication button, then choose the Manage button under Export Directories.
4. Select the appropriate directory.
5. Choose Add Lock to keep the directory from being replicated. Deselect Wait Until Stabilized to disable the option.
6. Choose OK.

Another obvious change involves the Registry. Recall that, by default, the export server checks its directory structure and announces itself every 5 minutes. This length of time is known as the *interval* value, and you can set it from one to 60 minutes or more on the export server. The import computer maintains a *pulse* value of 2 minutes (default)—not to be confused with the pulse value that you can modify on a PDC for account database synchronization. This pulse value controls how often the import computer contacts the export server directly according to the formula *pulse* * *interval*. This means that, by default, if the import computer does not hear from the export server after 10 minutes (pulse 2 * interval 5), it will initiate a connection with the export server to see whether it needs to copy anything. By increasing the pulse value, you increase the period of time within which the export server can contact the import computer to notify it of a change.

Summarizing and Planning Network Traffic

Throughout this chapter, you have looked at various common events, processes, and services that generate network traffic. You have analyzed their effect on the network and offered suggestions for their optimization. As you can probably guess, predicting network traffic is hardly an exact science. By now, however, you have a better idea of what kinds of traffic to expect and what to look for. The following is a check list of things to look for when trying to analyze or project traffic patterns, bottlenecks, and growth.

- Begin by determining the traffic generated by the event or service when it is started; focus on the computers involved, the frequency of the frames generated, and the average size of the frames.
- Identify any variables relating to the event or service. For example, the number of BDCs in the domain will effect how much synchronization traffic is generated.
- Identify how many client and server computers will participate in the traffic generated. Determine the amount of traffic generated between one set of computers, determine the frequency of the traffic generated, then extrapolate that number to the total number of computers involved.
- Determine whether you can optimize the service or event.
- Weigh the benefits provided by the service or event against the traffic that is generated.

Table 23.3 summarizes the services discussed in this chapter by the traffic each generates and its frequency. The values stated are approximate and will vary depending on your network implementation.

Table 23.3 Traffic Summary by Service

Service	Frequency of	Traffic Generated
DHCP service		
Obtain IP Address	Once when client boots	4 frames, 1368 bytes
Renew IP address lease	At startup and at 1/2 lease interval	2 frames, 684 bytes

Service	Frequency of	Traffic Generated
WINS service		
Registration	Once for every computer, service, and application	2 frames, 214 bytes
Renewal	At 1/2 the TTL value	2 frames, 214 bytes
Name resolution	When a connection needs to be established and the resolved name is not in cache	2 frames, 196 bytes
Address resolution	When connecting to another TCP/IP host and address is not in ARP cache	2 frames, 120 bytes
TCP session	Once per TCP host connection	3 frames, 180 bytes
NetBIOS session	Once per NetBIO host connection	2 frames, 186 bytes
SMB protocol negotiation	Once per SMB connection to target host	2 frames, 350 bytes
Connection sequence	Once per resource access	2 frames, 350 bytes
Session disconnect	Once at final disconnection from TCP host	5 frames, 360 bytes
Session Establishment	Whenever a user logs on	15 frames, 2000 byte
NT-based validation	Whenever a user logs on	20 frames, 3700 byte
Session breakdown	Whenever a user logs on	5 frames, 360 bytes
Implementing logon scripts, profiles, and policies	Whenever a user logs on	traffic varies

continues

Table 23.3 Continued

Service	Frequency of	Traffic Generated
Computer browser service		
Host announcement	From every computer with resources, once every announcement period (12 minutes, by default)	1 frame, 243 bytes
Master browser announcement	Whenever requested by a computer or backup browser and after every election	1 frame, 250 bytes
Workgroup announcement	From each master browser, once every announcement period (15 minutes, by default)	1 frame, 250 bytes
Master Browser Election	Whenever a computer or backup browser determines that the master browser is unavailable or when a computer that can become a master browser starts up	frames depend on the number of computers taking part in the election; each frame 225 bytes
Requesting a backup browser	When browsing is first initiated at a computer	2 frames, 450 bytes
Retrieving a browse list	Whenever the client browses for resources or whenever the backup browser updates its list from the master browser (every 12 minutes, by default)	20 frames, 2150 byte
Retrieving a list of shared resources from Windows NT servers	Whenever the client accesses a server in the browser list	19 frames, 3300 byte
Account database synchronization		
Request for PDC	Whenever the BDC starts up	4 frames, 745 bytes

Service	Frequency of	Traffic Generated
Account database synchronization		
Establish a session between PDC and BDC	Every time synchronization takes place	11 frames, 1280 byte
Establish a secure channel between PDC and BDC	Whenever the BDC starts up	
Verify the databases	Whenever the BDC starts up	6 frames, 1,350 byte
Update the PDC	Every time synchronization takes place	1 frame, 400 bytes
Synchronize the databases	Every time synchronization takes place; value based per user change	2 frames, 1,400 byte
Establishing a trust relationship	When the trust relationship is first created	110 frames, 16,000 bytes
Using accounts across a trust	Every time an account is selected at a computer in a trusting domain	12 frames, 1,550 bytes per trusted account
Verifying trusted accounts	Every time you view an ACL or local group membership that contains a trusted account; value based per trusted account	45 frames, 7,000 bytes
Pass-through authentication	Whenever user logs on to a domain across the trust or accesses a resource on a computer in the trusting domain	20 frames, 3,700 bytes
Directory replication		
Export server announcement	Whenever the directory tree is updated on a given interval (5 minutes, by default)	1 frame, 340 bytes

continues

Table 23.3 Continued

Service	Frequency of	Traffic Generated
Directory replication		
Establish session from import to export computer	Whenever the import computer needs to copy an updated directory tree from the export server	9 frames, 1,300 bytes
Verify the directory	Whenever the import computer needs to copy an updated directory tree from the export server	30 frames, 5,100 bytes
Update the import computer directory tree	Whenever the import computer needs to copy an updated directory tree from the export server; traffic depends on amount of data to be updated	30 frames, 5,100 bytes

Taking the Disc Test

If you have read and understood the material in the chapter, you are ready to test your knowledge. Insert the CD-ROM that comes with this book and run the self-test software as described in Appendix K, "Using the Self-Test Software."

From Here...

In this chapter, you took a rather detailed look at some common network traffic generated between Windows NT computers. You saw how the Network Monitor utility can help you identify traffic patterns and provide some insight into how the network is being used. This utility, together with Performance Monitor, are the two best tools in Windows NT 4.0 to analyze and troubleshoot network systems. The next chapter, "Advanced Troubleshooting," rounds out this section's discussion of monitoring and optimization techniques. It will discuss such topics as how to interpret the dreaded blue screen and how to use the kernel debugger tool.

Chapter Prerequisite

The reader should have a good knowledge of PC hardware, Windows NT installation and configuration, Windows NT architecture, and the boot process.

24

Advanced Troubleshooting

This chapter introduces you to Kernel Stop Errors, also referred to as blue screen errors (of death) or trap errors, and describes and identifies the data areas of a stop error that are pertinent to finding the cause of the problem. The precise time that a stop error occurs is also relevant to isolating the cause of the malfunction, such as during installation, after installation, or during the Windows NT initialization or boot process, and is discussed in this chapter. Software problems that cause stop errors are also discussed in this chapter.

Another topic of interest discussed in this chapter is crash dumps. You will learn how to configure the Windows NT Recovery options and how to configure the required memory resources. Tools to check, analyze, and copy a crash dump, such as Dumpchk, Dumpexam, and Dumpflop, are also presented.

Next, the Kernel debugger programs and options are discussed along with how to configure Windows NT systems to do live debugging procedures both at local sites and from remote sites. Discussions include setting up and connecting the host and target computers, locating the kernel debugger programs, and locating, expanding, and using the symbols files.

The last topic of discussion in this chapter is Event Viewer. The three types of event logs, event details, log settings, and other pertinent event viewer information is presented.

Topics in this chapter include the following:

- Windows NT kernel messages
- Stop errors
- Crash dumps
- Kernel debugger
- Remote troubleshooting
- Event Viewer

Windows NT Kernel Messages

There are three types of Windows NT kernel messages: hardware malfunction messages, status messages, and stop messages. Stop messages, also referred to as blue screens or traps, will be discussed in detail in this chapter.

Hardware Malfunction Messages

Hardware malfunction messages are caused by a hardware condition that the processor detects. The Windows NT Executive will display a message such as `Hardware malfunction: Call your hardware vender for support`; the actual message depends on the manufacturer. Other information is also displayed to indicate the nature of the problem, such as a memory parity error, a bus-data error, or a specific adapter error (with slot number), which again depends on the type of error and the hardware manufacturer.

Status Messages

Status messages, in most cases, are not as critical. This type of message is displayed when the Windows NT Executive detects a condition within a process or application in which the action required is simply clicking OK to terminate the process or application. Messages indicating the action are displayed in a window or dialog box on the screen.

There are three types of status messages: system-information, warning, and application-termination messages. System-information messages could include indications of an invalid current directory, a suspended thread, or a working set range error. Warning messages indicate information such as buffer overflow, a busy device, or an out-of-paper message. Application-termination messages range from access denied to a corrupt disk to a data error. Missing system files and out-of-virtual-memory messages are other examples.

Stop (Blue Screen/Trap) Messages

Stop messages, on the other hand, are probably the most severe. They always require you to restart the computer because the Windows NT Executive cannot recover from the error. Also provided is a mechanism for dumping memory information into a memory dump file if you configure the mechanism before the error occurs.

Stop errors can happen virtually at any time: during and after installation, during and after initialization (booting), or from a specific software condition.

Stop Messages During Installation

Stop errors that occur during installation are usually a result of incompatible hardware. Refer to the latest version of an HCL to determine whether all hardware on the computer is listed. You can find the latest HCL by doing a search on HCL from Microsoft Corporation's home Web page, **www.microsoft.com**.

Tip

If specific hardware is not on the HCL, contact the manufacturer for information on new hardware or updated BIOS and firmware revisions.

Another approach to determining the specific piece of hardware causing the problem is to configure the system to minimize requirements and try the installation again.

Stop Messages After Installation

It is very apparent that various hardware problems can happen after Windows NT is installed and operational. Also, any drivers, such as device drivers or file system drivers, can cause the Windows NT Executive to generate a stop error. You can fix problems of this nature by replacing hardware or reinstalling Windows NT components.

Tip

In some cases, Microsoft NT Service Packs can solve various types of stop error problems. To obtain service packs, access Microsoft Corporation's home Web page at **www.microsoft.com**.

Stop Messages Only During Windows NT Executive Initialization

A small group of stop errors can happen only during Phase 4 of the boot process, part of which is when the Windows NT Executive initializes. There are two parts to the initialization of the Windows NT Executive, phase 0 and phase 1. During phase 0, interrupts are disabled and only a few Executive components are initialized. One component initialized during phase 0 is the Hardware Abstraction Layer (HAL). During phase 1, the Executive is fully operational and the Windows NT subcomponents are initialized.

Key Concept

If you experience a phase 0 initialization stop message, run all the hardware diagnostic routines to try to solve the problem. If you find no hardware errors, reinstall Windows NT 4.0 and reinitialize to see whether the problem persists.

If you obtain a phase 1 initialization stop message, reinstall Windows NT and reinitialize the system.

Tables 24.1 and 24.2 display the Windows NT Executive phase 0 and phase 1 Initialization stop messages, respectively.

Table 24.1 Windows NT Executive Phase 0 Initialization Stop Error Messages

Error Code	Error Code Meaning
0x0031	PHASE0_INITIALIZATION_FAILED
0x005C	HAL_INITIALIZATION_FAILED
0x005D	HEAP_INITIALIZATION_FAILED
0x005E	OBJECT_INITIALIZATION_FAILED
0x005F	SECURITY_INITIALIZATION_FAILED
0x0060	PROCESS_INITIALIZATION_FAILED

Table 24.2 Windows NT Executive Phase 1 Initialization Stop Error Messages

Error Code	Error Code Meaning
0x0032	PHASE1_INITIALIZATION_FAILED
0x0061	HAL1_INITIALIZATION_FAILED
0x0062	OBJECT1_INITIALIZATION_FAILED
0x0063	SECURITY1_INITIALIZATION_FAILED
0x0064	SYMBOLIC_INITIALIZATION_FAILED
0x0065	MEMORY1_INITIALIZATION_FAILED
0x0066	CACHE_INITIALIZATION_FAILED
0x0067	CONFIG_INITIALIZATION_FAILED
0x0068	FILE_INITIALIZATION_FAILED
0x0069	IO1_INITIALIZATION_FAILED
0x006A	LPC_INITIALIZATION_FAILED
0x006B	PROCESS1_INITIALIZATION_FAILED
0x006C	REFMON_INITIALIZATION_FAILED
0x006D	SESSION1_INITIALIZATION_FAILED
0x006E	SESSION2_INITIALIZATION_FAILED
0x006F	SESSION3_INITIALIZATION_FAILED
0x0070	SESSION4_INITIALIZATION_FAILED
0x0071	SESSION5_INITIALIZATION_FAILED

Stop Messages Caused by Software Problems

Software conditions that the processor detects in a system can also produce stop error messages. This event, also called a *software trap*, is caused by the processor executing an instruction in a process or application when it encounters an error, such as a divide by zero or a memory segment not present. All 12 software traps produce the same stop error message format, as follows:

```
*** STOP: 0X0000007F (0x0000000n, 0x00000000, 0x00000000,
0x00000000) UNEXPECTED_KERNEL_MODE_TRAP
```

In the first parameter `0x0000000n`, *n* indicates which of the 12 stop messages has been encountered. These messages are displayed in Table 24.3.

Table 24.3 Windows NT Executive Software Trap Stop Error Messages

Parameter	Stop Message Meaning
`0x00000000`	An attempt to divide by zero
`0x00000001`	A system-debugger call
`0x00000003`	A debugger breakpoint
`0x00000004`	An arithmetic operation overflow
`0x00000005`	An array index that exceeds the array bounds
`0x00000006`	Invalid operands in an instruction or an attempt to execute a protected-mode instruction while running in real mode
`0x00000007`	A hardware coprocessor instruction with no coprocessor present
`0x00000008`	An error while processing an error (also known as a double fault)
`0x0000000A`	A corrupted Task State Segment
`0x0000000B`	An access to a memory segment that was not present
`0x0000000C`	An access to memory beyond the limits of a stack
`0x0000000D`	An exception not covered by some other exception; a protection fault that pertains to access violations for applications

Normal User Stop Messages Procedures

You cannot expect normal users to diagnose the causes of stop errors. When stop errors occur, you should instruct these users to record the first few lines of the message and then restart the system. If the stop error happens again, you can invoke a Last Known Good configuration; as the system administrator, however, you should ensure that the Recovery option is properly configured in the system to obtain memory dump information. You can then analyze the dumps to determine the cause of the error message.

General Stop Message Troubleshooting Procedures

Microsoft recommends that you follow the following procedure when you encounter stop errors:

1. Gather information about the problem.
2. Determine whether the problem is a known issue.
3. Determine whether the problem is caused by hardware.
4. Troubleshoot well-known stop codes.
5. Determine whether the problem is caused by non-HCL hardware.
6. Contact Microsoft Service Advantage.

Step 1: Gather Information About the Problem

Record, at a minimum, the following information when experiencing stop errors:

- The top four lines of a stop error, which include the stop error codes and other pertinent information. An example of the information to record follows:

```
STOP:
0X0000000A(0x0000000B,0x00000002,0x00000000,0xFE34C882)
IRQL_NOT_LESS_OR_EQUAL
ADDRESS 0xFE34C882 has base at 0xFE000000:
NTOSKRNL.EXE
```

- All hardware information, including system statistics, such as BIOS, CMOS settings, and controllers/adapters installed and their BIOS version.
- The platform and version of Windows NT installed, including any service packs, hotfixes, or third-party drivers, such as a Novell redirector.
- How often and when the stop error is occurring (whether it is random or when a specific operation is performed, such as a certain application or process).

Step 2: Determine Whether the Problem Is a Known Issue

The next step is to see whether someone has been there before. Try to determine whether this error has been a common occurrence and whether there is an already established workaround or hotfix.

Search Microsoft's Knowledge Base (from Microsoft's home Web page, choose support then technical support) by searching for the word stop, followed by the stop error code, followed by the program module name. An example follows:

```
STOP 0x0000000A NTOSKRNL.EXE
```

If you receive no results, search for just the word stop and try to locate any general stop error troubleshooting methods.

Step 3: Determine Whether the Problem Is Caused by Hardware

Stop errors are caused by hardware errors and outdated BIOS even if the hardware is on the HCL. Hardware configurations may also cause stop errors. The following examples indicate various situations.

- A system is working properly, but when the user performs a specific operation, such as booting the system, formatting a disk, or performing a backup operation, stop errors occur. Check the specific hardware involved for that operation. A software problem usually occurs only when a certain set of conditions are present. Try to isolate exactly what conditions are present when the failure happens.
- A system is working fine until the user installs a new piece of hardware, then stop errors begin to occur. Check the HCL for the new piece of hardware. Check for IRQs, IO addresses, and Direct Memory Access (DMA) conflicts. Check BIOS versions, driver versions, and configuration settings.

Step 4: Troubleshoot Well-Known Stop Codes

Some common stop errors are listed here for your information. Most of the illustrated stop error descriptions indicate the specific reason or cause of the problem.

- `STOP 0x0000000A IRQL_NOT_LESS_OR_EQUAL`
- `STOP 0x00000019 BAD_POOL_HEADER`
- `STOP 0x0000001E KMODE_EXCEPTION_NOT_HANDLED`
- `STOP 0x00000024 NTFS_FILE_SYSTEM`
- `STOP 0x0000002E DATA_BUS_ERROR`
- `STOP 0x0000003E MULTIPROCESSOR_CONFIGURATION_NOT_SUPPORTED`
- `STOP 0x00000051 REGISTRY_ERROR`
- `STOP 0x00000058 FTDISK_INTERNAL_ERROR`
- `STOP 0x00000077 KERNEL_STACK_OVERFLOW`
- `STOP 0x00000079 MISMATCHED_HAL`
- `STOP 0x0000007A KERNEL_DATA_INPAGE_ERROR`
- `STOP 0x0000007B INACCESSIBLE_BOOT_DEVICE`
- `STOP 0x0000007F USEXPECTED_KERNEL_MODE_TRAP`

- STOP 0x00000080 NMI_HARDWARE_FAILURE
- STOP 0x0000008B MBR_CHECKSUM_MISMATCH
- STOP 0x00000218 STATUS_CANNOT_LOAD_REGISTRY_FILE
- STOP 0x0000021A STATUS_SYSTEM_PROCESS_TERMINATED
- STOP 0x00000221 STATUS_IMAGE_CHECKSUM_MISMATCH

Step 5: Determine Whether the Problem Is Caused by Non-HCL Hardware

Microsoft, as a rule, does not totally support stop errors from hardware such as motherboards, disk drive controllers, network or video adapter cards, or multimedia devices that are not on the HCL. Because hardware that is not on the HCL has not been tested with Windows NT 4.0, diagnostic information is not available.

The first thing to do is to contact the manufacturer of the device for any information regarding Windows NT 4.0, such as device drivers.

Two articles in the Microsoft Knowledge Base on the Internet provide information concerning Microsoft's policy for supporting hardware that is not on the HCL. The two articles are Q142865 and Q143244.

The first article, Q142865 Microsoft PSS Support Policy on Hardware Not on Windows NT HCL, discusses details on troubleshooting problems with non-HCL hardware.

The second article, Q143244 How to Check If Unsupported Hardware Allows Windows NT Install, provides troubleshooting tips on hardware that will allow Windows NT 4.0 to be installed.

Step 6: Contact Microsoft Service Advantage

If you have not found a solution to the stop error by performing the previous Steps 1 through 5, contact Microsoft Service Advantage for support. You can find the Microsoft Service Advantage home page on the Internet at **http://www.microsoft.com/servad/**.

Stop Error Screen Layout and Section Meanings

Probably one of the most intimidating errors that Windows NT can produce is a stop error. The entire screen turns blue and a mass of numbers and letters appear, which usually causes panic and disillusion to the user. Enterprising administrators and support personnel, on the other hand, accept a stop error as a challenge and proceed to interpret the information presented to locate the cause of the error.

The first objective in diagnosing stop errors is to define the areas or sections of a stop error screen. Use Figure 24.1 and the following paragraphs to locate and define the five distinct sections:

- Debug port status indicators
- BugCheck information
- Driver information
- Kernel build number and stack dump
- Debug port information

FIG. 24.1⇒
An illustration of a Windows NT 4.0 Stop Error Screen (Blue Screen).

```
                                                                     DSR CTS SND
*** STOP,  0x0000000A  (0x00000060, 0x0000001C, 0x00000000, 0x80114738)
IRQL_NOT_LESS_OR_EQUAL

p4-0300 irql:1f   SERVER:0xf000030e

Dll Base DateStmp - Name               Dll Base DateStmp - Name
80100000 2e53fe55 - ntoskrl.exe        80400000 2e53eba6 - hal.dll
80010000 2e418846 - aha154x.sys        80013000 2e4bc29a - SCSIPORT.SYS
8001b000 2e4e7b6b - Scsidisk.sys       80220000 2e53f238 - Ntfs.sys
fe420000 2e406607 - Floppy.SYS         fe430000 2e406618 - Scsicdrm.SYS
fe440000 2e406659 - Fs_Rec.SYS         fe450000 2e40660f - Null.SYS
fe460000 2e4065f4 - Beep.SYS           fe470000 2e406634 - Sermouse.SYS
fe480000 2e42a4a4 - I8042prt.SYS       fe490000 2e40660d - Mouclass.SYS
fe4a0000 2e40660c - Kbdclass.SYS       fe4c0000 2e4065e2 - VIDEOPORT.SYS
fe4b0000 2e53d49d - ati.SYS            fe4d0000 2e4065e8 - vga.sys
fe4e0000 2e406655 - Msfs.SYS           fe4f0000 2e414f30 - Npfs.SYS
fe510000 2e53f222 - NDIS.SYS           fe500000 2e40719b - elnkii.sys
fe550000 2e406697 - TDI.SYS            fe530000 2e47c740 - nbf.sys
fe560000 2e5279d9 - nwlnkipx.sys       fe570000 2e53a89e - nwlnknb.sys
fe580000 2e494973 - tcpip.sys          fe5a0000 2e5257b8 - afd.sys
fe5b0000 2e5279d3 - netbt.sys          fe5d0000 2e4167f7 - netbios.sys
fe5e0000 2e4066b3 - mup.sys            fe5f0000 2e4f9f51 - rdr.sys
fe630000 2e53f24a - srv.sys            fe660000 2ef16062 - nwlnkspx.sys

Address   dword dump Build [1381]                                     Name
FF541E4c  fe5105df fe5105df 00000001 ff640128 fe4a8228  000002fe - NDIS.SYS
ff541E60  fe501368 fe501368 00000246 00004002 00000000  00000000 - elnkii.sys
ff541eb4  fe481509 fe481509 ff6688c8 ff668288 00000000  ff668138 - i8042prt.sys
ff541ee0  fe481ea8 fe481ea8 fe482078 00000000 ff541f04  8013c58a - i8042prt.sys
ff541ee4  fe482078 fe482078 00000000 ff541f04 8013c58a  ff6688c8 - i8042prt.sys
ff541ef0  8013c58a 8013c58a ff6688c8 ff668040 80405900  00000031 - ntoskrl.exe
ff541efc  80405900 80405900 00000031 06060606 06060606  06060606 - hal.dll

Restart and set the recovery options in the system control panel
or the /CRASHDEBUG system start option if this message reappears,
contact your system administrator or technical support group.
CRASHDUMP: Initializing miniport driver
```

Debug Port Status Indicators

If a modem or null modem cable is connected to the computer and the Kernel Debugger program is running, indicators will appear in the upper-right corner of the stop screen on the top line. These indicators will show the serial communication port status of the communication between a host and target computer. The following is a list of the various port status indicators that can appear in this section:

- MDM Debugger is using modem controls
- CD Carrier detected
- RI Ring indicator
- DSR Data set ready
- CTS Clear to send
- SND Byte of information being sent
- RCV Byte of information being received
- FRM Framing error
- OVL Overflow
- PRT Parity error

BugCheck Information

The next four lines (beginning with the line that starts with `*** STOP`) contain the error code (or BugCheck code) and other pertinent error code information. This information is critical to finding the cause of the error and, as mentioned previously in the section "General Stop Error Troubleshooting Procedures," should be recorded. In the example shown in Figure 24.1, the first line is as follows:

```
*** STOP: 0x0000000A (0x0000006c, 0x0000001c, 0x00000000,
0x80114738) IRQL_NOT_LESS_OR_EQUAL
```

- The `0x0000000A` indicates the stop error.
- The parameter `0x0000006c` identifies the address that was not referenced correctly.
- The parameter `0x0000001c` identifies the Interrupt Request Level (IRQL) that was required to access memory.
- The parameter `0x00000000` indicates that a Read operation was in progress. (A value of 1 would indicate a Write operation.)
- The parameter `0x80114738` indicates the instruction address that tried to access memory referenced in the first parameter.

Driver Information

The next section begins with the line `Dll Base` and continues for a number of lines, depending on the error. The example in Figure 24.1 displays an area of 17 lines and lists 34 drivers. Three columns of information are displayed on the left half of the screen, and three more columns are displayed on the right half of the screen. The first column in each half displays the base address of the driver in memory with the second column displaying the time stamp information. The third column in each half will display the names of all drivers loaded in the system at the time of the error.

Kernel Build Number and Stack Dump

Section 4 contains the version and build level of the Windows NT 4.0 Kernel, `Ntoskrnl.exe`. Any service pack or third-party driver information is *not* displayed in this section. This section can be extremely useful because it may indicate, depending on the stop error, the driver that failed and caused the stop error.

Debug Port Information

If Kernel Debugger is running, additional COM port information, such as what port and the speed of the port, is displayed here. Other data in this area will confirm whether a memory dump has been created or give instructions on how to further troubleshoot the problem.

Crash Dumps (Memory Dumps)

Once you analyze the stop error and cannot determine the solution to the error, you must obtain more data and information about the problem. One way to retrieve more information concerning a particular stop error is to have the computer dump the entire contents of memory at the time of the error. From this point, either an administrator or a support team can analyze the memory dump to determine the solution for the error.

The first step in initiating a memory dump if you encounter a stop error is to ensure that the Recovery option is configured correctly. You can configure this option to invoke a number of different procedures, but you should configure it to take memory dumps if the error persists.

You configure the Recovery option from the System Properties sheet on the Startup/Shutdown tab. The Recovery configuration options are shown in Figure 24.2.

The following is a list of the options available in the Setup/Shutdown tab of the System Properties dialog box:

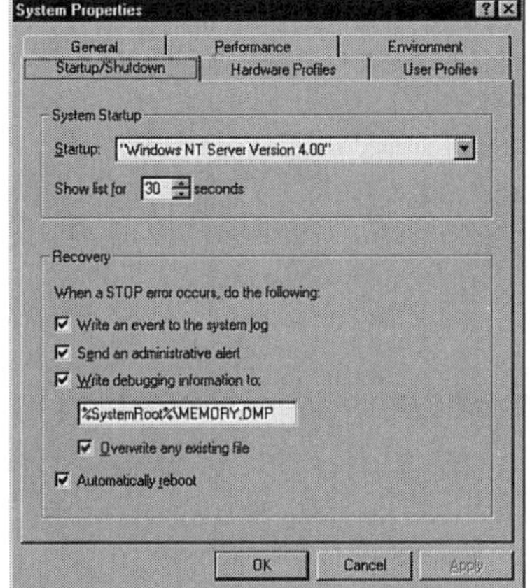

FIG. 24.2⇒
The Windows NT 4.0 Recovery option configuration location.

- Write an Event to the System Log

  If you select this option, an event will be written to the system log when a stop error occurs.

- Send an Administrative Alert

  If you select this option and have configured alerts in Server Manager or from the Server icon in the Control Panel, an administrative alert is sent to a designated computer on the network if a stop error occurs.

- Write Debugging Information To:

  This option, when selected, enables the entire contents of system memory to be written to a file specified in the space provided. This file will be written to `%SystemRoot%\MEMORY.DMP` by default. You can then use a Dumpexam utility to analyze the memory dump to isolate the cause of the error.

  In addition to selecting this option, you must meet four other requirements, which are listed here, to provide for a memory dump.

  - A pagefile must exist on the same partition where Windows NT 4.0 has been installed (the boot partition).
  - The pagefile must be at least 1M larger than the physical size of RAM in the system.
  - The boot partition must have at least as much free space as the size of the pagefile.
  - Automatically Reboot should be selected.

> **Caution**
> You *must* meet the preceding first three requirements to obtain a memory dump of the system. The memory dump process will put the entire contents of RAM memory in the pagefile on the boot partition. Before the reboot process, the pagefile information will be written to the specified `.DMP` file.

- Overwrite any Existing File

  If you select this option and a `MEMORY.DMP` file exists in the `%SystemRoot%` folder, that file will be overwritten.

- Automatically Reboot

  Select this option to invoke a reboot operation following a stop error. If you also have selected the memory dump option, that operation will take place before the reboot.

Crash Dump Analysis Utilities

The Windows NT 4.0 Server and Workstation CD-ROMs include three utilities that you can use to analyze the results of a memory dump. A copy of each of these utilities is located in a platform-specific folder (Alpha, I386, Mips, and PPC) under the Support\Debug folder. These utilities are:

- `Dumpchk.exe`
- `Dumpexam.exe`
- `Dumpflop.exe`

Dumpchk.exe

This utility is used to verify the validity of a memory dump and to assure it can be read by a debugger application. It verifies all the virtual and physical memory addresses and displays basic information about the memory dump. It will also display any errors found in the memory dump. The command-line syntax is shown in Figure 24.3.

You can use resultant information from this utility to determine which stop error occurred and which version of Windows NT was being used when the error occurred. An example of Dumpchk results using the `-v` and `-q` options is shown in Listing 24.1.

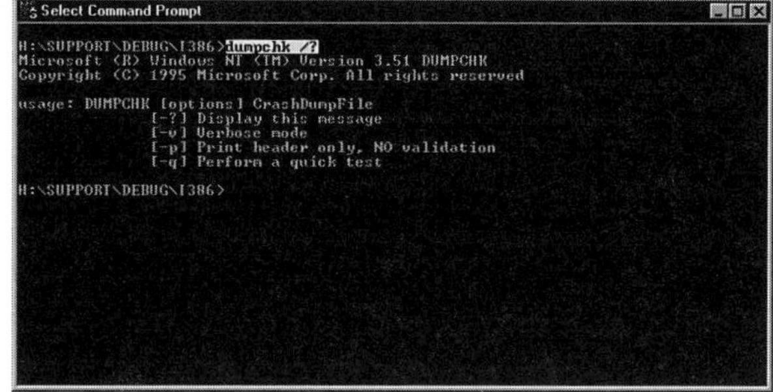

FIG. 24.3⇒ An example of the `Dumpchk.exe` utility command-line syntax.

Ch 24

Listing 24.1 An Example of *Dumpchk* Results

```
D:\>dumpchk -v -q memory.dmp
Filename . . . . . . .memory.dmp
Signature. . . . . . .PAGE
ValidDump. . . . . . .DUMP
MajorVersion . . . . .free system
MinorVersion . . . . .1381
DirectoryTableBase . .0x00030000
PfnDataBase. . . . . .0x81fcf000
PsLoadedModuleList . .0x8014dd90
PsActiveProcessHead. .0x8014dc88
MachineImageType . . .I386
NumberProcessors . . .1
BugCheckCode . . . . .0x0000000a
BugCheckParameter1 . .0xfed7a026
BugCheckParameter2 . .0x00000002
BugCheckParameter3 . .0x00000000
BugCheckParameter4 . .0xfed7a026
ExceptionCode. . . . .0x80000003
ExceptionFlags . . . .0x00000001
ExceptionAddress . . .0x8013f46c
NumberOfRuns . . . . .0x3
NumberOfPages. . . . .0x1f9d
Run #1
 BasePage . . . . . .0x1
 PageCount. . . . . .0x9e
Run #2
 BasePage . . . . . .0x100
 PageCount. . . . . .0xeff
Run #3
 BasePage . . . . . .0x1000
 PageCount. . . . . .0x1000

**************
**************—> Validating the integrity of the PsLoa
**************
```

continues

Listing 24.1 Continued

```
validating ntoskrnl.exe 0x80100000 0x000d4cc0
validating hal.dll 0x80010000 0x0000c920
validating atapi.sys 0x80001000 0x00006000
validating SCSIPORT.SYS 0x80007000 0x00007e80
validating Disk.sys 0x801d5000 0x00003a60
validating CLASS2.SYS 0x801d9000 0x000032e0
validating Ftdisk.sys 0x801dd000 0x00007b60
validating Ntfs.sys 0x801e5000 0x00058000
validating Floppy.SYS 0xfc6f8000 0x00005000
validating Null.SYS 0xfc9c9000 0x00001000
validating KSecDD.SYS 0xfc874000 0x00003000
validating Beep.SYS 0xfc9ca000 0x00001000
validating i8042prt.sys 0xfc738000 0x00007000
validating mouclass.sys 0xfc87c000 0x00003000
validating kbdclass.sys 0xfc884000 0x00003000
validating VIDEOPRT.SYS 0xfc750000 0x00006000
validating cirrus.SYS 0xfc420000 0x0000c000
validating Msfs.SYS 0xfc780000 0x00006000
validating Npfs.SYS 0xfc430000 0x0000a000
validating NDIS.SYS 0xff09c000 0x0001f000
validating win32k.sys 0xa0000000 0x00133000
validating cirrus.dll 0xfc580000 0x0000d000
validating Fastfat.SYS 0xfef29000 0x00023000
validating TDI.SYS 0xff084000 0x00003000
validating sfmatalk.sys 0xfeee2000 0x0001f000
validating nbf.sys 0xfeec9000 0x00019000
validating tcpip.sys 0xfeea6000 0x00023000
validating netbt.sys 0xfee89000 0x0001d000
validating amdpcn.sys 0xfc770000 0x00008000
validating afd.sys 0xfc640000 0x00010000
validating netbios.sys 0xfc7b0000 0x00008000
validating Parport.SYS 0xfef54000 0x00003000
validating Parallel.SYS 0xfef4c000 0x00004000
validating ParVdm.SYS 0xfc924000 0x00002000
validating Serial.SYS 0xfc410000 0x0000b000
validating srv.sys 0xfee28000 0x00039000
validating rdr.sys 0xfede9000 0x0003f000
validating mup.sys 0xfedb0000 0x00011000
validating sfmsrv.sys 0xfed67000 0x00021000
**************
**************—> Performing a quick check (^C to end)
**************
**************
**************—> Validating all physical addresses
**************
**************
**************—> Validating all virtual addresses
**************
**************
**************—> This dump file is good!
**************
```

Run this utility before you analyze and send a memory dump to Microsoft Support.

Dumpexam.exe

The Dumpexam utility is used to analyze a memory dump, extract specific information from the memory dump file, and create a text file containing specific memory dump information. This text file is considerably smaller than the raw memory dump file, `MEMORY.DMP` (recall that a raw memory dump file can be at least the size of physical memory). The default file that Dumpexam creates will be named `Memory.txt` and located in the `%SystemRoot%` folder. The `Memory.txt` file can provide, in some cases, a solution to the problem.

Two other files besides `Dumpexam.exe` are required to analyze a memory dump. One file is `Imagehlp.dll` and the other file depends on the platform being used: `Kdextx86.dll`, `Kdextalp.dll`, `Kdextmip.dll`, or `Kdextppc.dll` for x86, Alpha, MIPX, or PowerPC computers, respectively. You can find all files on a Windows NT 4.0 Server or Workstation CD-ROM in the `Support\Debug\<platform>` folder.

Ch 24

The command-line syntax is shown in Figure 24.4.

```
Select Command Prompt

H:\SUPPORT\DEBUG\I386>dumpexam /?
Microsoft (R) Windows NT (TM) Version 3.51 DUMPEXAM
Copyright (C) 1995 Microsoft Corp. All rights reserved

usage: DUMPEXAM [options] [CrashDumpFile]
         [-?]              Display this message
         [-v]              Verbose mode
         [-p]              Print header only
         [-f File name]    Specify output file name
         [-y Path]         Set the symbol search path

         If the crashdump filename is empty the name
         specified in the registry is used.

         If the symbol search path is empty the cdrom
         is used for symbols

H:\SUPPORT\DEBUG\I386>
```

FIG. 24.4⇒
An example of the `Dumpexam.exe` utility command-line syntax.

Examples and Explanations of Command-Line Syntax for the Dumpexam Utility

Dumpexam will examine a memory dump file named `MEMORY.DMP` located in the `%System%` folder and use the platform-specific Symbols files located on the CD-ROM.

continues

continued

```
Dumpexam -y d:\sp1\symbols;f:\support\debug\i386 -f
d:\memdump\m1dump.txt d:\memdump\memory.dmp
```

will examine a memory dump file named `MEMORY.DMP` located in the `d:\memdump` folder and use the symbols files located in the `d:\sp1\symbols` folder first, then use the symbols files located in `f:\support\debug\i386` folder. It will place an output file named `m1dump.txt` in the `d:\memdump` folder.

Note Symbols files are used in the order in which they are listed in the command-line syntax; therefore, the most recently installed service pack or hot fix symbols files must be listed in the order in which Windows NT was updated.

A partial example of `Memory.txt` is shown in Listing 24.2. The intent here is to display the various areas of the `Memory.txt` file, not to show an error indication.

Listing 24.2 A Partial Example of Memory.txt

```
****************************************************************
** Windows NT Crash Dump Analysis
****************************************************************
Filename . . . . . . .memory.dmp
Signature. . . . . . .PAGE
ValidDump. . . . . . .DUMP
MajorVersion . . . . .free system
MinorVersion . . . . .1381
DirectoryTableBase . .0x00030000
PfnDataBase. . . . . .0x81fcf000
PsLoadedModuleList . .0x8014dd90
PsActiveProcessHead. .0x8014dc88
MachineImageType . . .I386
NumberProcessors . . .1
BugCheckCode . . . . .0x0000000a
BugCheckParameter1 . .0xfed7a026
BugCheckParameter2 . .0x00000002
BugCheckParameter3 . .0x00000000
BugCheckParameter4 . .0xfed7a026
ExceptionCode. . . . .0x80000003
ExceptionFlags . . . .0x00000001
ExceptionAddress . . .0x8013f46c
****************************************************************
** Symbol File Load Log
****************************************************************
****************************************************************
** !drivers
****************************************************************
Loaded System Driver Summary
Base Code Size Data Size Driver Name Creation Time
****************************************************************
```

```
** !locks -p -v -d
*****************************************************************
**** Dump Resource Performance Data ****
0012fec8: No resource performance data available
*****************************************************************
** !memusage
*****************************************************************
*****************************************************************
** !vm
*****************************************************************
*** Virtual Memory Usage ***
        Physical Memory: 0 ( 0 Kb)
************ NO PAGING FILE ********************
        Available Pages: 0 ( 0 Kb)
        Modified Pages: -2146140568 (5372320 Kb)
        ********** High Number Of Modified Pages ********
        ********** High Number Of Modified No Write Pages ********
        Modified No Write Pages: -18306857 (-73227428 Kb)
Running out of physical memory
        NonPagedPool Usage: -515849464 (-2063397856 Kb)
        ********** Excessive NonPaged Pool Usage *****
        PagedPool Usage: 0 ( 0 Kb)
        Shared Commit: -59289440 (-237157760 Kb)
        Shared Process: 0 ( 0 Kb)
        PagedPool Commit: 0 ( 0 Kb)
        Driver Commit: 0 ( 0 Kb)
        Committed pages: 0 ( 0 Kb)
        Commit limit: 0 ( 0 Kb)
        ********** Number of committed pages is near limit ********
*****************************************************************
** !errlog
*****************************************************************
*****************************************************************
** !irpzone full
*****************************************************************
*****************************************************************
** !process 0 0
*****************************************************************
**** NT ACTIVE PROCESS DUMP ****
*****************************************************************
** !process 0 7
*****************************************************************
**** NT ACTIVE PROCESS DUMP ****
*****************************************************************
** !process
*****************************************************************
*****************************************************************
** !thread
*****************************************************************
*****************************************************************
** Register Dump For Processor #0
*****************************************************************
```

continues

Ch 24

Listing 24.2 Continued

```
eax=00143ce0 ebx=77f02a81 ecx=00000000 edx=00140000 esi=0012ff04
edi=00000665
eip=732deba0 esp=77f13f17 ebp=0526e190 iopl=0 nv up di pl nz na pe nc
cs=0000 ss=0000 ds=77f028fa es=12ff00 fs=0000 gs=0000 efl=732d0000
cr0=0012fed4 cr2=00000000 cr3=0012ff28 dr0=77f3be08 dr1=ffffffff
dr2=0012ff38
dr3=05262c22 dr6=00143ce0 dr7=00000001 cr4=77f3ae5c
gdtr=00000000 gdtl=0014 idtr=0012ff10 idtl=0014 tr=ff34 ldtr=0012
*******************************************************************
** Stack Trace
*******************************************************************
ChildEBP RetAddr Args to Child
fffffffc 00000000 00000000 00000000 00000000 0x00143ce0+0x12d0e4
 FFFFFFB0: 00 00 add byte ptr [eax],al
 FFFFFFB2: 00 00 add byte ptr [eax],al
 FFFFFFB4: 00 00 add byte ptr [eax],al
 FFFFFFB6: 00 00 add byte ptr [eax],al
 FFFFFFB8: 00 00 add byte ptr [eax],al
 FFFFFFBA: 00 00 add byte ptr [eax],al
 FFFFFFBC: 00 00 add byte ptr [eax],al
 FFFFFFBE: 00 00 add byte ptr [eax],al
 FFFFFFC0: 00 00 add byte ptr [eax],al
 FFFFFFC2: 00 00 add byte ptr [eax],al
 FFFFFFC4: 00 00 add byte ptr [eax],al
 FFFFFFC6: 00 00 add byte ptr [eax],al
 FFFFFFC8: 00 00 add byte ptr [eax],al
 FFFFFFCA: 00 00 add byte ptr [eax],al
 FFFFFFCC: 00 00 add byte ptr [eax],al
 FFFFFFCE: 00 00 add byte ptr [eax],al
 FFFFFFD0: 00 00 add byte ptr [eax],al
 FFFFFFD2: 00 00 add byte ptr [eax],al
 FFFFFFD4: 00 00 add byte ptr [eax],al
 FFFFFFD6: 00 00 add byte ptr [eax],al
 FFFFFFD8: 00 00 add byte ptr [eax],al
 FFFFFFDA: 00 00 add byte ptr [eax],al
 FFFFFFDC: 00 00 add byte ptr [eax],al
 FFFFFFDE: 00 00 add byte ptr [eax],al
 FFFFFFE0: 00 00 add byte ptr [eax],al
 FFFFFFE2: 00 00 add byte ptr [eax],al
 FFFFFFE4: 00 00 add byte ptr [eax],al
 FFFFFFE6: 00 00 add byte ptr [eax],al
 FFFFFFE8: 00 00 add byte ptr [eax],al
 FFFFFFEA: 00 00 add byte ptr [eax],al
 FFFFFFEC: 00 00 add byte ptr [eax],al
 FFFFFFEE: 00 00 add byte ptr [eax],al
 FFFFFFF0: 00 00 add byte ptr [eax],al
 FFFFFFF2: 00 00 add byte ptr [eax],al
 FFFFFFF4: 00 00 add byte ptr [eax],al
 FFFFFFF6: 00 00 add byte ptr [eax],al
 FFFFFFF8: 00 00 add byte ptr [eax],al
```

```
 FFFFFFFA: 00 00 add byte ptr [eax],al
 FFFFFFFC: 00 00 add byte ptr [eax],al
 FFFFFFFE: 00 00 add byte ptr [eax],al
--->00000000: 00 00 add byte ptr [eax],al
 00000002: 00 00 add byte ptr [eax],al
 00000004: 00 00 add byte ptr [eax],al
 00000006: 00 00 add byte ptr [eax],al
 00000008: 00 00 add byte ptr [eax],al
 0000000A: 00 00 add byte ptr [eax],al
 0000000C: 00 00 add byte ptr [eax],al
 0000000E: 00 00 add byte ptr [eax],al
 00000010: 00 00 add byte ptr [eax],al
 00000012: 00 00 add byte ptr [eax],al
 00000014: 00 00 add byte ptr [eax],al
 00000016: 00 00 add byte ptr [eax],al
 00000018: 00 00 add byte ptr [eax],al
 0000001A: 00 00 add byte ptr [eax],al
 0000001C: 00 00 add byte ptr [eax],al
 0000001E: 00 00 add byte ptr [eax],al
 00000020: 00 00 add byte ptr [eax],al
 00000022: 00 00 add byte ptr [eax],al
 00000024: 00 00 add byte ptr [eax],al
 00000026: 00 00 add byte ptr [eax],al
 00000028: 00 00 add byte ptr [eax],al
 0000002A: 00 00 add byte ptr [eax],al
 0000002C: 00 00 add byte ptr [eax],al
 0000002E: 00 00 add byte ptr [eax],al
 00000030: 00 00 add byte ptr [eax],al
 00000032: 00 00 add byte ptr [eax],al
 00000034: 00 00 add byte ptr [eax],al
 00000036: 00 00 add byte ptr [eax],al
 00000038: 00 00 add byte ptr [eax],al
 0000003A: 00 00 add byte ptr [eax],al
 0000003C: 00 00 add byte ptr [eax],al
 0000003E: 00 00 add byte ptr [eax],al
 00000040: 00 00 add byte ptr [eax],al
 00000042: 00 00 add byte ptr [eax],al
 00000044: 00 00 add byte ptr [eax],al
 00000046: 00 00 add byte ptr [eax],al
 00000048: 00 00 add byte ptr [eax],al
 0000004A: 00 00 add byte ptr [eax],al
 0000004C: 00 00 add byte ptr [eax],al
 0000004E: 00 00 add byte ptr [eax],al
```

Dumpflop.exe

The Dumpflop utility is used to copy a dump file in pieces to floppy disks to send to support personnel to analyze. This method is probably the least efficient way to send information, but it may be the only way to do so at a particular time because of other problems.

Compression is used when copying information to the floppies. A 16M memory dump will fit on five or six floppy disks. The command-line syntax is shown in Figure 24.5.

```
Select Command Prompt

H:\SUPPORT\DEBUG\I386>dumpflop /?
Microsoft (R) Windows NT (TM) Version 3.51 DUMPFLOP
Copyright (C) 1995 Microsoft Corp. All rights reserved

Usage:
DUMPFLOP [opts]                              - Store default dump thru Drive A:
DUMPFLOP [opts] <CrashDumpFile> [<Drive>:] - Store crash dump onto floppies
DUMPFLOP [opts] <Drive>: [<CrashDumpFile>] - Assemble crash dump from floppies
        [-?] display this message
        [-p] only prints crash dump header on assemble operation
        [-v] show compression statistics
        [-q] formats floppy when necessary during store operation
             overwrites existing crash dump file during assemble operation

H:\SUPPORT\DEBUG\I386>
```

FIG. 24.5⇒
An example of the `Dumpflop.exe` utility command-line syntax.

Kernel Debugger Sessions

If a system is continually crashing during the boot process, the Kernel Debugger option to find the cause of the crash configures a Kernel Debugger session. Before you can dive into the process of configuring and using the Windows NT 4.0 Kernel Debugger programs, however, you must understand debugging terminology.

Host Computer

A host computer is one that is used to troubleshoot a failing computer (target computer). The host computer is the system that runs the debugger programs and has access to the Symbols files. It is physically attached to the target computer by a null modem cable or a modem connection. It must also be running at least the same version of Windows NT software as the target computer.

Target Computer

A target computer is the system on which stop errors are occurring. It is the system that is connected to the host computer by a null modem cable or a modem connection and configured to send information to the host computer to be analyzed. It is the system that needs to be debugged.

Symbols Files and Trees

When source code for executable programs, drivers, dynamic-link libraries, and various other files is compiled for Windows NT, the resultant object code is in two forms or versions: a debug or checked version and a nondebug or free version. All files that Windows NT normally uses are a much smaller version of the object code, the nondebug version. Each and every nondebug file has a corresponding debug version used for troubleshooting, however. The debug versions of the files are referred to as *Symbols files*: they contain debug codes and are only used as reference codes to debug a broken system.

Symbols files are located on the CD-ROM for both Windows NT Server and Workstation in the `Support\Debug\<platform>\Symbols` folder. Also note that Symbols files exist for both service packs and hot fixes and must be obtained to troubleshoot stop errors if Windows NT updates are installed.

The Symbols folder for each platform contains a number of subfolders that contain the actual compressed Symbols (`.db_`) files. There is a subfolder for each type of Symbols file, such as `.exe` or `.dll`. You must decompress these files before using them. To decompress Symbols files, run a program called `Expndsym.cmd`, located in the `Support\Debug` folder on the Windows NT 4.0 Server and Workstation CD-ROMs.

Figure 24.6 presents the directory structure of a Windows NT 4.0 Server CD-ROM with the `Support\Debug\I386\Symbols\Exe` folder displayed.

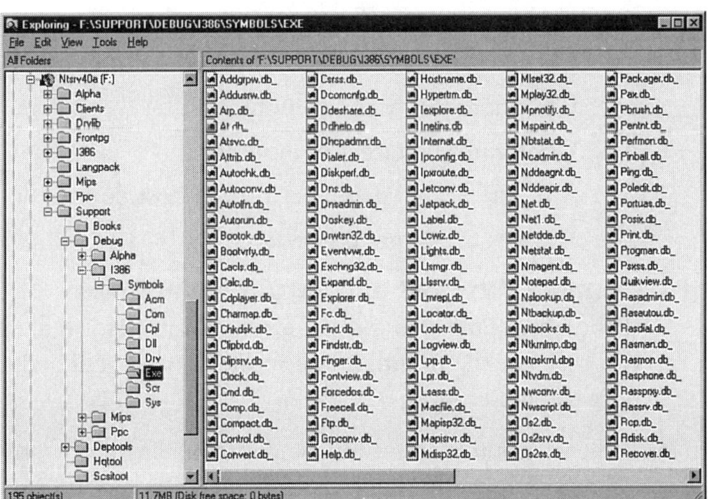

FIG. 24.6⇒
An example of the Symbols files and the Symbols tree structure.

Kernel Debugger Programs and Files

You need a number of executable files to perform kernel debugging. These programs are executed on a host computer and are used to debug the kernel on a target computer. You can find the programs listed in Table 24.4 on the Windows NT Server or Workstation CD-ROM in the `Support\Debug\<platform>` folder (`<platform>` = Alpha, I386, Mips, or Ppc).

Table 24.4 Kernel Debugger Programs

Program/File	Usage
`Alphakd.exe`	Kernel debugger for Alpha computers
`I386kd.exe`	Kernel debugger for Intel computers
`Mipskd.exe`	Kernel debugger for MIPS computers
`Ppckd.exe`	Kernel debugger for PowerPC computers

Configuring the Kernel Debugger Session

To configure a kernel debugger session, you must use a minimum of two computers: a host computer and the target computer. The two computers must be connected either locally with a null modem cable or remotely with a modem connection. The host computer must be running the same platform and version of Windows NT software as the target computer. Use the following steps to enable kernel debugging.

1. Connect the host computer and the target computer.
2. Configure the host computer.
3. Configure the target computer.
4. Start the kernel debugger on the host computer.
5. Reboot the target computer.

Connect the Host and Target Computers

If the host computer and the target computer are in close proximity, you can connect them with a null modem cable attached to an unused COM port in each computer.

If the computers are in remote locations from one another, you can connect them using modems. Select the Modem icon in the Control Panel and ensure the following options are configured:

Auto Answer	On
Hardware Compression	Disabled
Error Detection	Disabled
Flow Control	Hardware

The default baud for Intel computers is 9,600 baud; for RISC computers, it is 19,200 baud.

Configure the Host Computer

The host computer, during the debugger process, requires access to the Symbols files. To copy these files to the host computer, use the `Expndsym.cmd` program found on the Windows NT 4.0 Server and Workstation CD-ROMs in the `Support\Debug` folder. An example of the required syntax for `Expndsym.cmd` follows:

```
expndsym <Windows NT CDROM drive> <destination path>
```

`expndsym f: c:\debug` Will copy and expand the Symbols files from a CD-ROM drive `f:` to the `c:\debug\symbols` folder.

The next step in the kernel debugger process is to either set up a batch file or run the required commands from the command prompt to start the platform-specific kernel debugger program. An example batch file is illustrated later in the section "Start the Kernel Debugger."

The following list describes kernel debugger startup options:

- `-b` Causes the debugger to stop execution on the target computer as soon as possible by causing a debug breakpoint (INT 3)
- `-c` Causes the debugger to request a resync on connect
- `-m` Causes the debugger to monitor modem control lines
- `-n` Causes symbols to be loaded immediately rather than in a deferred mode
- `-v` Verbose mode; displays more information
- `-x` Causes the debugger to break in when an exception first occurs rather than letting the application or module that caused the exception deal with it

Note The most common used startup options are the `-m` and `-v` options.

Ch 24

Configure the Target Computer

If the target computer with which you're working is an Intel system, you start the debugger process simply by configuring the `boot.ini` file to include one of the following options at the end of the specific `boot.ini` selection used to start the system.

`/debug`	Causes the kernel debugger to be loaded during the boot process and is kept in memory. Because the kernel debugger stays in memory, the system can be accessed remotely and debugged.
`/debugport`	Specifies the serial port to be used by the kernel debugger. Default is com2 for Intel computers and com1 for RISC computers.
`/crashdebug`	Causes the kernel debugger to be loaded during boot but swapped out to the pagefile after the boot process. Remote access and debugging cannot be done in this mode.
`/baudrate`	Sets the speed that the `kernel debugger` will use in bits per second. Default is 9,600 for Intel computers and 19,200 for RISC computers.

If you use the `/baudrate` option, the `/debug` option is assumed and you do not have to enter it. ■

If your target computer is a RISC system, you must edit one line in the startup file; you would access that file differently on an Alpha system than on a MIPS or PowerPC system, however.

On an Alpha or PowerPC system, access the Boot Selections menu by selecting the Supplementary choice from the System Boot menu, then selecting the Setup the System choice from the Supplementary menu.

On a MIPS system, select the Run Setup choice to access the Setup menu, then select Manage Startup to display a boot options menu.

Start the Kernel Debugger

You can start the kernel debugger program from the command line or from a preconfigured batch file. An example batch file, which follows, will configure the COM port, make a path to the Symbols files, open a `debug.log` file, start a remote session, and execute the I386 debugger program with the `v` (verbose) and `m` (modem monitoring) options using the

Remote utility, which also starts a session named `debug`. The results of the batch file are shown in Figure 24.7

FIG. 24.7⇒
An example of how to start a kernel debugger session.

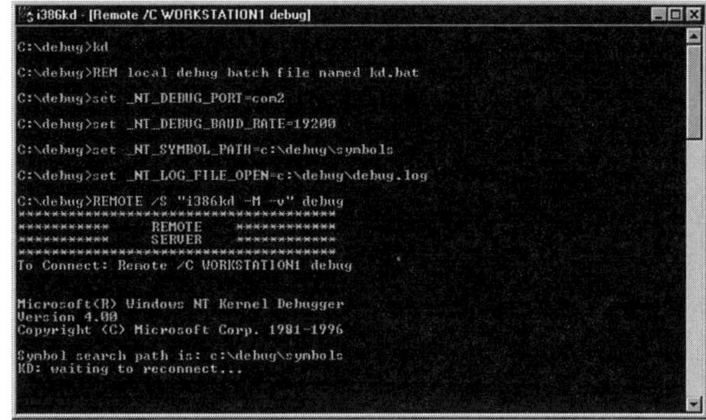

Once the kernel debugger program is running, you can enter commands to view various types of information or get a list of options. Before you can enter any of the following commands at the host computer, you must enter the `Ctrl+C` key sequence (see Table 24.5).

Table 24.5 Kernel Debugger Commands Entered at the Host Computer

Command	Action
`!reload`	Reloads the Symbol files
`!kb`	Displays a stack trace from the last frame dumped by `!trap` (see !trap as follows)
`!errlog`	If not empty, will display information about the component or process that caused the STOP error
`!process`	Lists information about the process running on the active processor
`!thread`	Lists currently running threads
`!kv`	Verbose stack trace used to find the trap frame
`!trap <trap frame address>`	Dumps the computer state when the trap frame occurred
`!process 0 0`	Lists all processes and their headers

continues

Table 24.5 Continued

Command	Action
`!drivers`	Lists the drivers currently loaded
`!vm`	Lists the system's virtual memory usage
`.reboot`	Restarts the target computer
`g`	Releases the target computer

If you start the kernel debugger by using the Remote utility as in the following example, other computers on the network can connect to the session `debug` and view the debugger information. You can find the Remote utility on the Windows NT 4.0 Resource Kit utility CD-ROM. Example syntax for the Remote utility is shown in Figure 24.8.

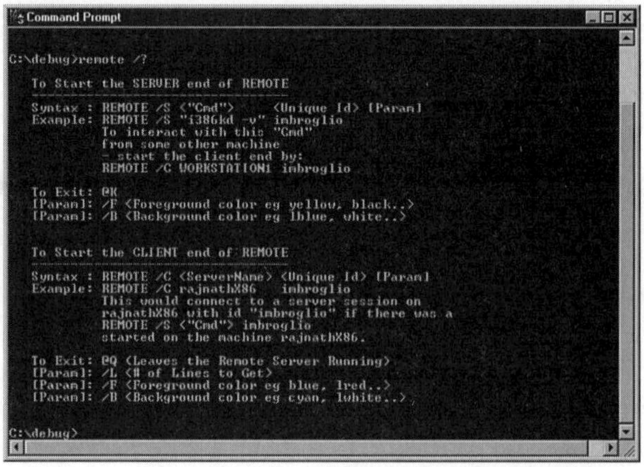

FIG. 24.8⇒
Examples of the Remote utility command-line syntax.

Reboot the Target Computer

To start recording the boot information on the host computer, simply reboot the target computer. As various drivers and dynamic link libraries load, they are displayed on the host computer. When the target computer halts with a stop error, you can determine the exact point of failure.

Listing 24.3 shows the results of a Kernel Debugger session retrieved during the boot process of a Windows NT 4.0 Workstation, Build Level 1381, with Service Pack 2 installed without a failure.

Listing 24.3 Results of a Kernel Debugger Session

```
KD: waiting to reconnect
Kernel Version 1381 UP Free
Kernel base = 0x80100000 PsLoadedModuleList = 0x8014dd90
KD ModLoad: 80100000 801d4cc0 ntoskrnl.exe
KD ModLoad: 80010000 8001c920 hal.dll
KD ModLoad: 80001000 80007000 atapi.sys
KD ModLoad: 80007000 8000ee80 SCSIPORT.SYS
KD ModLoad: 801d5000 801d8a60 Disk.sys
KD ModLoad: 801d9000 801dc2e0 CLASS2.SYS
KD ModLoad: 80086000 800872e0 Diskperf.sys
KD ModLoad: 801dd000 801ff000 Fastfat.sys
KD ModLoad: 77f60000 77fbc000 ntdll.dll
KD ModLoad: f96e0000 f96e48e0 Floppy.SYS
KD ModLoad: f9900000 f9901fa0 Sfloppy.SYS
KD ModLoad: f985c000 f985e500 Scsiscan.SYS
KD ModLoad: f96f0000 f96f5560 Cdrom.SYS
KD ModLoad: f9906000 f9907c40 Changer.SYS
KD ModLoad: f9708000 f970d0a0 Cdaudio.SYS
KD ModLoad: f990a000 f990b820 Fs_Rec.SYS
KD ModLoad: f99c9000 f99c99e0 Null.SYS
KD ModLoad: f9864000 f9866380 KSecDD.SYS
KD ModLoad: f99ca000 f99caea0 Beep.SYS
KD ModLoad: f9400000 f940ae40 sndblst.SYS
KD ModLoad: f9870000 f9873720 sermouse.sys
KD ModLoad: f9730000 f9736120 i8042prt.sys
KD ModLoad: f987c000 f987e340 mouclass.sys
KD ModLoad: f9884000 f9886340 kbdclass.sys
KD ModLoad: f9748000 f974d3e0 VIDEOPRT.SYS
KD ModLoad: f988c000 f988f840 vga.sys
KD ModLoad: f9760000 f97670e0 tgiul40.sys
KD ModLoad: f9894000 f9897840 vga.sys
KD ModLoad: f9778000 f977d680 Msfs.SYS
KD ModLoad: f9410000 f9419360 Npfs.SYS
KD ModLoad: fec44000 fec62fc0 NDIS.SYS
KD ModLoad: f989c000 f989e020 ndistapi.sys
KD ModLoad: febe9000 fcc435c0 Ntfs.SYS
KD ModLoad: a0000000 a0132580 win32k.sys
KD ModLoad: febab000 febc00c0 vga.dll
KD ModLoad: f97d8000 f97dde00 tgiul40.dll
KD ModLoad: f98c8000 f98ca1a0 framebuf.dll
KD ModLoad: febab000 febc00c0 vga.dll
KD ModLoad: f97e8000 f97ede00 tgiul40.dll
KD ModLoad: f9620000 f962eec0 Cdfs.SYS
KD ModLoad: f998c000 f998dea0 rasacd.sys
KD ModLoad: feab5000 feab74e0 TDI.SYS
KD ModLoad: fea52000 fea70820 sfmatalk.sys
KD ModLoad: fea39000 fea51560 nbf.sys
KD ModLoad: fea27000 fea38560 nwlnkipx.sys
KD ModLoad: fea16000 fea261a0 nwlnknb.sys\
KD ModLoad: fe9f5000 fea15820 tcpip.sys
```

Ch 24

continues

Listing 24.3 Continued

```
KD ModLoad: fe9d9000 fe9f4040 netbt.sys
KD ModLoad: f9430000 f94397e0 asyncmac.sys
KD ModLoad: febe1000 febe4f40 ne2000.sys
KD ModLoad: f9440000 f944de00 ndiswan.sys
KD ModLoad: f9450000 f945f6c0 afd.sys
KD ModLoad: f9710000 f97170c0 netbios.sys
KD ModLoad: fea7d000 fea7f640 Parport.SYS
KD ModLoad: fea75000 fea78900 Parallel.SYS
KD ModLoad: f99a8000 f99a9780 ParVdm.SYS
KD ModLoad: f98e0000 f98e25a0 Scsiprnt.SYS
KD ModLoad: f94a0000 f94aaf20 Serial.SYS
KD ModLoad: f9780000 f9785ee0 nwlnkrip.sys
KD ModLoad: fe922000 fe960d60 rdr.sys
KD ModLoad: fe835000 fe8595c0 nwrdr.sys
KD ModLoad: fe7fc000 fe834ba0 srv.sys
KD ModLoad: f9550000 f955e3c0 nwlnkspx.sys
KD ModLoad: fe7eb000 fe7fb700 mup.sys
LDR: Automatic DLL Relocation in Explorer.exe
LDR: Dll SHLWAPI.dll base bfe50000 relocated due to collision with
Dynamically Allocated Memory
KD ModLoad: fe621000 fe632be0 RASDD.DLL
```

Note The `Explorer.exe` file started after the login process and `RASDD.DLL` was loaded when a word processor was started in the host computer.

Remote Troubleshooting

As mentioned previously, the host computer and the target computer can be near each other and connected using a null modem cable; if the systems are apart from each other, however, modems can be used. This type of troubleshooting scenario implies that someone from a support team is available to diagnose the error. If this is not the case, you can establish a remote session with technical support, such as Microsoft Technical Support team through RAS.

The procedure is very similar to the one covered previously with some additions. You must either configure RAS on the host computer or some other system on the network that can access the host server, and another computer is required at some remote technical support area. Here are the steps required to access a kernel debugger session from a remote location.

1. The target computer is connected to a host computer. The host computer is either a RAS server or can access a RAS server.
2. The host computer is configured as previously mentioned in the section "Configure the Host Computer."
3. The target computer is configured as previously mentioned in the section "Configure the Target Computer."
4. The kernel debugger program is started on the host computer with the Remote utility as previously mentioned in the section "Start the Kernel Debugger." The example given was `REMOTE /s "i386kd -m -v"` debug.
5. From the Remote computer, establish a RAS session with the RAS server (the host computer if it is a RAS server or a RAS server that has access to the host computer).
6. From the Remote computer, establish a connection with the kernel debugger session from the Remote computer by using the Remote utility. An example would be

   ```
   REMOTE /c <host computer name> debug
   ```

7. Then reboot the target computer as previously mentioned in the section "Reboot the Target Computer."
8. You can now monitor the kernel debugger session and the technical support person can control it at the remote computer.

Events and Event Log Viewer

An *event* is defined as a significant incident in the system, in the security of the system, or in an application that requires someone to be notified.

Some events, such as a disk drive becoming full, are considered critical events and cause a message to be presented on the screen immediately to alert the user of the problem. Other events that do not need immediate attention are recorded in one of three types of event logs and can be viewed through the *Event viewer.*

Event viewer is a diagnostic tool within Windows NT 4.0 that can be extremely useful in troubleshooting various types of problems encountered with the system, with security, or with applications. You also can view events of each type from other computers on the network.

Event logging is a service in Windows NT 4.0 and is, by default, started each time Windows NT is booted. As stated previously, events are logged in three categories: system, security, and application.

- System — The system log contains entries logged by system components or services, such as a network adapter card or the browser service.
- Security — The security log contains entries caused by activities such as someone accessing a resource or logging on to the system. By default, security log auditing is disabled. You must enable auditing from User Manager for Domains before a security log will be produced. How to enable auditing and what events are available for security log auditing will be covered later in this chapter.
- Application — An application log contains entries logged from various applications being run in the system. You can find Dr. Watson and Autochk events in this log.

Key Concept

Everyone, including normal users, can view the system and application logs, but only administrators can view security logs. If a normal user tries to access the security log, an `Access is Denied` message is displayed.

Event Log Options

You start Event viewer from the Start, Programs, Administrative Tools program group. Once you start Event viewer, select the Log drop-down menu to select either the System, the Security, or the Applications log. Figure 24.9 displays the Log drop-down menu.

Other options available from the Log drop-down menu follow:

- Open — Allows you to open and view any `.evt` file that was previously saved.
- Save As — Allows you to save a log file.
- Clear All Events — Allows you to clear an event log. Before the log is cleared, a message is displayed asking you if you want to save the log.

FIG. 24.9⇒
The Event viewer Log drop-down menu.

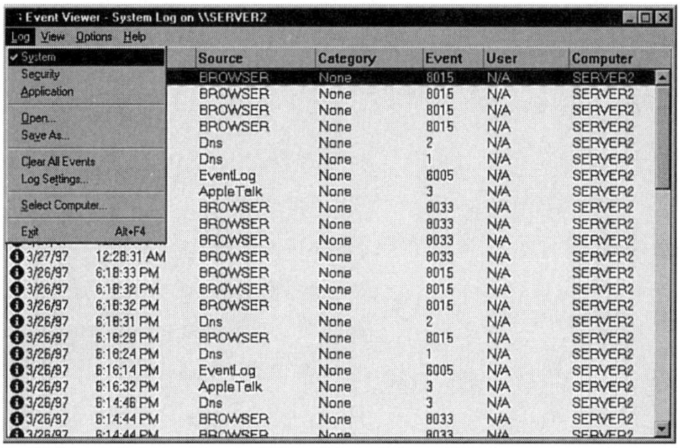

- **Log Settings** — Allows you to change the default log settings. You can adjust settings for each log independently and include size and wrapping settings. Default maximum log size is 512K with a range of 64K to 4,194,240K in 64K increments. Wrapping settings include Overwrite Events as Needed, Overwrite Events Older Than <days> Days, or Do Not Overwrite Events (Clear Manually). The default setting is to overwrite events older than seven days.
- **Select Computer** — Allows you to select any Windows NT computer on the network. You also can select LAN Manager 2.x servers to view system and security logs only. When you choose Select Computer, a Select Computer dialog box appears. If the computer you selected is available over a slow WAN link, select Low Speed Connection on the dialog box.
- **Exit** — Exit Event Viewer.

The View drop-down menu has the following options:

- **All Events** — The default setting; Event viewer will list all events in the selected log.
- **Filter Events** — From this option, you can specify time ranges of when events should be displayed. You can also select event types to be displayed and from what source, category, user, computer, or by event ID.

- Newest First — The default setting. As events occur, they are put on top of the list and displayed that way.
- Oldest First — Select this option to list the oldest events first.
- Find — Used to search for events by type or by source, category, ID, computer, user, or description.
- Detail — Displays more information about the selected event. You also can access the Event Detail dialog box by double-clicking any event in the Event Viewer display box.
- Refresh — Refreshes the Event Viewer display box.

With the Options drop-down menu, you can select low-speed connections, save settings on exit (set by default), or a different font for the Event viewer display. Select Low-speed Connection if you are analyzing event logs from other computers over a slow WAN connection. The only other drop-down menu is Help.

Event Log Headings

Once you display an Event Log using Event viewer, various headings will appear across the top of the display. The headings' meanings are displayed in Figure 24.10 and described in the following list.

Event Viewer - System Log on \\SERVER2

Log View Options Help

Date	Time	Source	Category	Event	User	Computer
3/30/97	1:29:01 PM	BROWSER	None	8015	N/A	SERVER2
3/30/97	1:29:01 PM	BROWSER	None	8015	N/A	SERVER2
3/30/97	1:29:01 PM	BROWSER	None	8015	N/A	SERVER2
3/30/97	1:29:01 PM	BROWSER	None	8015	N/A	SERVER2
3/30/97	1:28:57 PM	Dns	None	2	N/A	SERVER2
3/30/97	1:28:50 PM	Dns	None	1	N/A	SERVER2
3/30/97	1:27:00 PM	AppleTalk	None	3	N/A	SERVER2
3/30/97	1:26:37 PM	EventLog	None	6005	N/A	SERVER2
3/29/97	10:54:57 PM	BROWSER	None	8033	N/A	SERVER2
3/29/97	10:54:56 PM	BROWSER	None	8033	N/A	SERVER2
3/29/97	10:54:55 PM	BROWSER	None	8033	N/A	SERVER2
3/29/97	10:54:55 PM	BROWSER	None	8033	N/A	SERVER2
3/29/97	11:20:12 AM	BROWSER	None	8015	N/A	SERVER2
3/29/97	11:20:12 AM	BROWSER	None	8015	N/A	SERVER2
3/29/97	11:20:10 AM	BROWSER	None	8015	N/A	SERVER2
3/29/97	11:20:09 AM	BROWSER	None	8015	N/A	SERVER2
3/29/97	11:20:05 AM	Dns	None	2	N/A	SERVER2
3/29/97	11:19:57 AM	Dns	None	1	N/A	SERVER2
3/29/97	11:17:44 AM	EventLog	None	6005	N/A	SERVER2
3/29/97	11:18:06 AM	AppleTalk	None	3	N/A	SERVER2
3/27/97	12:28:34 AM	BROWSER	None	8033	N/A	SERVER2
3/27/97	12:28:33 AM	BROWSER	None	8033	N/A	SERVER2
3/27/97	12:28:33 AM	BROWSER	None	8033	N/A	SERVER2

FIG. 24.10⇒ A display of the Event Log screen headings.

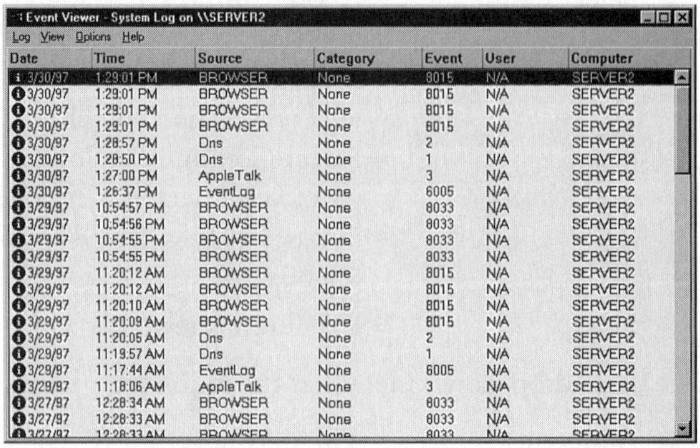

- Date — Date the event occurred.
- Time — Time the event occurred.
- Source — Software that logged the event. This software could be an application, a network adapter driver, a service, and so on.

- **Category** This heading has meaning mostly in the security log but also is used in the application log. It is how the event source has classified the event. In the security log, whatever classification of event was configured in User Manager for Domains will appear in this column. For example, if the logon/logoff service logged the event, logon/logoff will appear in this column.
- **Event** Identifies an event type or ID. This column relates back to source code and can be used by support personnel to cross-check events with the source code.
- **User** The user logged on to the system or the client name if the event was caused by the server service when a client was accessing this computer.
- **Computer** The name of the computer where the event occurred. This value is usually the local computer; if you are looking at an event log from another computer on the network, however, that computer name will be displayed.

A number of icons are displayed in front of the events under the Event column. The five different icons and their meanings are described in Table 24.6.

Table 24.6 Event Icons and Their Meanings

Icon	Symbol	Meaning
Error	Stop Sign	Serious Problem. If services did not load because of network adapter card settings, the services will be displayed with this type of error.
Warning	Exclamation Point	Not as serious as Error events, but problem could cause more serious problems at a later time, such as disk space getting low on a particular disk drive.

continues

Table 24.6 Continued

Icon	Symbol	Meaning
Information	Blue Circle	Usually describes successful operations, such as browser, DNS, and AppleTalk events. This icon offers information only.
Success Audit	Padlock	A security event that was successful, such as a successful logon.
Failed Audit	Key	A security event that was not successful, such as an unsuccessful logon attempt.

Event Details

Select an event in the Event viewer display screen and press Enter, double-click the selected event, or select the View drop-down menu and choose the Details selection. In any case, an Event Detail screen is displayed. This screen, in addition to the information already displayed on the Event Viewer display, will show a description window with additional information about the selected event. This information varies depending on the selected event; for example, a master browser was successfully elected, a duplicate IP address was detected on the network, an unsuccessful logon attempt was made in the security log, or a printer became available to the AppleTalk network in the application log.

The Data window at the bottom of the Event Detail screen can contain optional data in the form of either bytes or words. It is additional data created by the event source and is displayed in hexadecimal format. Support personnel familiar with the source application can interpret the meaning of these data. Not all events display information in this area. On the very bottom of the Event Detail screen are the Close, Previous, Next, and Help buttons. An example of the Event Detail screen is shown in Figure 24.11.

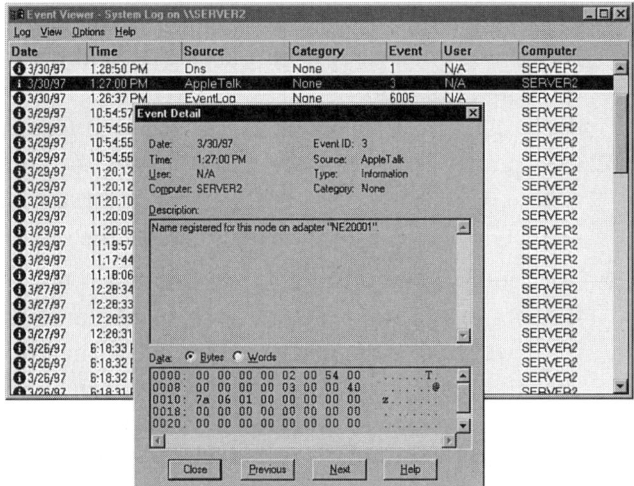

FIG. 24.11⇒ An example of an Event Detail dialog box for an event log.

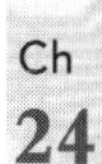

Ch 24

Troubleshooting Problems Using Event Viewer

To mention or display each and every possible event would be impossible. However, mentioning some general guidelines for using Event Viewer to troubleshoot system, security, and application problems can be done here.

- Monitor the system event log regularly on file and print servers to look for low-disk space warning errors and bad sector retry warnings.
- Monitor the application event log if an application is crashing and you need to try to find out why by searching for any events concerning that application.
- Monitor the security event log for any of the security event choices selected in User Manager or User Manager for Domains by choosing Policies, Audit selection.
- When analyzing events, always look for events that happened in a specific time frame. Start viewing detailed information of these events from the newest to the oldest, which will give you a complete picture of a failure. For example, the browser did not start because the workstation or server service did not start because the network adapter card settings were detected wrong. In this case, the browser was not the problem—the network adapter card setting configuration was the problem.
- Through Registry editing, you can halt the computer if the security log is full. First of all, you must select either the default Overwrite

Events Older Than x Days setting or the Do Not Overwrite Events (Clear Log Manually) from the Log drop-down menu, Settings option. Next, in the `HKEY_LOCAL_MACHINE\System\CurrentControlSet\Control\Lsa` key, add the `CrashOnAuditFail` value, and type `REG_WORD` to set it to 1. If the system halts, it has to be restarted by an administrator, the auditing security events must be turned off, and the security log cleared.

- You can save an event log three different ways: in an Event Log File (.EVT), a regular Text file (.TXT), or in a Comma-delimited Text (.TXT) file. If you save a log in Event Log File format, you can view the log later through Event Viewer. If you save it in a regular Text file, you can incorporate it into a word processor application; and if you save it in a Comma-delimited Text file, you can incorporate it into a spreadsheet or database application. You will lose all hexadecimal data if you save it in any of the three types of text format.

Taking the Disc Test

If you have read and understood the material in the chapter, you are ready to test your knowledge. Insert the CD-ROM that comes with this book and run the self-test software as described in Appendix K, "Using the Self-Test Software."

From Here...

This is the final chapter in the book. Following this chapter are a number of appendixes, including the "Glossary," "Certification Checklist," "How Do I Get There from Here?," "Testing Tips," "Contacting Microsoft," "Suggested Reading," "Internet Resources for Windows NT Server," "Lab Exercises," "Self-Test Questions and Answers," "Using the Self-Test Software," and "TechNet Sampler."

Good luck on your test!

Glossary

A

access-control entry (ACE) An entry in an access-control list that defines a set of permissions for a group or user.

access-control list (ACL) A list containing access-control entries. An ACL determines the permissions associated with an object, which can be anything in a Win32 environment.

access time The last time a file was run (if the file is executable). Otherwise, it is the last time the file was read or written to.

ACE See *access-control entry.*

ACK Short for acknowledgment. A control character sent to the other computer in a conversation. It usually is used to indicate that transmitted information has been received correctly, when using a communications protocol such as Xmodem.

ACL See *access-control list.*

active window The window the user is currently working with. Windows identifies the active window by highlighting its title bar and border.

Advanced Program-to-Program Communications (APPC) A method of interprogram communication, usually used by applications that are intended for use with IBM SNA-based networks.

Advanced Research Project Agency (ARPA) The agency responsible for the formation of the forerunner of the Internet. See *Defense Advanced Research Projects Agency.*

agent Software that runs on a client computer for use by administrative software running on a server. Agents are typically used to support administrative actions, such as detecting system information or running services.

Alerter Service A Windows NT Executive service that notifies selected users or computers of system-generated administrative alerts.

American National Standards Institute (ANSI) A computer standards-making organization based in the U. S.

American Standard Code for Information Interchange (ASCII) A scheme that assigns letters, punctuation marks, and so on, to specific numeric values. The standardization of ASCII-enabled computers and computer programs to support exchange of data.

ANSI See *American National Standards Institute.*

ANSI character set An 8-bit character set used by Microsoft Windows that enables you to represent up to 256 characters (0–255) by using your keyboard. The ASCII character set is a subset of the ANSI set. See *American National Standards Institute.*

API See *application programming interface.*

APPC See *Advanced Program-to-Program Communications.*

application A computer program that is designed to perform some specific type of work. An application is different from a utility, which performs some type of maintenance (such as formatting a disk).

application programming interface (API) A list of supported functions. Windows NT 4.0 supports the MS-DOS API, Windows API, and Win32 API. If a function is a member of the API, it is said to be a supported, or documented, function. Functions included with Windows, but are not part of the API, are referred to as undocumented functions. An API can also be a low-level software routine that programmers can use to send requests to the operating system.

ARPA See *Advanced Research Project Agency.*

ASCII See *American Standard Code for Information Interchange.*

ASCII character set A 7-bit character set that is widely used to represent letters and symbols found on a standard U.S. keyboard. The ASCII character set is identical to the first 128 characters in the ANSI character set.

association The process of assigning a file name extension to a particular application. When an extension has been associated with an application, Windows NT 4.0 starts the application when you choose to open the file from Windows Explorer. Associations are critical to the concept of document-centric computing.

attributes A characteristic of a file that indicates whether it is hidden, system, read-only, archive, or compressed.

Audio Video Interleaved (AVI) The format of the full-motion video files used by Windows NT 4.0.

Audit Policy A definition of the type of security-related events that are recorded by the Event Viewer.

authentication The validation of a user's access to a computer or domain either by the local computer (local validation) or by a backup domain controller for the domain that the user is accessing.

Autoexec.bat A file in the root directory of the boot disk that contains a list of MS-DOS commands that are automatically executed when the system is started. Autoexec.bat can be created either by the user or by the operating system. Windows NT 4.0 Setup examines the Autoexec.bat file to search for configuration information, such as user-environment variables.

auxiliary audio device Audio devices whose output is mixed with the *Musical Instrument Digital Interface* (MIDI) and waveform output devices in a multimedia computer. An example of an auxiliary audio device is the compact disc audio output from a CD-ROM drive.

AVI See *Audio Video Interleaved.*

B

background window Any window created by a thread other than the thread running in the foreground.

Backup Domain Controller The Windows NT controller server that performs the validation of user logon requests. The Backup Domain Controller obtains a copy of the master account database for the domain from the Primary Domain Controller.

Basic Input/Output System (BIOS) The bootstrap code of a PC. The low-level routines that support the transfer of information between the various parts of a computer system, such as memory, disks, and the monitor. Usually built into the machine's read-only memory (ROM). The BIOS can significantly affect the performance of the computer system.

batch program A file that contains one or more commands that are executed when you type the file name at the command prompt. Batch programs have the .BAT extension.

binding The process that links a protocol driver with a network adapter driver.

BIOS See *Basic Input/Output System.*

BIOS enumerator In a Plug and Play system, the BIOS enumerator is responsible for identifying all of the hardware devices on the computer's motherboard.

bit Short for binary digit, the smallest unit of data a computer can store. Bits are expressed as 1 or 0.

bitmap Originally an array of bits, but now expanded to include arrays of bytes, or even 32-bit quantities that specify the dot pattern and colors that describe an image on the screen or on printed paper.

BMP The extension used for Windows bitmap files.

Boot Loader This defines the location of the Windows NT boot and system files.

Boot Partition The partition that contains the Windows NT system files.

Bootstrap Protocol (BOOTP) This is an internetworking protocol that is used to configure TCP/IP networks across routers.

branch A segment of the directory tree, representing a directory and any subdirectories it contains.

browse To look through a list on a computer system. Lists include directories, files, domains, or computers.

buffer A temporary holding place reserved in memory, where data is held while in transit to or from a storage device or another location in memory.

buffering The process of using buffers, particularly to or from I/O devices, such as disk drives and serial ports.

bus enumerator A driver that is responsible for building the hardware tree on a Plug and Play system.

byte 8 binary digits (bits) combined to represent a single character or value.

C

cascading menu A menu that is a submenu of a higher level menu item. Also known as a hierarchical menu. The menus accessed via the Windows NT 4.0 Start Button are cascading menus.

CCITT See *International Telephone and Telegraph Consultative Committee.*

CD-DA See *Compact Disc-Digital Audio.*

CD-ROM See *Compact Disc-Read-Only Memory.*

CD-ROM/XA See *Compact Disc-Read-Only Memory Extended Architecture.*

CD-XA See *Compact Disc-Extended Architecture.*

CDFS See *Compact Disc File System.*

central processing unit (CPU) The computational and control unit of a computer; the device that interprets and executes instructions. The CPU, or microprocessor in the case of a microcomputer, has the capability to fetch, decode, and execute instructions and to transfer information to and from other resources over the computer's main data-transfer path, the bus. The CPU is the chip that functions as the "brain" of a computer.

character A letter, number, punctuation mark, or a control code, which is usually expressed in either the ANSI or ASCII character set.

character mode A mode of displaying information on the screen, where all information is displayed by using text characters (as opposed to graphical symbols). MS-DOS applications run in character mode.

check box In the Windows NT 4.0 interface, a square box that has two or three states from which the user selects or deselects an option from a set of options. A standard check box is a toggle, with two states: checked and unchecked. A three-state check box has an additional state: disabled (grayed).

class For OLE, a data structure and the functions that manipulate that data structure. An object is a member of a class. For hardware, a grouping of devices and buses for the purpose of installing and managing devices and device drivers, and allocating the resources used by them. The Windows NT 4.0 hardware tree is organized by device class.

clear-to-send A signal sent from the computer to a modem in a communications conversation to indicate readiness to accept data.

client A computer that accesses shared network resources provided by another computer, called a server. See also *server*.

code names A name that is assigned for the purpose of concealing the identity or existence of something or someone. The code name for Microsoft Windows NT 4.0 was "SUR," which sometimes appears as an identifier in several places in the released product, including hardware setup files. The next major release of Windows NT is code named "Cairo."

codec Compression/decompression technology for digital video and stereo audio.

communications protocol The rules that govern a conversation between two computers that are communicating via an asynchronous connection. The use of a communications protocol ensures error-free delivery of the data being communicated.

communications resource A device that provides a bidirectional, asynchronous data stream. Examples include serial and parallel ports, and modems. Applications access the resource through a service provider.

Compact Disc-Digital Audio (CD-DA) An optical data-storage format that provides for the storage of up to 73 minutes of high-quality, digital-audio data on a compact disc. Also known as Red Book audio or music CD.

Compact Disc-Extended Architecture (CD-XA) See *Compact Disc-Read-Only Memory Extended Architecture (CD-ROM/XA).*

compact disc file system (CDFS) Controls access to the contents of CD-ROM drivers.

Compact Disc-Read-Only Memory (CD-ROM) A form of storage characterized by high capacity (roughly 600 megabytes) and the use of laser optics rather than magnetic means for reading data.

Compact Disc-Read-Only Memory Extended Architecture (CD-ROM/XA) An extended CD-ROM format developed by Philips, Sony, and Microsoft. CD-ROM/XA format is consistent with the ISO 9660 (High Sierra) standard, with further specification of ADPCM (adaptive differential pulse code modulation) audio, images, and interleaved data.

Computer Browser Service This Executive Service identifies those Windows NT clients that have resources available for use within a workgroup or domain.

computer name A unique name that identifies a particular computer on the network. Microsoft networking uses NetBIOS names, which can have up to 15 characters, and cannot contain spaces.

Config.sys An ASCII text file that contains configuration commands. Used by MS-DOS, OS/2, and Windows NT 4.0 to load real-mode device drivers.

Configuration Manager One of three central components of a Plug and Play system (one for each of the three phases of configuration management). The configuration managers drive the process of locating devices, setting up the hardware tree, and allocating resources.

context menu The menu displayed at the location of a submenu that is displayed when you right-click. It is called the context menu because the contents of the menu depend upon the context in which it is invoked.

Control Panel The primary Windows NT 4.0 configuration tool. Each option that you can change is represented by an icon in the Control Panel window.

Controller See *Domain Controller.*

conventional memory The first 640K of memory in your computer that is used to run real-mode MS-DOS applications.

cooperative multitasking A form of multitasking in which threads cooperate with each other by voluntarily giving up control of the processor. Contrast this with *pre-emptive multitasking.*

CPU See *central processing unit.* (CPU)

crash A serious failure of the software being used.

CTS See *clear-to-send.*

cursor A bitmap whose location on the screen is controlled by a pointing device, such as a mouse, pen, or trackball. See also *bitmap.*

D

DARPA See *Defense Advanced Research Projects Agency* (DARPA).

data frame The structured packets into which data is placed by the Data Link layer.

datagram A packet of information and delivery data that is routed on a network.

default An operation or value that the system assumes, unless the user makes an explicit choice.

Defense Advanced Research Projects Agency (DARPA) An agency of the U.S. Department of Defense that sponsored the development of the protocols that became the TCP/IP suite. DARPA was previously known as ARPA, the *Advanced Research Project Agency*, when ARPANET was built.

desktop The background of your screen, on which windows, icons, and dialog boxes appear.

destination directory The directory to which you intend to copy or move one or more files.

device A generic term for a computer component, such as a printer, serial port, or disk drive. A device frequently requires its own controlling software (called a *device driver*).

device contention The method that Windows NT 4.0 uses to allocate access to peripheral devices when multiple applications are attempting to use them.

device driver A piece of software that translates requests from one form into another. Most commonly, drivers are used to provide a device-independent way to access hardware.

device ID A unique ASCII string created by enumerators to identify a hardware device and to cross-reference data about the device stored in the Registry.

device node One of the data structures that make up the hardware tree, a device node is built by the Configuration Manager into memory at system startup. Device nodes contain information about a given device, such as the resources it is using.

DHCP See *Dynamic Host Configuration Protocol (DHCP).*

dialog box The type of window that is displayed by Windows NT 4.0 when user input is needed. Usually contains one or more buttons, edit controls, option buttons, and drop-down lists.

dial-up networking Provides remote access to networks. Dial-up networking enables a remote user to access their network. Once connected, it is as if the remote computer is logically on the network—the user can do anything that he or she can do when physically connected to the network.

DIP switch Short for Dual In-line Package Switch. Used to configure hardware options, especially on adapter cards.

Direct Memory Access (DMA) A technique used by hardware adapters to store and retrieve information from the computer's RAM memory without involving the computer's CPU.

directory Part of a structure for organizing your files on a disk. A directory can contain files and other directories (called subdirectories).

Directory Replication Service This service provides a means of copying a directory and file structure from a source Windows NT Server to a target Windows NT Server or Workstation.

disk caching A method to improve performance of the file system. A section of memory is used as a temporary holding place for frequently accessed file data. Windows NT 4.0 dynamically allocates its disk cache.

disk operating system (DOS) See *MS-DOS.*

DLL See *dynamic-link library.*

DMA See *Direct Memory Access.*

DMA channel A channel for DMA transfers, those that occur directly between a device and memory, without involving the CPU.

DNS See *Domain Name Service.*

DNS name servers The servers that hold the DNS name database, and supply the IP address that matches a DNS name in response to a request from a DNS client. See also *Domain Name Service.*

dock To insert a portable computer into a base unit. Cold docking means the computer must begin from a power-off state and restart before docking. Hot docking means the computer can be docked while running at full power.

docking station The base computer unit into which a user can insert a portable computer to expand it to a desktop equivalent. Docking stations usually include drives, expansion slots, AC power, network and SCSI connections, and communication ports.

domain For DNS, a group of workstations and servers that share a single group name. For Microsoft networking, a collection of computers that share a security context and an account database stored on a Windows NT Server domain controller. Each domain has a unique name. See also *Domain Name System.*

Domain Controller The Windows NT Server computer that authenticates domain logons and maintains a copy of the security database for the domain.

Domain Name Service (DNS) A static, hierarchical name service for TCP/IP hosts. Do not confuse DNS domains with Windows NT domains.

DOS See *Microsoft Disk Operating System.*

DOS Protected Mode Interface (DPMI) A technique used to allow MS-DOS-based applications to access extended memory.

dpi Short for dots per inch, a measurement of the resolution of a monitor or printer.

DPMI See *DOS Protected Mode Interface.*

drag and drop Selectively moving or copying one or more objects between dialog boxes by using a mouse or other pointing device.

DRAM See *Dynamic Random-Access Memory.*

Dynamic Data Exchange (DDE) A form of interprocess communication (IPC) implemented in the Microsoft Windows family of operating systems. DDE uses shared memory to exchange data. Most DDE functions have been superseded by OLE.

Dynamic Host Configuration Protocol (DHCP) A protocol for automatic TCP/IP configuration that provides static and dynamic address allocation and management.

dynamic-link library (DLL) File functions that are compiled, linked, and saved separately from the processes that use them. Functions in DLLs can be used by more than one running process. The operating system maps the DLLs into the process's address space when the process is starting up or while it is running. Dynamic-link libraries are stored in files with the .DLL extension.

Dynamic Random-Access Memory (DRAM) A computer's main memory.

E

Eform See *electronic mail form.*

EISA See *Extended Industry Standard Architecture.*

electronic mail (e-mail) A message sent across a network between two or more store-and-forward messaging systems.

electronic mail form (Eform) A programmed form used to send e-mail in an electronic mail system.

Electronic Messaging System (EMS) A system that enables users or applications to correspond using a store-and-forward system.

e-mail See *electronic mail.*

EMM See *Expanded Memory Manager.*

EMS See *Expanded Memory Specification* and *Electronic Messaging System.*

Encapsulated PostScript (EPS) A file format used to represent graphics written in the PostScript page-description language.

enumerator A Plug and Play device driver that detects devices below its own device node, creates unique device IDs, and reports to Configuration Manager during startup.

environment variable A symbolic variable that represents some element of the operating system, such as a path, a file name, or other literal data. Typically used by batch files, environment variables are created with the `SET` command.

EPROM See *Erasable Programmable Read-Only Memory.*

EPS See *Encapsulated PostScript.*

EPS file A file containing code written in the Encapsulated PostScript printer programming language. Often used to represent graphics for use by desktop publishing applications.

Erasable Programmable Read-Only Memory (EPROM) A computer chip containing non-volatile memory. It can be erased (for reprogramming) by exposure to an ultraviolet light.

event An action or occurrence to which an application might respond, such as mouse clicks, key presses, mouse movements, or a system event. System events are any significant occurrences that may require user notification, or some other action by an application.

expanded memory Memory that complies with the Lotus-Intel-Microsoft Expanded Memory specification. Used by MS-DOS-based spreadsheet applications.

Expanded Memory Manager (EMM) The device driver that controls access to expanded memory.

Expanded Memory Specification (EMS) The specification that controls and defines Expanded Memory. Also known as the Lotus-Intel-Microsoft (LIM) specification, after the three major companies that designed it.

Extended Industry Standard Architecture (EISA) An enhancement to the bus architecture used on the IBM PC/AT, which allows the use of 32-bit devices in the same type of expansion slot that is used by an ISA adapter card. EISA slots and adapters were formerly common in server computers, but have been mostly replaced with PCI slots.

extended memory Memory that occupies physical addresses above the 1-megabyte mark.

Extended Memory Manager (XMM) The MS-DOS device driver that provides access to XMS memory.

Extended Memory Specification (XMS) The specification for the application program interfaces that allow an application to access and use extended memory.

F

family name The name of a given font family. Windows employs five family names—*Decorative, Modern, Roman, Script,* and *Swiss.* A sixth family name, *Dontcare*, specifies the default font. See also *font family*.

FAT See *file allocation table.*

FAT file system A file system based on a file allocation table. Windows NT 4.0 uses a 32-bit implementation called VFAT. See also *file allocation table* and *virtual file allocation table.*

FIFO See *First In, First Out.*

file A collection of information stored on a disk, and accessible by using a name.

file allocation table (FAT) A table or list maintained by some operating systems to keep track of the status of various segments of disk space used for file storage. See also *virtual file allocation table.*

file attribute A characteristic of a file that indicates whether the file is read-only, hidden, system, archived, a directory, or normal.

file sharing The capability of a network computer to share files or directories on its local disks with remote computers.

file system In an operating system, the overall structure in which files are named, stored, and organized.

file time A 64-bit value representing the number of 100-nanosecond intervals that have elapsed since January 1, 1601.

File Transfer Program (FTP) A utility defined by the TCP/IP protocol suite that is used to transfer files between dissimilar systems.

File Transfer Protocol (FTP) The standard method of transferring files by using TCP/IP. FTP allows you to transfer files between dissimilar computers, with preservation of binary data, and optional translation of text file formats.

First In, First Out (FIFO) Used to describe a buffer, where data is retrieved from the buffer in the same order it went in.

floppy disk A disk that can be inserted in, and removed from, a disk drive.

focus The area of a dialog box that receives input. The focus is indicated by highlighted text, or a button enclosed in dotted lines.

folder In Windows Explorer, an object that can contain other objects (a container object). Examples include disk folders, the fonts folder, and the printers folder.

font A collection of characters, each of which has a similar appearance. For example, the Arial font characters are all sans serif characters.

font family A group of fonts that have similar characteristics.

font mapper The routine within Windows that maps an application's request for a font with particular characteristics to the available font that best matches those characteristics.

frame See *data frame*.

free space Unused space on a hard disk.

friendly name A human-readable name that is used to give an alternative to the often cryptic computer, port, and share names. For example, "Digital 1152 Printer In The Hall" as opposed to "HALLPRT."

FTP See *File Transfer Program* and *File Transfer Protocol*.

G

gateway A computer that is connected to multiple networks and is capable of moving data between networks using different transport protocols.

GDI See *graphics device interface.*

graphical user interface (GUI) A computer system design in which the user interacts with the system by using graphical symbols, tools, and events, rather than text-based displays and commands, such as the normal Windows NT 4.0 user interface.

graphics device interface (GDI) The subsystem that implements graphic drawing functions.

GUI See *graphical user interface.*

H

handle An interface (usually a small black square) added to an object to enable the user to move, size, reshape, or otherwise modify the object.

hardware branch The hardware archive root key in the Registry, which is a superset of the memory-resident hardware tree. The name of this key is Hkey_Local_Machine\Hardware.

hardware tree A record in RAM of the current system configuration, based on the configuration information for all devices in the hardware branch of the Registry. The hardware tree is created each time the computer is started or whenever a dynamic change occurs to the system configuration.

high memory area (HMA) A 64K memory block located just above the 1M address in a Virtual DOS Machine (VDM). Originally made possible by a side effect of the 80286 processor design, the memory is usable when the A20 address line is turned on.

High-Performance File System (HPFS) A File System that is primarily used with OS/2 operating system version 1.2 or later. It supports long file names but does not provide security. Windows NT 4.0 does not support HPFS.

hive A discrete body of Registry information, usually stored in a single disk file.

HKEY_CLASSES_ROOT The Registry tree that contains data relating to OLE. This key is a symbolic link to a subkey of HKEY_LOCAL_MACHINE\SOFTWARE.

HKEY_CURRENT_USER The Registry tree that contains the currently logged-in user's preferences, including desktop settings, application settings, and network connections. This key maps to a subkey of HKEY_USERS.

HKEY_LOCAL_MACHINE The Registry tree that contains configuration settings that apply to the hardware and software on the computer.

HKEY_USERS The Registry tree that contains the preferences for every user that ever logged on to this computer.

HMA See *high memory area.*

home directory A directory that is accessible to a particular user and contains that user's files and programs on a network server.

host Any device that is attached to the internetwork and uses TCP/IP.

host ID The portion of the IP address that identifies a computer within a particular network ID.

host name The name of an Internet host. It may or may not be the same as the computer name. In order for a client to access resources by host name, it must appear in the client's HOSTS file, or be resolvable by a DNS server.

host table The HOSTS and LMHOSTS files, which contain mappings of known IP addresses mapped to host names.

HOSTS file A local text file in the same format as the 4.3 Berkeley Software Distribution (BSD) UNIX /etc/hosts file. This file maps host names to IP addresses. In Windows NT 4.0, this file is stored in the \WINNT directory.

hotkey Letters or combinations of keystrokes used in place of mouse clicks as shortcuts to application functions.

HPFS See *High-Performance File System.*

I-J

I/O addresses One of the critical resources used in configuring devices. I/O addresses are used to communicate with devices. Also known as *port.*

I/O bus The electrical connection between the CPU and the I/O devices. There are several types of I/O buses: ISA, EISA, SCSI, VLB, and PCI.

I/O device Any device in, or attached to, a computer that is designed to receive information from, or provide information to, the computer. For example, a printer is an output-only device, while a mouse is an input-only device. Other devices, such as modems, are both input and output devices, transferring data in both directions. Windows NT 4.0 must have a device driver installed to be able to use an I/O device.

ICMP See *Internet Control Message Protocol.*

icon A small bitmap (usually 16×16 pixels or 32×32 pixels) that is associated with an application, file type, or a concept.

IEEE See *Institute of Electrical and Electronic Engineers.*

IETF See *Internet Engineering Task Force.*

IFS See *installable file system.*

IHV See *independent hardware vendor.*

independent hardware vendor (IHV) A manufacturer of computer hardware. Usually used to describe the makers of add-on devices, rather than makers of computer systems.

Industry Standard Architecture (ISA) A computer system that is built on the Industry Standard Architecture is one that adheres to the same design rules and constraints that the IBM PC/AT adhered to.

INF file A file, usually provided by the manufacturer of a device, that provides the information that Windows NT 4.0 Setup needs to set up a device. INF files usually include a list of valid logical configurations for the device, the names of driver files associated with the device, and other information.

INI files Initialization files used by Windows-based applications to store configuration information. Windows NT 4.0 incorporates .INI files into its Registry when upgrading from previous versions of Windows.

installable file system (IFS) A file system that can be installed into the operating system as needed, instead of just at startup time. Windows NT 4.0 can support multiple installable file systems at one time, including the *FAT file system* and *NTFS*, network redirectors, and the *CD-ROM file system (CDFS).*

instance A particular occurrence of an *object*, such as a window, module, named pipe, or DDE session. Each instance has a unique *handle* that distinguishes it from other instances of the same type.

Institute of Electrical and Electronic Engineers (IEEE) An organization that issues standards for electrical and electronic devices.

Integrated Services Digital Network (ISDN) A digital communications method that permits connections of up to 128Kbps. ISDN requires a special adapter for your computer. An ISDN connection is available in most areas of the United States for a reasonable cost.

internal command Commands that are built in to the cmd.exe file.

International Organization for Standardization (ISO) The organization that produces many of the world's standards. Open Systems Interconnect (OSI) is only one of many areas standardized by the ISO.

International Telephone and Telegraph Consultative Committee (CCITT) International organization that creates and publishes telecommunications standards, including X.400. The initials CCITT actually stand for the real name of the organization, which is Comité Consultatif International Téléphonique et Télégraphique in French.

Internet The worldwide interconnected wide-area network, based on the TCP/IP protocol suite.

Internet Control Message Protocol (ICMP) A required protocol in the TCP/IP protocol suite. It allows two nodes on an IP network to share IP status and error information. ICMP is used by the ping utility.

Internet Engineering Task Force (IETF) A consortium that introduces procedures for new technology on the Internet. IETF specifications are released in documents called Requests for Comments (RFCs).

Internet group names A name known by DNS servers that includes a list of the specific addresses of systems that have registered the name.

Internet protocol (IP) The Network layer protocol of TCP/IP, responsible for addressing and sending TCP packets over the network.

interprocess communications (IPC) A set of mechanisms used by applications to communicate and share data.

interrupt An event that disrupts normal processing by the CPU, and results in the transfer of control to an interrupt handler. Both hardware devices and software can issue interrupts—software executes an INT instruction, while hardware devices signal the CPU by using one of the *interrupt request lines (IRQ)* to the processor.

interrupt request level (IRQL) Interrupts are ranked by priority. Interrupts can be masked (ignored), with the exception of a motherboard-generated Non-Maskable interrupt.

interrupt request lines (IRQ) Hardware lines on the CPU that devices use to send signals to cause an interrupt. Normally, only one device is attached to any particular IRQ line.

IP See *Internet protocol.*

IP address Used to identify a node on a network and to specify routing information on an internetwork. Each node on the internetwork must be assigned a unique IP address, which is made up of the network ID, plus a unique host ID assigned by the network administrator. The subnet mask is used to separate an IP address into the host ID and network ID. In Windows NT 4.0, you can either assign an IP address manually, or automatically by using DHCP.

IP router A system connected to multiple physical TCP/IP networks that can route or deliver IP packets between the networks. See also *gateway*.

IPC See *interprocess communications.*

IPX/SPX Internetworking Packet eXchange/Sequenced Packet eXchange. Transport protocols used in Novell NetWare networks. Windows NT 4.0 includes the Microsoft IPX/SPX-compatible transport protocol (NWLINK).

IRQ See *interrupt request level.*

IRQL See *interrupt request lines.*

ISA See *Industry Standard Architecture.*

ISDN See *Integrated Services Digital Network.*

ISO See *International Organization for Standardization.*

ISO Development Environment (ISODE) A research tool developed to study the upper layer of OSI. Academic and some commercial ISO products are based on this framework.

ISODE See *ISO Development Environment.*

K

K Standard abbreviation for kilobyte; equals 1,024 bytes.

Kbps Kilobits per second

kernel The Windows NT 4.0 core component responsible for implementing the basic operating system functions of Windows NT 4.0, including virtual memory management, thread scheduling, and File I/O services.

L

LAN See *local area network.*

legacy Hardware and device cards that don't conform to the Plug and Play standard.

link A connection at the LLC layer that is uniquely defined by the adapter's address and the destination service access point (DSAP). Also, a connection between two objects, or a reference to an object that is linked to another.

list box In a dialog box, a box that lists available choices. For example, a list of all files in a directory. If all the choices do not fit in the list box, there is a scroll bar.

LLC See *logical link control.*

LMHOSTS file A local text file that maps IP addresses to the computer names of Windows networking computers. In Windows NT 4.0, LMHOSTS is stored in the WINNT directory. (LMHOSTS stands for Lan Manager Hosts.)

local area network (LAN) A computer network confined to a single building or campus.

local printer A printer that is directly connected to one of the ports on your computer, as opposed to a network printer.

localization The process of adapting software for different countries, languages, or cultures.

logical drive A division of an extended partition on a hard disk, accessed by using a drive letter.

logical link control (LLC) One of the two sublayers of the Data Link layer of the OSI reference model, as defined by the IEEE 802 standards. See "Logical Link Control (LLC) Sublayer" in Chapter 15 for more information.

login The process by which a user is identified to the computer in a Novell NetWare network.

logon The process by which a user is identified to the computer in a Microsoft network.

logon script In Microsoft networking, a batch file that runs automatically when a user logs in to a Windows NT Server. Novell networking also uses logon scripts, but they are not batch files.

M

M Standard abbreviation for megabyte, or 1,024 kilobytes.

MAC See *media access control.*

MAC address The address for a device as it is identified at the media access control layer in the network architecture. MAC addresses are usually stored in ROM on the network adapter card, and are unique.

mailslot A form of interprocess communications used to carry messages from an application on one network node to another. Mailslots are one-way.

mailslot client A process that writes a message to a mailslot.

mailslot server A process that creates and owns a mailslot and can read messages from it. See also *process.*

management information base (MIB) A set of objects used by *SNMP* to manage devices. MIB objects represent various types of information about a device.

mandatory user profile This represents a user environment profile that cannot be changed by the user. If the profile is unavailable, the user will be unable to log on to the Windows NT enterprise.

map To translate one value into another.

MAPI See *Messaging Application Programming Interface.*

mapped I/O (or **mapped file I/O**) This is the file I/O that is performed by reading and writing to virtual memory that is backed by a file.

MDI See *multiple document interface.*

media access control (MAC) The lower of the two sublayers of the data-link layer in the IEEE 802 network model.

Media Control Interface (MCI) High-level control software that provides a device-independent interface to multimedia devices and media files. MCI includes a command-message interface and a command-string interface.

memory A temporary storage area for information and applications.

memory object A number of bytes allocated from the heap.

message A structure or set of parameters used for communicating information or a request. Every event that happens in the system causes a message to be sent. Messages can be passed between the operating system and an application, different applications, threads within an application, and windows within an application.

message loop A program loop that retrieves messages from a thread's message queue and then dispatches them.

Messaging Application Program Interface (MAPI) A set of calls used to add mail-enabled features to other Windows-based applications. One of the WOSA (Windows Open Systems Architecture) technologies.

metafile A collection of structures that stores a picture in a device-independent format. (There are two metafile formats—the enhanced format and the Windows format.)

MIB See *management information base.*

Microsoft Disk Operating System (MS-DOS) The dominant operating system for personal computers from the introduction of the IBM Personal Computer, until the introduction of Windows 95 and Windows NT 4.0.

MIDI See *Musical Instrument Digital Interface.*

minidriver The part of the device driver that is written by the hardware manufacturer and that provides device-specific functionality.

MS-DOS See *Microsoft Disk Operating System.*

MS-DOS-based application An application designed to run under MS-DOS. Windows NT 4.0 supports most MS-DOS-based applications, except those that communicate directly to hardware devices.

Multiple Document Interface (MDI) A specification that defines the standard user interface for Windows-based applications. An MDI application enables the user to work with more than one document at the same time. Microsoft Word is an example of an MDI application. Each of the documents is displayed in a separate window inside the application's main window.

multitasking The process by which an operating system creates the illusion that many tasks are executing simultaneously on a single processor. See also *cooperative multitasking* and *preemptive multitasking.*

multithreading The capability of a process to have multiple, simultaneous paths of execution (*threads*).

Musical Instrument Digital Interface (MIDI) A standard protocol for communication between musical instruments and computers.

N

name registration The way a computer registers its unique name with a name server on the network, such as a *WINS* server.

name resolution The process used on the network to determine the address of a computer by using its name.

named pipe A one-way or two-way pipe used for communications between a server process and one or more client processes. A server process specifies a name when it creates one or more instances of a named pipe. Each instance of the pipe can be connected to a client. Microsoft SQL Server clients use named pipes to communicate with the SQL Server.

NBF transport protocol NetBEUI frame protocol. A descendant of the NetBEUI protocol, which is a transport layer protocol, not the programming interface NetBIOS.

NCB See *network control block.*

NDIS See *network device interface specification.*

NetBEUI transport NetBIOS (Network Basic Input/Output System) Extended User Interface. A transport protocol designed for use on small subnets. It is not routable, but it is fast.

NetBIOS interface A programming interface that allows I/O requests to be sent to, and received from, a remote computer. It hides networking hardware from applications.

NetBIOS over TCP/IP The networking module that provides the functionality to support NetBIOS name registration and resolution across a TCP/IP network.

network A group of computers and other devices that can interact by means of a shared communications link.

network adapter driver Software that implements the lower layers of a network, providing a standard interface to the network card.

network basic input/output system (NetBIOS) A software interface for network communication. See *NetBIOS interface.*

network control block (NCB) A memory structure used to communicate with the NetBIOS interface.

Network DDE DSDM service The Network DDE DSDM (DDE share database manager) service manages shared DDE conversations. It is used by the *Network DDE service.*

Network DDE service The Network DDE (dynamic data exchange) service provides a network transport and security for DDE conversations. Network DDE is supported in Windows NT 4.0 for backwards compatibility, as most of its functions are superseded by OLE.

network device driver Software that coordinates communication between the network adapter card and the computer's hardware and other software, controlling the physical function of the network adapter cards.

network device interface specification (NDIS) In Windows networking, the interface for network adapter drivers. All transport drivers call the NDIS interface to access network adapter cards.

network directory See *shared directory.*

Network File System (NFS) A service for distributed computing systems that provides a distributed file system, eliminating the need for keeping multiple copies of files on separate computers. Usually used in connection with UNIX computers.

network ID The portion of the IP address that identifies a group of computers and devices located on the same logical network. Separated from the Host ID by using the *subnet mask*.

Network Information Service (NIS) A service for distributed computing systems that provides a distributed database system for common configuration files.

network interface card (NIC) An adapter card that connects a computer to a network.

network operating system (NOS) The operating system used on network servers, such as Windows NT Server or Novell NetWare.

network provider The Windows NT 4.0 component that allows Windows NT 4.0 to communicate with the network. Windows NT 4.0 includes providers for Microsoft networks and for Novell NetWare networks. Other network vendors may supply providers for their networks.

network transport This can be either a particular layer of the OSI Reference Model between the network layer and the session layer, or the protocol used between this layer on two different computers on a network.

network-interface printers Printers with built-in network cards, such as Hewlett-Packard laser printers equipped with Jet Direct cards. The advantage of network-interface printers is that they can be located anywhere on the network.

New Technology File System (NTFS) The native file system used by Windows NT 4.0 that supplies file and directory security, sector sparing, compression, and other performance characteristics.

NIC See *network interface card.*

NIS See *Network Information Service.*

NOS See *network operating system.*

NTFS See *Windows NT file system.*

O

object A particular instance of a class. Most of the internal data structures in Windows NT 4.0 are objects.

object linking and embedding (OLE) The specification that details the implementation of Windows objects, and the interprocess communication that supports them.

OCR See *Optical Character Recognition.*

OEM See *original equipment manufacturer.*

OLE See *object linking and embedding.*

Open Systems Interconnect (OSI) The networking architecture reference model created by the ISO.

operating system (OS) The software that provides an interface between a user or application and the computer hardware. Operating system services usually include memory and resource management, I/O services, and file handling. Examples include Windows NT 4.0, Windows NT, and UNIX.

Optical Character Recognition (OCR) A technology that is used to generate editable text from a graphic image.

original equipment manufacturer (OEM) Software that is sold by Microsoft to OEMs includes only the operating system versions that are preloaded on computers before they are sold.

OS See *operating system.*

OSI See *Open Systems Interconnect.*

P-Q

PAB See *personal address book.*

packet A transmission unit of fixed maximum size that consists of binary information representing both data-addressing information and error-correction information, created by the data-link layer.

page A unit of memory used by the system in managing memory. The size of a page is computer-dependent (the Intel 486 computer, and therefore, Windows NT 4.0, uses 4K pages).

page map An internal data structure used by the system to keep track of the mapping between the pages in a process's virtual address space and the corresponding pages in physical memory.

paged pool The portion of system memory that can be paged to disk.

paging file A storage file (PAGEFILE.SYS) that the system uses to hold pages of memory that are swapped out of RAM. Also known as a swap file.

parity Refers to an error-checking procedure in which the number of 1s must always be the same (either even or odd) for each group of bits transmitted without error. Also used in the main RAM system of a computer to verify the validity of data contained in RAM.

partition A partition is a portion of a physical disk that functions as though it is a physically separate unit. See also *system partition.*

partition table The partition table contains entries showing the start and end point of each of the primary partitions on the disk. The partition table can hold four entries.

password A security measure used to restrict access to computer systems. A password is a unique string of characters that must be provided before a logon or an access is authorized.

path The location of a file or directory. The path describes the location in relation to either the root directory or the current directory; for example, C:\WINNT\System32. Also, a graphic object that represents one or more shapes.

PCI See *Peripheral Component Interconnect.*

PCMCIA See *Personal Computer Memory Card International Association.*

performance monitoring The process of determining the system resources an application uses, such as processor time and memory. Done with the Windows NT 4.0 Performance Monitor.

Peripheral Component Interconnect (PCI) The local bus being promoted as the successor to VL. This type of device is used in most Intel Pentium computers and in the Apple PowerPC Macintosh.

persistent connection A network connection that is restored automatically when the user logs on. In Windows NT 4.0, persistent connections are created by selecting the Reconnect at Logon check box.

personal address book (PAB) One of the information services provided with the Microsoft Exchange client that is included with Windows NT 4.0. It is used to store the name and e-mail addresses of people with whom you correspond.

Personal Computer Memory Card International Association (PCMCIA) The industry association of manufacturers of credit-card sized adapter cards (PC cards).

PIF See *program information file.*

pixel Short for picture element, a dot that represents the smallest graphic unit of measurement on a screen. The actual size of a pixel is screen-dependent, and varies according to the size of the screen and the resolution being used. (Also known as pel.)

platform The hardware and software required for an application to run.

Plug and Play A computer-industry specification, intended to ease the process of configuring hardware.

Plug and Play BIOS A BIOS with responsibility for configuring Plug and Play cards and system-board devices during system power-up, it provides runtime configuration services for system board devices after startup.

p-node A NetBIOS implementation that uses point-to-point communications with a name server to resolve names as IP addresses.

Point-to-Point protocol (PPP) The industry standard that is implemented in dial-up networking. PPP is a line protocol used to connect to remote networking services, including Internet Service Providers (ISPs). Prior to the introduction of PPP, another line protocol, *SLIP*, was used.

pointer The arrow-shaped cursor on the screen that follows the movement of a mouse (or other pointing device) and indicates which area of the screen will be affected when you press the mouse button. The pointer may change shape during certain tasks.

port The socket to which you connect the cable for a peripheral device. See also *I/O address*.

port ID The method TCP and UDP use to specify which application that is running on the system is sending or receiving the data.

Postoffice The message store used by Microsoft Mail to hold the mail messages. It exists only as a structure of directories on disk, and does not contain any active components.

PostScript A page-description language, developed by Adobe Systems, Inc., that offers flexible font capability and high-quality graphics. PostScript uses English-like commands to control page layout and to load and scale fonts.

PPP See *Point-to-Point protocol.*

preemptive multitasking A multitasking technique that breaks up time into timeslices, during which the operating system allows a particular program thread to run. The operating system can interrupt any running thread at any time. Preemptive multitasking usually results in the best use of CPU time, and overall better-perceived throughput. See also *cooperative multitasking.*

primary partition A primary partition is a portion of a physical disk that can be marked for use by an operating system. There can be up to four primary partitions (or up to three, if there is an extended partition) per physical disk. A primary partition cannot be sub-partitioned.

print device Refers to the actual hardware device that produces printed output.

print monitor Keeps track of printers and print devices. Responsible for transferring information from the print driver to the printing device, including any necessary flow control.

print provider A software component that allows the client to print to a network printer. Windows NT 4.0 includes print providers for Microsoft networks and Novell networks.

printer driver The component that translates GDI objects into printer commands.

printer fonts Fonts that are built into your printer.

priority class A process priority category (high, normal, or idle) used to determine the scheduling priorities of a process's threads. Each priority class has five levels. See also *thread.*

private memory Memory owned by a process, and not accessible by other processes.

privileged instruction Processor-privileged instructions have access to system memory and the hardware. Privileged instructions can be executed only by Ring 0 components.

process The virtual address space, code, data, and other operating system resources, such as files, pipes, and synchronization objects that make up an executing application. In addition to resources, a process contains at least one thread that executes the process's code.

profile A set of data describing a particular configuration of a computer. This information can describe a user's preferences (user profile) or the hardware configuration. Profiles are usually stored in the Registry; for example, the key HKEY_USERS contains the profiles for the various users of the computer.

program file A file that starts an application or program. A program file has an .EXE, .PIF, .COM, or .BAT file name extension.

program information file (PIF) Windows NT 4.0 stores information about how to configure the VM for running MS-DOS applications in PIF files.

Programmable Read-Only Memory (PROM) A type of integrated circuit, usually used to store a computer's BIOS. PROM chips, once programmed, can only be read from, not written to.

PROM See *Programmable Read-Only Memory.*

properties In Windows NT 4.0, the dialog boxes that are used to configure a particular object.

protocol A set of rules and conventions by which two computers pass messages across a network. Protocols are used between instances of a particular layer on each computer. Windows NT 4.0 includes NetBEUI, TCP/IP, and IPX/SPX-compatible protocols. See *communications protocol.*

provider The component that allows Windows NT 4.0 to communicate with the network. Windows NT 4.0 includes providers for Microsoft and Novell networks.

R

RAM See *random access memory.*

random access memory (RAM) The RAM memory in a computer is the computer's main memory, where programs and data are stored while the program is running. Information stored in RAM is lost when the computer is turned off.

read-only A device, document, or file is read-only if changes to it are not permitted.

read-write A device, document, or file is read-write if changes can be made to it.

reboot To restart a computer. To reboot a Windows NT 4.0 computer, click the Start Button, choose Shutdown, and then choose Restart Your Computer.

redirector The networking component that intercepts file I/O requests and translates them into network requests. Redirectors (also called network clients) are implemented as installable file-system drivers in Windows NT 4.0.

REG_BINARY A data type for Registry value entries that designates binary data.

REG_DWORD A data type for Registry value entries that designates data represented by a number that is 4 bytes long.

REG_SZ A data type for Registry value entries that designates a data string that usually represents human-readable text.

Registry Windows NT 4.0's and Windows NT's binary system-configuration database.

Registry Editor (REGEDT32.EXE) A utility supplied with Windows NT 4.0 that enables the user to view and edit Registry keys and values.

Registry key A Registry entry that can contain other Registry entries.

remote access service (RAS) A Windows NT Executive service that provides remote networking access to the Windows NT Enterprise for telecommuters, remote users system administrators, and home users. See also *Dial-up Networking.*

remote administration The process of administrating one computer from another computer across a network.

remote initiation program load (RIPL) A technique that allows a workstation to boot by using an image file on a network server rather than a disk.

remote procedure call (RPC) An industry-standard method of interprocess communication across a network. Used by many administration tools.

Requests for Comments (RFCs) The official documents of the Internet Engineering Task Force that specify the details for protocols that are included in the TCP/IP family.

requirements The conceptual design and functional description of a software product, and any associated materials. Requirements describe the features, user interface, documentation, and other functions the product provides.

resource Windows resources include icons, cursors, menus, dialog boxes, bitmaps, fonts, keyboard-accelerator tables, message-table entries, string-table entries, version data, and user-defined data. The resources used by an application are either part of the system, or private resources stored in the application's program file. Also, a part of a computer system that can be assigned to a running process, such as a disk drive or memory segment.

RFCs See *Requests for Comments.*

RIP See *Routing Information Protocol.*

RIPL See *remote initiation program load.*

root directory See *directory tree.*

router A computer with two or more network adapters, each attached to a different subnet. The router forwards packets on a subnet to the subnet that they are addressed to.

routing The process of forwarding packets until they reach their destination.

Routing Information Protocol (RIP) A protocol that supports dynamic routing. Used between routers.

RPC See *remote procedure call.*

RPC server The program or computer that processes remote procedure calls from a client.

S

SAM Database The Registry database that contains the user and group account information, as well as user account policies. It is managed by the User Manager or User Manager for Domains utility.

screen buffer A memory buffer that holds a representation of an MS-DOS VM's logical screen.

screen saver Pictures or patterns that appear on your screen when your computer has not been used for a certain amount of time. Originally, screen savers were intended to protect the monitor from damage, but modern screen savers are used mostly for their entertainment value.

scroll To move through text or graphics (up, down, left, or right) to see parts of the file that are not currently displayed on the screen.

scroll arrow An arrow on each end of a scroll bar that is used to scroll through the contents of the window or list box.

scroll bar A bar that appears at the right and bottom edge of a window or list box whose contents are not completely visible. The scroll bar consists of two scroll arrows and a scroll box, which you use to scroll through the contents.

scroll box In a scroll bar, a small box that shows where the information currently visible is located, relative to the contents of the entire window.

SCSI See *Small Computer System Interface.*

Security ID (SID) The unique, randomly generated alphanumeric identifier assigned by Windows NT when a new user, group, trust or other security object is created.

sequence numbers Used by a receiving node to properly order packets.

Serial Line Internet Protocol (SLIP) The predecessor to PPP, SLIP is a line protocol supporting TCP/IP over a modem connection. SLIP support is provided for Windows NT 4.0. See also *Point-to-Point protocol.*

server A computer or application that provides shared resources to clients across a network. Resources include files and directories, printers, fax modems, and network database services. See also *client.*

server message block (SMB) A block of data that contains a work request from a workstation to a server, or the response from the server to the workstation. SMBs are used for all network communications in a Microsoft network.

server service An Executive Service that makes resources available to the workgroup or domain for file, print, and other RPC services.

service A process that performs a specific system function and often provides an application programming interface (API) for other processes to call. Windows NT 4.0 services include Computer Browser, Server, and Workstation.

session A layer of the OSI reference model that performs name recognition and the functions needed to enable two applications to communicate over the network. Also, a communication channel established by the session layer.

share In Microsoft networking, the process of making resources, such as directories and printers, available for network users.

share name The name by which a shared resource is accessed on the network.

shared directory A directory that is shared so that network users can connect to it.

shared memory Memory that two or more processes can read from and write to.

shared network directory See *shared directory.*

shared resource Any device, data, or program that is used by more than one other device or program. Windows NT 4.0 can share directories and printers.

sharepoint A shared network resource, or the name that one is known by.

shell The part of an operating system with which the user interacts. The Windows NT 4.0 shell is Windows Explorer.

shortcut key a combination of keys that result in the execution of a program, or selection of an option, without going through a menu.

shut down The process of properly terminating all running programs, flushing caches, and preparing the system to be powered off.

signaled One of the possible states of a mutex semaphore.

SIMM See *Single In-Line Memory Module.*

Simple Mail Transfer Protocol (SMTP) The application layer protocol that supports messaging functions over the Internet

Simple Network Management Protocol (SNMP) A standard protocol for the management of network components. Windows NT 4.0 includes an SNMP agent.

Single In-Line Memory Module (SIMM) One of the types of RAM chips.

SLIP See *Serial Line Internet Protocol.*

Small Computer System Interface (SCSI) Pronounced "scuzzy," a standard for connecting multiple devices to a computer system. SCSI devices are connected together in a daisy chain, which can have up to seven devices (plus a controller) on it.

SMB See *server message block.*

SMTP See *Simple Mail Transfer Protocol.*

SNMP See *Simple Network Management Protocol.*

socket A channel used for incoming and outgoing data that is defined by the Windows Sockets API. Usually used with TCP/IP.

socket services The protected-mode VxD that manages PCMCIA sockets adapter hardware. It provides a protected-mode PCMCIA Socket Services 2.x interface for use by Card Services. A socket services driver is required for each socket adapter.

source directory The directory from which files in a copy or move operation start out.

spooler A scheduler for the printing process. It coordinates activity among other components of the print model and schedules all print jobs arriving at the print server.

static VxD A VxD that is loaded at system startup.

string A sequence of characters that represents human-readable text.

subdirectory A directory within a directory.

subkey A Registry key contained within another Registry key. All Registry keys are subkeys, except for the six top-level keys.

subnet On the Internet, any lower network that is part of the logical network identified by the network ID.

subnet mask A 32-bit value that is used to distinguish the network ID portion of the IP address from the host ID.

swap file A special file on your hard disk that is used to hold memory pages that are swapped out of RAM. Also called a paging file.

syntax The order in which you must type a command, and the elements that follow the command.

system directory The directory that contains the Windows DLLs and drivers. Usually c:windows\system.

system disk A disk that contains the files necessary to start an operating system.

system partition The volume that contains the hardware-specific files needed to load Windows NT 4.0.

T

TAPI See *Telephony Application Program Interface.*

TCP See *Transmission Control Protocol.*

TCP/IP transport *Transmission Control Protocol/Internet Protocol.* The primary wide area network (WAN) transport protocol used on the worldwide Internet, which is a worldwide internetwork of universities, research laboratories, government and military installations, organizations, and corporations. TCP/IP includes standards for how computers communicate, conventions for connecting networks and routing traffic, as well as specifications for utilities.

TDI See *transport driver interface.*

Telephony Application Program Interface (TAPI) An API that enables applications to control modems and telephony equipment in a device-independent manner. TAPI routes application function calls to the appropriate "Service Provider" DLL for a modem.

telnet The application layer protocol that provides virtual terminal service on TCP/IP networks.

Terminate and Stay-Resident (TSR) A technique used by MS-DOS applications that enables more than one program to be loaded at a time.

text file A file containing only ASCII letters, numbers, and symbols, without any formatting information except for carriage return/linefeeds.

thread The basic entity to which the operating system allocates CPU time. A thread can execute any part of the application's code, including a part currently being executed by another thread (re-entrancy). Threads cannot own resources; instead, they use the resources of the process to which they belong.

thread local storage A storage method in which an index can be used by multiple threads of the same process to store and retrieve a different value for each thread. See also *thread.*

thunking The transformation between 16-bit and 32-bit formats, which is carried out by a separate layer in the VDM.

time-out If a device is not performing a task, the amount of time the computer should wait before detecting it as an error.

toolbar A frame containing a series of shortcut buttons that provides quick access to commands, usually located below the menu bar, although many applications provide "dockable" toolbars that may be moved to different locations on the screen.

Transmission Control Protocol (TCP) A connection-based protocol that is responsible for breaking data into packets, which the IP protocol then sends over the network. This protocol provides a reliable, sequenced communication stream for internetwork communication.

Transmission Control Protocol/Internet Protocol (TCP/IP) The primary wide area network used on the worldwide Internet, which is a worldwide internetwork of universities, research laboratories, military installations, organizations, and corporations. TCP/IP includes standards for how computers communicate, conventions for connecting networks and routing traffic, as well as specifications for utilities.

transport driver interface (TDI) The interface between the session layer and the network layer, used by network redirectors and servers to send network-bound requests to network transport drivers.

transport protocol Defines how data should be presented to the next receiving layer in the networking model, and packages the data accordingly. It passes data to the network adapter-card driver through the NDIS Interface, and to the redirector through the Transport Driver Interface.

TrueType fonts Fonts that are scalable, and that are sometimes generated as bitmaps or soft fonts, depending on the capabilities of your printer. TrueType fonts can be sized to any height, and they print exactly as they appear on the screen. They are stored as a collection of line and curve commands, together with a collection of hints that are used to adjust the shapes when the font is scaled.

trust relationship A security relationship between two domains, in which the resource domain "trusts" the user of a trusted account domain to use its resources. Users and groups that form a trusted domain can be given access permissions to resources in a trusting domain.

TSR See *Terminate and Stay-Resident.*

U

UDP See *user datagram protocol.*

UNC See *universal naming convention.*

Unimodem The universal modem driver used by TAPI to communicate with modems. It uses modem-description files to control its interaction with VCOMM.

uninterruptible power supply (UPS) A battery-operated power supply connected to a computer to keep the system running during a power failure.

universal naming convention (UNC) Naming convention, including a server name and share name, used to give a unique name to files on a network. The format is as follows: \\servername\sharename\path\filename.

UPS See *uninterruptible power supply.*

UPS service A software component that monitors an uninterruptible power supply, and shuts the computer down gracefully when line power has failed, and the UPS battery is running down.

usability A determination of how well users can accomplish tasks by using a software product. Usability considers the characteristics of a product, such as software, manuals, tutorials, help, and so on.

user account Refers to all the information that identifies a user to Windows NT 4.0, including user name and password, group membership, and rights and permissions.

user datagram protocol (UDP) The transport protocol offering a connectionless-mode transport service in the Internet suite of protocols. See also *Transport Control Protocol.*

user name A unique name identifying a user account in Windows NT 4.0. User names must be unique, and cannot be the same as another username, workgroup name, or domain name.

V

value entry A parameter under a key or subkey in the Registry. A value entry has three components: name, type, and value. The value component can be a string, binary data, or a DWORD.

VDM See *virtual DOS machine.*

VFAT See *virtual file allocation table.*

virtual DOS machine (VDM) A virtual machine provides a complete MS-DOS environment and a character-based window in which to run an MS-DOS based application. Every MS-DOS application runs in its own VDM.

virtual file allocation table (VFAT) See *file allocation table.*

virtual machine (VM) An environment created by the operating system in memory. By using virtual machines, the application developer can write programs that behave as though they own the entire computer. This leaves the job of sorting out which application is receiving keyboard input at the moment to Windows NT 4.0.

virtual memory The technique by which Windows NT 4.0 uses hard disk space to increase the amount of memory available for running programs.

visual editing The ability to edit an embedded object in place, without opening it into its own window. Implemented by OLE.

VL VESA local-bus standard for a bus that enables high-speed connections to peripherals, which preceded the PCI specification. Due to limitations in the specification, usually used only to connect video adapters into the system.

VM See *virtual machine.*

volume A partition that has been formatted for use by the file system.

VxD Virtual device driver. The *x* represents the type of device—for example, a virtual device driver for a display is a VDD and a virtual device driver for a printer is a VPD.

W

wildcard A character that is used to represent one or more characters, such as in a file specification. The question mark (?) wildcard can be used to represent any single character, and the asterisk (*) wildcard can be used to represent any character or group of characters that might match that position in other file names.

Win32 API The 32-bit application-programming interface used to write 32-bit Windows-based applications. It provides access to the operating system and other functions.

window handle A 32-bit value that uniquely identifies a window to Windows NT 4.0.

window name A text string that identifies a window for the user.

Windows Internet Name Service (WINS) A name-resolution service that resolves Windows networking computer names to IP addresses in a routed environment. A WINS server handles name registrations, queries, and releases.

Windows NT The portable, secure, 32-bit preemptive-multitasking member of the Microsoft Windows Operating system family. Windows NT Server provides centralized management and security, advanced fault tolerance, and additional connectivity. Windows NT Workstation provides operating system and networking functionality for computers without centralized management.

Windows NT File System (NTFS) The native file system used by Windows NT. Windows NT 4.0 can detect, but not use, NTFS partitions.

WINS See *Windows Internet Name Service.*

wizard A Windows NT 4.0 tool that asks you questions, and performs a system action according to your answers. For example, you can use the Add Printer Wizard to add new printer drivers or connect to an existing network printer.

workgroup A collection of computers that are grouped for viewing purposes or resource sharing, but that do not share security information. Each workgroup is identified by a unique name. See also *domain.*

workstation service This is the Windows NT computer's redirector. It redirects requests for network resources to the appropriate protocol and network card for access to the server computer.

WYSIWYG Stands for "What You See Is What You Get."

X-Z

X.121 The addressing format used by X.25 base networks.

X.25 A connection-oriented network facility.

X.400 An international messaging standard that is used in electronic mail systems.

x86-based computer A computer using a microprocessor equivalent to an Intel 80386 or higher chip.

XModem/CRC A communications protocol for transmitting binary files that uses a cyclic redundancy check (CRC) to detect any transmission errors. Both computers must be set to transmit and receive eight data bits per character.

XMS See *Extended Memory Specification.*

Certification Checklist

In addition to a resource like this book, this list of tasks tells you what you need to know to get on with the certification process.

Get Started

Once you have decided to start the certification process, you should use the following list as a guideline for getting started:

1. Get the Microsoft Roadmap to Education and Certification. (See "The Certification Roadmap" sidebar at the end of this appendix.)
2. Use the Roadmap Planning Wizard to determine *your* certification path.

Get Prepared

Getting started is one thing, but getting prepared to take the certification exam is a rather difficult process. The following guidelines will help you prepare for the exam:

1. Use the training materials listed in the Planning Wizard:
   - Microsoft Online Institute (MOLI). (See "The Microsoft Online Training Institute," in Appendix C.)
   - Self-Paced Training (see "Self-Paced Training," in Appendix C).
   - Additional study materials listed in the Roadmap.
2. Review the Exam Prep Guide on the Roadmap.
3. Gain experience with Windows NT 4.0.

Get Certified

Call Sylvan Prometric at 1-800-755-EXAM to schedule your exam at a location near you. (See "How Do I Register for the Exam?" in Appendix C; and Appendix D, "Testing Tips.")

Get Benefits

Microsoft will send your certification kit approximately two to four weeks after passing the exam. This kit qualifies you to become a Microsoft Certified Professional. (See "Benefits Up Close and Personal," in the Introduction to this book.)

The Certification Roadmap

The Microsoft Roadmap to Education and Certification is an easy-to-use Windows-based application that includes all the information you need to plan a successful training and certification strategy. The roadmap:

- Provides comprehensive information on the requirements for Microsoft Certified Professional certifications, with detailed exam topic outlines and preparation guidelines.
- Includes detailed outlines and prerequisites for Microsoft courses that are related to specific certification exams, helping you determine which courses teach the skills you need to meet your certification goals.
- Includes information on related Microsoft products and services.
- Helps you create a personal training and certification plan and print a to-do list of required certification activities.

You can request the Roadmap from Microsoft. In the U.S. and Canada, call 1-800-636-7544. Outside the U.S. and Canada, contact your local Microsoft office.

Or you can download it at the following online addresses:

- The Internet: **www.microsoft.com/train_cert/**
- The Microsoft Network (MSN): Go To MOLI, Advising Building, E&C Roadmap.
- Microsoft TechNet: Search for Roadmap and install from the built-in setup link.

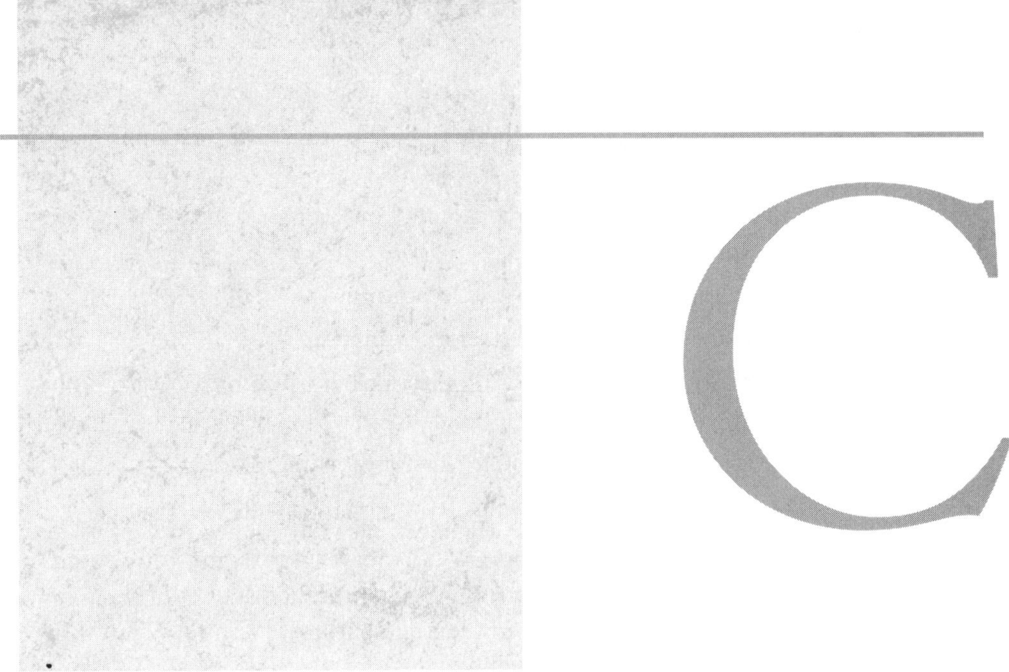

How Do I Get There from Here?

Becoming certified requires a certain level of commitment. The information in this appendix will answer some of the questions you may have about the certification process.

What Will I Be Tested On?

You should be able to apply your knowledge and experience with Windows NT 4.0 to perform the following tasks:

- Plan for, install, and troubleshoot Windows NT Server 4.0.
- Install software or hardware and run applications.
- Answer "how-to" questions from users.
- Tune and optimize your Windows NT Server 4.0.

- Customize the Windows NT Server 4.0 system and user environments.
- Install, manage, and configure the network components of Windows NT Server 4.0.
- Create and manage domain user accounts.
- Create, manage, and secure network resources.
- Troubleshoot systems and solve network hardware or software problems.
- Recommend software products, versions, or upgrades.
- Collect requests for additional software features and functions.

To successfully complete the Windows NT Server 4.0 Exam, you should be able to apply, according to Microsoft, "a comprehensive set of skills to the tasks necessary to administer, implement, and troubleshoot Microsoft Windows NT Server 4.0."

Analysis Is Good, but Synthesis Is Harder

Microsoft Certified Professional exams test for specific cognitive skills needed for the job functions being tested. Educational theorists postulate a hierarchy of cognitive levels, ranging from most basic (knowledge) up to the most difficult (evaluation), and a set of skills associated with each level:

- *Knowledge* is the lowest cognitive level at which you can identify, define, locate, recall, state, match, arrange, label, outline, and recognize items, situations, and concepts. Questions that ask for definitions or recitation of lists of characteristics test at this level.
- *Comprehension*, the level built immediately upon knowledge, requires that you translate, distinguish between, give examples, discuss, draw conclusions, estimate, explain, indicate, and paraphrase, rather than simply play back answers learned by rote.
- *Application* is the level at which hands-on activities come into play. Questions at this level ask you to apply, calculate, solve, plot, choose, demonstrate, change, interpret, operate, and design a procedure.
- *Analysis*, one of the top three levels, requires a thorough grounding in the skills required at the lower levels. You operate at this level when you analyze, state conclusions, detect logic errors, compare and contrast, break down, make an inference from, map one situation or problem to another, diagnose, diagram, or discriminate.

- *Synthesis* (which is harder than analysis) requires some creativity and the ability to rebuild and reintegrate what may have been disassembled during analysis. This level requires you to construct a table or graph, design, formulate, integrate, generalize, predict, arrange, propose, tell in your own words, or show the relationship between.
- *Evaluation*, the highest cognitive level, is based on all the skills accumulated at the lower levels. At this level, you assess, apply standards, decide, indicate fallacies, weigh, show the relationship between, summarize, decide, look at situations and tell what is likely to occur, or make a judgment.

Exam Objectives

The following list of objectives defines the specific skills Microsoft wants the exam to measure. As you review the list, you can see the level at which the Windows NT Server 4.0 Exam tests your knowledge and ability to implement, maintain, and troubleshoot the operating system. When an objective or item on the exam includes a verb or verb phrase associated with a given cognitive level (see the preceding section, "Analysis Is Good, but Synthesis Is Harder"), it is asking you to perform at that cognitive level.

For example, the exam objective "Installing Windows NT Server 4.0 to perform various server roles" asks you to perform at the Analysis level because it asks you to make a determination between three server roles—primary domain controller, backup domain controller, and member server. It's a good idea to be prepared to be tested at the Analysis level or higher for each objective.

You should review the following objectives and be able to apply the listed skills to the tasks described earlier in the section "What Will I Be Tested On?"

Planning

You will be tested for the following planning skills:

- Planning the implementation of a directory services architecture, considering appropriate domain models, single logon access, and resource access across domains.
- Configure disk drives for various requirements such as fault tolerance.

- Install and configure protocols as appropriate for the domain including TCP/IP, DHCP, WINS, NWLINK, DLC, and AppleTalk.

Installation and Configuration

You will be tested for your understanding of the installation process, as well as the various methods and tools available to configure the Windows NT system and user environment. Specific topics include:

- Choosing and installing the appropriate server role for Windows NT Server 4.0—for example, primary or secondary domain controller, and member server
- Configuring and binding protocols
- Configuring core services such as Directory Replicator and Computer Browser
- Configuring hard disks to provide redundancy, fault tolerance, and improved performance
- Creating, adding, and configuring printers, including setting up printer pools and setting printer priorities
- Configuring Windows NT Server 4.0 for client support such as Windows NT Workstation, Windows 95, and Macintosh

Managing Resources

You will be tested on your ability to manage disk, file, and print resources, and to create and manage user and group accounts. Specific topics include:

- Managing user and group accounts including user rights, account policies, and auditing changes to the account database
- Creating and managing policies and profiles for local and roaming users, as well as system policies
- Remotely administering servers from Windows 95 and NT Workstation clients
- Managing disk resources through sharing, permissions, file and folder security and auditing

Connectivity

You will be tested for your understanding of Windows NT 4.0 Networking and interoperability issues, including:

- Configuring interoperability among Windows NT Server and Novell NetWare servers through Gateway Services and Migration Tool
- Installing and configuring multiprotocol routing for the Internet, the BOOTP/DHCP Relay Agent, and IPX
- Installing and configuring Internet Information Server and other Internet services including Web services, DNS, and the intranet
- Installing and configuring Remote Access Service including implementing communications access, protocols, and security

Monitoring and Optimization

You will be tested on your ability to track and optimize system performance using a variety of tools. Specific topics include:

- Implementing and using Performance Monitor to measure system performance through the use of baseline measurement object tracking (processor, memory, disk, and network)
- Implementing and using Network Monitor to monitor network traffic through data collection, analysis, and filtering
- Identifying performance bottlenecks
- Optimizing server performance to achieve specific results, such as controlling network traffic and server load balancing

Troubleshooting

You will be tested on your understanding of basic Windows NT 4.0 concepts, processes, and functions, and your ability to choose the correct course of action to resolve problem situations. Specific topics include:

- Choosing the appropriate course of action to take to resolve installation failures
- Choosing the appropriate course of action to take to resolve boot failures

- Choosing the appropriate course of action to take to resolve configuration errors such as backing up and restoring the NT Registry, and editing the Registry
- Choosing the appropriate course of action to take to resolve printing problems
- Choosing the appropriate course of action to take to resolve RAS problems
- Choosing the appropriate course of action to take to resolve connectivity problems
- Choosing the appropriate course of action to take to resolve resource access and permission problems
- Choosing the appropriate course of action to take to resolve fault-tolerance failures such as backup, mirroring, and striping with parity
- Diagnosing and interpreting blue-screen problems, configuring a memory dump, and using Event Viewer (Event Log service)

What Kinds of Questions Can I Expect?

The Windows NT Server 4.0 Certification Exam includes two types of multiple choice item: single-answer and multiple-answer.

Single-Answer Multiple-Choice Item

A *single-answer multiple-choice item* presents a problem and a list of possible answers. You must select the best answer to the given question from a list. Each answer is preceded by an `OptionButton` control.

For example: You will be supporting a group of 10 account executives all running Windows NT Workstation on their computers. Occasionally, each account executive will need to share files with some or all of the other account executives. Two of the account executives have printers that all of them will use. You do not expect the group to grow by any more than five more persons. Which computing model will best meet their needs?

a) The Workgroup Model

b) The Single Domain Enterprise Model

c) The Master Domain Enterprise Model

d) The Complete Trust Enterprise Model

Your response to a single-answer multiple-choice item is scored as either correct (1 or more points) or incorrect (0 points).

The answer to the above question is A, The Workgroup Model.

Multiple-Answer Multiple-Choice Item

A *multiple-answer multiple-choice item* presents a problem and a list of possible answers. You must select the best answer to the given question from a list. The question is often (but not always) followed by a phrase indicating the number of correct answers, such as "Pick two." Each answer is preceded by a `CheckBox` control.

For example: Which of the following is part of the Kernel mode of the Windows NT architecture? (Select three)

a) WIN32 Subsystem

b) HAL

c) Executive Services

d) Device Driver support

Your response to a multiple-answer multiple-choice item is also scored as either correct (1 or more points) or incorrect (0 points). Your response scores all points only if all the correct answers are selected.

The answer to the above question is B, HAL; C, Executive Services; and D, Device Driver support.

How Should I Prepare for the Exam?

The best way to prepare for the Windows NT Server 4.0 Enterprise Certified Exam is to study, learn, and master Windows NT Server 4.0. If you'd like a little more guidance, Microsoft recommends these specific steps:

1. Identify the objectives you'll be tested on. (See "Exam Objectives" earlier in this appendix.)
2. Assess your current mastery of those objectives.
3. Practice tasks and study the areas you haven't mastered.

Following are some tools and techniques, in addition to this book, that may offer a little more help.

Assessment Exams

Microsoft provides self-paced practice, or assessment exams, that you can take at your own computer. *Assessment exams* let you answer questions that are very much like the items in the actual certification exams. Your assessment exam score doesn't necessarily predict what your score will be on the actual exam, but its immediate feedback lets you determine the areas requiring extra study. And the assessment exams offer an additional advantage: They use the same computer-based testing tool as the certification exams, so you don't have to learn how to use the tool on exam day.

An assessment exam exists for almost every certification exam. You can find a complete list of available assessment exams in the Certification Roadmap available from Microsoft.

How Do I Register for the Exam?

Registering for the Windows NT Server 4.0 Enterprise certification exam is simple:

1. Contact Sylvan Prometric at (800) 755-EXAM, with the examination number (70-68), your Social Security number, and credit card ready.
2. Complete the registration procedure by phone. (Your SSN becomes the ID attached to your private file; the credit card takes care of the $100 test fee.) Request contact information for the testing center closest to you.
3. After you receive the registration and payment confirmation letter from Sylvan Prometric, call the testing center to schedule your exam. When you call to schedule, you'll be provided with instructions regarding the appointment, cancellation procedures, ID requirements, and information about the testing center location.

You can verify the number of questions and time allotted for your exam at the time of registration. You can schedule exams up to six weeks in advance, or as late as one working day ahead, but you must take the exam within one year of your payment. To cancel or reschedule your exam, contact Sylvan Prometric at least two working days before your scheduled exam date.

Note At some locations, same-day registration (at least two hours before test time) is available, subject to space availability.

Testing Tips

You've mastered the required tasks to take the exam. After reviewing and re-reviewing the exam objectives, you're confident that you have the skills specified in the exam objectives. You're ready to perform at the highest cognitive level. And it's time to head for the testing center. This appendix covers some tips and tricks to remember.

Before the Test

Make sure you take care of the following items:

- Wear comfortable clothing. You want to focus on the exam, not on a tight shirt collar or pinching pair of shoes.
- Allow plenty of travel time. Get to the testing center 10 or 15 minutes early; nothing's worse than rushing in at the last minute. Give yourself time to relax.
- If you've never been to the testing center before, make a trial run a few days before to make sure that you know the route to the center.

- Carry with you at least two forms of identification, including one photo ID (such as a driver's license or company security ID). You will have to show them before you can take the exam.

Remember that the exams are closed-book. The use of laptop computers, notes, or other printed materials is not permitted during the exam session.

At the test center, you'll be asked to sign in. The test administrator will give you a Testing Center Regulations form that explains the rules that govern the examination. You will be asked to sign the form to indicate that you understand and will comply with its stipulations.

When the administrator shows you to your test computer, make sure that:

- The testing tool starts up and displays the correct exam. If a tutorial for using the instrument is available, you should be allowed time to take it.

Note If you have any special needs, such as reconfiguring the mouse buttons for a left-handed user, you should inquire about them when you register for the exam with Sylvan Prometric. Special configurations are not possible at all sites, so you should not assume that you will be permitted to make any modifications to the equipment setup and configuration. Site administrators are *not* permitted to make modifications without prior instructions from Sylvan.

- You have a supply of scratch paper for use during the exam. (The administrator collects all scratch paper and notes made during the exam before your leave the center.) Some centers are now providing you with a wipe-off board and magic marker to use instead of paper. You are not permitted to make any kind of notes to take with you, due to exam security.
- Some exams may include additional materials or exhibits. If any exhibits are required for your exam, the test administrator will provide you with them before you begin the exam and collect them from you at the end of the exam.
- The administrator tells you what to do when you complete the exam.
- You get answers to any and all of your questions or concerns before the exam begins.

As a Microsoft Certification examination candidate, you are entitled to the best support and environment possible for your exam. If you experience any problems on the day of the exam, inform the Sylvan Prometric test administrator immediately.

During the Test

The testing software lets you move forward and backward through the items, so you can implement a strategic approach to the test:

1. Go through all the items, answering the easy questions first. Then go back and spend time on the harder ones. Microsoft guarantees that there are no trick questions. The correct answer is always among the list of choices. Also, test questions can be marked and returned to later. If you encounter a question that you are not sure about, mark it and go back to it later. Chances are that you may gain some insight into how to answer the marked question from another subsequent question.
2. Eliminate the obviously incorrect answer first to clear away the clutter and simplify your choices.
3. Answer all the questions. You aren't penalized for guessing, so it can't hurt.
4. Don't rush. Haste makes waste (or substitute the cliché of your choice).

After the Test

When you have completed an exam:

- The testing tool gives you immediate, online notification of your pass or fail status, except for beta exams. Because of the beta process, your results for a beta exam are mailed to you approximately 6–8 weeks after the exam.
- The administrator gives you a printed Examination Score Report indicating your pass or fail status and your exam results by section. These embossed sheets should be kept in case you ever need to verify your score.
- Test scores are automatically forwarded to Microsoft within five working days after you take the test. If you pass the exam, you receive confirmation from Microsoft within two to four weeks.

If you don't pass a certification exam:

- Review your individual section scores, noting areas where your score must be improved. The section titles in your exam report generally correspond to specific groups of exam objectives.
- Review the exam information in this book; then get the latest Exam Preparation Guide and focus on the topic areas that need strengthening.
- Intensify your effort to get your real-world, hands-on experience and practice with Windows NT 4.0.
- Try taking one or more of the approved training courses.
- Review the suggested readings listed at the end of this appendix or in the Exam Preparation Guide.
- Take (or retake) the Windows NT 4.0 Assessment Exam.
- Call Sylvan Prometric to register, pay, and schedule the exam again.

Contacting Microsoft

Microsoft encourages feedback from exam candidates, especially suggestions for improving any of the exams or preparation materials.

To provide program feedback, to find out more about Microsoft Education and Certification materials and programs, to register with Sylvan Prometric, or to get other useful information, check the following resourccs.

Outside the United States or Canada, contact your local Microsoft office or Sylvan Prometric testing center.

Microsoft Certified Professional Program

(800) 636-7544

E-mail to **mcp@msprograms.com**

For information about the Microsoft Certified Professional program and exams, and to order the Microsoft Roadmap to Education and Certification.

Sylvan Prometric Testing Centers

(800) 755-EXAM

To register to take a Microsoft Certified Professional exam at any of more than 700 Sylvan Prometric testing centers around the world.

Microsoft Sales Fax Service

(800) 727-3351

For Microsoft Certified Professional Exam Preparation Guides and Microsoft Official Curriculum course descriptions and schedules.

Education Program and Course Information

(800) SOLPROV

For information about Microsoft Official Curriculum courses, Microsoft education products, the Microsoft Solution Provider Authorized Technical Education Center (ATEC) program (where you can attend a Microsoft Official Curriculum course), and to obtain the Microsoft Roadmap to Education and Certification.

Microsoft Certification Development Team

Fax: (206) 936-1311

To volunteer for participation in one or more exam development phases or to report a problem with an exam. Address written correspondence to:

Certification Development Team
Microsoft Education and Certification
One Microsoft Way
Redmond, WA 98052

Microsoft TechNet Technical Information Network

(800) 344-2121

For support professionals and system administrators to obtain information about or order the Microsoft TechNet CD series subscription. (Outside the U.S. and Canada, call your local Microsoft subsidiary for information.)

Microsoft Developer Network (MSDN)

(800) 759-5474

The official source for software development kits, device driver kits, operating systems, and information about developing applications for Microsoft Windows and Windows NT.

Microsoft Technical Support Options

(800) 936-3500

For information about the technical support options available for Microsoft products, including technical support telephone numbers and Premier Support options. (Outside the U.S. and Canada, call your local Microsoft subsidiary for information.)

Microsoft Online Institute (MOLI)

(800) 449-9333

E-mail to **MOLI_Quest@MSN.COM**

Internet site: **http://moli.microsoft.com**

For information about Microsoft's new online training program.

Suggested Reading

Titles from Que

Que Corporation offers a wide variety of technical books for all levels of users. Following are some recommended titles, in alphabetical order, that can provide you with additional information on many of the exam topics and objectives.

Note The final version of Windows NT 4.0 Workstation and Server were released in late August, 1996. Books with a publisher's date earlier than this were probably written based on the beta versions of the Windows NT 4.0 software. This note should by no means discourage you from considering these books for purchase, nor is it meant to reflect negatively on the authorship or content, especially where Windows NT concepts are concerned. However, the final versions of software sometimes introduce subtle changes in look and feel which may not exactly match a description given in the book.

Tip

To order any books from Que Corporation or other imprints of Macmillan Computer Publishing (SAMS, New Riders Publishing, Ziff-Davis Press, and others), call 800-428-5331, visit Macmillan's Information SuperLibrary on the World Wide Web (**http://www.mcp.com**), or check your local bookseller.

Windows NT 4.0 Installation and Configuration Handbook

Author: Jim Boyce

ISBN: 0-7897-0818-3

Special Edition Using Windows NT Server 4.0

Author: Roger Jennings

ISBN: 0-7897-0251-7

Other Titles

Advanced Windows, by Jeffrey Richter (Microsoft Press; ISBN 1-55615-677-4)

Inside Windows NT Server 4.0, by Drew Heywood (New Riders Publishing; ISBN: 1-56205-649-2)

Managing Windows NT Server, by Howard F. Hilliker (New Riders Publishing; ISBN: 1-56205-576-3)

Microsoft Windows NT Server 4.0 Resource Kit (Microsoft Press; ISBN: 1-57231-344-7)

Microsoft Windows NT Workstation Resource Kit (Version 4.0) (Microsoft Press; ISBN: 1-57231-343-9)

Professional Windows NT Server Resource Kit, by New Riders Publishing (New Riders Publishing; ISBN: 1-56205-703-0)

Windows NT Registry Troubleshooting, by Rob Tidrow (New Riders Publishing; ISBN: 1-56205-660-3)

Windows NT Server 4 Security, Troubleshooting, and Optimization, by New Riders Publishing (New Riders Publishing; ISBN: 1-56205-601-8)

Windows NT Server Professional Reference, by Karanjit S. Siyan, Ph.D. (New Riders Publishing; ISBN: 1-56205-659-X)

Windows NT 4 Server Unleashed, by Jason Garms, et al. (SAMS Publishing; ISBN: 0-672-30933-5)

Internet Resources for Windows NT Server

Here is a list of additional resources to help you prepare for your test.

Microsoft Resources

A number of useful resources available from Microsoft are:

- *Windows NT Server 4.0.* A key component of your exam preparation is your actual use of the product. Gain as much real-world experience with Windows NT 4.0 as possible. As you work with the product, study the online and printed documentation, focusing on areas relating to the exam objectives.
- *Microsoft TechNet.* An information service for support professionals and system administrators. If you're a TechNet member, you receive a monthly CD-ROM full of technical information.

Note To join TechNet, refer to the TechNet section in the Microsoft Education and Certification Roadmap (see "The Certification Roadmap" sidebar in Appendix B).

- *The Microsoft Developer Network.* A technical resource for Microsoft developers. If you're a member of the Developer Network, you can receive information on a regular basis through the Microsoft Developer Network CD, *Microsoft Developer Network News*, or the Developer Network forum on CompuServe.

Note To join the Microsoft Developer Network, refer to the Microsoft Developer Network section in the Certification Roadmap.

- The *Implementing and Supporting Microsoft Windows NT Server 4.0 in the Enterprise Exam Preparation Guide.* A Microsoft publication that provides important specific about the Windows NT Server 4.0 Enterprise test. The *Exam Preparation Guide* is updated regularly to reflect changes and is the source for the most up-to-date information about Exam 70-68. It can be obtained through Microsoft's World Wide Web site at **www.microsoft.com**.

Note The exam preparation guide can change at any time without prior notice, solely at Microsoft's discretion. Before you register for an exam, make sure that you have the current exam preparation guide by contacting one of the following sources:

- *Microsoft Sales Fax Service.* Call 800-727-3351 in the United States and Canada. Outside the U.S. and Canada, contact your local Microsoft office.
- *CompuServe.* **GO MSEDCERT**, Library Number 5.
- *Internet.* Anonymous FTP to **ftp.microsoft.com**, /Services/MSEdCert/Certification/ExamPreps.
- *Sylvan Prometric.* Call 800-755-EXAM in the U.S. and Canada. Outside the U.S. and Canada, contact your local Sylvan office.

Microsoft Online Training Institute (MOLI)

The *Microsoft Online Training Institute (MOLI)* on The Microsoft Network (MSN) is an interactive learning and information resource where Learning Advisors (instructors) pair their expert knowledge, guidance, and motivation with electronic self-study materials.

You may access MOLI at its main Classroom Building site on the Internet at **http://moli.microsoft.com**.

You enroll in a class, pay a small tuition fee (to cover the cost of materials and the Learning Advisor's time and expertise), and then receive a shortcut to the classroom. As a student, you can participate in class by interacting with a Learning Advisor and fellow students online via Exchange (e-mail), bulletin boards, forums, or other online communication services available through MSN. You control your own time by studying when and where you choose, working at your own speed, and attending the virtual "class" as often or as little as you want.

Only students enrolled in a class can participate in its online chat sessions and view the contents of the classroom, such as courseware and other materials provided by the Learning Advisor. In addition to MOLI campus resources, you have access to several other resources:

- The Assignments BBS give you access to courseware assignments, test questions that measure subject-matter comprehension, chapter review guides, lab assignments, and information about certification exam topics. You can take advantage of these resources anytime.
- One or more chat sessions per week allow you to supplement class courseware, interact with other classmates to solve real-life situations, and get expert advice.
- The Notes BBS lets students download and play files, tips and tools, and resources available through Microsoft.

Self-Paced Training

If you prefer to learn on your own, you can obtain Microsoft Official Curriculum training (as well as non-Microsoft Official Curriculum courses) in self-paced formats. Self-paced training kits are available through courses offered on the Microsoft Online Training Institute with materials available in book, computer-based training (CBT), and mixed-media (book and video) formats.

Microsoft Approved Study Guides, such as this book, are self-paced training materials developed by Independent Courseware Vendors (ICVs) to help you prepare for MCP exams. The Study Guides include both single self-paced training courses and series of training courses that map to one or more MCP exams.

Self-training kits and study guides are often available through Microsoft authorized training centers, or you can purchase them where books from Microsoft Press are sold.

Other Online Resources

Both MSN and CompuServe (**GO MECFORUM**) provide access to technical forums for open discussions and questions about Microsoft products. Microsoft's World Wide Web site (**http:\\www.microsoft.com**) also allows you to access information about certification and education programs.

Training Resources

Microsoft product groups have designed training courses to support the certification process. The Microsoft Official Curriculum is developed by Microsoft course designers, product developers, and support engineers to help you prepare for MCP exams.

Authorized Technical Education Centers (ATECs), such as Productivity Point International, are approved by Microsoft to provide training on Microsoft products and related technologies. By enrolling in a course taught by a Microsoft Solution Provider ATEC, you receive high-end technical training on the design, development, implementation, and support of enterprise-wide solutions using Microsoft operating systems, tools, and technologies.

You also may take MOC courses via face-to-face training offered by *Microsoft Authorized Academic Training Program* (AATP) institutions. AATP schools use authorized materials and curriculum designed for the MCP program and deliver Microsoft authorized materials, including the Microsoft Official Curriculum, over an academic term.

Supporting Microsoft Windows NT Server 4.0-Enterprise Technologies, course number 689, available from Microsoft authorized training institutions, may help you prepare for the exam. Course 689 is five days long.

For a referral to an AATP or Productivity Point ATEC in your area, call 800-SOLPROV.

Internet Resources

Microsoft's Windows operating system series (Windows 95, Windows NT 4.0 Workstation, Windows NT Server 4.0) has become quite popular. The amount of new information and programs that becomes available each day is staggering. If you don't want to wait for the next super book or next month's magazine, you can go online to get new information. You can get a lot of information through commercial online services such as CompuServe, America Online, or The Microsoft Network (MSN). You'll find more variety, and potentially more useful information, on the Internet, however.

That's where this appendix comes in. It points you to some of the best resources on the Internet for Windows NT information and programs, and earlier versions, as well as version 4.0. Keep in mind that there are hundreds of Internet sites for each Windows NT site that you find in this appendix. Most of these are not included because they contain links to the other sites. The result is a Web of Windows NT pages, all linked together, that contains nothing but links.

This appendix teaches you about:

- *FTP Servers.* It's usually easier to find shareware programs on the World Wide Web, but this sample of FTP sites collects so many programs in a few areas that they're worth checking out.
- *Mailing lists.* Sometimes it's easier to let the information you want come to you, instead of going out onto the Internet to look for it. Mailing lists deliver information directly to your mail box.
- *World Wide Web.* There's little doubt that the Web is the hottest resource on the Internet. You find a variety of Web pages dedicated to Windows NT, including personal and corporate Web pages.

On The Web

You can find shortcuts to the Internet address described here at Que's Web site at

http://www.quecorp.com

FTP Servers

The FTP servers in this section contain large collections of Windows NT shareware programs. They are all well organized, so you can quickly find the program you're looking for. Note that most of these sites are indexed by **Shareware.com**. See "Shareware.com" later in this chapter for more information.

Tip
If you don't have an FTP client, you can use your Web browser to access FTP servers. Type **ftp://** followed by the FTP address in your Web browser's address bar.

Microsoft

FTP address: **ftp://ftp.microsoft.com**

This is the place to look for updated drivers, new files for Windows NT, and sometimes free programs. My favorite part of this FTP site is the Knowledge Base articles that answer common questions about most of Microsoft's programs. If you're having trouble finding your way around, look for a file called DIRMAP.TXT, which tells you what the different folders have in them. Here's what you find under each of the folders on this site:

- **/BUSSYS.** Files for business systems, including networking, mail, SQL Server, and Windows NT. Here you can find some knowledge base links specific to NT. The Knowledge Base entries related to Windows NT reflect all versions of Windows NT.
- **/DESKAPPS.** Files for all of Microsoft's desktop applications, including Access, Excel, PowerPoint, Project, and Word. You can also find information for the Home series, including games and Works.
- **/DEVELPR.** The place to look if you're a developer. There are folders for Visual C++, Visual Basic, various utilities, the Microsoft Developer Network, and more. If you subscribe to the *Microsoft Systems Journal*, check here to find the source code for articles.
- **/KBHELP.** Microsoft's Knowledge Base folder. A *knowledge base*, in this context, is a help file that contains common questions and answers about Microsoft products. This folder contains one self-extracting, compressed file for each Microsoft product. There is not a

lot of information here as yet about Windows NT 4.0. However, this is still a good area to keep scanning for the newest data.

- **/SOFTLIB.** The folder to check out if you're looking for updated drivers, patches, or bug fixes. This folder contains more than 1,500 files, though, so you need to check out INDEX.TXT to locate what you want.
- **/PEROPSYS.** For personal operating systems. If you're looking for back issues of *WINNEWS*, look in the **WIN_NEWS** folder. There are other folders relating to all versions of Windows, MS-DOS, and Microsoft hardware.
- **/SERVICES.** Contains information about TechNet, Microsoft educational services, sales information, and so on.

Note Many of the folders on the Microsoft FTP site have two files that you should read: README.TXT and INDEX.TXT.

README.TXT describes the type of files you find in the current folder and any subfolders. It also may describe recent additions and files that have been removed.

INDEX.TXT describes each file in the folder. It's a good idea to search for the file you want in INDEX.TXT before trying to pick it out of the listing. Note that Microsoft's site is constantly changing, so you'll want to check back here often.

Walnut Creek

FTP address: **ftp://ftp.cdrom.com**

I consider myself lucky to get on this FTP site. It's incredibly popular. Walnut Creek sells CD-ROMs that are packed with freeware and shareware programs. Files from these CD-ROMs are available from the Walnut Creek FTP site, too. Here are some folders that you can find for Windows NT:

alpha
incoming
intel

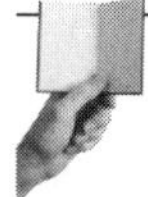

Tip

This site is usually very crowded. If you get onto this site, don't let yourself get disconnected by taking a coffee break; it could be a while before you get on again.

Mailing Lists

Windows NT-related mailing lists keep your mailbox full of messages. There's a lot of noise generated by these lists, but you can find a lot of gems, too. This section describes two of the most popular ones: DevWire and WinNews.

Microsoft DevWire

This is for Windows programmers. You'll find news and product information, such as seminar schedules and visual tool release schedules. To subscribe, send an e-mail to **DevWire@microsoft.nwnet.com** with **subscribe DevWire** in the body of your message.

Microsoft WinNews

This weekly newsletter keeps you up-to-date on the latest happenings at Microsoft. You also find product tips and press releases. To subscribe, send an e-mail to **enews99@microsoft.nwnet.com** and type **subscribe winnews** in the body of your message.

World Wide Web

The explosive growth of Windows Web pages is evident if you search for the keyword **Windows NT** using Yahoo!, WebCrawler, Excite, or Lycos. You can find thousands of Web pages dedicated to Windows NT, some from the corporate community such as Microsoft or Symantec. Many more exist from individuals who want to make their mark on the world by sharing what they know about Windows NT.

The Web pages in this section are only a start. Many contain links to other Windows NT sites. Before you know it, your Windows NT favorite places list will grow by leaps and bounds.

Microsoft Corporation

URL address: **http://www.microsoft.com**

Microsoft's Web site contains an amazing amount of information about its products, services, plans, job opportunities, and more. You can find the two most useful Windows NT Web pages by clicking the Products link or the Support link.

Here's what you find on each:

- *Products link.* This Web page contains links for most Microsoft products, including Windows NT. You find links to Microsoft pages for Windows 95, Office, BackOffice, Windows NT Workstation, and more. The bulletin board on this page also contains the latest information about Microsoft products.
- *Support link.* The Support Desktop Web page provides access to the Microsoft Knowledge Base, which you can use to search for articles based on keywords that you specify. It also contains links to the Microsoft Software Library and Frequently Asked Questions (FAQ) Web pages.

On The Web

This site is best viewed with Microsoft's Internet Explorer. You can get your own copy of Internet Explorer at **http://www.microsoft.com/windows/ie/ie.htm**.

And it's free, too.

Other NT-Related Web Sites

Chancellor and Chancellor Windows NT Resource Site

URL address: **http://www.chancellor.com/ntmain.html**

Info Nederland Windows NT Information Site

URL address: **http://nt.info.nl/english/default.htm**

Windows NT Magazine

URL address: **http://www.winntmag.com**

Windows NT Administration FAQ

URL address: **http://ftech.com/classes/admin/admin.htm**

Windows NT 4.0 Overview

This appendix provides an overview of the features and functionality of Microsoft Windows NT Workstation and Server 4.0. Topics discussed in this appendix include:

- Providing a list of features and functionality common to the Windows NT product line past and present, and exploring certain specific characteristics in more detail.
- Understanding when an installation of Windows NT Workstation or Server is appropriate given the needs of the clients involved, the level of administration desired, and the level of security required.
- Introducing the basic architecture of the Windows NT operating system and explaining the features and functions that are new to version 4.0.
- Comparing Microsoft's Workgroup model with its Enterprise model of network communication.

Microsoft Windows NT Features Overview

Microsoft Windows NT is a 32-bit operating system designed to provide fast and efficient performance for power computer users such as software developers, CAD programmers, and design engineers. Because it provides better performance for existing 16-bit applications (both MS-DOS and Windows), as well as 32-bit applications developed specifically for the operating system, Windows NT is increasingly found on the desks of the business user. These performance enhancements include:

- Multiple platform support
- Preemptive multitasking
- Expanded processing support
- Expanded memory support
- Expanded file system support
- Enhanced security
- Network and communications support

Multiple Platform Support

Microsoft Windows NT is engineered to run on several hardware platforms. The *Hardware Abstraction Layer,* or *HAL*, component of the Windows NT architecture isolates platform specific information for the operating system—for example, how to interact with a RISC-based processor as opposed to an Intel x86 processor. This makes Windows NT a highly portable system through the recompilation of only few pieces of code such as the HAL. Windows NT supports Intel x86 and Pentium-based computers and RISC-based computers such as MIPS R4000, DEC Alpha AXP, and PowerPC.

Preemptive Multitasking

All processes in Windows NT are given at least one thread of operation. A *thread* represents a piece of code relating to a process. Loading a file may require several threads to carry out the process—for example, locating the file on disk, allocating RAM for the file, and moving it into that allocated memory space. Many processes and applications written for Windows and Windows NT have multiple threads associated with them. Windows NT can treat each thread of a process independently of the others, providing a greater degree of control over the overall performance of the system.

Each thread also is given a processing priority based on its function. For example, an operating system process such as memory allocation receives a higher priority for its threads than a file save process. Each thread is given a specific amount of time with the processor. This is sometimes called *time-slicing*. Higher priority threads are processed ahead of lower priority threads. All the threads of one priority are processed first before those of the next priority and so on. This process is called *preemptive multitasking*.

In addition, certain threads, primarily those that are system-related, are processed in the protected mode of the processor (known as *ring 0*) and thus are protected from other processes and crashes. Other threads, those relating to application functions such as file printing, run in the unprotected mode of the processor. This means that while they may be given their own memory space, other "poorly written" applications (and their threads) might try to "butt in" and result in what is generally referred to as a *General Protection* or *GP fault*.

Microsoft and Windows NT have taken several precautions to ensure that this does not happen in Windows NT. Supporting both multitasking and multithreading gives applications excellent processing support and protection against system hangs and crashes.

Expanded Processing Support

Microsoft Windows NT provides *symmetric multiprocessing* with support for OEM implementations of up to 32 processors. Every process that runs under Windows NT has at least one thread of operation or programming code associated with it. A process might be user-generated such as the writing of a file to disk or printing a document, or system-generated such as validating a user logon or providing read access to a file.

Symmetric multiprocessing enables the Windows NT operating system to load balance process threads across all available processors in the computer, as opposed to *asymmetric multiprocessing* in which the operating system takes control of one processor and directs application threads to other available processors.

Expanded Memory Support

Windows NT supports computers with up to 4G of RAM and theoretic file or partition sizes of up to 16 exabytes (though this number will vary depending on the type of hardware you have). An *exabyte* is one billion gigabytes. You might consider that to be a theoretical number, and to a certain extent it is. However, it was not that long ago that MIS departments debated the wisdom of purchasing 10M disk drives for their users' computers because they felt that the drives would never be filled up.

Expanded File System Support

Windows NT provides support for the MS-DOS File Allocation Table (FAT) file system as well as its own New Technology File System (NTFS). Previous versions of Windows NT also supported OS/2's High Performance File System (HPFS). Version 4.0 no longer provides support for HPFS.

NTFS provides a high level of security in the form of file and directory level permissions similar to those found in other network operating systems such as trustee rights used in Novell's NetWare. NTFS also provides transaction tracking to help recover data in the event of system failure and *sector sparing*, which identifies potentially bad disk storage space and moves data to good storage. NTFS also provides data compression implemented as a file or directory property.

Enhanced Security

Security begins with Windows NT's WINLOGON and NETLOGON processes which authenticate a user's access to a computer, workgroup, or enterprise by validating the user name and password and assigning each with his own security identifier. In addition to this mandatory logon, Windows NT offers share-level resource control, security auditing functions, and file and directory level permissions (in NTFS partitions).

Network and Communications Support

Windows NT is designed to provide several internetworking options. The NetBEUI, NWLINK (IPX/SPX), TCP/IP, AppleTalk, and DLC protocols are all supported and included. Windows NT also is supported on Novell NetWare networks, Microsoft LAN Manager, IBM LAN Server and SNA networks, Banyan VINES, and DEC PATHWORKS.

Through *Remote Access Service* (RAS), Windows NT offers a secure dial-up option for clients and servers. RAS clients can remotely access any shared network resource to which they have been given access through RAS gateway functions, such as shared folders and printers.

In a Windows NT network valid workstation, clients include Microsoft Windows NT workstations and servers, Windows 3.x, MS-DOS, Windows for Workgroups, Windows 95, OS/2, Novell NetWare (client/server), and Macintosh.

Choosing Windows NT Workstation or Server

The difference in choosing when to use Windows NT Workstation or Windows NT Server is not necessarily the difference between desktop and enterprise computing. Both Windows NT Workstation and Windows NT Server provide the capability to make resources available on the network and thus act as a "server." For that matter, a Windows NT Server could be made part of a workgroup of Windows NT Workstations to act as the resource server for that workgroup. Choosing Windows NT Workstation or Windows NT Server really comes down to the features specific to each product and the type of network model that will be implemented. The following sections discuss the differences between Windows NT Workstation and Windows NT Server.

Microsoft Windows NT Workstation

Microsoft Windows NT Workstation is designed for the so-called power user, such as developers or CAD designers, but is increasingly becoming the desktop operating system of choice for end-user business computing because of its robust feature set as described in the last section. In addition to those features and functions which are common to both Windows NT workstation and Windows NT server, Windows NT Workstation offers the following specific characteristics:

- Unlimited outbound peer-to-peer connections
- Ten inbound client connections for resource access
- Can be a RAS client or server, but supports only one remote dial-in session

- Retail installation supports two processors for symmetric multiprocessing
- Acts as an import server for Directory Replication Services

Microsoft Windows NT Server

Windows NT Server is designed to provide file, print, and application service support within a given network model. While it also can be used as a desktop system, it is engineered to provide optimum performance when providing network services—for example, by optimizing memory differently for application servers than for domain controllers. In addition to the features and functions described previously, Windows NT Server offers the following:

- Allows as many inbound connections to resources as there are valid client licenses (virtually unlimited)
- Support for as many as 256 remote dial-in RAS sessions
- Retail installation supports as many as four processors for symmetric multiprocessing
- Provides a full set of services for application and network support such as:
  - Services for Macintosh allowing client support for Macintosh computers
  - Gateway Service for NetWare allowing Windows NT clients to access Novell NetWare file and print resources
  - Directory Replication Service for copying of directory structures and files from a source Windows NT server computer to a target Windows NT server or workstation computer
- Provides full integration into the Microsoft BackOffice suite including System Management Server, SNA Server, and SQL Server

New Features and Functions in Windows NT 4.0

This newest version of Windows NT continues Microsoft's commitment to reliable, performance-driven network-ready operating systems by incorporating the power, features, and functions of the Windows NT operating system with the object-oriented Windows 95 user interface. Enhanced features and functions common to both Windows NT 4.0 Workstation and Server include:

- Windows 95 user interface
- Windows Explorer
- Hardware profiles
- Enhanced dial-up networking support
- NDS-aware client services for Novell NetWare 4.x
- Integrated Microsoft Exchange Client
- Internet Explorer 2.0
- Web services

Windows 95 User Interface

All the basic features of Microsoft's Windows 95 interface have been integrated into Windows NT 4.0. This includes updated or enhanced system utilities such as the Task Manager (called the System Monitor in Windows 95), as well as additional utilities such as the Windows Explorer, Network Neighborhood, Briefcase, Desktop shortcuts, Microsoft Network support, and the Recycle Bin.

Windows Explorer

This feature of the interface replaces the File Manager utility. It provides excellent browsing capabilities for management of drives, directories, files, and network connections. The Explorer presents the user's data access information as a hierarchy of drives, desktop, network connections, folders, and files. The browsing capabilities of the Explorer offer not only browsing of file and directory names, but also of data strings within files. Throughout this book, you used Windows Explorer to access files and folders, set permissions, create and manage shared folders, and so on.

Note Though Windows Explorer replaces the File Manager utility by default, File Manager is still available and can be launched by the user.

File Manager can be run by following these simple steps:

continues

continued

1. Choose Start from the taskbar.
2. Choose Run from the Start menu.
3. Enter the File Manager file name: **winfile.exe**.
4. Choose OK.

Microsoft recommends using File Manager only until you become comfortable with Windows Explorer. File Manager is still available for transition purposes only. ■

Hardware Profiles

Perhaps one of the most useful enhancements to Windows NT 4.0 is the support for multiple hardware profiles. First introduced in Windows 95, this feature enables you to create hardware profiles to fit various computing needs. The most common example for using hardware profiles would be with portable computers. You can create separate profiles to support the portable when it is in use by itself, and for when it is positioned in a docking station.

Note Plug and Play is a much appreciated feature of Windows 95. Note that while the Plug-and-Play service has been included with Windows NT 4.0, "hot" plug and play—that is to say, the ability for the operating system to recognize a configuration change on-the-fly and implement it—will not be fully supported until the next major release of Windows NT. Windows NT 4.0 does, however, recognize some hardware changes when it restarts. For example, additional memory or a new hard disk will be automatically detected by Windows NT the next time you boot up. ■

Enhanced Dial-Up Networking Support

The RAS Client service now is installed as *Dial-Up Networking*. In addition, Windows NT 4.0 provides the Dial-Up Networking Monitor for monitoring user connections and devices as well as Remote Access Admin for monitoring remote user access to a RAS Server.

Windows NT 4.0 also offers Telephony API version 2.0 (TAPI) and universal modem driver (Unimodem) support which provides communications technology for Fax applications, the Microsoft Exchange client, the Microsoft Network (MSN), and Internet Explorer.

NDS Aware Client Service for Novell NetWare 4.x

Microsoft provides an enhanced version of its Client Services for NetWare (CSNW) with Windows NT 4.0 which supplies compatibility with Novell NetWare servers (versions 3.x and later) running NetWare Directory Services (NDS). This allows users to view NetWare shared resources organized in a hierarchical tree format.

Integrated Microsoft Windows Messaging

Microsoft *Windows Messaging* is Microsoft's newest electronic mail product. Windows Messaging has been included with Windows NT 4.0 and enables users to send and receive mail, embed objects in mail messages, and integrate mail functionality into Microsoft applications.

Internet Explorer 2.0

Microsoft's Internet Explorer 2.0 is included with Windows NT 4.0 to enable users access to the Internet. However, Microsoft now has Internet Explorer 4.0 available through its various Internet sites (**www.microsoft.com**, for example). Watch for Microsoft to continue to enhance this product and make upgrades widely (and inexpensively) available.

Note Internet Explorer requires that the TCP/IP protocol be installed, and a connection made to the Internet or an organization's intranet for file and htm searching and connection.

Web Publishing

Microsoft includes Web publishing services in Windows NT 4.0 which allow you to develop, publish, and manage Web pages, FTP, and Gopher services for your company's intranet, or for smaller peer-to-peer networks. With Windows NT 4.0 Workstation, Microsoft provides *Peer Web Services* (PWS) for smaller workgroup-based Web publishing. With Windows NT 4.0 Server, Microsoft provides *Internet Information Services* (IIS) designed for heavy intranet and Internet usage.

Integrated Network Monitor Agent

Windows NT Server 4.0 includes a version of the Network Monitor utility which is included with Microsoft's System Management Server BackOffice product. Network Monitor provides a full range of network analysis tools for tracking and interpreting network traffic, frames, and so forth.

Last but Certainly Not Least

Of all the features contained in Windows NT 4.0, there is one from which you will obtain the most productivity. It also is a example of enhancements made to Windows NT's Open GL and direct draw video support. This is, of course, PINBALL! Yes, there is a new game added to Windows NT 4.0 and it is quite an addition. As mentioned, it does take full advantage of changes to Windows NT's architecture and enhancements for video support. Try it out!

Note Pinball is installed in the Games folder which can be found by choosing Start, Programs, Accessories, Games. If you have not installed your games, you can use the Add/Remove Programs applet in Control Panel to add them. In the applet, choose the Windows Setup tab, highlight Accessories, choose Details and select Games. Choose OK. Be sure to have your source files or CD handy because Windows NT will prompt you for them. ■

In addition to these features which Windows NT Workstation and Server 4.0 share, Windows NT Server 4.0 offers the following specific list of features and functions:

- DNS Name Server and enhanced support
- Integrated Support for Multiprotocol routing
- Enhanced support for BOOTP and DHCP routing
- Remote Reboot Support for Windows 95 clients
- New remote server administration tools for Windows 95 clients
- Installation wizards for most utility program installations

Basic Architecture of Windows NT 4.0

An integral part of any understanding of Windows NT is a discussion of the internal architecture of the Windows NT operating system. There are several resources available for a in-depth coverage of this topic. This basic overview provides the building blocks and concepts needed to comprehend Windows NT security, service support, and other topics covered in this book.

The Windows NT 4.0 architecture consists of two primary processing areas: user or application mode, and kernel or privileged processor mode. The user mode, as it implies, provides operating system support primarily for user applications and the environment.

The kernel mode provides operating system support services for just about everything else including kernel processing, memory management, hardware access, and so forth. These kernel mode services are referred to as the *Executive Services.*

User (Application) Mode

The user mode of the operating system provides application processing support. Applications in Windows NT run in one of three subsystems provided by the operating system: WIN32, OS/2, and POSIX. The primary subsystem, and that which is loaded at boot time, is WIN32. Win32 supports both 32-bit Windows and Win95 applications as well as 16-bit DOS and Windows applications.

Note OS/2 was designed and implemented by IBM to support 32-bit applications in an object-oriented environment. POSIX stands for *Portable Operating System Interface for UNIX* and was originally an IEEE effort to standardize portability of applications across UNIX-based environments.

The OS/2 subsystem provides support for 1.x character-based OS/2 applications. POSIX provides support for POSIX-based applications. Any application program calls from these two subsystems that read/write to the display are forwarded to the WIN32 subsystem. Any other calls to drivers or other executive services are communicated directly to the kernel mode.

In Windows NT version 3.51, the USER and Graphics Device Interface (GDI) portions of the operating system were included in the WIN32 subsystem, thus in user mode. The USER is the Window Manager and responds to user input on-screen. The GDI processes graphics primitives such as pixels, lines, fills, and so on. The GDI also performs graphics rendering for print files.

If an application needed either the user or GDI for processing, it would have to create an *InterProcess Communication* (IPC) to it. This would involve a context switch from user mode to kernel mode (ring 0 to ring 3 of the processor) as well as 64K buffering. Then, another context switch would take place back to user mode. This, obviously, involves some time and decreases overall performance.

Windows NT version 4.0 moves the USER and GDI into the kernel mode. This move significantly improves application performance by eliminating the 64K buffer and leaving only a kernel transition. The benefit can be seen particularly in those applications that involve direct draw to the screen such as Pinball as well as in multimedia applications such as QuickTime.

Kernel (Privileged Processor) Mode

Kernel mode provides support for all major operating system functions. It controls access to memory and the execution of privileged instructions. All kernel mode processes run in the protected mode of the processor, ring 0. As such, the applications running in user mode are effectively buffered from direct access to hardware. Thus, 16-bit applications which are designed to access hardware directly will not run successfully under Windows NT. These would have to be rewritten to "talk" to the Windows NT kernel mode services.

The kernel mode consists of three parts: Executive Services, HAL, and Windows NT kernel.

Executive Services

This is the largest part of kernel mode. The Executive Services provides support for processes, threads, memory management, I/O, IPC, and security. It is here that most Windows NT services and process managers execute. It also is here where device driver support is provided, including Windows NT's network architecture support drivers, protocols, and so forth. It is written mostly in portable C code which helps make Windows NT portable across platforms. It is this C code that needs to be recompiled in order to accommodate different platforms such as Dec Alpha, PowerPC, and MIPS.

Windows NT Kernel

The Windows NT kernel provides support for thread management and context switching, synchronization among services and processes in

Executive Services, multiprocessor load balancing, and exception and interrupt handling.

HAL (Hardware Abstraction Layer)

The HAL provides hardware platform support. It isolates specific platform details from the Executive and the Windows NT kernel. It is largely due to the HAL, which those 16-bit applications that like to talk directly to hardware are unable to run. It can be said, therefore, that users applications are effectively isolated from base hardware interaction under Windows NT. HAL does it for you.

Windows NT Virtual Memory Management

One of the Executive Services managers is the *Virtual Memory Manager.* The memory architecture of Windows NT is a 32-bit, demand-based flat model. This model allows the Virtual Memory Manager to access up to 4G of RAM—generally far more than the amount of physical RAM installed in most computers.

If you recall Windows' swap file model, you're aware of two types of swap files: permanent and temporary. Both swap files managed available RAM in 4K pieces using an internal Windows algorithm called the *Least Recently Used* (LRU). Essentially, the LRU said that the piece of code in memory that was least recently accessed by a process was liable to be swapped to disk when more RAM was needed for a current process. On computers with the minimal required RAM for Windows, there could be a considerable amount of swapping that takes place.

The main difference between permanent and temporary swap files is that a permanent swap file has a pre-allocated amount of space reserved on the disk. Temporary swap files begin at 2M and then "grow" as needed to a predetermined amount. Thus, while a permanent swap file actually provided better swap performance because the space was always there and available, it also reduced the amount of available disk storage. Similarly, while temporary swap files did not reduce the amount of disk storage available up front, more resource was expended in finding additional storage space when the swap file needed to "grow."

Windows NT combines the "best" of these swap files. The Windows NT pagefile (PAGEFILE.SYS) is created when Windows NT is installed and generally defaults to an initial, pre-allocated size (permanent swap files) of 12 plus physical RAM and a maximum size of three times physical RAM (depending on the amount of disk space available). So, on a computer with 16M of physical RAM, the default initial pagefile size would be 28M (12+16M) and the maximum size would be about 48M (3*16M). Windows NT will boot with the initial size pagefile available. The pagefile subsequently grows as applications are loaded and demands for physical RAM increase.

It is important to realize that while Windows NT allows addressing of up to 4G of physical RAM, the Virtual Memory Manager can allocate up to 2G of virtual storage for each application. Another 2G is allocated for all system (kernel mode) processing. The Virtual Memory Manager addresses application memory.

1. When an application is loaded, the Virtual Memory Manager assigns it virtual memory addresses in physical RAM.
2. The data is then moved in pages out of physical RAM and into the pagefile.
3. As the data is needed by the application, it calls for the virtual memory addresses.
4. The Virtual Memory Manager moves those pages on demand into available locations in physical RAM.

This process of assigning virtual addresses to the application effectively hides the organization of physical RAM from the application. The various pages of the application may wind up in non-contiguous space in physical RAM (that is, in sectors which may be distributed at different locations on the disk rather than next to each other). But as the Virtual Memory Manager is providing it with its addresses, it really doesn't care—because it doesn't know. This allows Windows NT to make the most efficient use of available physical RAM, and provide an overall performance increase for application processing.

Windows NT Cache Manager

The final aspect of the Windows NT Architecture to discuss is the Windows NT Cache Manager. As one might expect by now, the tried-and-true Windows and DOS SMARTDrive disk cache manager is no more. It has been replaced by an operating system-driven Cache Manager that runs as part of the Executive Services, and thus in kernel mode. Its actual physical size depends on the amount of physical RAM installed. Windows NT's cache competes for RAM with other applications and processes and thus is automatically sized by the Cache Manager working in sync with the Memory Manager.

The Cache Manager provides an intelligent read-ahead/write-back operation. It predicts the next read location based on the history and locations of the last three reads. It also performs *lazy writes*—that is, using the processor when it is not being accessed by any other process—to update the file on disk while maintaining data in memory for quick access.

Lab Exercises

Getting Started

The best way to become familiar with the installation process is to install NT 4.0 Server a few times and pay close attention to what is happening. Later in this book, you will need at least two computers running Windows NT 4.0 Server in order to understand the way NT handles access security. If you have two computers available, install one using the **Custom** option and the other using **Typical**. The Preparation Checklist has been included once again as follows. Double-check your hardware configuration against the checklist before beginning setup. Then follow the process as outlined in Chapter 2, "Understanding Microsoft Windows NT 4.0." Specific instructions have been included in the steps outlined as follows. As you proceed with installation, **be sure to read each screen** for your own edification.

PREPARATION CHECKLIST

Read all NT documentation files.

Assess system requirements.

Assess hardware compatibility. Refer to Hardware Compatibility List.

Assess necessary drivers and configuration data:

◆ Video	Display Type, Adapter and chipset type
◆ Network	Card type, IRQ, I/O Address, DMA, Connector, and so on
◆ SCSI Controller	Adapter and chipset type, IRQ, bus type
◆ Sound/Media	IRQ, I/O Address, DMA
◆ I/O Ports	IRQ, I/O Address, DMA
◆ Modems	Port, IRQ, I/O Address, Modem Type

Before installing, backup your current configuration and data files. Make sure you have answers to all of these questions:

- What type of initial setup will be performed (you may need three blank formatted disks before running setup)?
- Where are the installation files located?
- What partition will NT system files be installed on?
- What file system will you install?
- Will you create an Emergency Repair Disk (if so, you need 1 blank disk available before running setup)?
- What is your installation CD Key?
- What is the unique computer name?
- What is the workgroup or domain name that the computer joins?
- Network connection data: IP addresses, IPX card numbers, and so on.
- What time zone is the computer located in?

Recommended Computer Configuration

- At least 2 486/66 or higher computers with 32M RAM
- Working network connection between these computers
- If you are part of a larger network, try to have your computer isolated onto its own network. If you cannot, be sure to inform your network

administrator of what you intend to do so that you can both take all necessary precautions to preserve security on the network.

- FAT formatted C: Primary Partition
- At least 300M free space on same or other drive
- Two or more physical disk drives to demonstrate disk striping
- CD-ROM drive for installation
- Optional 4 blank formatted disks—3 for startup disks and 1 for Emergency Repair
- 1 printer attached to either computer

Exercise 1—Setting Up Your Computers for This Book's Labs

1. If you have your own installation CD-ROM and a compatible CD-ROM, run setup from the CD-ROM. If you are accessing the installation files over the network, you must make a connection to the installation directory first. Connect as you normally would on your network or consult with your network administrator for appropriate access.
2. If you have four formatted blank 3.5" disks available (three for startup disks and one for Emergency repair), run **WINNT.EXE** from the installation directory and follow the directions on the screen. If you choose not to create the startup disks, run **WINNT /B**.

Note If you are installing NT on a RISC-based system, be sure to create a minimum 2M FAT partition and a large enough system partition for NT before starting setup. Then follow the guidelines outlined in the Notes and Sidebars of Chapter 3, "Windows NT Server 4.0 Setup," relating to RISC installations.

3. Press **ENTER** to install NT.
4. If you have any additional storage devices other than what NT detects, add them.
5. Verify that your basic hardware settings are correct and press **ENTER**.
6. Create a 250M partition out of the free space during installation, format it as FAT, and install the NT system partition there in a directory called **WINNT40**.

7. Let NT do an exhaustive scan of your disk drive and then reboot the computer.
8. For your first installation, choose **CUSTOM**. For your second, choose **TYPICAL**. Read all screens as you go along. Explore all buttons. It is impossible to create an exercise for all possible permutations that one might encounter, so it is up to you to explore.
9. When prompted for the User and Company Name, use your own.
10. When prompted for a Computer name use:

    COMPUTER1 for the first installation and **COMPUTER2** for the second (and so on for additional installations). You may, of course, name the computers anything you like. Future labs will refer to these suggested names. Just remember to substitute your own. If you are part of a larger network, be sure your computer names are unique.
11. Enter **studynt** as your password just as it appears—in lowercase. Again, you may choose your own password. Just don't forget it!
12. If you receive a message regarding the floating point error, do not choose the workaround.
13. If you have a formatted disk handy, create the Emergency Repair Disk. Remember that you can create it later.
14. Look at all the Optional Component lists and sublists to understand your choices. Install as many additional options as you like. Install at least the recommended options that NT displays. If you are low on disk space, then deselect games and other unessential accessories.
15. Let NT detect your network card, or if you have an OEM driver disk, install your card from the disk.
16. Deselect TCP/IP and select NETBEUI as your protocol. Also keep the default Network Services and Bindings.
17. You will create a workgroup called **STUDYGROUP**. As before, you can call the workgroup anything you like so long as you remember what you called it for future exercises, and so long as it does not conflict with any other workgroup on your network.
18. Enter the appropriate date and time zone values.
19. Select the appropriate settings for your monitor.
20. Complete the installation and let NT restart the system.

OPTIONAL EXERCISE

Follow the instructions in the Troubleshooting section of Chapter 3, "Windows NT Server 4.0 Setup," and run the NTHQ utility to see how it works. Log and print a report.

Chapter 4—Configuring Windows NT Server 4.0

There is no better practice at getting acquainted with the new NT 4.0 interface than by trying out the new features, exploring ALL object properties sheets, and having fun. Here is an exercise that uses all the more significant features of the interface. You will need one blank formatted disk.

Exercise—Navigating the Interface-Taskbar, Explorer, Shortcuts, and Briefcase

1. Start Windows Help and click the Contents tab.
2. From the topic list, choose HOW TO, Change Windows Settings, Change Taskbar Settings. Following the directions, make it so the taskbar does not display on top of all other windows.
3. Open My Computer. Select Options from the View menu and choose the option that replaces previous windows.
4. Right-click the A: drive icon and drag it to the desktop. Choose Create shortcut from the pop-up menu.
5. Open the C: drive icon. From the File menu choose NEW and create a new folder called LAB2.
6. From the Start menu, choose Programs, Accessories and then start the WordPad program.
7. Create a file called MEMO.DOC with the following text:

   This is the first draft of my memo.
8. From the File menu, choose Save As. Use its browse feature to find the LAB2 directory and save the MEMO.DOC file there. Minimize WordPad.
9. Open Windows Explorer and select the LAB2 directory. Right-click the file and drag it to the Briefcase icon on the desktop. Choose Create Synch Copy from the pop-up menu.

10. Place the formatted blank disk in the A: drive.
11. Drag the Briefcase from the desktop to the A: drive shortcut icon.
12. Move your mouse to the bottom of the screen until the taskbar appears. Select WordPad. Open the MEMO.DOC file in the Briefcase on the A: drive. Add the following text: **This is the second draft of my memo**, and save the file.
13. Open the A: drive shortcut icon and drag the briefcase back to the desktop.
14. Open the Briefcase and choose Update from the Briefcase menu option. Notice the window displaying the documents that have changed, and the suggestion to update the older document.
15. Choose Update All. Close Briefcase.
16. Start WordPad and open the MEMO.DOC file in the LAB2 directory. Verify that it has been updated.
17. Start the Find program. From the Advanced tab, search for all files on the C: drive containing the following text: "first draft." In the results window, verify that both copies appear.

Exercise 1—Using Control Panel to Configure Windows NT

1. Use Control Panel to modify the wallpaper on your computer to LEAVES.BMP, and change your WAIT mouse pointer to the animated cursor BANANA.ANI. Note that these changes take effect immediately.
2. Close Control Panel and open the Registry Editor (ex: Start\RUN\REGEDT32.EXE).
3. Click in the HKEY_CURRENT_USER subtree window to make it active.
4. Select View\Find Key and search for "cursors." When the Cursors key is found, close the FIND dialog box and select the Cursors key. Notice that the WAIT cursor parameter on the right side of the window shows that BANANA.ANI has been selected.
5. Change the WAIT value from BANANA.ANI to HORSE.ANI by double-clicking the WAIT value and typing in **HORSE.ANI** (using the appropriate path).

6. Choose EDIT\ADD VALUE and enter the value name **APPSTARTING** with a data type of REG_SZ. Choose OK and enter the file name and path to DINOSAUR.ANI.
7. Use Find Key again to find the WALLPAPER key. Were you able to? Recall that wallpaper is a feature of the desktop. Search for DESKTOP.
8. Select the DESKTOP key and view the right side of the window for entries related to wallpaper. You should find two: WALLPAPER and TILEWALLPAPER.
9. Modify the WALLPAPER entry (currently leaves.bmp) to WINNT40\FURRYD~1.BMP (check the path for this file before making the change—hint: Use FIND).
10. Modify the TileWallpaper entry to the value 1.
11. Close the registry. When do these changes take effect? Log off and then log back in and see if the changes have taken effect. If not, shut down and restart.

Exercise 2—Using the Registry

1. Open the Registry Editor.
2. Click in the HKEY_LOCAL_MACHINE subtree window to make it active.
3. Expand through the SOFTWARE hive to find the WINLOGON key: SOFTWARE\Microsoft\Windows NT\Current Version\Winlogon.
4. Double-click the parameter *Legal Notice Caption* on the right side of the window and enter the caption **Legal Notice**.
5. Double-click the parameter Legal Notice Text and enter the following: **Unauthorized access will be punished!**
6. Choose EDIT\ADD VALUE and enter the value name **DontDisplayLastUserName** with a data type of REG_SZ. Choose OK and enter the value 1 for "yes."
7. Close the Registry. When do these changes take effect? Log off and then log back in and see if the changes have taken effect. If not, shut down and restart.

Exercise 3—Using the Registry, Part 2

1. Open the Registry editor and make the HKEY_USERS subtree window active.
2. Expand through the .DEFAULT key to find DESKTOP: .DEFAULT\Control Panel\Desktop.
3. Modify the Wallpaper entry with the value LEAVES.BMP and the TileWallpaper entry to 1. This will change the default wallpaper that displays on booting NT.
4. Close the Registry. When do these changes take effect? Log off and then log back in and see if the changes have taken effect. If not, shut down and restart.

Exercise 4—System Policy Editor

1. Log in to the server as Administrator.
2. Start the System Policy Editor. (Start\Programs\Administrative Tools\System Policy Editor.)
3. If an existing NTCONFIG.POL file exists in WINNT40\SYSTEM32\REPL\IMPORT\SCRIPTS, open it. Otherwise, select File\New Profile.
4. Choose Edit\Add User and enter your valid user account.
5. Double-click your new user icon to display the policies.
6. Select Desktop, click the Wallpaper check box, and enter the path and file name to your favorite wallpaper in the lower part of the window (i.e., WINNT40\leaves.bmp).
7. Select System\Restrictions and check Disable Registry Editing Tools.
8. Choose Shell\Restrictions and check Remove Run Command from Start Menu and Don't Save Settings at Exit.
9. Close the policy and save it as NTCONFIG.POL in the WINNT40\SYSTEM32\REPL\IMPORT\SCRIPTS subdirectory.
10. Log off and log back on as the user account whose policy you modified. You should note the changes that have taken effect: The wallpaper should now be LEAVES, you should be unable to run REGEDT32, you should not have RUN as a Start menu option, and any changes you make to the environment, i.e., colors, cursors, will not be saved.

11. Log back on as Administrator and make further changes to experiment, or delete the policy.

Chapter 5—Managing Users and Groups

These exercises are most helpful if you have two computers available.

Exercise 1—Creating Users and Groups

Complete this exercise on both workstations if you have two.

1. Using Notepad, create the following logon script called KITE.BAT and save it in the WINNT40\SYSTEM32\REPL\IMPORT\SCRIPTS subdirectory.

   @echo Welcome to the Kite Flyers network!

   @echo off

   Pause

2. Use User Manager to create the following user accounts on both workstations. Require each to change their password when they log on (check User Must Change Password at Next Logon). In the Profiles button for each, enter the KITE.BAT logon script you created in Step 1, and enter the following home directory: **c:\users\%USERNAME%** using the drive in which you installed NT and that contains the USERS directory.

New Users

Username	Full Name	Description	Password
BrownC	Chris Brown	Chairperson	password
KreskeL	Lois Kreske	Secretary General	password
BarnesD	David Barnes	Marketing Manager	password
Donovan	Donovan	MIS Manager	password

3. Create the following group accounts:

Group Name	Description	Members
Managers	Kite Flyers Management Team	BrownC KreskeL BarnesD Donovan
Marketing	Marketing Team	BarnesD
MIS	MIS Team	Donovan

4. Create the following template accounts. Require the user to change password at next logon. Choose the Groups button, remove the Users group for each and add in the corresponding group you created in Step 3 (Sales for SalesTemp, Marketing for MarketingTemp, MIS for MISTemp). Choose the Profile button for each and enter in the login script you created (kite.bat) and the following home directory: c:\users\%USERNAME% using the drive in which you installed NT that contains the USERS directory (use Windows Explorer to confirm it).

Username	Full Name	Description	Password
SalesTemp	Sales Template	Sales Representative	stemplate
MarketingTemp	Marketing Template	Account Manager	mtemplate
MIStemp	MIS Template	System Analyst	itemplate

5. Create the following accounts by copying the appropriate template you created in Step 4. Notice what elements of the template account are copied (description, password options, group and profile information) and which you need to fill in username, full name, password).

   Sales

   FlagL, Lois Flag, password

   BarnesD, David Barnes, password

   Marketing

   Doggie, Doggie, password

   MIS

   GatesB, William Gates, password

   BaileyG, George Bailey, password

6. Use Windows Explorer to confirm that the home directories for each account were created.

Exercise 2—Managing User Profiles

Complete this exercise from Computer1.

1. Log on as GatesB. Change the password as instructed. Modify your environment settings by changing the screen colors, adding a wallpaper, and creating a shortcut to Solitaire on the desktop.
2. Log off and log on again as Administrator.
3. Use Windows Explorer to find the WINNT40\PROFILES directory. Notice the new subdirectory structure for GatesB with the file NTUSER.DAT in the GATESB subdirectory. Expand GATESB to find the Desktop subdirectory and notice the shortcut to Solitaire located there.
4. Find the WINNT40\PROFILES\Default User subdirectory. Expand it to display the Desktop subdirectory. Create a shortcut here for Solitaire (right-click and drag the Solitaire icon from WINNT40\SYSTEM32). Also, rename the NTUSER.DAT file in Default User to NTUSER.OLD and copy the NTUSER.DAT file from GATESB.
5. Create a new user called PAT with no password and no password options selected.
6. Log on as PAT. Notice that the Solitaire shortcut and the environment settings became part of PAT's profile. This will be true not only for each new user you create, but also for any previous user who has not yet logged on for the first time and thus created their own profile.
7. Log back on as Administrator. Use Windows Explorer to delete the NTUSER.DAT file from WINNT40\PROFILES\Default User and rename NTUSER.OLD back to NTUSER.DAT.

Exercise 3—Managing User Profiles–Part 2

1. Use Windows Explorer to create a new directory called Profiles in the root directory of Computer2. Right-click it and select Sharing, Shared As, and select OK. (If you do not have two computers installed, complete this exercise from the same computer and adjust the directions accordingly.)

2. On the first computer, Start User Manager. Delete the account PAT. Create a new user account called MEG with no password and no password options selected. Choose Profile and in User Profile Path enter the following: **\\Computer2\profiles\ntuser.dat**.
3. Start the System applet from the Control Panel and switch to the User Profiles tab. You will note an entry for Account Deleted. This was PAT that you deleted in Step 2. Select this entry and choose Delete and Yes.
4. In the list, select the entry for GATESB and choose Copy To.
5. In the Copy Profile To text box enter **\\computer2\profiles**, or choose Browse to find the directory in Network Neighborhood. In Permitted to use, select Change and choose MEG from the list (be sure to select Show Users). Choose OK and exit from System.
6. Log on as MEG. Notice that MEG received her profile from the second computer and that her environment settings match GATESB.
7. On the first computer, log off and log back in again as Administrator. Open the properties for MEG in User Manager and change the profile file reference from NTUSER.DAT to NTUSER.MAN.
8. Log on as MEG. Notice that you are unable to log in because you have referenced a mandatory profile that does not exist.
9. Log back in as Administrator. Delete the account MEG.

Chapter 6—Security and Permissions

This set of labs will be most effective if you use both computers, and if you have one NTFS partition created on each computer.

If you do not currently have an NTFS partition, but have an existing FAT partition that you can convert to NTFS (other than the boot partition), use the following Steps to convert it to NTFS:

1. Open a DOS prompt window.
2. At the prompt type CONVERT D: /FS:NTFS, where D: represents the letter of the partition that you are converting.
3. Press ENTER. If there are any files in use by NT on that partition such as the pagefile, you will see a message to the effect that you must reboot for the conversion to take effect. Do so. Otherwise, NT will convert the partition when you press ENTER.

If you do not have a partition that you can convert, but do have at least 50M of free disk space available, you can use Disk Administrator to create an NTFS partition. Follow these steps.

1. Start Disk Administrator. If this is the first time you are starting this utility, press OK to the start up message.
2. Click the free disk space available in the graphic screen provided.
3. From Partition on the menu, choose CREATE.
4. Specify the total size of the partition and choose OK. It should be at least 50M, but can be no smaller than 10M.
5. Choose Partition, Commit Changes Now.
6. From Tools, choose Format and NTFS.
7. When format is complete, exit Disk Administrator.

Exercise 1—Using Shares-Part 1

Log on as Administrator.

1. Using Windows Explorer, create the following folders and files on both computers in the NTFS partition. Place a couple lines of text in each file (you don't need to get fancy now).

\TOOLS	DOOM.TXT (Create new text file)
	BUDGET97.DOC (Create new Wordpad file)
\TOOLS\DATA	MEMO.DOC
	WELCOME.TXT

2. Share TOOLS as TOOLS.
3. Remove Everyone from the ACL for the share and add the Managers group with Change, and the Sales group with Read.
4. Create a new user called SimmonsB on Computer1. Add this user to the Sales group on Computer1.
5. Log on as SimmonsB on Computer1.
6. Using Network Neighborhood, access the TOOLS share on Computer2. Can you access it? NT should tell you that you do not have a valid account or password on Computer2. Recall that in a workgroup

environment, you must either create a valid account for every user that needs access to shared resources on a computer, or be able to connect as a valid user.

7. Create the account SimmonsB on Computer2 using the same password as you did on Computer1. Make this account a member of the Sales group on Computer2.
8. On Computer1, access the TOOLS share again. Your access should now be successful because you have a valid account on Computer2 that matches the username and password of the account on Computer1. Disconnect from the share.
9. On Computer2, change SimmonsB's password to something else.
10. On Computer1, right-click Network Neighborhood and choose Map Network Drive.
11. Choose the TOOLS share from the list displayed, or type in the path \\Computer2\TOOLS.
12. In the Connect As box, enter SimmonsB and choose OK. NT will request the password for SimmonsB on Computer2. Enter it in to gain access to the share. If you know the name and password of a valid user account on another computer, you can access the share on that computer.

Exercise 2—Using Shares–Part 2

1. On Computer1, log on as BrownC.
2. Connect to the TOOLS share on Computer2.
3. Open the file DOOM.TXT and make a change to the file and close it.
4. Log off, and log in as BarnesD.
5. Connect to the TOOLS share on Computer2.
6. Open the file DOOM.TXT and make a change to the file. Can you save the file? Note that NT will not let you save changes made to the file because BarnesD is a member of the Sales group which has been given Read access to the file. Do not close the file.
7. On Computer2, make BarnesD a member of the Managers group.
8. On Computer1, try to access the file and save changes again. Can you do it? Note that you will not be able to save your changes because

BarnesD's access token for the file still reflects the old group membership.

9. Close the file, and try to access it again and save changes. Could you do it? Disconnect from the share and reconnect, modify the file and save the changes. Were you successful? Note for yourself at which point after group membership changes that the change took effect.

Exercise 3—Hidden Shares

1. Share the DATA folder on Computer2 as DATA$. Give only Managers Change permission to the share.
2. Log on as BrownC on Computer1.
3. Using Network Neighborhood, look for the DATA share in the list of shares for Computer2. You should not see it since the $ makes it a hidden share.
4. Right-click Network Neighborhood and choose Map Network Drive. In the path box type **\\Computer2\DATA$** and choose OK. You should have been able to access the share.
5. Modify the file MEMO.DOC and save your changes.
6. Disconnect from the share and log off.

Exercise 4—File and Folder Permissions

Log on to both computers as Administrator and make the following changes:

- Modify the NTFS permissions for the TOOLS folder. Remove Everyone and add Managers with Read and Administrators with Full Control.
- Modify the NTFS permissions for the DATA folder. Remove Everyone and add Sales with Change and MIS with Add.

1. Log on to Computer1 as BrownC.
2. Use Windows Explorer to expand the NTFS partition. Open the file BUDGET97.DOC in TOOLS and modify it.
3. Can you save your changes? Note that the NTFS permission for Managers is Read. Since BrownC is a member of Managers, he also gets Read access to the file and therefore cannot save changes.

4. Log off and log back on as Donovan, a member of the MIS and Managers group.
5. Use Windows Explorer to access the DATA folder. Since MIS has only Add permission, you cannot access the DATA folder.
6. Use Notepad to create a document called DONOVAN.TXT. Try to save it in the DATA folder. (Access denied.) Try to save it in the TOOLS folder. (Only have READ access, so can't write a file to this folder.) Save it in the root directory of the NTFS partition.
7. Open a DOS prompt window. At the prompt, copy the file DONOVAN.TXT from the root of the NTFS partition to the TOOLS\DATA directory. Note that you can do this since you have ADD permission to the DATA folder.
8. Log off.

Exercise 5—File and Folder Permissions–Part 2

1. Log on as BrownC.
2. Access the TOOLS share on Computer2.
3. Open the file DOOM.TXT and modify it.
4. Save your changes. Can you do it? Not this time. The share permission is Change for Managers, and the NTFS permission is Read for Managers. When accessing a resource through a share, the more restrictive of the permissions will become the effective permissions. Thus, your effective permission is Read and you cannot save changes.
5. Log on as Administrator on Computer2.
6. Change the NTFS permission for Managers on TOOLS to Full Control.
7. On Computer1, reconnect to the share and try to modify and save the file again. This time, you can since the effective permission is Change (the more restrictive of the share permission—Change—and the NTFS permission—Full Control.)
8. As BrownC, create a new file called BrownC.TXT in the TOOLS directory on Computer2.
9. Log off.
10. As Administrator on Computer2, change the NTFS permission for managers on TOOLS to Change.

Exercise 6—File and Folder Permissions–Part 3

1. Log on as Donovan on Computer2.
2. Locate the TOOLS folder on Computer2.
3. Locate the file BrownC.TXT and display its Security properties (right-click, Properties, Security).
4. Choose Ownership to see that BrownC is the owner.
5. Can you take ownership of the file? No, because you only have Change permission.
6. Log off and log back on as Administrator.
7. Add Donovan to the ACL for the file BrownC.TXT with the NTFS Special Access Take Ownership permission.
8. Log on as Donovan again, and try to take ownership of the file. This time you can, because you have the permission to do so. Verify that Donovan is now the owner of BrownC.TXT.

Chapter 8—Remote Server Management

The first exercise of this lab assumes that at least one Windows NT server installation is available to use Network Client Administrator to create a shared folder to be used to install server tools on client computers on the network.

If a Windows NT 4.0 Workstation is available, Exercise 2 has you install server tools on that platform. If a Windows 95 platform is available, Exercise 3 has you install server tools on that platform.

Exercise 1

Complete this exercise from your domain controller.

1. Log on to your PDC and start the Network Client Administrator utility. (Start, Programs, Administrative Tools, Network Client Administrator.)
2. When the Network Client Administrator selection box appears, select Copy Client-based Network Administration Tools and choose Continue.
3. When the Share Client-based Network Administration Tools appears, enter the path where the server tools source files are located.

(Example: F:\Clients.) Accept the default destination path and share name and click OK.

4. When the files are copied to the selected folder, a Network Client Administrator information box appears. Read the message and choose OK.
5. Another Network Client Administrator information box appears stating that the Network Administration Tools are now available, choose OK.
6. On the Network Client Administrator selection box, select Exit.

Exercise 2

Complete this exercise from a Windows NT Workstation computer if available on the network.

1. Log on to a Windows NT 4.0 Workstation on the network with the administrator account.
2. Map to the network share created in Exercise 1.
3. Double-click the Winnt folder.
4. Double-click Setup.bat.
5. An MS-DOS prompt will start and the server tools files will be copied to your computer. Record the server tools .exe files that were copied in the following spaces:

   ____________________, ____________________,

   ____________________,

   Dhcpadmin.exe Poledit.exe Rasadmin.exe

   ____________________, ____________________,

   ____________________,

   Rplmgr.exe Srvmgr.exe Usrmgr.exe

   ____________________.

   Winsmgr.exe
6. Press any key to continue.
7. Right-click the Start button and choose Open.
8. When the Start menu appears, choose the File drop-down menu, select New, Folder, and type **Server Tools**.
9. Open Explorer and locate the <winntroot>\System32 folder.

10. Locate the server tools .exe files one at a time as recorded in Step 5. With the primary mouse button, drag each file to the Server Tools folder created in Step 9.

    Hint: Position the Explorer window and the Start menu window so each can be viewed.
11. Click the Start button, hover over the Server Tools selection, and choose Shortcut to Usrmgr.exe.
12. From the User drop-down menu, choose Select Domain and from the Select Domain window, select Domain A.
13. View the user and group accounts from that domain.
14. Close User Manager.

Exercise 3

Complete this exercise from a Windows 95 computer if available on the network.

1. Start Windows 95, open the Control Panel, and select the Add/Remove Programs icon.
2. Select the Windows Setup tab from the Add/Remove Programs Properties sheet and click the Have Disk button.
3. When the Install from Disk dialog box appears, enter the path to the server tools source files created in Exercise 1. (Example: <computername>\SetupAdm\Win95.)
4. When the Have Disk property sheet appears, select the check box next to the Windows NT Server Tools item and click Install.
5. After the server tools are installed, choose Start, Programs, Windows NT Server Tools, and select User Manager for Domains.
6. From the User drop-down menu, choose Select Domain and from the Select Domain window, select Domain A.
7. View the user and group accounts from that domain.
8. Close User Manager.

Chapter 9—Managing Disk Resources

These exercises are designed for computers which have two physical disk drives, and at least 100M of free space outside of an extended partition on one or more drives. If you have less, or if the free space includes an area of an extended partition, you will need to modify the exercise according to your configuration.

Exercise 1—Using Disk Administrator

1. Start Disk Administrator.
2. Select an area of free space.
3. Choose Partition, Create and create a new primary partition of 20M.
4. Create another primary partition of 50M.
5. Commit the changes.
6. Change the drive letter for the 50M partition to X and the 20M partition to Y through Tools, Assign Drive Letter.
7. Format drive Y as FAT and drive X as NTFS.
8. Close Disk Administrator and save your changes.

Exercise 2—Using Compression

1. Start Windows Explorer.
2. Select drive Y and create a new folder called TRUMP.
3. Copy WINNT256.BMP from the WINNT40 directory into TRUMP.
4. Look at the properties sheet for the file. Is there a Security tab? Is there a Compress attribute on the General tab? (NO! It's a FAT partition!)
5. Copy the folder and its file from drive Y to drive X.
6. Look at the file's properties sheet again. Is there a Security tab and Compress attribute option? (YES! It's an NTFS partition!)
7. Enable the compress attribute for the file and choose apply. What is its compressed size?
8. Close Windows Explorer.
9. Open a DOS Prompt window (Start, Programs, DOS Prompt).
10. At the prompt, type **CONVERT Y: /FS:NTFS** and press ENTER. NT will proceed to convert the partition from FAT to NTFS. (If it tells you to restart, do so.)

11. Start Windows Explorer.
12. Select drive Y and look at the properties of the file in TRUMP. You should now see the Security tab and Compress attribute option since the partition is now NTFS.

Exercise 3—Using Volume Sets

1. Start Disk Administrator.
2. Select drive Y and delete it. Note the confirmation message.
3. Select that area of free space (20M) and the remaining free space on the drive.
4. Choose Partition, Create Volume Set from the menu. Note the change in legend information indicating the new volume set.
5. Commit your changes, assign it drive letter Y, and format the volume set as FAT.
6. Close Disk Administrator.
7. Start Windows Explorer and select drive Y. Can you tell that it is a volume set? (NO! Not even through properties!) NT treats the volume set as a single drive.
8. Copy X:\TRUMP to Y.
9. Close Windows Explorer and start Disk Administrator.
10. Select the second member of Y and choose Partition, Delete. Note the confirmation message, and delete it. What did you delete? (The entire volume set.)
11. Close Disk Administrator and start Windows Explorer.
12. Confirm that drive Y is gone.

Exercise 4—Extended Volume Sets

1. Start Disk Administrator.
2. Select any FAT partition on your computer, and an area of free space on the same or another drive.
3. Choose Partition, Extend Volume Set from the menu. Can you do it? (NO! You cannot extend FAT partitions!)
4. Select the NTFS partition drive X and an area of free space on the same drive or another drive.

5. Choose Partition, Extend Volume set. Can you do it? (YES! You can extend NTFS partitions!) What else do you notice? (The extended set is automatically formatted as NTFS.)
6. Delete drive X. Notice that if you delete any member of the extended volume set, you delete the entire volume set.

Exercise 5—Using Stripe Sets

(Only if you have at least two physical disks with free space on each.)

1. Start Disk Administrator.
2. Select an area of free space on one disk, and an area of free space on another. (If you have additional disks, select free space on these as well.)
3. Choose Partition, Create Stripe Set from the menu.
4. Create the largest stripe set that you are allowed.
5. Notice in Disk Administrator how the stripe set is evenly distributed across the free space on the disks.
6. Delete the stripe set.

Exercise 6—Backup and Restore

(Only if you have a working tape drive attached to your computer.)

1. Use Disk Administrator to create a 50M NTFS partition (drive Z).
2. Use Windows Explorer to create a folder called BITMAPS in it and copy the bitmap files from the WINNT40 directory to BITMAPS.
3. Insert a new tape in the tape backup device.
4. Start Backup (Start, Programs, Administrative Tools, Backup).
5. Select the Z drive and check the check box in front of it to select all its contents. Double-click it to verify that the bitmap folder and all its files have been selected.
6. Choose BACKUP. Enter in a tape name, select Verify Files, keep all other defaults and proceed.
7. When backup is complete, exit the utility.
8. Use Notepad to view the BACKUP.LOG file created in the WINNT40 directory.
9. Start Windows Explorer.

10. Select drive Z and delete the BITMAPS folder.
11. Start Backup. The existing tape will be displayed in the window with the backup set you created listed.
12. If you appended to an existing tape, select Operations, Catalog to find and load the backup set for the BITMAPS files and folder. Otherwise, double-click the backup set in the tapes window to load the catalog for the backup set.
13. Select all files from the backup set including the BITMAPS folder.
14. Choose RESTORE and keep all defaults. Be sure the restore path is pointing to drive Z.
15. After the restore completes, exit the utility.
16. Start Windows Explorer and verify that the files and folder have been restored.

Chapter 10—Performance Monitor

Exercise 1—Using Performance Monitor

1. At a command prompt type: **DISKPERF -Y**.
2. If your computer has more than 16M RAM installed, modify the boot.ini file so that you boot only with 16M of RAM:

   To the line under [Operating Systems] that contains the location of the NT 4.0 workstation system files add the switch: /MAXMEM:16. (Remember, Boot.ini is a read-only file.)
3. Shut down and restart NT to enable the Performance Monitor disk objects and their counters.
4. Start the Windows Explorer utility and Pinball.
5. Start the Performance Monitor from the Administrative Tools group and add the following objects and counters to a new chart.
6. Track the values of each of the counters you added to the chart especially noting the working set values for Performance Monitor, Windows Explorer and Pinball (about 2.2M, 175K, and 184K, respectively). Note also the Commit Limit for the pagefile (will vary). Hint: Press Ctrl+H to highlight each line graph.
7. Switch to Explorer and create a new folder called PERFMON. Switch to Pinball and start the demo game.

8. Track the activity of the chart again and note the average values for each of the counters in the chart. Note any significant changes. In particular, you should have noticed a spike for %Processor Time for the processor and each of the three processes driven proportionately as each one performed its activity (creating the folder, running the demo game, updating the chart with the new statistics). Notice the flurry in disk counter activity initially, and then how it settles once the actions were performed. Notice, too, the increased amount of memory required by Pinball and Performance Monitor to correspond with their activities. Multiply Pages/Sec and Avg. Disk sec/Transfer to obtain the percent of Disk I/O related to pagefile activity. It will be well below Microsoft's suggested 10 percent threshold.
9. Switch to Windows Explorer. Copy the files only from the WINNT40 directory into the Perfmon folder. While the copy is taking place, switch to the Performance Monitor and note the Pages/Sec and Avg. Disk sec/Transfer. These have all peaked at or near the top of the scale. Multiply the average value for each together to obtain a percentage. This should be just over 10 percent and indicates that for this activity, the percent of disk I/O related to pagefile activity was greater than Microsoft's recommended 10 percent. If this was consistently above 10 percent, you might consider adding more RAM.
10. Open the BOOT.INI file and remove the /MAXMEM:16 switch. Restart NT.
11. If you have more than 16M RAM installed, repeat Steps 4-9 and note the differences (all disk values and %processor times should be less, though they will vary depending on the amount of additional RAM you have).
12. Close Windows Explorer and Pinball.

Exercise 2—Performance Monitor Logs

1. With Performance Monitor still running, select View from the menu, then LOG. Choose Add to Log and add each of the following objects to the log. Then choose Done.

   Logical Disk, Memory, Process, Processor
2. Select Options from the menu, then choose LOG. Enter PERF1.LOG for the log name and save it in the PERFMON folder. Set the interval to 1 second and choose Start Log.

3. Start Pinball and run the demo. Start Windows Explorer and create a new folder called PERFMON2. Copy everything from Perfmon into Perfmon2.
4. Switch to Performance Monitor. Wait another minute, then select Options, LOG, then Stop Log. Save the log file.
5. Select File from the menu, then New Chart to clear and reset the chart view for new values.
6. Select Options from the menu, then Data From. Under Log File, find and select the PERF1.LOG file you just created. Choose OK.
7. Select Edit from the menu, then Add To Chart. Note the entries listed represent those you collected during the log process. Add the following objects and counters to the chart as you did before. This time, the chart will represent static data collected from the log.

Object	Processor	Instance
Processor	%Processor Time	0
Process	%Processor Time	Perfmon, Explorer, Pinball
Process	Working Set	Perfmon, Explorer, Pinball
Memory	Commit Limit	N/A
Memory	Pages/Sec	N/A
Logical Disk	Avg. Disk sec/ Transfer	pagefile drive
Logical Disk	%Disk Time	pagefile drive

8. Note the average values for each during the log period.
9. Use Edit, Time Window to change the time range to show only the period of peak activity. Note how the average values change.
10. Close Performance Monitor.
11. Use Windows Explorer to delete the folders Perfmon and Perfmon2.

Chapter 11—Printing

This lab requires that you have one printer attached to one of your computers and assumes it is connected to Computer1. Installing Windows 95 print drivers is also an option if you have the Windows 95 CDROM handy.

Exercise 1—Creating a Printer

Even if you have installed your printer already, complete this exercise on Computer1. Pay close attention to the screens and messages and options available to you. Refer back to the chapter text to highlight and clarify screens.

1. Start the Add Printer wizard. (My Computer, Printers, Add Printer.)
2. You will install the printer on your local computer. Choose My Computer.
3. Select the port that your print device is attached to.
4. Select the manufacturer and model of the print device connected to your computer.
5. Set this to be your print default.
6. Call it Managers Printer and share the printer as NTPRINT. If you have the Windows 95 source CD-ROM available, select Windows 95 from the list of additional print drivers to support.
7. Print a test page to verify your configuration works.
8. If necessary, enter the appropriate path to the NT source files to complete installation.

Exercise 1A—Optional

If you have a network TCP/IP printer available that you can use and are allowed to manage, be sure to add the TCP/IP protocol to your computer and repeat Exercise 1. For Step 3, choose Add Port and select local port. Enter in the IP address of the network printer.

Exercise 2—Connecting to a Network Printer

1. On Computer2, start the Add Printer Wizard.
2. This time, choose Network Printer Server to connect to the printer you just created on Computer1.
3. From the Connect to Printer browse screen, expand through the Microsoft Windows Network entries to find the printer you created on Computer1 called NTPRINT and select it.

   OR

   Type in the UNC path to the printer as follows: **\\COMPUTER1\NTPRINT**.

4. Make this the default printer on Computer2.
5. Complete the installation. A network printer icon will be displayed in the Printers folder.
6. Use Notepad to create and save a short text document called PRINT.TXT. Suggested content: **If you can read this, printing was successful**.
7. Print PRINT.TXT to the network printer you just connected to. Was printing successful? YES.
8. On Computer1, open the NTPRINT print manager window and pause the shared printer.
9. Resubmit PRINT.TXT on Computer2.
10. In the NTPRINT window, select the PRINT.TXT print job and explore the Document Properties. Schedule the job to print at the next half-hour.
11. Resume the printer and wait until the next half-hour to see your print job print.

Exercise 3—Managing Printer Properties

1. On Computer1, open the NTPRINT properties sheet and select the Scheduling tab.
2. Set the priority to the highest setting (99).
3. On the Security tab, choose Permissions.
4. Remove Everyone and add Managers with Print permission.
5. Close NTPRINT properties.
6. Create another printer for the same print device on the same port. Call it Staff Printer and share it as STAFFPRT.
7. After it is created, open its properties and select the Scheduling tab.
8. Set the priority to the lowest setting (1).
9. On the Security tab, choose Permissions.
10. Remove Everyone and add MIS with Print permission.
11. Close STAFFPRT properties.
12. Make Donovan a member of the Power Users group on Computer1.
13. Log on to Computer1 as a Manager account—Donovan.
14. Open both NTPRINT and STAFFPRT windows. Pause NTPRINT and STAFFPRT.

15. Create a text document called TESTP1.TXT with the text **This is a test print - 1** and print to NTPRINT. You should see it queued up in the NTPRINT window.
16. On Computer2, log on as GatesB.
17. Connect to STAFFPRT and make it default.
18. Create a text document called Staffp1.TXT with the text **This is a staff test print - 1** and print to STAFFPRT. You should see it queued up in the STAFFPRT window on Computer1.
19. Create two more documents on Computer1 (TESTP2.TXT and TESTP3.TXT with similar text) and on Computer2 (Staffp2.TXT and Staffp3.TXT with similar text) and print them to their respective printers. You will see them queued up.
20. Resume STAFFPRT then NTPRINT. In what order did the print jobs print? Chances are that since STAFFPRT was resumed first, its low priority STAFFp1.TXT job was sent to the print device ahead of TESTP1.TXT. Nevertheless, before any other staff jobs print, the Managers' jobs will print first since their print queue associated with the same printer has a higher priority than staff print jobs.

If your computer had a previous printer setup, restore it as your default now if you like.

Chapter 12—Windows NT 4.0 Architecture

Portions of this lab require that you have installed at least two 16-bit Windows 3.1 applications. These might be earlier versions of Microsoft Office, or even your favorite Windows games.

Exercise 1—Running DOS and Windows 16-Bit Applications

1. Right-click the Task Bar and start the Task Manager. From View, Select Columns choose Base Priority. Resize the Task Manager window so that you can see the Base Priorities column.
2. Switch to Processes. Unless you started a Win 16 application earlier, you will see no entries for NTVDM.

3. Choose Start, Run and start the MS-DOS application EDIT.COM. This is the 16-bit MS-DOS Editor and comes with NT in the WINN40\SYSTEM32 directory.
4. Switch back to Task Manager and notice the addition of a new NTVDM entry. Notice the amount of memory allocated for it and its priority.
5. Start one of your Windows 16-bit applications.
6. Switch back to Task Manager and notice a new NTVDM entry with subentries for the application and the WOWEXEC.EXE. Notice also its Memory Usage and CPU Usage and priority.
7. Start another Windows 16-bit application. Make a mental note of the speed with which it loaded. Since it is being loaded into an existing WOW NTVDM, it will load rather quickly.
8. Switch back to Task Manager and notice its subentry in the WOW NTVDM as well as the memory and CPU changes.
9. Close the DOS application and both of the Win 16 applications and note the changes in Task Manager. The WOW NTVDM remains loaded against the event of a new Win 16 application starting, but the closed application entries have been removed.
10. Leave Task Manager running.

Exercise 2—Running 16-Bit Windows Applications in Their Own Memory Space

1. Start both of the Win 16 applications.
2. Switch to Task Manager and notice the WOW NTVDM sub-entries. On the Performance tab, note the total physical RAM in use.
3. Close one of the Win 16 applications and notice the change in physical RAM.
4. Create a shortcut on your desktop for the Win 16 application you closed. Right-click it and display its properties. On the Shortcut tab, select Run in Separate Memory Space.
5. Start the Win 16 application from its shortcut. Notice that it takes a little longer to load than in the last exercise. This is because NT must create a new WOW NTVDM for this application.

6. Switch back to Task Manager and confirm that a new WOW NTVDM has been created. Note its memory, CPU, and priority statistics.
7. Switch to the Task Manager Performance tab and note the total physical RAM in use. It is noticeably higher than when both applications ran in the same WOW NTVDM.
8. Close each Win 16 application and monitor the decrease in physical RAM used. How many WOW NTVDM entries remain on the Processes tab? One.

Exercise 3—Managing Process Priorities

1. Start Pinball from Start, Programs, Accessories, Games. If it is not available, load it through the Add Programs applet in Control Panel. (A quick way to activate a Pinball game and notice changes in this exercise is to run a demo game from the Game menu.)
2. Switch to Task Manager and find its entry. Notice its priority is set to Normal.
3. Close Pinball. Open a DOS Command Prompt window.
4. Start Pinball with a low priority by typing:

   START /LOW PINBALL
5. Switch to Task Manager and verify that Pinball is running with low priority. Pinball itself should appear to be running a bit sluggishly, though on fast Pentium systems, the change may not be noticeable.
6. On the Processes tab in Task Manager, right-click the Pinball entry and choose Set Priority. Change it to normal. Switch to the Performance tab and arrange Pinball so that you can see part of the Performance charts in the background. Notice that the charts continue to record data while you play Pinball.
7. Switch to Task Manager. On the Processes tab, right-click Pinball and change its priority to high. Switch to the Performance tab and arrange the screens as before. Notice that the chart ceases to record, or records very slowly while you play Pinball in the foreground.
8. Close Pinball and Task Manager.

Chapter 17—Windows NT Networking Services

Exercise 1—Managing Network Properties

Complete this exercise from both Computer1 and Computer2.

1. Start the Network applet from Control Panel (or right-click Network Neighborhood and view its Properties).
2. Select the Adapters tab to view your installed network adapter card.
3. Select the adapter card from the list and choose Properties. Note the properties of your adapter.
4. Close the adapter properties window and select the Bindings tab. Record the bindings for NetBEUI under NetBIOS, Workstation, and Server.
5. Select the Protocols tab and note that only NetBEUI is installed (unless you did something you weren't told to do in another lab).
6. Choose Add, and select TCP/IP protocol from the network protocols list. Be sure to have the source CD-ROM available. When prompted, enter the drive and path to the source files.
7. After the protocol is installed, choose OK. NT will prompt you for TCP/IP protocol settings. For Computer1, enter 121.132.4.1 with subnet mask 255.255.255.0, and for Computer2, enter 121.132.4.2 with subnet mask 255.255.255.0. (If you are connected to your company network and are using TCP/IP, use your company's recommended IP address and subnet mask, if appropriate. If you have a DHCP server available, and can use it, configure the computers to obtain their IP addresses from the DHCP server.)
8. Restart NT when prompted. After NT reboots, open the Network applet again.
9. On the Bindings tab, note the additional bindings for TCP/IP. Record these and compare them against the NetBEUI bindings. Notice that both bindings are bound to the Workstation and Server service. This means that you can connect to network resources on any server using NetBEUI or TCP/IP, and that your computer can service requests from any computer using NetBEUI or TCP/IP.

10. At a command prompt, enter the command IPCONFIG. What information is displayed? (IP address, subnet mask, and default gateway.) Record the information.
11. Now enter the command **IPCONFIG /ALL**. What additional information is displayed? (Host, DNS, node, and other NT IP configuration parameters, and the description and physical address of the adapter card.) Record the adapter information.
12. At the command prompt, PING the other computer's address. For example, on Computer1 type: PING 121.132.4.1. You should receive four "Reply from..." messages indicating that communication is established between the computers.
13. Through Windows Explorer, map a network drive to a resource on Computer2. You should be successful. Disconnect the mapping.
14. In the Network applet on Computer1, select the Protocols tab and remove NetBEUI. Restart NT when prompted.
15. After NT reboots, use Windows Explorer to map a drive to the same resource on Computer2. You should be successful. Why? (NT used TCP/IP to establish the connection. Computer2 has both NetBEUI and TCP/IP installed.) Disconnect the mapping.
16. In the Network applet on Computer2, select the Protocols tab and display the properties for TCP/IP.
17. Change the subnet mask to 255.255.0.0. Restart NT when prompted.
18. When Computer2 reboots, use Windows Explorer on Computer1 to map a drive to the same resource on Computer2. You should be unsuccessful this time. Why? (Even though both computers are using TCP/IP and are on the same subnet, they have different subnet masks and so are treated as though they were on different subnets. Therefore, they cannot communicate with each other.)
19. At a command prompt, try the PING command again. You should be unsuccessful (for the same reason as in Step 18).
20. Change the subnet mask on Computer2 back to 255.255.255.0. After the computer reboots, verify that communications can be established between the computers. (Use PING and Windows Explorer.)
21. Reinstall NetBEUI on Computer1. Restart NT when prompted.

Exercise 2—Workstation Bindings

1. In the Network applet on Computer1, select the Bindings tab and expand the Workstation bindings. Highlight Workstation in the list and choose Disable to disable its bindings. Choose OK and restart NT when prompted.
2. When Computer1 reboots, you will probably receive a service message error. Use Event Viewer to note which service failed to start (Workstation), and what other services dependent on it also failed to start (Computer Browser, Messenger).
3. Use Network Neighborhood to locate Computer2. Were you successful? No, because the Workstation service is used to perform this network request, and its bindings have been disabled.
4. Use Network Neighborhood to locate Computer1. Were you successful? Yes. Connect to a shared folder on Computer1 and copy a file to your desktop. Were you successful? Yes. Why? (The Server service on Computer1 handles requests for resources from other computers. These bindings are still enabled, so Computer1 can't browse the network, but it can still share its own resources. This tactic can be used to optimize bindings and improve network performance for NT computers which only need to make their resources available to other computers, but not establish connections of their own.)
5. Re-enable the Workstation bindings on Computer1 and restart NT when prompted.

Chapter 18—TCP/IP and Windows NT

Exercise 1

This exercise is intended to have you install the TCP/IP protocol and to manually configure an IP address and subnet mask. This exercise assumes that only the NetBEUI protocol is presently installed and the source files are located on your computer in a folder ntsrv on your C drive.

1. Log on to your domain controller as the administrator and open up the Network application by selecting Start, Settings, Control Panel, Network Icon.

2. Select the Protocols tab in the Network Properties dialog box and choose the Add button.
3. From the list of available protocols in the Select Network Protocol dialog box, select the TCP/IP Protocol and choose OK.
4. A TCP/IP Setup dialog box appears asking you if you want to use a DHCP server. Answer NO to continue.
5. When the Windows NT Setup dialog box appears, type the location of the source file in the space provided (**C:\ntsrv**) and choose Continue.

   Files will be copied and the TCP/IP protocol and related services will be installed. Notice that the TCP/IP protocol appears in the network protocols window on the Network properties sheet.
6. Choose Close on the Network properties sheet. (Bindings will be reviewed and configured.)
7. A Microsoft TCP/IP properties sheet appears to manually configure an IP address, subnet mask, and default gateway. Enter an IP Address of **131.107.2.x**, where *x* is a unique assigned number. Change the default subnet mask from 255.255.0.0 to **255.255.255.0**. Leave the Default Gateway entry blank.

Note You may require a different IP address and subnet mask because of your local network characteristics. Make sure that you supply a unique IP address, or error messages indicating a duplicate IP address on the network will result.

8. When the Networks Settings Change dialog box appears asking you to shut down and restart your computer, select YES.

Exercise 2

This exercise is intended to have you install the DHCP service to become a DHCP server and to configure a scope of address. You will also designate a group of addresses to be excluded from the scope and add an address reservation. This exercise assumes that the NetBEUI and TCP/IP protocols are presently installed and the source files are located on your computer in a folder ntsrv on your C drive.

1. Log on to your domain controller as the administrator and open up the Network application by selecting Start, Settings, Control Panel, Network Icon.

2. Select the Services tab in the Network properties dialog box and choose the Add button.
3. From the list of available services in the Select Network Services dialog box, select Microsoft DHCP Server and choose OK.
4. When the Windows NT Setup dialog box appears, type the location of the source file in the space provided (**C:\ntsrv**) and choose Continue.

   Files will be copied and the DHCP server service will be installed.

   An information box appears stating that if any adapters are using DHCP to obtain an IP address, they are now required to use a static IP address.
5. Press OK.

   Notice that the DHCP server appears in the network services window on the Network properties sheet.
6. Choose Close on the Network properties sheet. (Bindings will be reviewed and configured.)
7. When the Networks Settings Change dialog box appears asking you to shut down and restart your computer, select YES.
8. When your computer restarts, log on to your domain controller as the administrator and open up the DHCP Manager application by selecting Start, Programs, Administrative Tools, DHCP Manager**.** The DHCP Manager application dialog box appears.
9. From the Scope drop-down menu, select Create. A Create Scope (Local) configuration sheet appears.
10. In the IP Address Pool Start Address text box, enter **131.107.2.150** and in the IP Address Pool Stop Address text box, enter **131.107.2.199**. In the IP Address Pool Subnet Mask text box, enter **255.255.255.0**.
11. In the Exclusion Range Start Address text box, enter **131.107.2.170** and in the Exclusion Range Start Address text box, enter **131.107.2.180** and select Add. The range of address will appear in the Exclusion Addresses window.
12. In the Lease Duration area of the screen, ensure the Limited To radio button is selected and change the lease duration from the default value of 3 days to 1 day. Click OK.

13. A DHCP Manager message box appears telling you the scope was created successfully but is not activated yet. It then asks if you would like to activate the scope now. Click YES.
14. The new scope will appear under the Local Machine entry on the DHCP Manager dialog box with the light bulb on (this means the scope is active). If the new scope does not appear automatically, double-click the Local Machine entry.
15. On the DHCP Manager dialog box, select the newly created scope. From the Scope drop-down menu, select Add Reservations. The Add Reserved Clients information screen appears.
16. Review the required information for this screen. Notice the network number automatically appears in the IP Address portion of the screen. Why did this happen?

    (Because the starting address and subnet mask values were entered when the scope was created.)
17. Enter a value of your IP address used in Exercise 1, Step 7 in the IP Address text box.

    For the next step, a unique identifier is required to associate a specific network card with this reservation. To obtain a network card unique MAC address, perform the following steps:

    - Start up a command prompt.
    - Type **ipconfig /all**.
    - Record the Physical Address (this is the unique identifier).
18. Enter your 12-digit MAC address in the Unique Identifier text box.
19. Enter your computer name in the Client Name text box and choose Add, Close.
20. From the DHCP Manager dialog box, select the Scope drop-down menu and select Active Leases. Ensure the reservation you added is present. Remove the reservation by selecting Delete and Close DHCP Manager.

Exercise 3

This exercise is intended to have you install the WINS service on your computer to become a WINS server. This exercise assumes that the NetBEUI and TCP/IP protocols are presently installed and the source files are located on your computer in a folder ntsrv on your C drive.

1. Log on to your domain controller as the administrator and open up the Network application by selecting Start, Settings, Control Panel, Network Icon.
2. Select the Services tab in the Network properties dialog box and choose the Add button.
3. From the list of available services in the Select Network Services dialog box, select Windows Internet Name Service and choose OK.
4. When the Windows NT Setup dialog box appears, type the location of the source file in the space provided (**C:\ntsrv**) and choose Continue.

   Files will be copied and the WINS server service will be installed.
5. Choose Close on the Network properties sheet. (Bindings will be reviewed and configured.)
6. When the Networks Settings Change dialog box appears asking you to shut down and restart your computer, select YES.
7. When your computer restarts, log on to your domain controller as the administrator and open up the WINS Manager application by selecting Start, Programs, Administrative Tools, WINS Manager. The DHCP Manager application dialog box appears.
8. Your IP address should appear in the WINS Manager under the WINS Server window. Double-click your IP address. The statistics screen on the right side of the dialog box should refresh.
9. From the Mappings drop-down menu, select Show Database. View the Show Database [Local] Mappings window. How many entries are in the database pertaining to your computer? ________________________. List the entries in the database for your computer in the spaces provided below.

   (Answers will vary; however, at least two entries should be registered in the database pertaining to the local computer. There may be a browser entry, a domain entry, a computer entry, and a user entry.)
10. Choose Close and then exit from WINS Manager.

App I

Exercise 4

This exercise is intended to have you install the DNS service and to manually configure an alias computer name. You will then PING the alias to ensure proper configuration. This exercise assumes that the NetBEUI and

TCP/IP protocols are presently installed, and the source files are located on your computer in a folder ntsrv on your C drive.

1. Log on to your domain controller as the administrator and open up the Network application by selecting Start, Settings, Control Panel, Network Icon.
2. Select the Services tab in the Network properties dialog box and choose the Add button.
3. From the list of available services in the Select Network Services dialog box, select Microsoft DNS Server and choose OK.
4. When the Windows NT Setup dialog box appears, type the location of the source file in the space provided (**C:\ntsrv**) and choose Continue.

   Files will be copied and the DNS server service will be installed.
5. Choose Close on the Network properties sheet. (Bindings will be reviewed and configured.)
6. When the Networks Settings Change dialog box appears asking you to shut down and restart your computer, select YES.
7. When your computer starts, log on to your domain controller as the administrator and open up the Network application by selecting Start, Settings, Control Panel, Network Icon.
8. Select the Protocols tab in the Network properties dialog box, choose the TCP/IP protocol, and choose Properties.
9. In the Microsoft TCP/IP Properties sheet, select DNS.
10. In the Domain box, type **<your first name>.com**. Your computer name appears in the Host Name box; do not alter your computer name.
11. Select the Add button below the DNS Service Search Order window and enter your IP address in the TCP/IP DNS Server dialog box. Then click Add.
12. Select OK to close the Microsoft TCP/IP Properties window and choose OK again to close the Network application.
13. Open the DNS Manager application by selecting Start, Programs, Administrative Tools, DNS Manager. The DNS Manager application dialog box appears.
14. Select the DNS drop-down menu and select New Server. The Add DNS Server dialog box appears. Enter your computer name or your

IP address in the space provided and click OK. Your DNS server should appear under the Server List and Cache should appear under your DNS Server name or IP address.

15. Select the DNS drop-down menu and select New Zone. The Creating New Zone for <computer name> dialog box appears. Select the Primary option button and select Next.
16. In the Creating New Zone for <computer name> dialog box, type the same name entered in Step 10 (**your first name.com**) and press the Tab key. Verify that `<your first name>.com.dns` appears in the Zone File box. Select Next, Finish.

    Verify that your new zone name appears under your server name on the left pane of the dialog box, and that an NS record and an SOA record appear under Zone Info on the right pane in the dialog box.
17. Right-click your zone name in the left pane and select New Record. In the Record Type window, select the ARecord. Enter your host name and your host IP address and clear the Create Associated PTR Record check box. Click OK.
18. Right-click your zone name in the left pane and select New Record. In the Record Type window, select the CNAME Record. Enter an alias name of your choice in the Alias Name box and click OK.
19. In the For Host DNS box, type your computer name and your DNS domain name separated by a period (Example: **<computer name>.<your first name>.com.**) and click OK.
20. Close the Domain Name Service Manager application.
21. Start a command prompt window.
22. Type **Ping <alias name>**.

Chapter 19—Novell NetWare and Windows NT

Exercise 1—NetWare Connectivity

Complete this exercise if you have access to a NetWare server. Create an account on your NT Workstation that matches your account and password on the NetWare server. Make this account a member of the Administrators local group on your NT workstation.

1. Start the Network applet on Computer1. On the Protocols tab, select Add and choose NWLink from the list. Be sure to have the source files available. On the Services tab, select Add and choose Client Services for NetWare from the list. Choose OK and restart NT when prompted.
2. When NT restarts, logon as the NT account you created to match the account on the NetWare server. You will be prompted for a preferred NetWare server. Select the NetWare server that you have access to and choose OK. You will be logged in to the NetWare server.
3. Start the newly added GSNW applet in Control Panel. Review the options that are available. If your NetWare server is version 4.x, enter any NDS information that is appropriate.
4. From Windows Explorer, choose Tools, Map Network Drive. Notice the new entry for NetWare or Compatible Network. Expand this entry and find your server in the list.
5. Expand the server entry and select a directory that you have access to. Connect to it. If there is another server on which you have an account, select it from the list, choose a folder, and in the Connect As box, enter the logon ID for that NetWare server. CSNW will complete the connection, no doubt asking you for a password for that server.
6. Disconnect from both NetWare servers.
7. In the CSNW applet, set the preferred server to <NONE>.

Chapter 21—Remote Access Support

Exercise 1—Using RAS

To complete this exercise, you must have either a null modem cable to connect to the COM1 port on both computers, or modems installed in both computers and a separate working phone line and number for each.

Perform these steps on both computers. Log on as Administrator.

1. Start the Network Applet and select the Services tab.
2. Choose Add and select Remote Access Service from the list. Be sure to have the source files ready and provide NT with the installation path when prompted.

3. The New Modem wizard will appear. If you are using a modem, let NT detect it. Otherwise, choose to select it yourself, and pick Dial-up networking Serial Cables between 2 PCs. As you continue through the wizard, choose COM1, specify your country and area code, and finish the modem installation.
4. Next, you will need to configure the COM port. In the RAS Setup dialog box, choose the COM port from the list and select Configure. On Computer1, choose Dial Out only and on Computer2, select Dial Out and Receive calls. Then choose OK.
5. Select the Network button and verify that all protocols are selected for both computers. For each protocol on Computer2 under server settings, be sure that the Entire Network option is selected. For TCP/IP, select Use Static Address Pool and enter **121.132.4.100** and **121.132.4.110** as the begin and end addresses.
6. Choose OK and complete RAS installation. Choose NO when asked if you want to enable NetBIOS Broadcast Propagation. Restart NT when prompted.
7. After NT reboots, start the Remote Access Admin program on Computer2 (from the Administrative Tools folder).
8. Choose Users, Permissions from the menu and choose Grant All to grant permission to all users.
9. On Computer1, start the Dial-Up Networking program from Accessories. Create a phonebook entry for Computer2 (be creative). Leave the phone number blank if using a null modem cable, or the actual phone number if you are configured with modems and separate phone lines.
10. Disconnect Computer1's network cable connection.
11. Connect the null modem cable to the COM1 port on both computers.
12. Restart NT on Computer1. When the logon box appears, select Logon using Dial-Up networking. Select the phonebook entry you created for Computer2 as your dial-up number and choose Dial. If prompted for a password, enter the appropriate password for your account. RAS will connect you to Computer2.
13. Use Windows Explorer to connect to a resource on Computer2. Were you successful? Yes. You are connected using RAS.

14. Note the connection statistics recorded in the Remote Access Admin utility on Computer2.
15. Start the Dial-Up Networking program again and choose Hang Up.
16. Remove RAS from both computers by starting the Network Applet, selecting Remote Access Service from the Services tab, choosing Remove, and answering YES to the warning message. Restart NT when prompted.
17. Reconnect Computer1 to the network and remove the null modem cable from both computers.

Chapter 22—Multiprotocol Routing

This lab assumes that only the NetBEUI and TCP/IP protocols have been installed on your systems. The first exercise of this lab has you install the NWLink IPX/SPX Compatible transport protocol in order to later install RIP for IPX and use the IPXRoute utility. If for some reason that NWLink has already been installed, skip Exercise 1 and proceed to Exercise 2.

Exercise 1

Complete this exercise from your domain controller.

1. Access the Network Properties dialog box, select the Protocols tab, and choose the Add button.
2. Select the NWLink IPX/SPX Compatible Transport and choose OK.
3. When prompted, shut down and restart your computer.

Exercise 2

Complete this exercise from a domain controller that has TCP/IP installed.

1. Access the Network Properties dialog box, select the Services tab, and choose the Add button.
2. Select the RIP for Internet Protocol service and choose OK.
3. When prompted, shut down and restart your computer.
4. After your computer restarts, start a command prompt.

5. From the command line, type **route print**. View the displayed information. Are your domain controller IP Address and Subnet Mask present in the route table?

Exercise 3

Complete this exercise from a domain controller that has NWLink installed.

1. Access the Network Properties dialog box, select the Services tab, and choose the Add button.
2. Select the RIP for NWLink IPX/SPX Compatible Transport service and choose OK.
3. When prompted, shut down and restart your computer.
4. After your computer restarts, start a command prompt.
5. From the command line, type **ipxroute servers**. View the displayed information. In the space provided below, indicate your network number, MAC address, and your computer name.
6. From the command line, type **ipxroute table** and view the displayed information.

Chapter 24—Advanced Troubleshooting

Exercise 1—Using Event Viewer to Troubleshoot

1. Use the Services applet in Control Panel to change the startup value for the Messenger Service to Manual.
2. Restart NT. You should receive the message: `At least one service or driver failed to start.`
3. Start Event Viewer and look for the first Eventlog entry for the approximate time you restarted NT. Look at the message for the first Stop error right above it. This entry will probably say that some service that depends on the Messenger failed to start.
4. Use Services in Control Panel to set the Messenger Service startup value back to Automatic and restart the computer.
5. The error message should not now occur.

Exercise 2—Viewing Audit Events

1. If you haven't already, start User Manager. From Policy, Audit, enable auditing for successful and failed Logons and Logoffs.
2. Log on to the workstation as BrownC with the wrong password.
3. Try again with the correct password.
4. Log off and log back on as Administrator.
5. Start the Event Viewer and switch to the Security Log.
6. Locate, or filter if you wish, Logon/Logoff entries.
7. Find the entry for the incorrect password (hint: Look for the "lock" icon). What information does it provide you? (Reason for the failure, the user account involved, and the workstation on which the logon attempt took place, among other things.)
8. Review the entries for the successful logons.
9. Close Event Viewer.

The following lab exercises will require you to have a null modem connection between your two computers. One computer will be configured as a host computer; the other as a target computer. If a null modem cable is not available, Exercises 1 and 4 cannot be accomplished.

Exercise 3

Complete this exercise from both domain controllers.

1. Verify the COM port settings on each computer match by checking the settings from the Ports icon in the Control Panel. The following settings should be used on both computers:

Baud Rate	19,200 or 9,600
Auto Answer	On
Hardware Compression	Disabled
Error Detection	Disabled

2. Using a null modem cable, connect the two domain controllers together using any available COM port.

Exercise 4

Complete this exercise from the host computer.

1. Create a folder on drive C named Debug (use another drive if less than 100M of free space is available on C:).
2. Place the Windows NT 4.0 Server CD-ROM in the CD-ROM drive.
3. Copy the file Expndsym.cmd from the <cdrom>:\Support\Debug folder to C:\Debug.
4. Copy the contents of the <cdrom>:\Support\Debug\I386 folder to C:\Debug (excluding the Symbols folder).
5. From a command prompt window, display the C:\Debug folder and run the expand symbols files program by typing **expndsym <cdrom>: c:\debug**.
6. When the Symbols files are copied to the host computer, from the command prompt window, enter the following commands:

   set _nt_debug_port=com<port number>
   set _nt_debug_baud_rate=<baud rate>
   set _nt_symbol_path=c:\debug\symbols
   i386kd -m -v
7. Verify the command prompt window reads `KD: waiting to reconnect...`

Exercise 5

Complete this exercise from the target computer.

1. From Explorer, right-click the boot.ini file in the c:\ folder and select Properties.
2. If selected, clear the hidden and read-only attributes and click OK to close the boot.ini properties sheet.
3. From Explorer, double-click the boot.ini file and add **/debug** to the first line of the [operating systems] section of the file.
4. Reboot the target computer by selecting the [debugger enabled] selection.

Exercise 6

Complete this exercise from the host computer.

1. Verify communications between the two computers when blue screen appears.

2. From the host computer screen, press Ctrl+C to stop the Kernel Debugger and list, in the spaces below, the first five software modules loaded. (Answers may vary depending on hardware used.)

   ______**ntoskrnl.exe**______________________________

   ______**hal.dll**___________________________________

   ______**atapi.sys**_________________________________

   ______**scsiport.sys**______________________________

   ______**disk.sys**__________________________________
3. Press the g key and then the Enter key to continue the boot process.
4. When the boot process completes, type **@k** to exit the Kernel Debugger.

Exercise 7 (Optional)

If a file called Memory.dmp is available in the %SystemRoot% folder, complete this exercise.

1. From the command prompt window, display the c:\debug folder.
2. Enter the command **dumpchk -v**.
3. View the results. (Hint: You may want to make the command prompt window larger by adjusting the height of the window from the Command Prompt Layout tab on the properties sheet.)
4. Enter the command **dumpexam -v**.
5. View the result by opening the Memory.txt file in the %SystemRoot% folder.

Self-Test Questions and Answers

Using the Self-Tests

The tests in this appendix are performance-based questions designed to test your problem-solving capabilities. The questions are divided into three main test structures:

- *Self-Assessment Test.* This would typically be the test you take first. This test is meant to give you a sense of where your strengths and weaknesses are regarding Windows NT Server 4.0 in the Enterprise.
- *Chapter-End Test.* After reading a chapter from the study guide, you will have the option to take a mini-test consisting of questions relevant only to the given chapter. These questions are listed in order of the chapters in this book.
- *Mastery Test.* This test simulates the exam situation, so you will give answers to all questions and then get your overall score.

All test questions are of multiple choice type offering four possible answers. The answers are all labeled A, B, C and D. There will always be either one best answer or two or more options representing the correct answer. For example, a right answer might be "A" if you are asked to provide the best answer, or "A and D" if you are asked for the two best answers.

Note These questions are also included on the CD-ROM that accompanies this book. See Appendix K, "Using the Self-Test Software," for information on how to access these questions and run the software included with the CD. Also refer to Appendix C, "How Do I Get There from Here?" for examples of single and multiple answer questions.

Self-Assessment Test

Question #1

When the directory replicator service is configured, a user account must be created. Why is a user account required?

A. The administrator must log on to the computer with the user account and manually start and stop the replicator service.

B. The replicator service will log on to the computer as the user and use the account to perform directory replication.

C. The replicator service will not log on to the computer as the user, but will use the account in case the replicator service fails.

D. The administrator uses this account to perform administrative duties once the replicator service is configured.

Question #2

All companies building network products are required to implement all layers of the OSI model.

A. TRUE

B. FALSE

Question #3

You are analyzing network activity between your network clients and a server. You plan to use Network Monitor to monitor network traffic generated by and received by the server, and Performance Monitor to track system performance relating to network traffic. What types of objects would facilitate your analysis? Choose all that apply.

A. Redirector

B. Server

C. Protocol

D. Frame

Question #4

On a RISC-based computer, which of the following statements is true regarding Windows NT installation?

A. Execute setup from either the CD-ROM or over the network by typing WINNT32 and any optional switches.

B. You must have a 2M FAT minimum system partition before starting setup.

C. Execute setup only from a CD-ROM by running WINNT /ARC.

D. Run SETUPLDR from the I386 subdirectory on the CD-ROM.

Question #5

To install server tools on a Windows NT Workstation, Intel platform:

A. Run Setup.bat from the server CD-ROM, Clients folder.

B. Run Setup.bat from the server CD-ROM, Clients\Srvtools folder.

C. Run Setup.bat from the server CD-ROM, Clients\Srvtools\Winnt folder.

D. Run Setup.bat from the server CD-ROM, Clients\Srvtools\Winnt\I386 folder.

Question #6

Which of the following actions can serve to optimize network traffic associated with Directory Replication? Choose all that apply.

A. Lock directories that are not replicated frequently, or that you do not want to have replicated.

B. Maintain a shallow export directory tree structure.

C. Modify the interval value on the export server so that it does not check for changes in the export tree as frequently.

D. Remove the password from the Directory Replication service account.

Question #7

The major cause of STOP errors during the installation process is?

A. Incompatible software

B. Incompatible hardware

C. Incompatible Windows NT setup program

D. It is impossible to get STOP errors during installation.

Question #8

Team Leaders need to be able to modify files contained in the share TOOLS. While you were on vacation, your trusted sidekick modified the permissions for the share and the folder. The two exhibits show what the permissions look like now. Team Leaders complain that they are unable to modify their files. What should you do?

A. Fire your trusted sidekick.

B. Change the TOOLS NTFS permission for Team Leaders to Change, and the share permission to Read.

C. Change the TOOLS NTFS permission for the Team Leaders to Change.

D. Remove Team Leaders from the ACL for the TOOLS share.

Question #9

Which of the following Directory Services goals are met by trust relationships? Select all that apply.

A. Provide users a single logon account that can be used anywhere within the enterprise to log on to the network.

B. Centralize management of accounts and resources.

C. Maintain separate user accounts for resource access on each resource server in the enterprise.

D. Facilitate access to network resources regardless of their domain location.

Question #10

You suspect that someone is trying to log on to the network unauthorized. What is the best step you can take to increase security and determine who might be doing this?

A. Enable Account Lockout in the Account Policy requiring the Administrator to unlock the account.

B. Enable Account Lockout in the Account Policy requiring the Administrator to unlock the account. Enable auditing of unsuccessful logons and logoffs and monitor these events in the Event Viewer.

C. Advise users to change their passwords more frequently and not to use obvious passwords.

D. Increase the minimum password length in Account Policy.

Question #11

Which of the following are requirements for setting up a successful trust relationship? Choose all that apply.

A. The primary domain controller in each domain must be up and accessible.

B. There can be no current sessions between the PDCs of each domain.

C. You must have an administrator-level account.

D. You must have access to a computer running User Manager for Domains.

Question #12

Token rings are more efficient than Ethernet on heavily loaded networks because

A. token ring network cards are faster

B. Ethernet was originally designed for the Internet

C. collisions are frequent on heavily loaded Ethernet networks

D. token rings cannot be wired in a star topology

Question #13

The ABCCorp domain is configured as a Master Domain model. 5,000 user accounts are managed in the ABC-MIS domain in Chicago. Resource domains trust ABC-MIS. At the ABC-WEST resource domain, the print administrator is managing access to her printers by adding the appropriate user accounts from ABC-MIS to the ACL for each of five printers. Access will be managed for 300 users. ABC-WEST is connected to ABC-MIS via a slow WAN link. Every time she accesses the ABC-MIS account domain to display the list of users, the list takes several seconds to generate. The process is taking longer than she thinks it should. What can you suggest to improve performance and minimize network traffic? Choose the best answer.

A. Upgrade the WAN link to a higher speed.

B. Create local groups on the print servers in ABC-WEST and add the users to the local groups. Use the local groups to assign printer permissions.

C. Create global groups in ABC-MIS for the users that need printer access in ABC-WEST. Add the global groups to local groups on the print servers in ABC-WEST, and assign printer permissions to the local groups.

D. There is nothing you can do to improve performance. The same amount of trust traffic is generated whether you use user accounts or group accounts across the trust.

Question #14

The manager of the Accounting department wants to make next year's budget templates available for the staff accountants to review beginning next month. Staff accountants are already members of a global group called Accountants in CORPDOMAIN. The templates will be stored on the department resource server called ACCT1 in a folder called BUDGET97 on an NTFS partition. The folder has been shared with the default permission, which you do not want to change. How would you further secure the folder's contents so that it is available only to the Accounting department staff?

A. Use User Manager for Domains to create a local group on the resource server called Accountants. Make the global accountants group a member of the local accountants group. Assign the Accountants group permission to use the folder through User Manager for Domains.

B. Use User Manager for Domains to create a local group on the resource server called Accountants. Make the global accountants group a member of the local accountants group. Assign the appropriate User Rights to the Accountants group to access the BUDGET97 share.

C. Use User Manager for Domains to create a local group on the resource server called Accountants. Make the global accountants group a member of the local accountants group. Use the Security tab on the properties sheet for the folder to assign permissions to the Accountants group.

D. Use User Manager for Domains to create a local group on the resource server called Accountants. Make the global accountants group a member of the local accountants group. Use the Sharing tab on the properties sheet for the folder to assign permissions to the Accountants group.

Question #15

Of the following, which functions as part of the user mode of Windows NT 4.0?

A. CSR Subsystem

B. HAL

C. USER

D. WOW

Question #16

To install server tools on a Windows 95 client computer, the following resources and services are required.

A. Client for Novell Networks installed

B. 3M of free disk space

C. 8M of memory

D. Client for Microsoft Networks installed

Question #17

You are creating multiple user accounts for salespersons, marketers, and programmers. Each set of accounts belongs to the same relative groups (sales users in SALES, marketing users in MARKETING, and programmer users in PROGRAMMERS), uses the same logon scripts (SALES.BAT, MARKET.BAT, PROGRAM.BAT), and saves data in a home directory relative to each group (sales users under USERS\SALES, marketing users under USERS\MARKETERS, programmer users under USERS\PROGRAMMERS). What is the most efficient way to create these users?

A. Create a separate account for each user. As you create the user, use the %USERNAME% environment variable when specifying the home directory to let Windows NT create it for you.

B. Create a template for each type of user. Make the appropriate choices and entries for groups, logon script, and home directory. Use the %USERNAME% environment variable when specifying the home directory to let Windows NT create them for you. Then, create each user by copying the appropriate template.

C. Create all the users without specifying group membership. After they are all created, select each group of users by Ctrl+clicking them and create the appropriate group.

D. You must create each user individually.

Question #18

The default share name for the server tools share is:

A. SrvTools

B. ClientTools

C. SetupAdm

D. ServerTools

Question #19

Within a single workgroup, there will be a master browser elected for:

A. Each protocol

B. Every 32 computers

C. Every 12 users

D. Only one protocol

Question #20

Which of the following parameters can be configured manually with the NWLink protocol?

A. IP address

B. Frame type

C. Subnet mask

D. DHCP scope

Question #21

A DHCP reservation is assigned to a:

A. Computer

B. Network Adapter Card

C. Domain

D. Workgroup

Question #22

Kite Flyers Corporation has experienced tremendous growth and now has between 10,000 and 15,000 employees located across its three global locations: Chicago, London, and Tokyo. Resources are managed in each location as well as the users located in those offices. Which model best suits this organization?

A. Single domain model

B. Master domain model

C. Multiple Master domain model

D. Complete Trust domain model

Question #23

What server tool is NOT installed on a Windows NT 3.5/3.51 Workstation platform?

A. Services for Macintosh

B. System Policy Editor

C. Remote Access Administrator

D. User Profile Editor

Question #24

Routers work up to the __________________ layer in the OSI Network Model.

A. Physical

B. Data Link

C. Network

D. Transport

Question #25

The Finance domain users need to access a laser printer in the Marketing domain. The Marketing domain users need to access a scanner in the Finance domain. How many trust relationships need to be created to facilitate the sharing of these two network resources?

A. Create one two-way trust relationship between Finance and Marketing.

B. Create two one-way trust relationships, one from Finance to Marketing and the other from Marketing to Finance.

C. Create two one-way trust relationships from Finance to Marketing. One for the shared laser printer, and the other the scanner.

D. Create one trust relationship between Finance and Marketing. A trust relationship is always bidirectional.

Question #26

Which of the following steps is appropriate to take when troubleshooting a failed print job?

A. Verify that the appropriate print port has been defined and configured by printing a test page.

B. Delete and re-create the printer.

C. Determine whether the print device is online and connected.

D. Resubmit the print job to a file and then copy the file to a printer port to see if it is successful.

Question #27

The CSNW redirector will allow a Windows NT Workstation to communicate with:

A. Novell Servers

B. Windows NT Workstations

C. Macintosh Workstations

D. Novell Clients for client/server applications

Question #28

Once server tools are installed on a Windows NT Workstation, they can be run from:

A. The <winntroot>\System32 folder

B. The Start Menu, Programs, Server Tools group

C. The Start Menu, Programs, Administrative Tools group

D. Any manually made program group provided the executables are placed in that group

Question #29

The TOOLS folder has been shared to the Developers group with Change permission. DOOM is a subdirectory under TOOLS. Team Leaders should have access only to DOOM with Read permissions. What can you do to accomplish this?

A. Add Team Leaders to the TOOLS share with Read permission.

B. Create a new share called DOOM and give Team Leaders Read permission to it.

C. Add Team Leaders to the TOOLS share with Change permission.

D. Add Team Leaders to the TOOLS share with No Access and to the DOOM subdirectory with Read.

Question #30

What types of traffic are associated with the WINS service?

A. WINS Registration

B. WINS Time Out

C. WINS Query Request

D. WINS Address Request

Question #31

What are the differences between a local group and a global group? Choose all that apply.

A. Local groups can be created on workstations, servers, and domain controllers, while global groups can only be created and maintained on a domain controller.

B. Local groups can contain local users, domain users, and global groups, while global groups can contain only users from their domain.

C. Local groups can contain local users, domain users, global groups, and other local groups, while global groups can contain only users from their domain.

D. Local groups can be used for managing resources only on the local computer, while global groups can be used to manage resources on any computer that participates in the domain.

Question #32

Audit events are placed in the ________________ log in Event Viewer.

A. System

B. Security

C. Application

D. Audit

Question #33

RIP for IP and DHCP Relay can support ____________ hops.

A. 4

B. 8

C. 16

D. 32

Question #34

Under which of the following situations would you disable the user account rather than deleting it?

A. JaneD has left the company on maternity leave and plans to return in three months.

B. JohnB has taken an emergency medical leave of absence for possibly six or more months, but hopes to return full time.

C. JaniceD has left the company to take a job at Microsoft.

D. FrankP has taken a temporary team leader position in another department and will return when the project is completed.

Question #35

In your network, you would like to remotely monitor traffic on all your Windows NT 4.0 Server and Workstation computers, as well as your Windows 95 computers. Which of the following steps needs to take place?

A. Install the Network Monitor agent on all the computers and the Windows NT Server 4.0 version of Network Monitor on the computer that will remotely monitor the computers.

B. Install the Network Monitor agent on all the computers and the SMS full version of Network Monitor on the computer that will remotely monitor the computers.

C. Install only the Windows NT Server 4.0 version of Network Monitor on the computer that will remotely monitor the computers.

D. Install only the SMS full version of Network Monitor on the computer that will remotely monitor the computers.

Question #36

The reason that server tools are not installed by default on Windows NT Server installations is:

A. The server tools applications and utilities are already installed but must be run from a domain controller.

B. The server tools applications and utilities are not available for member servers.

C. The server tools applications and utilities cannot be run from the server platform.

D. The server tools applications and utilities are already installed and available for use.

Question #37

There are 300 Windows NT and Windows 95 client computers that print to five printers on a print server. You have received upgraded print drivers for two of the print devices connected to this print server. What must you do to ensure that all clients can continue to access all the print devices?

A. Install the upgraded print drivers on all the client computers that need to use those print devices.

B. Install the upgraded print drivers on all the client computers.

C. Install the upgraded print drivers only on the Windows NT client computers.

D. Do nothing. The print server can download the new drivers to the clients the next time they make a print request.

Question #38

By default, events are ordered in all event logs?

A. By oldest first

B. By event importance

C. By newest last

D. By newest first

Question #39

By default, all BDCs on the same subnet in a domain will become:

A. A domain master browser

B. A potential browser

C. A backup browser

D. A non-browser

Question #40

Which of the following sets of Windows NT network clients do not require print drivers to be manually installed on the local computer?

A. All Microsoft Network clients

B. Windows NT and Windows 95

C. Windows NT, Windows 95, Windows for Workgroups 3.11

D. Windows NT, Windows 95, LAN Manager v2.x for DOS

Question #41

The KITEMASTERS corporate network consists of 6,000 users located across five regional locations, each on its own subnet. About half the users have Windows NT Workstation 4.0 computers, and the rest have Windows 95 computers. These computers are frequently restarted throughout the day. There is one PDC and BDC located in the MIS department, and a BDC in each regional location. Each location also has one or more Windows NT Server 4.0 computers for resource management.

Using Network Monitor, you have noticed that there is an unusually high percentage of Browser traffic generated throughout the day. How can you optimize traffic associated with the Browser while letting users continue to browse for resources? Choose the best two answers.

A. You cannot configure Browser parameters.

B. Configure the Windows 95 and Windows NT Workstation 4.0 computers to never become browsers.

C. Disable the Server service on user computers which will not be sharing resources in the network.

D. Disable the Computer Browser service on all user computers.

Question #42

Kite Flyers Corporation has configured a Multiple Master domain model with accounts managed by MIS in the KFCORPA and KFCORPB domains. Resource domains are located in Seattle, Houston, and Boston. Certain users—whose accounts might be in either KFCORPA or KFCORPB—have been selected to provide backup functions for all the domains. Which of the following represents the most flexible solution for this scenario?

A. Create a global backup group called KFBACKUP in KFCORPA and in KFCORPB. Add the user accounts that reside in KFCORPA to its KFBACKUP global group, and add the users that reside in KFCORPB to its KFBACKUP global group. Add both KFCORPA\KFBACKUP and KFCORPB\KFBACKUP to the local Backup Operators groups in each resource domain.

B. Create a global backup group called KFBACKUP in KFCORPA. Add the users from KFCORPA and KFCORPB to KFBACKUP. Add KFBACKUP from KFCORPA to the local Backup Operators groups in each resource domain.

C. Create a global backup group called KFBACKUP in KFCORPA and in KFCORPB. Add the user accounts that reside in KFCORPA to its KFBACKUP global group, and add the users that reside in KFCORPB to its KFBACKUP global group. Add both KFCORPA\KFBACKUP and KFCORPB\KFBACKUP to the local Backup Operators groups in each resource domain and to the local Backup Operators groups for KFCORPA and KFCORPB.

D. Create a global backup group called KFBACKUP in KFCORPA. Add the users from KFCORPA and KFCORPB to KFBACKUP. Add KFBACKUP from KFCORPA to the local Backup Operators groups in each resource domain and to the local Backup Operators groups in KFCORPA and KFCORPB.

Question #43

What is the purpose of the print monitor SFMMON.DLL?

A. SFMMON.DLL monitors Macintosh print jobs routed using AppleTalk protocol to network print devices.

B. SFMMON.DLL is the System File Manager print monitor which tracks print jobs sent directly to or printed directly from a file.

C. SFMMON.DLL is the software print job compression DLL which compresses the print job before it is sent from the local print spooler to the print server.

D. SFMMON.DLL is not a valid print monitor.

Question #44

The Finance domain trusts the Marketing domain. You would like the administrators of the Marketing domain to be able to administer the servers in the Finance domain. What should you do to facilitate this?

A. Make the Domain Admins group from the Marketing domain a member of the local Administrators group on each server on the Finance domain.

B. Make the Administrators group from the Marketing domain a member of the local Administrators group on each server in the Finance domain.

C. Make the Domain Admins group from each server in the Finance domain a member of the local Administrators group in the Marketing domain.

D. Do nothing. When a trust is established, the Administrators group from the trusted domain is automatically added to the local administrator groups on the servers in the trusting domain.

Question #45

Which of the following network services generate traffic between a client and a server computer? Choose all that apply.

A. NetBIOS name registration with a WINS server

B. Logon validation

C. Account database synchronization

D. DHCP IP address requests

Question #46

Which of the following dialogs takes place as part of the Setup Wizard?

A. Personal information

B. Detection and configuration of storage devices

C. Request for network card settings

D. Video display setup

Question #47

Under what circumstances might a full database synchronization take place between a PDC and a BDC? Choose the best two.

A. Every synchronization event replicates the entire account databases.

B. Full synchronization occurs when the BDC is first installed.

C. Full synchronization may occur when the change log on the PDC becomes full and begins to overwrite existing information before the PDC can contact the BDC for updates.

D. Only changes are copied whenever synchronization occurs.

Question #48

A print job can be routed directly to a UNIX host print device and its status checked using which two command-line utilities?

A. LPD and LPR

B. LPD and LPQ

C. LPR and IPCONFIG

D. LPR and LPQ

Question #49

Which of the following steps need to take place before a file session can be established between two computers using the TCP/IP protocol? Choose all that apply.

A. The user must register its name with the WINS server.

B. Name resolution must take place.

C. Address resolution must take place.

D. A TCP Session must be established.

Question #50

Which files are read before NT displays the blue screen (check all that apply)

A. boot.ini

B. config.sys

C. ntldr

D. command.com

Question #51

Which of the following sets of usernames and passwords are acceptable for Windows NT ?

Username—Password

A. First Ass't Comptroller—FirstComp

B. FirstAsstCompt—1stComp

C. FirstAss*tCompt—COMP1

D. AssComp1—123COMPTROLLER1

Question #52

Bernadette has a math-intensive program that runs calculations while in the background. She wants to work with other program files while this application cranks away, but she does not want to sacrifice its CPU time. What do you advise?

A. Through the Systems applet in Control Panel, set the foreground response time to None. This will let foreground and background applications run at the same base priority level.

B. Through the Systems applet in Control Panel, set the background response time to Maximum. This will increase background base priority two levels.

C. From the Start, Run dialog box, start the math-intensive program with the /Realtime switch.

D. Do nothing. You cannot change application priorities.

Question #53

For CrashDumps to be obtained, a pagefile must exist on the

A. System partition
B. Boot partition
C. NTFS partition
D. Data partition

Question #54

Kite Flyers Corporation has two global locations, London and New York. MIS manages the users in both locations in two account domains. There are five departments: Accounting, Marketing, MIS, HR, and Corporate. Each has its own set of network resources that its staff accesses, and some resources that everyone in the company uses.

Primary Goals: Give all employees a single logon account that they can use to access their resources. Let MIS be able to manage the account domains from any location. Let each department manage its own resources. Let certain delegated users act as print operators for printers in each department.

Secondary Goals: Centralize resources by department. Let all delegated users be able to manage any domain's printers. Allow as much flexibility as possible for printer management.

Solution: Implement a Multiple Master Domain model. Have all resource domains trust the account domain, and let the account domains trust one another. Create a global group called KFPRINT in each account domain and add the delegated users to it. Add KFPRINT from both account domains to the local Print Operators groups on the print servers in each domain.

A. The solution satisfies none of the goals.
B. The solution satisfies all the primary goals and all the secondary goals.
C. The solution satisfies both primary goals, but only one secondary goal.
D. The solution satisfies two primary goals and two secondary goals.

Question #55

There is one high-speed network print device connected to the print server in MIS. MIS Managers and Project Leaders should always be able to print to this printer regardless of who has submitted print jobs. Help Desk staff should be able to print ahead of Developers. What will best accomplish this task?

A. Create three printers, each associated with the device, and assign the appropriate groups access only to their printer. Give the Manager's printer a priority of 1, Help Desk's printer a priority of 50, and Developer's printer a priority of 99.

B. Create three printers, each associated with the device, and assign the appropriate groups access only to their printer. Give the Manager's printer a priority of 99, Help Desk's printer a priority of 50, and Developer's printer a priority of 1.

C. Create three printers, each associated with the device, and assign the appropriate groups access only to their printer. Make the Manager's printer a printer pool by associating it with each print device.

D. Create three printers associated with the device and assign the appropriate groups access only to their printer. Make each printer a printer pool by associating it with each print device.

Question #56

Indicate the utility used from the command prompt to manually maintain an IPX routing table.

A. Route

B. IPXRoute

C. IPConfig

D. PING

Question #57

Kernel Debugger commands can be entered after a ________________ key sequence is entered.

A. Ctrl+G

B. Ctrl+C

C. Ctrl+K

D. Ctrl+Q

Question #58

To install server tools on a Windows 95 platform:

A. Run Setup.bat from the CD-ROM, Clients\Srvtools\Win95 folder.

B. Run Setup.bat from the CD-ROM, Clients\Srvtools\Windows folder.

C. Run Setup.exe from the CD-ROM, Clients\Srvtools\Windows folder.

D. Access Control Panel on the Windows 95 client computer and select the Add/Remove Programs ICON.

Question #59

Ned is a member of the Developers group at Springfield Technologies. He has been promoted to team leader for his group. He needs to edit the DOOM.DOC file in the Tools folder, but does not have Write access. What must you do to give Ned access to DOOM.DOC?

A. Do nothing. The next time Ned logs on, his permissions will change.

B. Change the Developers group permission to Change.

C. Add Ned to the Team Leaders group and have him log in again.

D. Change the Team Leaders group permission to Full Control.

Question #60

Which of the following statements is true about the default user accounts created in Windows NT Server 4.0?

A. The Administrator account is enabled and can be renamed; the Guest account is enabled and cannot be renamed.

B. The Administrator account is enabled and cannot be renamed; the Guest account is disabled and cannot be renamed.

C. The Administrator account is enabled and can be renamed; the Guest account is disabled and can be renamed.

D. The Administrator account is disabled and cannot be renamed; the Guest account is enabled and can be renamed.

Question #61

Kite Flyers Corporation consists of 300 employees located in a single office complex. Which domain model would best suit this organization?

A. Single domain model

B. Master domain model

C. Multiple Master domain model

D. Complete Trust domain model

Question #62

RIP for IPX can support ___________ hops.

A. 4

B. 8

C. 16

D. 32

Question #63

User, group, and computer accounts are contained in which accounts database?

A. SAM Accounts Database

B. Local Security Accounts Database

C. SAM Built-In Database

D. Account Synchronization Database

Question #64

When a TCP session is established, three frames are generated known as the TCP three-way handshake. Which of the following frames are part of the three-way handshake? Choose all that apply.

A. TCP Request from the client to the server.

B. TCP Name resolution request from the client to the WINS server.

C. TCP Request Acknowledgment from the server to the client.

D. TCP Session establishment from the client to the server.

Question #65

A DHCP server eliminates the need to manually configure:

A. A DHCP scope

B. A WINS database

C. An IP address and subnet mask for DHCP clients

D. An IP address and subnet mask for non-DHCP clients

Question #66

Which of the following steps applies to the Windows NT 4.0 print process on Windows NT computers? Select all that apply.

A. The GDI component of the client computer generates an enhanced metafile print job.

B. The bulk of the print process completes in the spooler on the client computer before forwarding the print job to the print server.

C. The print monitor controls access to the print devices and device ports and monitors status of the print job.

D. The local printer spooler makes a remote connection to the print server spooler and copies the print job there.

Question #67

The administrator of the TOOLS shared folder wants to limit access to the folder only to the Developers group. To accomplish this, she gives the Everyone group NO ACCESS, and the Developers group Change access. The Developers complain that they cannot access any file in TOOLS. What else must the administrator do?

A. Share the files in the TOOLS folder.

B. Remove the Everyone group.

C. Give the Developers group Full Control.

D. Format the partition as NTFS and assign NTFS permissions in addition to the share permissions.

Question #68

The person that created DOOM.DOC on server ACCT1 is no longer with the company. Cathy, a member of Team Leaders, will be assuming responsibility for the DOOM project, and needs to become the owner of DOOM.DOC. How can this be accomplished? Choose all that apply.

A. Give Cathy the Take Ownership of Files and Folders User Right on the server ACCT1.

B. Give Cathy the Take Ownership permission on the file DOOM.DOC.

C. Tell Cathy to just take ownership of the file.

D. Give the Team Leaders group the Take Ownership permission for DOOM.DOC.

Question #69

The Finance domain trusts the Marketing domain. What NetLogon function allows a user from the Marketing domain to log on and validate from a computer that participates in the Finance domain?

A. Directory Replication

B. Pass-Through Authentication

C. Trust Validation

D. Access Control Lists

Question #70

Nicole calls to say that her print jobs seem to have stopped running. You check the printer that she sent the jobs to and see that the jobs are stuck in queue. What steps should you take to clear the stuck jobs? Select all that apply.

A. Select the stuck jobs and choose Document, Cancel.

B. Select Printer, Purge Printer.

C. Use the Control Panel applet Services to stop and restart the Spooler service.

D. Select each stuck job and change its priority.

Question #71

When configuring GSNW on Windows NT Server, a group called _________________ must be set up on the Novell Server.

A. NTUserGateway

B. NovellGateway

C. NetBIOSGateway

D. NTGateway

Question #72

One factor that will definitely affect the type of domain model that you implement is:

A. The number of user and group accounts

B. The physical location and grouping of users

C. The type of wide area network connections you have in place

D. The location of network servers

Question #73

Your boss has advised you that BrownC has left the company and asks that you delete his account. Later, your boss hires BrownC back as a consultant and tells you to put his account back on the network. BrownC calls you the next day and informs you gruffly that he can no longer access any of the network resources that he used to. How do you troubleshoot?

A. Use the Registry to set BrownC's SID back to what it was before you deleted his account. He will then be able to access all the old resources.

B. Deleting BrownC's account also deleted his SID. Because security in Windows NT is linked to the user's SID, you will need to reestablish all the network resource access that BrownC used to have.

C. Use the Emergency Repair Disk or your last network backup to copy BrownC's old account back to the Registry.

D. Install a backup copy of the account database that contains his old account.

Question #74

The Finance domain trusts the Marketing domain. Sheila has just joined the Marketing group as a short-term contractor. Sheila needs access to a Finance database to complete her project. What type of account would you create for Sheila?

A. Create a global account for Sheila in the Marketing domain.

B. Create a local account for Sheila in the Marketing domain.

C. Create a global account for Sheila in the Marketing Domain and a global account for Sheila in the Finance domain.

D. Create a local account for Sheila in the Marketing domain and a global account for Sheila in the Finance domain.

Question #75

By default, CrashDump will be placed in the ____________________ folder.

A. %systemRoot%\System32

B. %systemRoot%\System32\Debug

C. %systemRoot%\System32\MemoryDump

D. %systemRoot%\

Question #76

You suspect that someone is trying to log in to various workstations unauthorized. What is the best step you can take to increase security and determine who might be doing this?

A. Enable Account Lockout in the Account Policy requiring the Administrator to unlock the account.

B. Enable Account Lockout in the Account Policy requiring the Administrator to unlock the account. Enable auditing of unsuccessful logons and logoffs and monitor these events in the Event Viewer.

C. Advise users to change their passwords more frequently and not to use obvious passwords.

D. Increase the minimum password length in Account Policy.

Question #77

ABCCorp network consists of 5,000 users located in three office locations: New York, Chicago, and San Francisco. The current plan is to locate one PDC and one BDC in the corporate headquarters in Chicago. How could you optimize this configuration to make logging on more efficient for the users and minimize network traffic? Choose the best two answers.

A. Create two more BDCs to accommodate the 5,000 users. Microsoft recommends one BDC for every 2,000 users.

B. Create a trust relationship among all the offices.

C. Locate one BDC in each location so that logon validation takes place locally.

D. Do nothing. This configuration is optimized.

Question #78

Frederick has recently loaded two more C++ applications to modify on his Windows NT 4.0 Workstation. He has noticed that when he boots and loads all his applications, Windows NT takes longer to respond to application requests. You use Performance Monitor and notice that pagefile usage has increased and that the Commit Limit for the pagefile increases rapidly when the applications are loaded. What is the best solution you can offer Frederick based on this data?

A. Purchase more RAM for Frederick's computer.

B. Move the pagefile to another disk partition.

C. Increase the initial size of the pagefile so that it doesn't have to grow right away as the applications load.

D. Move the C++ applications to another disk partition.

Question #79

The Registry location for the NetBEUI protocol parameters is HKEY_LOCAL_MACHINE\System\CurrentControlSet\Services\...:

A. NetBEUI\Parameters

B. NetBIOS\Parameters

C. NBF\Parameters

D. NetBEUI\NBF\Parameters

Question #80

The printer for a network print device has been configured to print documents at all times. Pam plans to send a large complex graphics document that she would like to have tomorrow morning. This job will take at least one hour to complete. What can you do to minimize the effect that printing this document will have on other documents in the queue?

A. Select Pam's document and pause it. Resume printing after hours when print jobs are at a minimum.

B. Modify the printer schedule so that it prints documents only after hours.

C. Modify the document schedule for Pam's document so that it prints only between 1:00 A.M. and 3:00 A.M.

D. Do nothing. The printer automatically holds long jobs until short jobs finish spooling and printing.

Question #81

You plan to use Performance Monitor to help predict and troubleshoot server activity under various conditions. Which of the following would be the best way to begin?

A. Create and monitor a real-time chart during peak activity and note the percent of processor usage during these periods.

B. Create a series of baseline logs of specific objects (processor, memory, disk, and network), each representing a different condition. Use these to predict activity under those conditions and to troubleshoot abnormal system activity.

C. Create a baseline log measuring system activity during periods of average activity. Compare this against real-time charts created during peak activity on the system.

D. Network Monitor would be a better tool to predict system activity.

Question #82

Which of the following characteristics can be applied to a domain? Choose all that apply.

A. A domain is a logical grouping of computers.

B. A domain depends entirely on the physical layout of the network.

C. A domain provides the foundation for implementing Directory Services.

D. A domain does not depend on the physical location of computers and users.

Question #83

A user is having problems logging on to the network and is seeing a variety of messages. Which of the following things would you check to troubleshoot?

A. The user is entering the correct username and password.

B. The username is case-sensitive.

C. The domain controller is up and accessible.

D. The user's account requires a mandatory profile that is accessible.

Question #84

To provide a greater level of security, you have decided to create an account policy that requires a minimum password length of eight characters, requires that users change their passwords at least once a month, and does not allow users to use the same password twice in two months. Which Account Policy settings are appropriate?

A. Max Password Age: 60; Min Password Age: 30; Min Password Length: 8; Password Uniqueness: 2

B. Max Password Age: 30; Min Password Age: 30; Min Password Length: 8; Password Uniqueness: 6

C. Max Password Age: 30; Min Password Age: 10; Min Password Length: 8; Password Uniqueness: 6

D. Max Password Age: 60; Min Password Age: 30; Min Password Length: 8; Password Uniqueness: 1

Question #85

What service must be installed on a Windows NT 4.0 Server to allow it to function as an AppleTalk router?

A. RPC

B. GSNW

C. FDDI

D. SFM

Question #86

The Finance domain users need to access a printer resource in the Marketing domain. You are going to set up a trust relationship to facilitate the sharing of this resource. Which two steps need to take place?

A. The Finance domain must identify the Marketing domain as its trusted domain.

B. The Marketing domain must permit the Finance domain to trust it—the Marketing domain must make Finance its trusting domain.

C. The Finance domain must permit the Marketing domain to trust it—the Finance domain must make Marketing its trusting domain.

D. The Marketing domain must identify the Finance domain as its trusted domain.

Question #87

Which three of the following four features are a part of the Services applet in Control Panel?

A. Running status

B. Load order

C. Hardware profile assignments

D. Startup options

Question #88

On a Windows NT Server in DomainA, you have stored a sales database and a marketing database, and have also shared a color printer. Five of the users in the domain are salespersons, five are marketers, and the rest are programmers. The users should be able to access their respective databases, but only the team leaders for sales, marketing, and programmers should be able to access the color printer. Which group strategy is the best?

A. Create local groups for sales, marketing, and team leaders and assign the appropriate user accounts to the appropriate groups. Then, assign permissions for each resource to the appropriate group.

B. Create global groups for sales, marketing, and team leaders and assign the appropriate user accounts to the appropriate groups. Then, assign permissions for each resource to the appropriate global group.

C. Create global groups for sales, marketing, and team leaders and assign the appropriate user accounts to the appropriate groups. Then create local groups for each and assign the global group to the local group. Then assign permissions for each resource to the appropriate local group.

D. Simply assign the appropriate users access to the resources that they need access to.

Question #89

After monitoring your heavily accessed file and print server, you determine that both the Server>Pool Paged Failures and Server>Pool Nonpaged Failures counters are unusually and consistently higher than normal. The Server service memory property is configured for Balanced memory usage. What should you do to reduce the number of Pool Paged and Pool Nonpaged failures?

A. Add more memory. Balanced is an appropriate setting for a file and print server.

B. Change the Server service memory configuration to Minimize Memory Used.

C. Change the Server service memory configuration to Maximize Throughput for File Sharing.

D. Change the Server service memory configuration to Load Balance Throughput for Virtual Memory.

Question #90

Server tools are designed to be installed on which of the following clients?

A. Windows 95

B. Windows for Workgroups 3.11

C. Windows NT 4.0 and 3.5/3.51 Workstations

D. Windows NT 4.0 Server

Question #91

The operating system choices displayed during bootup are stored in

A. the registry

B. the master boot record

C. boot.ini

D. config.sys

Question #92

What kind of connection can be established between the Host computer and the Target computer for the Host computer to monitor the Boot process on the Target computer?

A. Null Modem connection using a COM port

B. Normal Network connection using a Network Adapter Card

C. Modem connection using a COM port

D. Modem connection using an LPT port

Question #93

There are three downward-compatible print devices connected to the print server in MIS. MIS Managers and Project Leaders should always be able to print to the first available printer. Help Desk staff and Developers should be able to print only to their specified print device. What will best accomplish this task?

A. Create a printer for each device and assign the appropriate groups access only to their printer. Give the Manager's printer a priority of 1, Help Desk's printer a priority of 50, and Developer's printer a priority of 99.

B. Create a printer for each device and assign the appropriate groups access only to their printer. Give the Manager's printer a priority of 99, Help Desk's printer a priority of 50, and Developer's printer a priority of 1.

C. Create a printer for each device and assign the appropriate groups access only to their printer. Make the Manager's printer a printer pool by associating it with each print device.

D. Create a printer for each device and assign the appropriate groups access only to their printer. Make each printer a printer pool by associating it with each print device.

Question #94

If Windows NT is configured for Auto frame type detection and multiple IPX frame types are detected on the network, Windows NT will:

A. Automatically default to 802.3

B. Automatically default to 802.2

C. Automatically configure itself to all IPX frame types detected

D. Automatically default to the first IPX frame type detected

Question #95

A broadcast frame:

A. Is always directed to a specific computer by its IP, IPX, or MAC address.

B. Is sent to all hosts on the network via the unique destination address FFFFFFFF.

C. Is sent to a subset of computers on the network depending on how the computer has registered itself on the network.

D. Is a multicast frame that is directed to a specific computer on the network.

Question #96

The manager of the Accounting department wants to make next year's budget templates available for the staff accountants to review beginning next month. Staff accountants are all members of the Accountants global group in CORPDOMAIN. The templates will be stored on the department resource server called ACCT1 in a folder called BUDGET97. None of the partitions on ACCT1 are formatted with NTFS. How would you make the folder available only to the Accounting department staff?

A. Use User Manager for Domains to create a local group on the resource server called Accountants. Make the global Accountants group a member of the local Accountants group. Assign permission to use the folder to the Accountants group through User Manager for Domains.

B. Use User Manager for Domains to create a local group on the resource server called Accountants. Make the global Accountants group a member of the local Accountants group. Assign the appropriate User Rights to the Accountants group to access the BUDGET97 share.

C. Use User Manager for Domains to create a local group on the resource server called Accountants. Make the global Accountants group a member of the local Accountants group. Use the Security tab on the properties sheet for the folder to assign permissions to the Accountants group.

D. Use User Manager for Domains to create a local group on the resource server called Accountants. Make the global Accountants group a member of the local Accountants group. Use the Sharing tab on the properties sheet for the folder to assign permissions to the Accountants group.

Question #97

Network types can have network numbers or network ranges associated with them. Which type of network can have only one network number associated with it?

A. LocalTalk

B. EtherTalk

C. TokenTalk

D. FDDI

Question #98

You have created four printers. Each of them will be used by a specific group of users. Name all the steps which are required to successfully make the printer available to the appropriate users.

A. Share each printer.

B. Set the share permissions for each printer so that only the appropriate group has access.

C. Set the printer permissions for each printer so that only the appropriate group has access.

D. Create a printer pool so that each group can access all the print devices.

Question #99

Everyone should be able to read the files in a certain directory. However, the user who created the file should be able to modify it. What do you need to do?

A. Do nothing. By default, only the creator of a file has access to it. Windows NT restricts resource access by default.

B. Give the group Everyone read access and the Creator Owner group change access. By default, Windows NT allows everyone complete access to resources.

C. Give the group Everyone read access and the Creator Owner group change access. By default, Windows NT restricts resource access.

D. Give the group Everyone read access and the Users group change access. Windows NT will automatically determine who the owner of the file is and restrict the other users.

Question #100

Kite Flyers Corporation has its corporate headquarters in New York and branch offices in Chicago and San Francisco. Resource domains have been set up in each location and all accounts are managed by MIS in New York. The main goals of directory services are met. Which domain model does this represent and how many trusts need to be established?

A. **Master domain model.** The account domain in New York must trust each resource domain in each location; therefore, three one-way trusts need to be established.

B. **Complete Trust model.** All domains must trust one another. Because there are four domains, 4*(4-1) or 12 trusts must be established.

C. **Master domain model.** Each resource domain must trust the account domain in New York; therefore, three one-way trusts need to be established.

D. **Master domain model.** The account and resource domains must trust each other. Therefore, two one-way trusts must be established between each resource domain and the account domain, or six total.

Question #101

Fred is a member of the Developers group. The Developers group has been given the NTFS permission Full Control to the TOOLS folder. Fred is changing jobs and has been given NO ACCESS to the file DOOM.DOC, which is contained in the TOOLS folder. Later, Fred logs on and deletes the file DOOM.DOC. Luckily, you can restore the file from your tape backup. How can you prevent Fred from deleting the file again, but still maintain the original level of access for him and the Developers group?

A. Fire Fred.

B. Give the Developers group Special Access with all options selected for the TOOLS folder. Then give Fred NO ACCESS to the file.

C. Give the Developers group Change access at the folder level.

D. Give Fred NO ACCESS at the folder level.

Question #102

Built-in local groups and their members are contained in which accounts database?

A. SAM Accounts Database

B. Local Security Accounts Database

C. SAM Built-In Database

D. Account Synchronization Database

Question #103

Arlo, a member of the Developers group, is currently editing the file DOOM.DOC in the share TOOLS. The administrator of the share changes permission to the Developers group from Change to Read. Arlo continues to make changes to the document. What else must the administrator do to restrict Arlo's access?

A. Take Arlo out of the Developers group.

B. Give Arlo No Access explicitly.

C. Send Arlo a message to get his authorization.

D. Nothing. Arlo must disconnect from the share and then reconnect before the new permission will take effect.

Question #104

You created a trust between Finance and Marketing so that users in the Marketing domain can access resources managed in the Finance domain. However, Marketing users are unable to access resources. What would you check?

A. Has the trust been completed by both domains?

B. Was the trust broken?

C. Has appropriate access been granted to the users?

D. Is the trust set up in the correct direction?

Question #105

Kite Flyers Corporation has opened offices in London and Tokyo. Each office maintains its own resources, though all users are managed in the corporate headquarters. Which domain model is best suited to this organization?

A. Single domain model

B. Master domain model

C. Multiple Master domain model

D. Complete Trust domain model

Question #106

When planning a large wide area network for an enterprise, Microsoft advocates implementing a structure that supports the following characteristics: (Choose all that apply.)

A. Single network logon regardless of location or domain affiliation

B. Easy user access to network resources regardless of the location of the user or the resource in the enterprise

C. Decentralized account and resource administration

D. Synchronization of account and security information across the enterprise

Question #107

On your Windows NT 4.0 development workstation, you have concluded that performance as a whole has decreased. You are not sure which process is driving this, but you have noticed that your disk drive has had a lot more activity lately. What objects should you monitor through Performance Monitor to help you troubleshoot this situation?

A. Check the Processor>%Processor Time counter, determine the percent of disk I/O used for paging through the Memory>Pages/Sec counter and the Logical Disk>Avg. Disk sec/Transfer counter, and the Process>Working Set for every process running.

B. Check the Processor>%Processor Time counter, determine the percent of disk I/O used for paging through the Memory>Pages/Sec counter and the Logical Disk>Avg. Disk sec/Transfer counter. Track the Process>%Processor Time counter for every process running to determine which processes are pushing the processor excessively. Monitor the Process>Working Set counter for these processes in particular.

C. Check the Processor>%Processor Time counter, determine the percent of disk I/O used for paging through the Logical Disk>Disk Queue Length counter, and the Process>Working Set for every process running.

D. Check the Processor>%User Time counter, determine the percent of disk I/O used for paging through the Logical Disk>%Disk Time counter, and the Memory>Commit Limit counter for the pagefile.

Question #108

You are deciding whether to support long file names on FAT partitions for your server. You have a variety of client platforms that connect to the server, including MS-DOS and Windows 95. Some of the platforms support older 16-bit applications. Which of the following considerations would you make?

A. There are no significant concerns. All applications support long file names on all platforms in a Microsoft network.

B. Most Microsoft applications will support the long file names, but some older applications save changes by deleting the old file and renaming a temporary file to the original file name. This could eliminate the long file name.

C. Long file names saved in the root of the drive require one directory entry for the alias, and one for up to every 13 characters of the name. Because the root is hard-coded for 512 directory entries for FAT partitions, you could run out of entries.

D. If long file name support is disabled for the FAT partition, it is disabled for all partitions on that computer, including NTFS.

Question #109

The print device associated with a particular printer has failed. Several print jobs are waiting in queue in that printer. How can you service these print jobs?

A. Connect to another remote printer. Open the printer manager window for the printer and drag the waiting print jobs to the remote printer manager window.

B. Use the Ports tab properties for the printer to add a port for another remote printer. Deselect the current print port associated with the printer and select the remote port. Resume the printer.

C. Do nothing. You must replace the failed print device before printing can resume.

D. Use the Control Panel applet Services to stop the spooler service, configure it to connect to another remote printer, and restart it.

Question #110

From the following choices, indicate the step that is NOT required when installing and configuring a printing device using the TCP/IP protocol.

A. Enter the IP address of the remote controller servicing the print device in the Add LPR Compatible Printer dialog box.

B. Enter the name of the remote controller servicing the print device in the Add LPR Compatible Printer dialog box.

C. Enter the IP address of the print device in the Add LPR Compatible Printer dialog box.

D. Enter the IP address of the print server in the Add LPR Compatible Printer dialog box.

Question #111

What types of network traffic are associated with the DHCP service?

A. DHCP Address Request

B. DHCP Lease Renewal

C. DHCP Time Out

D. DHCP Replication

Question #112

While tracking the performance of disk activity on a system, you notice that the measured value is always 0 although the disk appears to be heavily used. What is your evaluation of this situation?

A. The disk is a high performance unit and can handle the heavy disk I/O.

B. The wrong disk objects and counters have been selected for Performance Monitor.

C. The disk counters had not been enabled by typing DISKPERF -Y at a command prompt.

D. The disk has crashed.

Question #113

Which tool(s) can you use to remotely manage file and folder permissions across the domain?

A. User Manager for Domains

B. Server Manager

C. Windows Explorer

D. Network Neighborhood

Question #114

Which of the following counters will provide you with the total number of bytes transferred during disk I/O for all the disks in your computer?

A. Logical Disk>Disk Bytes/sec, Total instance

B. Logical Disk>Disk Bytes/sec, for each partition instance

C. Physical Disk>Disk Bytes/sec, Total instance

D. Physical Disk>Disk Bytes/sec, for each disk instance

Question #115

The Finance domain trusts the Marketing domain. You would like to give Sheila, Frank, and Pat the responsibility of backing up all the domain controllers and servers in the Finance Domain. Which is the best course of action?

A. Add Sheila, Frank, and Pat to the Backup Operators group in the Marketing domain, and then add that Backup Operators group to the local Backup Operators groups on each domain controller and server in the Finance domain.

B. Create a global group in the Marketing domain called Global Backup and add Sheila, Frank, and Pat to it. Add Global Backup to the local Backup Operators groups on each domain controller and server in the Finance domain.

C. Create a global group in the Marketing domain called Global Backup and add Sheila, Frank, and Pat to it. Add Global Backup to the local Backup Operators group on the primary domain controller and the local Backup Operators groups on each server in the Finance domain.

D. Create new accounts for Sheila, Frank, and Pat on each domain controller and server in the Finance domain and add them to the local Backup Operators groups on each domain controller and server in the Finance domain.

Question #116

Which print monitor is loaded with TCP/IP and tracks print jobs targeted for TCP/IP print hosts?

A. IPMON.DLL

B. LPDMON.DLL

C. LPRMON.DLL

D. LOCALMON.DLL

Question #117

Which of the following features is provided by the full version of Network Monitor that comes with Microsoft's System Management Server? Choose all that apply.

A. Direct monitoring of remote computer traffic.

B. Determining which protocol consumed the most bandwidth.

C. Identifying which physical disk has the most I/O activity for a network session.

D. Capturing local network traffic to and from the computer running the utility.

Question #118

RIP for NWLink will allow a Windows NT computer to act as a:

A. IP Router

B. AppleTalk Router

C. IPX Router

D. DLC Router

Question #119

From the following choices, list the steps required to install a network interface printer using the DLC protocol.

A. Install the DLC protocol on the print server and shut down and restart.

B. Start the Print Wizard, select Add Printer, then select Add Port.

C. Select the Hewlett-Packard Network Port and click the New Port button.

D. Select a MAC address from the available addresses and supply a printer name in the Add Hewlett-Packard Network Peripheral Port dialog box.

Question #120

Which Windows NT Server service allows a user to log on at computers in domains in which they have no account through the trust relationship to a computer or domain in which they do have an account?

A. NetLogon Service

B. Directory Replication Service

C. Account Synchronization Service

D. Self Service

Question #121

Flora, the MIS director, wants company employees to be able to access the company's network through their personal Internet providers. However, she has concerns about the security of the company's network from unauthorized Internet access. What is your solution? Choose all that apply.

A. Use Point-to-Point Tunneling on the RAS server.

B. Enable callback security for Internet connections.

C. Connect only the RAS server to the Internet.

D. Enable filtering for PPTP on the RAS server.

Question #122

A user's effective access to a resource is determined by:

A. Comparing the rights of the user with the permissions assigned through the ACL of the resource.

B. Comparing the permissions in the access token of the user with the permissions assigned through the ACL of the resource.

C. Comparing the user and group SID entries in the user's access token with the permissions assigned through the ACL of the resource.

D. Comparing the user and group SID entries in the user's access token with the user rights listed in the ACL of the resource.

Question #123

For CrashDumps to be obtained, the pagefile must be at least ________ megabytes larger than the physical size of memory.

A. 1

B. 2

C. 4

D. 8

Question #124

Jeanette calls to say that her print jobs seem to have stopped running. You check the printer that she sent the jobs to and see that the jobs are stuck in queue. What steps should you take to clear the stuck jobs? Choose all that apply.

A. Select the stuck jobs and choose Document, Cancel.

B. Select Printer, Purge Print Documents.

C. Use the Control Panel applet Service to stop and restart the Spooler service.

D. Select each stuck job and change its priority.

Question #125

Kite Flyers Corporation is a relatively small company with about 1,000 employees. They are located in the same office complex. There are five departments: Accounting, Marketing, MIS, HR, and Corporate. Each has its own set of network resources that its staff accesses, and some resources that everyone in the company uses.

Primary Goals: Give all employees a single logon account that they can use to access their resources. Let each department manage its own resources.

Secondary Goal: Centralize resources by department.

Solution: Implement a single domain model and make all resource servers members of the domain.

A. The solution satisfies none of the goals.

B. The solution satisfies both primary goals and the secondary goal.

C. The solution satisfies both primary goals, but not the secondary goal.

D. The solution satisfies one primary goal and the secondary goal.

Question #126

Which of the following characteristics best apply to a domain network model? Choose two.

A. Resource access is provided by permitting access to users and groups that are members of the domain.

B. User and group accounts are maintained on each workstation that is a member of the domain.

C. A domain network model provides a relatively low level of resource security.

D. Resource and account management is centralized.

Question #127

Kite Flyers Corporation was formed from three different regional companies located in San Francisco, Chicago, and Atlanta. Each company already had its own Windows NT network configured as a Single Domain model. It is necessary that all the users in the new company be able to log on to the network, no matter which office they work from, and still be able to access their resources. Which domain model provides the best solution for this scenario?

A. Multiple Master domain model. Create two one-way trusts between San Francisco and Chicago, and between Chicago and Atlanta.

B. Master domain model. Have San Francisco and Atlanta create one-way trusts to Chicago.

C. Complete Trust model. Have all domains trust one another for a total of three trusts.

D. Complete Trust model. Have all domains trust one another for a total of six trusts.

Question #128

Which objects would be most beneficial to include in a log file when creating a baseline measurement of your system's performance? Choose the best three.

A. Memory

B. TCP/IP

C. Processor

D. Physical and Logical Disk

Question #129

Elaine was the print administrator for the LotsOf Print Corporation, but has left the country to pursue a career as an opera singer. You need to assign a new print administrator. What will you need to do concerning ownership of the LotsOf Print Corporation printers that Elaine created and managed?

A. Do nothing. Printers are not owned by a user; they are owned by the system.

B. Make the new print administrator a Print Operator. The new print administrator can then take ownership of the printers in LotsOf Print Corporation.

C. Give ownership of the printers to the new print administrator.

D. Give the new administrator Full Control permission over the printers. Full Control automatically assigns ownership to that user.

Question #130

The first four lines of the ____________________ section are critical to finding the cause of the STOP error.

A. BugCheck Information

B. Driver Information

C. Kernel Build Number and Stack Dump

D. Debug Port Information

Question #131

Desiree, a Visual Basic developer, has noticed that her system's performance has decreased since she began work on a large VB application. You have used Performance Monitor to determine that the pagefile usage has increased. You also notice that the pagefile, Windows NT system files, and the VB application are all stored on the same partition. In addition, the working set for the VB application shows that it consistently requires 16M for itself. What solutions can you recommend? Name all that apply.

A. Add more RAM in the computer.

B. Move the pagefile to a disk partition other than the system or application partition.

C. Increase the maximum size for the pagefile.

D. Create multiple pagefiles.

Question #132

A WINS database is used to:

A. Dynamically map IP addresses to network adapter card names

B. Dynamically map IP addresses to subnet masks

C. Dynamically map IP addresses to NetBIOS names

D. Dynamically map IP addresses to a user name

Question #133

The utility to verify the validity of a CrashDump is

A. Dumpflop.exe

B. Dumpexam.exe

C. Dumpchk.exe

D. Dump.exe

Question #134

You are using a RISC-based computer as your print server. All your clients are either MS-DOS, Windows for Workgroups, Windows 95, or Windows NT running on Intel-based computers. What must you do to ensure that all your clients can print to the print devices managed by the RISC-based print server?

A. Install both RISC-based and Intel print drivers on the RISC-based print server. Install the appropriate print drivers only on the MS-DOS and Windows for Workgroups computers.

B. Install both RISC-based and Intel print drivers on the RISC-based print server. The client computers will receive the appropriate platform driver from the print server when they make a print request.

C. Install RISC-based print drivers on the RISC-based print server and Intel print drivers on the client computers. Windows NT will do the platform translation.

D. Install the Intel print drivers on the RISC-based print server and RISC-based print drivers on the client computers.

Question #135

Which of the following features is provided by the version of Network Monitor that comes with Microsoft Windows NT Server 4.0?

A. Direct monitoring of remote computer traffic.

B. Determining which protocol consumed the most bandwidth.

C. Identifying which physical disk has the most I/O activity for a network session.

D. Capturing local network traffic to and from the computer running the utility.

Question #136

Which Process object counter would be useful in determining the amount of memory required by an application?

A. %Application Memory

B. Commit Limit

C. Working Set

D. Avg. Disk sec\Transfer

Question #137

The manager of the Accounting department wants to make next year's budget templates available for the staff accountants to review beginning next month. Staff accountants are already members of a global group called Accountants in CORPDOMAIN. The templates will be stored on the department resource server called ACCT1 in a folder called BUDGET97 on an NTFS partition. The folder has been shared with the default permission. The global accountants group has been added to a local group called Accountants on ACCT1. You would like everyone to be able to see the files, but only the accounting staff should be able to make changes. What do you need to do?

A. Change the share permission to only Accountants with Change permission.

B. Assign the Accountants group the NTFS permission Change to the BUDGET97 folder.

C. Change the share permission to Everyone with No Access and assign the Accountants group the NTFS permission Change for the BUDGET97 folder.

D. Change the share permission to Everyone with Read and assign the Accountants group the NTFS permission Change for the BUDGET97 folder.

Question #138

Protocols are installed by accessing the network icon in the Control Panel and:

A. Selecting the Protocol tab and selecting the Add button.

B. Selecting the Protocol tab and selecting the protocol.

C. Selecting the Protocol tab and choosing all protocols.

D. Selecting the Protocol tab, nothing else has to be selected.

Question #139

What server administrative tool is used to copy the server tools from the CD-ROM and automatically create a shared folder?

A. Network Server Tools Administrator

B. Network Client Administrator

C. Network Server Tools Manager

D. Network Server Manager

Question #140

The Advanced button on the Microsoft TCP/IP Properties sheet allows for the addition of:

A. 5 additional WINS server IP addresses

B. 10 additional default gateways

C. 5 additional DHCP server IP addresses
D. 5 additional default gateways

Question #141

Following the power-on self-test, NT loads

A. Environment settings
B. Master boot record
C. OS Kernel
D. OS system file

Question #142

Which of the following are components of an Ethernet 802.3 frame? Choose all that apply.

A. Source and Destination address
B. Length of the frame
C. Data contained in the frame such as IP and TCP information
D. Type of frame

Question #143

Michelle has been selected to assist you as a print administrator in the Dry Gulch office, since you, yourself, are unable to travel there frequently, though you'd really like to. What is the minimum level of access you need to give Michelle so that she can perform basic print management tasks such as creating and sharing printers and managing print jobs?

A. Make Michelle a member of the Print Operators local group on her print server.
B. Make Michelle a member of the Server Operator local group on her print server.
C. Make Michelle a member of the Administrators local group on her print server.
D. Give Michelle Full Control permission for each printer on her print server.

Question #144

A print job can be directed directly to a UNIX host print device, and its status checked using which two command-line utilities?

A. LPD and LPR
B. LPD and LPQ
C. LPR and IPCONFIG
D. LPR and LPQ

Question #145

Which Processor object counter would be useful to determine how much processor time is being utilized by application requests?

A. %Processor Time
B. %User Time
C. %Application Time
D. %Privileged Time

Question #146

Which tool(s) can you use to remotely manage shares across the domain?

A. User Manager for Domains
B. Server Manager
C. Windows Explorer
D. Network Neighborhood

Question #147

When a computer registers with a WINS server, how many name registration frames are generated?

A. One name is registered for each computer.
B. A name is registered for the computer and for every service or application that supports the NetBIOS API. One frame registers all these names.

C. A name is registered for the computer and for every service or application that supports the NetBIOS API. One frame is generated for each name that needs to be registered.

D. NetBIOS names are not registered with the WINS server.

Question #148

You want to give a particular domain user the ability to back up files on a server, but not be able to restore files. How can you accomplish this?

A. Make the domain user a member of the Backup Operators group on the server.

B. Make the domain user a member of the Server Operators group on the server.

C. Create a new local group called BACKUP ONLY on the server and make the domain user a member of it. Assign this new group to the Backup Files and Directories User Right.

D. Give the user read-only access to all the files.

Question #149

The manager of the Accounting department wants to make next year's budget templates available for the staff accountants to review beginning next month. Staff accountants are all members of the global group Accountants in the domain CORPDOMAIN. The templates will be stored on the department resource server called ACCT1 in a folder called BUDGET97. A local group called Budget has been created to manage access to the budget templates. None of the partitions on ACCT1 are formatted with NTFS. How would you make the folder available only to the Accounting department staff? Choose all that apply.

A. Share the BUDGET97 directory.

B. Add the Accountants group to the ACL for the share.

C. Remove the Everyone group from the ACL for the share.

D. Give the Accountants group read and write permissions at the folder level.

Question #150

Your workstations are members of a domain called Titan. You need to create user accounts so that two shifts of temporary employees can log on to the same computer, but only during their shift.

A. Use User Manager for domains on each local Windows NT Workstation to create the temporary accounts and assign each the appropriate logon hours.

B. Use User Manager on each local Windows NT Workstation to create the temporary accounts and assign each the appropriate logon hours.

C. Use User Manager for domains on the domain controller for Titan to create domain accounts for the temporary employees and assign each the appropriate logon hours.

D. Use User Manager on the domain controller for Titan to create local group accounts for the temporary employees and assign each the appropriate logon hours.

Question #151

Which type of frames are involved in connecting to a shared resource once the session has been established?

A. SMB session frames

B. WINS resolution frames

C. NBT broadcast frames

D. TCP request frames

Question #152

If the AppleTalk protocol is installed on a Windows NT Server, other Windows NT users on the network can access the server:

A. To create Macintosh Accessible Volumes on Macintosh computers

B. To access Macintosh Accessible Volumes on Macintosh computers

C. To access Macintosh Accessible Volumes on the workstation and share files with Macintosh users

D. As a print server

Question #153

The permission list defining access to a resource resides:

A. With the resource and is called the Access Control List.

B. With the user and is called the User Rights Policy.

C. With the user and is called the Access Control List.

D. With the resource and is called the User Rights Policy.

Question #154

The Finance domain trusts the Marketing domain. What implication can you draw from this relationship?

A. The Finance domain is the trusted domain and the Marketing domain is the trusting domain. Users from the Marketing domain can access resources in the Finance domain, but only log on at their own domain computers.

B. The Finance domain is the trusting domain and the Marketing domain is the trusted domain. Users from the Marketing domain can access resources in the Finance domain, but only log on at their own domain computers.

C. The Finance domain is the trusted domain and the Marketing domain is the trusting domain. Users from the Finance domain can access resources in the Marketing domain, and log on at computers in the Marketing domain.

D. The Finance domain is the trusting domain and the Marketing domain is the trusted domain. Users from the Finance domain can only access their own resources and log on at computers in their domain. Users from the Marketing domain can access resources in the Finance domain, and log on at computers in either the Finance domain or their own domain.

Question #155

An IP address consists of what two parts in the order from left to right?

A. A network address and a workstation address
B. A workstation address and a network address
C. A subnet mask address and a default gateway address
D. A default gateway address and a subnet mask address

Question #156

Indicate the utility used from the command prompt to manually maintain a static IP routing table.

A. Route
B. IPXRoute
C. IPConfig
D. PING

Question #157

You need to be able to remotely manage the account database on two trusted domains. Which steps must take place for this to happen successfully?

A. Do nothing. You can remotely manage accounts through a trust by default.
B. Use User Manager for domains and choose User, Select Domain from the menu to choose the remote domain you want to administer.
C. Make your account a member of the Account Operators group in the trusted domains.
D. Give your user account Full Control access to the SAM hive file in WINNT\SYSTEM32\CONFIG.

Question #158

If a group of workstations on a network are never to contain any shared resources, how can you optimize these workstations so they will never send host announcements to the master browser?

A. Disable the workstation service
B. Disable the server service
C. Disable the browser service
D. Disable the alerter service

Question #159

Kite Flyers Corporation has two global locations, London and New York. MIS manages the users in both locations in two account domains. There are five departments: Accounting, Marketing, MIS, HR, and Corporate. Each has its own set of network resources that its staff accesses, and some resources that everyone in the company uses.

Primary Goals: Give all employees a single logon account that they can use to access their resources. Let MIS be able to manage the account domains from any location. Let each department manage its own resources. Let certain delegated users act as print operators for printers in each department.

Secondary Goals: Centralize resources by department. Let all delegated users be able to manage any domain's printers. Allow as much flexibility as possible for printer management.

Solution: Implement a Single Domain model. Have all resource servers become members of the domain. Create a global group called KFPRINT. Add KFPRINT to the local Print Operators groups on the print servers in each domain.

A. The solution satisfies none of the goals.
B. The solution satisfies all the primary goals and all the secondary goals.
C. The solution satisfies all primary goals but only one secondary goal.
D. The solution satisfies two primary goals and two secondary goals.

Question #160

If the final print output is corrupted, what print process component should you check?

A. Spooler service on the client computer.
B. Spooler service on the print server.
C. Print processor on the print server.
D. Print monitor on the client computer.

Question #161

Kite Flyers Corporation has two global locations, London and New York. MIS manages the users in both locations in two account domains. There are five departments: Accounting, Marketing, MIS, HR, and Corporate. Each has its own set of network resources that its staff accesses, and some resources that everyone in the company uses.

Primary Goals: Give all employees a single logon account that they can use to access their resources. Let MIS be able to manage the account domains from any location. Let each department manage its own resources. Let certain delegated users act as print operators for printers in each department.

Secondary Goals: Centralize resources by department. Let all delegated users be able to manage any domain's printers. Allow as much flexibility as possible for printer management.

Solution: Implement a Multiple Master Domain model. Have all resource domains trust the account domain, and let the account domains trust each other. In each account domain, create a global group for print operators for each department's resource domain called, for example, ACCT-PRINT, MARK-PRINT, MIS-PRINT, HR-PRINT and CORP-PRINT. Add the appropriate global group to the local Print Operators groups on the print servers in their respective domains.

A. The solution satisfies none of the goals.

B. The solution satisfies all the primary goals and all the secondary goals.

C. The solution satisfies all primary goals but only one secondary goal.

D. The solution satisfies two primary goals and two secondary goals.

Question #162

Which of the following characteristics best apply to a workgroup network model? Choose two.

A. A workgroup network model provides a high level of security for resource access.

B. The workgroup model is best applied to smaller (fewer than 20) workstation groups.

C. A workgroup model is identified by its domain controller.

D. Each Windows NT computer participating in a workgroup must maintain a list of users that will be accessing the resources on that computer.

Question #163

Which of the following statements best represents Microsoft's groups strategy for the Master Domain model?

A. Create global groups in the resource domains to manage local resources. Create local groups in the account domains to manage users. Add the resource domains' global groups to the account domain's local groups.

B. Create local groups on the resource servers in the resource domains to manage access to resources. Group users into appropriate global groups in the account domain. Add the global groups from the account domain to the local groups in the resource domains.

C. Create local groups on the resource servers in the resource domains to manage access to resources. Create global groups in the resource domains and add to them global users from the account domain. Make the global groups from the resource domain members of the local groups on the resource servers.

D. Create local groups on the resource servers in the resource domains to manage access to resources. Add global users from the account domain to the local resource groups.

Question #164

Why is NetBEUI protocol routing not supported in Windows NT 4.0 installations?

A. Because NetBEUI maintains its own route tables and requires no additional services to handle routing.

B. Because NetBEUI cannot be installed on Windows NT 4.0 Server.

C. Because NetBEUI uses either RIP for IP or RIP for IPX, whichever is installed.

D. Because NetBEUI is not a routable protocol.

Question #165

Reference to the most recently installed Service pack Symbols files must be listed __________ in the Dumpexam utility command line.

A. Last

B. First after the normal Symbols files reference

C. Second

D. First

Question #166

Kite Flyers Corporation is a relatively small company with about 1,000 employees. They are located in the same office complex. There are five departments: Accounting, Marketing, MIS, HR, and Corporate. Each has its own set of network resources that its staff accesses, and some resources that everyone in the company uses.

Primary Goals: Give all employees a single logon account that they can use to access their resources. Let each department manage their own resources.

Secondary Goal: Centralize resources by department.

Solution: Give each department its own domain and let each manage its own users and resources.

A. The solution satisfies none of the goals.

B. The solution satisfies both primary goals and the secondary goal.

C. The solution satisfies both primary goals, but not the secondary goal.

D. The solution satisfies the secondary goal.

Question #167

The third major area of a STOP screen displays:

A. Debug Port Status Indicator Information

B. BugCheck Information

C. Driver Information

D. Kernel Build Number and Stack Dump Information

Question #168

Which statement best represents Microsoft's recommended group strategy for managing resources effectively?

A. Create a local group in the domain database and add the users from the domain to that local group. Create a local group on the resource computer and make the domain local group a member of the resource local group.

B. Create a global group in the domain database and add the users from the domain to that global group. Create a global group on the resource computer and make the domain global group a member of the resource global group.

C. Create a global group in the domain database and add the users from the domain to that global group. Create a local group on the resource computer and make the domain global group a member of the resource local group.

D. Create a local group on the resource computer and add the domain users directly to the local group.

Question #169

The Finance domain trusts the Marketing domain. The Finance domain shares a color laser printer that the CAD users in Marketing need to use from time to time. There is a global group in Marketing called CAD USERS. There is a local group on the print server in Finance called COLOR USERS that has Print permission to the color laser printer. How would you grant the Marketing CAD users permission to the color laser printer? Select the best answer (Microsoft's recommended solution).

A. In the Permissions dialog box for the color laser printer, choose Add and select the Marketing domain from the list of valid domains. Then select CAD USERS from the list of global groups in the Marketing database.

B. Add the CAD USERS global group from Marketing to the COLOR USERS local group on the print server.

C. Create a global group in Finance called MARKETING CAD USERS. Add the CAD USERS global group from Marketing to the MARKETING CAD USERS global group in Finance. Then add the MARKETING CAD USERS global group to the COLOR USERS local group on the print server.

D. You can't do this because the trust is in the wrong direction.

Question #170

The Finance domain trusts the Marketing domain. The Marketing domain trusts the Accounting domain. Users in the Accounting domain need to access a database resource in the Finance domain. What needs to happen to facilitate the sharing of that resource?

A. Nothing. Because Finance already trusts Marketing and Marketing already trusts Accounting, Finance can share the database resource directly to Accounting users through the trusts.

B. Create a one-way trust from the Accounting domain to the Finance domain.

C. Create a one-way trust from the Finance domain to the Accounting domain.

D. Create a reverse trust from Accounting to Marketing, and from Marketing to Finance.

Question #171

Which of the following protocols is not considered routable?

A. TCP/IP

B. NetBEUI

C. NWLink

D. AppleTalk

Question #172

Which counter will provide you with the total percent of time spent servicing disk requests for a given partition on a disk?

A. Logical Disk>%Disk Time

B. Logical Disk>Disk Queue Length

C. Physical Disk>%Disk Time

D. Physical Disk>Disk Queue Length

Question #173

The DLC protocol is used on Windows NT 4.0 computers to:

A. Communicate with HP JetDirect printing devices

B. Communicate with AppleTalk Postscript printing devices

C. Communicate with Novell file servers and client computers

D. Communicate with IBM mainframes and front end processors

Question #174

The Sales department recently acquired a laser quality printer with an envelope feed that has been installed on their print server called SalesPrint. The sales staff is already a member of the local group SALES on SalesPrint. The print operator shared the printer with the default permission. The sales staff can access the printer, but so can everyone else in the domain. What else must you do to ensure that only sales staff can access the printer?

A. Assign the Sales group print access to the printer.

B. Assign the Sales group print access to the printer, and remove the Everyone group.

C. Do nothing else.

D. Assign the Sales group print access to the printer, and give the Everyone group Read access.

Question #175

An IP address of 191.191.191.191 will have a default subnet mask of:

A. 255.255.255.0

B. 255.255.0.0

C. 255.0.0.0

D. 0.0.0.0

Question #176

Kite Flyers Corporation is a relatively small company with about 1,000 employees. They are located in the same office complex. There are five departments: Accounting, Marketing, MIS, HR, and Corporate. Each has its own set of network resources that its staff accesses, and some resources that everyone in the company uses.

Primary Goals: Give all employees a single logon account that they can use to access their resources. Let each department manage its own resources.

Secondary Goal: Centralize resources by department.

Solution: Implement a master domain model and have all resource domains trust the account domain.

A. The solution satisfies none of the goals.
B. The solution satisfies both primary goals and the secondary goal.
C. The solution satisfies both primary goals, but not the secondary goal.
D. The solution satisfies one primary goal and the secondary goal.

Question #177

Which Memory object counter would help to identify when to right-size the pagefile?

A. %Pagefile
B. Commit Limit
C. Working Set
D. %Disk Time

Question #178

Several users have called you within the past half-hour to complain that their print jobs are not printing. In fact, they get system messages that tell them that the spooler is not responding. You have verified that the spooler directory partition does not have adequate free space to hold all the print jobs sent to it. What steps should you take to resolve this situation?

A. Use the Control Panel applet Services to more frequently stop and restart the Spooler service to keep the print jobs from becoming fragmented.

B. Change the location of the spool directory to a partition with enough disk space by modifying the HKEY_LOCAL_MACHINE\System\CurrentControlSet\Control\Print\Printers DefaultSpoolDirectory parameter.

C. Change the location of the spool directory to a partition with enough disk space by modifying the HKEY_Current_User\Control\Print\Printers\Spool SpoolDirectory parameter.

D. If the partition is formatted with NTFS, compress the spool directory.

Question #179

From the following choices, indicate which are considered functions of a router.

A. They can pass information packets from one protocol to another such as TCP/IP to IPX.

B. They cannot pass information packets from one protocol to another such as TCP/IP to IPX.

C. They can pass information packets from one network segment to another, even though each segment may use a different media type such as Ethernet or Token Ring.

D. They can pass information packets from one network segment to another, but only if each segment is the same media type such as Ethernet or Token Ring.

Question #180

Indicate, from the following choices, which routing options are available with a Windows NT 4.0 Server installation.

A. IP Routing

B. IPX Routing

C. DHCP Relay

D. AppleTalk Routing

Question #181

The NWLink protocol by itself can be used to communicate with:

A. Novell Servers

B. Windows NT Workstations

C. Macintosh Workstations

D. Novell Clients for client/server applications

Answer Key for Self-Assessment Test

Question #	Correct Answer(s)	Question #	Correct Answer(s)
1	B	92	A, C
2	B	93	C
3	A, B, C	94	B
4	B	95	B
5	C	96	D
6	A, B, C	97	A
7	B	98	A, C
8	C	99	B
9	A, B, D	100	C
10	B	101	B
11	B, C, D	102	C
12	C	103	D
13	C	104	A, B, C, D
14	C	105	B
15	A, D	106	A, B, D
16	B, C, D	107	B
17	B	108	B, C
18	C	109	B
19	A	110	D
20	B	111	A, B
21	B	112	C

Question #	Correct Answer(s)	Question #	Correct Answer(s)
22	C	113	C, D
23	B	114	C
24	C	115	C
25	B	116	C
26	A, C, D	117	A, B, D
27	A	118	C
28	A, D	119	A, B, C, D
29	B	120	A
30	A, D	121	A, C, D
31	A, B, D	122	C
32	B	123	A
33	C	124	A, B, C
34	A, B, D	125	C
35	B	126	A, D
36	D	127	D
37	D	128	A, C, D
38	D	129	B
39	C	130	A
40	B	131	A, B, D
41	B, C	132	C
42	C	133	C
43	A	134	A
44	A	135	D
45	A, B, D	136	C
46	A, C, D	137	A, B
47	B, C	138	A
48	D	139	B
49	B, C, D	140	D
50	A, C	141	B
51	B	142	A, B, C, D

continues

continued

Question #	Correct Answer(s)	Question #	Correct Answer(s)
52	A	143	A
53	B	144	D
54	B	145	B
55	B	146	B
56	B	147	C
57	B	148	C
58	D	149	A, B, C
59	C	150	C
60	C	151	A
61	A	152	D
62	B	153	A
63	A	154	D
64	A, C, D	155	A
65	C	156	A
66	A, C, D	157	B, C
67	B	158	B
68	A, B, D	159	D
69	B	160	C
70	A, B, C	161	C
71	D	162	B, D
72	A	163	B
73	B	164	D
74	A	165	D
75	D	166	D
76	B	167	C
77	A, C	168	C
78	C	169	B
79	C	170	C
80	C	171	B

Question #	Correct Answer(s)	Question #	Correct Answer(s)
81	B	172	A
82	A, C, D	173	A, D
83	A, C, D	174	B
84	C	175	B
85	D	176	B
86	C, D	177	B
87	A, C, D	178	B
88	C	179	B, C
89	C	180	A, B, C, D
90	A, B, C	181	B, D
91	C		

Chapter Tests

The numbering for the questions in this section indicates the chapter which contains the material being tested. For example, Question #05-04 is testing your knowledge of material covered in Chapter 5.

Question #02-01

Which of the following are characteristics of NTFS? Choose three.

A. Transaction tracking

B. File- and directory-level permissions

C. Auto-defragmentation of files

D. Data compression

Question #02-02

Choose three features of Windows NT Server 4.0.

A. Windows 95 Interface

B. Peer Web Services

C. Plug and Play

D. Hardware Profiles

Question #02-03

Which of the following characteristics best apply to a workgroup network model? Choose two.

A. A workgroup network model provides a high level of security for resource access.

B. The workgroup model is best applied to smaller (fewer than 20) workstation groups.

C. A workgroup model is identified by its domain controller.

D. Each Windows NT computer participating in a workgroup must maintain a list of users that will be accessing the resources on that computer.

Question #02-04

Which of the following characteristics best apply to a domain network model? Choose two.

A. Resource access is provided by permitting access to users and groups that are members of the domain.

B. User and group accounts are maintained on each workstation that is a member of the domain.

C. A domain network model provides a relatively low level of resource security.

D. Resource and account management is centralized.

Question #02-05

When planning a large wide area network for an enterprise, Microsoft advocates implementing a structure that supports the following characteristics: (Choose all that apply.)

A. Single network logon regardless of location or domain affiliation.

B. Easy user access to network resources regardless of the location of the user or the resource in the enterprise.

C. Decentralized account and resource administration.

D. Synchronization of account and security information across the enterprise.

Question #03-01

You are planning to roll out Windows NT Server 4.0 to a division that has the following computer configurations. On which computers can you install Windows NT Server 4.0 successfully?

A. 3 386/25, 150M free space, 8M RAM, VGA, Windows 3.1

B. 2 386/33, 120M free space, 16M RAM, VGA, Windows for Workgroups

C. 5 486/66DX, 200M free space, 16M RAM, Super VGA, Windows for Workgroups

D. 2 Pentium/120, 100M free space, 16M RAM, Super VGA, Windows NT 3.51

Question #03-02

Which of the following dialogs take place during the text mode of the Setup process? Choose three.

A. Detection and configuration of storage devices

B. Initial hardware verification

C. Request for network card settings

D. Choice of file system for the system partition

Question #03-03

Which of the following dialogs takes place as part of the Setup Wizard?

A. Personal information

B. Detection and configuration of storage devices

C. Request for network card settings

D. Video display setup

Question #03-04

Which of the following switches will allow you to install Windows NT without creating the three startup disks?

A. WINNT /B
B. WINNT /O
C. WINNT /OX
D. WINNT /T:c

Question #03-05

On a RISC-based computer, which of the following statements is true regarding Windows NT installation?

A. Execute setup from either the CD-ROM or over the network by typing WINNT32 and any optional switches.
B. You must have a 2M FAT minimum system partition before starting setup.
C. Execute setup only from a CD-ROM by running WINNT /ARC.
D. Run SETUPLDR from the I386 subdirectory on the CD-ROM.

Question #03-06

You have begun the setup process and have been queried for mass storage devices. Setup presents you with a blank list of devices, but you know that you have a 1.2G IDE drive installed.

A. IDE devices are detected but generally not displayed in the list.
B. Windows NT has incorrectly identified your devices. Press F3 to exit setup and double-check your drive configuration.
C. Type S to add the drive configuration to the list.
D. Exit setup and run NTHQ to verify hardware detection.

Question #03-07

You must preconfigure your installation drive before starting setup.

A. TRUE
B. FALSE

Question #03-08

During the text mode phase, Windows NT displays a dialog box that shows you two drive partitions, and 600M free space on one drive. You would like to install Windows NT on the free space, but want to use only 200M.

A. You must preconfigure the free space before starting setup.

B. You can select the free space during setup, but you cannot change its size.

C. Select the free space and choose ENTER.

D. Select the free space and choose C to create the new partition. Then select the new partition and continue with installation.

Question #03-09

Which of the following statements does not apply to NTFS?

A. NTFS supports file and directory permissions security and access auditing.

B. NTFS supports transaction tracking and sector sparing for data recovery.

C. NTFS supports file and partition sizes of up to 4G.

D. NTFS provides file and directory compression.

Question #03-10

You are installing Windows NT on a computer that also must support and boot OS/2.

A. Windows NT supports OS/2's High Performance File System (HPFS) so there are no problems installing the Windows NT system files in the same partition as OS/2.

B. Windows NT 4.0 no longer supports HPFS, so you must install Windows NT in another partition. When Windows NT restarts the system, you can use the OS/2 boot manager to manage both partitions.

C. Windows NT 4.0 no longer supports HPFS, so you must install Windows NT in another partition. When Windows NT restarts the system, it will disable the OS/2 boot manager, but you can re-enable it by marking the Boot Manager partition active while in Windows NT and restarting the computer.

D. Windows NT and OS/2 cannot coexist on the same computer.

Question #03-11

Name the three main phases of the Setup Wizard.

A. Installing Windows NT Networking

B. Finishing Setup (Time Zone, Display, and final file copy)

C. Setup Options

D. Gathering Information About Your Computer

Question #03-12

What network information is necessary for you to supply during the Network portion of the Setup Wizard?

A. Network Protocols, Network Services, Network Bindings, Network Card settings, Network Model

B. Network Protocols, Network Card Settings, Workgroup or Domain membership

C. Computer Name, Network Card Settings, Workgroup or Domain membership

D. Windows NT self-detects all network settings.

Question #03-13

You have just completed the text mode portion of Windows NT setup and have rebooted to start the GUI Setup Wizard. Windows NT displays the message Missing or Corrupt NTOSKRNL. What should you check?

A. Check the Hardware Compatibility List to see whether the hard disk is compatible with Windows NT.

B. Your Installation CD-ROM may be corrupted. Contact Microsoft for a replacement CD-ROM.

C. Windows NT may have misdetected the SCSI drive. Boot to DOS and edit the BOOT.INI file changing SCSI to MULTI for this installation and verifying the partition number.

D. This happens occasionally on SCSI drives. You must reinstall Windows NT.

Question #04-01

Fred would like to modify his desktop wallpaper, screen saver, and screen colors. How does he get to the dialog to change these settings?

A. Choose Display from the Control Panel.
B. Right-click the desktop and choose Properties.
C. Right-click My Computer and choose Properties, Display.
D. Choose Start, Programs, Display.

Question #04-02

Which three of the following four features are a part of the Services applet in Control Panel?

A. Running status
B. Load order
C. Hardware profile assignments
D. Startup options

Question #04-03

Which Control Panel applet creates and manages accounts?

A. Disk Administrator
B. User Manager
C. Accessibility Options
D. There is no Control Panel Applet that does this.

Question #04-04

Janice is a hearing-impaired account manager who has asked if Windows NT provides any options appropriate for her. What can you do to help?

A. Select Control Panel, Sounds and increase the volume for system sounds.
B. Select My Computer, Properties and select the Accessibilities tab to set Sound options.

C. Select Control Panel, Accessibility Options and set the Sound options.

D. Windows NT does not provide options for physically challenged persons.

Question #04-05

Antonio frequently travels for the company and accesses the network on his laptop via modem while on the road. When he is at the office, he docks his laptop at his workstation and uses the network card in the docking station to access the network. How can you facilitate the boot process between these two hardware configurations?

A. Hardware profiles are a feature of Windows 95, not Windows NT 4.0.

B. Create a hardware profile for each configuration—docked and undocked—and set a default timeout value for the most frequently used configuration.

C. Modify the BOOT.INI file and include a boot menu choice for a second hardware configuration using the \PROFILE:filename boot switch.

D. Use Control Panel, Services and create a new profile from the HW Profiles button.

Question #04-06

Martha wants to modify her mouse pointers. What is the most appropriate procedure for doing this?

A. Choose Control Panel, Mouse and select the pointers through the Pointers tab.

B. Right-click the desktop, choose Properties, and select the Settings tab.

C. Start the Registry Editor, select HKEY_CURRENT_USER, and modify the Cursors subkey.

D. Start the Registry Editor, select HKEY_LOCAL_MACHINE, and modify the System\CurrentControlSet subkey.

Question #04-07

Which of the following hives in HKEY_LOCAL_MACHINE have corresponding directory files in the Windows NT system directory?

A. System

B. Software

C. Hardware

D. Security

Question #04-08

I need to add the company's logo to the default Windows NT boot-up screen. From which Registry subtree(s) can I make this modification?

A. HKEY_LOCAL_MACHINE

B. HKEY_CURRENT_USER

C. HKEY_USERS

D. This change can only be made through Control Panel, Service, Startup.

Question #04-09

Which of the following boot files is essential to the Boot Phase of the boot process?

A. NTLDR

B. NTDETECT.COM

C. NTOSKRNL.EXE

D. BOOT.INI

Question #04-10

While looking at the files on my RISC-based computer, I notice that NTLDR, NTDETECT.COM, and BOOT.INI are missing. What impact will this have on the boot process on this computer?

A. The boot process relies on these files to govern the Boot and Load Phases. Missing or corrupt files will result in error messages and failed boots.

B. It will have no impact on the boot process because RISC-based computers do not rely on these files.

C. The BOOT.INI is not an essential file. Windows NT will look for the default Windows NT system directory.

D. NTLDR is always needed to direct the boot process. NTDETECT.COM and BOOT.INI are not necessary on RISC-based computers.

Question #04-12

Jonas accidentally deleted the BOOT.INI file from his C: drive. Windows NT has been installed in the WINNT subdirectory on C:. What effect will the missing BOOT.INI have?

A. There will be no noticeable effect on the boot process. Windows NT will boot as always.

B. The BOOT.INI file provides the ARC path information that Windows NT needs to find the Windows NT system files. If it is missing, Windows NT will display a message that it cannot find the NTOSKRNL file and fail to boot.

C. If the BOOT.INI file is missing, Windows NT will not display the boot menu during bootup. Windows NT will look for the Windows NT system files on the boot partition in the default directory name (WINNT).

D. The BOOT.INI file is not needed on RISC-based systems.

Question #04-13

I have booted Windows NT and receive the message:

Windows NT could not start because the following file is missing or corrupt: \winnt\system32\ntoskrnl.exe.

How can I recover this file?

A. Boot with the Emergency Repair Disk and choose Verify Windows NT System Files.

B. Boot with the Windows NT Startup disk, choose Repair, and then Verify Windows NT System Files from the Emergency Repair Disk.

C. Find a working Windows NT computer and use the EXPAND command to expand the compressed version of this file from the installation source directory. Then copy the file to the system directory on the problem computer.

D. Boot with a Windows NT Boot Disk and copy the file from this disk.

Question #05-01

Which of the following statements is true about the default user accounts created in Windows NT Server 4.0?

A. The Administrator account is enabled and can be renamed; the Guest account is enabled and cannot be renamed.

B. The Administrator account is enabled and cannot be renamed; the Guest account is disabled and cannot be renamed.

C. The Administrator account is enabled and can be renamed; the Guest account is disabled and can be renamed.

D. The Administrator account is disabled and cannot be renamed; the Guest account is enabled and can be renamed.

Question #05-02

Everyone should be able to read the files in a certain directory. However, the user who created the file should be able to modify it. What do you need to do?

A. Do nothing. By default, only the creator of a file has access to it. Windows NT restricts resource access by default.

B. Give the group Everyone read access and the Creator Owner group change access. By default, Windows NT allows everyone complete access to resources.

C. Give the group Everyone read access and the Creator Owner group change access. By default, Windows NT restricts resource access.

D. Give the group Everyone read access and the Users group change access. Windows NT will automatically determine who the owner of the file is and restrict the other users.

Question #05-03

On a Windows NT Server in DomainA, you have stored a sales database and a marketing database, and have also shared a color printer. Five of the users in the domain are salespersons, five are marketers, and the rest are programmers. The users should be able to access their respective databases, but only the team leaders for sales, marketing, and programmers should be able to access the color printer. Which group strategy is the best?

A. Create local groups for sales, marketing, and team leaders and assign the appropriate user accounts to the appropriate groups. Then, assign permissions for each resource to the appropriate group.

B. Create global groups for sales, marketing, and team leaders and assign the appropriate user accounts to the appropriate groups. Then, assign permissions for each resource to the appropriate global group.

C. Create global groups for sales, marketing, and team leaders and assign the appropriate user accounts to the appropriate groups. Then create local groups for each and assign the global group to the local group. Then assign permissions for each resource to the appropriate local group.

D. Simply assign the appropriate users access to the resources that they need access to.

Question #05-04

What are the differences between a local group and a global group? Choose all that apply.

A. Local groups can be created on workstations, servers, and domain controllers, while global groups can only be created and maintained on a domain controller.

B. Local groups can contain local users, domain users, and global groups, while global groups can contain only users from their domain.

C. Local groups can contain local users, domain users, global groups, and other local groups, while global groups can contain only users from their domain.

D. Local groups can be used for managing resources only on the local computer, while global groups can be used to manage resources on any computer that participates in the domain.

Question #05-05

Which of the following sets of usernames and passwords are acceptable for Windows NT?

Username—Password

A. First Ass't Comptroller—FirstComp

B. FirstAsstCompt—1stComp

C. FirstAss*tCompt—COMP1

D. AssComp1—123COMPTROLLER1

Question #05-06

Your workstations are members of a domain called Titan. You need to create user accounts so that two shifts of temporary employees can log on to the same computer, but only during their shift.

A. Use User Manager for domains on each local Windows NT Workstation to create the temporary accounts and assign each the appropriate logon hours.

B. Use User Manager on each local Windows NT Workstation to create the temporary accounts and assign each the appropriate logon hours.

C. Use User Manager for domains on the domain controller for Titan to create domain accounts for the temporary employees and assign each the appropriate logon hours.

D. Use User Manager on the domain controller for Titan to create local group accounts for the temporary employees and assign each the appropriate logon hours.

Question #05-07

Your boss has advised you that BrownC has left the company and asks that you delete his account. Later, your boss hires BrownC back as a consultant and tells you to put his account back on the network. BrownC calls you the next day and informs you gruffly that he can no longer access any of the network resources that he used to. How do you troubleshoot?

A. Use the Registry to set BrownC's SID back to what it was before you deleted his account. He will then be able to access all the old resources.

B. Deleting BrownC's account also deleted his SID. Because security in Windows NT is linked to the user's SID, you will need to reestablish all the network resource access that BrownC used to have.

C. Use the Emergency Repair Disk or your last network backup to copy BrownC's old account back to the Registry.

D. Install a backup copy of the account database that contains his old account.

Question #05-08

Under which of the following situations would you disable the user account rather than deleting it?

A. JaneD has left the company on maternity leave and plans to return in three months.

B. JohnB has taken an emergency medical leave of absence for possibly six or more months, but hopes to return full time.

C. JaniceD has left the company to take a job at Microsoft.

D. FrankP has taken a temporary team leader position in another department and will return when the project is completed.

Question #05-09

You are creating multiple user accounts for salespersons, marketers, and programmers. Each set of accounts belongs to the same relative groups (sales users in SALES, marketing users in MARKETING, and programmer users in PROGRAMMERS), uses the same logon scripts (SALES.BAT, MARKET.BAT, PROGRAM.BAT), and saves data in a home directory relative to each group (sales users under USERS\SALES, marketing users under USERS\MARKETERS, programmer users under USERS\PROGRAMMERS). What is the most efficient way to create these users?

A. Create a separate account for each user. As you create the user, use the %USERNAME% environment variable when specifying the home directory to let Windows NT create it for you.

B. Create a template for each type of user. Make the appropriate choices and entries for groups, logon script, and home directory. Use the %USERNAME% environment variable when specifying the home directory to let Windows NT create them for you. Then, create each user by copying the appropriate template.

C. Create all the users without specifying group membership. After they are all created, select each group of users by Ctrl+clicking them and create the appropriate group.

D. You must create each user individually.

Question #05-10

To provide a greater level of security, you have decided to create an account policy that requires a minimum password length of eight characters, requires that users change their passwords at least once a month, and does not allow users to use the same password twice in two months. Which Account Policy settings are appropriate?

A. Max Password Age: 60; Min Password Age: 30; Min Password Length: 8; Password Uniqueness: 2

B. Max Password Age: 30; Min Password Age: 30; Min Password Length: 8; Password Uniqueness: 6

C. Max Password Age: 30; Min Password Age: 10; Min Password Length: 8; Password Uniqueness: 6

D. Max Password Age: 60; Min Password Age: 30; Min Password Length: 8; Password Uniqueness: 1

Question #05-11

You suspect that someone is trying to log on to the network unauthorized. What is the best step you can take to increase security and determine who might be doing this?

A. Enable Account Lockout in the Account Policy requiring the Administrator to unlock the account.

B. Enable Account Lockout in the Account Policy requiring the Administrator to unlock the account. Enable auditing of unsuccessful logons and logoffs and monitor these events in the Event Viewer.

C. Advise users to change their passwords more frequently and not to use obvious passwords.

D. Increase the minimum password length in Account Policy.

Question #05-12

You want to give a particular domain user the ability to back up files on a server, but not be able to restore files. How can you accomplish this?

A. Make the domain user a member of the Backup Operators group on the server.

B. Make the domain user a member of the Server Operators group on the server.

C. Create a new local group called BACKUP ONLY on the server and make the domain user a member of it. Assign this new group to the Backup Files and Directories User Right.

D. Give the user read-only access to all the files.

Question #05-13

A user is having problems logging on to the network and is seeing a variety of messages. Which of the following things would you check to troubleshoot?

A. The user is entering the correct username and password.

B. The username is case-sensitive.

C. The domain controller is up and accessible.

D. The user's account requires a mandatory profile that is accessible.

Question #05-14

You need to be able to remotely manage the account database on two trusted domains. Which steps must take place for this to happen successfully?

A. Do nothing. You can remotely manage accounts through a trust by default.

B. Use User Manager for domains and choose User, Select Domain from the menu to choose the remote domain you want to administer.

C. Make your account a member of the Account Operators group in the trusted domains.

D. Give your user account Full Control access to the SAM hive file in WINNT\SYSTEM32\CONFIG.

Question #06-01

The manager of the Accounting department wants to make next year's budget templates available for the staff accountants to review beginning next month. Staff accountants are all members of the Accountants global group in CORPDOMAIN. The templates will be stored on the department resource server called ACCT1 in a folder called BUDGET97. None of the partitions on ACCT1 are formatted with NTFS. How would you make the folder available only to the Accounting department staff?

A. Use User Manager for Domains to create a local group on the resource server called Accountants. Make the global Accountants group a member of the local Accountants group. Assign permission to use the folder to the Accountants group through User Manager for Domains.

B. Use User Manager for Domains to create a local group on the resource server called Accountants. Make the global Accountants group a member of the local Accountants group. Assign the appropriate User Rights to the Accountants group to access the BUDGET97 share.

C. Use User Manager for Domains to create a local group on the resource server called Accountants. Make the global Accountants group a member of the local Accountants group. Use the Security tab on the properties sheet for the folder to assign permissions to the Accountants group.

D. Use User Manager for Domains to create a local group on the resource server called Accountants. Make the global Accountants group a member of the local Accountants group. Use the Sharing tab on the properties sheet for the folder to assign permissions to the Accountants group.

Question #06-02

The manager of the Accounting department wants to make next year's budget templates available for the staff accountants to review beginning next month. Staff accountants are all members of the global group Accountants in the domain CORPDOMAIN. The templates will be stored on the department resource server called ACCT1 in a folder called BUDGET97. A local group called Budget has been created to manage access to the budget templates. None of the partitions on ACCT1 are formatted with NTFS. How would you make the folder available only to the Accounting department staff? Choose all that apply.

A. Share the BUDGET97 directory.

B. Add the Accountants group to the ACL for the share.

C. Remove the Everyone group from the ACL for the share.

D. Give the Accountants group read and write permissions at the folder level.

Question #06-03

A user's effective access to a resource is determined by:

A. Comparing the rights of the user with the permissions assigned through the ACL of the resource.

B. Comparing the permissions in the access token of the user with the permissions assigned through the ACL of the resource.

C. Comparing the user and group SID entries in the user's access token with the permissions assigned through the ACL of the resource.

D. Comparing the user and group SID entries in the user's access token with the user rights listed in the ACL of the resource.

Question #06-04

The Sales department recently acquired a laser quality printer with an envelope feed that has been installed on their print server called SalesPrint. The sales staff is already a member of the local group SALES on SalesPrint. The print operator shared the printer with the default permission. The sales staff can access the printer, but so can everyone else in the domain. What else must you do to ensure that only sales staff can access the printer?

A. Assign the Sales group print access to the printer.

B. Assign the Sales group print access to the printer, and remove the Everyone group.

C. Do nothing else.

D. Assign the Sales group print access to the printer, and give the Everyone group Read access.

Question #06-05

The permission list defining access to a resource resides:

A. With the resource and is called the Access Control List.

B. With the user and is called the User Rights Policy.

C. With the user and is called the Access Control List.

D. With the resource and is called the User Rights Policy.

Question #06-06

Arlo, a member of the Developers group, is currently editing the file DOOM.DOC in the share TOOLS. The administrator of the share changes permission to the Developers group from Change to Read. Arlo continues to make changes to the document. What else must the administrator do to restrict Arlo's access?

A. Take Arlo out of the Developers group.
B. Give Arlo No Access explicitly.
C. Send Arlo a message to get his authorization.
D. Nothing. Arlo must disconnect from the share and then reconnect before the new permission will take effect.

Question #06-07

The administrator of the TOOLS shared folder wants to limit access to the folder only to the Developers group. To accomplish this, she gives the Everyone group NO ACCESS, and the Developers group Change access. The Developers complain that they cannot access any file in TOOLS. What else must the administrator do?

A. Share the files in the TOOLS folder.
B. Remove the Everyone group.
C. Give the Developers group Full Control.
D. Format the partition as NTFS and assign NTFS permissions in addition to the share permissions.

Question #06-08

Ned is a member of the Developers group at Springfield Technologies. He has been promoted to team leader for his group. He needs to edit the DOOM.DOC file in the Tools folder, but does not have Write access. What must you do to give Ned access to DOOM.DOC?

A. Do nothing. The next time Ned logs on, his permissions will change.
B. Change the Developers group permission to Change.
C. Add Ned to the Team Leaders group and have him log in again.
D. Change the Team Leaders group permission to Full Control.

Question #06-09

The TOOLS folder has been shared to the Developers group with Change permission. DOOM is a subdirectory under TOOLS. Team Leaders should have access only to DOOM with Read permissions. What can you do to accomplish this?

A. Add Team Leaders to the TOOLS share with Read permission.

B. Create a new share called DOOM and give Team Leaders Read permission to it.

C. Add Team Leaders to the TOOLS share with Change permission.

D. Add Team Leaders to the TOOLS share with No Access and to the DOOM subdirectory with Read.

Question #06-10

The manager of the Accounting department wants to make next year's budget templates available for the staff accountants to review beginning next month. Staff accountants are already members of a global group called Accountants in CORPDOMAIN. The templates will be stored on the department resource server called ACCT1 in a folder called BUDGET97 on an NTFS partition. The folder has been shared with the default permission, which you do not want to change. How would you further secure the folder's contents so that it is available only to the Accounting department staff?

A. Use User Manager for Domains to create a local group on the resource server called Accountants. Make the global accountants group a member of the local accountants group. Assign the Accountants group permission to use the folder through User Manager for Domains.

B. Use User Manager for Domains to create a local group on the resource server called Accountants. Make the global accountants group a member of the local accountants group. Assign the appropriate User Rights to the Accountants group to access the BUDGET97 share.

C. Use User Manager for Domains to create a local group on the resource server called Accountants. Make the global accountants group a member of the local accountants group. Use the Security tab on the properties sheet for the folder to assign permissions to the Accountants group.

D. Use User Manager for Domains to create a local group on the resource server called Accountants. Make the global accountants group a member of the local accountants group. Use the Sharing tab on the properties sheet for the folder to assign permissions to the Accountants group.

Question #06-11

The manager of the Accounting department wants to make next year's budget templates available for the staff accountants to review beginning next month. Staff accountants are already members of a global group called Accountants in CORPDOMAIN. The templates will be stored on the department resource server called ACCT1 in a folder called BUDGET97 on an NTFS partition. The folder has been shared with the default permission. The global accountants group has been added to a local group called Accountants on ACCT1. You would like everyone to be able to see the files, but only the accounting staff should be able to make changes. What do you need to do?

A. Change the share permission to only Accountants with Change permission.

B. Assign the Accountants group the NTFS permission Change to the BUDGET97 folder.

C. Change the share permission to Everyone with No Access and assign the Accountants group the NTFS permission Change for the BUDGET97 folder.

D. Change the share permission to Everyone with Read and assign the Accountants group the NTFS permission Change for the BUDGET97 folder.

Question #06-12

Team Leaders need to be able to modify files contained in the share TOOLS. While you were on vacation, your trusted sidekick modified the permissions for the share and the folder. The two exhibits show what the permissions look like now. Team Leaders complain that they are unable to modify their files. What should you do?

A. Fire your trusted sidekick.

B. Change the TOOLS NTFS permission for Team Leaders to Change, and the share permission to Read.

C. Change the TOOLS NTFS permission for the Team Leaders to Change.

D. Remove Team Leaders from the ACL for the TOOLS share.

Question #06-13

The person that created DOOM.DOC on server ACCT1 is no longer with the company. Cathy, a member of Team Leaders, will be assuming responsibility for the DOOM project, and needs to become the owner of DOOM.DOC. How can this be accomplished? Choose all that apply.

A. Give Cathy the Take Ownership of Files and Folders User Right on the server ACCT1.

B. Give Cathy the Take Ownership permission on the file DOOM.DOC.

C. Tell Cathy to just take ownership of the file.

D. Give the Team Leaders group the Take Ownership permission for DOOM.DOC.

Question #06-14

Fred is a member of the Developers group. The Developers group has been given the NTFS permission Full Control to the TOOLS folder. Fred is changing jobs and has been given NO ACCESS to the file DOOM.DOC, which is contained in the TOOLS folder. Later, Fred logs on and deletes the file DOOM.DOC. Luckily, you can restore the file from your tape backup. How can you prevent Fred from deleting the file again, but still maintain the original level of access for him and the Developers group?

A. Fire Fred.

B. Give the Developers group Special Access with all options selected for the TOOLS folder. Then give Fred NO ACCESS to the file.

C. Give the Developers group Change access at the folder level.

D. Give Fred NO ACCESS at the folder level.

Question #06-15

Which tool(s) can you use to remotely manage shares across the domain?

A. User Manager for Domains

B. Server Manager

C. Windows Explorer

D. Network Neighborhood

Question #06-16

Which tool(s) can you use to remotely manage file and folder permissions across the domain?

A. User Manager for Domains
B. Server Manager
C. Windows Explorer
D. Network Neighborhood

Question #07-01

You are creating multiple user accounts for salespersons, marketers, and programmers. Each set of accounts belongs to the same relative groups (sales users in SALES, marketing users in MARKETING, and programmer users in PROGRAMMERS), uses the same logon scripts (SALES.BAT, MARKET.BAT, PROGRAM.BAT), and saves data in a home directory relative to each group (sales users under USERS\SALES, marketing users under USERS\MARKETERS, programmer users under USERS\PROGRAMMERS). What is the most efficient way to create these users?

A. Create a separate account for each user. As you create the user, use the %USERNAME% environment variable when specifying the home directory to let Windows NT create it for you.
B. Create a template for each type of user. Make the appropriate choices and entries for groups, logon script, and home directory. Use the %USERNAME% environment variable when specifying the home directory to let Windows NT create them for you. Then create each user by copying the appropriate template.
C. Create all the users without specifying group membership. After they are all created, select each group of users by Ctrl+clicking them and create the appropriate group.
D. You must create each user individually.

Question #07-02

To provide a greater level of security, you have decided to create an account policy that requires a minimum password length of eight characters, that users change their passwords at least once a month, and does not allow users to use the same password twice in two months. Which Account Policy settings are appropriate?

A. Max Password Age: 60; Min Password Age: 30; Min Password Length: 8; Password Uniqueness: 2

B. Max Password Age: 30; Min Password Age: 30; Min Password Length: 8; Password Uniqueness: 6

C. Max Password Age: 30; Min Password Age: 10; Min Password Length: 8; Password Uniqueness: 6

D. Max Password Age: 60; Min Password Age: 30; Min Password Length: 8; Password Uniqueness: 1

Question #07-03

You suspect that someone is trying to log in to various workstations unauthorized. What is the best step you can take to increase security and determine who might be doing this?

A. Enable Account Lockout in the Account Policy requiring the Administrator to unlock the account.

B. Enable Account Lockout in the Account Policy requiring the Administrator to unlock the account. Enable auditing of unsuccessful logons and logoffs and monitor these events in the Event Viewer.

C. Advise users to change their passwords more frequently and not to use obvious passwords.

D. Increase the minimum password length in Account Policy.

Question #07-04

You want to give a particular user the ability to back up files on a workstation, but not be able to restore files. How can you accomplish this?

A. Make the user a member of the Backup Operators group on the workstation.

B. Make the user a member of the Server Operators group on the workstation.

C. Create a new local group called BACKUP ONLY on the local workstation and make the user a member of it. Assign this new group to the Backup Files and Directories User Right.

D. Give the user Read Only access to all the files.

Question #07-05

There are five summer interns joining the company this year for a three-month period. You want to give them access to the network, but you want to restrict their environment settings to specific programs, colors, and so on. They should not be able to change the settings. What steps are involved?

A. Change the NTUSER.DAT file in the shared directory to NTUSER.MAN.

B. Copy the account through the User Profiles tab in the System applet to a shared directory on a central server.

C. Create a user account and make the appropriate changes to that account's environment settings.

D. Specify the location and file name of the profile in each summer intern's account properties.

Question #07-06

As you create new users, you would like them to assume the same default environment settings, such as common application groups, startup programs, and company logo, as wallpaper. Which steps will achieve this end?

A. Modify the appropriate changes in the Default User and All Users profile folders in WINNT40\Profiles. When a new user is created, that user's profile will begin with the settings from these two.

B. Create a System Policy file that contains the appropriate settings for the Default user and save it in the WINNT40\SYSTEM32\REPL\IMPORT\SCRIPTS subdirectory on the validating computer.

C. Create a template user account and modify the settings for that account. Create new accounts by copying the template.

D. Create a system policy file for each set of users modifying the settings as appropriate for each user.

Question #07-07

Profiles can be stored

A. in the registry

B. in boot.ini

C. on the server

D. on disks

Question #07-08

Mandatory profiles may cause problems with remote users because (check all that apply)

A. The logon process can take a long time.

B. Users may be prevented from logging on if the connection goes down.

C. A user's changes are stored on the local workstation.

D. Remote users need more freedom.

Question #08-01

Server tools are designed to be installed on which of the following clients?

A. Windows 95

B. Windows for Workgroups 3.11

C. Windows NT 4.0 and 3.5/3.51 Workstations

D. Windows NT 4.0 Server

Question #08-02

The reason that server tools are not installed by default on Windows NT Server installations is:

A. The server tools applications and utilities are already installed but must be run from a domain controller.

B. The server tools applications and utilities are not available for member servers.

C. The server tools applications and utilities cannot be run from the server platform.

D. The server tools applications and utilities are already installed and available for use.

Question #08-03

To install server tools on a Windows 95 client computer, the following resources and services are required.

A. Client for Novell Networks installed

B. 3M of free disk space

C. 8M of memory

D. Client for Microsoft Networks installed

Question #08-04

To install server tools on a Windows NT Workstation, Intel platform:

A. Run Setup.bat from the server CD-ROM, Clients folder.

B. Run Setup.bat from the server CD-ROM, Clients\Srvtools folder.

C. Run Setup.bat from the server CD-ROM, Clients\Srvtools\Winnt folder.

D. Run Setup.bat from the server CD-ROM, Clients\Srvtools\Winnt\I386 folder.

Question #08-05

Once server tools are installed on a Windows NT Workstation, they can be run from:

A. The <winntroot>\System32 folder.

B. The Start Menu, Programs, Server Tools group.

C. The Start Menu, Programs, Administrative Tools group.

D. Any manually made program group provided the executables are placed in that group.

Question #08-06

What server administrative tool is used to copy the server tools from the CD-ROM and automatically create a shared folder?

A. Network Server Tools Administrator

B. Network Client Administrator

C. Network Server Tools Manager

D. Network Server Manager

Question #08-07

The default share name for the server tools share is:

A. SrvTools

B. ClientTools

C. SetupAdm

D. ServerTools

Question #08-08

To install server tools on a Windows 95 platform:

A. Run Setup.bat from the CD-ROM, Clients\Srvtools\Win95 folder.

B. Run Setup.bat from the CD-ROM, Clients\Srvtools\Windows folder.

C. Run Setup.exe from the CD-ROM, Clients\Srvtools\Windows folder.

D. Access Control Panel on the Windows 95 client computer and select the Add/Remove Programs ICON.

Question #08-09

What server tool is NOT installed on a Windows NT 3.5/3.51 Workstation platform?

A. Services for Macintosh

B. System Policy Editor

C. Remote Access Administrator

D. User Profile Editor

Question #09-02

You need to extend a FAT partition to allow more space for a growing database. Which option best explains your strategy?

A. Use Disk Administrator to select the FAT partition and an area of free space and choose Partition, Create Volume Set.

B. Use Disk Administrator to select the FAT partition and an area of free space and choose Partition, Extend Volume Set.

C. Use Disk Administrator to select the FAT partition and an area of formatted space and choose Tools, Combine Volume Sets.

D. Convert the drive to NTFS and create a volume set

Question #09-04

You need to convert a partition from FAT to NTFS with no loss of data. How can you best accomplish this task?

A. Use Disk Administrator to select the partition and choose Tools, Format. Then select NTFS.

B. Use the command-line utility CONVERT.EXE to convert the partition.

C. Use the Windows NT Backup utility to back up the partition data to disk. Then format the partition for NTFS and restore the data.

D. You cannot convert a FAT partition to NTFS without loss of data.

Question #09-05

Which of the following statements are true regarding Volume Sets and Stripe Sets? Choose all that apply.

A. Stripe sets can contain the system partition and volume sets cannot.

B. Stripe sets must combine areas of equal size while volume sets can combine areas of any size.

C. Stripe sets cannot contain the system partition and volume sets can.

D. Stripe sets write to all members of the set concurrently while volume sets fill each member of the set in turn.

Question #09-06

Windows NT calls the active primary partition its:

A. Boot partition

B. System partition

C. Startup partition

D. Extended partition

Question #09-08

Which of the following statements is true regarding FAT and NTFS? Choose all that apply.

A. FAT supports long file names and so does NTFS.

B. NTFS supports long file names but FAT does not.

C. FAT supports a maximum partition size of 4G and NTFS supports a maximum partition size of 16E.

D. Formatting a partition as FAT requires less than 1M of overhead, while NTFS formatting requires at least 4M.

Question #09-09

Which of the following statements accurately describes NTFS? Choose all that apply.

A. NTFS provides built-in transaction tracking.

B. NTFS supports file compression as a file property.

C. NTFS requires less than 4M of overhead for formatting.

D. NTFS offers file and folder level security.

Question #09-10

You are deciding whether to support long file names on FAT partitions for your server. You have a variety of client platforms that connect to the server, including MS-DOS and Windows 95. Some of the platforms support older 16-bit applications. Which of the following considerations would you make?

A. There are no significant concerns. All applications support long file names on all platforms in a Microsoft network.

B. Most Microsoft applications will support the long file names, but some older applications save changes by deleting the old file and renaming a temporary file to the original file name. This could eliminate the long file name.

C. Long file names saved in the root of the drive require one directory entry for the alias, and one for up to every 13 characters of the name. Because the root is hard-coded for 512 directory entries for FAT partitions, you could run out of entries.

D. If long file name support is disabled for the FAT partition, it is disabled for all partitions on that computer, including NTFS.

Question #09-11

Lucy has been appointed the backup coordinator for the network. What must you do to enable her to accomplish this task and still maintain security on the data? Choose all that apply.

A. Make Lucy a member of the local Backup Operators group on each computer that needs to be backed up.

B. Make Lucy a member of the Server Operators group on each server computer that needs to be backed up.

C. Assign Lucy the Backup Files and Directories user right.

D. Give Lucy Full Control over all files and folders.

Question #09-12

You have been asked to implement a backup strategy that backs up all files each Monday to a tape, and then only files that are new or have changed each day since the Monday backup to subsequent tapes on Tuesday through Friday. In addition, on Friday, you must create an archive tape for off-site storage. Which solution will meet this requirement?

A. Perform a normal backup on Monday, then a differential backup Tuesday through Friday. On Friday, perform an additional Copy backup for archival off-site.

B. Perform a normal backup on Monday, then an incremental backup Tuesday through Friday. On Friday, perform an additional Copy backup for archival off-site.

C. Perform a normal backup on Monday and Friday and an incremental backup each day.

D. Perform a normal backup on Monday and Friday and a differential backup each day.

Question #09-13

You are ready to implement your backup strategy and want to back up files from all Windows NT computers remotely to an archive directory on your local computer. All remote shares have been implemented. What is the best solution?

A. Connect to the shares, start Backup, and select the files and folders to be backed up. Choose Backup and enter the UNC path to the target archive directory in the Backup Path text box.

B. Connect to the shares, start Backup, and choose Operations, Select Target from the menu. Enter the path to the archive directory in the Backup Path text box.

C. Connect to the shares, start Backup and redirect the backup path using the Tools, Options menu.

D. You cannot back up to disk.

Question #09-14

You need to recover a lost folder for a user. Before you do so, what can you do to minimize errors?

A. Review the backup set catalog for any corrupted files before proceeding with the backup.

B. Review the backup log file to see if any files were missed during the backup process.

C. Select the verify files restore option.

D. Do nothing. Windows NT automatically verifies files while restoring to disk.

Question #10-01

Frederick has recently loaded two more C++ applications to modify on his Windows NT 4.0 Workstation. He has noticed that when he boots and loads all his applications, Windows NT takes longer to respond to application requests. You use Performance Monitor and notice that pagefile usage has increased and that the Commit Limit for the pagefile increases rapidly when the applications are loaded. What is the best solution you can offer Frederick based on this data?

A. Purchase more RAM for Frederick's computer.

B. Move the pagefile to another disk partition.

C. Increase the initial size of the pagefile so that it doesn't have to grow right away as the applications load.

D. Move the C++ applications to another disk partition.

Question #10-02

Desiree, a Visual Basic developer, has noticed that her system's performance has decreased since she began work on a large VB application. You have used Performance Monitor to determine that the pagefile usage has increased. You also notice that the pagefile, Windows NT system files and the VB application are all stored on the same partition. In addition, the working set for the VB application shows that it consistently requires 16M for itself. What solutions can you recommend? Name all that apply.

A. Add more RAM in the computer.
B. Move the pagefile to a disk partition other than the system or application partition.
C. Increase the maximum size for the pagefile.
D. Create multiple pagefiles.

Question #10-03

Which Processor object counter would be useful to determine how much processor time is being utilized by application requests?

A. %Processor Time
B. %User Time
C. %Application Time
D. %Privileged Time

Question #10-04

Which Process object counter would be useful in determining the amount of memory required by an application?

A. %Application Memory
B. Commit Limit
C. Working Set
D. Avg. Disk sec\Transfer

Question #10-05

Which Memory object counter would help to identify when to right-size the pagefile?

A. %Pagefile
B. Commit Limit
C. Working Set
D. %Disk Time

Question #10-06

On your Windows NT 4.0 development workstation, you have concluded that performance as a whole has decreased. You are not sure which process is driving this, but you have noticed that your disk drive has had a lot more activity lately. What objects should you monitor through Performance Monitor to help you troubleshoot this situation?

A. Check the Processor>%Processor Time counter, determine the percent of disk I/O used for paging through the Memory>Pages/Sec counter and the Logical Disk>Avg. Disk sec/Transfer counter, and the Process>Working Set for every process running.

B. Check the Processor>%Processor Time counter, determine the percent of disk I/O used for paging through the Memory>Pages/Sec counter and the Logical Disk>Avg. Disk sec/Transfer counter. Track the Process>%Processor Time counter for every process running to determine which processes are pushing the processor excessively. Monitor the Process>Working Set counter for these processes in particular.

C. Check the Processor>%Processor Time counter, determine the percent of disk I/O used for paging through the Logical Disk>Disk Queue Length counter, and the Process>Working Set for every process running.

D. Check the Processor>%User Time counter, determine the percent of disk I/O used for paging through the Logical Disk>%Disk Time counter, and the Memory>Commit Limit counter for the pagefile.

Question #10-07

Which counter will provide you with the total percent of time spent servicing disk requests for a given partition on a disk?

A. Logical Disk>%Disk Time

B. Logical Disk>Disk Queue Length

C. Physical Disk>%Disk Time

D. Physical Disk>Disk Queue Length

Question #10-08

Which of the following counters will provide you with the total number of bytes transferred during disk I/O for all the disks in your computer?

A. Logical Disk>Disk Bytes/sec, Total instance
B. Logical Disk>Disk Bytes/sec, for each partition instance
C. Physical Disk>Disk Bytes/sec, Total instance
D. Physical Disk>Disk Bytes/sec, for each disk instance

Question #10-09

Which objects would be most beneficial to include in a log file when creating a baseline measurement of your system's performance? Choose the best three.

A. Memory
B. TCP/IP
C. Processor
D. Physical and Logical Disk

Question #10-10

You plan to use Performance Monitor to help predict and troubleshoot server activity under various conditions. Which of the following would be the best way to begin?

A. Create and monitor a real-time chart during peak activity and note the percent of processor usage during these periods.
B. Create a series of baseline logs of specific objects (processor, memory, disk and network), each representing a different condition. Use these to predict activity under those conditions and to troubleshoot abnormal system activity.
C. Create a baseline log measuring system activity during periods of average activity. Compare this against real-time charts created during peak activity on the system.
D. Network Monitor would be a better tool to predict system activity.

Question #10-11

While tracking the performance of disk activity on a system, you notice that the measured value is always 0 although the disk appears to be heavily used. What is your evaluation of this situation?

A. The disk is a high performance unit and can handle the heavy disk I/O.

B. The wrong disk objects and counters have been selected for Performance Monitor.

C. The disk counters had not been enabled by typing DISKPERF -Y at a command prompt.

D. The disk has crashed.

Question #10-12

You are analyzing network activity between your network clients and a server. You plan to use Network Monitor to monitor network traffic generated by and received by the server, and Performance Monitor to track system performance relating to network traffic. What types of objects would facilitate your analysis? Choose all that apply.

A. Redirector

B. Server

C. Protocol

D. Frame

Question #10-13

After monitoring your heavily accessed file and print server, you determine that both the Server>Pool Paged Failures and Server>Pool Nonpaged Failures counters are unusually and consistently higher than normal. The Server service memory property is configured for Balanced memory usage. What should you do to reduce the number of Pool Paged and Pool Nonpaged failures?

A. Add more memory. Balanced is an appropriate setting for a file and print server.

B. Change the Server service memory configuration to Minimize Memory Used.

C. Change the Server service memory configuration to Maximize Throughput for File Sharing.

D. Change the Server service memory configuration to Load Balance Throughput for Virtual Memory.

Question #11-01

Which of the following sets of Windows NT network clients do not require print drivers to be installed on the local computer?

A. All Microsoft Network clients

B. Windows NT and Windows 95

C. Windows NT, Windows 95, and Windows for Workgroups 3.11

D. Windows NT, Windows 95, and LAN Manager v2.x for DOS

Question #11-02

Which of the following steps applies to the Windows NT 4.0 print process on Windows NT computers? Choose all that apply.

A. The GDI component of the client computer generates an enhanced metafile print job.

B. The bulk of the print process completes in the spooler on the client before forwarding the print job to the print server.

C. The print monitor controls access to the print devices and device ports, and monitors status of the print job.

D. The local printer spooler makes a remote connection to the print server spooler and copies the print job there.

Question #11-03

Jeanette calls to say that her print jobs seem to have stopped running. You check the printer that she sent the jobs to and see that the jobs are stuck in queue. What steps should you take to clear the stuck jobs? Choose all that apply.

A. Select the stuck jobs and choose Document, Cancel.

B. Select Printer, Purge Print Documents.

C. Use the Control Panel applet Service to stop and restart the Spooler service.

D. Select each stuck job and change its priority.

Question #11-04

Several users have called you within the past half-hour to complain that their print jobs are not printing. In fact, they get system messages that tell them that the spooler is not responding. You have verified that the spooler directory partition does not have adequate free space to hold all the print jobs sent to it. What steps should you take to resolve this situation? Choose two.

A. Use the Control Panel applet Services to more frequently stop and restart the Spooler service to keep the print jobs from becoming fragmented.

B. Change the location of the spool directory to a partition with enough disk space by modifying the HKEY_LOCAL_MACHINE\System\CurrentControlSet\Control\Print\Printers DefaultSpoolDirectory parameter.

C. Change the location of the spool directory to a partition with enough disk space by modifying the HKEY_Current_User\Control\Print\Printers\Spool SpoolDirectory parameter.

D. If the partition is formatted with NTFS, compress the spool directory.

Question #11-05

If the final print output is corrupted, what print process component should you check?

A. Spooler service on the client computer

B. Spooler service on the print server

C. Print processor on the print server

D. Print monitor on the client computer

Question #11-06

Which print monitor is loaded with TCP/IP and tracks print jobs targeted for TCP/IP print hosts?

A. IPMON.DLL

B. LPDMON.DLL

C. LPRMON.DLL

D. LOCALMON.DLL

Question #11-07

What is the purpose of the print monitor SFMMON.DLL?

A. SFMMON.DLL monitors Macintosh print jobs routed using AppleTalk protocol to network print devices.

B. SFMMON.DLL is the System File Manager print monitor that tracks print jobs sent directly to or printed directly from a file.

C. SFMMON.DLL is the software print job compression DLL that compresses the print job before it is routed from the local print spooler to the print server.

D. SFMMON.DLL is not a valid print monitor.

Question #11-08

A print job can be routed directly to a UNIX host print device and its status checked using which two command-line utilities?

A. LPD and LPR

B. LPD and LPQ

C. LPR and IPCONFIG

D. LPR and LPQ

Question #11-09

Nelson has been selected to assist you as a printing administrator in the Dry Gulch office, because you are unable to travel there frequently, though you'd really like to. What is the minimum level of access you need to give Nelson so that he can perform basic print management tasks such as creating and sharing printers and managing print jobs?

A. Make Nelson a member of the Print Operators local group on his print server.
B. Make Nelson a member of the Server Operator local group on his print server.
C. Make Nelson a member of the Administrators local group on his print server.
D. Give Nelson Full Control permission for each printer on his print server.

Question #11-10

You have created four printers. Each of them will be used by a specific group of users. Name all the steps that are required to successfully make the printer available to the appropriate users.

A. Share each printer.
B. Set the share permissions for each printer so that only the appropriate group has access.
C. Set the printer permissions for each printer so that only the appropriate group has access.
D. Create a printer pool so that each group can access all the print devices.

Question #11-11

Rosemarie was the print administrator in Ulan Bator, but has left the country to pursue a career as an opera singer. You need to assign a new print administrator. What will you need to do concerning ownership of the Ulan Bator printers that Rosemarie created and managed?

A. Do nothing. Printers are not owned by a user; they are owned by the system.
B. Make the new print administrator a Print Operator. The new print administrator can then take ownership of the printers in Ulan Bator.
C. Give ownership of the printers to the new print administrator.
D. Give the new administrator Full Control permission over the printers. Full Control automatically assigns ownership to that user.

Question #11-12

The print device associated with a particular printer has failed. Several print jobs are waiting in queue in that printer. How can you service these print jobs?

A. Connect to another remote printer. Open the printer manager window for the printer and drag the waiting print jobs to the remote printer manager window.

B. Use the Ports tab properties for the printer to add a port for another remote printer. Deselect the current print port associated with the printer and select the remote port. Resume printing.

C. Do nothing. You must replace the failed print device before printing can resume.

D. Use the Control Panel applet Services to stop the spooler service, configure it to connect to another remote printer, and restart it.

Question #11-13

There are three downward-compatible print devices connected to the print server in MIS. MIS Managers and Project Leaders should always be able to print to the first available printer. Help Desk staff and Developers should be able to print only to their specified print device. What will best accomplish this task?

A. Create a printer for each device and assign the appropriate groups access only to their printer. Give the Managers' printer a priority of 1, Help Desk's printer a priority of 50, and Developers a priority of 99.

B. Create a printer for each device and assign the appropriate groups access only to their printer. Give the Managers' printer a priority of 99, Help Desk's printer a priority of 50, and Developers a priority of 1.

C. Create a printer for each device and assign the appropriate groups access only to their printer. Make the Managers' printer a printer pool by associating it with each print device and give managers priority over other jobs.

D. Create a printer for each device and assign the appropriate groups access only to their printer. Make each printer a printer pool by associating it with each print device.

Question #11-14

There is one high-speed network print device connected to the print server in MIS. MIS Managers and Project Leaders should always be able to print to this printer regardless of who else has submitted print jobs. Help Desk staff should be able to print ahead of Developers. What will best accomplish this task?

A. Create three printers, each associated with the device, and assign the appropriate groups access only to their printer. Give the Managers' printer a priority of 1, Help Desk's printer a priority of 50, and Developers a priority of 99.

B. Create three printers, each associated with the device, and assign the appropriate groups access only to their printer. Give the Managers' printer a priority of 99, Help Desk's printer a priority of 50, and Developers a priority of 1.

C. Create three printers, each associated with the device, and assign the appropriate groups access only to their printer. Make the Managers' printer a printer pool by associating it with each print device.

D. Create three printers associated with the device and assign the appropriate groups access only to their printer. Make each printer a printer pool by associating it with each print device.

Question #11-15

The printer for a network print device has been configured to print documents at all times. Farley plans to print a large, complex graphics document that he would like completed tomorrow morning. This job will take at least one hour to complete. What can you do to minimize the effect that printing this document will have on other documents in the queue?

A. Select Farley's document and pause it. Resume printing after hours when print jobs are at a minimum.

B. Modify the printer schedule so that it only prints documents after hours.

C. Modify the document schedule for Farley's document so that it only prints between 1:00 A.M. and 3:00 A.M.

D. Do nothing. The printer automatically holds long jobs until short jobs finish spooling and printing.

Question #11-16

Which of the following steps are appropriate to take when troubleshooting a failed print job?

A. Verify that the appropriate print port has been defined and configured by printing a test page.

B. Delete and re-create the printer.

C. Determine whether the print device is online and connected.

D. Resubmit the print job to a file and then copy the file to a printer port to see if it is successful.

Question #11-17

You are using a RISC-based computer as your print server. All your clients are either MS-DOS, Windows for Workgroups, Windows 95, or Windows NT running on Intel-based computers. What must you do to ensure that all your clients can print to the print devices managed by the RISC-based print server?

A. Install both RISC-based and Intel print drivers on the RISC-based print server. Install the appropriate print drivers only on the MS-DOS and Windows for Workgroups computers.

B. Install both RISC-based and Intel print drivers on the RISC-based print server. The client computers will receive the appropriate platform driver from the print server when they make a print request.

C. Install RISC-based print drivers on the RISC-based print server and Intel print drivers on the client computers. Windows NT will do the platform translation.

D. Install the Intel print drivers on the RISC-based print server and RISC-based print drivers on the client computers.

Question #11-18

There are 300 Windows NT client computers that print to five printers on a print server. You have received upgraded print drivers for two of the print devices connected to this print server. What must you do to ensure that all clients can continue to access all the print devices?

A. Install the upgraded print drivers on all the clients that need to use those print devices.
B. Install the upgraded print drivers on all the client computers.
C. Install the upgraded print drivers only on the Windows NT client computers.
D. Do nothing. The print server can download the new drivers to the clients the next time they make a print request.

Question #12-01

Of the following, which functions as part of the Kernel mode of Windows NT 4.0?

A. CSR Subsystem
B. HAL
C. GDI
D. Thread prioritization

Question #12-02

Of the following, which functions as part of the user mode of Windows NT 4.0?

A. CSR Subsystem
B. HAL
C. USER
D. WOW

Question #12-03

Which two subsystems are loaded when Windows NT boots?

A. CSR and Security Subsystems
B. CSR and OS/2 Subsystems
C. Environment and Security Subsystems
D. OS/2 and POSIX Subsystems

Question #12-04

Bernadette obtained a WIN32 application from a friend through e-mail but has not been able to successfully load and run it on her Power PC. You have checked for the usual things—memory, disk space, and so on—and all looks fine. What else can you do?

A. Run the WIN32 application in its own memory space.

B. Check the platform for which the application was compiled. Bernadette must use a version compiled for the PowerPC platform.

C. Shut down and restart Windows NT to free up application resources.

D. Tell her to read the manual.

Question #12-05

Mandy is running Pinball, the DOS Editor, Word 6, Excel 5, and Microstomp, a 16-bit, third-party Windows Web surfing program. Microstomp has hung up due to low resource memory. What other applications will be affected?

A. All other applications

B. All other applications except the DOS Editor

C. All other applications except Pinball

D. All other applications except Pinball and DOS Editor

Question #12-06

Mandy is running Pinball, the DOS Editor, Word 6, Excel 5, and Microstomp, a 16-bit, third-party Windows Web surfing program. Microstomp has been configured to run in its own memory space. Microstomp has hung up due to low resource memory. What other applications will be affected?

A. No other applications

B. No other applications except the DOS Editor

C. No other applications except Pinball

D. No other applications except the other Win 16 applications

Question #12-07

Which of the following statements is true about the NTVDM?

A. Each NTVDM has one thread of operation associated with it.

B. Each NTVDM is designed to emulate the Windows memory environment and provides a set of support files to do so.

C. Each NTVDM is configurable by modifying the properties of the MS-DOS application.

D. Each NTVDM is configurable through one AUTOEXEC.BAT and CONFIG.SYS file that is read when Windows NT boots.

Question #12-08

Angela has an older MS-DOS program that she needs to run on her Windows NT 4.0 workstation. The application requires a specific environmental variable set and device driver loaded. How can you help Angela configure her program to run successfully?

A. Configure the program to run in its own memory space.

B. Create an AUTOEXEC.BAT and CONFIG.SYS with the appropriate settings to load when Windows NT boots.

C. Create a specific AUTOEXEC and CONFIG for the application and reference it in the applications properties (PIF).

D. Install the application using the ADD Application applet in Control Panel and reference the environment variable and device driver during installation.

Question #12-09

Which of the following statements accurately describes a Win 16 application running under Windows NT 4.0?

A. All Win 16 applications run in the same NTVDM by default.

B. All Win 16 applications are non-preemptively multitasked within the NTVDM.

C. 16-bit calls are translated into 32-bit calls through a process called thunking.

D. WOW emulates the Windows 3.1 memory environment for Win 16 applications.

Question #12-10

Mandy is running Pinball, the DOS Editor, Word 6, Excel 5, and Microstomp, a 16-bit, third-party Windows Web surfing program. Microstomp occasionally hangs up due to low resource memory. This affects her other Windows applications. What can you suggest to alleviate this problem?

A. Configure Microstomp to run in its own memory space.

B. Configure each Win 16 application to run in its own memory space.

C. Modify the PIF for Microstomp to increase its resource memory allocation.

D. Modify the PIF for the WOW NTVDM to increase resource memory allocations for all the Windows applications.

Question #12-11

Bernadette is running Microstomp, which has been configured to run in its own memory space to prevent its affecting other applications when it hangs. When Microstomp ran in the same NTVDM, Bernadette could run her Word 6 scripts that used DDE to communicate with Microstomp. Now her scripts no longer work. What can she do?

A. Do nothing. Windows NT does not support OLE and DDE across multiple WOW NTVDMs.

B. Windows NT does not support OLE and DDE across multiple WOW NTVDMs. Bernadette must run Microstomp in the same WOW NTVDM as the other Windows applications.

C. Windows NT does not support OLE and DDE across multiple WOW NTVDMs for poorly behaved applications. Bernadette should run Microstomp and Word 6 in the same WOW NTVDM to preserve OLE and DDE for these two applications, and configure the other two Windows applications to each run in its own memory space.

D. Modify the PIF for Microstomp to support OLE and DDE.

Question #12-12

Len occasionally needs to run an OS/2 database program on his Windows NT 4.0 workstation. He configured a CONFIG.SYS prior to running the application for the first time, and the changes took. He now needs to modify the CONFIG.SYS file. He used WordPad to make the changes, but they do not seem to be read by the OS/2 application. What two options do you advise?

A. Use Notepad to modify the CONFIG.SYS file.

B. The OS/2 subsystem obtains information for its CONFIG.SYS file from the Windows NT Registry. Use an OS/2-based text editor to modify the OS/2 CONFIG.SYS after starting the OS/2 application.

C. Use the OSCONFIG command-line utility to update the Windows NT Registry information.

D. Modify the entries in the Windows NT Registry.

Question #12-13

Mandy has recently upgraded to Windows NT Workstation 4.0 from MS-DOS. When she tries to run his favorite disk optimization utility, the application fails. What do you advise?

A. Reinstall the application under Windows NT so that the Registry can be updated.

B. Modify the application's properties to allow hardware interaction (Advanced tab).

C. Remove the application or dual boot and run it only from DOS. Applications that directly access hardware devices will not run successfully under Windows NT 4.0.

D. Do nothing. You can never run this application.

Question #12-14

Bernadette has a math-intensive program that runs calculations while in the background. She wants to work with other program files while this application cranks away, but she does not want to sacrifice its CPU time. What do you advise?

A. Through the Systems applet in Control Panel, set the foreground response time to None. This will let foreground and background applications run at the same base priority level.

B. Through the Systems applet in Control Panel, set the background response time to Maximum. This will increase background base priority 2 levels.

C. From the Start, Run dialog box, start the math-intensive program with the /Realtime switch.

D. Do nothing. You cannot change application priorities.

Question #12-15

Len is running Pinball, the DOS Editor, Word 6, Excel 5, and Microstomp, a 16-bit, third-party Windows Web surfing program. He says that he has configured Microstomp to run in its own memory space. However, it has failed and the other Windows applications are also unresponsive. How can you unload Microstomp and try to return control to the other Windows applications?

A. Shut down and restart Windows NT Workstation 4.0.

B. Click the X button in the upper-right corner of the Microstomp window.

C. Start Task Manager, select Microstomp from the list of applications, and choose End Task.

D. Start Task Manager, select the WOW NTVDM entry on the Processes tab, and select End Process.

Question #12-16

Mandy is running Pinball, the DOS Editor, Word 6, Excel 5, and Microstomp, a 16-bit, third-party Windows Web surfing program. She says that she has configured Microstomp to run in its own memory space. However, it has failed and the other Windows applications are also unresponsive. How can you tell if Microstomp has been configured to run in its own memory space?

A. Start Task Manager and look for a second WOW NTVDM entry with a reference to the Microstomp application on the Processes tab.

B. Display the properties of the shortcut for Microstomp and see whether Run in Separate Memory Space has been selected on the Shortcut tab.

C. Start Task Manager and look for duplicate occurrences of WOWEXEC on the Applications tab.

D. You cannot tell without restarting the application.

Question #13-01

Which two subsystems are loaded when Windows NT boots?

A. CSR and Security Subsystems

B. CSR and OS/2 Subsystems

C. Environment and Security Subsystems

D. OS/2 and POSIX Subsystems

Question #13-02

Following the power-on self-test, NT loads

A. Environment settings

B. Master boot record

C. OS Kernel

D. OS system file

Question #13-03

The two primary phases of the NT boot sequence are

A. Boot and load

B. Boot and initialize

C. Load and initialize

D. Startup and shutdown

Question #13-04

The operating system choices displayed during bootup are stored in

A. the registry
B. the master boot record
C. boot.ini
D. config.sys

Question #13-05

Which files are read before NT displays the blue screen (check all that apply)?

A. boot.ini
B. config.sys
C. ntldr
D. command.com

Question #13-06

On a RISC computer, which of the following files are NOT needed during bootup (check all that apply)?

A. OSLOADER
B. BOOT.INI
C. NTLDR
D. NTOSKRNL

Question #13-07

Boot.ini contains switches to control which of these properties?

A. operating systems displayed
B. boot drive letter
C. amount of memory used by NT
D. modem settings

Question #14-01

The ISO OSI model contains

A. seven layers
B. six layers
C. eight layers
D. more layers every year

Question #14-02

All companies building network products are required to implement all layers of the OSI model.

A. TRUE
B. FALSE

Question #14-03

The lowest layer in the OSI model is

A. Applications
B. Transport
C. Error detection
D. Physical

Question #14-04

A frame is created/processed by which layer?

A. Physical
B. Data-link
C. Transport
D. Error detection

Question #14-05

Packet routing is managed by which layer?

A. Physical
B. Network
C. Transport
D. Applications

Question #14-06

Session multiplexing is handled by which layer?

A. Physical
B. Network
C. Transport
D. Session

Question #14-07

The presentation layer is primarily used to (check all that apply)

A. redirect file accesses over the network
B. translate data formats
C. control what appears on the computer monitor
D. create names for use by the application layer

Question #14-08

IEEE 802 standards are compatible with the OSI model.

A. TRUE
B. FALSE

Question #14-09

Media Access Control and Logical Link are layers of the OSI model.

A. TRUE

B. FALSE

Question #14-10

Token rings are more efficient than Ethernet on heavily loaded networks because

A. token ring network cards are faster

B. Ethernet was originally designed for the Internet

C. collisions are frequent on heavily loaded Ethernet networks

D. token rings cannot be wired in a star topology

Question #14-11

When an ethernet collision is detected,

A. a central server selects a winner

B. each workstation waits a random amount of time and tries again

C. all workstations switch to token ring mode

D. repeat the transmission immediately

Question #14-12

A protocol is considered routable if

A. it can be used over the Internet

B. it is approved by the IEEE

C. can be used to send information through a router

D. can pass through a LAN bridge

Question #15-01

Which of the following Directory Services goals are met by trust relationships? Select all that apply.

A. Provide users a single logon account that can be used anywhere within the enterprise to log on to the network.

B. Centralize management of accounts and resources.

C. Maintain separate user accounts for resource access on each resource server in the enterprise.

D. Facilitate access to network resources regardless of their domain location.

Question #15-02

The Finance domain users need to access a laser printer in the Marketing domain. The Marketing domain users need to access a scanner in the Finance domain. How many trust relationships need to be created to facilitate the sharing of these two network resources?

A. Create one two-way trust relationship between Finance and Marketing.

B. Create two one-way trust relationships, one from Finance to Marketing and the other from Marketing to Finance.

C. Create two one-way trust relationships from Finance to Marketing. One for the shared laser printer, and the other the scanner.

D. Create one trust relationship between Finance and Marketing. A trust relationship is always bidirectional.

Question #15-03

The Finance domain trusts the Marketing domain. What implication can you draw from this relationship?

A. The Finance domain is the trusted domain and the Marketing domain is the trusting domain. Users from the Marketing domain can access resources in the Finance domain, but only log on at their own domain computers.

B. The Finance domain is the trusting domain and the Marketing domain is the trusted domain. Users from the Marketing domain can access resources in the Finance domain, but only log on at their own domain computers.

C. The Finance domain is the trusted domain and the Marketing domain is the trusting domain. Users from the Finance domain can access resources in the Marketing domain, and log on at computers in the Marketing domain.

D. The Finance domain is the trusting domain and the Marketing domain is the trusted domain. Users from the Finance domain can only access their own resources and log on at computers in their domain. Users from the Marketing domain can access resources in the Finance domain, and log on at computers in either the Finance domain or their own domain.

Question #15-04

The Finance domain trusts the Marketing domain. The Marketing domain trusts the Accounting domain. Users in the Accounting domain need to access a database resource in the Finance domain. What needs to happen to facilitate the sharing of that resource?

A. Nothing. Because Finance already trusts Marketing and Marketing already trusts Accounting, Finance can share the database resource directly to Accounting users through the trusts.

B. Create a one-way trust from the Accounting domain to the Finance domain.

C. Create a one-way trust from the Finance domain to the Accounting domain.

D. Create a reverse trust from Accounting to Marketing, and from Marketing to Finance.

Question #15-05

Which of the following are requirements for setting up a successful trust relationship? Choose all that apply.

A. The primary domain controller in each domain must be up and accessible.

B. There can be no current sessions between the PDCs of each domain.

C. You must have an administrator-level account.

D. You must have access to a computer running User Manager for Domains.

Question #15-06

The Finance domain users need to access a printer resource in the Marketing domain. You are going to set up a trust relationship to facilitate the sharing of this resource. Which two steps need to take place?

A. The Finance domain must identify the Marketing domain as its trusted domain.

B. The Marketing domain must permit the Finance domain to trust it—the Marketing domain must make Finance its trusting domain.

C. The Finance domain must permit the Marketing domain to trust it—the Finance domain must make Marketing its trusting domain.

D. The Marketing domain must identify the Finance domain as its trusted domain.

Question #15-07

Which Windows NT Server service allows a user to log on at computers in domains in which they have no account through the trust relationship to a computer or domain in which they do have an account?

A. NetLogon Service

B. Directory Replication Service

C. Account Synchronization Service

D. Self Service

Question #15-08

The Finance domain trusts the Marketing domain. What NetLogon function allows a user from the Marketing domain to log on and validate from a computer that participates in the Finance domain?

A. Directory Replication

B. Pass-Through Authentication

C. Trust Validation

D. Access Control Lists

Question #15-09

The Finance domain trusts the Marketing domain. Sheila has just joined the Marketing group as a short-term contractor. Sheila needs access to a Finance database to complete her project. What type of account would you create for Sheila?

A. Create a global account for Sheila in the Marketing domain.

B. Create a local account for Sheila in the Marketing domain.

C. Create a global account for Sheila in the Marketing Domain and a global account for Sheila in the Finance domain.

D. Create a local account for Sheila in the Marketing domain and a global account for Sheila in the Finance domain.

Question #15-10

Which statement best represents Microsoft's recommended group strategy for managing resources effectively?

A. Create a local group in the domain database and add the users from the domain to that local group. Create a local group on the resource computer and make the domain local group a member of the resource local group.

B. Create a global group in the domain database and add the users from the domain to that global group. Create a global group on the resource computer and make the domain global group a member of the resource global group.

C. Create a global group in the domain database and add the users from the domain to that global group. Create a local group on the resource computer and make the domain global group a member of the resource local group.

D. Create a local group on the resource computer and add the domain users directly to the local group.

Question #15-11

The Finance domain trusts the Marketing domain. You would like the administrators of the Marketing domain to be able to administer the servers in the Finance domain. What should you do to facilitate this?

A. Make the Domain Admins group from the Marketing domain a member of the local Administrators group on each server on the Finance domain.

B. Make the Administrators group from the Marketing domain a member of the local Administrators group on each server in the Finance domain.

C. Make the Domain Admins group from each server in the Finance domain a member of the local Administrators group in the Marketing domain.

D. Do nothing. When a trust is established, the Administrators group from the trusted domain is automatically added to the local administrator groups on the servers in the trusting domain.

Question #15-12

The Finance domain trusts the Marketing domain. You would like to give Sheila, Frank, and Pat the responsibility of backing up all the domain controllers and servers in the Finance Domain. Which is the best course of action?

A. Add Sheila, Frank, and Pat to the Backup Operators group in the Marketing domain, and then add that Backup Operators group to the local Backup Operators groups on each domain controller and server in the Finance domain.

B. Create a global group in the Marketing domain called Global Backup and add Sheila, Frank, and Pat to it. Add Global Backup to the local Backup Operators groups on each domain controller and server in the Finance domain.

C. Create a global group in the Marketing domain called Global Backup and add Sheila, Frank, and Pat to it. Add Global Backup to the local Backup Operators group on the primary domain controller and the local Backup Operators groups on each server in the Finance domain.

D. Create new accounts for Sheila, Frank, and Pat on each domain controller and server in the Finance domain and add them to the local Backup Operators groups on each domain controller and server in the Finance domain.

Question #15-13

The Finance domain trusts the Marketing domain. The Finance domain shares a color laser printer that the CAD users in Marketing need to use from time to time. There is a global group in Marketing called CAD USERS. There is a local group on the print server in Finance called COLOR USERS that has Print permission to the color laser printer. How would you grant the Marketing CAD users permission to the color laser printer? Select the best answer (Microsoft's recommended solution).

A. In the Permissions dialog box for the color laser printer, choose Add and select the Marketing domain from the list of valid domains. Then select CAD USERS from the list of global groups in the Marketing database.

B. Add the CAD USERS global group from Marketing to the COLOR USERS local group on the print server.

C. Create a global group in Finance called MARKETING CAD USERS. Add the CAD USERS global group from Marketing to the MARKETING CAD USERS global group in Finance. Then add the MARKETING CAD USERS global group to the COLOR USERS local group on the print server.

D. You can't do this because the trust is in the wrong direction.

Question #15-14

You created a trust between Finance and Marketing so that users in the Marketing domain can access resources managed in the Finance domain. However, Marketing users are unable to access resources. What would you check?

A. Has the trust been completed by both domains?

B. Was the trust broken?

C. Has appropriate access been granted to the users?

D. Is the trust set up in the correct direction?

Question #16-01

Which of the following characteristics can be applied to a domain? Choose all that apply.

A. A domain is a logical grouping of computers.
B. A domain depends entirely on the physical layout of the network.
C. A domain provides the foundation for implementing Directory Services.
D. A domain does not depend on the physical location of computers and users.

Question #16-02

One factor that will definitely affect the type of domain model that you implement is:

A. The number of user and group accounts.
B. The physical location and grouping of users.
C. The type of wide area network connections you have in place.
D. The location of network servers.

Question #16-03

Kite Flyers Corporation consists of 300 employees located in a single office complex. Which domain model would best suit this organization?

A. Single domain model
B. Master domain model
C. Multiple Master domain model
D. Complete Trust domain model

Question #16-04

Kite Flyers Corporation has opened offices in London and Tokyo. Each office maintains its own resources, though all users are managed in the corporate headquarters. Which domain model is best suited to this organization?

A. Single domain model
B. Master domain model
C. Multiple Master domain model
D. Complete Trust domain model

Question #16-05

Kite Flyers Corporation has experienced tremendous growth and now has between 10,000 and 15,000 employees located across its three global locations: Chicago, London, and Tokyo. Resources are managed in each location as well as the users located in those offices. Which model best suits this organization?

A. Single domain model

B. Master domain model

C. Multiple Master domain model

D. Complete Trust domain model

Question #16-06

Kite Flyers Corporation has its corporate headquarters in New York and branch offices in Chicago and San Francisco. Resource domains have been set up in each location and all accounts are managed by MIS in New York. The main goals of directory services are met. Which domain model does this represent and how many trusts need to be established?

A. Master domain model. The account domain in New York must trust each resource domain in each location; therefore, three one-way trusts need to be established.

B. Complete Trust model. All domains must trust one another. Because there are four domains, 4*(4-1) or 12 trusts must be established.

C. Master domain model. Each resource domain must trust the account domain in New York; therefore, three one-way trusts need to be established.

D. Master domain model. The account and resource domains must trust each other. Therefore, two one-way trusts must be established between each resource domain and the account domain, or six total.

Question #16-07

Kite Flyers Corporation was formed from three different regional companies located in San Francisco, Chicago, and Atlanta. Each company already had its own Windows NT network configured as a Single Domain model.

It is necessary that all the users in the new company be able to log on to the network, no matter which office they work from, and still be able to access their resources. Which domain model provides the best solution for this scenario?

A. Multiple Master domain model. Create two one-way trusts between San Francisco and Chicago, and between Chicago and Atlanta.

B. Master domain model. Have San Francisco and Atlanta create one-way trusts to Chicago.

C. Complete Trust model. Have all domains trust one another for a total of three trusts.

D. Complete Trust model. Have all domains trust one another for a total of six trusts.

Question #16-08

Which of the following statements best represents Microsoft's groups strategy for the Master Domain model?

A. Create global groups in the resource domains to manage local resources. Create local groups in the account domains to manage users. Add the resource domains' global groups to the account domain's local groups.

B. Create local groups on the resource servers in the resource domains to manage access to resources. Group users into appropriate global groups in the account domain. Add the global groups from the account domain to the local groups in the resource domains.

C. Create local groups on the resource servers in the resource domains to manage access to resources. Create global groups in the resource domains and add to them global users from the account domain. Make the global groups from the resource domain members of the local groups on the resource servers.

D. Create local groups on the resource servers in the resource domains to manage access to resources. Add global users from the account domain to the local resource groups.

Question #16-09

Kite Flyers Corporation has configured a Multiple Master domain model with accounts managed by MIS in the KFCORPA and KFCORPB domains. Resource domains are located in Seattle, Houston, and Boston. Certain users—whose accounts might be in either KFCORPA or KFCORPB—have been selected to provide backup functions for all the domains. Which of the following represents the most flexible solution for this scenario?

A. Create a global backup group called KFBACKUP in KFCORPA and in KFCORPB. Add the user accounts that reside in KFCORPA to its KFBACKUP global group, and add the users that reside in KFCORPB to its KFBACKUP global group. Add both KFCORPA\KFBACKUP and KFCORPB\KFBACKUP to the local Backup Operators groups in each resource domain.

B. Create a global backup group called KFBACKUP in KFCORPA. Add the users from KFCORPA and KFCORPB to KFBACKUP. Add KFBACKUP from KFCORPA to the local Backup Operators groups in each resource domain.

C. Create a global backup group called KFBACKUP in KFCORPA and in KFCORPB. Add the user accounts that reside in KFCORPA to its KFBACKUP global group, and add the users that reside in KFCORPB to its KFBACKUP global group. Add both KFCORPA\KFBACKUP and KFCORPB\KFBACKUP to the local Backup Operators groups in each resource domain and to the local Backup Operators groups for KFCORPA and KFCORPB.

D. Create a global backup group called KFBACKUP in KFCORPA. Add the users from KFCORPA and KFCORPB to KFBACKUP. Add KFBACKUP from KFCORPA to the local Backup Operators groups in each resource domain and to the local Backup Operators groups in KFCORPA and KFCORPB.

Question #16-10

Kite Flyers Corporation is a relatively small company with about 1,000 employees. They are located in the same office complex. There are five departments: Accounting, Marketing, MIS, HR, and Corporate. Each has its own set of network resources that its staff accesses, and some resources that everyone in the company uses.

Primary Goals: Give all employees a single logon account that they can use to access their resources. Let each department manage its own resources.

Secondary Goal: Centralize resources by department.

Solution: Implement a single domain model and make all resource servers members of the domain.

A. The solution satisfies none of the goals.
B. The solution satisfies both primary goals and the secondary goal.
C. The solution satisfies both primary goals, but not the secondary goal.
D. The solution satisfies one primary goal and the secondary goal.

Question #16-11

Kite Flyers Corporation is a relatively small company with about 1,000 employees. They are located in the same office complex. There are five departments: Accounting, Marketing, MIS, HR, and Corporate. Each has its own set of network resources that its staff accesses, and some resources that everyone in the company uses.

Primary Goals: Give all employees a single logon account that they can use to access their resources. Let each department manage its own resources.

Secondary Goal: Centralize resources by department.

Solution: Implement a master domain model and have all resource domains trust the account domain.

A. The solution satisfies none of the goals.
B. The solution satisfies both primary goals and the secondary goal.
C. The solution satisfies both primary goals, but not the secondary goal.
D. The solution satisfies one primary goal and the secondary goal.

Question #16-12

Kite Flyers Corporation is a relatively small company with about 1,000 employees. They are located in the same office complex. There are five departments: Accounting, Marketing, MIS, HR, and Corporate. Each has its own set of network resources that its staff accesses, and some resources that everyone in the company uses.

Primary Goals: Give all employees a single logon account that they can use to access their resources. Let each department manage their own resources.

Secondary Goal: Centralize resources by department.

Solution: Give each department its own domain and let each manage its own users and resources.

A. The solution satisfies none of the goals.
B. The solution satisfies both primary goals and the secondary goal.
C. The solution satisfies both primary goals, but not the secondary goal.
D. The solution satisfies the secondary goal.

Question #16-13

Kite Flyers Corporation has two global locations, London and New York. MIS manages the users in both locations in two account domains. There are five departments: Accounting, Marketing, MIS, HR, and Corporate. Each has its own set of network resources that its staff accesses, and some resources that everyone in the company uses.

Primary Goals: Give all employees a single logon account that they can use to access their resources. Let MIS be able to manage the account domains from any location. Let each department manage its own resources. Let certain delegated users act as print operators for printers in each department.

Secondary Goals: Centralize resources by department. Let all delegated users be able to manage any domain's printers. Allow as much flexibility as possible for printer management.

Solution: Implement a Multiple Master Domain model. Have all resource domains trust the account domain, and let the account domains trust each other. Create a global group called KFPRINT in each account domain and add the delegated users to it. Add KFPRINT from both account domains to the local Print Operators groups on the print servers in each domain.

A. The solution satisfies none of the goals.
B. The solution satisfies all the primary goals and all the secondary goals.
C. The solution satisfies both primary goals, but only one secondary goal.
D. The solution satisfies two primary goals and two secondary goals.

Question #16-14

Kite Flyers Corporation has two global locations, London and New York. MIS manages the users in both locations in two account domains. There are five departments: Accounting, Marketing, MIS, HR, and Corporate. Each has its own set of network resources that its staff accesses, and some resources that everyone in the company uses.

Primary Goals: Give all employees a single logon account that they can use to access their resources. Let MIS be able to manage the account domains from any location. Let each department manage its own resources. Let certain delegated users act as print operators for printers in each department.

Secondary Goals: Centralize resources by department. Let all delegated users be able to manage any domain's printers. Allow as much flexibility as possible for printer management.

Solution: Implement a Single Domain model. Have all resource servers become members of the domain. Create a global group called KFPRINT. Add KFPRINT to the local Print Operators groups on the print servers in each domain.

A. The solution satisfies none of the goals.

B. The solution satisfies all the primary goals and all the secondary goals.

C. The solution satisfies all primary goals but only one secondary goal.

D. The solution satisfies two primary goals and two secondary goals.

Question #16-15

Kite Flyers Corporation has two global locations, London and New York. MIS manages the users in both locations in two account domains. There are five departments: Accounting, Marketing, MIS, HR, and Corporate. Each has its own set of network resources that its staff accesses, and some resources that everyone in the company uses.

Primary Goals: Give all employees a single logon account that they can use to access their resources. Let MIS be able to manage the account domains from any location. Let each department manage its own resources. Let certain delegated users act as print operators for printers in each department.

Secondary Goals: Centralize resources by department. Let all delegated users be able to manage any domain's printers. Allow as much flexibility as possible for printer management.

Solution: Implement a Multiple Master Domain model. Have all resource domains trust the account domain, and let the account domains trust each other. In each account domain, create a global group for print operators for each department's resource domain called, for example, ACCT-PRINT, MARK-PRINT, MIS-PRINT, HR-PRINT and CORP-PRINT. Add the appropriate global group to the local Print Operators groups on the print servers in their respective domains.

A. The solution satisfies none of the goals.

B. The solution satisfies all the primary goals and all the secondary goals.

C. The solution satisfies all primary goals but only one secondary goal.

D. The solution satisfies two primary goals and two secondary goals.

Question #17-01

Which of the following protocols is not considered routable?

A. TCP/IP

B. NetBEUI

C. NWLink

D. AppleTalk

Question #17-02

Protocols are installed by accessing the network icon in the Control Panel and:

A. Selecting the Protocol tab and selecting the Add button.

B. Selecting the Protocol tab and selecting the protocol.

C. Selecting the Protocol tab and choosing all protocols.

D. Selecting the Protocol tab, nothing else has to be selected.

Question #17-03

The Registry location for the NetBEUI protocol parameters is HKEY_LOCAL_MACHINE\System\CurrentControlSet\Services\...:

A. NetBEUI\Parameters

B. NetBIOS\Parameters

C. NBF\Parameters

D. NetBEUI\NBF\Parameters

Question #17-04

If the AppleTalk protocol is installed on a Windows NT Server, other Windows NT users on the network can access the server:

A. To create Macintosh Accessible Volumes on Macintosh computers

B. To access Macintosh Accessible Volumes on Macintosh computers

C. To access Macintosh Accessible Volumes on the workstation and share files with Macintosh users

D. As a print server

Question #17-05

By default, all BDCs on the same subnet in a domain will become:

A. A domain master browser

B. A potential browser

C. A backup browser

D. A non-browser

Question #17-06

Within a single workgroup, there will be a master browser elected for:

A. Each protocol

B. Every 32 computers

C. Every 12 users

D. Only one protocol

Question #17-07

If a group of workstations on a network are never to contain any shared resources, how can you optimize these workstations so they will never send host announcements to the master browser?

A. Disable the workstation service

B. Disable the server service

C. Disable the browser service

D. Disable the alerter service

Question #17-08

When the directory replicator service is configured, a user account must be created. Why is a user account required?

A. The administrator must log on to the computer with the user account and manually start and stop the replicator service.

B. The replicator service will log on to the computer as the user and use the account to perform directory replication.

C. The replicator service will not log on to the computer as the user, but will use the account in case the replicator service fails.

D. The administrator uses this account to perform administrative duties once the replicator service is configured.

Question #18-01

An IP address of 191.191.191.191 will have a default subnet mask of:

A. 255.255.255.0

B. 255.255.0.0

C. 255.0.0.0

D. 0.0.0.0

Question #18-02

An IP address consists of what two parts in the order from left to right?

A. A network address and a workstation address

B. A workstation address and a network address

C. A subnet mask address and a default gateway address

D. A default gateway address and a subnet mask address

Question #18-03

The Advanced button on the Microsoft TCP/IP Properties sheet allows for the addition of:

A. 5 additional WINS server IP addresses

B. 10 additional default gateways

C. 5 additional DHCP server IP addresses

D. 5 additional default gateways

Question #18-04

A DHCP server eliminates the need to manually configure:

A. A DHCP scope

B. A WINS database

C. An IP address and subnet mask for DHCP clients

D. An IP address and subnet mask for non-DHCP clients

Question #18-05

A DHCP reservation is assigned to a:

A. Computer

B. Network Adapter Card

C. Domain

D. Workgroup

Question #18-06

A WINS database is used to:

A. Dynamically map IP addresses to network adapter card names

B. Dynamically map IP addresses to subnet masks

C. Dynamically map IP addresses to NetBIOS names

D. Dynamically map IP addresses to a user name

Question #18-07

The DLC protocol is used on Windows NT 4.0 computers to:

A. Communicate with HP JetDirect printing devices
B. Communicate with AppleTalk Postscript printing devices
C. Communicate with Novell file servers and client computers
D. Communicate with IBM mainframes and front end processors

Question #19-01

The NWLink protocol by itself can be used to communicate with:

A. Novell Servers
B. Windows NT Workstations
C. Macintosh Workstations
D. Novell Clients for client/server applications

Question #19-02

Which of the following parameters can be configured manually with the NWLink protocol?

A. IP address
B. Frame type
C. Subnet mask
D. DHCP scope

Question #19-03

If Windows NT is configured for Auto frame type detection and multiple IPX frame types are detected on the network, Windows NT will:

A. Automatically default to 802.3
B. Automatically default to 802.2
C. Automatically configure itself to all IPX frame types detected
D. Automatically default to the first IPX frame type detected

Question #19-04

The CSNW redirector will allow a Windows NT Workstation to communicate with:

A. Novell Servers
B. Windows NT Workstations
C. Macintosh Workstations
D. Novell Clients for client/server applications

Question #19-05

When configuring GSNW on Windows NT Server, a group called __________________ must be set up on the Novell Server.

A. NTUserGateway
B. NovellGateway
C. NetBIOSGateway
D. NTGateway

Question #19-06

RIP for NWLink will allow a Windows NT computer to act as a:

A. IP Router
B. AppleTalk Router
C. IPX Router
D. DLC Router

Question #20-01

Which of the following sets of Windows NT network clients do not require print drivers to be manually installed on the local computer?

A. All Microsoft Network clients
B. Windows NT and Windows 95
C. Windows NT, Windows 95, Windows for Workgroups 3.11
D. Windows NT, Windows 95, LAN Manager v2.x for DOS

Question #20-02

Which of the following steps applies to the Windows NT 4.0 print process on Windows NT computers? Select all that apply.

A. The GDI component of the client computer generates an enhanced metafile print job.

B. The bulk of the print process completes in the spooler on the client computer before forwarding the print job to the print server.

C. The print monitor controls access to the print devices and device ports and monitors status of the print job.

D. The local printer spooler makes a remote connection to the print server spooler and copies the print job there.

Question #20-03

Nicole calls to say that her print jobs seem to have stopped running. You check the printer that she sent the jobs to and see that the jobs are stuck in queue. What steps should you take to clear the stuck jobs? Select all that apply.

A. Select the stuck jobs and choose Document, Cancel.

B. Select Printer, Purge Printer.

C. Use the Control Panel applet Services to stop and restart the Spooler service.

D. Select each stuck job and change its priority.

Question #20-04

Several users have called you within the past half-hour to complain that their print jobs are not printing. In fact, they get system messages that tell them that the spooler is not responding. You have verified that the spooler directory partition does not have adequate free space to hold all the print jobs sent to it. What steps should you take to resolve this situation?

A. Use the Control Panel applet Services to more frequently stop and restart the Spooler service to keep the print jobs from becoming fragmented.

B. Change the location of the spool directory to a partition with enough disk space by modifying the HKEY_LOCAL_MACHINE\System\CurrentControlSet\Control\Print\Printers DefaultSpoolDirectory parameter.

C. Change the location of the spool directory to a partition with enough disk space by modifying the HKEY_Current_User\Control\Print\Printers\Spool SpoolDirectory parameter.

D. If the partition is formatted with NTFS, compress the spool directory.

Question #20-05

If the final print output is corrupted, what print process component should you check?

A. Spooler service on the client computer

B. Spooler service on the print server

C. Print processor on the print server

D. Print monitor on the client computer

Question #20-06

Which print monitor is loaded with TCP/IP and tracks print jobs targeted for TCP/IP print hosts?

A. IPMON.DLL

B. LPDMON.DLL

C. LPRMON.DLL

D. LOCALMON.DLL

Question #20-07

What is the purpose of the print monitor SFMMON.DLL?

A. SFMMON.DLL monitors Macintosh print jobs routed using AppleTalk protocol to network print devices.

B. SFMMON.DLL is the System File Manager print monitor which tracks print jobs sent directly to or printed directly from a file.

C. SFMMON.DLL is the software print job compression DLL which compresses the print job before it is sent from the local print spooler to the print server.

D. SFMMON.DLL is not a valid print monitor.

Question #20-08

A print job can be directed directly to a UNIX host print device, and its status checked using which two command-line utilities?

A. LPD and LPR

B. LPD and LPQ

C. LPR and IPCONFIG

D. LPR and LPQ

Question #20-09

Michelle has been selected to assist you as a print administrator in the Dry Gulch office, since you, yourself, are unable to travel there frequently, though you'd really like to. What is the minimum level of access you need to give Michelle so that she can perform basic print management tasks such as creating and sharing printers and managing print jobs?

A. Make Michelle a member of the Print Operators local group on her print server.

B. Make Michelle a member of the Server Operator local group on her print server.

C. Make Michelle a member of the Administrators local group on her print server.

D. Give Michelle Full Control permission for each printer on her print server.

Question #20-10

You have created four printers. Each of them will be used by a specific group of users. Name all the steps which are required to successfully make the printer available to the appropriate users.

A. Share each printer.

B. Set the share permissions for each printer so that only the appropriate group has access.

C. Set the printer permissions for each printer so that only the appropriate group has access.

D. Create a printer pool so that each group can access all the print devices.

Question #20-11

Elaine was the print administrator for the LotsOf Print Corporation, but has left the country to pursue a career as an opera singer. You need to assign a new print administrator. What will you need to do concerning ownership of the LotsOf Print Corporation printers that Elaine created and managed?

A. Do nothing. Printers are not owned by a user; they are owned by the system.

B. Make the new print administrator a Print Operator. The new print administrator can then take ownership of the printers in LotsOf Print Corporation.

C. Give ownership of the printers to the new print administrator.

D. Give the new administrator Full Control permission over the printers. Full Control automatically assigns ownership to that user.

Question #20-12

The print device associated with a particular printer has failed. Several print jobs are waiting in queue in that printer. How can you service these print jobs?

A. Connect to another remote printer. Open the printer manager window for the printer and drag the waiting print jobs to the remote printer manager window.

B. Use the Ports tab properties for the printer to add a port for another remote printer. Deselect the current print port associated with the printer and select the remote port. Resume the printer.

C. Do nothing. You must replace the failed print device before printing can resume.

D. Use the Control Panel applet Services to stop the spooler service, configure it to connect to another remote printer, and restart it.

Question #20-13

There are three downward-compatible print devices connected to the print server in MIS. MIS Managers and Project Leaders should always be able to print to the first available printer. Help Desk staff and Developers should be able to print only to their specified print device. What will best accomplish this task?

A. Create a printer for each device and assign the appropriate groups access only to their printer. Give the Manager's printer a priority of 1, Help Desk's printer a priority of 50, and Developer's printer a priority of 99.

B. Create a printer for each device and assign the appropriate groups access only to their printer. Give the Manager's printer a priority of 99, Help Desk's printer a priority of 50, and Developer's printer a priority of 1.

C. Create a printer for each device and assign the appropriate groups access only to their printer. Make the Manager's printer a printer pool by associating it with each print device.

D. Create a printer for each device and assign the appropriate groups access only to their printer. Make each printer a printer pool by associating it with each print device.

Question #20-14

There is one high-speed network print device connected to the print server in MIS. MIS Managers and Project Leaders should always be able to print to this printer regardless of who has submitted print jobs. Help Desk staff should be able to print ahead of Developers. What will best accomplish this task?

A. Create three printers, each associated with the device, and assign the appropriate groups access only to their printer. Give the Manager's printer a priority of 1, Help Desk's printer a priority of 50, and Developer's printer a priority of 99.

B. Create three printers, each associated with the device, and assign the appropriate groups access only to their printer. Give the Manager's printer a priority of 99, Help Desk's printer a priority of 50, and Developer's printer a priority of 1.

C. Create three printers, each associated with the device, and assign the appropriate groups access only to their printer. Make the Manager's printer a printer pool by associating it with each print device.

D. Create three printers associated with the device and assign the appropriate groups access only to their printer. Make each printer a printer pool by associating it with each print device.

Question #20-15

The printer for a network print device has been configured to print documents at all times. Pam plans to send a large complex graphics document that she would like to have tomorrow morning. This job will take at least one hour to complete. What can you do to minimize the effect that printing this document will have on other documents in the queue?

A. Select Pam's document and pause it. Resume printing after hours when print jobs are at a minimum.

B. Modify the printer schedule so that it prints documents only after hours.

C. Modify the document schedule for Pam's document so that it prints only between 1:00 A.M. and 3:00 A.M.

D. Do nothing. The printer automatically holds long jobs until short jobs finish spooling and printing.

Question #20-16

Which of the following steps is appropriate to take when troubleshooting a failed print job?

A. Verify that the appropriate print port has been defined and configured by printing a test page.

B. Delete and re-create the printer.

C. Determine whether the print device is online and connected.

D. Resubmit the print job to a file and then copy the file to a printer port to see if it is successful.

Question #20-17

You are using a RISC-based computer as your print server. All your clients are either MS-DOS, Windows for Workgroups, Windows 95, or Windows NT running on Intel-based computers. What must you do to ensure that all your clients can print to the print devices managed by the RISC-based print server?

A. Install both RISC-based and Intel print drivers on the RISC-based print server. Install the appropriate print drivers only on the MS-DOS and Windows for Workgroups computers.

B. Install both RISC-based and Intel print drivers on the RISC-based print server. The client computers will receive the appropriate platform driver from the print server when they make a print request.

C. Install RISC-based print drivers on the RISC-based print server and Intel print drivers on the client computers. Windows NT will do the platform translation.

D. Install the Intel print drivers on the RISC-based print server and RISC-based print drivers on the client computers.

Question #20-18

There are 300 Windows NT and Windows 95 client computers that print to five printers on a print server. You have received upgraded print drivers for two of the print devices connected to this print server. What must you do to ensure that all clients can continue to access all the print devices?

A. Install the upgraded print drivers on all the client computers that need to use those print devices.

B. Install the upgraded print drivers on all the client computers.

C. Install the upgraded print drivers only on the Windows NT client computers.

D. Do nothing. The print server can download the new drivers to the clients the next time they make a print request.

Question #20-19

From the following choices, list the steps required to install a network interface printer using the DLC protocol.

A. Install the DLC protocol on the print server and shut down and restart.

B. Start the Print Wizard, select Add Printer, then select Add Port.

C. Select the Hewlett-Packard Network Port and click the New Port button.

D. Select a MAC address from the available addresses and supply a printer name in the Add Hewlett-Packard Network Peripheral Port dialog box.

Question #20-20

From the following choices, indicate the step that is NOT required when installing and configuring a printing device using the TCP/IP protocol.

A. Enter the IP address of the remote controller servicing the print device in the Add LPR Compatible Printer dialog box.

B. Enter the name of the remote controller servicing the print device in the Add LPR Compatible Printer dialog box.

C. Enter the IP address of the print device in the Add LPR Compatible Printer dialog box.

D. Enter the IP address of the print server in the Add LPR Compatible Printer dialog box.

Question #21-01

Which communication protocol can be used to establish RAS connections between Windows NT 4.0 workstations and RAS servers? Choose all that apply.

A. SLIP

B. PPP

C. X-Link

D. PPP Multilink

Question #21-02

Users in remote offices need to connect through dial-up networking to various resources on the company network. The resource servers use a variety of protocols for various performance reasons. What must you do to ensure that users dialing in can access any resource server that they have been given access to?

A. Assign dial-in permission for each user to each resource server.

B. Install every protocol on every resource server.

C. Install all the protocols on the RAS server only.

D. Install all the protocols on each user's remote computer.

Question #21-03

Flora, the MIS director, wants company employees to be able to access the company's network through their personal Internet providers. However, she has concerns about the security of the company's network from unauthorized Internet access. What is your solution? Choose all that apply.

A. Use Point-to-Point Tunneling on the RAS server.

B. Enable callback security for Internet connections.

C. Connect only the RAS server to the Internet.

D. Enable filtering for PPTP on the RAS server.

Question #21-04

The marketing department staff travels a lot and dials in to the company network while visiting client offices to obtain product information. Elvira, the marketing director, wants the company to assume the dial-up costs rather than the client. What do you advise?

A. Enable callback security on the RAS server and let the marketer provide the callback number.

B. Enable callback security on the RAS server and specify a number the server should always call back.

C. Do nothing. Charges are always assumed by the RAS server.

D. Select the Reverse Charges option on the RAS server Callback properties.

Question #21-05

The marketing department staff travels a lot and dials in to the company network while visiting client offices to obtain product information. There are several numbers that can be used for dialing in. The marketers do not want to have to take the additional time during their client presentations to configure area code and country code information for each dial-in number. What do you advise?

A. Enable callback security on the RAS server and let the marketer provide the callback number.

B. Have the marketers create a TAPI location before their client call that includes the area code and country code. This location can then be applied to any of the dial-in numbers when Dial-Up networking is loaded.

C. You must change the country and area codes each time you select a dial-in number.

D. Create separate phone book entries for each area code and country code.

Question #21-06

For security reasons, you want to restrict access for dial-up users only to the RAS server when they dial in, but not restrict their access when at the office. What must you do?

A. Do nothing. This is the default setting.

B. Disable gateway access for each RAS server network protocol setting.

C. Configure the permissions on each of the resource servers in the network to restrict the users.

D. Configure the dial-in permissions for each user on the RAS server to restrict access to the RAS server.

Question #22-01

Indicate, from the following choices, which routing options are available with a Windows NT 4.0 Server installation.

A. IP Routing

B. IPX Routing

C. DHCP Relay

D. AppleTalk Routing

Question #22-02

Why is NetBEUI protocol routing not supported in Windows NT 4.0 installations?

A. Because NetBEUI maintains its own route tables and requires no additional services to handle routing.

B. Because NetBEUI cannot be installed on Windows NT 4.0 Server.

C. Because NetBEUI uses either RIP for IP or RIP for IPX, whichever is installed.

D. Because NetBEUI is not a routable protocol.

Question #22-03

Routers work up to the __________________ layer in the OSI Network Model.

A. Physical
B. Data Link
C. Network
D. Transport

Question #22-04

From the following choices, indicate which are considered functions of a router.

A. They can pass information packets from one protocol to another such as TCP/IP to IPX.
B. They cannot pass information packets from one protocol to another such as TCP/IP to IPX.
C. They can pass information packets from one network segment to another, even though each segment may use a different media type such as Ethernet or Token Ring.
D. They can pass information packets from one network segment to another, but only if each segment is the same media type such as Ethernet or Token Ring.

Question #22-05

RIP for IP and DHCP Relay can support ____________ hops.

A. 4
B. 8
C. 16
D. 32

Question #22-06

RIP for IPX can support ____________ hops.

A. 4
B. 8
C. 16
D. 32

Question #22-07

Indicate the utility used from the command prompt to manually maintain a static IP routing table.

A. Route
B. IPXRoute
C. IPConfig
D. PING

Question #22-08

Indicate the utility used from the command prompt to manually maintain an IPX routing table.

A. Route
B. IPXRoute
C. IPConfig
D. PING

Question #22-09

What service must be installed on a Windows NT 4.0 Server to allow it to function as an AppleTalk router?

A. RPC
B. GSNW
C. FDDI
D. SFM

Question #22-10

Network types can have network numbers or network ranges associated with them. Which type of network can have only one network number associated with it?

A. LocalTalk
B. EtherTalk
C. TokenTalk
D. FDDI

Question #23-01

Which of the following features is provided by the full version of Network Monitor that comes with Microsoft's System Management Server? Choose all that apply.

A. Direct monitoring of remote computer traffic.

B. Determining which protocol consumed the most bandwidth.

C. Identifying which physical disk has the most I/O activity for a network session.

D. Capturing local network traffic to and from the computer running the utility.

Question #23-02

Which of the following features is provided by the version of Network Monitor that comes with Microsoft Windows NT Server 4.0?

A. Direct monitoring of remote computer traffic.

B. Determining which protocol consumed the most bandwidth.

C. Identifying which physical disk has the most I/O activity for a network session.

D. Capturing local network traffic to and from the computer running the utility.

Question #23-03

A broadcast frame:

A. Is always directed to a specific computer by its IP, IPX, or MAC address.

B. Is sent to all hosts on the network via the unique destination address FFFFFFFF.

C. Is sent to a subset of computers on the network depending on how the computer has registered itself on the network.

D. Is a multicast frame that is directed to a specific computer on the network.

Question #23-04

Which of the following are components of an Ethernet 802.3 frame? Choose all that apply.

A. Source and Destination address

B. Length of the frame

C. Data contained in the frame such as IP and TCP information

D. Type of frame

Question #23-05

In your network, you would like to remotely monitor traffic on all your Windows NT 4.0 Server and Workstation computers, as well as your Windows 95 computers. Which of the following steps needs to take place?

A. Install the Network Monitor agent on all the computers and the Windows NT Server 4.0 version of Network Monitor on the computer that will remotely monitor the computers.

B. Install the Network Monitor agent on all the computers and the SMS full version of Network Monitor on the computer that will remotely monitor the computers.

C. Install only the Windows NT Server 4.0 version of Network Monitor on the computer that will remotely monitor the computers.

D. Install only the SMS full version of Network Monitor on the computer that will remotely monitor the computers.

Question #23-06

Which of the following network services generate traffic between a client and a server computer? Choose all that apply.

A. NetBIOS name registration with a WINS server

B. Logon validation

C. Account database synchronization

D. DHCP IP address requests

Question #23-07

What types of network traffic are associated with the DHCP service?

A. DHCP Address Request
B. DHCP Lease Renewal
C. DHCP Time Out
D. DHCP Replication

Question #23-08

What types of traffic are associated with the WINS service?

A. WINS Registration
B. WINS Time Out
C. WINS Query Request
D. WINS Address Request

Question #23-09

When a computer registers with a WINS server, how many name registration frames are generated?

A. One name is registered for each computer.
B. A name is registered for the computer and for every service or application that supports the NetBIOS API. One frame registers all these names.
C. A name is registered for the computer and for every service or application that supports the NetBIOS API. One frame is generated for each name that needs to be registered.
D. NetBIOS names are not registered with the WINS server.

Question #23-10

Which of the following steps need to take place before a file session can be established between two computers using the TCP/IP protocol? Choose all that apply.

A. The user must register its name with the WINS server.
B. Name resolution must take place.

C. Address resolution must take place.

D. A TCP Session must be established.

Question #23-11

When a TCP session is established, three frames are generated known as the TCP three-way handshake. Which of the following frames are part of the three-way handshake? Choose all that apply.

A. TCP Request from the client to the server.

B. TCP Name resolution request from the client to the WINS server.

C. TCP Request Acknowledgment from the server to the client.

D. TCP Session establishment from the client to the server.

Question #23-12

Which type of frames are involved in connecting to a shared resource once the session has been established?

A. SMB session frames

B. WINS resolution frames

C. NBT broadcast frames

D. TCP request frames

Question #23-13

ABCCorp network consists of 5,000 users located in three office locations: New York, Chicago, and San Francisco. The current plan is to locate one PDC and one BDC in the corporate headquarters in Chicago. How could you optimize this configuration to make logging on more efficient for the users and minimize network traffic? Choose the best two answers.

A. Create two more BDCs to accommodate the 5,000 users. Microsoft recommends one BDC for every 2,000 users.

B. Create a trust relationship among all the offices.

C. Locate one BDC in each location so that logon validation takes place locally.

D. Do nothing. This configuration is optimized.

Question #23-14

The KITEMASTERS corporate network consists of 6,000 users located across five regional locations, each on its own subnet. About half the users have Windows NT Workstation 4.0 computers, and the rest have Windows 95 computers. These computers are frequently restarted throughout the day. There is one PDC and BDC located in the MIS department, and a BDC in each regional location. Each location also has one or more Windows NT Server 4.0 computers for resource management.

Using Network Monitor, you have noticed that there is an unusually high percentage of Browser traffic generated throughout the day. How can you optimize traffic associated with the Browser while letting users continue to browse for resources? Choose the best two answers.

A. You cannot configure Browser parameters.

B. Configure the Windows 95 and Windows NT Workstation 4.0 computers to never become browsers.

C. Disable the Server service on user computers which will not be sharing resources in the network.

D. Disable the Computer Browser service on all user computers.

Question #23-15

Under what circumstances might a full database synchronization take place between a PDC and a BDC? Choose the best two.

A. Every synchronization event replicates the entire account databases.

B. Full synchronization occurs when the BDC is first installed.

C. Full synchronization may occur when the change log on the PDC becomes full and begins to overwrite existing information before the PDC can contact the BDC for updates.

D. Only changes are copied whenever synchronization occurs.

Question #23-16

Built-in local groups and their members are contained in which accounts database?

A. SAM Accounts Database

B. Local Security Accounts Database

C. SAM Built-In Database

D. Account Synchronization Database

Question #23-17

User, group, and computer accounts are contained in which accounts database?

A. SAM Accounts Database

B. Local Security Accounts Database

C. SAM Built-In Database

D. Account Synchronization Database

Question #23-18

The ABCCorp domain is configured as a Master Domain model. 5,000 user accounts are managed in the ABC-MIS domain in Chicago. Resource domains trust ABC-MIS. At the ABC-WEST resource domain, the print administrator is managing access to her printers by adding the appropriate user accounts from ABC-MIS to the ACL for each of five printers. Access will be managed for 300 users. ABC-WEST is connected to ABC-MIS via a slow WAN link. Every time she accesses the ABC-MIS account domain to display the list of users, the list takes several seconds to generate. The process is taking longer than she thinks it should. What can you suggest to improve performance and minimize network traffic? Choose the best answer.

A. Upgrade the WAN link to a higher speed.

B. Create local groups on the print servers in ABC-WEST and add the users to the local groups. Use the local groups to assign printer permissions.

C. Create global groups in ABC-MIS for the users that need printer access in ABC-WEST. Add the global groups to local groups on the print servers in ABC-WEST, and assign printer permissions to the local groups.

D. There is nothing you can do to improve performance. The same amount of trust traffic is generated whether you use user accounts or group accounts across the trust.

Question #23-19

Which of the following actions can serve to optimize network traffic associated with Directory Replication? Choose all that apply.

A. Lock directories that are not replicated frequently, or that you do not want to have replicated.

B. Maintain a shallow export directory tree structure.

C. Modify the interval value on the export server so that it does not check for changes in the export tree as frequently.

D. Remove the password from the Directory Replication service account.

Question #24-01

The major cause of STOP errors during the installation process is?

A. Incompatible software.

B. Incompatible hardware.

C. Incompatible Windows NT setup program.

D. It is impossible to get STOP errors during installation.

Question #24-02

The third major area of a STOP screen displays?

A. Debug Port Status Indicator Information

B. BugCheck Information

C. Driver Information

D. Kernel Build Number and Stack Dump Information

Question #24-03

The first four lines of the ____________________ section are critical to finding the cause of the STOP error.

A. BugCheck Information

B. Driver Information

C. Kernel Build Number and Stack Dump

D. Debug Port Information

Question #24-04

By default, CrashDump will be placed in the ____________________ folder.

A. %systemRoot%\System32

B. %systemRoot%\System32\Debug

C. %systemRoot%\System32\MemoryDump

D. %systemRoot%\

Question #24-05

For CrashDumps to be obtained, a pagefile must exist on the

A. System partition

B. Boot partition

C. NTFS partition

D. Data partition

Question #24-06

For CrashDumps to be obtained, the pagefile must be at least ________ megabytes larger than the physical size of memory.

A. 1

B. 2

C. 4

D. 8

Question #24-07

The utility to verify the validity of a CrashDump is

A. Dumpflop.exe

B. Dumpexam.exe

C. Dumpchk.exe

D. Dump.exe

Question #24-08

Reference to the most recently installed Service pack Symbols files must be listed __________ in the Dumpexam utility command line.

A. Last

B. First after the normal Symbols files reference

C. Second

D. First

Question #24-09

What kind of connection can be established between the Host computer and the Target computer for the Host computer to monitor the Boot process on the Target computer?

A. Null Modem connection using a COM port

B. Normal Network connection using a Network Adapter Card

C. Modem connection using a COM port

D. Modem connection using an LPT port

Question #24-10

Kernel Debugger commands can be entered after a ________________ key sequence is entered.

A. Ctrl+G

B. Ctrl+C

C. Ctrl+K

D. Ctrl+Q

Question #24-11

Audit events are placed in the ________________ log in Event Viewer.

A. System

B. Security

C. Application

D. Audit

Question #24-12

By default, events are ordered in all event logs?

A. By oldest first

B. By event importance

C. By newest last

D. By newest first

Answer Key for Chapter Tests

Question #	Correct Answer(s)	Question #	Correct Answer(s)
02-01	A, B, D	13-01	A
02-02	A, D	13-02	B
02-03	B, D	13-03	A
02-04	A, D	13-04	C
02-05	A, B, D	13-05	A, C
03-01	C	13-06	B, C
03-02	A, B, D	13-07	A, B, C
03-03	A, C, D	14-01	A
03-04	A	14-02	B
03-05	B	14-03	D
03-06	A	14-04	B
03-07	B	14-05	B
03-08	D	14-06	C
03-09	C	14-07	A, B
03-10	C	14-08	A
03-11	A, B, D	14-09	B
03-12	A	14-10	C
03-13	C	14-11	B
04-01	A, B	14-12	C
04-02	A, C, D	15-01	A, B, D

Question #	Correct Answer(s)	Question #	Correct Answer(s)
04-03	D	15-02	B
04-04	C	15-03	D
04-05	B	15-04	C
04-06	A	15-05	B, C, D
04-07	A, B, D	15-06	C, D
04-08	C	15-07	A
04-09	A	15-08	B
04-10	B	15-09	A
04-12	C	15-10	C
04-13	B, C	15-11	A
05-01	C	15-12	C
05-02	B	15-13	B
05-03	C	15-14	A, B, C, D
05-04	A, B, D	16-01	A, C, D
05-05	B	16-02	A
05-06	C	16-03	A
05-07	B	16-04	B
05-08	A, B, D	16-05	C
05-09	B	16-06	C
05-10	C	16-07	D
05-11	B	16-08	B
05-12	C	16-09	C
05-13	A, C, D	16-10	C
05-14	B, C	16-11	B
06-01	D	16-12	D
06-02	A, B, C	16-13	B
06-03	C	16-14	D
06-04	B	16-15	C
06-05	A	17-01	B

continues

continued

Question #	Correct Answer(s)	Question #	Correct Answer(s)
06-06	D	17-02	A
06-07	B	17-03	C
06-08	C	17-04	D
06-09	B	17-05	C
06-10	C	17-06	A
06-11	A, B	17-07	B
06-12	C	17-08	B
06-13	A, B, D	18-01	B
06-14	B	18-02	A
06-15	B	18-03	D
06-16	C, D	18-04	C
07-01	B	18-05	B
07-02	C	18-06	C
07-03	B	18-07	A, D
07-04	C	19-01	B, D
07-05	A, B, C, D	19-02	B
07-06	A, B	19-03	B
07-07	C	19-04	A
07-08	A, B	19-05	D
08-01	A, B, C	19-06	C
08-02	D	20-01	B
08-03	B, C, D	20-02	A, C, D
08-04	C	20-03	A, B, C
08-05	A, D	20-04	B
08-06	B	20-05	C
08-07	C	20-06	C
08-08	D	20-07	A
08-09	B	20-08	D
09-02	D	20-09	A

Question #	Correct Answer(s)	Question #	Correct Answer(s)
09-04	B	20-10	A, C
09-05	B, D	20-11	B
09-06	B	20-12	B
09-08	A, C, D	20-13	C
09-09	A, B, D	20-14	B
09-10	B, C	20-15	C
09-11	A, B, C	20-16	A, C, D
09-12	B	20-17	A
09-13	D	20-18	D
09-14	A, B, C	20-19	A, B, C, D
10-01	C	20-20	D
10-02	A, B, D	21-01	A, B, D
10-03	B	21-02	C
10-04	C	21-03	A, C, D
10-05	B	21-04	A
10-06	B	21-05	B
10-07	A	21-06	B
10-08	C	22-01	A, B, C, D
10-09	A, C, D	22-02	D
10-10	B	22-03	C
10-11	C	22-04	B, C
10-12	A, B, C	22-05	C
10-13	C	22-06	B
11-01	B	22-07	A
11-02	A, C, D	22-08	B
11-03	A, B, C	22-09	D
11-04	B, D	22-10	A
11-05	C	23-01	A, B, D
11-06	C	23-02	D
11-07	A	23-03	B

continues

continued

Question #	Correct Answer(s)	Question #	Correct Answer(s)
11-08	D	23-04	A, B, C, D
11-09	A	23-05	B
11-10	A, C	23-06	A, B, D
11-11	B	23-07	A, B
11-12	B	23-08	A, D
11-13	C	23-09	C
11-14	B	23-10	B, C, D
11-15	C	23-11	A, C, D
11-16	A, C, D	23-12	A
11-17	A	23-13	A, C
11-18	D	23-14	B, C
12-01	B, C, D	23-15	B, C
12-02	A, D	23-16	C
12-03	A	23-17	A
12-04	B	23-18	C
12-05	D	23-19	A, B, C
12-06	A	24-01	B
12-07	A, C	24-02	C
12-08	C	24-03	A
12-09	A, B, C, D	24-04	D
12-10	A	24-05	B
12-11	C	24-06	A
12-12	B, D	24-07	C
12-13	C	24-08	D
12-14	A	24-09	A, C
12-15	C	24-10	B
12-16	A, B	24-11	B
		24-12	D

Mastery Test

Question #1

Which of the following are requirements for setting up a successful trust relationship? Choose all that apply.

A. The primary domain controller in each domain must be up and accessible.

B. There can be no current sessions between the PDCs of each domain.

C. You must have an administrator-level account.

D. You must have access to a computer running User Manager for Domains.

Question #2

Which of the following statements does not apply to NTFS?

A. NTFS supports file and directory permissions security and access auditing.

B. NTFS supports transaction tracking and sector sparing for data recovery.

C. NTFS supports file and partition sizes of up to 4G.

D. NTFS provides file and directory compression.

Question #3

When a TCP session is established, three frames are generated known as the TCP three-way handshake. Which of the following frames are part of the three-way handshake? Choose all that apply.

A. TCP Request from the client to the server.

B. TCP Name resolution request from the client to the WINS server.

C. TCP Request Acknowledgment from the server to the client.

D. TCP Session establishment from the client to the server.

Question #4

You need to convert a partition from FAT to NTFS with no loss of data. How can you best accomplish this task?

A. Use Disk Administrator to select the partition and choose Tools, Format. Then select NTFS.

B. Use the command-line utility CONVERT.EXE to convert the partition.

C. Use the Windows NT Backup utility to back up the partition data to disk. Then format the partition for NTFS and restore the data.

D. You cannot convert a FAT partition to NTFS without loss of data.

Question #5

The Finance domain users need to access a laser printer in the Marketing domain. The Marketing domain users need to access a scanner in the Finance domain. How many trust relationships need to be created to facilitate the sharing of these two network resources?

A. Create one two-way trust relationship between Finance and Marketing.

B. Create two one-way trust relationships, one from Finance to Marketing and the other from Marketing to Finance.

C. Create two one-way trust relationships from Finance to Marketing. One for the shared laser printer, and the other the scanner.

D. Create one trust relationship between Finance and Marketing. A trust relationship is always bidirectional.

Question #6

The third major area of a STOP screen displays:

A. Debug Port Status Indicator Information

B. BugCheck Information

C. Driver Information

D. Kernel Build Number and Stack Dump Information

Question #7

There are three downward-compatible print devices connected to the print server in MIS. MIS Managers and Project Leaders should always be able to print to the first available printer. Help Desk staff and Developers should be able to print only to their specified print device. What will best accomplish this task?

A. Create a printer for each device and assign the appropriate groups access only to their printer. Give the Managers' printer a priority of 1, Help Desk's printer a priority of 50, and Developers a priority of 99.

B. Create a printer for each device and assign the appropriate groups access only to their printer. Give the Managers' printer a priority of 99, Help Desk's printer a priority of 50, and Developers a priority of 1.

C. Create a printer for each device and assign the appropriate groups access only to their printer. Make the Managers' printer a printer pool by associating it with each print device and give managers priority over other jobs.

D. Create a printer for each device and assign the appropriate groups access only to their printer. Make each printer a printer pool by associating it with each print device.

Question #8

What is the purpose of the print monitor SFMMON.DLL?

A. SFMMON.DLL monitors Macintosh print jobs routed using AppleTalk protocol to network print devices.

B. SFMMON.DLL is the System File Manager print monitor which tracks print jobs sent directly to or printed directly from a file.

C. SFMMON.DLL is the software print job compression DLL which compresses the print job before it is sent from the local print spooler to the print server.

D. SFMMON.DLL is not a valid print monitor.

Question #9

Which tool(s) can you use to remotely manage shares across the domain?

A. User Manager for Domains

B. Server Manager

C. Windows Explorer

D. Network Neighborhood

Question #10

Team Leaders need to be able to modify files contained in the share TOOLS. While you were on vacation, your trusted sidekick modified the permissions for the share and the folder. The two exhibits show what the permissions look like now. Team Leaders complain that they are unable to modify their files. What should you do?

A. Fire your trusted sidekick.

B. Change the TOOLS NTFS permission for Team Leaders to Change, and the share permission to Read.

C. Change the TOOLS NTFS permission for the Team Leaders to Change.

D. Remove Team Leaders from the ACL for the TOOLS share.

Question #11

The printer for a network print device has been configured to print documents at all times. Pam plans to send a large complex graphics document that she would like to have tomorrow morning. This job will take at least one hour to complete. What can you do to minimize the effect that printing this document will have on other documents in the queue?

A. Select Pam's document and pause it. Resume printing after hours when print jobs are at a minimum.

B. Modify the printer schedule so that it only prints documents after hours.

C. Modify the document schedule for Pam's document so that it only prints between 1:00 A.M. and 3:00 A.M.

D. Do nothing. The printer automatically holds long jobs until short jobs finish spooling and printing.

Question #12

Audit events are placed in the ________________ log in Event Viewer.

A. System

B. Security

C. Application

D. Audit

Question #13

Which of the following characteristics best apply to a workgroup network model? Choose two.

A. A workgroup network model provides a high level of security for resource access.

B. The workgroup model is best applied to smaller (fewer than 20) workstation groups.

C. A workgroup model is identified by its domain controller.

D. Each Windows NT computer participating in a workgroup must maintain a list of users that will be accessing the resources on that computer.

Question #14

The manager of the Accounting department wants to make next year's budget templates available for the staff accountants to review beginning next month. Staff accountants are already members of a global group called Accountants in CORPDOMAIN. The templates will be stored on the department resource server called ACCT1 in a folder called BUDGET97 on an NTFS partition. The folder has been shared with the default permission, which you do not want to change. How would you further secure the folder's contents so that it is available only to the Accounting department staff?

A. Use User Manager for Domains to create a local group on the resource server called Accountants. Make the global accountants group a member of the local accountants group. Assign the Accountants group permission to use the folder through User Manager for Domains.

B. Use User Manager for Domains to create a local group on the resource server called Accountants. Make the global accountants group a member of the local accountants group. Assign the appropriate User Rights to the Accountants group to access the BUDGET97 share.

C. Use User Manager for Domains to create a local group on the resource server called Accountants. Make the global accountants group a member of the local accountants group. Use the Security tab on the properties sheet for the folder to assign permissions to the Accountants group.

D. Use User Manager for Domains to create a local group on the resource server called Accountants. Make the global accountants group a member of the local accountants group. Use the Sharing tab on the properties sheet for the folder to assign permissions to the Accountants group.

Question #15

You are creating multiple user accounts for salespersons, marketers, and programmers. Each set of accounts belongs to the same relative groups (sales users in SALES, marketing users in MARKETING, and programmer users in PROGRAMMERS), uses the same logon scripts (SALES.BAT, MARKET.BAT, PROGRAM.BAT), and saves data in a home directory relative to each group (sales users under USERS\SALES, marketing users under USERS\MARKETERS, programmer users under USERS\PROGRAMMERS). What is the most efficient way to create these users?

A. Create a separate account for each user. As you create the user, use the %USERNAME% environment variable when specifying the home directory to let Windows NT create it for you.

B. Create a template for each type of user. Make the appropriate choices and entries for groups, logon script, and home directory. Use the %USERNAME% environment variable when specifying the home directory to let Windows NT create them for you. Then, create each user by copying the appropriate template.

C. Create all the users without specifying group membership. After they are all created, select each group of users by Ctrl+clicking them and create the appropriate group.

D. You must create each user individually.

Question #16

Which of the following protocols is not considered routable?

A. TCP/IP

B. NetBEUI

C. NWLink

D. AppleTalk

Question #17

User, group, and computer accounts are contained in which accounts database?

A. SAM Accounts Database

B. Local Security Accounts Database

C. SAM Built-In Database

D. Account Synchronization Database

Question #18

Kite Flyers Corporation is a relatively small company with about 1,000 employees. They are located in the same office complex. There are five departments: Accounting, Marketing, MIS, HR, and Corporate. Each has its own set of network resources that its staff accesses, and some resources that everyone in the company uses.

Primary Goals: Give all employees a single logon account that they can use to access their resources. Let each department manage its own resources.

Secondary Goal: Centralize resources by department.

Solution: Implement a master domain model and have all resource domains trust the account domain.

A. The solution satisfies none of the goals.
B. The solution satisfies both primary goals and the secondary goal.
C. The solution satisfies both primary goals, but not the secondary goal.
D. The solution satisfies one primary goal and the secondary goal.

Question #19

If the final print output is corrupted, what print process component should you check?

A. Spooler service on the client computer
B. Spooler service on the print server
C. Print processor on the print server
D. Print monitor on the client computer

Question #20

Which of the following actions can serve to optimize network traffic associated with Directory Replication? Choose all that apply.

A. Lock directories that are not replicated frequently, or that you do not want to have replicated.
B. Maintain a shallow export directory tree structure.

C. Modify the interval value on the export server so that it does not check for changes in the export tree as frequently.

D. Remove the password from the Directory Replication service account.

Question #21

An IP address of 191.191.191.191 will have a default subnet mask of:

A. 255.255.255.0

B. 255.255.0.0

C. 255.0.0.0

D. 0.0.0.0

Question #22

To provide a greater level of security, you have decided to create an account policy that requires a minimum password length of eight characters, requires that users change their passwords at least once a month, and does not allow users to use the same password twice in two months. Which Account Policy settings are appropriate?

A. Max Password Age: 60; Min Password Age: 30; Min Password Length: 8; Password Uniqueness: 2

B. Max Password Age: 30; Min Password Age: 30; Min Password Length: 8; Password Uniqueness: 6

C. Max Password Age: 30; Min Password Age: 10; Min Password Length: 8; Password Uniqueness: 6

D. Max Password Age: 60; Min Password Age: 30; Min Password Length: 8; Password Uniqueness: 1

Question #23

As you create new users you would like them to assume the same default environment settings, such as common application groups, startup programs, and company logo, as wallpaper. Which steps will achieve this end?

A. Modify the appropriate changes in the Default User and All Users profile folders in WINNT40\Profiles. When a new user is created, that user's profile will begin with the settings from these two.

B. Create a System Policy file that contains the appropriate settings for the Default user and save it in the WINNT40\SYSTEM32\REPL\IMPORT\SCRIPTS subdirectory on the validating computer.

C. Create a template user account and modify the settings for that account. Create new accounts by copying the template.

D. Create a system policy file for each set of users modifying the settings as appropriate for each user.

Question #24

Which of the following steps is appropriate to take when troubleshooting a failed print job?

A. Verify that the appropriate print port has been defined and configured by printing a test page.

B. Delete and re-create the printer.

C. Determine whether the print device is online and connected.

D. Resubmit the print job to a file and then copy the file to a printer port to see if it is successful.

Question #25

Which of the following counters will provide you with the total number of bytes transferred during disk I/O for all the disks in your computer?

A. Logical Disk>Disk Bytes/sec, Total instance

B. Logical Disk>Disk Bytes/sec, for each partition instance

C. Physical Disk>Disk Bytes/sec, Total instance

D. Physical Disk>Disk Bytes/sec, for each disk instance

Question #26

The administrator of the TOOLS shared folder wants to limit access to the folder only to the Developers group. To accomplish this, she gives the Everyone group NO ACCESS, and the Developers group Change access. The Developers complain that they cannot access any file in TOOLS. What else must the administrator do?

A. Share the files in the TOOLS folder.

B. Remove the Everyone group.

C. Give the Developers group Full Control.

D. Format the partition as NTFS and assign NTFS permissions in addition to the share permissions.

Question #27

From the following choices, indicate which are considered functions of a router.

A. They can pass information packets from one protocol to another such as TCP/IP to IPX.

B. They cannot pass information packets from one protocol to another such as TCP/IP to IPX.

C. They can pass information packets from one network segment to another, even though each segment may use a different media type such as Ethernet or Token Ring.

D. They can pass information packets from one network segment to another, but only if each segment is the same media type such as Ethernet or Token Ring.

Question #28

Arlo, a member of the Developers group, is currently editing the file DOOM.DOC in the share TOOLS. The administrator of the share changes permission to the Developers group from Change to Read. Arlo continues to make changes to the document. What else must the administrator do to restrict Arlo's access?

A. Take Arlo out of the Developers group.

B. Give Arlo No Access explicitly.

C. Send Arlo a message to get his authorization.

D. Nothing. Arlo must disconnect from the share and then reconnect before the new permission will take effect.

Question #29

To install server tools on a Windows NT Workstation, Intel platform:

A. Run Setup.bat from the server CD-ROM, Clients folder.

B. Run Setup.bat from the server CD-ROM, Clients\Srvtools folder.

C. Run Setup.bat from the server CD-ROM, Clients\Srvtools\Winnt folder.

D. Run Setup.bat from the server CD-ROM, Clients\Srvtools\Winnt\I386 folder.

Question #30

Mandy is running Pinball, the DOS Editor, Word 6, Excel 5, and Microstomp, a 16-bit, third-party Windows Web surfing program. Microstomp occasionally hangs up due to low resource memory. This affects her other Windows applications. What can you suggest to alleviate this problem?

A. Configure Microstomp to run in its own memory space.

B. Configure each Win 16 application to run in its own memory space.

C. Modify the PIF for Microstomp to increase its resource memory allocation.

D. Modify the PIF for the WOW NTVDM to increase resource memory allocations for all the Windows applications.

Question #31

The NWLink protocol by itself can be used to communicate with:

A. Novell Servers

B. Windows NT Workstations

C. Macintosh Workstations

D. Novell Clients for client/server applications

Question #32

In your network, you would like to remotely monitor traffic on all your Windows NT 4.0 Server and Workstation computers, as well as your Windows 95 computers. Which of the following steps needs to take place?

A. Install the Network Monitor agent on all the computers and the Windows NT Server 4.0 version of Network Monitor on the computer that will remotely monitor the computers.

B. Install the Network Monitor agent on all the computers and the SMS full version of Network Monitor on the computer that will remotely monitor the computers.

C. Install only the Windows NT Server 4.0 version of Network Monitor on the computer that will remotely monitor the computers.

D. Install only the SMS full version of Network Monitor on the computer that will remotely monitor the computers.

Question #33

Under what circumstances might a full database synchronization take place between a PDC and a BDC? Choose the best two.

A. Every synchronization event replicates the entire account databases.

B. Full synchronization occurs when the BDC is first installed.

C. Full synchronization may occur when the change log on the PDC becomes full and begins to overwrite existing information before the PDC can contact the BDC for updates.

D. Only changes are copied whenever synchronization occurs.

Question #34

Your boss has advised you that BrownC has left the company and asks that you delete his account. Later, your boss hires BrownC back as a consultant and tells you to put his account back on the network. BrownC calls you the next day and informs you gruffly that he can no longer access any of the network resources that he used to. How do you troubleshoot?

A. Use the Registry to set BrownC's SID back to what it was before you deleted his account. He will then be able to access all the old resources.

B. Deleting BrownC's account also deleted his SID. Because security in Windows NT is linked to the user's SID, you will need to reestablish all the network resource access that BrownC used to have.

C. Use the Emergency Repair Disk or your last network backup to copy BrownC's old account back to the Registry.

D. Install a backup copy of the account database that contains his old account.

Question #35

Which of the following steps applies to the Windows NT 4.0 print process on Windows NT computers? Choose all that apply.

A. The GDI component of the client computer generates an enhanced metafile print job.

B. The bulk of the print process completes in the spooler on the client before forwarding the print job to the print server.

C. The print monitor controls access to the print devices and device ports, and monitors status of the print job.

D. The local printer spooler makes a remote connection to the print server spooler and copies the print job there.

Question #36

Which Windows NT Server service allows a user to log on at computers in domains in which they have no account through the trust relationship to a computer or domain in which they do have an account?

A. NetLogon Service

B. Directory Replication Service

C. Account Synchronization Service

D. Self Service

Question #37

What kind of connection can be established between the Host computer and the Target computer for the Host computer to monitor the Boot process on the Target computer?

A. Null Modem connection using a COM port
B. Normal Network connection using a Network Adapter Card
C. Modem connection using a COM port
D. Modem connection using an LPT port

Question #38

You created a trust between Finance and Marketing so that users in the Marketing domain can access resources managed in the Finance domain. However, Marketing users are unable to access resources. What would you check?

A. Has the trust been completed by both domains?
B. Was the trust broken?
C. Has appropriate access been granted to the users?
D. Is the trust set up in the correct direction?

Question #39

Users in remote offices need to connect through dial-up networking to various resources on the company network. The resource servers use a variety of protocols for various performance reasons. What must you do to ensure that users dialing in can access any resource server that they have been given access to?

A. Assign dial-in permission for each user to each resource server.
B. Install every protocol on every resource server.
C. Install all the protocols on the RAS server only.
D. Install all the protocols on each user's remote computer.

Question #40

For CrashDumps to be obtained, the pagefile must be at least ________ megabytes larger than the physical size of memory.

A. 1

B. 2

C. 4

D. 8

Question #41

ABCCorp network consists of 5,000 users located in three office locations: New York, Chicago, and San Francisco. The current plan is to locate one PDC and one BDC in the corporate headquarters in Chicago. How could you optimize this configuration to make logging on more efficient for the users and minimize network traffic? Choose the best two answers.

A. Create two more BDCs to accommodate the 5,000 users. Microsoft recommends one BDC for every 2,000 users.

B. Create a trust relationship among all the offices.

C. Locate one BDC in each location so that logon validation takes place locally.

D. Do nothing. This configuration is optimized.

Question #42

You have begun the setup process and have been queried for mass storage devices. Setup presents you with a blank list of devices, but you know that you have a 1.2G IDE drive installed.

A. IDE devices are detected but generally not displayed in the list.

B. Windows NT has incorrectly identified your devices. Press F3 to exit setup and double-check your drive configuration.

C. Type S to add the drive configuration to the list.

D. Exit setup and run NTHQ to verify hardware detection.

Question #43

Nelson has been selected to assist you as a printing administrator in the Dry Gulch office, because you are unable to travel there frequently, though you'd really like to. What is the minimum level of access you need to give Nelson so that he can perform basic print management tasks such as creating and sharing printers and managing print jobs?

A. Make Nelson a member of the Print Operators local group on his print server.

B. Make Nelson a member of the Server Operator local group on his print server.

C. Make Nelson a member of the Administrators local group on his print server.

D. Give Nelson Full Control permission for each printer on his print server.

Question #44

While tracking the performance of disk activity on a system, you notice that the measured value is always 0 although the disk appears to be heavily used. What is your evaluation of this situation?

A. The disk is a high performance unit and can handle the heavy disk I/O.

B. The wrong disk objects and counters have been selected for Performance Monitor.

C. The disk counters had not been enabled by typing DISKPERF -Y at a command prompt.

D. The disk has crashed.

Question #45

There are three downward-compatible print devices connected to the print server in MIS. MIS Managers and Project Leaders should always be able to print to the first available printer. Help Desk staff and Developers should be able to print only to their specified print device. What will best accomplish this task?

A. Create a printer for each device and assign the appropriate groups access only to their printer. Give the Manager's printer a priority of 1, Help Desk's printer a priority of 50, and Developer's printer a priority of 99.

B. Create a printer for each device and assign the appropriate groups access only to their printer. Give the Manager's printer a priority of 99, Help Desk's printer a priority of 50, and Developer's printer a priority of 1.

C. Create a printer for each device and assign the appropriate groups access only to their printer. Make the Manager's printer a printer pool by associating it with each print device.

D. Create a printer for each device and assign the appropriate groups access only to their printer. Make each printer a printer pool by associating it with each print device.

Question #46

A DHCP reservation is assigned to a:

A. Computer

B. Network Adapter Card

C. Domain

D. Workgroup

Question #47

Under which of the following situations would you disable the user account rather than deleting it?

A. JaneD has left the company on maternity leave and plans to return in three months.

B. JohnB has taken an emergency medical leave of absence for possibly six or more months, but hopes to return full time.

C. JaniceD has left the company to take a job at Microsoft.

D. FrankP has taken a temporary team leader position in another department and will return when the project is completed.

Question #48

Kite Flyers Corporation has two global locations, London and New York. MIS manages the users in both locations in two account domains. There are five departments: Accounting, Marketing, MIS, HR, and Corporate. Each has its own set of network resources that its staff accesses, and some resources that everyone in the company uses.

Primary Goals: Give all employees a single logon account that they can use to access their resources. Let MIS be able to manage the account domains from any location. Let each department manage its own resources. Let certain delegated users act as print operators for printers in each department.

Secondary Goals: Centralize resources by department. Let all delegated users be able to manage any domain's printers. Allow as much flexibility as possible for printer management.

Solution: Implement a Single Domain model. Have all resource servers become members of the domain. Create a global group called KFPRINT. Add KFPRINT to the local Print Operators groups on the print servers in each domain.

A. The solution satisfies none of the goals.
B. The solution satisfies all the primary goals and all the secondary goals.
C. The solution satisfies all primary goals but only one secondary goal.
D. The solution satisfies two primary goals and two secondary goals.

Question #49

Once server tools are installed on a Windows NT Workstation, they can be run from:

A. The <winntroot>\System32 folder.
B. The Start Menu, Programs, Server Tools group.
C. The Start Menu, Programs, Administrative Tools group.
D. Any manually made program group provided the executables are placed in that group.

Question #50

Which print monitor is loaded with TCP/IP and tracks print jobs targeted for TCP/IP print hosts?

A. IPMON.DLL

B. LPDMON.DLL

C. LPRMON.DLL

D. LOCALMON.DLL

Question #51

The Finance domain trusts the Marketing domain. The Finance domain shares a color laser printer that the CAD users in Marketing need to use from time to time. There is a global group in Marketing called CAD USERS. There is a local group on the print server in Finance called COLOR USERS that has Print permission to the color laser printer. How would you grant the Marketing CAD users permission to the color laser printer? Select the best answer (Microsoft's recommended solution).

A. In the Permissions dialog box for the color laser printer, choose Add and select the Marketing domain from the list of valid domains. Then select CAD USERS from the list of global groups in the Marketing database.

B. Add the CAD USERS global group from Marketing to the COLOR USERS local group on the print server.

C. Create a global group in Finance called MARKETING CAD USERS. Add the CAD USERS global group from Marketing to the MARKETING CAD USERS global group in Finance. Then add the MARKETING CAD USERS global group to the COLOR USERS local group on the print server.

D. You can't do this because the trust is in the wrong direction.

Question #52

There are 300 Windows NT and Windows 95 client computers that print to five printers on a print server. You have received upgraded print drivers for two of the print devices connected to this print server. What must you do to ensure that all clients can continue to access all the print devices?

A. Install the upgraded print drivers on all the client computers that need to use those print devices.
B. Install the upgraded print drivers on all the client computers.
C. Install the upgraded print drivers only on the Windows NT client computers.
D. Do nothing. The print server can download the new drivers to the clients the next time they make a print request.

Question #53

The DLC protocol is used on Windows NT 4.0 computers to:

A. Communicate with HP JetDirect printing devices
B. Communicate with AppleTalk Postscript printing devices
C. Communicate with Novell file servers and client computers
D. Communicate with IBM mainframes and front end processors

Question #54

Which three of the following four features are a part of the Services applet in Control Panel?

A. Running status
B. Load order
C. Hardware profile assignments
D. Startup options

Question #55

There is one high-speed network print device connected to the print server in MIS. MIS Managers and Project Leaders should always be able to print to this printer regardless of who has submitted print jobs. Help Desk staff should be able to print ahead of Developers. What will best accomplish this task?

A. Create three printers, each associated with the device, and assign the appropriate groups access only to their printer. Give the Manager's printer a priority of 1, Help Desk's printer a priority of 50, and Developer's printer a priority of 99.

B. Create three printers, each associated with the device, and assign the appropriate groups access only to their printer. Give the Manager's printer a priority of 99, Help Desk's printer a priority of 50, and Developer's printer a priority of 1.

C. Create three printers, each associated with the device, and assign the appropriate groups access only to their printer. Make the Manager's printer a printer pool by associating it with each print device.

D. Create three printers associated with the device and assign the appropriate groups access only to their printer. Make each printer a printer pool by associating it with each print device.

Question #56

A user is having problems logging on to the network and is seeing a variety of messages. Which of the following things would you check to troubleshoot?

A. The user is entering the correct username and password.

B. The username is case-sensitive.

C. The domain controller is up and accessible.

D. The user's account requires a mandatory profile that is accessible.

Question #57

If the AppleTalk protocol is installed on a Windows NT Server, other Windows NT users on the network can access the server:

A. To create Macintosh Accessible Volumes on Macintosh computers

B. To access Macintosh Accessible Volumes on Macintosh computers

C. To access Macintosh Accessible Volumes on the workstation and share files with Macintosh users

D. As a print server

Question #58

The first four lines of the ______________________ section are critical to finding the cause of the STOP error.

A. BugCheck Information

B. Driver Information

C. Kernel Build Number and Stack Dump

D. Debug Port Information

Question #59

The ABCCorp domain is configured as a Master Domain model. 5,000 user accounts are managed in the ABC-MIS domain in Chicago. Resource domains trust ABC-MIS. At the ABC-WEST resource domain, the print administrator is managing access to her printers by adding the appropriate user accounts from ABC-MIS to the ACL for each of five printers. Access will be managed for 300 users. ABC-WEST is connected to ABC-MIS via a slow WAN link. Every time she accesses the ABC-MIS account domain to display the list of users, the list takes several seconds to generate. The process is taking longer than she thinks it should. What can you suggest to improve performance and minimize network traffic? Choose the best answer.

A. Upgrade the WAN link to a higher speed.

B. Create local groups on the print servers in ABC-WEST and add the users to the local groups. Use the local groups to assign printer permissions.

C. Create global groups in ABC-MIS for the users that need printer access in ABC-WEST. Add the global groups to local groups on the print servers in ABC-WEST, and assign printer permissions to the local groups.

D. There is nothing you can do to improve performance. The same amount of trust traffic is generated whether you use user accounts or group accounts across the trust.

Question #60

The Sales department recently acquired a laser quality printer with an envelope feed that has been installed on their print server called SalesPrint. The sales staff is already a member of the local group SALES on SalesPrint. The print operator shared the printer with the default permission. The sales staff can access the printer, but so can everyone else in the domain. What else must you do to ensure that only sales staff can access the printer?

A. Assign the Sales group print access to the printer.

B. Assign the Sales group print access to the printer, and remove the Everyone group.

C. Do nothing else.

D. Assign the Sales group print access to the printer, and give the Everyone group Read access.

Question #61

Packet routing is managed by which layer?

A. Physical

B. Network

C. Transport

D. Applications

Question #62

If the final print output is corrupted, what print process component should you check?

A. Spooler service on the client computer

B. Spooler service on the print server

C. Print processor on the print server

D. Print monitor on the client computer

Question #63

Name the three main phases of the Setup Wizard.

A. Installing Windows NT Networking

B. Finishing Setup (Time Zone, Display, and final file copy)

C. Setup Options

D. Gathering Information About Your Computer

Question #64

Indicate the utility used from the command prompt to manually maintain an IPX routing table.

A. Route

B. IPXRoute

C. IPConfig

D. PING

Question #65

You suspect that someone is trying to log on to the network unauthorized. What is the best step you can take to increase security and determine who might be doing this?

A. Enable Account Lockout in the Account Policy requiring the Administrator to unlock the account.

B. Enable Account Lockout in the Account Policy requiring the Administrator to unlock the account. Enable auditing of unsuccessful logons and logoffs and monitor these events in the Event Viewer.

C. Advise users to change their passwords more frequently and not to use obvious passwords.

D. Increase the minimum password length in Account Policy.

Question #66

You have created four printers. Each of them will be used by a specific group of users. Name all the steps which are required to successfully make the printer available to the appropriate users.

A. Share each printer.
B. Set the share permissions for each printer so that only the appropriate group has access.
C. Set the printer permissions for each printer so that only the appropriate group has access.
D. Create a printer pool so that each group can access all the print devices.

Question #67

Which of the following parameters can be configured manually with the NWLink protocol?

A. IP address
B. Frame type
C. Subnet mask
D. DHCP scope

Question #68

After monitoring your heavily accessed file and print server, you determine that both the Server>Pool Paged Failures and Server>Pool Nonpaged Failures counters are unusually and consistently higher than normal. The Server service memory property is configured for Balanced memory usage. What should you do to reduce the number of Pool Paged and Pool Nonpaged failures?

A. Add more memory. Balanced is an appropriate setting for a file and print server.
B. Change the Server service memory configuration to Minimize Memory Used.
C. Change the Server service memory configuration to Maximize Throughput for File Sharing.
D. Change the Server service memory configuration to Load Balance Throughput for Virtual Memory.

Question #69

Fred is a member of the Developers group. The Developers group has been given the NTFS permission Full Control to the TOOLS folder. Fred is changing jobs and has been given NO ACCESS to the file DOOM.DOC, which is contained in the TOOLS folder. Later, Fred logs on and deletes the file DOOM.DOC. Luckily, you can restore the file from your tape backup. How can you prevent Fred from deleting the file again, but still maintain the original level of access for him and the Developers group?

A. Fire Fred.

B. Give the Developers group Special Access with all options selected for the TOOLS folder. Then give Fred NO ACCESS to the file.

C. Give the Developers group Change access at the folder level.

D. Give Fred NO ACCESS at the folder level.

Question #70

A print job can be directed directly to a UNIX host print device, and its status checked using which two command-line utilities?

A. LPD and LPR

B. LPD and LPQ

C. LPR and IPCONFIG

D. LPR and LPQ

Question #71

Which of the following sets of usernames and passwords are acceptable for Windows NT?

Username—Password

A. First Ass't Comptroller—FirstComp

B. FirstAsstCompt—1stComp

C. FirstAss*tCompt—COMP1

D. AssComp1—123COMPTROLLER1

Question #72

Which tool(s) can you use to remotely manage file and folder permissions across the domain?

A. User Manager for Domains
B. Server Manager
C. Windows Explorer
D. Network Neighborhood

Question #73

Elaine was the print administrator for the LotsOf Print Corporation, but has left the country to pursue a career as an opera singer. You need to assign a new print administrator. What will you need to do concerning ownership of the LotsOf Print Corporation printers that Elaine created and managed?

A. Do nothing. Printers are not owned by a user; they are owned by the system.
B. Make the new print administrator a Print Operator. The new print administrator can then take ownership of the printers in LotsOf Print Corporation.
C. Give ownership of the printers to the new print administrator.
D. Give the new administrator Full Control permission over the printers. Full Control automatically assigns ownership to that user.

Question #74

When configuring GSNW on Windows NT Server, a group called _________________ must be set up on the Novell Server.

A. NTUserGateway
B. NovellGateway
C. NetBIOSGateway
D. NTGateway

Question #75

Kite Flyers Corporation has experienced tremendous growth and now has between 10,000 and 15,000 employees located across its three global locations: Chicago, London, and Tokyo. Resources are managed in each location as well as the users located in those offices. Which model best suits this organization?

A. Single domain model
B. Master domain model
C. Multiple Master domain model
D. Complete Trust domain model

Question #76

What server administrative tool is used to copy the server tools from the CD-ROM and automatically create a shared folder?

A. Network Server Tools Administrator
B. Network Client Administrator
C. Network Server Tools Manager
D. Network Server Manager

Question #77

What are the differences between a local group and a global group? Choose all that apply.

A. Local groups can be created on workstations, servers, and domain controllers, while global groups can be created and maintained only on a domain controller.
B. Local groups can contain local users, domain users, and global groups, while global groups can contain only users from their domain.
C. Local groups can contain local users, domain users, global groups, and other local groups, while global groups can contain only users from their domain.
D. Local groups can be used for managing resources only on the local computer, while global groups can be used to manage resources on any computer that participates in the domain.

Question #78

Network types can have network numbers or network ranges associated with them. Which type of network can have only one network number associated with it?

A. LocalTalk

B. EtherTalk

C. TokenTalk

D. FDDI

Question #79

You need to be able to remotely manage the account database on two trusted domains. Which steps must take place for this to happen successfully?

A. Do nothing. You can remotely manage accounts through a trust by default.

B. Use User Manager for domains and choose User, Select Domain from the menu to choose the remote domain you want to administer.

C. Make your account a member of the Account Operators group in the trusted domains.

D. Give your user account Full Control access to the SAM hive file in WINNT\SYSTEM32\CONFIG.

Question #80

The manager of the Accounting department wants to make next year's budget templates available for the staff accountants to review beginning next month. Staff accountants are already members of a global group called Accountants in CORPDOMAIN. The templates will be stored on the department resource server called ACCT1 in a folder called BUDGET97 on an NTFS partition. The folder has been shared with the default permission. The global accountants group has been added to a local group called Accountants on ACCT1. You would like everyone to be able to see the files, but only the accounting staff should be able to make changes. What do you need to do?

A. Change the share permission to only Accountants with Change permission.

B. Assign the Accountants group the NTFS permission Change to the BUDGET97 folder.

C. Change the share permission to Everyone with No Access and assign the Accountants group the NTFS permission Change for the BUDGET97 folder.

D. Change the share permission to Everyone with Read and assign the Accountants group the NTFS permission Change for the BUDGET97 folder.

Question #81

Which type of frames are involved in connecting to a shared resource once the session has been established?

A. SMB session frames

B. WINS resolution frames

C. NBT broadcast frames

D. TCP request frames

Question #82

Ned is a member of the Developers group at Springfield Technologies. He has been promoted to team leader for his group. He needs to edit the DOOM.DOC file in the Tools folder, but does not have Write access. What must you do to give Ned access to DOOM.DOC?

A. Do nothing. The next time Ned logs on, his permissions will change.

B. Change the Developers group permission to Change.

C. Add Ned to the Team Leaders group and have him log in again.

D. Change the Team Leaders group permission to Full Control.

Question #83

An IP address consists of what two parts in the order from left to right?

A. A network address and a workstation address

B. A workstation address and a network address

C. A subnet mask address and a default gateway address

D. A default gateway address and a subnet mask address

Question #84

For CrashDumps to be obtained, a pagefile must exist on the

A. System partition

B. Boot partition

C. NTFS partition

D. Data partition

Question #85

The Finance domain trusts the Marketing domain. You would like the administrators of the Marketing domain to be able to administer the servers in the Finance domain. What should you do to facilitate this?

A. Make the Domain Admins group from the Marketing domain a member of the local Administrators group on each server on the Finance domain.

B. Make the Administrators group from the Marketing domain a member of the local Administrators group on each server in the Finance domain.

C. Make the Domain Admins group from each server in the Finance domain a member of the local Administrators group in the Marketing domain.

D. Do nothing. When a trust is established, the Administrators group from the trusted domain is automatically added to the local administrator groups on the servers in the trusting domain.

Question #86

You want to give a particular domain user the ability to back up files on a server, but not be able to restore files. How can you accomplish this?

A. Make the domain user a member of the Backup Operators group on the server.

B. Make the domain user a member of the Server Operators group on the server.

C. Create a new local group called BACKUP ONLY on the server and make the domain user a member of it. Assign this new group to the Backup Files and Directories User Right.

D. Give the user read-only access to all the files.

Question #87

The print device associated with a particular printer has failed. Several print jobs are waiting in queue in that printer. How can you service these print jobs?

A. Connect to another remote printer. Open the printer manager window for the printer and drag the waiting print jobs to the remote printer manager window.

B. Use the Ports tab properties for the printer to add a port for another remote printer. Deselect the current print port associated with the printer and select the remote port. Resume the printer.

C. Do nothing. You must replace the failed print device before printing can resume.

D. Use the Control Panel applet Services to stop the spooler service, configure it to connect to another remote printer, and restart it.

Question #88

Choose three features of Windows NT Server 4.0.

A. Windows 95 Interface

B. Peer Web Services

C. Plug and Play

D. Hardware Profiles

Question #89

Which Process object counter would be useful in determining the amount of memory required by an application?

A. %Application Memory

B. Commit Limit

C. Working Set

D. Avg. Disk sec\Transfer

Question #90

Which of the following hives in HKEY_LOCAL_MACHINE have corresponding directory files in the Windows NT system directory?

A. System

B. Software

C. Hardware

D. Security

Question #91

IEEE 802 standards are compatible with the OSI model

A. TRUE

B. FALSE

Question #92

To install server tools on a Windows 95 platform:

A. Run Setup.bat from the CD-ROM, Clients\Srvtools\Win95 folder.

B. Run Setup.bat from the CD-ROM, Clients\Srvtools\Windows folder.

C. Run Setup.exe from the CD-ROM, Clients\Srvtools\Windows folder.

D. Access Control Panel on the Windows 95 client computer and select the Add/Remove Programs ICON.

Question #93

The Finance domain trusts the Marketing domain. The Marketing domain trusts the Accounting domain. Users in the Accounting domain need to access a database resource in the Finance domain. What needs to happen to facilitate the sharing of that resource?

A. Nothing. Because Finance already trusts Marketing and Marketing already trusts Accounting, Finance can share the database resource directly to Accounting users through the trusts.

B. Create a one-way trust from the Accounting domain to the Finance domain.

C. Create a one-way trust from the Finance domain to the Accounting domain.

D. Create a reverse trust from Accounting to Marketing, and from Marketing to Finance.

Question #94

From the following choices, list the steps required to install a network interface printer using the DLC protocol.

A. Install the DLC protocol on the print server and shut down and restart.

B. Start the Print Wizard, select Add Printer, then select Add Port.

C. Select the Hewlett-Packard Network Port and click the New Port button.

D. Select a MAC address from the available addresses and supply a printer name in the Add Hewlett-Packard Network Peripheral Port dialog box.

Question #95

Which statement best represents Microsoft's recommended group strategy for managing resources effectively?

A. Create a local group in the domain database and add the users from the domain to that local group. Create a local group on the resource computer and make the domain local group a member of the resource local group.

B. Create a global group in the domain database and add the users from the domain to that global group. Create a global group on the resource computer and make the domain global group a member of the resource global group.

C. Create a global group in the domain database and add the users from the domain to that global group. Create a local group on the resource computer and make the domain global group a member of the resource local group.

D. Create a local group on the resource computer and add the domain users directly to the local group.

Question #96

Which of the following steps need to take place before a file session can be established between two computers using the TCP/IP protocol? Choose all that apply.

A. The user must register its name with the WINS server.

B. Name resolution must take place.

C. Address resolution must take place.

D. A TCP Session must be established.

Question #97

Your workstations are members of a domain called Titan. You need to create user accounts so that two shifts of temporary employees can log on to the same computer, but only during their shift.

A. Use User Manager for domains on each local Windows NT Workstation to create the temporary accounts and assign each the appropriate logon hours.

B. Use User Manager on each local Windows NT Workstation to create the temporary accounts and assign each the appropriate logon hours.

C. Use User Manager for domains on the domain controller for Titan to create domain accounts for the temporary employees and assign each the appropriate logon hours.

D. Use User Manager on the domain controller for Titan to create local group accounts for the temporary employees and assign each the appropriate logon hours.

Question #98

Which counter will provide you with the total percent of time spent servicing disk requests for a given partition on a disk?

A. Logical Disk>%Disk Time

B. Logical Disk>Disk Queue Length

C. Physical Disk>%Disk Time

D. Physical Disk>Disk Queue Length

Question #99

Within a single workgroup, there will be a master browser elected for:

A. Each protocol

B. Every 32 computers

C. Every 12 users

D. Only one protocol

Question #100

The person that created DOOM.DOC on server ACCT1 is no longer with the company. Cathy, a member of Team Leaders, will be assuming responsibility for the DOOM project, and needs to become the owner of DOOM.DOC. How can this be accomplished? Choose all that apply.

A. Give Cathy the Take Ownership of Files and Folders User Right on the server ACCT1.

B. Give Cathy the Take Ownership permission on the file DOOM.DOC.

C. Tell Cathy to just take ownership of the file.

D. Give the Team Leaders group the Take Ownership permission for DOOM.DOC.

Question #101

When planning a large wide area network for an enterprise, Microsoft advocates implementing a structure that supports the following characteristics: (Choose all that apply.)

A. Single network logon regardless of location or domain affiliation.

B. Easy user access to network resources regardless of the location of the user or the resource in the enterprise.

C. Decentralized account and resource administration.

D. Synchronization of account and security information across the enterprise.

Question #102

What types of network traffic are associated with the DHCP service?

A. DHCP Address Request

B. DHCP Lease Renewal

C. DHCP Time Out

D. DHCP Replication

Question #103

By default, events are ordered in all event logs?

A. By oldest first

B. By event importance

C. By newest last

D. By newest first

Question #104

A DHCP server eliminates the need to manually configure:

A. A DHCP scope

B. A WINS database

C. An IP address and subnet mask for DHCP clients

D. An IP address and subnet mask for non-DHCP clients

Question #105

Which of the following features is provided by the full version of Network Monitor that comes with Microsoft's System Management Server? Choose all that apply.

A. Direct monitoring of remote computer traffic.

B. Determining which protocol consumed the most bandwidth.

C. Identifying which physical disk has the most I/O activity for a network session.

D. Capturing local network traffic to and from the computer running the utility.

Question #106

You have been asked to implement a backup strategy that backs up all files each Monday to a tape, and then only files that are new or have changed each day since the Monday backup to subsequent tapes on Tuesday through Friday. In addition, on Friday, you must create an archive tape for off-site storage. Which solution will meet this requirement?

A. Perform a normal backup on Monday, then a differential backup Tuesday through Friday. On Friday, perform an additional Copy backup for archival off-site.

B. Perform a normal backup on Monday, then an incremental backup Tuesday through Friday. On Friday, perform an additional Copy backup for archival off-site.

C. Perform a normal backup on Monday and Friday and an incremental backup each day.

D. Perform a normal backup on Monday and Friday and a differential backup each day.

Question #107

On your Windows NT 4.0 development workstation, you have concluded that performance as a whole has decreased. You are not sure which process is driving this, but you have noticed that your disk drive has had a lot more activity lately. What objects should you monitor through Performance Monitor to help you troubleshoot this situation?

A. Check the Processor>%Processor Time counter, determine the percent of disk I/O used for paging through the Memory>Pages/Sec counter and the Logical Disk>Avg. Disk sec/Transfer counter, and the Process>Working Set for every process running.

B. Check the Processor>%Processor Time counter, determine the percent of disk I/O used for paging through the Memory>Pages/Sec counter and the Logical Disk>Avg. Disk sec/Transfer counter. Track the Process>%Processor Time counter for every process running to determine which processes are pushing the processor excessively. Monitor the Process>Working Set counter for these processes in particular.

C. Check the Processor>%Processor Time counter, determine the percent of disk I/O used for paging through the Logical Disk>Disk Queue Length counter, and the Process>Working Set for every process running.

D. Check the Processor>%User Time counter, determine the percent of disk I/O used for paging through the Logical Disk>%Disk Time counter, and the Memory>Commit Limit counter for the pagefile.

Question #108

The CSNW redirector will allow a Windows NT Workstation to communicate with:

A. Novell Servers

B. Windows NT Workstations

C. Macintosh Workstations

D. Novell Clients for client/server applications

Question #109

The TOOLS folder has been shared to the Developers group with Change permission. DOOM is a subdirectory under TOOLS. Team Leaders should have access only to DOOM with Read permissions. What can you do to accomplish this?

A. Add Team Leaders to the TOOLS share with Read permission.

B. Create a new share called DOOM and give Team Leaders Read permission to it.

C. Add Team Leaders to the TOOLS share with Change permission.

D. Add Team Leaders to the TOOLS share with No Access and to the DOOM subdirectory with Read.

Question #110

The KITEMASTERS corporate network consists of 6,000 users located across five regional locations, each on its own subnet. About half the users have Windows NT Workstation 4.0 computers, and the rest have Windows 95 computers. These computers are frequently restarted throughout the day. There is one PDC and BDC located in the MIS department, and a BDC in each regional location. Each location also has one or more Windows NT Server 4.0 computers for resource management.

Using Network Monitor, you have noticed that there is an unusually high percentage of Browser traffic generated throughout the day. How can you optimize traffic associated with the Browser while letting users continue to browse for resources? Choose the best two answers.

A. You cannot configure Browser parameters.

B. Configure the Windows 95 and Windows NT Workstation 4.0 computers to never become browsers.

C. Disable the Server service on user computers which will not be sharing resources in the network.

D. Disable the Computer Browser service on all user computers.

Question #111

What service must be installed on a Windows NT 4.0 Server to allow it to function as an AppleTalk router?

A. RPC

B. GSNW

C. FDDI

D. SFM

Question #112

A broadcast frame:

A. Is always directed to a specific computer by its IP, IPX, or MAC address.

B. Is sent to all hosts on the network via the unique destination address FFFFFFFF.

C. Is sent to a subset of computers on the network depending on how the computer has registered itself on the network.

D. Is a multicast frame that is directed to a specific computer on the network.

Question #113

The permission list defining access to a resource resides:

A. With the resource and is called the Access Control List.

B. With the user and is called the User Rights Policy.

C. With the user and is called the Access Control List.

D. With the resource and is called the User Rights Policy.

Question #114

Several users have called you within the past half-hour to complain that their print jobs are not printing. In fact, they get system messages that tell them that the spooler is not responding. You have verified that the spooler directory partition does not have adequate free space to hold all the print jobs sent to it. What steps should you take to resolve this situation?

A. Use the Control Panel applet Services to more frequently stop and restart the Spooler service to keep the print jobs from becoming fragmented.

B. Change the location of the spool directory to a partition with enough disk space by modifying the HKEY_LOCAL_MACHINE\System\CurrentControlSet\Control\Print\Printers DefaultSpoolDirectory parameter.

C. Change the location of the spool directory to a partition with enough disk space by modifying the HKEY_Current_User\Control\Print\Printers\Spool SpoolDirectory parameter.

D. If the partition is formatted with NTFS, compress the spool directory.

Question #115

If a group of workstations on a network are never to contain any shared resources, how can you optimize these workstations so they will never send host announcements to the master browser?

A. Disable the workstation service

B. Disable the server service

C. Disable the browser service

D. Disable the alerter service

Question #116

Reference to the most recently installed Service pack Symbols files must be listed __________ in the Dumpexam utility command line.

A. Last

B. First after the normal Symbols files reference

C. Second

D. First

Question #117

To provide a greater level of security, you have decided to create an account policy that requires a minimum password length of eight characters, that users change their passwords at least once a month, and does not allow users to use the same password twice in two months. Which Account Policy settings are appropriate?

A. Max Password Age: 60; Min Password Age: 30; Min Password Length: 8; Password Uniqueness: 2

B. Max Password Age: 30; Min Password Age: 30; Min Password Length: 8; Password Uniqueness: 6

C. Max Password Age: 30; Min Password Age: 10; Min Password Length: 8; Password Uniqueness: 6

D. Max Password Age: 60; Min Password Age: 30; Min Password Length: 8; Password Uniqueness: 1

Question #118

Which of the following statements accurately describes NTFS? Choose all that apply.

A. NTFS provides built-in transaction tracking.

B. NTFS supports file compression as a file property.

C. NTFS requires less than 4M of overhead for formatting.

D. NTFS offers file and folder level security.

Question #119

Which objects would be most beneficial to include in a log file when creating a baseline measurement of your system's performance? Choose the best three.

A. Memory

B. TCP/IP

C. Processor

D. Physical and Logical Disk

Question #120

Which Memory object counter would help to identify when to right-size the pagefile?

A. %Pagefile

B. Commit Limit

C. Working Set

D. %Disk Time

Question #121

Why is NetBEUI protocol routing not supported in Windows NT 4.0 installations?

A. Because NetBEUI maintains its own route tables and requires no additional services to handle routing.

B. Because NetBEUI cannot be installed on Windows NT 4.0 Server.

C. Because NetBEUI uses either RIP for IP or RIP for IPX, whichever is installed.

D. Because NetBEUI is not a routable protocol.

Question #122

What types of traffic are associated with the WINS service?

A. WINS Registration

B. WINS Time Out

C. WINS Query Request

D. WINS Address Request

Question #123

Built-in local groups and their members are contained in which accounts database?

A. SAM Accounts Database

B. Local Security Accounts Database

C. SAM Built-In Database

D. Account Synchronization Database

Question #124

Kernel Debugger commands can be entered after a ________________ key sequence is entered.

A. Ctrl+G

B. Ctrl+C

C. Ctrl+K

D. Ctrl+Q

Question #125

You plan to use Performance Monitor to help predict and troubleshoot server activity under various conditions. Which of the following would be the best way to begin?

A. Create and monitor a real-time chart during peak activity and note the percent of processor usage during these periods.

B. Create a series of baseline logs of specific objects (processor, memory, disk and network), each representing a different condition. Use these to predict activity under those conditions and to troubleshoot abnormal system activity.

C. Create a baseline log measuring system activity during periods of average activity. Compare this against real-time charts created during peak activity on the system.

D. Network Monitor would be a better tool to predict system activity.

Question #126

You are using a RISC-based computer as your print server. All your clients are either MS-DOS, Windows for Workgroups, Windows 95, or Windows NT running on Intel-based computers. What must you do to ensure that all your clients can print to the print devices managed by the RISC-based print server?

A. Install both RISC-based and Intel print drivers on the RISC-based print server. Install the appropriate print drivers only on the MS-DOS and Windows for Workgroups computers.

B. Install both RISC-based and Intel print drivers on the RISC-based print server. The client computers will receive the appropriate platform driver from the print server when they make a print request.

C. Install RISC-based print drivers on the RISC-based print server and Intel print drivers on the client computers. Windows NT will do the platform translation.

D. Install the Intel print drivers on the RISC-based print server and RISC-based print drivers on the client computers.

Question #127

Michelle has been selected to assist you as a print administrator in the Dry Gulch office, since you, yourself, are unable to travel there frequently, though you'd really like to. What is the minimum level of access you need to give Michelle so that she can perform basic print management tasks such as creating and sharing printers and managing print jobs?

A. Make Michelle a member of the Print Operators local group on her print server.

B. Make Michelle a member of the Server Operator local group on her print server.

C. Make Michelle a member of the Administrators local group on her print server.

D. Give Michelle Full Control permission for each printer on her print server.

Question #128

One factor that will definitely affect the type of domain model that you implement is:

A. The number of user and group accounts.

B. The physical location and grouping of users.

C. The type of wide area network connections you have in place.

D. The location of network servers.

Question #129

You are analyzing network activity between your network clients and a server. You plan to use Network Monitor to monitor network traffic generated by and received by the server, and Performance Monitor to track system performance relating to network traffic. What types of objects would facilitate your analysis? Choose all that apply.

A. Redirector

B. Server

C. Protocol

D. Frame

Question #130

When a computer registers with a WINS server, how many name registration frames are generated?

A. One name is registered for each computer.

B. A name is registered for the computer and for every service or application that supports the NetBIOS API. One frame registers all these names.

C. A name is registered for the computer and for every service or application that supports the NetBIOS API. One frame is generated for each name that needs to be registered.

D. NetBIOS names are not registered with the WINS server.

Question #131

Protocols are installed by accessing the network icon in the Control Panel and:

A. Selecting the Protocol tab and selecting the Add button.

B. Selecting the Protocol tab and selecting the protocol.

C. Selecting the Protocol tab and choosing all protocols.

D. Selecting the Protocol tab, nothing else has to be selected.

Question #132

Indicate, from the following choices, which routing options are available with a Windows NT 4.0 Server installation.

A. IP Routing

B. IPX Routing

C. DHCP Relay

D. AppleTalk Routing

Question #133

Kite Flyers Corporation consists of 300 employees located in a single office complex. Which domain model would best suit this organization?

A. Single domain model
B. Master domain model
C. Multiple Master domain model
D. Complete Trust domain model

Question #134

Boot.ini contains switches to control which of these properties?

A. operating systems displayed
B. boot drive letter
C. amount of memory used by NT
D. modem settings

Question #135

What server tool is NOT installed on a Windows NT 3.5/3.51 Workstation platform?

A. Services for Macintosh
B. System Policy Editor
C. Remote Access Administrator
D. User Profile Editor

Question #136

The default share name for the server tools share is:

A. SrvTools
B. ClientTools
C. SetupAdm
D. ServerTools

Question #137

The marketing department staff travels a lot and dials in to the company network while visiting client offices to obtain product information. There are several numbers that can be used for dialing in. The marketers do not want to have to take the additional time during their client presentations to configure area code and country code information for each dial-in number. What do you advise?

A. Enable callback security on the RAS server and let the marketer provide the callback number.

B. Have the marketers create a TAPI location before their client call that includes the area code and country code. This location can then be applied to any of the dial-in numbers when Dial-Up networking is loaded.

C. You must change the country and area codes each time you select a dial-in number.

D. Create separate phone book entries for each area code and country code.

Question #138

Which of the following statements best represents Microsoft's groups strategy for the Master Domain model?

A. Create global groups in the resource domains to manage local resources. Create local groups in the account domains to manage users. Add the resource domains' global groups to the account domain's local groups.

B. Create local groups on the resource servers in the resource domains to manage access to resources. Group users into appropriate global groups in the account domain. Add the global groups from the account domain to the local groups in the resource domains.

C. Create local groups on the resource servers in the resource domains to manage access to resources. Create global groups in the resource domains and add to them global users from the account domain. Make the global groups from the resource domain members of the local groups on the resource servers.

D. Create local groups on the resource servers in the resource domains to manage access to resources. Add global users from the account domain to the local resource groups.

Question #139

From the following choices, indicate the step that is NOT required when installing and configuring a printing device using the TCP/IP protocol.

A. Enter the IP address of the remote controller servicing the print device in the Add LPR Compatible Printer dialog box.

B. Enter the name of the remote controller servicing the print device in the Add LPR Compatible Printer dialog box.

C. Enter the IP address of the print device in the Add LPR Compatible Printer dialog box.

D. Enter the IP address of the print server in the Add LPR Compatible Printer dialog box.

Question #140

Which of the following Directory Services goals are met by trust relationships? Select all that apply.

A. Provide users a single logon account that can be used anywhere within the enterprise to log on to the network.

B. Centralize management of accounts and resources.

C. Maintain separate user accounts for resource access on each resource server in the enterprise.

D. Facilitate access to network resources regardless of their domain location.

Question #141

The Finance domain trusts the Marketing domain. What NetLogon function allows a user from the Marketing domain to log on and validate from a computer that participates in the Finance domain?

A. Directory Replication

B. Pass-Through Authentication

C. Trust Validation

D. Access Control Lists

Question #142

Routers work up to the ________________ layer in the OSI Network Model.

A. Physical

B. Data Link

C. Network

D. Transport

Answer Key for Mastery Test

Question #	Correct Answer(s)	Question #	Correct Answer(s)
1	B, C, D	72	C, D
2	C	73	B
3	A, C, D	74	D
4	B	75	C
5	B	76	B
6	C	77	A, B, D
7	C	78	A
8	A	79	B, C
9	B	80	A, B
10	C	81	A
11	C	82	C
12	B	83	A
13	B, D	84	B
14	C	85	A
15	B	86	C
16	B	87	B
17	A	88	A, D
18	B	89	C
19	C	90	A, B, D
20	A, B, C	91	A

Question #	Correct Answer(s)	Question #	Correct Answer(s)
21	B	92	D
22	C	93	C
23	A, B	94	A, B, C, D
24	A, C, D	95	C
25	C	96	B, C, D
26	B	97	C
27	B, C	98	A
28	D	99	A
29	C	100	A, B, D
30	A	101	A, B, D
31	B, D	102	A, B
32	B	103	D
33	B, C	104	C
34	B	105	A, B, D
35	A, C, D	106	B
36	A	107	B
37	A, C	108	A
38	A, B, C, D	109	B
39	C	110	B, C
40	A	111	D
41	A, C	112	B
42	A	113	A
43	A	114	B
44	C	115	B
45	C	116	D
46	B	117	C
47	A, B, D	118	A, B, D
48	D	119	A, C, D
49	A, D	120	B
50	C	121	D

continues

continued

Question #	Correct Answer(s)	Question #	Correct Answer(s)
51	B	122	A, D
52	D	123	C
53	A, D	124	B
54	A, C, D	125	B
55	B	126	A
56	A, C, D	127	A
57	D	128	A
58	A	129	A, B, C
59	C	130	C
60	B	131	A
61	B	132	A, B, C, D
62	C	133	A
63	A, B, D	134	A, B, C
64	B	135	B
65	B	136	C
66	A, C	137	B
67	B	138	B
68	C	139	D
69	B	140	A,B,D
70	D	141	B
71	B	142	C

Using the Self-Test Software

The tests on this CD-ROM consist of performance-based questions. This means that rather than asking you what function an item would fulfill (knowledge-based question), you will be presented with a situation and asked for an answer that shows your capability of solving the problem.

Using the Self-Test Software

The program consists of three main test structures:

- *Self-Assessment Test* This would typically be the test you take first. This test is meant to give you a sense of where your strengths and weaknesses are regarding Windows NT Server 4.0. You will get immediate feedback on your answer. It will either be correct and you will be able to go to next question, or it will be incorrect and the system will recommend what part of the study guide to research and you will be prompted to try again.

- *Chapter-End Test* After reading a chapter from the study guide, you will have the option to take a mini-test consisting of questions relevant only to the given chapter. You will get immediate feedback on your answer, as well as an indication of what subsection to find the answer should your response be incorrect.
- *Mastery Test* This is the big one. This test is different from the two others in the sense that feedback is not given on a question-by-question basis. It simulates the exam situation, so you will give answers to all questions and then get your overall score. In addition to the score, for all wrong answers you will get pointers as to where in the study guide you need to study further. You will also be able to print a report card featuring your test results.

All test questions are of the multiple choice type offering four possible answers. The answers are all labeled A, B, C, and D. There will always be either one or two alternatives representing the right answer; thus, a right answer might be "A and D" or any other combination.

Equipment Requirements

To run the self-test software, you must have *at least* the following equipment:

- IBM compatible PC I386
- Microsoft DOS 5.0
- Microsoft Windows 3.x
- 4M of RAM
- 256-color display adapter
- Double-speed CD-ROM drive

To take full advantage of the software and run it at a more acceptable speed, however, the following equipment is recommended:

- IBM Compatible I486 DX
- Microsoft Windows 3.1 or better
- 8M of RAM
- 256-color display adapter or better
- Quad speed CD-ROM drive

Running the Self-Test Software

The self-test software runs directly from the CD-ROM, and does not require you to install any files to your hard drive. After you have followed these simple start-up steps, you will find the software very intuitive and self-explanatory.

If you are using Windows 3.x, Windows NT 3.x, or Windows for Workgroups:

1. Insert the disk in your CD-ROM drive.
2. Select Run from the File menu of your Windows Program Manager, click Browse, and select the letter of your CD-ROM drive (typically D).
3. Double-click the file name dtique95.exe and the self-test program will be activated.

If you are using Windows 95 or Windows NT 4.0:

1. Insert the disk in your CD-ROM drive.
2. Click the Start button on the Windows taskbar, select Run, and click Browse. Select My Computer and double-click dtique95.exe.

As soon as dtique95 executes, you will be in the program and will just have to follow instructions or click your selections.

TechNet Sampler

What's on the TechNet Sampler CD-ROM?

The CD-ROM accompanying this book contains the Microsoft TechNet Sampler, the February 1997 edition, for a 30-day free trial.

TechNet is a CD-ROM-based document storage and retrieval system designed to provide the latest information on Microsoft's many software products. In addition to information about Microsoft's software, Microsoft also fills TechNet with practical planning and implementation suggestions for use of their products. These real-world case studies and architecture examples are a wealth of information for systems engineers, systems administrators, applications developers, and other serious professionals using Microsoft products.

Note Microsoft estimates that each update to TechNet contains over 60,000 new articles, building the database to an estimated total of 100,000 articles.

TechNet provides the latest Resource Kits, technical integration information, third-party tools, utilities, and training materials designed to help you build your business (see Figure L.1).

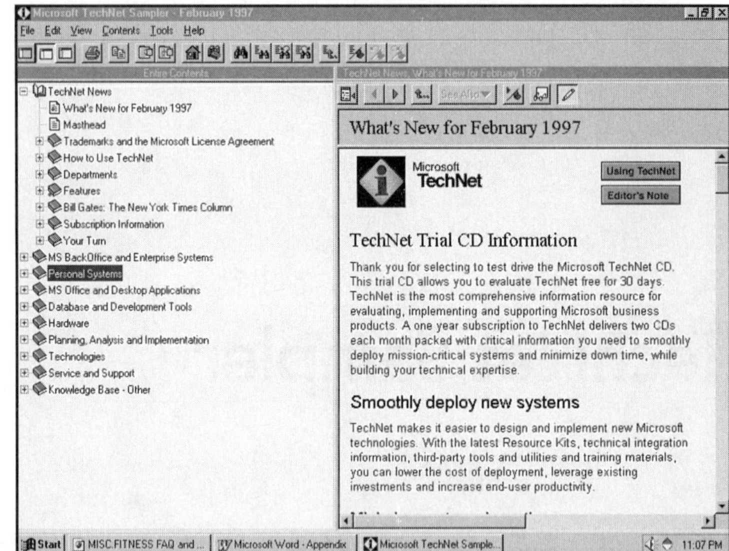

FIG. L.1 ⇒ The TechNet user interface.

The TechNet CD ROM contains ten major product databases to help you organize your search:

- TechNet News
- MS BackOffice and Enterprise Systems
- Personal Systems
- MS Office and Desktop Applications
- Database Development Tools
- Hardware
- Planning, Analysis, and Implemenation
- Technologies
- Service and Support
- Microsoft Knowledge Base

TechNet News

TechNet News provides information about the current version of TechNet you are using, as well as any features about the TechNet subscription itself. The articles cover the latest in Microsoft's innovations in computer software as well as a variety of articles on Bill Gates and Microsoft's market presence.

MS BackOffice and Enterprise Systems

The MS BackOffice and Enterprise Systems articles contain key information on *Microsoft's BackOffice, Windows NT Workstation,* and *Microsoft LAN Manager* products. To ease the integration and implementation of MS BackOffice products, also included is the Microsoft Windows NT Server Resource Kit, system implementation tools and utilities, and the Microsoft Consulting Technical Notes.

Personal Systems

Articles in the Personal Systems database deal with topics important to users and supporters of *Microsoft Windows 95, Internet Explorer, MS-DOS,* and the *Windows 3.x* family of operating systems. This includes the Windows 95 Resource Kit, a variety of Microsoft tools and utilities, and Microsoft Technical Notes on many of the features of Windows personal operating systems.

MS Office and Desktop Applications

This library contains important information on *Microsoft Office, Microsoft FrontPage, Microsoft Project, Microsoft Team Manager* and *Microsoft Works.* Additionally, patches, utilities, implementation suggestions, and case studies of real-world uses can be found here.

Database and Development Tools

Articles in the Database and Development Tools database provide valuable information for users of *Internet Studio, Visual Basic, FoxPro,* and *SourceSafe.* Important, time-saving articles can be found under Tips and Techniques, Technical Notes, and Tools and Utilities. For serious users of these applications, this CD-ROM database provides crucial updates and development code that makes programming professional applications easier.

Hardware

The Hardware database contains general articles on hardware implementation and configuration issues such as ISDN and other add-on hardware. Additionally, updated configuration information and replacement drivers can be found here for most Microsoft-compatible hardware. Look here for hardware driver updates, new drivers for newly manufactured hardware, and the latest software drivers for new technologies for the PC.

Planning, Analysis, and Implementation

The Planning, Analysis, and Implementation library contains literally hundreds of articles on getting set up with Microsoft products for business success. Discussions on client/server setup and methodologies, integrating current and new technologies, and software development suggestions are all examples of the articles in this database.

Technologies

Articles in the Technologies database include a complete update on the latest in Microsoft protocol and API innovations. Covering MAPI, TAPI, WOSA, and ODBC, and more, this database will appeal to serious applications developers looking to solve real-world problems. For instance, there is a complete tutorial here on interfacing your current business e-mail applications with software you develop using the MAPI e-mail interface API. Additionally, this section contains a complete tutorial to the new CryptoAPI including discussions of key generation and digital signatures.

Service and Support

The Service and Support articles contain valuable information on where to look for more personalized information, putting you in touch with hundreds of Microsoft solutions providers. The database includes InfoSource, a listing of Microsoft third-party product and partner information sources, and the Microsoft Solutions Provider Directory containing the addresses of thousands of independent Microsoft Certified Professionals.

Microsoft Knowledge Base

The Microsoft Knowledge Base (KB) is probably the second most valuable part of the TechEd CD-ROM, second only to the Resource Kits. The KB contains thousands of trouble resolution solutions already fielded and documented by Microsoft engineers. Problems that others have already encountered are documented, resolved, and provided to you in a CD-ROM format for easy browsing and retrieval. Additionally, Microsoft has included the software patches and utilities necessary to resolve the problems encountered.

Installing the TechNet Sampler CD-ROM

Microsoft TechNet is preconfigured for installation on Windows 95 and Windows NT on the CD-ROM that accompanies this book. To run the CD-ROM, you need Microsoft Windows 95 or later or Windows NT operating system and at least 4M of system RAM. Additionally, you will need at least 20M of hard drive space free to effectively use this application.

To install Microsoft TechEd on your computer, insert the CD-ROM into your CD-ROM drive. If you're installing for Windows 95, continue with the following section; if you're installing for Windows NT, please skip to the section titled "Installing TechNet on Windows NT."

Installing TechNet on Windows 95

After you insert the Microsoft TechNet Sampler CD-ROM into the CD-ROM drive on your computer and close the drive door, Windows 95 recognizes the disc. The Microsoft TechNet AutoPlay dialog box appears and prompts you to continue by selecting the setup for Microsoft TechNet Sampler and then clicking the TechNet button on the left side of the dialog box. This begins the installation process on your computer. Follow the dialog boxes through the installation process.

Note When installing TechNet on a Pentium workstation, you should install the "minimum" option in the installation dialog box since there is little decline in performance between the maximum and minimum options.

You may also use the Add/Remove Programs option in the Control Panel to install the TechNet Sampler on your Windows 95 computer.

App L

Installing TechNet on Windows NT

Windows NT will recognize the AutoStart feature of this CD-ROM. Insert the CD-ROM into the CD-ROM drive and AutoStart will check for a previous installation of the TechNet product and then offer you installation options. Alternatively, you may install TechNet on your Windows NT system by using the Add/Remove Programs option in the Control Panel.

Getting Started

Microsoft TechNet is designed to provide for rapid extraction of technical information with limited user interaction. It also is designed to allow for easy browsing in a familiar way, similar to the way in which most readers browse books and technical journals.

Navigating through the vast amounts of information provided with TechNet is simple and easy once you become familiar with its format. The following sections provide helpful information for searching the various databases.

Searching the TechNet Database

While it is easy to browse through TechNet to retrieve relevant information, it often is more time-efficient to search directly for the subject matter for which you are looking. Searching is one of the more advanced features of Microsoft TechNet.

Keyword Searches

You can accomplish simple searches for key terms of importance by using the keyword search feature of Microsoft TechNet. To access this feature, select Query from the Tools drop-down menu, or press Ctrl+F. When you do, the Query dialog box appears.

To limit the scope of your query, select any of the option buttons in the Query dialog box (see Figure L.2). The Scope of Search option determines the total number of databases in which the search query term will be searched.

Figure L.2, for example, demonstrates the use of the simple Query dialog box to locate the search term "MCSE." You can search the entirety of the TechNet database by selecting the "Entire Contents" option button or you can limit your search to a specific database topic by selecting the Subset of

Contents option button. After you enter the topic you want to search, click the Run Query button to begin the search.

Tip

Search query terms can be full words or partial words. To include the words *certified*, *certification*, and *certificate* in your query, for example, you would simply need to type the word piece `certifi` in the Query dialog box. Also, note that the query string is not case-sensitive. Any string of characters will be revealed regardless of their case status.

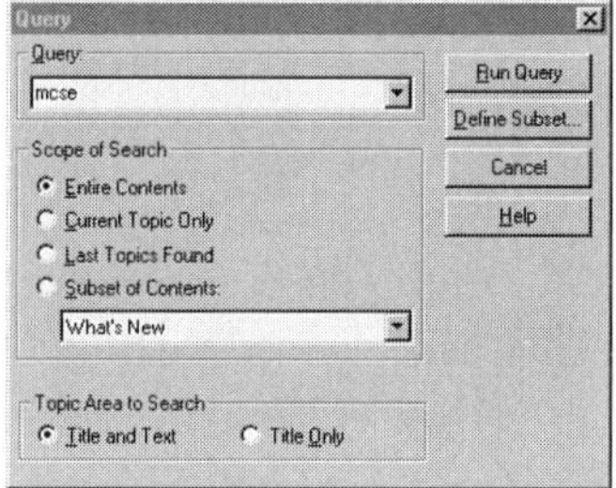

FIG. L.2 ⇒ The TechNet Query dialog box.

Query results appear in the Query Results dialog box (see Figure L.3). After you select the article you want to view, click the Display button, or press Alt+D, to display the article for viewing.

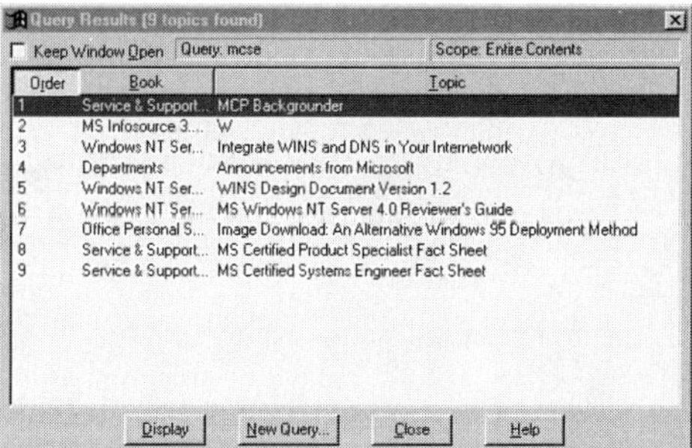

FIG. L.3 ⇒ The TechNet Query Results dialog box.

Complex Boolean Searches

Boolean operators, such as AND, OR, and NOT, add to the versatility of your queries. Boolean logic enables a query to pull articles from TechNet that match only the specific requirements of the logical query. The following examples clarify this concept:

The *AND* Operator

The `AND` operator works by combining the key terms you enter and displaying only those articles that contain *both* terms. The following query, for example, results in articles containing both "MCSE" and "certification."

```
MCSE AND certification
```

Note that both terms must be present in an article for it to be selected and appear in the Query Results dialog box as a result of your query.

The *OR* Operator

The `OR` operator works by including any article that contains any of the terms linked together by the `OR` operator, as in the following example:

```
MCSE OR certified OR certification
```

This query results in articles that contain any of the preceding query terms.

In the preceding example, because the `OR` operator is exclusive, only articles with the words "certified" and "certification" will be retrieved. If you want to lessen the exclusive search for those terms, use fewer letters in your search term. For instance, in order to find MCSE or any topic containing the words which start with certif-, use the following query:

```
MCSE or certif
```

This query returns articles with either the word MCSE or words such as certification, certify, certificate, or any others containing the letter sequence `certif`.

The *NOT* Operator

The `NOT` operator is a powerful method for excluding articles that you know you will not be interested in. Following is a simple example of this technique:

```
certifi NOT certificate
```

The preceding query results in all articles with any word starting with `certifi`, but would not return articles that contained the word `certificate`.

Complex Proximity Searches

Proximity searches find articles that contain word relationships. For instance, let us say you are looking for two words of importance and you want them to be discussed in relation to each other. Your search would need to be honed to identify articles where both words were in the same paragraph.

The *NEAR* Operator

The use of `NEAR` can help to limit your search to only those articles that have relevance to the topic for which you are searching. The term MCSE, for example, can apply to many Microsoft TechNet topics. Assume, however, that you want only those articles that contain MCSE and the word "exam" in the same paragraph. By typing the query as the following

```
MCSE NEAR exam
```

your search results will contain only those articles containing MCSE within the same paragraph as the word "exam." You will save yourself considerable time working with the `NEAR` operator feature.

Customizing Information

While TechNet is comprehensive, it does not provide for customized information relevant only to you. Adding this personal information to your Microsoft TechNet database, as you discover it, is one of the powerful features of TechNet.

To create personalized bookmarks on any TechNet screen, select Bookmarks from the Edit drop-down menu, or press Ctrl+Shift+B. This will mark your location for easy retrieval and reference later on when you have moved on to another page or topic. The Bookmarks feature allows you to later return to the exact same spot in your text as you left off (see Figure L.4).

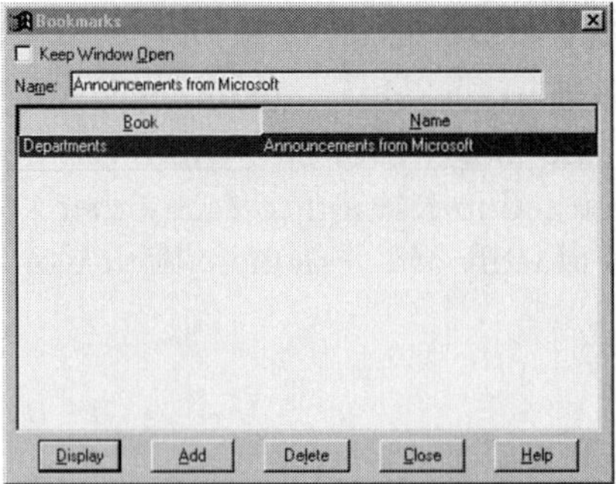

FIG. L.4 ⇒
The TechNet Bookmark dialog box.

You can also add personalized notes to the TechNet database. To add notes, simply select Annotation from the View drop-down menu, or press Ctrl+Shift+A. These notes will remain with the text of the database and will reappear anytime you retrieve the database article.

Index

Symbols

A

B

D

E

F

G

H

I

J-K

L

M

N

P

Q-R

U

X-Z

Complete and Return This Card for a *FREE* Computer Book Catalog

Thank you for purchasing this book! You have purchased a superior computer book written expressly for your needs. To continue to provide the kind of up-to-date, pertinent coverage you've come to expect from us, we need to hear from you. Please take a minute to complete and return this self-addressed, postage-paid form. In return, we'll send you a free catalog of all our computer books on topics ranging from word processing to programming and the Internet.

Mr. ☐ Mrs. ☐ Ms. ☐ Dr. ☐

Name (first) ☐☐☐☐☐☐☐☐☐☐☐ (M.I.) ☐ (last) ☐☐☐☐☐☐☐☐☐☐☐☐☐☐☐

Address ☐☐☐☐☐☐☐☐☐☐☐☐☐☐☐☐☐☐☐☐☐☐☐☐☐☐☐☐☐☐☐☐☐☐☐

☐☐☐☐☐☐☐☐☐☐☐☐☐☐☐☐☐☐☐☐☐☐☐☐☐☐☐☐☐☐☐☐☐☐☐

City ☐☐☐☐☐☐☐☐☐☐☐☐☐☐☐ State ☐☐ Zip ☐☐☐☐☐ ☐☐☐☐

Phone ☐☐☐ ☐☐☐ ☐☐☐☐ Fax ☐☐☐ ☐☐☐ ☐☐☐☐

Company Name ☐☐☐☐☐☐☐☐☐☐☐☐☐☐☐☐☐☐☐☐☐☐☐☐☐☐☐☐☐☐☐☐☐

E-mail address ☐☐☐☐☐☐☐☐☐☐☐☐☐☐☐☐☐☐☐☐☐☐☐☐☐☐☐☐☐☐☐☐☐

1. Please check at least three (3) influencing factors for purchasing this book.

Front or back cover information on book .... ☐
Special approach to the content .... ☐
Completeness of content.. ☐
Author's reputation .... ☐
Publisher's reputation .... ☐
Book cover design or layout .... ☐
Index or table of contents of book .... ☐
Price of book.. ☐
Special effects, graphics, illustrations .... ☐
Other (Please specify): ______________________________ ☐

2. How did you first learn about this book?

Saw in Macmillan Computer Publishing catalog .... ☐
Recommended by store personnel .... ☐
Saw the book on bookshelf at store .... ☐
Recommended by a friend .... ☐
Received advertisement in the mail .... ☐
Saw an advertisement in: ____________________________ ☐
Read book review in: ________________________________ ☐
Other (Please specify): ______________________________ ☐

3. How many computer books have you purchased in the last six months?

This book only .... ☐ 3 to 5 books .... ☐
2 books.................. ☐ More than 5 .... ☐

4. Where did you purchase this book?

Bookstore .... ☐
Computer Store .... ☐
Consumer Electronics Store .... ☐
Department Store .... ☐
Office Club .... ☐
Warehouse Club... ☐
Mail Order .... ☐
Direct from Publisher .... ☐
Internet site .... ☐
Other (Please specify): ______________________________ ☐

5. How long have you been using a computer?

☐ Less than 6 months ☐ 6 months to a year
☐ 1 to 3 years ☐ More than 3 years

6. What is your level of experience with personal computers and with the subject of this book?

	With PCs	With subject of book
New	☐	☐
Casual	☐	☐
Accomplished	☐	☐
Expert	☐	☐

Source Code ISBN: 0-7897-0990-2

7. Which of the following best describes your job title?

- Administrative Assistant ☐
- Coordinator ☐
- Manager/Supervisor ☐
- Director ☐
- Vice President ☐
- President/CEO/COO ☐
- Lawyer/Doctor/Medical Professional ☐
- Teacher/Educator/Trainer ☐
- Engineer/Technician ☐
- Consultant ☐
- Not employed/Student/Retired ☐
- Other (Please specify): ________________ ☐

8. Which of the following best describes the area of the company your job title falls under?

- Accounting ☐
- Engineering ☐
- Manufacturing ☐
- Operations ☐
- Marketing ☐
- Sales ☐
- Other (Please specify): ________________ ☐

9. What is your age?

- Under 20 ☐
- 21-29 ☐
- 30-39 ☐
- 40-49 ☐
- 50-59 ☐
- 60-over ☐

10. Are you:

- Male ☐
- Female ☐

11. Which computer publications do you read regularly? (Please list)

____

***Comments*:** ________________________________

Fold here and scotch-tape to mail.

NO POSTAGE NECESSARY IF MAILED IN THE UNITED STATES

BUSINESS REPLY MAIL

FIRST-CLASS MAIL PERMIT NO. 9918 INDIANAPOLIS IN

POSTAGE WILL BE PAID BY THE ADDRESSEE

ATTN MARKETING
MACMILLAN COMPUTER PUBLISHING
MACMILLAN PUBLISHING USA
201 W 103RD ST
INDIANAPOLIS IN 46290-9042

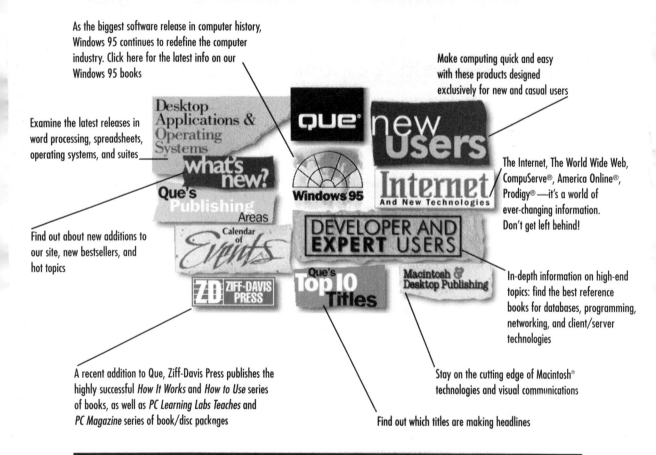

Before using any of the software on these discs, you need to install the software you plan to use. See Appendixes K and L, "Using the Self-Test Software" and "TechNet Sampler," for directions. If you have problems with these CD-ROMs, please contact Macmillan Technical Support at (317) 581-3833. We can be reached by e-mail at **support@mcp.com**.

Read This Before Opening Software

By opening this package, you are agreeing to be bound by the following:

This software is copyrighted and all rights are reserved by the publisher and its licensers. You are licensed to use this software on a single computer. You may copy the software for backup or archival purposes only. Making copies of the software for any other purpose is a violation of United States copyright laws. THIS SOFTWARE IS SOLD AS IS, WITHOUT WARRANTY OF ANY KIND, EITHER EXPRESSED OR IMPLIED, INCLUDING BUT NOT LIMITED TO THE IMPLIED WARRANTIES OF MERCHANTABILITY AND FITNESS FOR A PARTICULAR PURPOSE. Neither the publisher nor its dealers and distributors nor its licensers assume any liability for any alleged or actual damages arising from the use of this software. (Some states do not allow exclusion of implied warranties, so the exclusion may not apply to you.)

The entire contents of these discs and the compilation of the software are copyrighted and protected by United States copyright laws. The individual programs on the discs are copyrighted by the authors or owners of each program. Each program has its own use permissions and limitations. To use each program, you must follow the individual requirements and restrictions detailed for each. Do not use a program if you do not agree to follow its licensing agreement.

Exam Objective	Chapter	Chapter Topic Heading
Planning		
Planning the implementation of a directory services architecture, considering appropriate domain models, single logon access, and resource access across domains.	2, 3, 4, 5, 6	2 - Entire chapter 3 - Entire chapter 4 - Entire chapter 5 - Entire chapter 6 - Entire chapter
Configuring disk drives for various requirements, such as fault tolerance.	9	9 - Entire chapter
Installing and configuring protocols as appropriate for the domain, including TCP/IP, DHCP, WINS, NWLINK, DLC, and AppleTalk.	8, 16, 17	8 - Understanding Windows NT Protocol Choices and Configuration Options 17 - Windows NT 4.0 and Multiprotocol Routing - TCP/IP Routing - DHCP Relay - RIP for NWLink IPX Routing - AppleTalk Routing
Installation and Configuration		
Choosing and installing the appropriate server role for Windows NT Server 4.0; in other words, primary or secondary domain controller and member server.	5, 6	5 - Planning Effective WAN Performance - Planning the Size of the Directory Services Database - Planning the Type and Quantity of Enterprise Domain Controllers 6 - Entire chapter
Configuring and binding protocols.	8	8 - Entire chapter
Configuring hard disks to provide redundancy, fault tolerance, and improved performance.	9	9 - Entire chapter
Creating, adding, and configuring printers, including setting up printer pools and setting printer priorities.	10	10 - Entire chapter
Configuring Windows NT Server 4.0 for client support such as Windows NT Workstation, Windows 95, and Macintosh.	11	11 - Entire chapter
Configuring core services such as Directory Replicator and Computer Browser.	8	8 - Entire chapter
Managing Resources		
Managing user and group accounts including user rights, account policies, and auditing changes to the account database.	3, 12	3 - Managing Users and Groups Across Trusts 12 - Entire chapter, - Creating and Managing Account Policies, System Rights, and Auditing
Creating and managing policies and profiles for local and roaming users, as well as system policies.	14	14 - Entire chapter
Remotely administering servers from Windows 95 and Windows NT Workstation clients.	7, 12, 13, 15	7 - Accessing the Registry Remotely 12 - Remote Account Management Tips 13 - Managing Shares and Permissions Remotely 15 - Entire chapter
Managing disk resources through sharing, permissions, file and folder security, and auditing.	13	13 - Entire chapter

201 W. 103rd Street, Indianapolis, IN 46290 (317) 581-3500

Exam Objective	Chapter	Chapter Topic Heading
Connectivity		
Configuring interoperability among Windows NT Server and Novell NetWare servers through Gateway Services and Migration Tool.	16	16 - Entire chapter
Installing and configuring multiprotocol routing for the Internet, the BOOTP/DHCP Relay Agent, and IPX.	8, 17	8 - Protocol Choices and Configuration 17 - Entire chapter
Installing and configuring Internet Information Server and other Internet services, including Web services, DNS, and intranet.	18	18 - Entire chapter
Installing and configuring Remote Access Service, including implementing communications access, protocols, and security.	19	19 - Entire chapter
Monitoring and Optimization		
Implementing and using Performance Monitor to measure system performance through the use of baseline measurement, object tracking (processor, memory, disk, and network).	20	20 - Entire chapter
Implementing and using Network Monitor to monitor network traffic through data collection, analysis, and filtering.	21	21 - Entire chapter
Identifying performance bottlenecks.	20, 21	20 - Entire chapter 21 - Entire chapter
Optimizing server performance to achieve specific results such as controlling network traffic and server load balancing.	20, 21	20 - Summarizing Performance Monitoring and Optimization 21 - Exploring Browser Traffic, Analyzing Traffic between Domain Controllers (Database Synchronization, Trusts, Directory Replication), and Summarizing and Planning Network Traffic
Troubleshooting		
Choosing the appropriate course of action to take to resolve installation failures.	6	6 - Entire chapter
Choosing the appropriate course of action to take to resolve boot failures.	7, 22	7 - Troubleshooting the Boot Process - STOP Messages Only During Windows NT Boot 22 - Reboot the Target Computer
Choosing the appropriate course of action to resolve configuration errors such as backing up and restoring the Windows NT Registry and editing the Registry.	7	7 - Troubleshooting the Boot Process, Other Troubleshooting Tips, What Is the Last Known Good Control Set
Choosing the appropriate course of action to resolve printing problems.	10	10 - Troubleshooting Printing
Choosing the appropriate course of action to resolve RAS problems.	19	19 - Troubleshooting RAS
Choosing the appropriate course of action to resolve connectivity problems.	11	11 - Troubleshooting
Choose the appropriate course of action to resolve resource access and permission problems.	13	13 - Troubleshooting Security
Choose the appropriate course of action to resolve fault-tolerance failures, such as backup, mirroring, and striping with parity.	9	9 -Troubleshooting
Diagnosing and interpreting blue screen problems, configuring a memory dump, and using Event Viewer (Event Log service.)	22	22 - Windows NT Kernel Messages - STOP Error Screen Layout and Section Meanings - Kernel Debugger Sessions - CrashDumps (Memory Dumps) - Remote Troubleshooting - Events and Event Log Viewer

Productivity Point International Training Centers

Call 1 (800) 848-0980 or go to **http://www.propoint.com/que** for class schedules and registration information.

United States Locations

Arizona
Phoenix

California
Culver City
Fresno
San Diego
San Francisco
Santa Clara

Colorado
Denver

Florida
Boca Raton
Fort Lauderdale
Jacksonville
Maitland
Miami
Tallahassee
Tampa

Georgia
Atlanta

Illinois
Chicago
Deerfield
Hinsdale
Naperville
Rolling Meadows

Indiana
Indianapolis
Mishawaka

Iowa
Cedar Rapids
West Des Moines

Kansas
Overland Park

Kentucky
Florence
Louisville

Louisiana
Baton Rouge
Lafayette
New Orleans

Maine
Portland

Massachusetts
Boston
Marlboro
Newton Lower Falls

Michigan
Ann Arbor
Grand Rapids
Holland
Troy

Minnesota
Bloomington
Minneapolis

Missouri
St. Louis

Nevada
Las Vegas
Reno

New Hampshire
Bedford

New Jersey
Iselin
Mt. Laurel
Parsippany

New York
Melville
New York
Rochester

North Carolina
Durham
Greensboro
Raleigh

Ohio
Cincinnati
Dayton
Dublin
Maumee

Oklahoma
Oklahoma City

Oregon
Portland

Pennsylvania
Allentown
Blue Bell
Camp Hill

Philadelphia
Pittsburgh

Tennessee
Brentwood
Memphis

Texas
Austin
Dallas
Fort Worth
Houston
San Antonio

Utah
Murray
Salt Lake City

Virginia
Alexandria
Glen Allen
Richmond

Washington
Bellevue
Spokane

Washington D.C.

West Virginia
Charleston

Wisconsin
Green Bay
Neenah
Stevens Point
Wausau

Caribbean Locations

Puerto Rico
Hato Rey

Canadian Locations

Alberta
Calgary

British Columbia
Vancouver

Manitoba
Brandon
Thompson
Winnipeg

Ontario
Etobicoke
Hamilton
Kenora
Kitchener
London
Niagara
North Bay
Ottawa
Sarnia
Scarborough
Sudbury
Toronto

Quebec
Montreal

Saskatchewan
Regina
Saskatoon

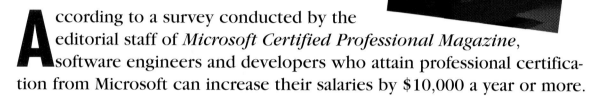

MCPS and MCSD Certification Requirements

The following exams are currently available for Microsoft Certified Product Specialist and Microsoft Certified Solution Developer certification tracks. For complete details, visit Microsoft's Training and Certification Web site at **http://www.microsoft.com/train_cert/**.

Test #	Exam Name	MCPS[1]	MCSD[2]
70-30	Microsoft Windows 3.1	C	
70-42	Implementing and Supporting Microsoft Windows NT Workstation 3.51	C	
70-43	Implementing and Supporting Microsoft Windows NT Server 3.51	C	
70-48	Microsoft Windows for Workgroups 3.11	C	
70-63	Implementing and Supporting Microsoft Windows 95	C	
70-67	Implementing and Supporting Microsoft Windows NT Server 4.0	C	
70-73	Implementing and Supporting Microsoft Windows NT Workstation 4.0	C	
70-150	Microsoft Windows Operating Systems and Services Architecture I	C	C
70-151	Microsoft Windows Operating Systems and Services Architecture II	C	C
70-38	Microsoft Project 4.0 for Windows	E	
70-39	Microsoft Excel 5.0 for Windows	E	
70-49	Microsoft Word 6.0 for Windows	E	
70-66	Microsoft Word for Windows 95	E	
70-21	Microsoft SQL Server 4.2 Database Implementation	E	
70-24	Developing Applications with C++ Using the Microsoft Foundation Class Library		
70-25	Implementing OLE in Microsoft Foundation Class Applications		E
70-27	Implementing a Database Design on Microsoft SQL Server 6.0		E
70-50	Microsoft Visual Basic 3.0 for Windows—Application Development		E
70-51	Microsoft Access 2.0 for Windows—Application Development		E
70-52	Developing Applications with Microsoft Excel 5.0 Using Visual Basic for Applications		E
70-54	Programming in Microsoft Visual FoxPro 3.0 for Windows		E
70-65	Programming with Microsoft Visual Basic 4.0		E
70-69	Microsoft Access for Windows 95 and the Microsoft Access Developer's Toolkit		E

[1]Microsoft Certified Product Specialist (MCPS)

Requires one operating system exam. Additional product specialties listed are electives.

[2]Microsoft Certified Solution Developer (MCSD)

Requires two core technology exams and two elective exams.

C = core *E = elective*

See other side for Microsoft Certified Systems Engineer requirements.

201 W. 103rd Street, Indianapolis, IN 46290 (317) 581-3500

MCSE Certification Requirements

The following exams are currently available for Microsoft Certified Systems Engineer certification tracks. For complete details, visit Microsoft's Training and Certification Web site at **http://www.microsoft.com/train_cert/**.

		MCSE[1]		NT 3.5 to NT
Test #	Exam Name	3.51 Track	4.0 Track	4.0 Migration Path[2]
70-42	Implementing and Supporting Microsoft Windows NT Workstation 3.51	C		
70-43	Implementing and Supporting Microsoft Windows NT Server 3.51	C		
70-30	Microsoft Windows 3.1	C	C	
70-46	Networking with Microsoft Windows for Workgroups 3.11	C	C	
70-47	Networking with Microsoft Windows 3.1	C	C	
70-58	Networking Essentials	C	C	
70-63	Implementing and Supporting Microsoft Windows 95	C	C	
70-48	Microsoft Windows for Workgroups 3.11		C	
70-73	Implementing and Supporting Microsoft Windows NT Workstation 4.0		C	
70-67	Implementing and Supporting Microsoft Windows NT Server 4.0		C	C
70-68	Implementing and Supporting Microsoft Windows NT Server 4.0 in the Enterprise		C	C
70-12	Microsoft SNA Server	E	E	
70-14	Implementing and Supporting Microsoft Systems Management Server	E	E	
70-21	Microsoft SQL Server 4.2 Database Implementation	E	E	
70-22	Microsoft SQL Server 4.2 Database Administration for Microsoft Windows NT	E	E	
70-26	System Administration of Microsoft SQL Server 6.0	E	E	
70-27	Implementing a Database Design on Microsoft SQL Server 6.0	E	E	
70-37	Microsoft Mail 3.2 for PC Networks—Enterprise	E	E	
70-53	Internetworking Microsoft TCP/IP on Microsoft Windows NT 3.5	E	E	
70-59	Internetworking Microsoft TCP/IP on Microsoft Windows NT 4.0	E	E	
70-75	Implementing and Supporting Microsoft Exchange	E	E	
70-77	Implementing and Supporting Microsoft Internet Information Server	E	E	
70-78	Implementing and Supporting Microsoft Proxy Server 1.0	E	E	

[1]***Microsoft Certified Systems Engineer (MCSE)***

Requires four operating system exams and two elective exams.

[2]***NT 3.5 to NT 4.0 Migration Path***

MCSEs certified under the Windows NT 3.51 track who want to upgrade their certification to Windows NT 4.0. Requires two operating system exams.

C = core *E = elective*

See other side for Microsoft Certified Product Specialist and Microsoft Certified Solution Developer requirements.